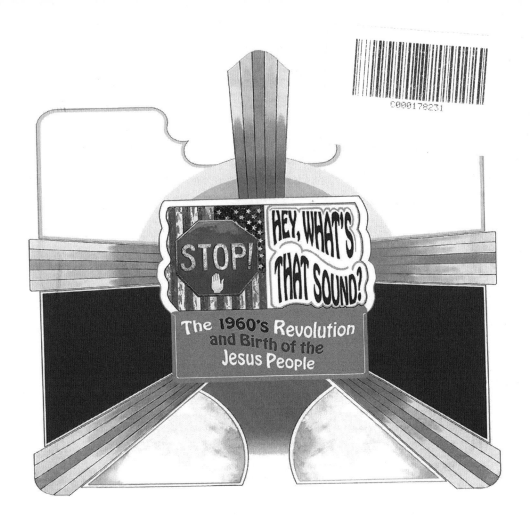

STOP! HEY, WHAT'S THAT SOUND?

The 1960's Revolution and Birth of the Jesus People

A Historical and Visual Journey
into the 1960's and 70's—in Pursuit
of Equality, Justice, Peace and
Truth

D.E. HOYT
AND FRIENDS

PSALM Press

1

STOP! HEY, WHAT'S THAT SOUND?

The 1960s Revolution and Birth of the Jesus People
A HISTORICAL AND VISUAL JOURNEY IN THE US AND UK

© 2019 D. E. Hoyt

Library of Congress 002-141-299

Psalm Press Albuquerque, NM

ISBN 978-1-7332991-1-4

MANAGING EDITOR
D.E. HOYT

ART & DESIGN EDITOR
I.H. HONOR

COVER ART: I.H. HONOR & D.E. HOYT

PROOF & PRE-FLIGHT EDITOR
VIRGINIA M. HOYT

REVISION EDITORS
ANDREW WHITMAN and TREVOR ALLEN

INDESIGN TECHNICAL ASSISTANCE / WEB DESIGN
HANS SUNDQUIST

ACKNOWLEDGMENTS FOR:
ILLUSTRATION, DESIGN, PHOTOGRAPHY, PHOTO & ART RESTORATION,
STORIES & PARABLES, POEMS, SONG LYRICS,
& CONTRIBUTING EYE-WITNESS ACCOUNTS
pp. IV, V

The Lonesome Stone Theatrical Musical CH 18-19 Produced by Deo Gloria Trust, Selsdon House 212-220 Addington Road, South Croydon, Surrey, CR2 8LD, United Kingdom

Publisher's Cataloging-in-Publication Data

Names: Hoyt, D. E., Editor

Title: Stop! Hey , what's that sound? : the 1960's revolution and birth of the Jesus People / D. E. Hoyt and friends

Description: "A historical and visual journey into the 1960s-70s, in pursuit of equality, justice, peace and truth." -from title page. | Includes bibliographical references. | Albuquerque, NM: Psalm Press, 2019.

Subjects: LCSH Jesus People. | Evangelicalism--United States. | Evangelistic work. | Youth--Religious life. Church history--20th century. | Christianity--20th century. | Christianity and culture. | Hippies--United States--History. United States-- History--20th century. | Social change--United States--History--20th century. | United States-- Social condtions --1960-1980. | United States--History--1961-1969. | BISAC HISTORY / United States / 20th Century | RELIGION / Christianity / History

Classification: LCC BV3793 .H69 2019 | DDC 269/.2--dc23

Dedication

A social and spiritual conscience, a questioning mind and a receptive heart to that which is true, are qualities that offer personal and generational hope.

A huge thanks to each of the contributors who join me in dedicating this book. In concert we encourage all who read, to search for truth with your whole heart. For those who embrace this journey— a promise awaits.

You will seek and find Me when you seek Me with all your heart. Jeremiah 29:13

- The True and Living God

ACKNOWLEDGMENTS

I could not have written this book without the help of many friends who have taken the time to compile their stories and place their trust in me to edit and synthesizing their important historical accounts in an understandable, truthful and honorable manner.

I am especially thankful for my wife Ginny Hoyt's support and enthusiastic encouragement. In addition, Val Skow Oliva, Sue Palosaari Cowper, Andrew Whitman and the late Lynn Malmberg have each lent their personal support and faithfully prayed for this project of many years to come to fruition for God's glory.

Illustrations

Clara Sörnäs 19
Rick Griffin 46
Pat McCormack 104
Julia North Richards 157
Debbie Wilcox 167, 641, 800
Ted Wise 187, 219
Stanislaw Zogorski 378
David Edward Byrd 378 464
Mad Arai-d Co., Ltd 411
William C. Ressler 366
Richard Sturdtevant 702
Johannes Gehrts 499
Dean Schendel 369, 379, 381, 491
I.H. Honor 694,
D.E.Hoyt 162, 165, 185, 195, 254, 256, 303, 310, 315, 368, 381, 397, 405, 409, 486, 704
I.H. Honor and D.E.Hoyt 686

Design

Ian McDonald/D.E. Hoyt 381

Photography By:

Am Stock Arc./Getty Images 15
Marc Riboud 40
Jim Marshall 46, 60
Old News Company 47
Art Greenspon 48
Bill Hudson 49
I.H. Honor 15, 22, 60, 65, 68, 79, 81,
Dennis L Manness 73, 74

San Francisco Chronicle 74
AFP/Getty Images 173
JFK Presidential Library 173
Time Magazine 271
Time Mag. / Leviton 262
H.C. Thoma 328
Chris Frampton 358, 403
Marjie Steinweiss 456
Marianne Sundquist 467
AD The Bible-film crew 517
Val Skow Oliva 526, 528
Ginny Hoyt 614
D.E. Hoyt 59, 66, 74, 81, 168, 195, 274, 610, 633, 635,
Jill Furmandusky 367, 371, 374, 375, 376, 383, 384, 385, 386, 387, 388, 389, 390, 391, 392, 393

Photo & Art Restoration

I.H. Honor

15, 22, 60, 65, 69, 71, 73, 74, 75, 77, 79, 82, 111, 118, 125, 133, 146, 153, 154, 160, 181, 183, 186, 189, 190, 192, 194, 197, 204, 218, 220, 232, 237, 243, 245, 246, 253, 256, 270, 274, 279, 280, 287, 292, 298, 307, 309, 311, 317, 328, 331, 333, 349, 352, 353, 354, 360, 368, 371, 375, 398, 406, 415, 417, 427, 442, 444, 445, 453, 456, 462, 464, 534, 535, 559, 561, 562, 571, 586, 715, 716, 717, 719, 720, 721, 722, 727, 730, 738, 784, 790

D.E. Hoyt

27, 30, 32, 33, 44, 52, 55, 58, 59, 77, 80, 83, 87, 94, 95, 124, 148, 153, 161, 163, 176, 200, 201, 216, 214, 217, 219, 222, 224, 227, 229, 231, 235, 249, 257, 275, 283, 290, 291, 310, 312, 318, 324, 325, 326, 338, 340, 345, 360, 363, 366, 367, 370, 374, 376, 395, 396, 399, 401, 402, 408, 413, 414, 416, 425, 431, 433, 441, 463, 464, 469, 475, 504, 520, 524, 532, 536, 541, 548, 549, 556, 564, 575, 578, 582, 583, 585, 588, 590, 595, 601, 604, 605, 609, 611, 621, 622, 623, 633, 635, 638, 678, 698, 707, 735, 738, 749, 774, 782, 799

Stories & Parables

'Lifesaving Station' 486
Dr. Theodore O. Wedel

'Go in Peace'- rewrite
I.H. Honor 480
original unknown

'God Leads a Pretty
Sheltered Life'
unknown 178

Poetry

I.H. Honor & D.E. Hoyt

Song Lyrics

One Day Came
Don Matthews

Lonesome Stone
Mike Damrow

San Francisco
John Phillips

Vegetables
Randy Stonehill

Where Do We Go From
Hear?
*Greg Nancarrow, Larry
Barker*

Bear Boogie
Mike Damrow

For What It's Worth
Buffalo Springfield

Goin Back
*Gerry Goffin & Carole King
rewrite Greg Nancarrow*

Changes
Rich Haas

He'll Set You Free
Dave Hoyt, Mike Damrow

Lives of Men
Mike Damrow

Come Jesus Come
Greg Nancarrow

Free
Mike Damrow

Rejoice
Joe Grier, David Eden

Take A Little Time
Andrae Crouch

Contributing Eyewitness Accounts

We are grateful for each contributor who wrote or shared by interview what they saw, heard and experienced firsthand during the 1960's–70s. During an era of widespread social turmoil and questioning—an unexpected spiritual in-breaking took place. This is the first publishing of the majority of these accounts. With the fleeting of days we offer them to the historical narrative of what we know to be true—in hopes of inspiring a coming generation.

Writer Accounts

Trevor Allen - Cambridge, England UK
Dale Alter - Contra Costa County, CA USA
Larry Barker - Milwaukee, WI USA
Karin Bienge - London, England UK
Michael Clark - Northwest JP USA
Michael Damrow - Lake Geneva, WI USA
Anne Clowser O'Donnell - Polick Pines, CA USA
Vic Clowser - Santa Cruz, CA USA
Edward Clowser - Polick Pines, CA USA
Ben & Rosalind Day - McMinnville, TN USA
Jack Fliehmann - Walnut Creek, CA USA
Kenneth P. Frampton - Purley Surrey England UK
Jenny Haas - Wisconsin, USA
Ginny Hoyt - Albuquerque, NM USA
Paul Jones - England, UK
Lynn Malmberg - Wisconsin, USA
Val Skow Oliva - Vacaville, CA USA
Sue Cowper Palosaari - Idlewild, CA USA
Kent Philpott - Mill Valley, CA USA
Jo Snappenfield - Oregon, USA
Stephen Spicer - England UK
Andrew Whitman - England UK

Interviewees

Caroline Green - Isle of Wight, England UK
Dan Pauly - Santa Fe, NM USA
Dan Scalf - Atlanta, WI USA

Interviewers / writers

George V.R. Smith - Atlanta Journal USA 1970
  'Lighting Candles in Downtown Atlanta'
Fiona Wilson - London, England UK [Caroline Green]
D.E. Hoyt - Albuquerque, NM USA [Dan Pauly]
Mary Held - News Service, Wisconsin USA [Dan Scalf]

Contents

VII

I am Human

I am human—of the earth; alive

I have eyes; arms, hands and feet

Nose, mouth, ears too, each a gift

If I don't have some of them, I'm still me

I am no better or worse than anyone

I am every color

I am Human—have a heart, feel it pound

I am Human—have breath, feel it go in and out

I'm aware of self and those around me

People come and go and things keep changing

I hope, search, dream and feel

I want to belong, be accepted

I sometimes sense loneliness, danger and fear

My inner spirit knows there is evil

But I seek what is good; to love and be loved

I believe there is something unknown

Greater than you, or me

I want to know what this is

Truth; a Creator?

I am human, made by God?

Made for what?

honor

Introduction

God Stuff?

For readers who are skeptical of spiritual things, God, or religion—you're in good company. Counterfeits abound and caution is wise! People question the existence of a True God amidst thousands of gods people worship which are permeated with human footprints and manipulation.

Both old and new religions claim divine origin, sacred doctrines, and adopt a range of traditions and rituals which are specific to each. Pleasing these gods and their leaders is another hoop seekers must jump through. A careful discerning of any path to substantiate if it's true is difficult and extremely hard work. In close second, the invisibility of God beyond our sensory perception creates the dilemma of how can we be sure of what is not verifiable through normal means? Unnumbered millions have asked, "Where is God? Can God be seen, or known?" This is the Great Search of the Ages.

Some seek truth or God and give up in frustration—weary of running into dead-ends. Others make a random choice to bring closure to being undecided. Those raised in a particular religion often adopt it as their own without questioning. For the non-religious, religion is tolerated but not practical; it's confusing, loaded with strife, the cause of wars and a mystery when it comes to actually making contact with God.

If you're unsure if God exists, is interested in humans, or has initiated a visit to planet earth—this book documents one such occurrence. It also intentionally points back to the main God visitation in human history. Honest evaluation and critical thinking is welcome as you draw your own conclusions.

If you have minimal exposure to the Bible and have been led to believe it's filled with human error and mistranslations—please push the Pause-Button on making a final judgment until you've read this book.

Many contributing authors have woven passages from the Bible into their accounts in response to their own questions and doubts, or to illuminate spiritual truths. As lifelong learners we hope readers will benefit by considering the spiritual compass from which these narratives and personal stories spring. The Bible verses below provide a historical overview that lots of people have never read.

> In the past God spoke to our ancestors through the prophets at many times and in various ways, but in these last days He has spoken to us by His Son, whom he appointed heir of all things, and through whom also He made the universe. The Son is the radiance of God's glory and the exact representation of His being, sustaining all things by his powerful Word. After he had provided purification for sins, he sat down at the right hand of the Majesty in heaven.   Hebrews 1:1-3

The Main God Visit

If these three verses from the New Testament book of Hebrews are true, nothing compares to Jesus Christ's visit to earth. If they are not, belief in Jesus as the Messiah-Savior is nothing more than a religious myth. These Bible verses claim Jesus radiates God's glory and is the exact representation of God's being. They also claim Jesus Christ provided purification of sin (through his death) and then rejoined God (after being raised from the dead) and now sits at the right hand of God's Majesty in heaven.

In the past 2000 + years since Jesus' advent, various God-visits linked to Jesus have taken place. Some spanned several continents; others were national or regional, while many remain unknown.

> Jesus said "My Father is always doing his work. He is working right up to this day. I am working too." John 5:17

Is God active in the present? Followers of Jesus claim one-on-one encounters is the predominant way God connects with humans. This means belief in Jesus Christ is subjective. Christ-followers say individuals pray, seek truth and look for answers about life and God-things and when the human heart and spirit is in the right place, a personally recognizable spiritual awakening takes place. They also believe man-made or demoniacally inspired religions are poised to divert honest seekers to a counterfeit path (I Timothy 4:1-2). To substantiate or disprove this claim we will investigate a number of these groups.

Some believe there is only one True and Living God capable of changing a person on the inside and igniting an awareness of divine Truth. This idea was not on the radar of most who tell their stories in this book. God was a mystery—until something otherworldly happened.

We came from various geographical locations. Some had Christian roots, while the majority had been oblivious to God and Jesus Christ before these events took place. From a handful of individuals responding to God, to localized prayer and worship gatherings hungry to know God—a torch was lit spreading across America, Europe, Africa, India, Central and South America, Australia, New Zealand and into Asia.

Literally, hundreds of thousands of individuals who had previously been unaware of God being real or accessible were transformed in mind and heart by God's Spirit. Most would have never imagined anything like this could have happened six months prior. The majority of those impacted by this God Visit had not been on any spiritual trajectory. I was one of the exceptions, but even then was surprised by the Almighty seeking me out.

Team of Authors

Within these pages contributing author-friends and I share our first person accounts and narratives with the aim of providing an insider's voice and vantage point from those who lived in the 1960's-1970's Counter-Culture times and were grafted into The Jesus People Movement. We hail from a variety of USA regions and European countries.

The early portion of this book is autobiographical—a thumbnail view of my life as a troubled youth, my sins and search for truth. Each contributor will share their own story, fleshing-out what their lives looked like prior to a transformation.

If you find yourself saying, "I can't believe these authors were this screwed up and made so many dumb mistakes," it's understandable. To balance this assessment, take a moment and think about your own worst sins. We all have skeletons. Some people's sins are in the open while others remain hidden; either way they will follow each of us to death and judgment (I Timothy 5:24).

As you read about some of us at our worst, with our faults in the open, perhaps you too will find hope. "All have sinned" (Romans 3:23) is a healthy reminder. Earthly glory and fame are swallowed up by human weaknesses. A Country Music Legend gives us a potent dose of the folly of trusting in the wrong things, or even people we admire.

> "And you could have it all, my empire of dirt. I will let you down, I will make you hurt." – Johnny Cash

A number of historian-type authors, reporters and news people have written on radical aspects of the Hippie and Jesus Movement days, sensationalizing the bizarre. Others have dissected and dissed some players, placing them in a negative historical tomb, while elevating others mistakenly. The fickleness of the media, writers and pundits was huge in the 60's as it is today. One day a person is a hero, the next, an unredeemable scoundrel! The highs and lows and failures of individuals during these days were akin to their critics. All of us are flawed in some way, all guilty of something!

The political Right and Left, both then and now can easily point out the weaknesses of the 60's generation. In self righteousness many attempt to erase the contributions made. Myopic sweeping judgments miss the nuances of a generation who had an active social conscience, the guts to stand up for what they believed, were less "I" centered and less materialistic. The 60's generational goal was to discover a better way of living which led to a battle against greed, prejudice, injustice, government deception and a War Machine mentality and practice. Our faults were also substantial.

Lots of political and social issues were on the table; critical for every thinking person of the day. People were grappling with what to believe and how to correct social ills. Evil was at work, sending out its tentacles of hate, prejudice, anarchy, god counterfeits and unpredictable new types of dangerous drugs. As lead author I can assure you this book has nothing to do with being pro any political side. **The poison of hypocrisy and duplicity is no respecter of political parties.**

The prologue and early chapters address the mood, frustration, courage, hopes and dreams of the turbulent 1960's. A short historical window is opened to provide a contextual understanding that will surprise some. When a nation, segment of society or group of people makes profoundly good or bad choices there are consequences and lessons which can be insightful to us and future generations. Bad choices come at a price, with repercussions affecting lives for generations to come.

In the mid to later chapters we offer a first-person narrative of a true spiritual outbreaking that swept across land and sea. Sadly, counterfeit imposters arose infiltrating what God birthed.

This writing dives deep into an authentic spiritual battle between the forces of Darkness and evil, Truth and Light—unveiling the path to the True and Living knowable God.

Some look for an adventure and a cause to live for beyond the mundane doldrums of materialism and status quo society. Others are happy with routines and the positives found within society. *Regardless of an individual's personal leanings, internal courage to seek truth and discover if there is a Living God should be revisited by every generation.*

As you read, keep your heart open. This is a more than a historical account. It's an opportunity to learn how God works, speaks and interacts with humans. You be the judge, as to whether God came close to a considerable segment of a generation who were wrestling with issues similar to what we face today.

We'll touch on the rise of the Civil Rights / Free Speech / Women's Rights Movements, the Radical Groups of the day, The Political Right and Left, The Peace & Love Generation, and the Jesus People Movement. Our in-depth focus will be on the inside history of the Peace & Love Generation, Counterfeit Religions, and the Jesus People Movement.

Due to the breadth of the Jesus People Movement we have chosen to cover only what contributing authors were in some way linked to, or saw and experienced firsthand. Since the inception of this writing a commitment for accuracy and authenticity has been our goal.

This is an eyewitness account from those who lived it.

Prologue

What's Going On?

The Backdrop

The siren split the air with such force our 3rd grade class was struck with fear. In a matter of moments we went from a peaceful learning setting, to organized panic—moving from sitting positions, to positioning ourselves under our desks. If your desk was near a window, as mine was; we went to the most interior wall in the room and curled in a ball with our heads down.

My heart was pounding. My breath was noticeably louder. Our teacher quickly turned on the classroom radio to listen for emergency information. Frozen in our assigned emergency positions, the piercing sound of the siren seems longer than four minutes.

The world was not a safe place. The Air-Raid or Nuclear-Threat

siren blasted out a warning of what was occurring, or could happen. We'd seen the news, heard from parents and teachers, that other countries might launch an attack on the USA.

We were "war babies" (Baby Boomers), born into a dangerous world. Life on planet earth was uncertain and peace was fragile.

> **Author's Note:** Revisiting of our not-too-distant past historically puts into context the events that led up to the need for social change. Simultaneously a God visit was on the way to provide answers and help.

Recovery from WW II

America, the United Kingdom, Europe and every country impacted by World War II were in a period of rebuilding their infrastructure and mourning the dead. The scar was fresh, but the war was over! US President Truman and British Prime Minister **Churchill** alongside leaders from Canada, Australia, New Zealand, South Africa, Russia and China had been successful in their joint-effort to stop Hitler and his allies. *The defeat of the Nazi war machine was crucial for the planet.* The hard facts that emerged regarding Hitler's ethnic cleansing campaigns and mass murders horrified the civilized world.

Hitler is directly responsible for 11 million holocaust deaths which took place in concentration and death camps—6 million Jews and 5 million others. Among these were at least 2 million Soviet POW's, who were starved, worked to death, or mass-murdered. Other deaths in the European WW II war-theater are conservatively estimated at 35 million, which include 20 million Germans. The remainder of deaths occurred in occupation and allied force battles. This brought the total of deaths related to Hitler's Nazi goal of world domination—to near 48 million!

German, Japanese, Italian and North Korean aggression had attempted to annihilate people groups and overthrow nations. Now Russia was flexing its nuclear muscle.

The Cold War

The US and other countries were arming themselves with powerful bombs, capable of mass destruction like the two atomic bombs the US dropped on Japan. Both the US and Russia were now developing hydrogen bombs with 1000 times the strength of atomic bombs and the arms race was on.

Desiring equal or greater power, Russia jumped ahead of the US, launching the first satellite, Sputnik, into orbit. The US concluded, if the Soviets put a satellite into , they could do the same thing with a nuclear ballistic missile warhead.

The Cold War was mysteriously veiled, a secretive buildup of super-weapons that could wipe out huge geographical areas. With Russia and the USA emerging from World War II as superpowers—a nuclear arms race was on; an era of testing and stockpiling thousands of nuclear war-

Nuclear Missiles

heads in an effort to be the strongest. The conclusion was, whoever had the best technology had the most power. The race was becoming more dangerous—with the potential of an all-out nuclear war.

The USA in the 1950's—60's

Though the 1950's would be good years for many countries, they would not be without problems for the USA. North Korea's communistic regime launched an attack on South Korea attempting to subjugate the population to communist rule. The Korean War drew in the newly formed United Nations with US troops representing 90% of those who came to the defense of South Korea. In support of North Korea, China sent troops and Russia provided supplies and weapons. An armistice was finally signed in July 1953 ending this conflict with the establishment of the Demilitrized zone between the North and South Korea, to be patrolled on both sides.

The booming prosperity of the 1950's nurtured a widespread sense of stability. The United States adds two more states, Alaska and Hawaii—and Puerto Rico becomes a commonwealth. Highways are built to make traveling easier and shopping centers are developed. TV is the "in-thing" with millions of families buying a set. Television and movie entertainment soar. The purchase of refrigerators, cars, homes and other conveniences are more affordable. Many new companies like McDonald's are launched.

American's love of sports like baseball, football, prize fighting, tennis and golf grow in popularity—a positive infusion to war recovery. Classical, country and folk music roots branch out to pop, rock-n-roll and jazz.

The sixties began with the election of America's youngest president, John F. Kennedy at age 44. Of Irish descent, a Roman Catholic by faith, having served in the military with honors, JFK demonstrated strong leadership and vision for our country. His thesis on the common enemy of man was: "Tyranny, poverty, disease, and war." The public sentiment under JFK was, "anything is possible."

He took intentional steps to lessen poverty and vigorous action in the cause of civil and human rights. Through the Alliance for Progress and the Peace Corps, he brought American idealism to the aid of developing nations and cast a vision for compassionate service.

The Cuban Missile Crisis was a test for JFK's young presidency. Armed Cuban exiles supported by the USA were defeated in an attempt to overthrow Fidel Castro's regime. Russia came to Cuba's aid and installed a nuclear missile site in western Cuba. When the Soviets' action was discovered by the US, JFK and Russian leader Khrushchev entered into "crisis dialogue." The US imposes a naval blockade of all offensive weapons bound for Cuba. Heightening the crisis, a USA U-2 plane is shot down over Cuba. The showdown intensified. Kennedy wants all nuclear weapons removed from Cuba. Khrushchev wants a public promise that the US will not invade Cuba. On the brink of a disastrous confrontation, both sides agree to the terms and a nuclear war is averted. These successful steps in diplomacy lead to a test ban treaty and a gradual slowing down of the nuclear arms race.

Civil Rights

The push for civil rights for all Americans was an important goal in the 1960s. Many US citizens had forgotten, ignored or defied the mandate of equality and freedom for African Americans. The abduction of Africans had brought wealth to slave trading nations. Over 50,000 abduction voyages were made—spanning three centuries. Millions of Africans died during capturing raids, death-marches to the coast, in holding prisons, in route by ship, or by cruelty and overwork till they dropped dead. Slaves were whipped, tortured, raped, underfed, uncared for when ill, slept in shacks exposed to the weather—often dying prematurely from these sub-human conditions while working from sun-up to sundown.

Africa Ravaged

The negative impact of the international slave trade on Africa was catastrophic. In addition to the millions of able-bodied individuals captured and uprooted from their tribes, the old and very young were often killed, or left to starve.

The entire infrastructure of multiple hundreds of tribal groups was destroyed. Social life was forever changed and traditional values subverted. The relationships between kingdoms, ethnic groups, religious communities, castes, rulers and subjects, peasants and soldiers, the enslaved and the free experienced a massive upheaval. The tyranny of the slave trade gave way to predatory regimes taking advantage of instability and widespread grief as Africa sunk into a state of regression and population growth became stagnant.

To compound the Slave Trading evils committed by America, South

Slave Memorial of Rememberance - Tanzania Africa

America, North Africa and Europe, European powers set out to control the political process in Africa to prevent the rise of African centralized states. This was done to prevent Africa from shutting down the lucrative slave trading business and other European business interests.

The aftermath of Africans being raped, starved, killed, or forced into slavery was an Africa left underdeveloped, disorganized, and vulnerable to the next phase of European colonialism. Let no one forget the beautiful continent of Africa and its people were subjected to the worst of human atrocities, both in their homeland and in other countries while slaves. What was perpetrated against them ranks among the highest levels of criminality!

The US Civil War was fought over the issue of slavery. The goal of the northern states was to give African and other ethnic groups the dignity they deserved, and honor our constitutional commitment to "liberty and justice for all." US blood flowed over the practice of slavery with approximately 620,000 deaths combined on both sides. On January 1, 1863 President Abraham Lincoln issued an executive order and signed into law the Emancipation Proclamation. This changed the legal status of 3 million slaves in the designated areas of the South from slave to free. Since this time, acceptance and honoring this proclamation of freedom and equal treatment of African Americans and minorities has been opposed by many. Blacks in the south have endured white prejudice, terrorism and inhumane treatment by those who tenaciously opposed the notion that African Americans and others were worthy of equal human status.

Dr. Martin Luther King Jr., a young pastor at Dexter Avenue Baptist Church in Montgomery, Alabama was called to address and bring national attention to the ongoing human-rights abuses of Blacks in southern states. Though US Africans were free constitutionally on paper, with full citizenship rights as Americans—it was not being honored or practiced.

Prejudice continued in many US southern states. The "colored" or "niggers" were considered unequal to whites. Some southern whites considered themselves genetically advanced in comparison to 'inferior' Blacks. Places of business, seating areas, toilets and drinking fountains for "Whites Only" were commonplace. Southerners resented being forced to give up slavery when the North won the Civil War. Generations of slave owners found a way to justify mistreating and exploiting African Americans and clung to their mind-set of superiority. Unfortunately, these generational attitudes and sins were passed down to their children and children's children.

The Civil Rights Movement wanted to revisit and obtain the freedoms issued in the Emancipation Proclamation Law and the North's victory in the Civil War. Peaceful "freedom marchers" encountered attack-dogs, fire hoses and brutal police violence. The precursor of these marches was severe abuse of Blacks in southern states; bombings, lynchings, killings, beatings, rape, property and cross burnings, threats of intimidation, exclusion from fair wages for work and denial of access to voting. Hundreds of bombs were placed and exploded, destroying or damaging Blacks' homes, cars, businesses and churches—killing or injuring innocent children and adults. The perpetrators' aim was to terrorize African Americans and white supporters. The Klu Klux Klan, white supremacy groups or racist individuals were responsible. Southern society as a whole, including law enforcement, was complicit in not providing protection and justice for African Americans. Sadly this occurred without restraint, guilt or legal ramifications in many cases.

The Civil Rights march on Washington D.C. in August of 1963 was for jobs, voting rights and "freedom of equality." Some 250,000 marchers showed up—25% white. On August 28, 1963, Martin Luther King, Jr., standing in front of the Lincoln Memorial, delivered his historic "I Have a Dream" speech in which he called for an end to racism. A coalition of civil rights groups organized the march which became the largest in US history. Before, during and after, Dr. Martin Luther King Jr. gained increasing public exposure as a prominent African American voice for the nation. President JF Kennedy was a strong supporter of the Civil Rights Act which remained stalled in congress.

Shock & Unrest

Three months later on Nov. 23, 1963 in Dallas, Texas, US President John F. Kennedy was assassinated. The shock of the JFK assignation was felt around the world. America was numb. Normal life in the US came to a halt. Like 9/11, the world stopped turning. Disbelief, horror and grief co-mingle. A tragic loss was complicated by unclear facts surrounding who was really behind the sniper killing. The Civil Rights Act was finally passed into law in 1964 after JFK's death, which included working rights for women.

The intensity of unrest was something you could feel. The USA war with Vietnam, forced draft, massive death counts and civil rights battle caused national distress. US anti-war demonstrators and civil rights marchers continued to take their causes to the streets. Police and civilian clashes escalate. When it appears things couldn't get any worse, Dr. Martin Luther King Jr. is assassinated by a sniper's bullet and shortly after Senator Robert F. Kennedy is killed by a solo assassin in a crowd.

What is going on? Each of these respected US leaders strongly supported civil rights and the needs of all US citizens regardless of race, religion, or social status. They were men of action with clear voices advocating an end to prejudice and promoted fair wages for women and minorities. They paid the ultimate price. In horror, America reeled with the assassination of all three. They were social and spiritual lights in a world that grew darker without their influence.

(L) Robert F. Kennedy, Attorney General
(R) US President John F. Kennedy
At a ceremony honoring
African Americans

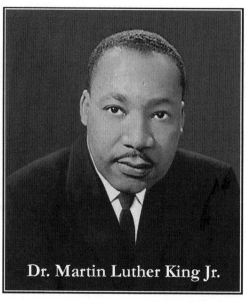

Dr. Martin Luther King Jr.

On the heels of these deaths, the radical Black leader Malcolm X was assassinated in New York City. Shortly after, the LA Watts riots broke out. Government war policies, harsh policing practices and racist hold-outs were fanning the flames of disillusionment and protest among growing numbers of Americans.

Meanwhile, the rise of a counter-culture in support of "peace and love" was in its germination stage, nurtured by a handful of poets, writers, music artists and bands. On its heels would come an unexpected unleashing of God's Spirit into the world.

The Mainstream Church

In the 1950s both Protestants and Catholics increased in numeric growth— though differences and distrust between the two groups remained. The authority of the Pope, praying to Mary and other saints was problematic for Protestants. Catholics were equally skeptical of Protestants. Catholic Church officials had concluded many Protestant doctrines were outside orthodoxy and encouraged their parishioners to stay away from their churches and limit close friendships with adherents.

During the 1950s attending church was popular though the depth of spirituality during this surge is difficult to determine. Mainline denominations expanded rapidly to almost every city. Liberal and legalistic expressions found their place. Evangelical and Pentecostal churches grew by leaps and bounds. Para-church ministries with targeted mission work garnered strong support. In the larger arena, evangelistic crusades and healing revivals were very popular. Billy Graham, Oral Roberts and a handful of others were in the lime-light of these larger venue events which were often televised.

A Melting Pot

The 60s church finds itself confronted with the Vietnam War, the Civil Rights Movement, the Sexual Revolution, Women's Liberation, Black Militant groups, Hippies, New Age Cults, world religions like Buddhism, Hinduism, Transcendental Meditation, Spiritism, the Occult and Satanism. In this milieu of diverse change, institutional Christianity, its teachings, leaders, actions and non-actions are challenged. Government, corporate business, police, hawkish military adherents and the church are lumped together as "the establishment." In this upheaval, many mainline church denominations yield to a softening and watering-down of their teaching. Embarrassed by Jesus' unpopularity and claims, a "social gospel" emerges, designed to fit-in and be more palatable.

Christianity in the 1960's

In short order, the gospel of Jesus Christ's life and death on a cross to save humankind is no longer taught in many mainline churches. As a precursor, an erosion of God and Christ-centered faith infiltrates seminaries. Jesus' sinless life, miracles, teachings and deeds are viewed with suspicion by professors who espouse these notions to their students. Jesus' death, resurrection and ascension, the reliability of the Scriptures of the Old and New Testaments are likewise in question. A myriad of questions surface— Is Jesus the Messiah? Is God a man or women type of deity, or is he or she mythical? Was Jesus a liar and deceiver, or a prophet, a good man, a gifted teacher, or the promised One? Was Jesus divine, or just a good man, or was he both? Was Jesus Christ raised from the dead, or did he fake his death and then disappear?

With these types of foundational issues up for grabs, many church leaders and attendees found themselves in a twilight zone of spiritual uncertainty. If the Bible is not reliable, or the God behind it, or the Savior it proclaims—what can be trusted? Long-held spiritual practices in many mainstream churches went by the wayside; like prayer gatherings, Bible preaching and group study, discipleship training and mission outreach.

I was invited to a Bible study led by a Christian pastor/chaplain in 1964, seeking any truth to be found in the Christian faith. To my surprise, the gathering had nothing to do with studying or learning about the Bible. The gathering was a Meditation Session with recorded sitar music by Ravi Shankar playing in the background. There was no prayer, Bible study or teaching. Encountering this type of scenario compelled those who were inquiring about Jesus Christ to look elsewhere.

The light of Christ within many churches which claimed to hold the power to save and transform people was growing dim. A large percentage of mainline Protestant churches with deep financial coffers embraced social activism and good works, church-school development, building programs, property maintenance and promoting an image of respectability in the community. The Christ-centered exceptions among both Protestant and Catholic churches were in the minority.

Because of this, it's not surprising that the majority of young adult seekers denounced the church of the 60s as materialistic, seeking social status, lacking in spiritual substance and role models, hung up on religious and denominational traditions and distinctives, aloof and standoffish to those outside the social status of parishioners.

In contrast, some churches remained loyal to the foundational truths but became timid regarding Jesus' claims and words to avoid offending hearers. Other remnant churches from varying denominations and independent churches held tenaciously to their convictions about the gospel of Christ. These Christ followers were the "keepers of the flame." Among these were Catholics and their charismatic wing, some Baptists, Evangelicals, Independents and a variety of Full Gospel churches. Many of these were praying with intensity, asking God to intervene and reveal Himself amidst these tumultuous times.

Integrated into the mix of spiritual choices were world religions, cults, gurus, new age religions and the occult, each vying to "recruit truth seekers" while gaining ever-widening recognition and acceptance in society worldwide.

The pages that follow document a God Visit outside the parameters of religious orchestration.

PLACES CONTRIBUTORS WILL VISIT IN THEIR NARRATIVES
USA, Canada, Nova Scotia, Mexico, England, Scotland,
Finland, Poland, Sweden, E. & W. Germany, Netherlands,
Soviet Georgia, Russia, Africa and China

1

What Is, Was and Is to Come

San Fran—My New Home

It was late summer 1966. San Francisco's Haight-Ashbury was in the early stages of becoming the epicenter of the USA Hippie counter-culture. I'd been in correspondence with an old buddy named Luther who was an investor and board member of the Straight Theater on the north side of Haight Street. He'd invited me to San Fran with a promise of work at the theater and a place to stay. He'd told me amazing things were unfolding in the Bay Area and thought I'd want to be in on the action.

It was a strange twist of fate that he'd found me. The invitation was luring. It would get me out of LA County which had been my downfall in the past. San Francisco was unchartered territory—with the exception of spending a few hours enroute as a young runaway. The smell and taste of fresh sourdough bread from Fisherman's Wharf was my only memory.

I saved for the trip to San Fran and was excited. A neighbor-family said they'd miss me. The wife Barbara had frequently cooked extra when making a stew, chicken, or baking cookies, sending some over with one of her boys. She'd invited me to church but I never went. It would have been too awkward with Eastern meditation as my spiritual focus. On the day of my departure for San Fran, Barbara drove me to the Greyhound bus stop and as she said goodbye, she urged me with concern in her voice,

"Your prayers to God will be heard, but there are counterfeits of the Living God. Stay open to Jesus Christ. He is the true Savior. Please write, I'll be praying." I thanked her and said goodbye. I didn't know what to think. I knew she was a Christian and a good person. She reminded me of my Grandma who'd shared similar words and prayed for me. My thoughts quickly returned to the bus trip north and San Francisco in anticipation of a new beginning. I was psyched!

On arrival, Luther met me as agreed and his description of the city was right-on. Walking in the Haight was like stepping into a different time period. Guys and ladies were dressed in renaissance or western pioneer type clothing. They seemed friendly, happy and hopeful.

According to Luther, some 15,000 free-spirited people had moved into the Haight, renting or buying spacious Victorian homes and apartments. Among these were prominent bands like Jefferson Airplane, The Charlatans, Big Brother and the Holding Company and the Grateful Dead.

After a quick tour of the Straight Theater we headed across the Golden Gate Bridge to Luther's house in Marin County. His pad was perched on a steep hill between San Anselmo and Fairfax. Luther had a rough looking house guest from Mexico with a large black mustache and beard—with a sizable stash of pot and hash (hashish).

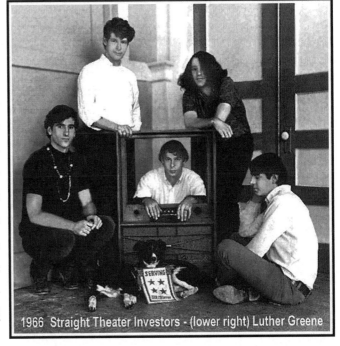

1966 Straight Theater Investors - (lower right) Luther Greene

After dinner we settled into the rustic living room, with the fireplace blazing and smoked dope. Our entertainment was Luther's Mexican house guest who told us wild drug adventure tales, sex exploits and superstitious Spiritism stories.

"YourMost days Luther and I drove into the city and worked at the theater. Luther ran errands, picked up supplies, helped with the work and supervised. He and his partners had undertaken the renovation of this venue with the goal of getting it up and running for smaller band concert events for the summer of 1967. I and a handful of workers had been hired to help restore the old theater. Huge amounts of debris, loose plaster, rotted wood and unusable old theater stuff had to be removed amidst lots of dust. We filled a number of large dumpsters.

I gradually figured out the Mexican dude at Luther's crib was on an extended visit. He was for sure a *Mi Vida Loca* (my crazy life) kind of guy, but different from the LA and institutional gang-bangers I'd known. He had a loud laugh, was pumped with adrenalin and given to non-stop storytelling. I couldn't figure out how he could keep talking given the amount of dope he smoked. The down side was he monopolized the conversations with Spiritism and the demonic making me feel polluted and trapped at Luther's.

In Southern Cal I'd been on a meditation routine, but it'd been out the window since moving north. I told Luther I wanted to move into the city and he was OK with it. On my last night at his pad, I was high on acid and hash and walked past a picture of Jesus Christ on the wall. As I stopped to look at it—I saw a tear of blood form under one of the eyes and a drop appear. Looking more carefully, it was still there with a faint second tear drop further down on his face. It looked real with watery edges around the drop. A tear of blood intrigued me. I stood starring at Jesus' face and eyes a long time and felt God might be saying something to me. I didn't know. In the morning I asked Luther if I could have the picture. "Yea, no problem, take it."

Move into the City

Luther paid me weekly for work at the theater and gave me extra to rent a room in the city. This, along with my small savings, would keep me afloat. The furnished room I rented was basic and cheap. It had a single bed, night stand, small dresser, linoleum floors, a small throw rug by the bed and three tall southern windows facing Haight Street. Showers and toilets were down the hallway. For a pittance of money I had privacy and was thankful. The peace of less noise at Luther's and not being to get high was a relief.

I was glad to still have work at the theater. Phase two of work at the Straight Theater involved patching larger wall holes, mudding them in with a plaster bonder, taping wall cracks with nylon and resurfacing all problem areas with a top coat of plaster. New wall build-outs were dry-walled, mudded, taped and sanded. The entire building was rewired and the heating and cooling replaced. The stage area was being restored and a new dance floor was being laid. Painting would follow. The plan for stage three was an install of a state-of-the-art lighting and sound system and theater screen. Things were coming together.

Tenants at my new digs stayed to themselves. We'd say "hey", but that was about it. The neighborhood was predominantly black with a strong criminal element coming out at night a few blocks east. One night, lying on my bed staring at the water marked ceiling in my digs, I thought about what life had been like—so far.

Bad choices, peer influence and becoming institutionalized over a span of years had contributed to a dark beginning. I couldn't place the blame elsewhere; *I'd screwed up and allowed my heart to become callused.* The school of hard knocks made me a survivor, but not a good person! In battling demons, sins and destructive choices, I'd failed. For years I'd been caught up in a revolving door of being in and out of trouble with the law. I wanted to change—and was ready to put the brakes on a life of being incarcerated. This was what motivated me to seek God and stay with it. I knew it was a long-shot, but I had nothing to lose!

A Wild and Dangerous Ride
Narrative of a Sinner

Born in Los Angeles, California—I grew up in the suburb city of Arcadia. As a kid I learned how to work and make things, did a variety of chores, had a paper route, played sports and helped care for our pets. Life was good until our parents' divorce when I was about 8. Shortly after, we moved.

Seeing Dad only on the weekends and being under Mom's new and demanding rules caused my brother and me to react in different ways. Over the next year or so we both fell into different types of mischief. Neither of us were bad or defiant kids, but with Mom working and gone most of the time—we gradually became discouraged by unreasonably long chore-lists that we couldn't finish if we did our school homework. Punishments and groundings increased. Over time, the strict rules got old and we both began looking for ways to avoid being home.

As an interim solution our parents decided to send both of us to Monte Vista Christian Boarding School in Watsonville, CA, several hundred miles away. The school was located in the boonies of the north-central part of the state surrounded by fruit orchards and agriculture with a co-ed population of about 80 kids. It was

Monte Vista Christian School
Watsonville, CA   1954

weirdly Pentecostal; aligned with the Assemblies of God Church during this period.

What I liked most about the place, was a friend I made named Niyol [Wind] a Native American my age. We'd throw knives in the stable's wood planks and ride horses when allowed. Nearing the end of the school year I was punished for a relatively minor infraction of the rules and received a severe whipping. A cherry switch was used on my bare-butt and upper thighs which drew blood. Angered and embarrassed—I ran away by night.

I hid in an orchard till dawn and hitch-hiked north to SF and then on to the logging town of Pollock Pines wanting to get as far away from Monte Vista as possible. Altitude sickness forced me to knock on a door and ask for help. The family let me use their phone to call my Mom. In short order money was wired so I could take a Greyhound back to LA with the promise I wouldn't be sent back to Monte Vista.

With summer vacation several weeks away, I had an invite from Niyol and family to visit them in Arizona for part of the summer. Surprisingly my parents agreed, which gave them additional time to figure out what to do with my brother and I.

A Greyhound took me from LA to the city of Chambers in Eastern Arizona where I met Niyol and his dad. We traveled by truck an hour or so north near Ganado. It was cool to be riding in an old truck on dirt roads and the southwest terrain was different than anything I'd ever seen. Niyol's family lived in a tiny house among a cluster of Hogan type structures on the Navajo Nation REZ (Reservation), surrounded by open land and huge skies. The men caught and broke in wild horses and the women wove rugs for part of their income. Niyol's house doubled as a store for the grouping of about fifty adults and children. They stocked non-perishable canned foods and a variety of practical items regularly needed. The water source was a well centrally located with a hand-pump.

Life was simple with work, play and worship integrated into daily life. We met in one of the Hogans for Christian worship and sat on a dirt floor with mats around the edges. The singing was mostly in Navajo with a few songs in English. Women nursed their little ones, babies cried and God was worshiped. The adults and kids were all friendly and patient with me. Niyol and I were given chores to do for an hour or so a day and the rest of the time we rode horses, shot his 22 for target practice and went on hiking or riding adventures. On Saturday or Sundays we'd play baseball in the afternoons while dodging prairie dog holes and wild brush. The teams were small but we made do. Arizona sunrises and sunsets were amazing! Canyon de Chelly was amazing. This adventure formed a life-long positive memory.

On returning to CA, my brother had already been placed in Lark Ellen Home for Boys in Azusa, CA and I joined him. This would be the longest of my placements—taking me up to attending Azusa junior high some three years later. I would never return home. Getting high with Lark Ellen homeboys was my downfall, landing me back in the L.A. Juvenile system. A failed placement at the Optimist Boys Home, resulted in being sent to Whittier Youth Authority, (CYA aka California Youth Authority) followed by two correctional forestry camps, Kenyon Scudder and Carl Holton. On release I was accepted into a foster home near Lark Ellen, reconnected with former "home boy" friends and attended Glendora High School. Disputes with my foster parent over hanging out with old friends and curfew times shot me back into the court system.

This parole violation catapulted me back into the California Youth Authority (CYA) system and I landed at Paso Robles. Seething with anger, I joined an institutional gang and began attacking those who mouthed off to us. This went under the radar as I worked my way up the gang ladder.

All was good until we attacked a 'snitch' who was hospitalized with life-threatening wounds. I was implicated and thrown into solitary confinement at the end of the marching yard.

Entering the 'hole' through a huge gray steel door, the pungent smell of urine and chlorine hit me. In the months to come I spent almost all of my time alone in a dingy cell on a mattress stained with somebody else's urine and used a funky gray wool blanket to keep warm. Food came through a metal slot in the door. Three times a week we were

CA Youth Authority - Paso Robles, Salinas Unit

taken out for fresh air to a center plot within the complex. We ran the parameter for varying periods of time, followed by digging deep holes in the hard soil—and then filling them in. I'd hoped to get shot back into the population, but the Youth Authority Review Board had something else in mind.

After 90 + days in the hole, I was transferred from Paso Robles to Preston School of Industry (CYA) with additional time on my sentence for a battery attack.

Preston Youth Authority

Preston's population was older and it had a reputation of being a dangerous place. Gang-banging, fights, race riots, guard attacks and tear-gas was the norm. It was a training ground for young gladiators who'd most likely be facing prison soon. The majority of the population didn't care if they lived or died. Life was expendable. Living up to being tough for your honor, gang, or race was a driving force. Whatever the fallout—didn't matter.

Spending a year and a half at Preston, staying alive and graduating high school while there was a big deal! On parole I had the best intentions of staying out of trouble.

Preston School of Industry 1894-1994

Adult Time

I keep my nose clean for almost a year until I got popped for drunk and disorderly behavior—a minor offence. My sentence should have been probation, but I got a six-month stay at LA's Wayside Honor Farm. While there, a young guard slammed my head into a cement wall while a bunch of us were spread eagle facing the wall over a security issue The guard accused me of attacking him when I drew a fist in reaction.

The Lock-Up at Wayside was extreme. No windows, furniture, sink or traditional toilet. A hole in the ground with push flush was it. The one dim light in the room was turned off. Accused of attacking a guard brought the wrath of guards working the unit. Without warning, guards would burst into the cell kicking me for several minutes and then leave abruptly. This happened 5-6 times during my week's stay. I thought a lot about trying to find the cop who'd bounced me on the bogus charge of attacking him and killing him once out. From the hole I was placed in an isolation unit called Siberia for three months. Unprovoked violence initiated by guards against inmates in Siberia was further reason to hate pigs that lived up to their name. I served my time and was finally released.

My next run-in with the law was the most serious of my life. A buddy and I cooked up the idea of going to Tijuana, Mexico to score kilos of weed and return to the States with a big stash. At a hot Mexican border these plans came to a screeching halt! Our vehicle was searched, the drugs were found and we were arrested for smuggling drugs into the USA. This was a serious offense. My continued bad choices and concern over me running—kept my parents from bailing me out. I couldn't blame them.

Hard-Time

I spent nine months in San Diego County Jail awaiting trial because my partner in crime jumped bail. I had a variety of cell mates. One of them was a forty year old heroin addict named Wally. I watched him kick his habit cold turkey. Over the course of months we became friends. Wally had lost his family and business due to heroin. He was a man in deep sorrow for what he'd put his family through. Knowing we were both heading to Federal prison, we made a pact to search for God and began while we were in SD County Jail. My sentence was 6 years with the possibility of early parole under the Youth Act. He went to Federal Prison in Leavenworth, Kansas and I went to Lompoc, in California.

I'd been a hard-nosed kid, no stranger to correctional institutions, violence, riots, been in jail—but landing in the adult prison population was different. It wasn't just the gun-towers, high walls, barbed fences and high security everywhere—it was what you saw and felt amidst a population of thugs, con-artists, gang-bangers and crazy time-bomb career criminals. The atmosphere in prison is filled with those who threaten anyone they can by intimidation or violence. Racial and gang lines are drawn. Intense levels of anger and unrest are something you can actually feel; like when a race riot is about to go down. Riots happen, inmates attack each other and some die. Personal security and alertness has to be maintained 24/7. The adrenalin in my body was always at work wherever I moved in the population. I'm a survivor by mercy from above. Trust me. Prison is a dark and dangerous place—not someplace you want to call home!

Sticking to the pact I'd made with Wally, I threw myself into an intense search for God and truth. I hung with a group of other inmates on a similar search. We shared holy books, meditated, and delved into the teachings of gurus, spiritual masters, world religions and philosophers. Some resources were in the prison library, others we ordered by mail. Most of them were not easy to decipher.

Some of the books we passed around were, *What Buddha Taught,* by Walpola Rahula, *The Forth Way,* by Gerjiief & Ospenski, *Autobiography of a Yogi,* by Paramahansa Yogananda, *Tibetan Book of the Dead,* by Padma Sambhava, *The Sleeping Prophet,* by Edgar Cayce, *Man Is Not Alone,* by Abraham

Heschel, *The Interior Castle*, by St. Teresa of Avila, *The Candle of Vision*, by George W. Russell, *The Gospel of Thomas*, by Marvin Meyer, *The Birth of Tragedy*, by Nietzsche, *The Decent of Man*, by Darwin, *The Seven Story Mountain*, by Thomas Merton, *Yi Jing – I Ching, the Book of Changes, Lectures by Lao Nai-hsuan*, translated into German by Richard Wilhelm and rendered into English by Cary F. Baynes, *Imitation of Christ*, by Thomas a Kempis, *Ethics*, by Dietrich Bonhoeffer, and *Christ and Culture*, By H. Ricard Niebuhr. There were more . . .

Mystery surrounded many of these teachings and paths. I only grasped a fraction of what I read. Many of the books were beyond my comprehension level; vague, sometimes contradictory and not easily applied. Woven into most were spiritual truths, unusual rituals with a smattering of suggestions. This collection of resources turned out to be a maze of possibilities pulling in different directions. It was weird. I'd get interested in one and quickly find it wasn't a good match.

Meditation, concentration and prayer were what I decided on. The goal was to attain the ability to live above the mundane, get rid of anger and have some peace of mind and heart. Purity and enlightenment was a lofty distant goal. I knew it was not going to be easy achieving this—as my sin-nature was strong.

The path of Hinduism as taught by Paramahansa Yogananda seemed to be the most understandable and devotionally inspiring path. Having read *Autobiography of a Yogi*, by Yogananda—I ordered a correspondence course entitled "Christ Consciousness" from Self Realization Fellowship and completed it. The discipline of meditation sitting on a folded blanket on my cell floor for 2-3 hours a day became a routine. Organically I became part of a small meditation band of 6 inmates. Two were well-connected gang bangers. One had been part of the Weathermen on the streets. The remaining three of us were nondescript seekers of truth. We hung out in the yard together and watched each other's backs.

Two and a half years into my sentence at Lompoc I was notified I could be expecting parole soon. Deciding where to live and obtaining employment was part of the plan. I secured both, and on the day of release offered up one of the most sincere prayers of my life, "Please God, help me to never be locked up again!"

A year or so had passed since this event. Luther's invite to San Francisco was an unexpected opportunity for change.

Back to San Fran

I continued working at the Straight Theater part-time and began checking into additional work. I applied to drive a city bus in SF, but found navigating a large bus in the hilly terrain of SF was not in my gift-set.

One day while returning to my flat in the Fillmore District, I met an older Black man who was headed down the main stairs to the basement of the building. He introduced himself as Mr. Davis. He told me he and his wife occupied a basement apartment near the boiler room. His job was building maintenance, keeping the furnace fired-up and fixing other things that broke. Over the course of the next month we became friends and he invited me to visit and share food with he and his wife. He and the Mrs. were the friendliest people I'd met in the city so far.

Walking into their tiny basement apartment was a cultural eye opener. The kitchen doubled for a living room 10x10 ft. in size with a small bedroom closet at the far end. That was it. The dining table took up most of their living space with two small basement windows. I can still hear Ma Davis say, "Come on in Mr. David, we need to puts some meat on your bones! How's ya doing. Now sits down right here and tell me everything. Now, don't be tellin me you ain't got some stories to tell. I wants to hear it all. I don't get out much." They knew I practiced meditation, studied eastern religions—but accepted me. It was awkward when they treated me as their son, or as some kind of royalty when I visited.

Looking around their sparse apartment, they had no extras, yet they were sharing their food out of their poverty. I was humbled and grateful at the same time. They were genuine in their love and interest in a southern California white-boy.

Without exception they bowed their heads and prayed before every meal. Their prayers were from the heart, something akin to this. "Dear Lord, we thank you today for every bountiful gift you have given to us in this life. For food and drink, for strength and Your mercy which is new with the rising of the sun. We lift ourselves before you, as we do David. Help us to see You for who You are. And thank you for the blood of Jesus Christ, shed to wash away every one of our sins! In the darkness and in the daylight keep us from the Evil One, let Your strong and mighty arm protect us in our comings and goings. Dear Lord receive our Thanksgiving for these Thy gifts in Jesus Christ's Holy Name. Amen."

Prayer was a sacred holy thing. I didn't know much about their style of prayer but knew they were sincere. I was still trying to figure out who to pray to and what to believe. Living in the Filmore among mostly African Americans was a contrast to the hippie Haight District several miles up the road. I spent equal time in both neighborhoods.

A gnawing unrest was in the air, even amidst the hopefulness in the Haight. Unresolved social issues loomed huge in the minds and hearts of many Americans. Individually and corporately the US had big questions, authentic pain and firm opposing opinions.

A Time of Questioning

Author's note: Political partisanship divisions have been the source of crippling ineffectiveness in national government passing laws and making wise decisions to benefit all Americans. Both Republicans and Democrats have a long history of political and social sins. This section is not intended to side with any political party. I write as an Independent. In every historical season of events there is plenty of blame to go around. Nobody's right, when everybody's wrong sometimes!

People were asking, "Is our country and world headed in the right direction? Am I?" Unrest was as real as an infected tooth, with pain increasing over the heated clashes of the 1960s. A throbbing of disillusionment, anger, distrust and unanswered questions was pushing large numbers of the populace to seek answers and relief. Protests and marches were regularly met with police or government violent reactions. An atmosphere of confrontation and anger was galvanizing both sides. Somewhere in the middle there were rumblings of a more peaceful middle ground.

People were asking lots of questions: "Should we be involved in the War in Vietnam? Is the US government telling us the whole truth? Are we being guided wisely from the heart of the constitution, or morphing into a police-state? Have we drifted from being a democratic society? Aren't we granted the constitutional right to peacefully protest against things we know are wrong for our personal or national well-being without being beaten, tear-gassed, or jailed? Can those who are guiding us be trusted? Who was responsible for President JF Kennedy's death? What should we do if our conscience doesn't support the direction our national leaders are taking? How do we voice our concerns? Why is alcohol legal and pot illegal?"

"Why aren't deeds of violence perpetrated by law enforcement against minorities and the poor brought to trial more often in our courts of law? Why are the rich and powerful given special treatment when it comes to breaking the law? Why shouldn't we opt out of the system if it's going in the wrong direction? Have our leaders lost their conscience about right and wrong—justice and equality? Are my parents' values, what I want to follow? Where is the truth in this world? What can I believe in and who can I trust?"

These and more questions were being asked both silently and publicly.

Where's USA Loyalty?

Other parts of the population had different questions or statements of conviction: "What is the problem with these protestors? Don't they see it's un-American and illegal to challenge the government in this way? They're just a bunch of trouble making communists! They're stirred up by radicals planted here from Russia! You'd think the niggers in the south would know their place and be thankful for what they got! Do you really think blacks are equal to whites? You got to be kidding!!"

"Whoever heard of kids not being interested in bettering themselves and gaining more possessions? So what if our troops are being killed in Vietnam? War makes men out of boys! We've always fought for what we got. And, as for those long-hair hippies, they're just a bunch of draft-card burning fagot cowards—a dishonor to our country! What's the matter with this world? What we oughta do is lock 'em all up, and let 'em rot! It's outrageous, the disrespect all these low-lifes are showing! Who do they think they are?!!"

Red-Neck bigotry and prejudice was not alone, with both Republicans and Democrat conservatives holding similar sentiments—unable to hear or consider populace concerns.

A less extreme and tempered response toward protestors and hippies might sound like this: "They're confused and don't realize how wonderful our country is. They've never seen how bad it is in other parts of the world. They're just young, unable to grasp the reasons our country has to be involved in wars. The rights of the poor and minorities are not as bad as people make it sound. Blacks and other minorities should stop expecting to be given everything on a platter. People on welfare need to get their butts back to work!"

Problems Everywhere—Solutions Elusive

This is only a smattering of comments and questions that were bouncing around in the minds and hearts of those of us who lived in the 1960s. The past and present in American history was a mix of what was good and decent, and that which was bad and crippling. Facing and turning from our less than humane past was a populace goal. But, many wondered, "Had America regressed to being cruel, harsh, intolerant, bigots, prejudiced, unjust, liars, murderers, haters and hypocrites—locked into a stubborn denial of these faults?" The truth is, we're all guilty of something!

In spite of this, some Americans still looked down on fellow citizens as second-class. Jews, African Americans, Hispanics, Japanese, Native Americans and other minorities were seen as inferior. Vietnam War or Civil-Rights protesters and hippies were labeled, targeted and suspected of being less than true Americans. This type of social branding, psychological rejection and shunning of non-whites or protestors of all colors was troubling.

Protestors were often jailed in peaceful demonstrations, resulting in the loss of jobs. Sympathizers of those beaten at peaceful protests were lumped in as agitators and anti-American. In a world minus cell-phone cameras, personal computers, the Internet, email and 24/7 television—the absence of accountability seemed more pronounced. Business owners could fire a person without cause. *Women and minorities were not paid equal wages. Local governments could deny African Americans voting rights, a place to sit, or eat. "Whites Only," "No Niggers," or "Hippies Not Welcome" signs could be posted without consequences.* [See Chapter 31 Photo Scrapbook for images of the times]

Law enforcement could look the other way, or be guilty of hate-crimes with no fear of prosecution. If a crime was committed by a prominent or wealthy white person in the south, it might be overlooked entirely.

Like today, local and national government politicians could boycott passing needed laws for political party reasons, regardless of their crucial and intrinsic value for the betterment of the nation. Sound familiar?!

Un-American to Question?

Belief in "True Liberty and Justice for all" and raising ethical and conscience questions is considered off-limits by die-hard loyalists who believe we should support government policies 100% without questioning. A worrisome mind-set!

President John F. Kennedy was a bright spot that had been snuffed-out too soon! Important work needed to be done! Who will stand for the greater good of our country? Martin Luther King Jr. and his team were attempting to be that voice—against stiff and violent opposition. Senator Robert Kennedy rallied on behalf of common people who were being exploited. Each of these men's voices and sphere of influence were sadly silenced by an assassin's bullet.

In the minds of concerned Americans, any government was capable of going down a destructive road and dragging the majority of the population with it. Hitler's Third Reich in Germany was a recent and glaring reminder of what blind loyalty could do to wreak havoc on a nation and the world at large. The hugeness of the topic of "human and civil rights for all" regardless of ethnicity, gender, or social status was confronting societies across the globe.

America had a lot of work to do in nurturing shared-wealth, letting minorities into business, government, white churches, schools, neighborhoods and their hearts. Embedded into the internal battle for the soul of a diverse nation—was the experimental side of young and old looking for solutions and a different emphasis in USA society.

As a participant in the generation of the 1960s, I recall how huge the issue of *Trust* was. *Many citizens were convinced we were being lied to by the government.* We wondered, "Is government representing the will of the American public? Or, have elected officials become two toxic parties of Republicans and Democrats embroiled in such bitter fights between each other that they're no longer able to accomplish governmental work for the good of the American people?

Have elected officials become blinded to their omissions of failing to solve critical problems and pass crucial and wise laws? Have they succumbed to the pressures of special interest groups? Are these interests so power and greed driven—they are unable to see the 'dark future' they have launched with an intrinsic myopic short-sightedness focused on financial gain, or partisanship?

Does government fail to understand that repressive violence against the public in reaction to peaceful protests and marches is never acceptable?

Jan Rose Kasmir appeals to American National Guard to consider Peace   Washington, DC 1967

The 1960s USA government was in trouble. The ruts and sin of racism was deep. Old ways of making a fortune on the backs of minorities and the powerless was running its course. All workers, including women, needed and deserved fair wages. In the 60s, United Farm Workers, led by Cesar Chavez in California, represented the struggle to obtain fair wages and adequate housing for migrant workers which became a bitter and long battle against the rich and powerful farm barons.

Social battles like this are rekindled by those who care, have a vision and put themselves in the shoes of those who suffer, desiring to be treated and compensated fairly for honest and hard work. People are not beasts of burden to be exploited!

The difficult struggle for social change was and is not, easily won. Through great sacrifice, injury and death, society may change, if leaders of any nation will acknowledge and work toward finding a remedy to ease the pain and suffering of its people. Only by yielding to a change of heart and conscience by actions that demonstrate it must be so—will a nation heal, be one and be healthy.   — Anonymous

2

San Francisco Dreaming

Rise of a Counter-Culture

The social shift and unifying goals that characterized the 1960s counter-culture were non-conformity, freedom to follow one's conscience, ecological awareness, natural childbirth, a search for higher consciousness and harmony with nature. Other unifying values were shared resources, eating healthier, vegetarianism, communal living, artistic and music experimentation and an aversion to materialism. Socially and politically, the counter-culture was firmly against the war in Vietnam, human and civil rights abuses, the absence of freedom of speech, and supported the right to demonstrate and protest when all else failed. For some, there was strong support for the 'sexual revolution' of non-binding sex. In addition to alcohol the preferred drugs of choice were marijuana, hashish, LSD (acid), Peyote buttons (magic mushrooms) or mescaline (a derivative of peyote).

Most hippies didn't buy into the entire counter-culture package, choosing only what they felt comfortable with. Many hippies were married and abstained from illicit-sex. Some distanced themselves from all drug and alcohol use, in favor of a natural high through exercise or meditation. Others abstained altogether from sex, drugs and eating meat in search of spiritual truth, enlightenment, or God. Though small in number, seekers of truth were visible and respected within the larger hippie culture.

Spiritual figures like Jesus Christ, Buddha, St. Francis, Gandhi, Martin Luther King Jr., gurus and other religious leaders were held in high esteem by many in the counter-culture. Poets, philosophers and various authors were also looked up to. These communicators confirmed or encouraged experimenting with different values and practices. They challenged hippies to consider doing something adventurous.

Authors widely read were, Jack Kerouac, *The Dharma Bums* and *On the Road*, "Howl" and other poems by Allan Ginsberg, the "Desiderata", a poem by Max Ehrmann, *Walden*, a memoir by Henry David Thoreau, *Another Roadside Attraction*, by Tom Robbins, *Been Down So Long It Looks Like Up to Me*, autobiography by Richard Fariña, and *The Drifters*, by James Michener. Adding to this list was *Psychedelic Prayers,* by Timothy Leary, *The Book - On the Taboo Against Knowing Who You Are*, by Alan Watts, and a smattering of books on world religions. Rock bands and solo artists were also a big deal to devoted groupies.

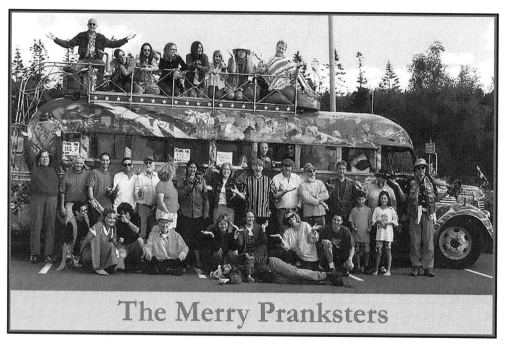

The Merry Pranksters

As early as 1964, author Ken Kesey who penned *One Flew Over the Cuckoo's Nest,* and a group of friends called the Merry Pranksters took a lengthy road-trip across the US in a colorfully painted school bus. Kesey had participated in CIA-sponsored LSD trials while a student at Stanford. Ironic! The humorous take was, "LSD was so widely used by CIA operatives, they became covert hippies." "Who'd thunk" the CIA was one of the first to conduct LSD experiments? The CIA's counterpart was other government agencies and various psychological testing which had been conducted since the mid 1940s.

Kesey and friends decided to make LSD available to others through a series of Electric Kool-Aid—Acid Tests, which were musical and multi-media events where those present were given a dose of LSD. Kesey believed psychedelics had the potential to transform society if a sufficient percentage of the populace had the psychedelic experience. He thought this could usher in beneficial social and political change. Timothy Leary had a similar vision. *LSD remained legal until the fall of 1966.*

The new Counter-Culture was mostly organic. Initial figures like Kesey, Leary, Ginsberg and others faded as new songwriters, bands and artists took their place. As "WWII war babies" we were ready to bring our own ideas, energy, music, art, writing and gifts to bear. Idealism was strong.

Who's Influencing?

When our kids go out to play, hang with friends, date, go off to university, or move away from home, influence plays a huge role in what happens next. Surely they will follow the norms of society, or maybe not?

The counter-culture pushed back against societal pressure to adhere to a materialistic lifestyle. Submission to dictated norms was met with resistance. Too many issues were on the table. Naive trust in the status quo had run its course and the blinders were off. Government corruption, lies, secrecy, contradictions and hypocrisy was in plain view.

January 1967 Human Be-In— Golden Gate Park, San Francisco

An estimated 30,000 showed up at the Polo Field on the south side of Golden Gate Park for a Gathering of the Tribes—Human Be-In on January 14, 1967. A variety of posters were designed to promote the event. San Francisco's underground newspaper, *The Oracle,* did its part; the word got out and a growing counter-culture showed up in droves.

Artist Michael Bowen, friend Allan Cohen and Allan Ginsberg were key organizers. The LSD Guru Timothy Leary set the tone for the event with his quote, "Turn-on, Tune-in and Drop-out." Underground chemist Owsley Stanley provided massive doses of LSD for the gathering. Allan Ginsberg and others spoke. Bands like Jefferson Airplane, The Grateful Dead, Big Brother and the Holding Company, Quicksilver Messenger Service and others contributed the music.

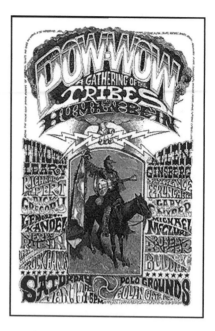

Berkeley's militant radicals opposed to the Vietnam War policies and the government intermingled with Haight-Ashbury

hippies at this event. Flower power hippies were not interested in a radical agenda, choosing peaceful war protests.

When this January Be-In was in motion, it felt like an invasion of enormous proportions in and around the Haight and in Golden Gate Park. There were a lot of people and drugs! I wondered what would happen next.

Social Activism

As events, protests, marches and rallies were planned and advertised, no one knew how many would show up. Activism through sacrifice of time, energy and money was prevalent in the 1960's. This was reflected in growing numbers of participants in causes that mattered. People were thinking and questioning. Bright and smart university students, hopeful youth and common citizens were being impacted, allowing a social conscience to be formed, as individuals took a stand for what they believed.

People were engaging in issues beyond the big "I" of personal and family survival. Cultural goals to improve our nation and world and make it a better place for everyone were the ideals that were being pursued. Voices like Mario Savio, Jerry Rubin, Abby Hoffman, SDS 'Students for a Democratic Society' activists Tom Hayden and author C. Wright Mills, who penned *The Power Elite* helped spawn and fuel a nationwide student movement for change. The Vietnam War was central in uniting students who wanted a voice in governmental war policies.

San Fran April 15, 1967
Spring Mobilization to End the Vietnam War

As the Vietnam War dragged on, body-bags of young American soldiers were being shipped home regularly.

This and massive Vietnamese civilian deaths was taking its toll on the conscience of America's populace. There were more questions than answers. The USA government was intentionally withholding accurate war information from the American people. The truth came out first in trickles and then in torrents. Revelations of US bombings in Cambodia and leaked information regarding the North and South Vietnam campaigns and increased American casualties fueled war protests.

Protest momentum grew from hundreds of participants to multiple thousands. Protest organizers promoted peaceful marches at bon-fires, in stadium venues, at free speech platforms on university campuses and sought media coverage to gain a national hearing. San Francisco was a stronghold of Anti-War protestors, hosting many anti-war marches. All across the land, American

citizens from all walks of life were united in asking the US government to stop the war.

I participated in the April 15, 1967 Peace March that went up Haight Street winding its way to Kezar Stadium in Golden Gate Park. 100,000 peaceful marchers made the trek from downtown's 2nd Street to the stadium. During the event I witnessed police singling out individuals and hitting them with night-sticks without cause.

Hippies and Blacks were targeted, though marchers represented a broad cross-section of society. Brutality witnessed or caught on camera, caused growing concern and embarrassment to local law enforcement and the American government as a whole. If we'd have had cell-phone cameras the public outcry would have been multiplied monumentally. Our home country of the 'free and the brave' wasn't as free as many Americans thought! Unprovoked police attacks on innocent citizens that made it to the national news outraged US citizens. [See Vietnam War facts at end of this chapter.]

Freedom Marchers

Police & National Guard brutality toward Civil Rights 'Freedom Marchers' and Anti-War demonstrators with attack dogs, fire hoses, night-sticks, tear gas, and bayonets became an epidemic. Arrests followed to intimidate protesters and their supporters.

In the picture to the right a number of Ullman High School students were bitten by police dogs on May 3, 1963, in downtown Birmingham

Alabama. The students remained passive to this police-inspired brutality.

For those sitting on the fence regarding the war, civil rights, women's rights, voting rights, fair wages, police and national guard brutality at peaceful demonstrations—a national conscience was being pricked. "We the People" was not being honored.

East Coast Be-In

On March 26, 1967 New York actors, artists, dancers, teachers, hippies and interested citizens came to Sheep Meadow in Central Park for their first "Be-In." Some 10,000 participated in the event, which would be a precursor to much larger gatherings and more anti-war demonstration rallies in the days to come.

Migration to San Francisco

When John Phillips of the Mamas and Papas penned the tune "San Francisco," sung by Scott McKenzie, released on May 13th 1967 a spark was ignited. The tune soared to number 4 in American charts and number 1 in Great Britain.

To kick off the Summer of Love, Radio KFRC sponsored the Fantasy Fair and Magic Mountain Music Festival on June 10-11. The entry fee was $2. All proceeds went to Hunter's Point Child Care Center in San Francisco. The festival was held in the 4000 seat amphitheater and surrounding woods on the high south face of Mt. Tamalpais in Marin County. 25-plus artists performed over a two-day period, many of whom were regulars at the Filmore and Avalon Ballroom. An estimated 35,000-plus attended. This music festival placed Psychedelic Rock front and center and is considered to be the first multi act outdoor Rock Festival on planet earth. Unlike many Rock and Pop Festivals that would follow—the entire amphitheater and wooded areas that were used by concert goers, were left just as they found them. All rubbish and trash was placed in or by dumpsters if full. Transportation from Mill Valley and the Marin County Civic Center was provided by Trans-Love Bus Lines.

A month later McKenzie sang "San Francisco" during a Mamas and Papas set at the Monterey Pop Festival of June 17–19 with over 50,000 in attendance. The popularity of this tune alongside other media and underground sources aided in promoting the 1967 Summer of Love to be held in San Francisco.

I remember the buzz in the air. "Thousands will be coming to San Francisco; it's going to be massive." Voices quickly weighed in on the positive or negative effects a mass pilgrimage to San Francisco might have. Some were sure such a gathering would ripple outward to the whole nation and beyond. Others felt it would be a disaster. Regardless of opinions—interest in being a part of a San Fran Summer of Love was growing. News of an upcoming SOL was in the national media. The invitation was filtering out over the air waves in song, in print and by word of mouth. Students from all over were eager for school to be over so they could make the trek to San Francisco's Haight-Ashbury.

The beat generation wore dark colors and guys grew goatees, coining the name "hip." From "hip" to "hippies" the transition and contrast had been made and it was striking. The beat generation kept a low profile, while hippies aka "flower children" were often outlandish, wearing unusual or bright clothing that expressed individuality. Non-conventional appearance was a statement of freedom and hippie identity in contrast to the straight mainstream segment of society that paid ridiculous prices to look "in fashion." Most hippie clothing was purchased at garage or rummage sales, flea markets or secondhand stores and modified. Brightly colored, ragged, rough, or tie-dyed clothes along with beads, jewelry and sandals or barefoot was "right on." Guys wore their hair long and typically wore beards and mustaches while the women wore little or no makeup—often bra-less. Feathers, ankle bells, outrageous hats and an assortment of unique attire including pioneer and Native American clothing were popular.

Infamous Streets—Haight & Ashbury

The music, friendly atmosphere, free concerts in the park and hundreds and then thousands of people flocking to the streets of San Francisco seemed to be changing the complexion of the city in positive ways. People in the Haight were friendly, less money driven, seeking answers; open to experience, truth and God. Many were willing to share what they owned. This was the hopeful side of a new counter-culture, a rebirth of sorts—a dream of how we were meant to live. New slogans of "Peace, Love and Brotherhood" accompanied those in search of this freedom. The duration of the positive aspects of the Hippie culture would be tested.

For the Greater Good— San Fran Artists, Dreamers & Workers

Bob Dylan's lyrics, 'The Times They Are A-Changin' (1964) summed up the mid to late 1960's. The music, dress, beliefs and attitudes about life, war and peace were being reshaped outside the traditional box. New artists, dreamers and workers were rising to do their part. Many counter-culture hippies alongside a growing number in mainstream society were unified in advocating for freedom of speech, equal and human rights, women's rights and the right for peaceful marches and protests. A growing number had a heart to improve the world by resisting a self-centered and selfish agenda. In spite of wide-spread media and government criticism toward the dreamers, we believed in our causes. Some efforts would succeed, others would fail.

Corrupt politicians would eventually be held accountable, racist violence would eventually be prosecuted, the war in Vietnam would finally end, and civil, human and women's rights issues would get a serious hearing. Freedom of speech and the right to protest governmental or law enforcement corruption and violence would remain an ongoing battle.

The Counsel for the Summer of Love

With the handwriting on the wall, a collection of groups and concerned individuals came together for the purpose of establishing a better infrastructure to accommodate a large influx of visitors that would be arriving in San Francisco for the Summer of Love.

The Counsel for the Summer of Love formed in early 1967 was a planning and action motivated group of concerned hippies, citizens, church leaders and local organizations—who pooled their energy, resources and influence to get ahead of a population explosion crisis. The SOL council would focus on action-based practical solutions with the aim of avoiding a meltdown of the Haight-District's infrastructure with an anticipated 50 thousand visitors heading our way in a few short months.

Chet Helms was the pivotal individual who brought together the diverse groups who would form the council for the SOL. Helms' other work was promoting concerts at the Fillmore Auditorium on alternating

weekends with Bill Graham until obtaining the 'Avalon Ballroom' dance hall on Sutter St. He was also an integral part of Family Dog cooperative, whose mission was to recruit local artists to design posters and conduct art workshops, and dance and drama troops to do street theater all over San Francisco.

Chet Helms

In addition, Helms was good friends with the Grateful Dead, Quick Silver Messenger Service and Big Brother and Holding Company. He was the one who made the match by inviting student-friend Janis Joplin who he'd known in Texas to come to San Fran and become the lead singer for the Big Brother. This and other shared musical ventures brought groups together. Many attribute the success of a number of SF bands including Jefferson Airplane to Helms inclusion and support.

Hamilton United Methodist Church & All Saints Episcopal Church and the SOL Council Team

Hamilton Methodist Church and All Saints Episcopal, both on Waller Street hosted early SOL meetings and lent their facilities for baking and food preparation. Each SOL participating group was gifted in their own way. The participants were the Diggers, the Oracle newspaper, the Straight Theater, the Family Dog, The Zen Center, a handful of local individuals and some staff members from Hamilton Methodist and All Saints Episcopal. My invite came via Luther Greene of the Straight Theater and a buddy from the Zen Center. Our initial meetings were 'think-tank' sessions.

Our goals were to enlist and coordinate volunteers, and to develop services and resources to meet specific anticipated needs. Food, water, safe housing, toilet and shower facilities, medical care and emergency crisis intervention were high priorities. The council would also provide event coordination for street theatre troops, dance teams, art shows, music performers and larger concerts in and around the Haight-Ashbury District and Golden Gate Park.

San Francisco's Underground Newspaper the 'Oracle' wrote:

> Americans loving love and hoping for peace and seeking wisdom and guidance have turned toward the Haight-Ashbury and are journeying here. Our best efforts have so far failed to gather civic support and material resources for the many thousands expected.
>
> If you want to journey to San Francisco you should bring in addition to flowers and bananas: 1) Money for rents and food 2) Sleeping bags, rucksacks, or backpacks 3) Extra food; brown rice and soy sauce (100 lb. bags of rice at mills costs $12.) 4) Camping equipment for living in wilderness and national parks 5) Warm clothing for very cold foggy San Francisco summer climate and 6) Proper identification. (The San Francisco Oracle, Vol. 1, Issue 8, p. 32 1967)

Life in the Haight

The Haight was an interesting and fascinating place to live. I'd made the move from the Fillmore district to Waller Street, a block south of Haight Street and was settled into a small room. I liked the Haight. The creative innovative artistic energy in San Francisco was something you could feel.

Incoming residents were primarily "Love and Peace—Flower Power" enthusiasts.

I enjoyed working on the Straight Theater part time—being involved in readying the theater to be functional again. The finishing touches of lights, sound, faux and mural painting were in progress.

The Haight had a long history of providing housing for Irish immigrants in years gone by. In the present, many properties in the Haight and nearby San Fran districts were in a renaissance of restoration. Buildings, adjoining row-flats and Victorian homes were being repainted using a vivid multi-color palette. Inside, floors, walls and ceilings were being restored to their former glory. The end results were remarkable!

Hoyt - Chanting 1966

Renovated storefront shops were also opening on Haight Street and adjoining side-streets with brightly colored signs and murals. The Free Clinic, Huckleberry House, The Switchboard, Family Dog Health Clinic and Free Store were up and running. These and other neighborhood projects and services gave a hopeful boost to our district's readiness for the upcoming Summer of Love. The Straight Theater was on schedule to open soon.

While at an SOL meetings I met a girl my age who taught Sunday school at Hamilton Methodist and developed a friendship with her and her family. She was beautiful with long blonde waist-length hair. Visiting them was a lift, and although my way of searching for God was strange—they accepted me.

At the top of my list of likes about the Haight District was Golden Gate Park, several blocks from my digs. Walking in this park was addictive in a good way. It's huge, peaceful and an amazing place to commune with nature, breathe in fresh air and pray. I also liked the diversity of people who'd moved to the Haight. Being a regular in the neighborhood I'd made a handful of casual acquaintances who knew me and said hey when we ran into each other. It seemed like a good fit.

The weekends were beginning to get busier with the hype about the SOL drawing nearer. Curiosity nudged an influx of weekend visitors to have a look-see. It was understandable but annoying. Week-enders cruising the Haight in their cars would cause standstill traffic jams as they gawked or yelled weird things. Some were supportive, others were rednecks and hippie-haters who'd concluded we were the scum of the earth!

Movers and Shakers

The co-operative of groups that comprised the Council for the SOL played an important role in planning ahead, securing volunteers and providing tangible services as the throngs of people began arriving. Many individuals representing these groups and the volunteers they attracted for the most part did so selflessly out of compassion for others. The core-groups were unique with their own vision and skills.

The Family Dog was a cooperative of orga-nizers, artists, printers and promoters for bay area concerts and major events. They were front and center in the Summer of Love planning and coordination. Chet Helms lent his many relational ties to nurture this artistic co-op. Almost every concert poster, flyer, or postcard bore their logo for Bay Area events—a tag or trade mark of psychedelic event authenticity.

The Diggers, an Improvisation Theater Team" founded by RC Davis, had morphed into a community. Their stage was the streets and parks of the Haight-Ashbury, and later the whole city of San Francisco. Part of their vision embraced the dream of a society free of owning private land. During the mid-to-late 1960s, the San Francisco Diggers opened a Free Store, Free Bakery and Free Medical Clinic. They launched the popular free Digger Bread using whole and wheat grains cooked in one and two pound coffee cans, distributed at the Free Bakery. They also provided an assortment of other free foods at their store, transportation, temporary housing, organized free music concerts and art-showings to support political art. The

A 'Digger' giving sandwiches

Diggers organized an additional means of aiding those in need by securing a commitment from San Fran merchants and rock bands to contributed 1% of their profits to the Free City Bank Fund, which supported Free Food Distribution in the city. The Diggers offered the full range of practical services for the SOL.

Haight Ashbury Free Clinic: As a freshly minted physician in the mid-1960s San Francisco, Dr. David E. Smith saw the psychedelic scene up close. With so many young people flooding the city to "tune in, turn on and drop out," he saw a healthcare need he couldn't ignore. In the summer

of 1967, he started the Haight Ashbury Free Clinic, providing free medical care largely funded by Grateful Dead benefit concerts and the clinic's neighbors.

The clinic was small and informal. Guiding principles for HAFC included an emphasis on non-judgmental, decentralized care, often delivered by volunteers in consultation with professionals. Distrust of traditional healthcare was high due to judgmental attitudes and shaming of clients with drug abuse or venereal disease problems. In most instances they were turned away. The Haight Ashbury Free Clinic served as an alternative type of healthcare that was more respectful and responsive to patient needs. This model would grow to over 500 free clinics nationwide logging over half a million patient visits.

Huckleberry House opened on June 18, 1967 in honor of Huck Finn. It offered a 24/7 crisis service and emergency shelter for high-risk youth

between the ages of 11 and 17. The Regional Young Adult Project hired two co-directors, **Rev. E. Larry Beggs and Barbara Brachman** to develop and implement the new runaway shelter project.

During its first three months of operation, Huckleberry for Runaways served a total of 211 youth in crisis, exceeding original expectations. By the end of its first full year of operation, 664 runaways had been served—with two-thirds hailing from outside the Bay Area. Their advertised description read, "We provide immediate runaway assistance—housing and protection."

Huckleberry House
1292 Page St. S.F. CA

The Huckleberry House program goals were to alleviate the problems that runaways and homeless youth faced on the streets by providing 24-hour crisis intervention. The services offered were: safe housing, food, clothing, resolution counseling, reuniting youth with their family if possible, and empowering youth to identify healthy lifestyle alternatives and develop positive decision-making. Huck House was an immediate alternative to incarceration. Though the San Fran Police disliked hippies, they knew runaways would receive superior care to that of the overcrowded Juvenile Hall County programs—so they used this resource. Like the Haight Free Clinic, Huckleberry House would grow and expand, destined to be a source of humanitarian compassion to aid young runaways for many years to come.

The Switchboard located at 1830 Fell Street in the Haight-Ashbury district was the vision of Al Rinker. The Switchboard offered a hot-line open evenings from 7-10 pm Mon.-Thurs. Advertising for the magazine or radio said, "We have case workers, social workers and counselors on hand to help. If you have problems securing your welfare, or similar needs, call us. We provide emergency resource connections based on availability and help for runaways. Call the Switchboard!" The Switchboard also launched *It's Happening Now*, an inexpensive small magazine which gave local writers a venue of expression—while directing those in need to the services of the Switchboard and other Summer of Love cooperatives.

The Straight Theater located at 1702 Haight Street at Cole Street had previously been a movie theater, later vaudeville, followed by other tenants, until it was stripped of its copper wiring, becoming useless. During its early years it was called the Haight Theater. In 1966 a handful of friends and investors took on the job of its restoration, renaming it the Straight Theater.

Gradually the building was brought up to code with new electrics, a refurbished stage and dance floor. On June 5, 1967 the theater reopened as a multipurpose

**The STRAIGHT THEATER on Haight Street - Summer of 1967
In the Haight-Ashbury near Golden Gate Park - San Francisco**

venue with a capacity of 1,500 for concerts. The Grateful Dead, Wildflower, Straight Theater Dancers, Lighting by Reginald, and a month later Quicksilver Messenger Service, Mount Rushmore, Salvation Army Banned and Mother Earth helped launch the theater as an SOL concert and theater venue. It was used for smaller local musical concerts, drama, poetry, dance, film, mixed media and community events.

My friend Luther Greene and other Straight Theater board members had accomplished their goal. They also remained invested in the Council for the SOL, hosting a number of community meetings to address SOL issues and problems as they unfolded.

Golden Gate Park

Dutch Windmill

Hosting the SOL in the Haight District of San Francisco would have likely been impossible without Golden Gate Park and it's entrance on the west end of Haight Street. The park was an incredible asset for events, concerts, and just hanging out in a nature setting. Hippie Hill became a scenic gathering-place during these days. Golden Gate Park, considered one of the nation's best urban parks, draws millions of visitors annually.

The park is 3 miles long with the Pacific Ocean bordering the west end. It is ½ mile wide and spans 1017 acres. It contains a museum, science academy, Japanese tea gardens, conservatory of flowers, botanical gardens, Strybing Arboretum, two windmills, several lakes, Kezar stadium, a polo field, a beach chalet and is beautifully planted with a wide variety of trees, shrubs, flowers and gardens. This resource, along with the rolling hills and beauty of Marin and Sonoma Counties to the north and their coastlines, and equally gorgeous coastline to the south meandering down to Santa Cruz, were all nearby gifts of nature for hippies to enjoy. With this peaceful backdrop surrounding us, an unanswered question loomed, "Could we live up to a better way of living without falling prey to our own vices, greed and hypocrisies?"

Generational Music Voices

Dylan, Hendrix, Janis Joplin, Donovan, the Grateful Dead, Jefferson Airplane, Big Brother and the Holding Company, Quicksilver Messenger Service, the Charlatans, Moby Grape, The Mamas and the Papas, Simon & Garfunkel, Cream, Pink Floyd, the Beatles, the Doors, Scott McKenzie,

JANIS JOPLIN

Bob Dylan

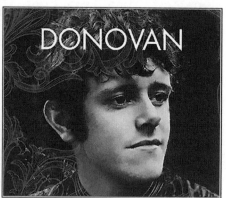

DONOVAN

GRATEFUL DEAD

JANIS JOPLIN & BIG BROTHER & HOLDING COMPANY

Joan Baez, 13th Floor Elevators, the Butterfield Blues Band and many more added their lyrics, music, dress and energy in support of the "love and peace generation."

Spiritual Buddies

I had two friends I hung with and shared meals as able. One was a Zen Buddhist who was an initiate at the San Fran Zen Center under Shunryu Suzuki Roshi, priest and abbot (Soto lineage). I visited the center on his request located on Page Street. It was ornate, spotless, with no furniture. A hardwood floor glistened from frequent use. Natural light came from windows on one side of the meditation room.

Zen Buddhism

In Zen there are sitting, walking and instructional gatherings. The word *Zen* is derived from the Sanskrit word *Dhyana* which means "meditation." Zen Buddhism is the practice of discovering enlightenment (*bodhi*) through meditation just as Siddharta Gautama, aka Buddha, is said to have attained.

Zen Buddhism teaches that all human beings have the Buddha-nature, or the potential to attain enlightenment within them, but the Buddha-nature has been clouded by ignorance. To overcome this ignorance, Zen rejects the study of scriptures, religious rites, devotional practices, and good works—in favor of meditation leading to a sudden breakthrough of insight and awareness of ultimate reality. A disciple's training in the Zen path is usually under the guidance of a Master aka Shífu, or Dai-Osho, or Zenji (founder of a school). The rules, called "Vinya" for Zen initiates, can be overwhelming. In Japanese Zen monasteries, senior monks watch over and correct novices non-stop. Monks arise long before sunrise for morning meditations. Rigid self-discipline follows throughout the day. Western Zen is said to be rigorous, but not to the extreme found in Zen monasteries in the East. The San Fran Zen Center is widely known for bridging the gap by welcoming lay participants, visitors and initiates—which is why I was allowed to visit.

Author's note: This following overview on Taoism is offered as a study of what may remain unknown about any spiritual path until researching its origins. Every seeker of Truth will benefit if you do something similar.

Taoism / Daoism

My other friend studied Taoism, aka Daoism. While camping on Mt. Tamal-pais in Marin County, CA, he relayed some of the basics. Taoism began in China around 600 BC through a spiritual teacher-sage named Lao Tzu aka Laozi, meaning old master. The 'Tao' is believed to be the eternal source behind everything that exists—the origin and law of all things in the universe. It is said to be Way-Path and Principle which holds the key to immortality. To follow Taoism is to enter into harmony with the universe by living simply, spontaneously and cultivating the Three Treasures: compassion, moderation and humility. Moral and ethical excellence and behaving in a completely natural, non-uncontrived way are virtues of honor in Taosim.

The principle of *'Action by Non-Action'* is equally essential. As water movement flows effortlessly, or planets revolve around the sun without struggle, or as trees grow without trying to grow—action through inaction is all around us. Taoism views life in an out-of-the-box way. The great sage Lao-Tzu teaches, "We turn clay to make a vessel; but it is in the space where there is nothing that the usefulness of the vessel depends. As we take advantage of what is, we should recognize the usefulness of what is not." I knew this was only the tip of the iceberg that lay beneath the surface of this teaching. I wondered if there was a downside to this path.

Hiking, resting, quiet-time and meditation consumed the remainder of our camping weekend, without further discussion on Taoism. Both of us were comfortable with silence. On a mountain surrounded by huge trees, an ocean and wildlife, it was peaceful; conducive to losing oneself in meditation and reflection. The absence of additional conversation was appropriate.

On returning to San Fran, curiosity nudged me to visit a library and read up on Taoism. My search for truth was still in progress and I wanted to know more. The founder of Taoism is said to have been an official record keeper and historian in the imperial archives of the eastern Zhou Dynasty which spanned 1046 to 256 BC. Sometime in the sixth century BC Laozi wrote the *Tao Te Ching* (*Daodejing, Dao De Jing*). In English the title is translated, *The Classic of the Way of Virtue* (some editions add *and the Power*), which is the first foundational text in Taoism. Laozi's spiritual lineage is believed to have been from ancient immortals. Laozi was a poet, historian, philosopher and spiritual sage. Copies of his writings have been excavated in a number of archaeological digs with the oldest dating back to the late 4th century BC.

Laozi's students were meticulous in recopying original documents and carrying forth his teachings. An early student named Zhuangzi interpreted and added to the original text outlining practical ways of weaving Taoist thought into everyday life. These two texts provide the philosophical foundation of Taoism. After Laozi and Zhuangzi, the literature of Taoism grew steadily and was compiled in form of a canon—called the *Daozang*, published in AD 748 by Emperor Tang Xuan-cong, who traced his ancestry to Laozi. The canon currently consists of around 1,400 newer texts that were collected by Taoist monks which attempt to bring together all of the teachings of Taoism, including all the commentaries and expositions of the various masters from the original teachings found in the *Tao Te Ching and Zhuang Zi.*

The Dark Side of Taoism gods

Taoism followers endeavor to live a simple life and integrate virtues in harmony with the universe. Digging deeper I learned Taoists worship and pray to a grouping of immortals called the Three Pure Ones. They are believed to be the highest of deities, along with Laozi "Ancestor of the Great Balance" and the "Heavenly Lord of the Great Oneness."

These are the highest of deity gods reverenced and prayed to. Under these higher gods is The Jade Emperor who rules the court over the lesser gods and spirits of the Taoist universe. These gods each hold an office with specific duties, such as the Three Divine Officials, responsible for pardoning sins, stopping disasters and bestowing blessings. A number of other gods are also in charge of natural phenomena; for example, the Father of Thunder and Mother of Lightning govern thunderstorms. Images or statues of these gods often adorn one section of the temple where Taoists can bow before them in veneration and prayer.

The number of additional lesser gods are many, like the god of happiness, good- luck, medicine, food, longevity, rain, wealth or homage and worship of ancestors. The ritual of food sacrifices to the spirits of the deceased, or any of these gods is widely practiced in Taoism. Priests frequently perform rituals and rites privately, in local temples, or during street festivals. Each ritual can take upwards of an hour or more to complete. These rituals contain incantations and prayers to the spirit world, fire sacrifices, and use of talisman objects said to contain magical and sacramental properties to provide benefits or protection for individuals or geographical provinces. In street parades lion and dragon dances are performed as Taoist priests invoke spirit mediums to embody the dancers who in a frenzied state may cut their flesh with knives in honor of the gods.

Every Taoist priest is mandated to have extensive training in exorcism to be able to kill ghosts, dispel illness and drive out evil spirits.

Taoism, Confucianism and Buddhism

Taoism and Confucianism arose side by side in China around 600 BC. They were joined by Buddhism a century or so later when it expanded into China's mainland from India. In China's dynasty history, one or more paths have been chosen as the religion of the country or state over the centuries.

For thousands of years these three spiritual paths have shared thought, beliefs and practices which have been passed back and forth. A resource accessed by adherents in each group is the *I-Ching* or *Book of Changes*—considered one of the oldest Chinese books in the world with origins thought to pre-date recorded history. Most agree the I-Ching promotes divination, fortune telling, ancient folk religion and Chinese philosophy. Sameness and

THE YEN-YANG SYMBOL
RELATED TO THE TAO

Confucianism

Life

Water

non-sameness exist in Taoism, Buddhism and Confucianism—each possessing intricate and multiple layers of beliefs and practices—some hidden, many overlapping. Complex rituals, personal striving, austerity and mysterious connections with the spirit world swim together.

Searching through the maze of religious thought in Taoism via immortals, mystical sages and multiple layers of lesser gods was eye opening. The practice of invoking spirit-mediums, contacting the dead and the expansive amount of gods reverenced or worshiped helped me decide against this path.

I remained uncertain of how far the sharing of beliefs and practices had intertwined between Taoism, Confucianism and Buddhism. How these three religions had melded together when one was chosen as the national religion in China was a complex question. I concluded it was dependent on regional application and emphasis through respected elder teachers, or enlightened (Bodhisattva) lead monks.

A Guru to Open a Temple in the Haight

One windy evening I headed down a side street, making my way to my flat. Noises of the city, colored posters on storefronts and walls lined the route. As I turned the corner, someone put a small flyer in my hand. To my surprise, it had a picture of a Swami from India, with a short story about him on the back. The flyer said he was setting up a Krishna Temple in our neighborhood. This could be worth looking into—a bona-fide Swami from India. Could he be part of the answer?

Swami A.C. Bhaktivedanta

It felt like I'd been in a searching mode forever; I was ready for some tangible spiritual direction. After years of looking on my own, I wondered how long it would take to get a break-through. Feeling impatient, I wondered what this Swami would be like. Would he be the real deal?

One afternoon I ran into a few of his followers. I listened as they sang their chants and talked with them afterwards. Their sincerity was compelling. On invitation I followed them back to the storefront being turned into a temple on Frederick Street. They seemed to be doing the right things, providing free meals for the needy

Swami A.C. Baktivedanta
Golden Gate Park Feb. 1967

and were pursuing God. The teaching was a type of Hinduism similar to what I'd practiced at Lompoc with a focus on chanting a mantra, rather than meditation. They considered the chant to be a springboard to entering into the presence of Krishna, i.e. God.

This Krishna group was intriguing, comprised of a handful of new devotees and a couple of US transplants from the NY temple. Visiting the temple, I hoped to connect with other seekers and compare notes. The first step was to attend the 7am worship gathering called Kirtan. It was a good discipline to get up early and start the day spiritually. A second Kirtan was held in the late afternoon which I also attended; food was provided at both.

The swami had been out of town, teaching at the NY temple. On his return, I was impressed. He dressed in light orange, was understandable, spoke good English and was extremely knowledgeable in the ancient teachings of the Hindu religion. At the end of each Kirtan he gave a teaching session on topics that pertained to the essence of the path he taught on achieving "Krishna consciousness" and took questions.

Entering a Krishna Temple prior to and during worship was like stepping into another world. In anticipation of Kirtan, disciples were feverishly fingering their large wooden red or blue beads and chanting the Hare Krishna mantra. As the worship began, the mantra would take on melodic form as a hand organ, cymbals and drums were added. I remember a young Jewish convert chanting his mantra and playing cymbals next to me. The intensity of his passion for chanting and then rising to dance spurred me on. Quickly the room would fill with incense as most devotees arose and danced into a frenzy until near exhaustion over the course of a 20-30 minute period. It was a spiritual natural high.

Gradually, the inside of the large storefront room on Fredrick Street was transformed into a close resemblance of a temple in India. Bright colorful pictures of Rama and Krishna (two Hindu lover-gods) were displayed on the walls. A tall altar was built with three large wooden statues called Juggernauts placed on a higher platform—representing various forms of God. Some devotees believed they symbolically embodied the Hindu trinity of Brahma, Vishnu and Shiva. Food and flowers were placed on this altar as an offering to these Hindu deities along with pictures of swami's spiritual teachers. It was a dramatic cultural shift for most new devotees who were born and raised in America.

Vietnam War Facts: The Vietnam War ran from 1954-1975. The countries involved were North and South Vietnam, Laos, Cambodia, the USA and Allied troops. The mid-range estimate of deaths in the larger war theater is 2,450,000. Among these deaths and casualties, 500,000 were South Vietnam civilians, many assassinated by the Viet Cong. Another 16,000 South Vietnamese, US and allied troops died in Viet Cong or Khmer Rouge Prisoner of War (POW) camps. Warring troops planted a large amount of land mines and bombs which continue to kill or maim civilians today. American deaths are estimated at 60,000 with an additional 155,000 who were wounded or disabled.

U.S. aircraft sprayed approximately 20 million gallons of herbicides over Vietnam, Cambodia and Laos from 1961 to 1971 to destroy leaves and food crops. AGENT ORANGE containing the poisonous chemical 'Dioxin' was the most commonly used. An estimated 2.8 million U.S. vets were exposed to this deadly chemical and 3.5 million Vietnamese people. The U.S. Department of Veteran Affairs has identified 13 deadly diseases and many cancers associated with exposure to Agent Orange. In addition, tens of thousands of individuals have suffered serious birth defects including missing and deformed limbs, cerebral palsy, spinal deterioration, and physical and mental disabilities. The debilitating affects of Agent Orange are now being passed to the third and fourth generation. Ongoing soil and river pollution continues to poison the regions food chain and thwart vegetation growth. [See chapter 31 pg. 684]

3

The Times They Are a Changin'

The City of San Francisco Refuses to Help

Volunteer service for the Summer of Love and involvement at the Krishna Temple kept me busy. The hard work of the SOL collaborative team was paying off with considerable preparedness in place. It amazed San Francisco residents how intentionally uninvolved San Fran City Hall and its many government departments had been. Their prejudice toward Vietnam War protestors, hippies and people of color had blinded them to an opportunity to step up and offer tangible assistance to help head off a social crisis and humanitarian need. The city's response to requests for help was, "We'll keep as many incoming Summer of Love visitors away as we can."

A Renewed Journey in Hindu Origins

The opportunity of having direct contact with a legitimate guru and spiritual master from India was alluring. My previous interest in Hinduism had been via a correspondence course from Self Realization Fellowship, founded by Swami Paramahansa Yogananda who was already deceased. His writings and lessons emphasized Kriya Yoga—a sacred spiritual path with origins said to date to millennia past.

Through meditation, Yogananda taught his followers how to deal with energy and consciousness in order to recharge the body, awaken the mind and experience the Divine. Yogananda traced his own spiritual awakening to his spiritual teacher and a succession of spiritual masters going back centuries. His legacy and teaching was being carried on by Sri Daya Mata, a female devotee, who had attained the mantle of spiritual master. She and others represented the next generation of leadership at Self Realization Fellowship.

This previous exposure to Hinduism was familiar territory when it came to considering Swami Bhaktivedanta and Krishna Consciousness.

Hinduism & Krishna Consciousness

There are three main Hindu gods; Brahma the Creator, Vishnu the Preserver, and Shiva the Destroyer. Brahma is not worshiped. Brahma is the personified form of an "indefinable and unknowable divine principle" called by Hindus "Brahman."

The symbol to the left represents Om, or Aum, the principal symbol of Hinduism. It is both a visual and an oral representation of Brahman-Creator God. This mark has another name, Pravana, which means "that by which God is effectively praised," and "that which is ever new." Some Hindus repeat the word Om in order to transcend their individual thoughts, aspiring to merge with God.

Vishnu is the preserver of order in the universe and is the most popular of Hindu gods. Krishna is believed to be the eighth Avatar of Vishnu. The term "Avatar" literally means "of divine descent" and refers to the manifestation of a Hindu deity on earth. It is similar to the Christian concept of incarnation, except an Avatar does not become human but simply appears in human form or some other mystical form during a particular historical event.

Avatars are said to appear in order to give guidance to humanity or to accomplish great deeds. Krishna's incarnation from Vishnu is depicted in paintings as a handsome young man playing a flute. He appears as a charioteer and advisor of Arjuna in the Bhagavad-Gita.

The name Krishna means all-attractive. Radha and Krishna are collectively known within Hinduism as the combination of both the feminine as well as the masculine aspects of God. Paintings of Radha and Krishna show a male and female deity side by side. It is believed the god Shree Krishna and Radha is that feeling of love which connects a living being to his creator. With Krishna, Radha is acknowledged as the supreme goddess, for it is said she controls Krishna. It's believed that Krishna enchants the world, but Radha enchants Him. Therefore she is the supreme goddess of all—Radha Krishna. Thus, the name on the Fredrick Street temple in San Francisco was called The Radha Krishna Temple. What I didn't know at that time was there are thousands of lesser gods under Vishnu and Shiva and their Avatars.

Swami Bhaktivedanta taught that by chanting and singing the divine name of Krishna, of direct decent from Vishnu, all would be set right in the universe and a devotee would become aligned with God over time. I would be remiss if I didn't at least mention the attributes of the other central god in the Hindu trinity, Shiva.

Shiva is thought to be the most important of gods—though extremely complex. Shiva may represent goodness, benevolence and serves as the "protector" but simultaneously is the one who can usher in destruction as the "destroyer" of all things. Paradoxically, Shiva is also associated with "creation." In Hinduism, the universe is thought to regenerate in cycles over the course of millions of years. Shiva destroys the universe at the end of each cycle which allows for a new creation. Shiva is the deity that is best aligned with the great "Ascetic"—all followers who abstain from all forms of indulgence and pleasure, concentrating on meditation as the vehicle to attain perfect peace and happiness. Shiva is the most important Hindu god for the Shaivism sect, the patron god of Yogis and Brahmins, and the protector of the Vedas and sacred texts.

Swami's emphasis on the Avatar Radha Krishna of decent from Vishnu was mysterious, profound and focused. The rarity of securing a guru in the flesh was the strongest drawing point for me.

Devotee Initiation

Settling into the temple felt good. Studying, chanting while maintaining the personal discipline of meditation helped me feel like I was making progress.

Over the course of a number of months a small group of us had been accepted for initiation into "Krishna Consciousness" by the Swami. The ceremony was scheduled to be integrated into an afternoon Kirtan service at the temple.

Swami A.C. Bhaktivedanta

Acceptance as a devotee by Swami A.C. Bhaktivedanta was huge! The initiation was conducted in an elaborate ceremony called Ritvik. At the center of the event was a five-foot wide by ten-inch high rounded thick metal pan—shaped like a wok. Swami carefully placed wood, kindling, food, bananas, flowers and other items inside the pan, chanting with Hindu words. When finished, he lit the fire and spent time chanting over each new devotee, marking them with ashes from the fire and giving each a new name. He gave me the name "Davikanandana" accompanied by personal comments to encourage and challenge me. This initiation bonded a devotee to his or her spiritual master and nurtured loyalty to lord Krishna and the Krishna Consciousness Movement. It was a great honor to be initiated by the Swami A.C. Bhaktivedanta Srila Prabhupada and we all felt gratitude and devotion to him.

He had come to the United States at age sixty-nine with only a few possessions to preach Krishna to the west. His teaching was sincere, convincing, and marked by many years of loyal devotion to Krishna. He'd already written a number of commentaries on Vaishnavas Scriptures and was currently working on the *Srimad-Bhagavatam* and a new translation of the Bhagavad-Gita. Swami was a scholar, teacher and devotional spiritual Master. He spoke a number of languages fluently, was sharp-witted and intellectually strong.

Swami's Teaching

He taught, "Human beings have forgotten their true relationship to Krishna, and their liberation lies in a return to Godhead through the grace of Krishna. Human beings can remove the obstacles to that grace by chanting the *Mahamantra*. It's not necesarry to understand it; its transcendental sound will have automatic results and raise one to a spiritual plane. It's also imperitive to engage in holy association. Associating with non-devotees will have a bad effect and result in an increase of sense gratification.

"One should also eat *prasadam* (food offered to Krishna). While preparing the food one should think only of Krishna. Eating the *prasadam* is a purifying act, equal to chanting the *Mahamantra*. It is crucial that one accept a bona-fide spiritual master who is in disciplic succession from Lord Krishna. One cannot return to Godhead without submitting to Krishna, and one can only approach Krishna through his representative."

Swami was that representative for us as devotees. I and other young devotees were amazed by his wisdom, knowledge and love of Krishna. We were in awe of this devotion. His regulations for disciples were strict which I didn't mind. There was to be no gambling. This included frivolous games or sports. The use of all forms of intoxicants or stimulants, including alcohol, drugs, tobacco, coffee and tea was prohibited. There were dietary prohibitions against eating meat, fish, or eggs. The diet was strictly vegetarian and consisted of food that had first been offered to Krishna. For the most part, all Krishna Consciousness converts willingly adhered.

San Francisco 1967 Summer of Love

San Francisco seemed to be the natural host for this hybrid experiment of a new counter culture. Golden Gate Park and the whole of the San Fran Bay Area stood in stark contrast to the coughing smog five hundred miles south in Los Angeles.

No one knew how many would come to San Francisco so the media poked fun calling it "The Invasion of the Flower Children." 1967s springbreak for college and university campuses brought hundreds of the earliest visitors to the Haight for a couple of days. Soon after, beginning in early May thousands began the trek to San Fran and they kept coming.

The atmosphere on the streets was charged with energy. Bell-bottom jeans, flowing dresses, and symbols of peace were everywhere. Old world or unusual attire and long hair among both sexes were prevalent. Girls wore flowers in their hair, and guys sought to have a stash of LSD, Pot, or Hash to pass around. Some wore rainbow colors and psychedelic scarves around their necks.

The pedestrian street and sidewalk traffic was massive like lunch-hour in Manhattan, NYC. Psychedelic music and the smell of incense and pot wafted everywhere. Those moving into the area were care-free, friendly and often high. Donovan's words, "They call me mellow yellow, quite rightly, born high forever to fly," fit the mood on the streets accurately.

The SOL was bigger than most expected. People came from Canada, Europe, South America, Australia and all over the USA. Instead of 50,000, 100,000 and upwards descended on San Francisco's Haight-Ashbury district, Golden Gate Park, nearby neighborhoods and Berkeley. The

idea of a "cultural utopia" comprised of free music concerts, food, sex and psychedelic drugs attracted a wide range of people, in search of some of the above under the wider umbrella of "the Peace and Love generation."

Janis Joplin hooked up with Big Brother and the Holding Company for a two year run that was explosive. Jimmy Hendrix scrambled resonant minor chords and notes into a sound unequaled called, the "Jimi Hendrix Experience." Music artists and groups with the right promotion rocked their way to stardom. Bill Graham and Chet Helms had a promoter's field-

Earth Ball Bouncing in Golden Gate Park
San Francisco, California - June 1967

day—booking Joplin and Hendrix and many more into The Filmore West, Winterland and Filmore East. The Avalon Ballroom was another popular venue. Artists and groups like The Who, Country Joe and The Fish, The Doors, The Birds, Quick-Silver Messenger Service, The Grateful Dead, Dylan, Jefferson Airplane and a slew of other musical troubadours performed at these venues.

"Love and Peace" and the name "Hippies" became synonymous. People came from far and wide; the die-hard drop-outs, draft-card burners, curious, vacationers, those hoping to experience a society of love and peace and meet beautiful people. Others came to change the world through politics, writing, music, dance, painting and poetry. Their agenda was to integrate new ideas, philosophy and artistic expression as a new cultural norm. Smaller in number were those like myself in search of God and truth. Still others came to work, build, dream and get things done. Among these, many worked as volunteers, cooks, servers and hosts for the SOL events to keep things running smoothly.

Some industrious craftsman hippies came with converted vehicles that doubled as workshops, offering to supply and sell leather products, metal art & useful objects, paintings, ceramics, candles, clothing apparel and other stuff. Lots of people brought music instruments with them and played together in the parks in random jam sessions. The overall mood was festive during April-June of 1967.

The media was "over the top" in covering the rise of the Hippie culture. They bounced around from the earliest Be-In, to concerts in the park, The Monterey Pop Festival, Fantasy Fair Magic Mountain Music Festival in Marin County, down to the Filmore venues, The Avalon Ballroom and street events for any news scoop! The swelling crowds at these events impressed them.

The promise of free events and concerts was real. I recall a Steve Miller Blues Band concert I stumbled on in Golden Gate Park. The band was set up on a flat-bed truck with a sizable crowd gathered, listening and dancing. This mid-size concert was typical of day-concerts alongside drama and dance team presentations throughout the park. Larger concerts were usually held on the weekends. Art exhibits, poetry and free speech events were held at other sites in the Haight, like the Straight Theater. All were a part of the SOL programming. The Haight and the adjoining Golden Gate Park had already hosted the infamous January 1967 one day "Be-In" and it was considered to be one of the best city venues for larger concerts and gatherings.

A San Fran Tsunami of People

The wave of humanity that came to San Fran seeking something was massive. A fresh way of looking at the world and "doing life" with others was a reason for many. Meeting new people and developing friendships with those who were different, yet held a similar world-view, was the cross-pollination many desired. This was reflected in the music, dress, ideas and dreams of the generation. The availability of more drugs in the cannabis genre and LSD was another drawing point.

Being in the San Fran Bay area hub where psychedelic rock bands could be seen and heard in person was huge. The possibility of having good sex was another draw. The majority of those who came were eighteen and older, but this didn't stop underage teens from joining the action. Runaways came by the hundreds; innocent, hopeful, sick of plastic sofa covers, oppressive parental control and materialism. Less than desirable drifters also showed up with a history of avoiding work like the plague and looking

for a handout. Degenerates and criminals emerged as well, more than happy to exploit the populace with rip-off drug pricing, bad-drugs, rape and violence to get what they wanted.

Overwhelmed

The Counsel for the SOL and local volunteers in Haight-Ashbury, and friends in Marin County and Berkeley quickly saw they were unable to accommodate the needs of the hordes of people arriving on a sustained basis. Once again, local residents in the Haight and SOL council members implored the City of SF to lend a helping hand. They declined, uninterested and unwilling. The police aligned with the attitude that trickled down from the city council and mayor's office.

The Oracle Newspaper wrote an article urging people to come to San Francisco prepared. Sadly, it was never read by most that came. The result was homelessness, hunger, overcrowding, drug and medical problems and crime. Those who came prepared had the time of their lives traveling in converted trucks, vans and buses painted wildly, with their own home on wheels. No worries about accommodations. Others who brought money could easily rent a house, or flat. Entrepreneurs could gather a group of individuals and go in on a house or flat rental.

For the less endowed, when the music was over and any altered state of consciousness wore off, it was back to the reality of survival. "Panhandling" (begging) was the outgrowth of this desperation. The have-nots needed food, a warm place to crash in San Fran's cold summer months, and sought safe places to avoid being hurt.

Living on the streets was risky and dangerous. Young runaways were often exploited. Girls could usually find a place to crash in exchange for sex. The aftermath was a common scenario; young ladies were either discarded like dirty laundry after sex parties or kept as pets. Lots of unprepared poorer hippies spent most of the summer hungry, begging, selling trinkets or themselves and drugs to survive.

Some lucky visitors came to the Haight for a short period of time; got high, tripped to amazing psychedelic rock, had mind-blowing sex, became a god on an acid trip and enjoyed a brief holiday in San Fran—oblivious to the tragic fate that fellow Flower Children were experiencing.

Those forced to live on the street routinely got beat-up, raped, ripped off, or poisoned by bad drugs. A number met their worst nightmare—experiencing a complete break with reality. Drugs that caused fear and panic ravaged many users. This happened to a friend. I went looking for him and was bummed to hear he'd taken some experimental drug that fried his brain. I found him in a SF psych-ward in the southern part of the city. He didn't recognize me and to my knowledge never recovered.

The Summer of Love was unfortunately not living up to its name for many who came.

Harder Drugs Infiltrating

Powerful drugs like STP, Speed, Crystal Meth, Heroine and Cocaine joined the ranks with LSD and Marijuana. STP, Speed and Crystal Meth were relatively cheap but bad news for Haight's population. STP was a drug that sent many hippies to the emergency room or the Free Clinic in a state of intense panic and fear. The effects of this drug were: substantial perceptual changes such as blurred vision, multiple images, vibration of objects, visual hallucinations, distorted shapes, enhancement of details, vivid contrasts, slowed passage of time and increased sexual drive and pleasure. STP also caused pupil dilation and a rise in blood pressure. As a long-acting drug, if a person's trip went bad—there was no way of stopping it!

The stimulant Speed (in powder or pill form) and Crystal Meth (a more potent purer version) were equally dangerous. Nazi Germany was the first nation to mass produce Crystal Meth which they named "Pervitin." They gave it to Nazi pilots, soldiers, doctors and nurses extensively throughout

World War II. The drug was used to increase energy and alertness for extended periods of time, reduce pain and make people feel good. Hitler used this to have an edge in the war theater. Dependency and side effects were not of interest to the German war machine.

As enticing as Crystal Meth aka Pervitin was, its long-term effects on the human body were devastating. Short rest periods weren't enough to make up for long stretches of wakefulness, and the soldiers quickly became addicted to the stimulant. With the addiction came sweating, dizziness, depression and hallucinations. Many Nazi soldiers died of heart failure—others shot themselves during psychotic episodes.

Heroine, Morphine and Cocaine were more expensive but also available. Injecting these was often the preferred practice. Dirty needles and multi-user bongs and hash pipes increased the transfer of diseases among users.

Peace and Love Implosion

The streets gradually began to change from care-free to sketchy, then dangerous.  Shootings over drug deals gone bad or arguments forced many hippies in the Haight into becoming security conscious. Once the sun went down the criminal element took to the streets. It reminded me of the Filmore District—not safe after dark. I turned up my survival radar for the first time since moving to the Haight. With digs now on Waller Street, just a block away from Haight Street, hearing gun-shots at night became more commonplace. Nobody liked it.

Walking the blocks, I saw the plight of street people unprepared for the harshness. Many were now penniless. I'd give directions to the nearest place to get help. On occasion I'd see girls crying on an apartment stoop. Inquiring what was going on, the response was usually that their boyfriend

or people in the house had kicked them out. I was glad I could give an immediate referral for emergency housing and food. The slogan of "Peace and Love" meant little to victims of street crime, exploitation and being dumped.

I lived in a 'closet' within an apartment unit rented by four girls. They offered this space rent-free in exchange for security, some light chores and pet-sitting when they were away. This arrangement was ideal with minimal personal belongings and the Krishna temple nearby.

Commune Ranch

To flee the rising crime rate, over-population and weekend circus of tourist coming to gawk—a core of early hippies decided to leave the city and start communes, ranches and farms. One, the largest and best known flew under several names; Morning Star Ranch, Morning-Star Commune, or the Digger Farm. It was located in rural Sonoma County CA near the towns of Occidental and Sebastopol. It was a host-site to many hippies wanting to live in a work-

ing-commune while still moving freely back and forth to San Fran for concerts, or to help with SOL events and concerts.

Increase of Panhandlers

Unfortunately there was a new surge of pan handlers in the Haight and they were everywhere! They emerged from seemingly thin air asking, "Spare change, man?" I had very little money and didn't know what to say or do. Sometimes I'd give them my food money, feeling sorry for them. Over time as their numbers increased, I had no choice but to refer them to SOL food bank resources, Digger food distribution locations, or Anchor Rescue Mission.

Counterfeits

Around the same time, self-appointed spiritual guides, teachers or spiritual masters showed up. Seeing my Hindu garb, I was regularly approached by people claiming to be a prophet, a guru, Jesus Christ, or God. It was annoying! I recalled my neighbor Barbara warning about "spiritual counterfeits" and would move around them as quickly as possible. Engaging in conversation was useless. Most of them just wanted to hear themselves talk.

A Spiritual Hope Unraveling

My concern about three wooden Juggernauts in the temple wasn't going away. I kept telling myself, "I should be thankful to have found a living Swami to teach me" and I was! In the beginning when the Juggernauts were erected on the temple's altar, the concept of food and flowers being offered to them seemed novel—but not anymore!

The Juggernauts were weird! Regardless of what I was told about them representing various forms of God. it seemed like pagan idol worship.

I couldn't bring this up to Swami directly, knowing he'd be offended, so I decided to talk it over with Wayne, a fellow devotee. Talking about it with Wayne seemed safe until I realized he wasn't open to discussing anything controversial which might put the Swami's teachings into question. Seeing this, I backed off.

This concern had to remain unspoken. I made a point of not looking at the Juggernauts and tried to block them out of my mind as much as possible. Thankfully someone had recently erected a circular curtain around the altar and they were only visible during worship.

After Kirtan services the Swami made a practice of fielding questions from those in attendance. As Christmas approached, I asked what he thought of Jesus Christ. He said, "He is a demi-god, one of the greatest sons of god." But he never celebrated or acknowledged the birth of Christ as he did other Hindu gurus' birthdays. When I asked why, he took someone else's question. This was his polite way of avoiding questions he didn't think were necessary to answer.

As the months passed Swami became noticeably impatient, abrupt and defensive while taking questions. Often he'd ignore a question, or firmly say, "Enough!" Gradually Swami's practice of fielding questions after Kirtan became less frequent. This change disturbed some, but I was more concerned about Juggernaut worship via food and flowers.

An accompanying frustration was the "Temple Commander" directly under Swami. He was a tall, dark-haired, bearded NY transplant who didn't like people! He made temple regulars feel like second-class devotees, unworthy of approaching him. He did the same with visitors, making them feel unwelcome. He reminded me of a mean Catholic priest I'd met years earlier—who didn't help God's cause as a front man! The combination of Juggernaut worship and an unfriendly temple commander made the temple less inviting for some of us.

When the environment at the temple became too tense, a group of us would share a meal and hang out away from the temple to offset the hostility of the temple commander.

Devotees didn't expect personal time with the Swami. The protocol was understood; most devotees would never meet one-on-one with the Swami unless summoned for a specific reason. He was busily engaged in a rewrite of the Bhagavad-Gita, other holy book translations—while traveling back and forth between the San Fran and NYC temples.

An Unexpected Visitor

One evening a guy named Kent came to the flat I shared, saying he'd heard I was a seeker of truth and wanted to ask some spiritual questions. He wore a plaid-shirt and jeans looking a bit out of place in the Haight. After a few minutes of small talk, I invited him into the common living area. He asked a lot of questions about my beliefs in God—listening intently to my answers. Toward the end of our visit, I asked him about his faith. He said, "I am a follower of Jesus Christ."

That's interesting, I thought, I've never heard anyone say it this way before. The opportunity to dialogue openly about spiritual beliefs was rare and we agreed to meet up again. On the next visit we easily picked up where we left off probing each other's thinking on different aspects of God and following him. Thankfully he didn't attack my beliefs. We were light-years apart in our views of God, but it was refreshing to be able to raise questions without feeling put-down, stupid, or that I was stirring up controversy.

As we continued to meet our friendship grew in a low-key way. On one occasion he brought me a pair of new house-slippers a family member had made. His generosity seemed genuine. During each visit, we'd talk about Jesus Christ, look at some verses in the Bible and I'd try and share something I was learning at the Krishna Temple.

He noted my interest in the Bible and asked if I would like to learn how to study it. I was intrigued. I'd never had anyone offer, or be willing to take the time to assist me in understanding the Bible, so I agreed. I had a small print old Bible in my collection of holy books, but it was unread.

Kent was enthusiastic, suggesting we begin in the New Testament book of Ephesians. Between studies, he encouraged me to read the Gospel of St. John—offering to answer questions when we connected again. He added, "If I don't know an answer, I'll research the subject and do my best to find an answer."

This sounded good. The Bible had been a closed book, and I didn't know why. Studying with someone and dialoguing seemed like an excellent way to begin. It was obvious Kent was extremely knowledgeable in the Bible and eager to share his beliefs and what he'd learned. I was appreciative, wanting to share something in return but couldn't think of anything. Then it hit me, "I'll invite Kent to the Krishna Temple so he'll learn about Krishna, chanting, our style of worship—which will help him understand my spiritual journey."

I was pleasantly surprised when he accepted the invitation and came to a Kirtan service. Devotees who'd arrived early were fingering their prayer beads and chanting the Krishna mantra with intensity and vigor. The chanting of all those present was like the humming of a bee-hive.

Kirtan began on time with some forty devotees and few visitors present. The temple quickly filled with incense as the Harmonium hand-organ, Manjira hand-cymbals and Tabla drums came to life. In the course of a few minutes Krishna followers were lost into singing, dancing and Krishna worship.

Watching Kent out of the corner of my eye I could tell he was experiencing something new. He appeared to be taking it all in—but I sensed it was uncomfortable for him as the pace of music grew faster and faster over the course of 20-30 minutes. The service climaxed with devotee dancers and musicians in near exhaustion. On this particular occasion the lecture portion was abbreviated due to Swami being at the NY Temple. In his place, our less than beloved temple commander gave a short talk. As people were leaving, I connected with Kent briefly and said goodbye. I'd wanted him to experience Kirtan and was very interested in his impressions and feedback.

Temple Residence

Shortly after Kent's visit, my Krishna friend Wayne asked if I wanted to live at the temple in exchange for assisting him with temple duties. He encouraged me to take the position, thinking it would give me more of a chance to interact with Swami and see what the temple was like on the inside. He emphasized, "The Temple Commander will be gone a lot, helping with the NY temple." This was good news, lessening one concern.

I wondered if living at the temple would help me face my Juggernaut phobia. Several days later, I told Wayne yes and made the move. My belongings were minimal, fitting easily into a tiny suitcase.

After moving to the temple I kept in touch with Kent. We put off meeting during the transition but agreed to have our next Bible study in the temple basement a few weeks later. I invited my Krishna buddy Wayne to the study. Swami lived above the temple and neither of us thought anyone would mind, so we set a study date for an evening time-slot.

Unfortunately, the dynamics of the study changed with both Wayne and I present. We fell into interrupting Kent and injecting our beliefs, rather than learning from the Bible and what it said. Kent was patient, but must have felt frustrated. It appeared our study time was cut short due to the awkward impasses of disagreement. I wondered, "Could the huge differences in philosophy and beliefs find any common ground?" Hesitantly,

Kent and I agreed to meet again.

What's Going On?

Between Bible studies, life at the temple was active. Two Kirtan services a day, keeping everything spotlessly clean, prepping and cooking for devotees and visitors was a lot of work.

One afternoon a nicely dressed older lady opened the front door and stepped into the temple. I'd been cleaning near the door and wondered what she might want. She looked around, we exchanged greetings and she said she had a few words for me. Lovingly she urged me, "Open your heart to Jesus Christ. God wants you to turn from idol worship and trust in His Son Jesus Christ!" Speaking with sincerity and urgency, I listened.

Overhearing the lady's words from the adjoining kitchen, our temple commander burst through the curtained doorway, walked quickly toward us, grabbed the woman by the arm, and pushed her forcibly out the front door. She almost fell, but regained her balance. I stepped outside immediately to help her—but she'd turned and started walking slowly away. Returning inside, I thought about punching the commander but gave him a dirty look instead.

A few days later I met a man in Golden Gate Park who went out of his way to talk to me. We talked a bit and before I said goodbye he told me that Jesus Christ was sent by God and was the true Savior of the world.

As I walked away, my mind traveled back to my Grandma who prayed and believed God would touch my life. She was a Christian, as was my former neighbor, Barbara, who was still praying for me. Then there was my new friend Kent. Now, two additional voices telling me about Jesus Christ.

I was puzzled by the collective emphasis on Jesus' critical role in spiritual matters and decided to revisit this privately with Kent.

4

An Appointment with God

Timothy

Recalling the awkwardness of the last Bible study with Kent—I felt unsettled, wondering if I should cancel, but didn't. When the evening arrived, Kent brought a Chinese guy named Timothy Wu. He was friendly, confident and had jet-black straight hair. Wayne opted out of attending this study, which was understandable. I didn't push it, thinking it was for the best.

Beginning in the book of Ephesians the study quickly moved to other New and Old Testament Scriptures with Timothy guiding the direction of the study. It appeared Kent had agreed to this in advance.

The passages we read and studied all seemed to focus on a sharp contrast between a "True God" and

false gods and their representatives. I bit my tongue and made a concerted effort to be a learner, rather than react. If it hadn't been for the fiasco of the previous study, I would have said more.

Confrontation

As the study progressed, the gist of what I was gleaning inferred Krishna Consciousness and most other religious paths were of human origin and false. No matter how hard I tried, the congenial back and forth dialogue with Kent and Timothy took a strained, confrontational turn. Having viewed many Bible verses, I noted the difference between a "Living God" and false religions developed by man. This new information challenged much of what I believed. Feeling boxed into a corner, I felt agitated. Timothy must have picked up on it because he abruptly ended the Bible Study and led us in a closing prayer. Relief was momentary.

He and Kent knew their Bibles inside and out, but Timothy seemed overly confident and narrow in his view of God. In the course of the study he'd politely suggested that Hinduism and the temple was pagan without actually saying it!

I realized 'World Religions' and Hinduism was a complex mixture of mythical and questionable gods—but seeing and hearing it spelled out in plain terms was a blow to my pride. I didn't like the Juggernauts in the temple and never would, but I still felt there was considerable merit in Swami's instruction!

Before Timothy left I initiated a rebuttal through these questions. *"Why would God exclude millions of people who seek him through world religions? How can he claim Jesus Christ is the only way to God? And, how can his explanation of a True God—be so narrow-minded!?"*

Timothy took a deep breath saying, "I'd like to attempt to answer these important questions, but this will take time and my ride home is waiting for me." Kent had already left to get the car.

"Go ahead!" I blurted out in anger, "The God you claim to follow must not be a God of love who cares about or is interested in all people! It's obvious He's not, since you've blasted the Hindu faith and all the religions of the world and now you won't take the time to explain why! Typical!"

"Wait a minute," Timothy urged, and was gone. In several minutes, he returned saying, "Kent will wait."

"Give me an answer!" I blurted out. "Why would God reject people from different religions who seek him? Millions are born into religions other than Christianity, or join them and worship God in their own way! If they are sincere—how could a loving and just God not accept them?"

"This is difficult to answer," Timothy replied with a noticeable pause. "Humans intuitively know there is a God and follow the urge to seek out something to worship. In ancient history people fashioned objects of wood, stone and metal to worship, or the sun, moon, stars and planets. In many cultures animal forms of gods were central to their worship. Powerful kings had images fashioned in their likeness and made people bow down and worship them. Fertility gods have been worshiped by many groups and tribes.

Thousands of temples have been erected to different gods. Egyptian, Greek, Roman and other cultures chose national gods to worship. Objects of worship have ranged from mythical gods and deities—to spiritual leaders, philosophies, power, material images and everything in between. Expansive religions have sprouted from human origins and none of these represent the True and Living God."

> Jesus taught, "True worshipers will worship the Father in spirit and truth, for they are the kind of worshipers the Father seeks."   John 4:23b NIV®

Timothy continued, "Many are sincere, clinging to their god beliefs with tenacity—practicing loyal devotion, disciplines and worship. Unfortunately, devout worship to a false god—does no good. It doesn't connect us to what is real and true. There is only one True God who created the universe and mankind in His image."

God Doesn't Want to Exclude Anyone!

Timothy went on to say, "In the earliest of commandments cited in the Bible, God urges humans not to worship anything but Him (Exodus 20:3-4). From then to now, people continue to worship things other than Him. I believe God is righteous and fair and will accept those who love and seek him. The important thing is that you are hearing about The True God now! You have the opportunity to discover for yourself if what I'm saying can be trusted."

I wasn't satisfied and interrupted sharply, "It's not acceptable to me that there is only one way to find God! According to you, the only door is through Jesus Christ. Why are you so narrow minded?!"

Calmly, Timothy responded in a softer tone, "If I opened my soul and spirit to all of the man-made gods and their religions—I would be sick spiritually."

He continued speaking about Jesus Christ as if he knew him as a friend, saying, "God loved His creation so much, that he sent His own Son to the world to be born as a human in the flesh. The reason I sound narrow-minded is—Jesus is the Messiah, the Savior, God's own Son, sent to earth to break the power of sin and death and to rescue humankind.

The battle we are engaged in is the result of a fallen angel who became evil. In rebellious pride he was banished to earth and deceived the human race. This deception caused the plague of sin to spread throughout the world. The angel in revolt against God is Lucifer, also known as Satan, the evil one. He is behind all the atrocities and evil in the world.

To set things right, God sent His own Son to earth. Jesus' blameless death was needed to defeat the curse of sin and death. When Jesus died, he paid the ultimate price by exchanging His holy life, to defeat this curse.

In obedience to His Father's plan, Jesus willingly died by crucifixion shedding His own blood to cover and remove all human sin, past present and future. Three days later Jesus was raised from the dead by His Father. Jesus conquered death! By these two events, Jesus demolished the curse of sin and death and the evil one's power over us!"

> Jesus said, "The work of God is this: to believe in the One He
> has sent."   John 6:29

Timothy added, "While Jesus was on earth He revealed what His Father was like. He taught truth, exposed evil, extended mercy and love and called people to turn from sin. Because Jesus is God's Son, He has the authority to free us and give eternal life!

"If you open your heart and mind to the True and Living God and His Son Jesus Christ, you will know these things for yourself! God will reveal them to you!"

God's Presence and Timothy's Directive

Taking a step closer to me, Timothy put his hand on my shoulder and looked me in the eyes asking, "Do you want to know the truth?" Taking in what he'd just said, I nodded, unable to find any words to counter his explanation of God's plan."

Emphatically he added, *"You have been deceived by a 'Spirit of Divination', but God is calling you. He has a place and work for you. In three weeks you will be taken out of this place, and you will come to know the True God."*

As he spoke, a presence came over me, similar to what I had experienced years earlier—a steady even power. I wondered, "Could God be speaking to me through Timothy?" I stood there stunned—feeling humbled and small.

"You need to stop chanting the Krishna mantra and call out directly to God!"

How can I do this while living in the temple? I wondered and blurted out, "How?"

Quickly Timothy responded, *"Call out to God, he will hear you! He sees you and has been listening to you throughout your search and has brought you to this moment, so you might find the truth!"*

A holy hush seemed to engulf us as I stood staring at Timothy. Without hesitation, he opened his Bible and read from the New Testament book of Romans, making sure I could see the words. "If you confess with your mouth, Jesus is Lord, and believe in your heart that God raised Him from the dead, you will be saved (Romans 10:9)."

"This is God's promise to you David. Invite Jesus Christ into your life. He is the way to God! When Jesus died, his blood covered your sin. His resurrection from the dead paved the way for you to share in eternity with God. God appointed Jesus Christ to be the go-between, mediator and doorway, to bring us back into a relationship with the True God.

"When we believe in Jesus Christ's work—our spiritual life is activated! When we invite Jesus Christ into our life—God does the rest by placing His Spirit in us." And,

> The Holy Spirit bears witness with our spirit that we have
> become children of the True God.   Rom. 8:16 NIV®

An Internal Battle Rages

Up to this point, I'd been listening. Suddenly a resistance to what Timothy was saying returned. Angered—I spoke firmly, "I think you should leave!"

He said, "OK. But first, let's pray." Saying a short prayer, he appealed to me one last time. "Just ask God to reveal Himself to you, and answer the question if Jesus Christ is the true Son of God. You've got nothing to lose! If what I'm saying is not the truth, you can forget this whole thing and go back to chanting. Give God a chance to speak to you. Go directly to Him, I know He will answer you!"

Abruptly, Timothy turned and left—and I was alone. With the events of the evening whirling in my head I decided to take a walk. The night air was cold and damp as I stepped out onto Frederick Street, but it felt good. Thinking about the study I was suddenly livid. I was angry at Timothy for some of the outrageous assertions he'd made and I was mad at myself for not speaking up more. I was frustrated with Kent for bringing Timothy and ticked at God for dragging me through this maze of yet another twist in my search for truth. When was it ever going to get clear!?

> From a distance moving rapidly
> The arrow flies swiftly to the center
> My soul is not content
> Engaged in the great search
> The pursuit of God and Truth!
> While searching—something is out there
> Someone—is seeking me out in return!
> Could it be the True God of all life?
> Is the unseen One reaching out to me?
> If so, how will I hear Him?
> Whose ear is tuned to His voice?
> What will He sound like?
> Will He speak audibly?
> How will I know it's truly Him?   DEH

The last Bible Study was like an unwanted tape-recording replaying in my head. Timothy's words and a few Bible verses we'd read, kept coming to mind over and over.

I knew I'd led a sinful life—lying, stealing, hating, getting high, battery, bad attitudes, cursing, lust, illicit sex and the list went on. Multiple thousands of sins! During my search for truth, some things had fallen away, but hate, anger and private sins remained strong. *Deep down I believed the true God could fix me.* I was no longer sure my devotion to Swami, chanting, or Krishna Consciousness could.

Pondering this, it hit me, *"Only God can forgive sin!"* Maybe I will stop chanting the Krishna mantra and go directly to God!

Troubling Images Appear and Vanish

One evening, several days after the Bible study, I saw two groupings of images while lying on my bed in the basement of the temple.

The first began in a huge marketplace with people from various parts of the world buying and selling. Many cultures and languages were represented—each dressed in their native clothing. Without warning, a piercing blast cut through the skies. Everything stopped—everyone stood still. Then I heard a song of worship in a language I didn't recognize. It was coming from different people scattered among the massive crowds. As they sang, they lifted their hands toward heaven and then their bodies began to rise. In a split second, my eyes saw a form filling the whole sky. It was the face and upper body of Jesus Christ with nail wounds in his hands, with arms outstretched. It looked like he was gathering his followers. Around him was a huge army of warrior angels on heavenly horses.

The image changed as if caught on film and now I saw myself standing with a group of truth-seekers. I looked up at the face of Jesus, then down at my feet. My feet were on the earth along with a group of seekers around me. I was troubled, realizing I was not ready—having not believed in Jesus. As quickly as these pictures came—they were gone.

Several minutes later, a second series of pictures came as clearly as the first. I saw the face of Paramahansa Yogananda first. He appeared radiant and glowing but as I kept watching, his face contorted, becoming evil. The same thing happened with several more spiritual teachers I'd studied, or looked up to, concluding with the face of my spiritual master Swami A.C. Bhaktivedanta.

"What's going on!? Why were images of my favorite gurus turning evil?" I lay there for a long time praying, asking God to help me figure this out—pleading for an answer. Suddenly, the word PRIDE came into my

PARAMAHANSA YOGANANDA   SWAMI A.C. BHAKTIVEDANTA

mind with this understanding accompanying it: "These spiritual masters are taking the place of God to their followers." The silence that followed was thick with something supernatural—darkness and light were at war.

I'd never experienced anything like this. "Where did these images come from? Was this a vision? Is God speaking to me?" I'd only cried once or twice as a kid—but this night in the stillness of the temple basement, my eyes swelled with tears as I called out to God and drifted into a restless sleep.

O God, Help Me!

I consciously chose to stop chanting from that evening on. As long as I was in the temple I appeared to chant, but began praying directly to God. I could lip the chants, but I wasn't saying them from my soul. I couldn't take the chance; I had to get this right. My prayer was urgent.

Help me to distinguish what is true.
Who is Jesus Christ?
Is he Your son?
Is he the door to finding you?
Can I be forgiven through him?
What is idol worship?
Is it wrong to follow a guru, or swami?
Is there a hidden evil I can't see?
Open the words of the Bible to me.
Show me what is real.
Rescue me—if I'm deceived.
Please—meet with me God!
Reveal your true self.
Protect me from what is evil!

A week past and I continued praying, asking God to show me the truth. It was weird going through the motions of outwardly lip-chanting while praying directly to God, but I was getting the hang of it. Into the second week of this I woke up one morning feeling something was different. On hearing the drone of the harmonium and morning chanting upstairs it was obvious I'd slept in. It was 7am and I was late for Kirtan! Dressing quickly, I splashed water on my face and dashed upstairs, slipping in as quietly as possible. Kirtan was progressing as usual, with the exception of a dirty look from the temple commander for my tardiness.

I gazed around, taking in the panorama of activity in the temple.

Fasting from food to obtain spiritual answers gave me a heightened awareness. The melody of the small harmonium organ, the sharp taps of the Tabla drum, and the ring of the Manjira hand-cymbals were more pronounced than usual. The smell of the pungent incense was pervasive and strong as I watched its smoke waft through the temple. The devotees and visitors danced and sang Hare Krishna, lost into the ecstatic ritual—oblivious to everything around them, but this morning their faces appeared strained and unnatural.

Fire in the Temple

I was beginning to feel like I was on a bad drug-trip, when a visitor began yelling, "Fire! Fire!!"

Immediately, the temple commander ran to the phone, calling the fire department. At the same time devotees and guests flooded out the front door in a panic. With the smoky haze from the incense I hadn't noticed that the ceiling of the temple was filled with a dark smoke. On a quick inspection, I saw smoke curling in the temple from the top of the basement door where Wayne and I lived. Dropping my cymbals I lunged for the door and opened it—letting a large billow of smoke into the temple. My buddy Wayne reached the door just after me and we both headed down the stairs with him in the lead. Taking a few steps we could see it was a wood altar in our living area that had caught fire, probably ignited by a candle or incense.

Burst of Light

Following Wayne, I reached the half-way point of the stairs when I felt the same presence I'd encountered when Timothy was talking to me after the last Bible study. An unusual calm came over me and I heard a voice saying twice, "Call on me now! Call on me now!"

I didn't know where the voice was coming from but knew it was speaking to me. Taking a deep breath I offered up an urgent silent prayer. "Lord, show me the truth. Jesus Christ, if you are the Son of God, help me. Forgive me!"

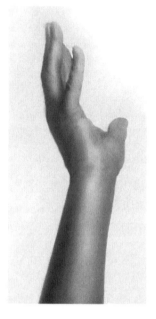

At once a burst of light entered my body and I was flooded with a presence from God. A brilliant light was around me and in me. Instantly, without words, there came a clear realization that Jesus Christ was God's Son, and he was freeing me. He was present! He was the true door to God. He was alive! Intuitively I knew my sins were being forgiven, God was receiving me; He'd heard my prayers and was rescuing me!

I remained aware of things around me, but everything seemed to move slowly. Wayne was throwing things away from the fire. I finished walking down the stairs, helped him and grabbed my Bible that had escaped the fire. Wayne had smothered the fire, but a large block of altar wood was still smoldering. Just then, the San Fran Fire Department arrived, feeding a hose to the basement, and finished dousing the smoldering wood, putting the fire out.

While they were wrapping things up, I walked slowly up the stairs, still feeling waves of God's presence. I felt clean on the inside for the first time since being a kid. The persistent, tormenting restlessness was gone. I felt at peace. The long search was over. I could tell something evil and confusing had left me. I'd come home to the True God, finally calling out to the right source.

Later that morning, I took off the initiation neck beads the swami had given me and threw my collection of expensive religious books into a large metal garbage can in the alley on the side of the temple. Doing this was a decisive step. These ties had to be broken; I was leaving the temple, just as Timothy had predicted. As a means of conveying what had happened, I wrote on the basement wall near where I slept, "Jesus Christ is the true way to The Living God."

As I packed a few possessions, several close temple friends wept. They didn't understand. I told them I had to leave. It was a sincere, loving and unusual goodbye. I knew things would never be the same. I was no longer a devotee of Swami Bhaktivedanta. I was thankful Swami was still visiting the NY Krishna Temple. I needed time before seeing him. It was a strange feeling walking out of the temple—knowing this was making a distinct break with the Swami and Krishna Consciousness.

Kent's Help

My first thought was to visit the flat of some nearby friends—to gather my thoughts, but they were out. Walking down Stanyan Street with my small suitcase in hand, I decided to call Kent. Finding a phone booth I gave him the news, "God has visited me and I know that Jesus is God's Son. Can you help me? I need to get out of the city."

Kent was surprised and elated saying, "Wow, I'll pick you up in twenty-five minutes in front of Golden Gate Park." On the drive to Mill Valley he offered me a temporary place to live with his family at Golden Gate Baptist Seminary.

I felt at peace in Kent's seminary apartment. I was in a safe setting to begin processing what had happened. Kent and Bobbie Philpott had two small girls, Dori and Gracie, who kept the place hopping when they were home. Kent's family welcomed and accepted me, taking the risk of helping a new Christian with a significantly different cultural background, and I was grateful.

The absence of Temple rituals and routines was a strange adjustment. I recall fashioning a small Christian shrine area in the living room, which I'm sure freaked them out, but Kent and Bobbie overlooked it, giving me time to debrief. I didn't miss the city's increased violence, dirty streets, pungent smells and craziness. I did miss my Krishna friends and a handful of other friends outside the temple.

When considering returning to the city for a visit, we both agreed it would be good for me to focus on getting more familiar with God and begin digging into the Bible. In doing so, I'd be more prepared to answer questions that could arise.

One Month Later—A Reflection

Nine years of being locked up had been a living hell, but the last three years of searching through a maze of esoteric, mystical, and world religions had been mentally, emotionally and spiritually exhausting. The drama and confusion was over. *I knew for certain, only God can forgive human sin!*

My quest for truth and peace had come to a conclusion in a way I would have never imagined. The unusual events, people I'd met, and circumstances which unfolded helped me understand this was an appointment arranged by God. He was the initiator. I hadn't done anything to earn or deserve mercy and forgiveness. I'd received a gift from God through His Son Jesus Christ (Ephesians 2:8-9)!

I finally got it—God had been seeking me, creating hunger. He saw me. I hadn't come to God on my own, but with His help! A long history of train-wrecks and bad choices had been my downfall. God knew about my battles with sin, guilt, anger, restlessness and a lack of peace. My predicament, all of it, was open to His view. Wanting to change, while being uncertain of truth and God, had kept me unsettled. The struggle and questions, doubts and frustrations, the longing to find the truth were all needed. They'd allowed me to reach my last spiritual low of uncertainty.

Emptied of being spiritually sure about what was true had created an opening for God to work. Finally I was listening, paying attention. Then came the hoped for but unexpected; I heard God's voice, "Call on Me now!" What followed was the miraculous stuff God can accomplish in a few moments in time when someone is birthed by His Holy Spirit.

The Power and Light of Jesus Christ had permeated every inch of my being, casting out darkness and freeing me from the grip of 'counterfeit religious spirits.' The evil spirits of divination were banished by the presence of Jesus Christ!

They were religious lying spirits that claimed they spoke for God. They offered morsels and fragments of truth to keep me enticed, but hadn't led me to the True God. It took a direct encounter with the "Living God" to remove the confusion and drive out these dark impostors. Amazing!

> "The Lord is the true God; he is the Living God, the eternal King."   Jeremiah 10:10a

> "You show that you are a letter from Christ, the result of our ministry, written not with ink but with the Spirit of the Living God, not on tablets of stone but on tablets of human hearts."   2 Corinthians 3:3

5

Launched into New Life

Surrounded by the True and Living God brought peace of mind and heart. The creative and powerful way I'd been rescued from darkness verified the reality of an All-seeing, All-knowing, Omnipresent God who is active. I was humbled by His intervention.

Rebirth Confirmation

On Kent's advice, I began reading the Gospel books in the New Testament of the Bible. I was blown away by Jesus' words and interactions with various types of people. A light switch had been turned on. The more I read, the harder it was to put the Bible down. I'd enjoyed reading books in the past, but had never experienced this type of hunger to understand the truth and what happened when Jesus Christ was on earth.

Reading Matthew, Mark, Luke and John was like taking a road-trip with Jesus. The spiritual truths that popped on the pages were direct and challenging, but not confusing. I found it easy to identify with those who Jesus met, whose hearts were changed and who decided to follow Him.

What surprised me and held my attention was nothing negative was edited out of the narrative. This was the real deal! Books I'd read about spiritual masters always had a positive story, discussing who influenced them spiritually (i.e. their spiritual masters), how they became enlightened and their life work, as in 'Autobiography of a Yogi' by Paramahansa Yogananda.

The Bible and Jesus' words were not like this! The passages I read revealed the inner motives of the human heart; anger, hatred, selfishness, unbelief and how people reacted to God speaking to them, or asking something of them. God's words went to the core of how a person treated the poor, the sick, the weak, their neighbors, or their view of spiritual matters and how they thought God should act.

I could tell that those chosen by God to record what was in the Scriptures of the Bible, did so by the 'Spirit of Truth.' Accuracy and honesty was everywhere! God's view on an absence of faith, love or truth, or living life with hardheartedness, prejudice and self-righteousness were clearly wrong. The more I read, an understanding was growing about what 'Good or Evil' was from God's vantage-point. Sin was an accurate word to describe undesirable behavior or attitudes. There were hundreds of examples jumping off the page. Prejudice is a sin, because no one is superior in God's eyes. Self-righteousness is a sin, for the same reason. No one is without sin. Insights like these were changing my entire spiritual outlook!

The mistakes Jesus' disciples made were in the open! They didn't always have faith, believe, or understand what was going on. Over time their ideas and lives changed. In the course of 3 ½ years of walking with Jesus, they still didn't grasp the big picture. It took Jesus' death and resurrection and God sending His Spirit to live inside them, to bring the full reality of what they'd been brought into. It took a rebirth by God's Spirit to open their spiritual understanding and it was the same for me.

Spiritual rebirth opened my spiritual eyes! Prior to being filled with Jesus Christ's Spirit in the Krishna Temple, my ability to understand spiritual things was almost non-existent. I didn't know Jesus was the Messiah sent by God to save this world. I didn't have a clue that we can never work or meditate our way to becoming acceptable to God. I had no idea there was a True and Living God amidst thousands of impostors. I couldn't understand the Bible. It was like trying to decipher a different language.

Jesus' Spirit in me was now illuminating the words in the Bible. Having studied other religious books, I quickly discovered the Scriptures of the Bible were in a league of their own. The Bible is Alive to those who read with eyes of faith. It, in conjunction with the Holy Spirit, has the ability to reach the deepest part of our being and instruct us in God's ways.

For the word of God is living and active and full of power
[making it operative, energizing, and effective]. It is sharper
than any two-edged sword, penetrating as far as the division
of the soul and spirit [the completeness of a person], and of
both joint and marrow [the deepest parts of our nature],
exposing and judging the very thoughts and intentions of
the heart.   Hebrews 4:12 Amplified Bible

Verification of a Heart Change & Living In Christ

Proof of God's work in my heart was multiplying. For years I'd struggled
with the emotion of hate. In the fires of a locked-up lifestyle of incarceration, I'd acquired a deep-seated hatred toward cops and guards. I'd come to
believe some were as corrupt as criminals. Cops and guards were notorious
for skimming drugs, taking bribes, using excessive force, unjustified assault
and murder. In uniform, cops got away with a lot of serious stuff. In the
past I'd viewed them as the enemy! When I saw a cop, or patrol vehicle,
emotions of hate surfaced. Not anymore. During the first few months as a
Christian, my hatred toward police simply vanished!

     In a similar way, being spiritually confused about what was true and
what wasn't was gone. Spiritual confusion had been a low-grade source of
frustration for a number of years. On receiving Jesus Christ's Spirit, God
drove out the spirits of divination and the fog of confusion was lifted!

     Other negative personal traits were in process, undergoing a more
gradual transformation. Restlessness and being on-edge was diminishing
significantly. Defensive aggressive behavior was still around but less pronounced. Since age 10, when my tour through youth institutions began, I
started acting crazy and explosive when confronted or threatened. These
reactions scared people and crippled friendships. This had grown into an
uncontrollable negative character trait. For years I'd been an over-reactive
time-bomb, which could explode over something dumb. Once, while on
parole from Preston, I'd punched a customer in the face who got too close
to me in a check-out line. It was crazy!

     The intensity and frequency of these outbursts was definitely on
the decline. Lying, selfishness, isolation were also on their way out. "God's
Peace" and presence was the replacement. As far as I could tell, spiritual

surgery had been successful and new life had taken root.

This didn't mean all my problems and repercussions from past sins were gone. It would take years to work through some things from the past. I quickly caught on, 'becoming more like Jesus'" was going to take time! Anger and lust were personal flaws that would hound me for years to come. I would need to resist these temptations, or repent and turn away from these sins if I missed the mark and gave in.

God's work in me was like the restoration of an old house. Some areas were cleaned and restored from top to bottom immediately. Other rooms would be restored gradually as I learned to surrender these areas to God and allow Him to help me clean these up. Surrendering to the Holy Spirit in obedience to the Word of God would be a lifelong endeavor.

The initial changes of seeing, feeling and thinking differently were significant in helping my faith to grow. I'd experienced a heart change, from a heart of stone to one that now felt and was alive. I read a passage in the Scriptures which addressed this miracle that only God performs.

> "I will give you a new heart and put a new spirit in you;
> I will remove from you your heart of stone and give you a
> heart of flesh."   Ezekiel 36:26 (NIV)

All, who place their trust in Jesus Christ receive this same spiritual surgery. I was in awe, when I reflected on this, feeling an immense sense of relief to be forgiven for all my past sins and know with certainty Jesus is the Son of God! Also, to realize I was now a part of God's eternal family!

A Book like No Other—The Bible

When reading the Bible, I knew my mind was being infused with life-changing truth. The precursor was, *the opening of my spiritual eyes* when Jesus' Holy Spirit entered my being at my spiritual birth in the temple..

The gift that followed was access to an accurate record of God's interaction with all types of people in the Bible. It was fascinating to be learning so much about God's nature, what He teaches and Jesus' advent on earth. The more I read, the stronger I felt spiritually.

Sometimes after reading the Scriptures for a season, I'd put the Bible down and sit in amazement thinking, "This book which points men and women to God, and reveals Jesus Christ as God's Son, is alive!"

When I brought this up to Kent, he explained it was the Holy Spirit inside of me, who was giving me understanding—allowing faith and new life to grow. He said, "It's your spiritual food. A lot of people read the Bible out of curiosity, some for intellectual stimulation, or perhaps to critique it, in an attempt disprove its spiritual origins. Some people have their spiritual eyes opened while doing so—others remain blinded. When we put our faith in God and call out to Him as you've done, God seals the deal by putting His Holy Spirit inside of us to be our teacher about lots of things as well as opening our understanding to the Words of God recorded in the Bible."

"Amazing!" I replied. I was still awed by how easy it was to understand compared to when I was not yet "born of the Spirit."

Listening to a recording by Billy Graham, he encouraged Christians to read in Psalms and Proverbs on a regular basis and incorporate this into daily study alongside other New or Old Testament books. Doing so, I saw the advantage immediately. Psalms gave me a sense of the personal relationship we have with God through dialogue, and Proverbs was loaded with practical wisdom. It was like a well balanced diet. Hundreds of these verses jumped off the pages giving me encouragement. Here's one, "He is my loving God and my fortress, my stronghold, my deliverer, my cover and shield, in whom I find shelter (Psalm 144:2 NIV®)."

Seminary Digs

I was thankful Kent and his wife invited me to stay with them until I could get my bearings. Life at seminary for Kent and family was busy, but peaceful for me. Bobbie and the kids headed out to work and school early. Kent had classes to attend, papers to write, a part-time job at JC Penney's and preaching prep for the weekends. I didn't know how he juggled it all, but he did. Positive events and breakthroughs were a regular occurrence as the weeks and months passed.

Kent and I endeavored to find time to connect daily to visit. We'd dialogue about what I was learning and he'd field questions that arose, or refer me to places in the Scriptures that explained the topic. When he was stumped, he'd say, "I don't know, but I'll try to find an answer." During prayer, we'd pray for each other, for friends of mine who were still in the city, for missionaries, places of need and lots of things. Intuitively, I knew I wasn't a bother to Kent, but instead he was excited to help me get established spiritually.

While he was in class I did a few chores around the house, took walks, and kept up with reading, studying and prayer. There was a lot going on inside of me. Truth that I'd looked for was now flooding my mind and heart. With seminary housing being compact, I slept on the living room couch. This was an adjustment for the family but they handled it well. There's no convenient time to have somebody become a Christian that you've been working with and praying for, and especially when they need housing.

Kent took me with him to a few seminary classes and other recreational activities at school. We also went to church and out to the streets, parks, and beaches surrounding San Francisco. He was outgoing and seemed to find it easy to start up conversations with people who were total strangers. He'd begin by discussing general topics or spiritual things and by asking questions to stimulate dialogue about beliefs and philosophies. Before long, Jesus Christ was at the center of the conversation. This approach was amazingly effective and not canned. I watched closely how naturally and effortlessly Kent was able to engage people by asking open ended questions.

In the beginning I'd listen, look up passages afterwards that arose in dialogue and think about how I might respond if asked tough questions, like those I put to Timothy. Tagging along with Kent was good for me, especially when we connected with someone who was seeking God. Listening to the back and forth dialogue was fascinating and educational. In doing so, it was shocking to discover the majority of people we talked to were either oblivious, or confused about spiritual things. Those who had a smattering of religious exposure were often uncertain what they believed. Most had no relationship with God.

My Friend Wayne

After a couple of months, Kent and I went back to the streets of San Francisco and hooked up with a number of my friends. I was especially interested in reconnecting with my buddy Wayne and a few others from the temple. To do so, I went solo, not wanting to scare off devotees with two of us present. I decided to visit immediately following a Kirtan service when devotees and visitors would be milling around.

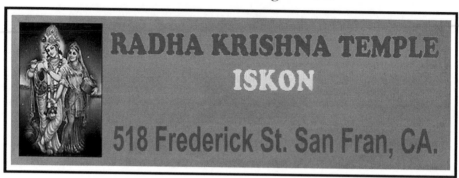

Doing so, I found Wayne and we walked far away enough from the front door of the temple so we wouldn't be overheard. He spoke in a whisper, "Swami issued a warning about Christians since you became a follower of Jesus. Bibles are now banned from temple grounds and everyone but fund-raisers are required to shave their heads. We are only allowed to leave a small pony tail in the center of the back of our head directly above our Chakra. It's called a 'Sikha.' Srila-Prabhupada (Swami) said Krishna will snatch us up by this lock of hair and we will attain to live in the high planets in the spiritual world. Swami also made these changes to make sure devotees were loyal to Krishna and to close the door on Christianity or any other religious influence."

Wayne was being upfront and honest, but this news thwarted my ability to gain much in the way of a hearing from him, or other temple friends. Noticing he was nervous being seen talking with me, I asked if we could take a short walk down Fredrick Street to get us out of direct view of other devotees who were hanging around the front of the temple. He agreed, saying we could only visit briefly.

He was dressed in the traditional light orange wrapped temple garb and fingering his mantra beads in a small pouch on his side. I urged him as a friend to at least listen to what had happened to me. He said he knew, adding, "Some of the temple devotees are still confused, not knowing what to think. And Swami was not happy to hear news of what happened to you."

Wayne had been a close friend, but one of the most loyal and devoted followers of Swami at the San Fran temple. Wayne knew I'd converted to Jesus Christ but not much more. I urged him to at least hear what had happened.

He didn't answer, so I proceeded. I told him about Jesus Christ's death for our sin and the gift of being forgiven and accepted by God because of Jesus' death in our place. I shared about Jesus' resurrection from physical death and the indwelling of God's Spirit which is given to every person who puts their trust in Jesus Christ. I explained briefly how a "spiritual rebirth" opens the door to a relationship with the True and Living God.

Wayne was trying to listen and understand, but something was blocking his concentration. It was visible in his eyes and facial expression. I sensed he was trying to honor our friendship-history by paying attention. At the same time he was taking a risk of being reprimanded for even talking to me. Wayne had joined the temple before me, and we were initiated at the same time. He'd voiced concerns in the past, mainly about the unfriendly temple commander, but perhaps this had blown over.

As I spoke, Wayne drifted in and out from listening to nervously fingering his prayer beads in the pouch on his waist, praying the Krishna mantra under his breath. I continued, hoping something would get through. "To find God, we need to go to the source, directly to Him. God is able to reveal to us the truth about who Jesus Christ is. Jesus is the bridge between God and man (2 Timothy 2:5). God has provided forgiveness and acceptance as a free gift to all who place their trust in Jesus. He is the Messiah!"

Standing close to Wayne, I saw his eyes were glazed, and his face grew pale. I suddenly realized he wasn't listening any longer; his look was distant as if miles away. When he refocused there was sadness in his eyes and I realized our close friendship was being separated by two distinctively different belief systems.

He'd chosen Swami Baktivedanta and was unknowingly turning away from the True and Living God. No words were used. We knew what was happening. We hugged and looked at each other one last time before he turned and walked back down Frederick Street. Watching him disappear into the Krishna Temple, I felt pain at the core of my being. I knew I hadn't come close to penetrating the Krishna mind-set and spiritual delusion he was locked into. The intensity of the spiritual battle being fought for the souls of men was evident through my short visit with Wayne. I felt sad. My heart was grieving for Wayne and the multitudes of sincere seekers following paths that would not yield what they hoped for.

I saw Swami A.C. Baktivedanta twice after I left the Krishna Consciousness Movement. The first time we spoke was following a Kirtan worship service at the temple. I shared with him briefly how I had experienced forgiveness through Jesus Christ, and how God's Spirit had visited me. He called me by my Hindu name saying, "I'm sorry you have chosen a lesser path." He then motioned with his hand and said, "That's enough!" The second time was from a distance when he was speaking at an event at Golden Gate Park. After my exodus from the temple—life for devotees became strict. They were more radical, less friendly and closed to outside input. No discussions were allowed or conversations entertained that didn't pertain to Krishna Consciousness.

I remained extremely concerned for Wayne and others at the temple. My heart ached when I thought about the power of the spirit-world to deceive sincere seekers. I was also concerned about other friends and acquaintances I'd known or lived with prior to hooking up with the Swami. Kent and I visited a handful of them. There was mild interest—but nothing came of it.

People in the Haight were open to drugs, alternative philosophies, psychedelic music and lots of weird stuff, but anything that represented the straight-world was suspect. For some hippies, the name of Jesus Christ was OK. To others, Jesus represented organized religion and a repressive reminder of childhood memories and forced legalism they wanted to shake off. When I first began telling people in the Haight about Jesus Christ, the majority thought Christianity equaled an out-dated religious model that smacked of "status quo" hypocrisy. This barrier needed to be shattered and God did it in His own timing.

Learning Curve

Reading the Bible regularly I was making significant headway in completing different books. Kent encouraged me to stay with it, saying this overview would give me an important foundation. I was learning a lot about God, how He worked in human history and His plan for humankind. It was exciting to discover what was important to God and on His heart.

Kent gave me the freedom to explore the Bible and didn't tell me exactly what to study after I completed reading the Gospels. He gave helpful advice when he thought it would benefit my spiritual understanding.

On one occasions, he said, "Not everyone has a dramatic encounter with God like you have. But, every person who claims to be a follower of Jesus Christ should have an awareness from God that they've been spiritually reborn. This inner witness confirms Jesus is God's Son, the Savior of the world and our relationship with Him. It is Jesus in conjunction with the Holy Spirit who forgives our sins and births us into "God's family."

Following Jesus is the true mark of belonging to God. Those who say they belong to God and never obey God are deceiving themselves. The Holy Spirit is the provider of the power to help us live as disciples, but we must keep listening, obeying and following.

The visions you received and how God reached you in the temple was God's way of helping you make a clean break from your religious search and Krishna worship. The convergence of people speaking to you about Jesus was not random, but part of God's way of preparing your heart and spirit so you'd be able to make the right decision to pray and seek the truth. Saul became the disciple Paul through a dramatic encounter with Jesus while he was out hunting down Christians. God knows exactly how to get our attention and reach our minds and hearts." I nodded in silent agreement.

Kent was a student pastor at a small church in Byron, California, some forty-five minutes north of Mill Valley. Attending Sunday worship with his family was a cultural shock for the congregation and me! I was not your typical visitor. I stood out like a hamburger at a vegetarian dinner with my street mannerisms, tattoos, and eastern religion appearance. We used song books in worship and some of the old hymns dragged on with five verses! The upside was you had another shot at catching the melody each time the song repeated. The entire package was new.

Kent wore a suit and tie on Sundays and was a good preacher. In the back of my mind, I hoped I wouldn't have to wear this type of straight clothing. The positive side of attending church was I continued to learn from the Bible. People in this small country church were friendly and glad I'd become a follower of Jesus Christ, but unsure what to say to me. I felt the same awkwardness and tried to avoid too much conversation. The smiles and warm hand-shakes were enough for now. As mismatched as I was among these rural folk, this was where I started attending worship as a follower of Jesus Christ.

In The Name of the Father, Jesus Christ and the Holy Spirit!

My first water baptism took place at this small little church. This step solidified my understanding of dying to my old life and being raised to new life in Jesus Christ. Before the baptism, Pastor Kent explained, "The work Jesus did by dying on the cross, made a way for us to come to God the Father and be forgiven. Jesus was the Savior and mediator between God and Man. When God raised Jesus from the dead, Satan was conquered! This miracle opened the door for anyone who would believe—to begin a new life. Jesus is the Son of God, sent to reveal God's fullness."

Kent continued, "Jesus was baptized by John the Baptist as an example, and taught his disciples to baptize all who believed, 'In the Name of the Father, Son, and Holy Spirit.'

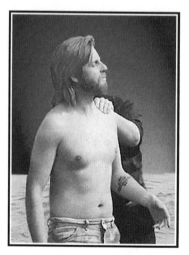

Baptism is an outward sign of the inward work of God in our lives. It's a picture of Jesus' burial and resurrection. When buried in the waters of baptism you are identifying with Jesus' death to forgive our sin. This visual image is about your conscious decision to die to your old life of habitually giving in to sin. Arising from the waters of baptism is a picture and reminder of God's power that raised Jesus from the dead—which is transferred to every believer who is raised out of the waters of baptism to a new life with God's Spirit living in you. Your job is to keep your heart open to God and obey the Holy Spirit's guidance and the instruction He gives you through the Bible."

The baptism service followed. It was exciting to see several adults, some teens and elementary age students each making this same commitment to follow Jesus. Being baptized publicly was a decisive step. I again sensed the presence of the Holy Spirit as I came up out of the waters of baptism. The mysterious working of God flowing into my life was undeniably real. To consider that God, who created the universe and everything in the world, was capable of visiting individuals who were seeking him was beyond my comprehension, but I now knew without any doubt it was true!

Thankfully, the dark side of my life was on the run! Years of bouncing around in youth and adult correctional institutions and a long search for truth in esoteric and eastern religions had culminated in spiritual rebirth. Who would have guessed I'd have an encounter with Jesus Christ in a Radha Krishna Hindu Temple in San Francisco?!

Timothy Wu Reconnect

On a chance encounter, Timothy spotted me in the Presidio District of San Fran and ran across the street with a warm smile and gave me a hug. This was the first time seeing him since the last Bible study at the temple. He said he'd heard from Kent what had happened and knew I was living on seminary grounds. He was elated that God had revealed Jesus Christ to me. Asking how things were for him, he quickly brought me up to speed on his life. He was pastor of a Chinese church in San Francisco and finishing up his studies at Seminary. All was good!

Seeing him caused an instant recall. Timothy's role in confronting the errors of religious counterfeits had been crucial in alerting and convicting me. Timothy's brazen boldness had been used by God to give me the push I needed. His words "Call out to God directly and ask Him if Jesus is the true Son of God." And, "God is going to take you out of this temple and you're going to come to know the True and Living God," lodged themselves firmly in my memory.

These and other things he'd said were troubling at the time—but effective as a final catalyst that pushed me to ask God, "Is Jesus Your Son, the Messiah?"

Seeing Timothy again was special! Curious about his use of prophetic words about me being taken out of the temple in several weeks, I asked him about this. Timothy smiled saying, "The words I found myself saying surprised me. I knew the Holy Spirit must have been using me to speak 'words of wisdom, or knowledge' which are gifts of the Spirit mentioned in I Corinthians 12:7–11 of the Bible."

In an almost embarrassed manner he added, "When you posed the question, 'How could a loving and righteous God turn away from and reject people from all the religions of the world except Christianity?' I didn't have an adequate answer. The explanation that came out of my mouth was wisdom beyond my ability. I realized immediately, it must have come from the Holy Spirit. I thought about this afterwards including the prediction of you being taken out of the temple. God had never used me in this way before. I wondered about our whole dialogue exchange that evening. Had I been too pushy and direct? I prayed God would use what came from Him for His glory and continued praying for you. "

I thanked Timothy for being open to the Holy Spirit, speaking the truth and praying for me. Timothy put his hand on my shoulder, said a short prayer and assured me he would continue praying for my new life in Christ. As was Timothy's manner, he said, "Got to go" and disappeared across the street.

A Questionable Idea

One day Kent and I came up with a plan to get me working and provide extra income for both of us, deciding on a "Handyman Service." We ran an ad in the local newspaper and waited for the phone to ring. Sure enough we landed a few jobs, but soon found out we needed a variety of tools along with the personal skill-set to accomplish most of this work.

One of our earliest jobs stands out as a memorable fiasco! A home owner called saying they needed a number of their doors shortened to accommodate a higher pile carpet they'd just installed. Sounded simple, a little shaving, power sanding and we'd have it done. On arriving at the home we learned each door required saw-cuts of ¼ to ½ inch depending on the door. "OK", Kent said, "We can do this." We bought a new blade for his old circular saw and started the job. From the very first door, we encountered problems with splintering and getting the cuts right, but kept at it.

As the job proceeded we cut a bit more than needed off of several interior doors—but way too much off the front door. Rehanging the expensive raised-panel hardwood front door, our jaws dropped in horror and panic. Within minutes of this discovery, the wife arrived home, walked up the front steps, and immediately saw the glaring problem. I can still see her closing the front door and bending down to see the size of the gap. It was about 1 ½-2 inches higher than it should have been. In alarm she blurted out, "You've cut the door too short! Lizards, chipmunks, spiders and mice can come right in!"

Kent and I were speechless, flush-red with embarrassment. Kent finally blurted out, "We'll make things right and pay for a new door." There went our wages on that job! After a few more sketchy outings we decided we'd try house painting and became good at it over time. The painting trade ended up being one of our better ideas among others that failed. Painting houses grew into a viable vocation which supported us in ministry ventures for many years to come. Meanwhile our excursions into the Haight continued.

The Haight—July-October 1967
Talons from the Dark-Side Pierce Deep

New Age religions were a hypnotic and enticing replacement for western churches that seemed outdated and distant. The occult and Satanism seemed to slip in the back-door of the Peace and Love Movement. I didn't realize how pervasive these influences were until I started seeing more of them on the streets.

The stage was set, the bands played, drug dealers dealt their potions—while a vulnerable generation tried to figure out what to believe. Light and darkness, freedom and confusion had been stirred together into a strange melting pot. Dark Spiritism influences were aggressively putting their talons into the hippie camp introducing different faces of the "Magic Arts." The expansive world of the occult caught many naive young hippies off-guard. Occult books, séances, Ouija board games, Tarot cards, palm reading, charms, omens and horoscopes became a fascination to many hippies. The pairing of psychedelic drugs and the occult formed an "unholy union of evil." Those going deeper, seeking to become witches or wizards would be mandated to invoke the Evil One and his demons openly.

The ability to differentiate between good and evil was for the most part foreign to Flower Children. Most hippies were blindsided by the darkness of the occult, violence and being ripped-off and taken advantage of. The original idea of 'Peace and Love', going with the flow, being friendly, sharing what you had and being happy was no longer matching reality for many hippies. Becoming victims of criminal activity was not what they'd come to San Francisco for. Backed into an alley by some street thug, a hippie's world came crashing in when they found themselves saying, "Just don't hurt me!"

The Haight District no longer looked like a Utopian Festival of Peace and Love. *The hope and vision was swallowed up by a sinister evil. Free love hedonism, the reckless use of dangerous and addictive drugs, and the beguiling influence of the dark-side had crushed the 'Flower Children' dream.* Peace and Love flowers lay scattered on dirty sidewalks, dead! Hopeful aspirations were no match for Satan's expansive bag of tricks, honing in on unsuspecting victims.

The Fickle Media

The media covering the Peace and Love Movement turned it into a spectacle—going wild in paparazzi fashion from January through July 1967. This nonstop circus-type of coverage contributed to the rapid population invasion into San Fran and the Haight. Now with things beginning to turn sour, these same reporters were quick to pounce on the movement, now that it had taken a nosedive. They went into attack mode poking harsh critiques at any and every Flower Children failure—while distancing themselves from any notable qualities.

They quickly forgot the greening vision among the counter-culture and their part in mobilizing huge 'anti-war protests', 'free speech' and 'freedom marches.' Reporters chose to ignore the Council for the Summer of Love and the work of, The Free Clinic, Huckleberry House, The Diggers, The Switchboard, Straight Theatre and all the volunteers who stepped up when the city of San Fran refused to lift a finger! The media turned its back on the arts explosion in the San Fran area which had swelled through the Peace and Love movement. Almost all of the positives were forgotten.

Ironically, San Fran touted the wisdom and foresight to not support the SOL knowing it was doomed to fail. The status-quo was again right in its own eyes! Any good that occurred—was dismissed.

The real story was not black or white. There were lots of incredibly talented people who emerged from the 60s Generation that would go on to make an impact on society and the world for good.

There was a lot that was wrong and evil about these days. Bad people exploited the 'Peace Generation' for profit or notoriety. Timothy Leary's slogan, "Turn On, Tune In and Drop-Out" was just another catch-phrase without substance to help the 'Summer of Love.' In a genuine social revolution there is massive work to be done. The SOL team and all those who assisted them were the hands and feet of meeting practical needs. They addressed the necessity of food and water, housing, hygiene and medical treatment when required. Hippies who became homeless were susceptible to many encroaching dangers, which necessitated the need for these services including crisis counseling.

I felt bad about the turn of events that had struck a near-death blow to the counter-culture. I knew evil had infiltrated! I saw and felt it, but didn't understand how it could have been avoided with so many oblivious to evil and the dangers of new drugs. I was glad to have been a part of the SOL Counsel, even if in a limited way. A lot of good had been done which continued.

Mock Death of a San Fran Peace and Love Venue

On October 6, 1967, those remaining in the Haight District, along with a handful of early Haight visionaries, staged a mock funeral. A coffin was paraded down Haight Street in symbolic fashion to announce the SOL had run its course and was officially over and dead. The demise of the San Fran "Flower Power" caused by drugs, crime and violence over-running the area necessitated this funeral ceremony to bring closure to those who organized it.

Some thought the mock funeral signified the "death of the hippie." Not so. Mary Kasper, an active resident in Haight Ashbury explained the reasoning and message of a mock funeral. "We wanted to signal that this was the end of the Summer of Love. Stay where you are! Bring the positive aspects of the revolution to where you live."

Most participants in the SOL had already returned to university, to jobs, their hometowns, or started businesses. Some had joined communes that were self-sustaining like MorningStar Ranch. The majority remained hippies and found ways to continue their alternative lifestyle elsewhere.

Some embraced foreign travel as a means of self-discovery. They traveled the world. Early hippie backpackers set off on what became known as 'The Hippie Trail' winding through Europe, the Middle East, through Kathmandu and the Nepal mountain pass and into India. They hitch-hiked, traveled by public transport, walked, or used revamped buses and camper vans—always living as cheaply as possible.

Finding truth, purpose and meaning was elusive for many young adults living in the 1960s & 1970s. Questions outnumbered answers. Drugs and war were both having a negative impact. Destructive drug highs, or walking the jungle mine-fields in Nam littered with dead bodies and lost limbs, were both a nightmare with repercussions to come. The weaknesses of 'War Power' and 'Flower Power' both laced with drugs, were flawed, unable to produce a lasting better way of life.

Social satirist and later activist Paul Krassner gave his take on the Peace and Love Generation saying:

> "It was sex, drugs and rock 'n' roll, and those were all fun—but at the core of the counter-culture was a spiritual revolution."

> If this was true—how would this play out?

6

An Incredible Teacher

I continued to be hungry to grow in the truth. One afternoon I asked Kent, "What do you think about me going to school to learn more about the Bible like you have?"

"Well, David, it would have to be a Bible College. That would be the next step for you since you've graduated from high school. Seminary is for those who've already been to college. We can look into it and write to a couple Bible Colleges and see what happens. I can be a reference and you can apply for work on campus to help pay your tuition."

After several months of prayer and mailing applications, I was accepted by a Baptist Bible college in southern California. The package included 25 + hours of campus work per week to cover room, board and tuition.

Spiritual Fishing—Stinson Beach

In the meantime Kent and I continued working together painting the exteriors of homes and connecting with people in Marin County and San Francisco. As was Kent's practice, we had places to go and people to meet. We went to a variety of venues sharing Jesus Christ. One such outing took us to Stinson Beach

Stinson Beach is part of the Golden Gate National Recreation Area,

Stinson Beach, CA

north of Golden Gate Bridge on the Pacific Ocean. On warm sunny days in Marin County, you can count on people heading out to the water and beaches. Kent decided we should do the same, with the aim of sharing our faith in Jesus at the beach. This stretch of coastline is spectacular with Mt. Tamalpais and Muir Woods nearby and rolling hills winding down to the ocean.

Our hope was to strike up conversations with anyone who was interested in spiritual dialogue. Usually I was paired with Kent, but he decided to walk up the beach heading north and then work his way back to wherever I ended up. Surprised, I said, "I'm not sure I'm ready!?"

"Just trust the Holy Spirit to speak through you," Kent replied."Let's pray." Kent led us in a short prayer and he was off walking up the coastline at a swift pace.

Connecting with people when they're in a relaxed or swim mode at the beach was awkward for me. I didn't want to interrupt their down-time. I tried to scope out who might be open and less engaged in recreational games, sand-castle building or swimming. Most of those I approached were friendly but not keen on any kind of discussion with a stranger. About twenty minutes into saying hey to different people I ran into a girl who was solo, looking at a magazine.

Approaching where she was sitting in the sand, she seemed deep in thought until she looked up smiling, and said, "Hi."

Asking if she was interested in talking about spiritual stuff she said, "Definitely!"

"Great!" I responded, "Can I sit down?"

"Sure."

This was the most receptive person I'd met thus far. As we talked, I learned she was a seeker of truth and had dipped into a number of mystical paths in search of God. She was more than eager to have someone to listen and bounce ideas off of. She began by highlighting some of the teachers she'd studied and the books she'd read. I affirmed having an understanding of some of them and continued listening.

She said she'd come to the beach to let her brain and spirit air out for the day. Her dilemma was discerning what was true and what wasn't. She too felt like she'd hit a brick wall when it came to knowing what to believe. It was amazing how parallel our paths were. She spoke for about a half an hour before saying, "As you can tell, my conclusions are blurry and uncertain. So, tell me about your take on spiritual truth."

"Wow! Talk about an open ended request!"

Not wanting to overwhelm her, I touched briefly on the highlights of my journey in seeking truth, a few of the frustrations, and how God began to convict me through two visions, which I described.

From her body language she was listening intently. I continued by telling her about the people who had told me about Jesus, including Kent and Timothy. Next, I shared what happened in the Krishna Temple and being flooded with the Spirit of Jesus Christ.

"Wow!" She said and then asked, "How did you know who was talking to you?"

"When I heard, "Call on me now" twice, I wasn't sure. But what occurred after my short prayer, was so powerful I couldn't move. The light inside and around me was beyond anything I'd ever seen in brightness and it was pulsing. I knew beyond doubt this was God's presence. *As His Spirit flowed into me in waves, a clear realization came; this was the True God and through Jesus Christ His Son I was being forgiven and accepted. It was true; Jesus was the Messiah— the Savior of the World!*

And while this was happening God drove the religious spirits of divination out of me! I felt like a kid, clean on the inside, like I'd never done anything wrong—which was far from the case!"

To affirm these things from the Scriptures, I opened my small pocket Bible and shared this verse out of the Gospel of John where she could see the words.

Jesus said, "I am the way and the truth and the life. No one comes to the Father except through me."   John 14:6 NIV®

Looking up from the passage, it was evident God's Spirit was doing something in her. She was teary-eyed, with eyes closed, head down and appeared to be praying. Not knowing what to do, I stopped talking and prayed silently. Some five minutes passed until she broke the silence with a question that blew my mind!

"Can I receive Jesus Christ into my life right now!?" I didn't know what to say or do. I'd never had anyone ask me this before. Being a new Christian, I'd never prayed with anyone for this to happen. With my mind racing I asked her two short questions. "Are you serious? Can you wait here while I get my friend who's just up the beach to explain how?"

"Yes, to both!" She replied.

Feeling unprepared and elated with excitement at the same time, I jumped up, told her I'd be back and headed north in search of Kent. I found him in about seven minutes, filled him in on the girl's request and both of us returned to where she was sitting.

I could tell Kent was excited for her and the decision she wanted to make. He assured her she was entering into the true plan God designed for mankind to enter into a relationship with God. To strengthen her understanding, He then gave a highlight of Jesus' life, teachings, death to absorb human sin and resurrection from the dead which verified Jesus being the true Savior and Messiah.

Kent said "this opened the way for God's Spirit to be placed inside everyone who received Him as LORD." He then asked her to read John 3:16 out of his Bible:

> For God so loved the world that he gave his one and only Son, that whoever believes in him shall not perish but have eternal life.

From there, Kent gave a few more basics to make sure she understood this was a heart decision that God would honor if she was sincere. Then without religious gimmicks or coercion, he asked if she would like to proceed by inviting Christ into her life. When she answered "Yes", he asked her to pray with him a simple prayer for forgiveness and reception of Jesus into her life. Glancing at her I could see tears of joy ripple down her cheeks as she prayed. After this prayer she shared a deep heart-felt "Thank you!" We stayed on visiting for 10-15 minutes, gave a contact phone number and said goodbye.

Shining & Letting God be God

On the way back to Kent's seminary apartment we talked about *the miracle of individuals being receptive and prepared by God for salvation.* Kent said, "Young Christians like yourself may not know everything, but you often 'shine the brightest' to those who are outside the faith and hungry for God. You know what's real, you've experienced being forgiven and accepted by God and it's all fresh! When you speak about God it's not some canned spiel, but genuine—and people know it's real!

"New Christians are like a high output light bulb. People see the Spirit of Jesus shining on you, in you, in your eyes or on your face. You may not be aware of any of this. This is how the word **Christian** came into existence. People outside the faith saw the Holy Spirit shining in believers. They lit up their corner of the world and people started calling them little Christs or Christians.

Many church leaders do a great disservice by quenching the light in new Christians by conveying they should be quiet, grab a pew and are not ready to do anything! These leaders forget that new life is what non-Christians are attracted to, not religious do's and don't s and man-made religious rules. Early Christians were excited and thankful, empowered by the Holy Spirit and they set the world on fire with the news of Jesus!

God has lots of ways of reaching people. His presence may touch them like the girl on the beach, or during some crisis, or they could see something spiritual, or they hear the Word of God and it becomes alive to them. Any of these and many more are the creative means God can use to help a person know He's speaking directly to them. The love or acceptance they feel from a Christian speaks volumes, or the love they experience among a group of Christians bears witness to God's existence.

When Timothy put his hand on your shoulder and began speaking words that God gave him, you recognized God's Spirit was present. The Holy Spirit works in ways that are often mysterious. All who believe in

Jesus Christ are co-workers with God. We sow the seeds of God's truth and God's Spirit does the supernatural work inside people's hearts and minds.

Next time, you'll know what to do if a situation arises and a person wants to receive Jesus Christ. This is the ideal situation. When a person decides of their own volition to receive Jesus Christ as Savior, spiritual rebirth is just a prayer away.

We can't forgive, or lead anyone to salvation by our cleverness, spiritual arguments, wisdom, or by use of a religious technique. It doesn't produce lasting results.

Spiritual Rebirth is God's territory, a miracle the Father, His Son Jesus Christ and the Holy Spirit accomplish. We can pray and be available to be God's hands, feet, arms, legs, mouth and voice; but its God alone who initiates the miracle of regeneration and salvation!"

"Wow, I hope I can remember this stuff, Kent!"

"The Lord will help you when the time comes."

Education or Mentoring?

In late August I said goodbye to Kent and family and headed south to attend Bible College, taking a Greyhound from San Fran to Los Angeles. From there I caught several more buses to reach the area in Riverside where the Bible school was located. Walking up the long driveway suitcase in hand my heart was pounding.

The campus buildings were Spanish style with arches, pillars, tile shingles and the grounds were well maintained. Following the signs, I made my way to the Admissions office. In route I saw a few other students who looked ultra-conservative.

In admissions, the secretary spoke in a formal tone, "Please take a seat and I'll notify the admissions director you're here."

Self conscious, I thought about my hair length and white clothing. Over the next forty-five minutes I waited. Finally the Dean of Admissions called me into his office. He began, "I'm sorry for the delay in meeting with you. I've been looking over the limited work exchange positions we offer to incoming students in need of financial aid. I'm sorry but they're all filled. It doesn't look like you'll be able to begin at our Bible College at this time."

"Could I have some time to try and secure funds from my family?"

"We feel it best that you take some additional time to be part of a local church before you attend school here."

"I applied and was accepted!"

"Yes I know, but the full-time job positions are currently filled. I'm sorry. You should consider working for a few years and get established in a local Baptist church and save for this. Then perhaps you will be ready to return."

"Does my appearance have anything to do with this decision?"

"Perhaps." He admitted. "But there are other reasons too, the ones I just mentioned to you. I'm sorry."

I swallowed hard, feeling the finality of his comments. Regaining some composure, I picked up my small suitcase and made my way to the door. This decision was obviously not going to be reversed and I had no control over it. There was nothing I could do but accept it.

Walking down the driveway to the main street my legs felt heavy and my gut was churning. After the long trip south, I hadn't expected this outcome. Simplifying what I'd just heard, "I wasn't a match for this conservative school until I looked and talked like them." Ouch! Rejection was something I never got used to. I tried not to take it personally—but did.

A Living God—Concerned and Active

Rehearsing what had just happened, my pace slowed to an aimless shuffle. I was bummed and didn't have a clue what to do next. My future was blank. While slipping to the next rung down on the ladder of discouragement, I heard a voice similar to the day I received Christ, saying, "That's all right, I will teach you." The same last four words came again. "I will teach you."

Wow! Who else could this be—but God? These concise words seemed to breathe hope into my being. Immediately my legs weren't so heavy and my steps regained energy. "I will teach you" was a completely different perspective to remedy the door that had just slammed shut. How could I do better, than having God for a teacher.

On an arid and scorching Riverside road, rejection and a closed door were replaced by a few words from the Almighty. It was amazing to consider, the Most High was interested in my situation! The idea of a Living God present everywhere throughout the universe at the same time, caring for and speaking to people was beyond my comprehension level, but it was real.

Where to go and which direction to take, was the next question at hand. As quickly as this thought formed, it hit me; I'll go to the small town of Monrovia. It was a place I was familiar with, where my Grandma had once lived and my former neighbor Barbara currently lived.

Within the first week I knew this was a good move. I rented a room by the week at a small hotel above Myrtle Avenue and found a job at a Holster Company.

Myrtle Ave. Downtown Monrovia, CA 1950's-60's

The first Sunday in town I attended the Assemblies of God Church I'd seen on one of my walks. Pastor Vinton Huffey was the first person I met at the door. He took an interest in me, offering to help me in a number of ways. He gave me landscaping work at his home and taught me a "Foundations of the Faith" class. This class was exactly what I needed along with worship and hearing good messages from the Word of God.

On more than one occasion Pastor admitted to me privately that his congregation was far too comfortable. "They're not as interested in reaching out as they should be, and I'm glad you're here, to remind me what I should be doing alongside the normal church work." He urged me to steer clear of the church youth group knowing they didn't welcome outsiders as he hoped they would. I was fine with this, as the group was Jr. and Sr. High age level and noticeably snobby.

Pastor Vinton Huffey

Pastor Huffey was a man of tall stature, balding, even-tempered and exuded wisdom and a prayerful approach to whatever he put his hand or energy into. From my perspective, God had put me exactly where He wanted me! In the months that followed Pastor Huffey became a spiritual mentor to me, taking me along with him, enjoying the company of someone committed to sharing Christ with others and open to spiritual guidance. He was totally comfortable with going to the local park to share in conversations with anyone willing to dialogue. In doing so, a number of people responded to Jesus' words.

Returning to Say "Thanks!"

In Monrovia I also reconnected with my former neighbor, Barbara. Her deeds of kindness in sharing food, taking me to the bus stop when I moved to San Fran, her faith, prayers and words about Jesus Christ had each been used by God. No kindness was wasted! Knocking on her door, I waited with excitement. The door opened and she recognized me instantly.

"David! It's so good to see you," she said as she hugged me. "Come on in and tell me all about what you're doing here. I've been wondering what had happened to you and was hoping to hear from you. Now tell me what's going on!"

"I've got some great news."

"Come on, tell me!"

"I've received Jesus as my Savior! And I know He's the true Son of God!"

"Praise God! This is wonderful news!"

"Do you remember when I was studying Eastern Religions?"

"Yes."

"One of the last things you told me before I moved to San Francisco was, 'Stay open to Jesus Christ because there are lots of fakes out there?

I remembered your words and this is exactly what I encountered. There were lots of spiritual paths I learned about in San Francisco. The last place I lived in San Francisco was the Haight-Ashbury District and it was loaded with self-appointed messiahs, prophets and spiritual guides claiming to have a corner on God. Ironically, the street prophets and messiahs were usually drunk on alcohol or high on some drug, and I knew they were bogus.

I continued to meditate and pray for God's help. About this time I heard about a Swami who had come to the USA from India who was opening a temple in our neighborhood. Tired of dead-ends and still searching, I visited the temple and heard the Swami teach. I was impressed by his expansive knowledge and devotion to God. He taught a "mantra" that was supposed to align seekers with God. I began chanting the mantra and was among the first group in San Fran temple to be initiated by swami into "Krishna Consciousness."

I paused to see if Barbara was bored. She wasn't, saying, "Please continue; I'm very interested!"

"OK! During this time, I met a Christian named Kent who offered to help me learn how to study the Bible. While doing so, two important truths from the Bible surfaced. First, there is a "True and Living God" among thousands of false gods. Secondly, Jesus Christ is God's Son, a part of God, sent into the world to teach the truth and by His sacrificial death and resurrection from the dead, He is able to free anyone who believes in Him from the power of sin and death. The clincher is Jesus Christ is the only mediator between God and us (I Timothy 2:5). He is God's appointed Messiah for all of humanity.

Being confronted with these two truths caused an internal war. I'd listen to Kent, or one of his friends named Timothy and then get mad. I'd think God was speaking to me and then fight it—thinking the claim of Jesus Christ being the only way to God could never be possible! This assertion was absent of compassion and spiritual justice. Surely, God wouldn't reject sincere seekers from different religious paths across the globe!?

This back and forth battle was raging when I came to the conclusion, "Only the true God could forgive human sin." This realization caused me to rethink my resistance to spiritual truths and comments Kent and Timothy had made. I recalled Timothy's challenge, "Stop chanting and ask God for the truth. Ask God if Jesus is the true Son of God, the Savior of the World, the Messiah!"

When things were the weirdest, I saw two sets of troubling images before going to sleep one night. They both indicated I was on the wrong path. This was followed by out-of-the-blue encounters with other Christians who said, "Jesus Christ is the way to God."

What followed about a week later was an amazing encounter with God in the Krishna temple. In the middle of worship a small fire broke out in the temple basement. In the middle of the chaos I heard an unknown voice say "Call on me now" twice. I couldn't tell where the voice was coming from. So, I prayed in silence, asking if Jesus was the Savior and to be forgiven if He was. In seconds I was flooded with the Spirit of Jesus Christ in such a powerful way I was speechless, in complete awe. I knew inside that God had received my prayer and Jesus Christ was God's own Son; the only One who could forgive my sins!"

Barbara chimed in, "That's so like God, He made it absolutely clear to you! This news is so awesome David! God is so great! He is able to do things that only He can! Over the past year, I've prayed for you! Now, seeing you, and hearing what God has done to set you on the right path increases my faith in God being able to do the seeming impossible.

So, David, what brings you back to Monrovia?"

"Well, I'd hoped to go to a Bible College in southern California and had been accepted, but when I got there, they didn't have a spot for me. It was discouraging, but I know God is teaching me and I feel at peace. I'm excited about what's going on now and what the future holds. Right now, I have a job at a holster company and I'm renting a room at a hotel by the week."

"Are you going to church anywhere?"

"Yes, I've been attending the Assemblies of God Church. Pastor Huffey has been helping me in different ways and I think it's a good match."

"That's great! I just wanted to make sure you knew that you're welcome to come to the church I attend anytime. It's the same Nazarene church I've always attended. The main thing is that you're in a church where you're accepted and growing.

Oh David, the news of Jesus saving you is the best news I've heard in a very long time! God really does work miracles in ways that are beyond our understanding and He is faithful to answers prayer in His own way and timing!"

"I know, Barbara! Each seed that was planted in my heart by you and other Christians, and every prayer offered up, helped defeat Satan's grip on my soul! I can hardly believe how different everything is, since receiving

Jesus into my life."

"I'm so happy to hear this, David, and so glad you came back to tell me what God has done for you. This strengthens my faith in a time when I really need it. Since you were here, my husband has been in and out of the hospital and has been unable to work. The kids are OK and growing, but things have been a lot harder. I know God will bring us through, so I keep praying and trusting. I'm working part-time now and this is helping pay the bills."

We sat and visited for awhile and I had a chance to see her kids, now 6 inches taller – as they bolted in and out of the house a couple of times. "Guess they keep you busy?"

"Sure do, but they've been a big help, with my husband sick and all. They do some of the chores and help me look after him. They're good kids and doing well in school too."

"Well Barbara, I'd better take off, but I'll come back and check in from time to time when I'm in the neighborhood. OK?"

"That would be terrific. And please remember to pray for us."

"I will Barbara."

Valuable Mentoring

Pastor Huffey's mentoring was practical and intentional in helping me to grow in a variety of ways. One Sunday after church he said, "David, I've been thinking that it might be good for you to bring us a message, or share part of your testimony one Sunday evening. What do you think? I'd like for you to pray about it."

I prayed and agreed to do it, asking Pastor for help. "I think I'll need some coaching, because speaking publicly makes me nervous. Would you look over what I come up with?"

"Sure my boy, I'll be glad to give you a few suggestions, but I think you'll do just fine. We all have to start somewhere and we'll be trusting God's Holy Spirit to anoint your words."

When the evening came for me to address the congregation I felt extremely nervous. Speaking to people on the streets was no problem, but talking to a larger group of people in a church setting was different. I invited my Mom, Dad and step-Mom having no idea if they'd show up, but they did. As the worship songs were being sung I thought about mounting the stairs to the pulpit that Pastor Huffey filled so well with his tall frame. The responsibility of presenting God's Word hit me right about the time pastor invited me to the platform. My legs suddenly began shaking uncontrollably and continued to do so throughout the talk. It was strange how speaking in a church setting caused this reaction. Thankfully the size of the pulpit hid my wobbling legs from most of the congregation!

Daniel Chapter 3 was my Bible text. I spoke about the three Hebrew young men who refused to bow down to Nebuchadnezzar's gold image and a supernatural deliverance which occurred after having been thrown into a fiery furnace. The courage of the Hebrews and the miraculous way God protected them was the transferable aspect of the talk. It was an honor to speak from God's Word and Pastor Huffey had given this opportunity. The level of nervousness, leg-shaking and sweating was surprising. When the message was over my shirt was literally sopping from perspiration.

Having my family present felt good and I thanked them for attending. A number from the congregation offered encouraging words afterwards. I knew I'd prepared and done my best and was relieved it was over. I liked Pastor Huffey's words about trying new things, "We all have to begin somewhere!"

Holy Spirit Baptism

At the Assemblies Church the infilling of the Holy Spirit was taught and opportunities were given to receive this gift. An invitation or alter call occurred at the latter part of each service where people could go to the front of the church to pray, or be prayed for. If requested, the pastor, elders, or older Christians would lay hands on our back, head, or shoulders and pray for our specific needs and requests. One of my ongoing requests was to receive the infilling of the Holy Spirit.

At the altar I heard others praying in tongues and I saw some being filled with the Spirit for the first time. How this happened was a mystery, but I'd read about it in the New Testament. On a few occasions I felt close to receiving this gift but a prayer language never came. Others had the same problem. The desire to be filled with the Holy Spirit prompted me to fast from food and give myself to God in intense personal prayer.

Arriving early at church for a Wednesday evening prayer meeting, an older Christian who knew I was seeking to be filled with the Holy Spirit, said to me privately, "Seek the Giver, not the gift! You will receive the Holy Spirit's infilling in God's timing and way." This made sense and his words stuck. I continued to fast and to pray over the next week or so.

My evening habit was to spend an hour or so worshiping God in praise, Bible reading and prayer. I was also reading a book entitled, *Aglow With the Spirit,* by Dr. Robert Frost. It was profound when it came to the ministry of the Holy Spirit and the infilling. It echoed the words of the elder who'd told me to "Seek the Giver, not the gift."

Then, it happened! I'd been singing songs of praise, when I heard the sound of a wind in my room which landed on me. The power I'd experienced on the day I received Jesus was filling me again and I began speaking in an unknown language. Waves of God's Spirit kept coming. In the beginning I was trembling, which turned to shaking. God's power was too great to contain—which caused praise in this new language to flow out of me. This was not a brief event. Over the next hour or so I heard a variety of languages and was amazed they were coming from my mouth. As I received the Holy Spirit, it flowed back to the God of heaven in mysterious heavenly languages. I felt transported spiritually into a deeper level of praise and awareness of God's holiness, majesty and glory.

I now knew what Jesus meant when He said:

> "Let anyone who is thirsty come to me and drink. Whoever believes in Me, as Scripture has said, rivers of living water will flow from within them."   John 7:37–38 NIV®

This Holy Spirit's infilling lasted in my waking hours on and off over the next several weeks. It was hard to concentrate on my job of making leather holsters without bursting into praise sporadically. I did so quietly, beneath the hum of the industrial seaming machines. As a result of this experience, I was led into intercessory prayer for others and began speaking more boldly in Jesus Christ's Name.

I was still young in the faith and had a lot to learn about walking in the flow of the Holy Spirit, but was significantly encouraged by being baptized into His Spirit. God used this infilling, the Bible, Pastor Huffey's preaching and teaching and a variety of people to help me grow; plus the voice of the Holy Spirit when I was able to hear it.

A Saint with a Heart of God

One of the people God used to encourage me was Mary Feister. She ran the Christian bookstore in Monrovia, CA. She'd worked as a missionary for many years prior to contracting a tropical virus while on the mission field. Near death she'd been flown home, placed in a US hospital and had gradually and miraculously regained her health. Post-recovery she'd started this Christian Bookstore with a few hundred dollars.

She saw the store as "The Lord's Store," a new mission field to help and encourage anyone who entered the doors. I'd been in the store a number of times buying tracts and looking over Bibles but couldn't afford to upgrade my second-hand Bible. Over the months Mary and I became friends. During this time my Bible became more raggedy, with pages starting to loosen from the bindings and I resorted to good old duct-tape!

Visiting the bookstore regularly, I'd share highlights of my week and she'd do the same. She was the kind of woman who had a deeper perspective about life and always had a fresh word of encouragement. One day when entering her store, she greeted me warmly, saying, "Well David I've been expecting you."

"Really? I didn't even know I was coming in."

"Well, I thought I'd be seeing you soon, because during prayer I saw you coming through the door. I won't keep you wondering what this is all about; I have something for you from the Lord."

As she was speaking she had already gone to the long glass counter display case and was taking Bible boxes out. One by one she laid them out on the counter-top; about ten in number of the best Bibles in the bookstore. Then she carefully opened each box and folded back the tissue paper that surrounded each Bible. As I stood there with my mouth hanging open she leaned over and patted me on the shoulder saying, "What are you waiting for? God wants you to have a new Bible. It's a gift from Him and being that we're partners, me too! Now look each one over, take your time and choose whichever one you like the best."

"Mary, I don't know what to say", I stammered.

"You don't have to say anything. Just rejoice in God's goodness and love for you!"

"I do. Praise you Lord! And thank you Mary for being His instrument!"

"This is the Lord's gift to you. He knows you don't have the money right now."

Mary was one of those ladies who could speak a word of wisdom that would ring in your soul and her gaze into my eyes reminded me of Christ looking at me, and through me.

"I've got some work to do, so just take your time looking them over."

I must have spent a half an hour looking over the selection of Bibles until deciding on a King James with a medium to large print. While starting to fold over the tissue paper on several of the Bibles and place them neatly back in there box, Mary showed up saying, "So David, have you made your choice?"

"Yes I have" pointing to one of the Bibles. "Thank you Mary!"

With a huge smile she said, "You're more than welcome young man! It's my privilege, just remember, this is God's gift to you. He knows each of our needs, cares about us and is our best friend!"

Mary was a genuine, wise and loving representative of God. She was like a spiritual mother to me and she had a heart of gold. An insight I caught from her was how she saw all Christians who comprised the Body of Christ and the lost. Church or denominational affiliation, or none at all, didn't lessen her view of anyone she met. When a person believed in God the Father, Jesus Christ His Son, and the Holy Spirit, they were of equal value, brothers and sisters in God's eternal family.

If a person wandered in her store with no spiritual background or understanding, or if they believed something erroneous, she always treated them as Jesus would have, with love, compassion and words of truth. Every living person was of great value in God's eyes! She taught me by example, *Every person needs to be loved, accepted, cared for, and helped at one time or another.*

Mary encouraged me to learn, hear and obey the voice of the Lord. She poured herself into others like me, through Christ's fullness living in her. She became an important spiritual mentor in my life. I will never forget the things Mary taught me by word and example. I still own and treasure the Bible God gave me as a gift through her, a sign of God's generosity and care.

Dan Pauly—A Brother in Christ

While in Mary's store, I ran into Dan Pauly a young Christian my age. Both of us had been converted around the same time. He'd previously lived in Newport Beach and was into the surfer scene, using LSD and pot until he had a supernatural encounter with the Lord.

Returning home to live with his family, Pastor Dr. Luther Meyer took Dan under his wing like Pastor Huffey had done when I showed up. Dr. Meyer encouraged Dan to develop an outreach to his friends. When I ran into Dan he had a number of designated call-in lines set up at Bethel Church for anyone to call-in and hear a message. I'd seen the phone number on a card and called to see what it was about. The recording was concise; Jesus Christ was alive! It was followed by gathering times. I was impressed. It was a creative vehicle that stirred people's interest and attracted a number of older teens.

In talking with Dan I learned he'd been invited to speak at several high schools and the youth group at his church was growing. As I didn't have wheels I never visited Bethel Union Church but continued to run into Dan and struck up a friendship. Little did I know that this friendship would continue for many decades to come.

A Conversion / Interview by DEH

Dan Pauly came to faith in Christ when he was 21 years old on February 12th 1967. The means God employed in reaching Dan were anything but normal—they were supernatural! How this unfolded will follow shortly in Dan's words.

God's Amazing Love

Previous to this, Dan told me about being eight years old and experiencing God's love. He recalls being in a small church with his parents standing in a Sunday School gathering singing songs before separating for study. While taking song requests, Dan remembers raising his hand and requesting 'The Old Rugged Cross.' "When we began to sing I sensed God's presence enter the church and then me. *God touched me and filled me with His love!* Though young, I knew Jesus' presence was love! Overwhelmed by this, I began to cry. At the time my parents were not committed Christians but attended church regularly. They were surprised and somewhat baffled to see me crying. Being filled with God's love was something that made me feel safe. I couldn't explain it, but knew it was real!

From this time till the age of 21 this experience drifted to the back-burner and had slipped from my memory."

A Drive that Changed Everything!

"I was driving to a surfer dance from Newport Beach to Harmony Park in Anaheim California. I had two friends with me. A girl riding shot-gun and a guy in the back seat. Suddenly God's presence filled the car and I was no longer aware of my passengers or that I was driving. God showed me my life was full of dark things. Next, I saw a picture of my parents standing in church praying with a small group and I knew they were praying for me. Then, I became aware of an amazing galaxy of light spinning over me. It was beyond anything I could describe, the most beautiful thing I'd ever seen! In response, I heard myself say, 'Jesus Christ, come into my life!' I said it twice.

An audible voice like no other voice I'd ever heard spoke to me saying, 'Is this what you really want?' A pause followed until I felt something deep in my belly rising up to my mouth saying, 'Yes!' As soon as I said this, the galaxy of light came inside me and I was aware of my surroundings and that I was driving.

The girl in the passenger seat was crunched up against the door with a look of terror in her eyes. My friend in the back seat looked to be in shock. I spoke to him later and he said, 'Don't ever ask me what happened, or talk to me again about this!'

We went on to the dance at Harmony Park where I was a regular and knew a lot of people. I told many of my friends I'd met Jesus Christ on the way to the dance. None of them argued, but listened intently with an awestruck look in their eyes. Visiting the restroom I saw myself in the mirror and was frightened by the way my face looked. I looked like an over-exposed photo filled with light shining everywhere!

On returning home that night I saw an old Bible I owned with a statue of Buddha sitting on top of it. A thought came, 'Take the Bible and read something before you go to sleep.' Another thought followed, "You're too tired, just go to bed." Going to bed won out.

The next morning I panicked, reflecting on all that had happened the night before, I feared becoming a social outcast rehearsing the worst, 'All my friends will think I'm crazy!' Not wanting this label, I tried to forget what had happened. And, somehow, I managed to blot the whole episode out of my thoughts for over a month. But, during this time I fell into depression and thought about committing suicide.

A month and a half later, on April 1, I saw a telephone pole that reminded me of a cross. For some reason, I got excited. My memory was jarred about what had happened a month earlier. I realized, I had left God out of my life and I needed Him!

A Duo Encounter with the Almighty

With this fresh in my thoughts, my roommate Sal returned home. He'd taken his girlfriend to Mexico for an abortion and looked depressed. In spite of this ordeal he asked, "How was your day?"

'I've left God out of my life and need Him', I said. In our bummed state of mind we were sitting on his bed talking, when both of us became aware of a swirling light in the room, the same galaxy light as I'd seen in the car. We both were in awe until we were both knocked off the bed. Sal said to God, 'Forgive me for everything I've done.' Both of us uttered similar repetitious pleading with God for forgiveness.

Following this, we saw two small dark clouds coming out of our stomachs and combining into one, accompanied by demonic squeaky noises. The dark cloud then moved rapidly toward and vanished out the front door. Amazed, we stood up, hugged and knew we were now brothers in Christ.

I called my parents, shared what had happened and they urged me to come for a visit. I did, and decided to move back home. By this time my parents were Christians and members of Bethel Union Baptist Church in Duarte, California." [Interview with Dan Pauly Continues]

Dr. Luther Meyer, Pastor-Mentor

Dan's parents' pastor, Dr. Luther Meyer, served the church and taught at Life Bible College in Los Angeles, founded by Aimee Semple McPherson who pioneered the Foursquare Gospel Churches. Interestingly, Dr. L. Meyer instructed Chuck Smith who was the founding pastor of Calvary Chapel when Smith was a student at Life Bible College and prayed with him when he received the baptism of the Holy Spirit.

At Bethel's prayer gatherings, Dr. Meyer could regularly be seen on his knees praying quietly and reverently in tongues before God. He was a Spirit-filled man with a heart for the church and the lost.

Dan's conversion was an answer to many prayers that were being offered through the broader church, including Dr. Meyer's small Baptist church in Duarte. Many Catholic and Protestant Christians had been praying for this same outpouring of God's Holy Spirit to awaken the church and reach the lost. What no one knew was how this outpouring would happen and what it would look like.

When Dr. Luther Meyer and his sister Audry Meyer saw and heard what God was doing in the lives of late teens who were receiving Christ outside the church, they knew God was doing something amazing in His own way!

Dr. Luther Meyer mentored Dan and gave him plenty of room to develop Bethel's youth ministry. Under this spiritual covering an important spiritual foundation was being laid for what would follow.

Outreach with Impact

Dan witnessed to lots of his old friends and the youth group at Bethel continued to grow to about eighty strong. The church call-in lines were also buzzing with more activity than ever. During this time, well known radio host Audry Meyer learned of Dan through her brother Luther and invited Dan and friends to share their testimonies on KHOF, broadcasting out of Glendale, CA. Through this and other exposure, many doors opened to speak at area High Schools including a full assembly at Duarte High School where Dan had previously attended. With drugs being a serious campus problem, many school officials accepted responsibility for allowing a strong Christ-centered message to be given, in hopes of helping students steer away from the dangers of drug use. The results were always positive! No one was brainwashed. Those who responded to the message of Jesus Christ being alive and the Savior of the world, found a new life and a natural "high" through the Holy Spirit—minus the brain-frying side effects of new and dangerous drugs flooding the market.

Pauly & Frisbee's Friendship in Christ

Around this time, Dan met Lonnie Frisbee at a beach gathering of new Christians and they became friends. On Dan's recommendation Lonnie's first outing to minister at a church was on the invite of Dr. Meyer, to speak at Bethel Union Church. Dan and Lonnie's friendship continued over the years.

Based in Monrovia, Dr. Charles Harden of United Evangelical Churches interacted with a number of young Jesus People who had been converted during the early stages of the Jesus Movement. He provided a spiritual umbrella and supported a handful of them as they launched into ministry. Dan Pauly and I were among these. Dr. Harden ordained Dan to the Gospel Ministry and licensed me as a "Christian Worker." Both of us were under the umbrella of United Evangelical Churches.

Pauly continued ministering in Duarte and Monrovia and would soon see a rapid expansion into other neighboring cities.

Our Father's Family—Christian House Ministries
Southern California

A number of friends who Dan had reached for Christ founded five Christian Houses called Our Father's Family in Southern California. One was in Duarte, two were in Pasadena, a fourth was in Burbank and another in Alhambra. Dan was active in preaching, teaching and outreach ministry with these houses and area High Schools that invited them to speak. Paul Dancheck was among the early leaders of these Christian houses.

Dan's Expanding Witness

Dan's interaction with the body of Christ as a young believer was broad. He interacted with Teen Challenge and made friends with Andre Crouch who directed the "Addicts Choir." He did things with Youth for Christ, Young Life, Hollywood Presbyterian Church and a variety of other churches who invited him to share his faith and testimony. An Episcopal church gave him the use of their sanctuary for larger youth meetings and outreach. He attended Kathryn Kuhlman healing meetings at the Shrine Auditorium in Los Angeles and was impacted by her faith and healing ministry.

Dan Pauly - Our Father's Family Christian House Ministries

Author's Note: Dan's continuing story and bio can be found in Bio's 2 Chapter 28. His Mission's journey with Lonnie Frisbee to Europe and Africa can be found in the Missions Chapter 24.

Early L.A. Teen Challenge Ministry

The Assembly of God church I attended offered opportunities to travel and hear special speakers that were in our area. One Friday evening, a group of us attended a Full Gospel Businessman's Dinner, held at a restaurant in downtown Los Angeles. The sponsoring organization was comprised of Christian businessmen in L.A. County. After the dinner, the event featured a concert by Andre Crouch and the Disciples, with testimonies from former heroin addicts who had been through, or were still living at, a Teen Challenge center in Los Angeles.

"We've Come This Far by Faith" was sung that night with such an anointing that I've never forgotten this tune. The songs and testimonies from the Teen Challenge individuals were simple yet powerful, a clear reminder that God continues to provide transformation for anyone who calls out to Him.

I said a prayer that night for friends I knew who were still trapped by destructive choices. I added a request to boldly proclaim God's Name, knowing *the power of Jesus Christ's blood can wash away the most addictive and darkest of human sins.*

7

Lancaster—a Desert Call

Spiritual Education

"I will teach you," were words still resounding in my heart, and God was doing just that! I was learning from a variety of sources—the Bible, the Holy Spirit, by listening and intercession prayer and through Pastor Huffey's preaching and teaching. In addition I was a recipient of Mary's mentoring, mission talks at my new workplace World Vision and access to Christian radio and books of faith. Discussing various topics with those inside and outside the faith was another means of gaining spiritual insight and nudging me to look things up in the Scripture.

Anytime I connected with someone who didn't know much about God or spiritual things I'd see how important it was for them to at least have the opportunity to hear about Jesus Christ. Thankfully, Pastor Huffey loved to carve out time to go to the local parks. Like Kent, he was great at weaving the subject of God and Jesus Christ into discussions.

I wondered why more Christians weren't out and about sharing their faith like the early disciples until I read Jesus' explanation. "The harvest is plentiful but the workers are few (Matthew 9:37b)." Pastor Huffey and I discussed this several times. He said, "Christians are afraid to leave the safety of the church to speak the name of Jesus in public, because they're fearful of being labeled a religious fanatic, laughed at, mocked, ridiculed, embarrassed or rejected." The idea of worrying what people may think, or about how we might be received was in Pastor Huffey's opinion a poor excuse for not sharing our faith and obeying Jesus' command to go into all the world with the "Good News."

I had similar fears and concerns, but had learned some resistance is normal. I would probably never interact and convey the gospel of Jesus if I let fear and intimidation put the kibosh on talking with people outside the church. Reading the parable of "The Sower" in Luke 8:4-15 gave me a better understanding of what happens when people hear about Jesus Christ and God's offer through Him. Some scoff and ridicule while seeds of truth are being sown. Others may show initial interest that fades and so forth. Jesus emphasized the importance of seeds falling on "good soil and bringing forth an abundant crop." He said only one out of four seeds, may end up doing so.

Kent explained this same truth, saying I should have realistic expectations and be tough when it came to push-back from those who were antagonistic toward Christ. "Christian's who live in countries that hate anything to do with Christ are persecuted regularly!" Kent added, "It's not about us, but about God! If three out of four people, laugh, spit and mock us; and the fourth person receives God into their lives, it's been a very good day! God is the one who opens hearts. Some individuals will be receptive and some won't, but may be later."

This was not difficult to understand, when I thought about how I fluctuated between being open and resistant, which over time culminated in my spiritual rebirth.

Benefits of Engaging with Others

I found going out to meet people and talking about God exciting! Like anything, it became easier with practice. Talking to total strangers can be fascinating; similar to what happens on random TV street interviews. People are interesting, funny, have unique life perspectives, enjoy having someone listen to them and have something to give us in return when we're paying attention. In one-on-one or smaller settings, openness often increases, which is a good thing. And it isn't like we are alone; God's Holy Spirit is with us.

In conversations I learned to ask open-ended questions and listen more carefully. Being patient with focused attention was crucial. By listening I learned a lot about a person; the reasons they might be leery of religion or God, the types of burdens, pain, doubts, fears or illnesses they were experiencing, or had in the past, and so on.

The simple truth, "It's not about us, but God" applied over and over again. People need love, hope, acceptance, peace, to be really heard, to find healing and forgiveness. Everyone needs to experience direct contact with God, His compassion and truth and find out how to be spiritually reborn.

Following almost every outing I'd find myself searching the Scriptures to better understand what had arisen in dialogue. Thinking through these things and praying about them was important, as well as praying for those I'd interacted with. Looking up verses, marking them in my Bible and beginning to use a Bible Concordance as a means of doing so, was an organizational vehicle that helped me learn and retain important truths.

God's Plans—Higher than Mine

With the passing of months, I realized it was for the best that I wasn't accepted into Bible College. Pastor Huffey and Mary Feister confirmed this by things they'd said. God had directed me away from an ultra-conservative Bible College which could have turned me into something I wasn't. Instead, He'd directed me into relational opportunities for growth which would broaden my spiritual perspective without quenching my passion to share the message of Jesus Christ. This made sense now!

> "As the heavens are higher than the earth, so are my ways higher than your ways and my thoughts than your thoughts."   – God (Isaiah 55:9 NIV®)

I was excited about the new job I'd secured at World Vision. The pay was better, employee chapel services were encouraging and I liked knowing I was making a difference in the world at the same time. My job was to pack relief barrels, which were shipped to places of need all over the world!

My spiritual habits were steady. I attended church three times a week and practiced Bible study and prayer daily. Additional spiritual support came from Mary Feister at the Christian bookstore and a Christian barber I could always chat with about the Bible. Work and chapel at World Vision five days a week and witnessing where people congregated filled out the rest of my schedule. Overall, things were good and I was thankful!

How Does God Speak to us in Prayer?

Practicing listening to God was my solitude prayer practice. Stilling my mind of random thoughts was an important step in preparing my heart for deeper levels of prayer and intercession. Listening was next. Following this, I'd offer prayer petitions for others.

Entering the Holy Place

Sitting quietly – hearing the silence
My own breath – a distant hum
Eyes closed – darkness becoming light
Seemingly important things—fading

Thoughts that dash about
Stilled by the will to listen
When unyielding—subdued again
Till quiet and peace rule

Till the heart and soul is ready
Quieted, attentive, willing to release
Selfishness, greed, fear, pride
Humbly preparing
Still – peaceful – patiently waiting

For the One who rules all
The Creator—The Almighty
Who in His own way
Speaks to His servants
By His Holy Spirit

Cleansing, renewing, transforming
Leading into Intercession
All with tender compassion and mercy
Welcoming – sincere, honest – prayer

Unveiling the big picture
Identifying what is 'Real'
Infusing His servants
With holy qualities
Hope, faith, truth and Love

In listening prayer I began hearing the name "Lancaster." It was weird! Was this a person, a place, something in the Bible? Over a month's time period the word "Lancaster" would pop into my thoughts at least once a week during prayer. I decided to borrow a map and located a city with this name in the high desert north of LA. Lancaster was a medium sized desert town near Palmdale. This was intriguing.

One Sunday after church I spoke with Pastor Huffey about it. "Pastor, over the past month, I've been hearing the name Lancaster during times of prayer. Have you ever had anything like this happen to you?"

"Well, yes." Pastor continued, "It's happened several times when God was calling us to do something, or let go of something. God can speak in any variety of ways David, but you have to be careful about what you act on. Was that all you heard?"

"Yes, just Lancaster. I've located a city with that name, north of LA in the desert."

"Well, David, you just can't take it for granted that this is God speaking, so go slow and keep listening. What exactly do you think God might be saying?"

"I don't know."

"You have a good job at World Vision, you're getting grounded spiritually and growing nicely. This could very well be Satan trying to uproot you before you're ready. I'll pray for you about this, but I wouldn't rush off into this just yet."

I knew Pastor had my best interest at heart and his caution was for my own good. I didn't know anyone in Lancaster, had no promise of work and had never been there before. I decided to give the whole subject a rest and go slow as pastor advised.

In the months that followed, Lancaster continued to surface on and off during listening prayer times.

Counsel from Mary

I decided to ask Mary at the Christian bookstore for her take. The door jingled as I entered. "Hi Mary", and she quickly appeared from the back room.

"Well hello David, what can I do for you today? How are things going for you?"

"Things are good. Church, work and witnessing are going well—and

I love the Bible you gave me! I'm reading and learning a lot."

"I knew you would. So what brings you in today? Do you need more tracts?"

"No, but I need to ask you a few questions about prayer and something that's been going on."

"Fire away!"

"Several months ago, the word **Lancaster** started coming to mind during prayer. I wasn't sure if it was a person, or a place and it kept happening. Out of curiosity I looked up the name on a map and found there is a city with this name in the high desert above Los Angeles. I'm wondering if God wants me to go there.

Pastor Huffey told me to be careful and not do anything rash and I respect and understand his concern. After talking things over with him, he told me to keep listening and go slow, reminding me that I have a good job at World Vision and am still getting grounded in the faith. The reason I've come to you is, *I need your input on how God speaks to us in prayer."*

"David, this is an important area of discernment for every Christian. If God never spoke to us about anything specific, as some believe, we would never know His fresh leading. So, yes David, God does speak to us individually and it's our job to verify if it's really Him. Pastor Huffey's caution is wise. If a person frequently says, "God told me this or that" there is a danger they're getting their own thoughts mixed up with thinking God is speaking to them. Many people have done this, usually doing what they wanted to do, attaching a "God told me" to justify going ahead with something. The results of this type of practice are disastrous!

On the other side of the coin, to be closed to God's voice, ignore what we hear, or conclude the voice of the Holy Spirit is just our own thinking, isn't much better! The safe choice most Christians make is to do nothing and God can't speak to them, because they are closed to hearing Him.

When I returned to the USA after many years in the mission field, the doctors didn't think I would survive the strain of malaria I'd picked up. After a lengthy recovery, I finally got well. Gradually, I began to think about a Christian Bookstore during prayer. My energy was still not up to par. So, I kept praying and listening and eventually became convinced that God was telling me to step out in faith and open this bookstore as a mission for Him. At the time I only had seven hundred dollars in savings, but somehow I have been able to pay all my bills and gradually grow this store with God's help. The full confirmation of this call came when I was actually doing what the Lord had spoken to me in prayer and seeing how He'd opened this new mission field.

God knows exactly how to speak to each of us in prayer. Our job is to ask God to reveal His plan for us in an obvious way. As a missionary I remember being called by God to go and proclaim Jesus' love and truth to a specific region and people group in a Third World country. This is an example of how detailed spiritual calls can be, but God speaks to each of us differently.

I appreciate Pastor Huffey's concern for you and agree with him for the most part, considering his caution and counsel to be wise. On the other hand, if the Lord persists in telling you something, which seems to be the case, it presents another possibility. Since you have no personal interest or selfish motive in going to Lancaster, it could be that God is calling you there. I don't know, but when God speaks, it is usually clear, persistent and doesn't go away. From what you've said, this is what's been happening with you. I cannot counsel you one way or the other, because this is one of those times when it's between you and God. You're the only one that can know how God is speaking to you."

"Is there a way I can be sure?"

"Well, you mentioned the Lord was teaching you about fasting and prayer. This would be an excellent question to fast and pray about. Ask God for a clear sign and confirmation that it's definitely His voice. Ask Him to reveal more to you about Lancaster. Ask Him if this is someplace where He has a work for you to do? When I think back to when I was your age, I was open to God's leading and this is what put me on the mission field. And being where God wanted me was the best place to be!

My parents feared for my safety and longed for me to have a secure life, but Jesus called me to walk with Him down a dusty dirt path among 'Tribes' people. When it's all said and done, it's all about listening to God and obeying His still small voice and doing what He has called and gifted us for in this life. Have you ever read about how God spoke to Elijah on a mountain and called him out of a cave where he was hiding?"

"I don't think so."

Taking her Bible, Mary turned to I Kings Chapter 19 saying, "I'll read a portion of this account, but it would be good for you to read this carefully on your own and the background of what had already occurred."

Mary read verses 11-13: 'So, God called to Elijah in the cave and told him to go out and stand on the mountain as the Lord Almighty was about to pass by but Elijah was afraid, and stayed inside the cave. Then a great and powerful wind tore the mountains apart and shattered the rocks before the Lord, but the Lord was not in the wind. After the wind there was an earthquake, but the Lord was not in the earthquake. After the earthquake came a fire, but the Lord was not in the  fire. And after the fire came a gentle whisper. When Elijah heard it, he pulled his cloak over his face and went out and stood at the mouth of the cave (I Kings 19:11-13)."

Mary then said, "This gentle whisper and Still Small Voice' was the voice of the Lord. The wind, earthquake and fire were powerful, but God's voice is heard in quietness. This is why Jesus taught us to go into our own private prayer closet and pray. Find a quiet place where you are not distracted. Invite His holy presence. Surrender you plans, ambitions and entire life to carry out God's will.

> When you pray, go into your room, close the door and pray to your Father, who is unseen. Then your Father, who sees what is done in secret, will reward you. – Jesus   Matthew 6:6 NIV®

It takes times to quiet our heart and spirit and still our random thoughts, but when we do, God can speak in ways we can be certain it's Him. Ask for His help in discerning His will. Every Christian should learn how to recognize God's voice if they hope to be led by Him.

Churches are full of people who do almost everything in their own steam, their own way. Seeking God and asking for His plans seems foolish to them. When people don't ask for God to reveal His will for their lives, the extent of their service and impact on the world for Christ is reduced to warming a pew and attending a church pot-luck!

So, pray to be able to hear His voice and recognize when He is speaking. No person can give you an answer about Lancaster, but I can encourage you to pray and keep praying. He'll show you! Allow the Word of God from the Scriptures to speak to you as well. Oftentimes we get a confirmation of something we're praying about from the Bible. Fasting will help you in this process and I'll be praying along with you. Keep the fire burning, David! Now, is there anything else I can help you with today?"

"I don't think so. Thanks Mary!"

Fasting and Praying

On Mary's advice, I began a fast and continued praying. Fasting was a good spiritual discipline. The first few days I'd get hungry sporadically and get distracted by hunger, but by the third or fourth day, hunger tapered off and food wasn't on my mind. I was sharper mentally, more aware of what I was doing. If I felt weak at work, I'd drink a vegetable drink. Overall, it was a cleansing feeling and my concentration and spiritual hunger sharpened considerably. One evening while reading the Scriptures, I came across the verses below:

> Some wandered in desert wastelands finding no way to a city where they could settle. They were hungry and thirsty and their lives ebbed away. Then they cried out to the Lord in their trouble and He delivered them from their distress. He led them to a straight way, to a city where they could settle. Let them give thanks to the Lord for His unfailing love and His wonderful deeds to men, for He satisfies the thirsty and fills the hungry with good things.   Psalm 107:4-9 NIV®

Reading further in Psalm 107 I saw that it was loaded with various stories of deliverance and God reaching out to those in desperate straits. It seemed like a long shot but I was open, sensing a responsibility to follow God's lead. Five months had passed since I first heard the word Lancaster in prayer. The more I prayed, the more convinced I became, believing I had a destiny with a place called 'Lancaster, California.'

The next time I saw Mary at the bookstore I told her about this decision and she was glad to hear that I'd taken adequate time to pray about making this move. She assured me she would be praying for me and the mission God had for me there.

It was a difficult subject to talk about with Pastor Huffey because I knew he would be sad to see me go, and probably with good reason feel I wasn't ready, so I kept praying for the right timing.

Slowly but surely a nest egg of savings had grown. During prayer the Lord gave me a peace about taking this step with Him into the unknown. I received a number of Bible verses that strengthened my resolution to press forward, trusting God to be with me. By now I had enough money to last a number of months, which was more than I was used to. The question that kept surfacing had to do with my immaturity as a person and a Christian.

Two weeks before leaving, I finally got enough courage to tell Pastor what my plans were. As expected, he wasn't excited, more worried than anything. We hugged on my last Sunday in church and he said he would not forget me in his prayers. I thanked him and we said goodbye. It seemed like my decision hurt him and I felt sad about this.

Lancaster Bound

Suitcase in hand I bought a one-way ticket and boarded a Greyhound Bus, destined for California's high desert and the city of Lancaster. Apprehensive, yet faith-filled, I'd be trying out my spiritual wings, testing what I believed to be God's voice sending me to do something.

Lancaster was a flat, spread-out town surrounded by a sandy, brush-filled terrain of browns and silver green, an ideal setting for more rabbits than I'd ever seen in my life. The first day in Lancaster I landed a job at the local car wash, not the ideal work, but it would do until I could find something better. It was early fall. The winds were cold, the pay was low and the work was hard, but I was thankful! It helped me rent a nice room by the week without dipping into what I had saved.

Not many people were out and about on the streets like other places I'd lived, but with the passing of each day I felt I was here for a purpose. Two more positive signs came in the way of finding a home church at the Foursquare Gospel where I was welcomed and the additional blessing of being invited to live with an older Christian couple, who attended there, for a very minimal rent.

The couple that invited me into their home were the Blazedales, but they insisted I call them Ma and Pa. They were among a growing list of unique Christian people God was bringing into my life. They believed in me and were excited about the vision of sharing the good news of Jesus Christ with those outside of the church.

A God Arrangement

In addition to a job, home church and a place to live, I met a guy my age named "Christian" who used to be a druggie in town, but had joined the military and found Jesus Christ while enlisted. Sitting in a coffee shop he told me about his journey and we both shared stories of our conversion to Jesus Christ. Amazingly, almost all of the local drug dealers were his old friends and he was hoping to find a way to share Christ with them. I told him how God had led me to Lancaster and we both sensed this was a teaming-up that God had arranged.

My new friend would only be in town on military leave for a week, so we decided to make the rounds connecting with as many of his old friends as possible and see what would happen. We prayed together and sensed a oneness of purpose to lift up the name of Jesus to them.

Christian had wheels, so he picked me up and we drove to one of his old buddy's house. Two of Christian's former friends were there and both were high on something. They offered us drugs; we declined and made some small talk to change the subject. Both of us shared a smattering of our testimonies and just as we began telling them why God sent His Son Jesus Christ to die for our sins, something bizarre happened to both of them. One began shaking intensely and the other crying uncontrollably.

"What's up?" I said, looking at Christian.

"I don't have a clue" he blurted out.

Had they taken some bad drugs!? We hoped the one who was shaking violently—wasn't overdosing! We talked about calling an emergency ambulance, but what if the police showed up and we got popped with them for a drug stash? There was also the possibility that the one convulsing could die. How would we explain this?

We prayed hard for both of them over the next 10 minutes until the symptoms amazingly subsided. Talk about relief!!

Is There Anything Too Hard for God?

Christian asked, "What's going on?!" Both told us they'd taken a hefty hit of drugs right before we arrived but were now straight. They couldn't figure out what brought them down so quickly. Then, the clincher came. They both wanted us to tell them what we knew about Jesus Christ and how they could know Him. Christian and I were shocked!

We'd only been talking with them for five minutes before they'd zoned out with bizarre symptoms. Wow! Talk about God showing up! The shaking and crying must have been God preparing them and bringing them down from whatever drugs they'd taken, so they'd be able to hear and receive Jesus Christ.

Immediately, Christian and I took turns sharing the account of Jesus' life, death and resurrection and both of Christian's friends asked to receive Jesus Christ. This was the beginning of a series of miracles that would shake the community of Lancaster.

> I am the LORD, the God of all mankind. Is anything too
> hard for me? – God   Jeremiah 32:27 NIV®

An Open House Party, God Visit

The next day Christian called to tell me that the two who'd received Christ had told some of their friends who were also into the local drug scene, and they too were interested in meeting us and hearing about God. I told my pastor's son Gary about this and he was psyched. He knew more of the Bible than Christian and I and we invited him to join us in answering any questions that might arise. We didn't know what to expect. The venue for this event would be an open house party thrown by friends of the first two guys who had received Christ.

From what we'd been told, news of the party was getting out. The idea was exciting, but we didn't know how we'd be able to share Christ in this setting? We prayed, tossed around a few ideas, but hadn't settled on anything. We didn't know what to expect, or what God might want to do.

On the night of the party people started arriving in a steady flow. The music was blasting, there was plenty of food and the house guests were quickly overflowing into the front and back yards. Our new friends made the rule, "Anybody doing drugs had to do them outside!" They decided that every half hour or so, they'd pull the plug on the music and have one of us who'd been a Christian for awhile share our testimony, or something from the Bible. We did this and the looks on everyone's faces but our host's revealed shock and amazement! Had they accidentally taken some religious drug! What was going on!?

In the middle of the evening, God's presence descended on the house! I'd never seen anything like it. It was like moving in a spiritual realm, walking in eternity with everything happening in slower motion.

> Without orchestration, God's Spirit was revealing to different ones, their sin and need, followed by a noticeable evidence of receiving Jesus Christ by their countenance of 'light' and their words. A number said, "We believe what we've heard about Jesus Christ being God's Son and we want to follow Him."
>
> In awe we were seeing the 'life and truth in Jesus Christ' being miraculously translated to those at the party.
>
> God is the giver of salvation! He always stands ready to reach into the minds and hearts of those who ask and open themselves to Him.

I will never forget this night! It's etched in my memory with a big, To God be the Glory! *God can do anything in any way He chooses!*

Too soon, Christian said goodbye and returned to the Army. Prior to this we'd invited a number of those who'd responded to Jesus Christ to the little Foursquare Gospel church I'd been attending. The proof of God's divine work was they came and continued as Jesus' followers.

From the night of the open house party, a core group was formed which would start a discipleship ministry called 'The Way Inn Ranch.' The Foursquare Church became our sponsor. Pastor Goodell Sr. was prepared by God because he and his wife and the congregation welcomed and accepted every person who entered the doors of the church and remained supportive of everything God was doing! Pastor Goodell Sr. and Jr. both helped baptize and teach many of the new believers in the ways of Jesus. As a relatively new Christian I was deeply awed by all that God had done in such a miraculous way!

The Enemy's Attack

Thanks to the Blazedales, I didn't have to worry about a roof over my head, or food. Ma Blazedale was a great cook, especially compared to what I'd been used to on my own. In time, I landed a job closer to the Blazedales' home doing heavy manual labor. The pay was significantly better. This job entailed busting up and carrying concrete out of a huge storage barn. I was also herding and loading turkeys on big trucks part-time when the work was there. Both were exhausting jobs, but it kept me fit.

One night after a grueling work day, I experienced a serious satanic attack shortly after going to bed. In a half-awake, half-asleep state, I sensed an evil presence in my room. Then I heard a voice whispering in a raspy voice, "I want you!" I knew it was Satan or one of his demons. I felt paralyzed with fear and I couldn't move to get up. My mouth seemed stopped. I couldn't even say the name of Jesus. I fought to gain control over my mouth, tongue and legs but they wouldn't move. The voice continued, in a cold and evil whisper, "I want you!" It was as if a dark cloud had settled over my room and I was under its power.

Fighting a paralysis of fear I managed to crawl out of the bed and locate the light switch. As I turned it on I managed to stammer out the words "In Jesus Name, the Lord rebuke you Satan!" In a cold sweat I stood there regaining my composure.

Hearing me from the living room, Pa Blazedale knocked on my door asking what had happened. I let him in and explained. He prayed with me and encouraged me to pray for God's protection every night before going to sleep. He challenged me to make an agreement with the Lord to read the Bible daily and memorize verses of protection.

He explained how perverse Satan is, seeking to torment us when we're tired, drowsy, or asleep. He suggested I ask for God's angelic protection over my sleeping hours. I took what he said to heart memorizing a collection of Bible verses on God's covering of protection. I never experienced this type of fear again.

Pa Blazedale also told me that the enemy would try to attack or intimidate us before or while God is doing something significant in our lives, or in ministry endeavors. I was grateful for his input, prayers and teaching me how to stand firm in Jesus Christ against the spiritual forces of darkness. The enemy was obviously angry about what was happening in Lancaster.

The Way Inn Ranch Team

Over the course of the next few months we providentially learned of an abandoned nursing home on the outskirts of Lancaster with spacious grounds. We visited as a group and saw the potential of a place where all of us could live. Pastor Goodell Sr. worked out a lease agreement with the owners and it was ours for the price of restoration and a modest rent. We were up for the challenge and began the process of cleaning and painting the living quarters, dining hall, newly designated chapel and other buildings. It appeared to be empty for many years.

We cleaned out an old chicken coop and pig pen—got a pig, laying hens and planted veggie gardens. We all chose larger projects to accom-

Left to Right - 1.Steve Armitage, 2.Dave Scanlon, 5.Kenny Hart, 6. D.E. Hoyt, 7. Gary Goodell 8. David Drake, 9. Don Matthews, 10. Rev. Goodell Sr.

plish alongside our daily chores. Restoring an old unoccupied property was an ambitious endeavor for a group of desert suburban ex-druggies, but God was in it. He'd already accomplished the main work of bringing conviction of sin, convincing of truth and changing hearts.

Repainting the living quarters with others and making and painting new signs for the property and chapel was one of my projects. I liked doing this with some painting experience from working with Kent.

Lancaster, CA 1968

The restoration of the buildings and grounds was similar to what was happening in each of us. Day by day, a well cared for ranch emerged from the rubble of an abandoned property in disrepair. We had partnered with God and were now occupying territory for His Kingdom. It was all very cool and amazing! Six of the early group enrolled in Life Bible College in Los Angeles. A few became full time pastors.

Dashed Hope

Up until now I'd never had a significant relationship with a woman, but in

Lancaster I met and fell for a beautiful Christian lady I'd met at church. To say that I was smitten is an understatement. In a relatively short time we became engaged. Unfortunately our engagement was short lived as my temper and jealousy spoiled things and she cut it off. Humbled and discouraged I was forced to acknowledge I was too immature for marriage and needed to wait.

The stability of the ranch was mainly due to Pastor Goodell Sr. and his son Gary who were in charge. I was more than OK with this. With the recent failed engagement in public view, I felt embarrassed and relieved that I didn't have much of a leadership role. I was still young in the faith with issues to work out. Anger was a tough nut to uproot—my nemesis, my thorn in the flesh.

Next Steps

A number of the early converts from The Way Inn would go on to Life Bible College in Los Angeles. Some wanted to become pastors, others teachers, or to be involved in outreach ministry in a local church. I never saw or heard from "Christian" again, but God had allowed us to sow a few seeds and He took it from there.

Lancaster had been a place on the heart of God. I learned it's better to listen and obey what God tells us persistently in prayer and step out in faith, than ignore God's "still small voice". What's safe and stable can be lifeless. Lancaster was a divine work, authenticated by how it went down via an otherworldly outpouring of the Holy Spirit. God had birthed a number of individuals into His family without human manipulation. All we could say was, "Yeah God!"

Satan's Den

While in Southern California I began thinking about Tom, a buddy from Lompoc who was a fellow seeker. We'd met on a correctional bus from L.A to Lompoc which led to a friendship that spanned several years of craziness in prison. We hung out in the yard, played handball, ran the track, shared holy books and watched each other's back.

On arrival at Lompoc one of Tom's best friends from the streets, John helped us make the transition from the receiving unit into the main population. John was an outrageously bold white guy who had a signifi-cant share of the drug-traffic at Lompoc. His partner in crime was Mike, a slender Italian Catholic, who wielded equal clout. The duo had all kinds of connections and thugs who stood behind them as security. Ironically, after Tom and I arrived, John and Mike's focus of selling drugs shifted to being "God seekers."

Several years had passed since then and I concluded Tom must surely be paroled by now. In trying to locate Tom, I spoke with his Mom by phone. She was cautious when learning I was a friend from Lompoc. Hearing concern in her voice about giving her son's phone number to a parolee, I shared how I'd come to faith in Jesus Christ and God and had begun a new life.

There was a pause, then an audible sigh of relief on her end! She went on to explain she and her husband were Christians and were very con-cerned about Tom. From seeing her son on occasion, she'd learned he was back into drugs and hanging around old friends.

When I reached Tom by phone I learned he, John and Mike from Lompoc were renting a house together in a canyon area. He was open to reconnecting and we set a day for me to visit. The drive south to Orange County brought back old memories, both good and bad. There was nothing legal parole-wise about my trio of friends living together.

As I entered the expansive home, it was obvious they were into drug distribution. Kilos of pot were in plain sight as well as weapons. Tom wasn't going straight. I'd suspected this from several things he'd said by phone. They'd all slipped back into wheeling and dealing. Tom told me the main drug they were selling and spreading for God was LSD, showing me a large quantity stored in the refrigerator.

If the police or narcs showed up I too could face a parole violation. I wasn't sure what to do, but having made the trip I decided to see how things went.

I wanted to talk with Tom alone, but it wasn't in the works initially. Over a brief lunch with the three, I tried to share my encounter with Jesus Christ. John was high, interrupting whenever he could. I knew each of them had experienced contact with Satan guised as God when high on acid and considered themselves "spiritually elevated and in tune with God."

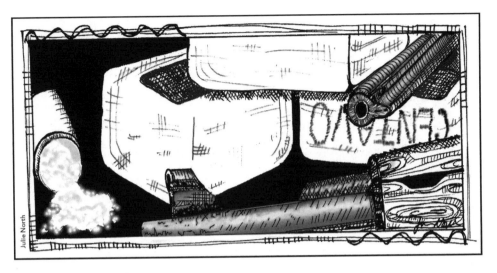

An Unwanted Message

When the subject came up again I said, "I think Acid-Highs create a spiritual illusion that seems real at the time, but it fades and everything goes back to the way it was before. Direct contact with God is different. Only God can change our heart and mind in a lasting way. And Jesus Christ is the only One who can forgive our sin and drive evil out of our lives."

I remember what happened on a lot of acid trips; I felt like I was entering eternity, seeing incredible things, or that I was an ancient seer, a god, or part of god. On other 'Trips' I could see demons and darkness everywhere! I wanted to shut it down but couldn't. Evil had people in its grips and wasn't about to let them go. They were slaves of the flesh and the world."

With John, Tom and Mike preoccupied with eating their sandwiches I continued, "You know what I'm talking about. On Acid it was easy to feel like I was one with nature, the ocean, the wind, the sky or moon, or have some mystical, spiritual or sensual experience. Taking Acid or Peyote creates other-worldly images and experiences, but are they real? Do they change us? Or are our old bad habits still in control?

I know Satan is present when I've dropped Acid, disguising himself as an angel of light, a great Seer, or God. The hook he leaves embedded in our spirit is the illusion of us making spiritual progress, but it's not real! Only God's Holy Spirit sent by Jesus Christ can cleanse our soul and free us! This is why God sent His Son into the world to lead us out of darkness."

Resistance

My take on LSD and Peyote brought an angered response from John, Mike and Tom. "You don't know what you're talking about!" John said. Mike chimed in with an articulate defense about them spreading spiritual awareness of God by dealing acid throughout Orange County. Tom was agitated and verbalized, "Your Jesus encounter is probably a leftover flashback from acid you've taken in the past!"

While Tom was talking John picked up a handgun and loaded it. I'd always reacted negatively to intimidation and this was no exception. Angered, I shared a few Bible Scriptures from Matthew chapter 24 where Jesus speaks about false Christs and their ability to deceive even spiritually-minded people. When I'd finished, John and Mike got up and left the room.

Tom stayed but didn't say anything. He was high on something. He grabbed a bag of pot and some papers—rolled a joint, lit it and asked if I wanted to get high. I declined. It appeared that further spiritual discussion wasn't going to happen unless acid was an acceptable part of the equation.

In the afternoon John and Mike were busy making drug transactions with a handful of customers who'd come by to score. Late afternoon, Tom and I scrounged up a meal in the kitchen and ate an early dinner. He continued to smoke dope and laced it with hash into the evening—causing him to drift into a sleep stupor. Tired from the drive south and the intensity of the setting, I crashed for the night on the living room couch.

The next morning I knew I should leave. For privacy, Tom and I went outside and sat in his car. "Tom, think about the promises you made to yourself in prison to stay away from dealing. Where do you think all this is heading?" I said, pausing. "Don't you see the risk? You could easily end up back in prison." Sitting in the passenger seat Tom grew angry, pulled a gun out of the glove box and put it to my head saying, "I'm telling you to shut-up! I don't want to hear any more of this bullshit!"

Angered by his threat, adrenalin pumping I didn't stop trying to reason with him. Finally, he put the gun down on his lap saying, "I think you'd better go."

Sensing I'd hit a wall—I said, "OK" and left.

Bad News

Eight months later I called Tom's family when I couldn't contact him by phone and his mom answered. When I asked how I could reach him, she gave me the news. "Tom's dead," she struggled to say in a broken voice. "He was shot in the head in Mexico, and drugs were involved. The police believe that an argument broke out, and one of Tom's friends may have killed him, but they haven't been able to prove it conclusively."

Tom's mom was broken as she went on, "Tom was a good student and everything was great in high school. If only he'd have let God help him and listen to those of us who loved him. I know you tried to talk to him too, because he told me about your visit. He was embarrassed about how he'd treated you." Her grief was still fresh and I sensed the pain of her son's death would never fully be healed. We spoke a little longer and quietly said good-bye. I felt mixed emotions of sadness, anger and awareness of how uncertain life is.

In the past when I'd called, I found out Tom's family were Christians. I shared with them how Jesus was changing my life. Knowing Tom and I had been close and that I was now a believer, helped Tom's mom open up to me. I was glad she did, but Tom's death was devastating news! It was hard to wrap my head around this. The possibility of John or Mike putting a bullet in Tom's head made my stomach churn. It was hard to believe that Tom's life had been snuffed out in this way. I knew drugs made people crazy, ruthless and killers. No one knew for certain who was responsible. It could have been Mexican drug dealers, John or Mike, or someone else with him.

The sobering reality of the brevity of life and uncertain time of death increased in my mind after Tom's death. It pushed me to value the relationships God was giving me and those that were to come. *No one has enough genuine life-time friends!*

Around this time, I received a postcard and then a phone call from Pastor Kent telling me about what was currently going on in the way of new outreach in the Bay area. An invite to return and help was added. With the break-up of my engagement it seemed like a good time to make a move.

Returning to San Fran would put me back into the thick of all the elements of life in a big city. Representing Jesus, God's true light for the world in the dark corners of San Francisco's street-life would have its challenges.

I have come into the world as a light, so that no one who believes in me should stay in darkness. - Jesus Christ

John 12:46

8

Back in San Fran

Monrovia and Lancaster had both been important in my spiritual formation. Leaving mentors and new friends was the hardest part of moving on, but I would not forget them. Monrovia had been foundational, via receiving excellent mentoring. Lancaster had boosted my confidence in God's ability to do the impossible, balanced by the humbling counterpart of personal immaturity.

On Kent's invitation I caught a Greyhound and returned to San Francisco. When I met with Kent he filled me in on his work in the city and new contacts he'd made in the Haight. He was excited, the perennial optimist, and it was catching.

Anchor Rescue Mission

My next stop after meeting with Kent was Anchor Rescue Mission in the Fillmore District. I'd called ahead and made arrangements for live-in volunteer work. Food and lodging would be provided in exchange for 25-30 hours of mission work. This freed me to do outreach with Kent in the

Haight.

Sisters Yvonne and Drayton who ran the mission were very excited to learn I'd received Christ. My first visit to the mission had been shortly after moving to San Francisco in 1966, which continued on-and-off until early 1967 when I joined the Krishna temple. I'd go to the Mission for a meal when I was hungry and broke, and usually stayed after to help wash dishes and clean up.

Anchor Rescue Mission, Fillmore District SF, CA

Sister Drayton had founded the mission in a needy part of the Fillmore District near the crossroads of Fillmore and McAllister. A few decades earlier this same district had been a well-kept, safe, African-American community known for musical creativity—hosting many up and coming musicians and singers like Ella Fitzgerald. A motto for the area at that time was "Give me your tired, your poor and your talented." With the passing of time, the Filmore's charm had faded. Crime, alcoholism, gambling, unemployment and vices of the flesh had infiltrated.

Over the years, the mission and neighborhood had gone through cycles. In previous days, the mission was able to provide overnight accommodations and showers for 15 men. When building codes were updated, the housing portion of the building had to be closed off. The mission now conducted a worship service, followed by a hot meal, six days a week for 40-60 visitors. Sister Drayton and close friend, Sister Yvonne, were the Christian women God chose to co-lead and carry out the bulk of the workload at the mission.

They had a vision and deep concern to aid those who'd fallen victim to temptation, addiction, or on hard times. If God had not called them, they would most likely have chosen a safer setting to serve in. Over time the Filmore District had turned dangerous, especially at night.

Small and large missions like this can be found the world over. They provide tangible help to the down-trodden of our world, while holding out spiritual hope. At the core of Anchor Rescue Mission was the message of God's love expressed through His Son, Jesus Christ. This mission was not state or federally funded, but sustained through prayer, faith and benevolent gifts given through a diversity of sources.

Sister Yvonne was a jubilant woman about forty years old with a smile and fresh word of encouragement that would brighten any body's day! Sister Drayton was a distinguished woman in her late fifties, always dressed tastefully. She had severe medical issues but never made mention of them at the mission. I learned of

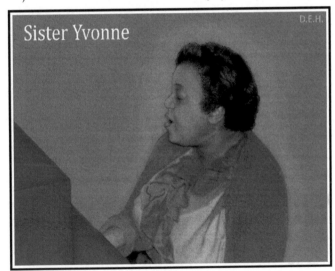

Sister Yvonne

this privately, through Sister Yvonne.

The duo was clear about their role at the mission. They were persistent and believing prayer warriors, administrators, did food procurement, food-prep and cooking. They also led the music portion of worship and provided special music unless guests were lined up to do so. Sister Yvonne played piano and sang. Both led music and did special numbers for the mission's worship services. In my heart and mind I can easily see and recall them singing "Love Lifted Me", one of the favorite hymns requested by guests.

Sister Drayton recruited speakers who had a heart for the lost. The speakers preached on a rotation basis for each mission service. In a pinch, both Sisters Drayton and Yvonne could fill-in and communicate the gospel clearly and passionately which they did from time to time when a speaker was ill, or had some other type of emergency.

While working at the mission, I met almost all of the volunteer speakers who came from different denominational and non-denominational backgrounds. Most were pastors, teachers, or evangelists. Without exception Christ-honoring sermons were combined with an invitation to receive Jesus Christ. When the mission service was over, a hot meal was provided to every guest.

The vision of the Mission was to make sure every person who entered the doors had an opportunity to hear the "good news of Jesus Christ" and hopefully understand, God's love and forgiveness is greater than any of our sins!

On a regular basis visitors would respond by opening up to God after years of running in the opposite direction, and the amazing miracle of salvation would occur.

The mission was housed in an old building comprised of two downstairs storefronts. On entering the mission there were rows of chairs with seating for approximately 60, which filled the mission's chapel. At the front of the chapel was a piano, a pulpit and a curtain which opened into a small prayer room, used by the staff and visiting speakers. Behind this was a spacious kitchen. The opposite side of the storefront housed freezers and clothing.

Sisters Yvonne and Drayton practiced deep intercession prayer for the salvation of all who came to the mission, the body of Christ and the many practical needs of the mission and their home church. For the most part they did so in the small Prayer Room on their knees. The frayed carpet in front of each chair bore distinct knee marks, a witness of their focused devotion, love of God and dependence on Him.

Of all the lessons these gifted women passed on to me, "the power of prayer offered in faith", was etched on my soul! They were consistent and disciplined about prayer. Jesus was the vine and they were His branches.

The only way to bear fruit was to abide in Him! Prayer and communion with the Father, Son and Holy Spirit was a top priority; the means of entering God's presence and standing up for those spiritually who couldn't stand up for themselves.

While working at the mission it was confirmed again, Satan and his demons were not a myth. The sisters and visiting speakers encountered the dark working of the enemy in many of the lives that entered the door of the mission. They were accustomed to demons speaking out. We all witnessed the oppressive grip the Evil One had on the vulnerable of this world. Sister Yvonne and Sister Drayton never gave in to the Evil One, but fought his forces through the powerful "blood of Jesus Christ." They prayed over the entire mission asking God to make it "holy ground" to all who came through the doors; requesting that men and women's hearts would surrender to God's love and grace. They also prayed with authority, binding the Evil One from controlling the lives of those who would come to the mission. They prayed in faith that the bondage caused by vices of the flesh would be broken in Jesus' Mighty Name!

The anchor logo rising from the deep represented God's power to rescue anyone who calls out to Him. The deliverance theme found in Psalm 107 fit the mission perfectly. The cross as part of the anchor represented the hope we find when we place our faith in Jesus Christ. Jesus is the One who anchors our soul in a relationship with God that is firm and secure!

In my mind's eye, I can see Sister Yvonne playing the piano and Sister Drayton leading the music; their voices filling the chapel with sweet praise and devotion. Those who entered the mission were always in for a

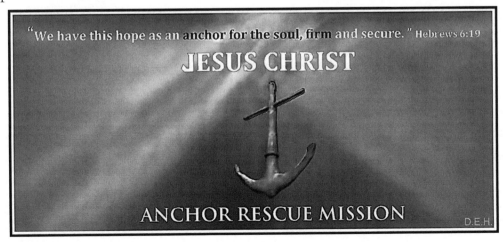

"We have this hope as an anchor for the soul, firm and secure." Hebrews 6:19

JESUS CHRIST

ANCHOR RESCUE MISSION

D.E.H.

treat. A meaningful worship experience for those with ears to hear and a hot meal prepared with love.

The guests of the mission were the homeless, hippies, alcoholics, vets, drug addicts and runaways. Foul breath, smelly clothes and the stench of tobacco and alcohol permeated many of those that shuffled in for respite from the harshness of street-life. The contrast of human despair and God's love were always present in this little mission. One by one, miracles occurred, prayers were answered and lives were changed. Many who end up on the streets feel worthless, but they are valuable to God!

> Are not five sparrows sold for two pennies? Yet not one of
> them is forgotten by God.   Luke 12:6 NIV®

I learned first-hand how God miraculously provided for this small mission that served the locals in need. There were times when the staple cupboards and freezers were near empty, until a gift of money, food, clothing, or other useful items came in at just the right time. This was not a well-endowed mission with back-up supplies. The miracles that occurred were similar to what took place at the orphanages led by George Muller of Bristol, England. *Real need and earnest prayer were the prelude to a miracle,* as it was in the feeding of the multitudes by Jesus.

Certain days of the week we visited the Farmers' Market. It was an eye-opening experience. The sisters prayed for specific needs and went to the large outdoor produce market, a couple of bakeries and a meat market or two, expecting and depending on God to provide.

They didn't go to buy or beg, but to receive whatever sellers chose to discard or give out of a simple act of charity for the Lord's work, or to help their fellow humans in need. As they walked the produce line with a large hand-wagon, I noticed the growers knew them. With a nod of the head, or a subtle face gesture it was apparent if they were able to donate that day. In the course of an hour the mission vehicle was overflowing. "To God be the glory, and God bless you", the sisters would say as each gift was given. *I gradually caught on; God's provisions were ample to meet the needs of those who truly represented Him.*

Working at the mission in the Filmore district was not without incidents. Unruly and violent guests showed up fairly regularly, but were not allowed to stay if they didn't calm down. Extracting them from the premises could easily turn into a scene where the police had to be called.

Security from Above

Getting to and from the mission safely was a challenge. The streets around the mission were thick with drug dealers, pimps, prostitutes, alcoholics, violence and crime, especially after dark. It was tricky navigating our movements, requiring common sense and heightened personal security. When I stepped off the bus from the Haight to the Fillmore district I could count on six dangerous blocks before I reached the front door to the mission. I purposely took a back route to avoid the concentration of street activity. As a white boy, I stood out more than I wanted to.

As careful as I was, a young thief cornered me at knife-point one evening, just as I'd reached the front door of the mission. "Give me your money, or I'm gonna stick you!" he said forcefully. He was desperate and nervous, but seemed serious. He looked to be about my age.

Looking at him squarely, I said, "I've only got change."

He persisted, "Come on man, I'll stick you if you don't give me all your money!"

"I work at this mission and everything we do is about Jesus Christ changing lives. I'm a servant of God and the truth is, you shouldn't be trying to rob anyone!"

He seemed stunned as our eyes locked in a stare. Then he folded his blade and took off down the street. I don't know what spooked him. My adrenalin gradually subsided after getting inside the mission and locking the door behind

DEBBIE WILCOX

me. A sense of relief swept over me and I thanked God for His security. Sisters Yvonne and Drayton were no strangers to these types of attacks having encountered many of these incidents over the years. It didn't cause them to waver, but made them stronger in Him. The important thing was, it didn't come close to touching their joy! Trials and tribulations in this world come and go, but Jesus Christ's presence in us is not diminished as we keep trusting Him in all circumstances, good or bad.

Helping with food-prep, kitchen clean-up, organizing donated food and clothing and providing security for out-of-control guests were my first assignments at the mission. As time passed Sister Drayton would allow me to share my testimony, or preach if a pastor canceled. Kent was also asked to join the speaker rotation at the mission. Working at the Mission was an incredible learning experience, leaving a positive spiritual imprint.

Openness in the Haight

Connecting with neighborhood locals and recent arrivals in the Haight, I saw more openness and softening among street-people to spiritual things that previously wasn't there! The erosion of good vibes in the Haight had deflated some of the counter-culture's arrogance and pride. This new receptivity was a good thing!

It felt good to be back in San Fran, but the noise and craziness would take some getting used to. Temptation, danger and darkness were more pervasive. Unfortunately the fading glory of Flower-Power didn't stop people from continuing to migrate to San Fran, unaware of what they would find.

The new wave of street people found dirty streets, the mixture of dog-poop and incense stench, burned out hippies lacking the energy to be friendly, and an eerie presence of something dead. The once hopeful atmosphere in the Haight had soured and turned bleak.

Greedy landlords contributed to the decline of the area by exploiting tenants with double to triple rent hikes, making it near impossible to find affordable lodging. This forced the have-nots to flounder on the streets, making them easy prey for criminals to swoop in and abuse.

The plague of 'Greed' is not isolated to landlords, but pervasive in all sectors of society worldwide. It exploits, abuses and harms all who encounter its scourge. In everyday life this evil contributes to homelessness, drug and alcohol abuse and crime. It's everywhere—even among the poor living on the streets.

Olivia braided wristbands and ankle bracelets with beads intertwined to eke out a meager existence on the streets. She did so with another girl and a guy who provided security for one another. Olivia had been abused, threatened and stolen from by bad street people. Crime forced many victims to rethink their exaggerated view of universal goodness. The bipolar opposites of 'Peace and Love' and 'Hate and Greed' were both present in places where hippies congregated.

Olivia

Visiting Ma & Pa Davis

I was excited to reconnect with Ma and Pa Davis. The Davis' were an amazing African-American couple in their mid-seventies who adopted and loved me when I'd first moved to San Francisco in 1966. Both were short in stature. Pa Davis was soft spoken and Ma Davis was joyous—with a double portion of love to go around! Pa Davis took care of the boiler room in the apartment building where I'd lived and Ma Davis did maid services in the neighborhood. The Davis' lived in a tiny basement apartment next to the boiler room, with a rent reduction in exchange for maintenance work. Neither drove.

Though they were as poor as dirt, it never ceased to amaze me how they'd plan ahead and share meals with me out of their poverty. They knew my room was without a stove or refrigerator and they wanted to share. In spite of their low income and physical problems, they were genuinely thankful—always praising Jesus!

A wave of thankfulness came over me as I thought of them. Before each meal they'd bow their heads and pray in gratitude for everything they had and for Jesus' power and love to be known in the world. I'd attended their church for worship and a potluck. I liked it but my interest was in world religions back then.

When I left San Fran for Bible College I'd missed seeing them and sharing my big news. Now, back in the city I was eager to see them, so I jumped on a bus and headed down to the Fillmore. When I entered the old stone building, memories flooded back, about where my head was at when I used to live here. I'd been searching without any clear direction, trying to find God on my own. Things were different now; I knew Jesus was Savior and Lord! Inside the building I took two short stair flights down to the Davis' apartment door and knocked firmly. "Who is it?" Ma Davis called out.

"David, who used to live upstairs" I spoke loudly.

"Oh, my Lord!" She exclaimed as the door swung open and she welcomed me with a big hug and kiss. Pa Davis got up from their small table, moving less steady and walked slowly over to grab me, holding on with a long bear-hug squeeze.

"So good to see you, my boy!" He whispered with a sigh of relief, "And to know you're OK."

Being young and caught up in my own life, I'd never obtained their address to stay in touch by mail and they'd obviously been worried.

"Come on in honey—we're just so glad to see you!" Ma Davis piped in.

Not able to hold it in, I said, "Guess what's happened to me?"

"Come on now boy, tell us! We want to hear everything!" Ma Davis blurted out.

"OK" I said with excitement. "I've received Jesus Christ into my life!"

"Oh my, oh my, oh my, Praise the Lord! Hallelujah! Hallelujah! Hallelujah! Praise the Lord! Oh, David—this is such wonderful news!" Ma Davis gleefully exclaimed.

"Praise You Sweet Jesus, Praise the wonderful Name of the Lord!" Pa Davis added.

"This is such wonderful news and we're so happy for you! So glad that Jesus saved you!" Ma Davis cooed.

By now she was beaming from ear to ear. They were so happy that it made me feel good. Gathering herself, Ma Davis sat down saying, "We're gonna have a good ole visit, now come on David, come over here and sit down." As I was sitting down Ma Davis leaned toward me and chuckled, "We're going to celebrate and you're gonna tell us all about how Jesus saved you. Now, what can I get you to drink? We want you to stay for lunch! Oh, David, this is the best news!"

"I'll have whatever your having to drink."

"You're just not picky enough" Pa Davis said grinning.

Ma Davis followed, "We gots to fatten you up a bit—and get some meat on your bones. But first, tell us how you found Jesus!"

"It was so many things that converged. When I thought of you and those who had shown the love of Jesus to me, I couldn't help but keep an open mind and heart. I knew you were praying for me like my Grandma had; so was my neighbor Barbara from Monrovia, Kent and family and his student friend Timothy from the seminary. The combined prayers of each of you were chipping away at the darkness which had a grip on me.

After I saw you last, I joined a Hindu temple in the Haight when a Swami from India moved into the neighborhood. In the beginning, I was impressed by his knowledge and devotion to God. Gradually the storefront was transformed into a temple and three large wooden idols were brought in and placed on an altar in the main worship room. The swami gave the directive to provide food and flower offerings to these "Juggernauts" or idols, daily. This was unexpected and troubling. I never felt good about these carved figures.

Shortly after, I met a seminary student named Kent and he offered to teach me how to study the Bible. We met and talked about God and the Bible and I sometimes shared what I was learning at the temple.

At one of the Bible studies Kent brought a fellow student named Timothy who was Chinese. As the study unfolded, the focus of the teaching was on the topic of pagan religions, false prophets and Jesus Christ being the only way to a relationship with God.

After the study, I voiced my opinion and resistance to God being that narrow in scope. Timothy gave his reasons and challenged me to call out to the True and Living God and ask if Jesus was His Son. He told me to stop chanting the Hindu mantra and go directly to God. At the time I reacted in anger and told him to leave!

The next day, after calming down, the thought hit me, "Only God can forgive human sin." This helped me decide to take Timothy up on his challenge. *I started praying silently to God, asking Him to reveal if Jesus Christ is His Son, the Messiah.*

A war was going on inside me! I didn't know it, but the war was between God and Satan's counterfeit religious spirits. I recalled Timothy's words, "You've been deceived by a spirit of divination. Keep calling out to God and ask Him to show you if Jesus Christ is the true door to finding Him." He said other things that cut to my heart, leaving me in turmoil. In desperation I prayed harder. One night before going to sleep I saw things that only God could show me about spiritual masters I'd admired—and about myself.

Timothy's words kept echoing in my mind, "Stop chanting your mantra, and call out to the True and Living God and He will show you the truth. He will show you that Jesus Christ is the Son of God and you will know for yourself!"

The more I thought about it the more convinced I became that Jesus Christ's identity was critical. If He was and is God's Son, a part of God, sent by God, He would be able to forgive my sin, and I would follow him.

Then, one morning in the middle of a worship service at the Krishna Temple, God showed up. There was a small fire in the basement putting everybody into a panic. Most people fled the temple in fear. Three of us stayed behind. In the middle of this confusion I heard a voice say, "Call on me now! Call on me now!" I whispered a short prayer and immediately God's spirit flooded my body with light!

I knew it was the spirit of Jesus Christ entering my body and that God was forgiving and cleansing me. In that moment Jesus cast out the evil religious spirits that had held me captive in confusion! It was beyond my human understanding that in such a short space of time, God was able to make things so clear.

"My, my Mama—it sounds like he's got the real thing! He's truly been saved! We're so glad you came back to let us know. Thank you Jesus! Thank you Jesus!"

"OK now David," Ma Davis spoke up, "We want to hear everything! Including what you've been up to since Jesus came into your heart. I'm gonna start putting out fix-ins for sandwiches."

Pa Davis leaned my way and put his hand on top of mine saying "David, this is a powerful thing that God has done for you. You've seen things lots of people never see!

With a laugh, Ma Davis said, "Now you know for sure—Jesus is the Son of God! God is good and he's good all the time! Praise you Jesus! Now, now, now, isn't God great and powerful, His ways are past finding out. It's an amazing thing what God can do in a human heart and spirit", Ma Davis exclaimed!

"What happened next?" Pa Davis queried.

"Kent invited me to live with his small family at Golden Gate Seminary. He helped me get into a regular habit of Bible reading and prayer and I was baptized in a small church in Byron where he was a student pastor."

"That sounds like a fine start that God has given you", Pa added.

"OK", Ma Davis said, "Let's pray and give thanks. Thank you Jesus for everything you have provided. All that we have comes from You. Thank You for bringing David to visit us today and for how You powerfully set him free! Praise you Jesus, Praise you God our Father! Bless and nourish us with this food so we can serve you. In Jesus' Holy Name, Amen!"

Breaking into a little melody, Ma Davis began to hum and then sing, "O happy day, O happy day, when Jesus washed, when Jesus washed, when Jesus washed—washed my sins away—O happy day!" This song led into a rich time of visiting and catching up, a happy day for the three of us, with Jesus at the center.

◇

Sobering News: Complicated National Grief

In April of 1968 Dr. Martin Luther King Jr., age 39, was shot and killed by a sniper in Memphis, Tennessee. *His death brought sorrow and anguish of soul the world over and all those on the side of equal rights for people of color in the USA. Martin Luther King Jr.'s social and spiritual imprint was irreplaceable!* Grief and disillusionment mingled as another bright US leader fell prey to assassination by a sniper's bullet. Similar to the questions that surrounded JFK's assassination, the truth of who may have been behind both assassinations remained veiled.

With the nation and world still in shock, just two months later, Senator Robert F. Kennedy was assassinated at age 43. In disbelief and sorrow it was near impossible for Americans to wrap their heads around this triple national tragedy. The convergence of these deaths caused unparalleled grief and an unraveling of hope. How could these three righteous political and social agents of change be snuffed out in this violent way? Who was really responsible? Unanswered questions loomed. Hearts across the globe were heavy.

*How could this happen in the Land of
the Free and the Home of the Brave?!*

In spite of these tragic events, life would slowly resume for Americans and others who grieved across the globe, but the loss and unanswered questions surrounding these assignations would live on and not be forgotten.

Outings in the Haight

Kent and I were both developing relationships with people we could revisit. Street people began to recognize us and see us in a positive way. We were Street Christians (later called Jesus People) viewed as good-guys by the locals, not out to run a scam or hurt them. If individuals were without food we'd invite them to Anchor Rescue Mission, or refer them to another downtown mission. We knew this wasn't ideal, because of the distance to these missions, but many made the trek anyway. We knew they'd hear the Good News of Jesus and receive a hot meal.

Surprisingly people were still coming to the Haight in a regular stream with overflow crowds on the weekends. What they were coming to see, had for the most part vanished. A handful of retail stores selling Hippie stuff were still around. Visitors dressed in hippie garb in the daytime hours made it seem like there was a resurgence of the Flower Power culture. It was as if the message of the "Summer of Love" was a year late in reaching those who were still migrating to San Fran. Runaways, wanna-be hippies, drug dealers, a new wave of free-love advocates and spiritual seekers were among the 1968 throng.

Weekday nights told the true story of a broken dream filled with danger and violence. Most good-will hippies steered clear of the streets during the night hours, especially Haight Street and the park. Daytime was safer. We also needed to be street-smart and conducted our outreach ministry in daylight hours.

A growing number of Haight residents and visitors were open to hear the truth, rather than listen to the lies and delusions of weird street counterfeits claiming to be a representative of God. Satan's disguise was for the most part becoming easier for street people to see through.

This was good for us and gave credence to our words. We would often contrast Jesus Christ who came to save and rescue, with the darkness of the evil One who attempts to deceive and destroy lives. To street people this was an understandable reality they were witnessing for themselves.

> Jesus said, "The thief comes only to steal and kill and destroy; I have come that they may have life, and have it to the full."   John 10:10 NIV®

The battle for the hearts and minds of a generation was real. Representing the True and Living God in this setting was crucial for those who needed to hear the truth and find peace of mind and heart.

The San Francisco Bay Area Jesus People Movement

Only One Way to Heaven?

This topic sparked interest, intense discussion and oftentimes anger. For those who thought all paths lead to heaven, this claim was an affront, "How dare you suggest you know or are following the 'Only Way' to God and I'm deceived!?" Responses like this were the norm.

Having fought against the idea of there being just "one way to access God", I understood the frustration of those who opposed this. I'd rejected this idea prior to grasping the difference between a "True God" and thousands of counterfeits.

In talking with a lot of street-people since I'd received Jesus Christ, I'd learned most of those I asked about God had come up with their own 'personal religion,' taking a little of this teaching, or a bit of this philosophy and arrived at their own God, or non-God concept. Some bought into pagan, occult, or demonic religions without questioning. A large number of street people were oblivious to anything spiritual, but were obstinate about anyone telling them anything. For these, the idea of God having parameters or rules didn't matter, because they did what they wanted and weren't interested!

Regardless of where people were in their head, I knew God was capable of getting anyone's attention. Resistance to the "True and Living God and His Son Jesus Christ" could easily change in a brief moment in time. God was capable of doing anything! I'd read the Bible verse below and could attest to it personally!

> "I am the LORD, the God of all mankind. Is anything too hard
> for me?"   Jeremiah 32:27 NIV®

When I realized how polarizing the truth of Jesus being the only One who was able to forgive human sin and bring us into a relationship with God, I wrote an article titled "Only One Way? How Narrow Minded!"

This had been my response when Timothy confronted me with Jesus Christ being the only mediator between God and man. I'd emphatically told him, "How narrow minded!"

This article was published in the San Fran street paper *The Oracle*, in handout form and later in Berkeley's *Right On* newspaper.

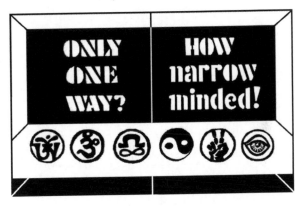

Dialogue on the topic, "One Way to God" raised lots of questions, drew conflicting opinions, and naturally led to discussion on Jesus' identity. Who was Jesus Christ? Was He God and Man? Was He the Messiah? If He was God's Son and the Savior of mankind, how did he impact the world, and what does this mean for me personally?

These pivotal questions created opportunities for God to speak to those who were open and listening. The meaning of "Messiah" and proof of him completing his mission were among other legitimate queries that also arose.

Having searched for God and truth, I remembered the dilemma of feeling unsure what to believe or trust. Around this time an anonymous short article surfaced that we put into handout form. It was titled 'God Leads a Pretty Sheltered Life.' *With many thinking God was either non-existent, asleep, or on a long vacation, it generated needed conversation regarding God's involvement in human affairs.*

God Leads A Pretty Sheltered Life

At the end of time, billions of people were scattered on a great plain before God. Some of the groups near the front talked heatedly, not with cringing shame, but with embittered belligerence.

"How can God judge us? How can he know about suffering?" snapped a brunette, jerking back a sleeve to reveal a tattooed number from a Nazi concentration camp. "We endured terror, beatings, torture, and death!"

In another group, a black man lowered his collar. "What about this?" He demanded, showing his rope burns. "Lynched for no crime but being black! We've suffocated in slave ships, were wrenched from loved ones, and toiled til only death gave us release."

Hundreds of such groups were visible across the plain. Each had complaints against God for the evil and suffering He'd permitted in His world. How lucky God was they all agreed, to be able to live in heaven where all is light, without weeping, fear hunger, hatred, torture, or harsh punishments. Indeed, what does God know about man? What does He know about being forced to endure unspeakable suffering? After all, "God leads a Sheltered Life!"

So each group sent out a leader, chosen because they had suffered the most. There was an African black male tortured for decades and then hanged to death by slave owners on trumped up charges, who represented 14 million slaves. There was a Jew who watched his entire family killed and buried in a mass grave and was then transported by train to a Nazi Death Camp, forced into hard labor, tortured for years and finally gassed to death. He represented 6 million Jews. There was a woman from Ethiopia who was viciously raped and forcefully mutilated in her genital area by her captors resulting in continuous pain. She became their slave working from sunup to sundown. While attempting to protect other women in the camp, she was tied to a stake and burned to death as an example. She represented 27 million middle-African women. There was a Native American from the Pequots tribe who traded with pilgrims until they became paranoid and attacked his tribe at night and captured him. In a barbarous massacre many in his tribe died. He and a handful of others were tortured by being 'flayed alive.' The skin on his face and head was torn off and he was then disemboweled while still alive. He represents one million Native Americans who were massacred, raped, forced into slavery, or driven from their lands in the 'Trail of Tears' marches.

Hundreds of other groups who had suffered atrocities were lined up across the great plain. Satisfied by their representatives; at last they were ready to present their case. Before God would be qualified to be their judge; He must endure similar horrendous suffering and pain to what they had endured.

Their decision was that God should be sentenced to live on earth as a man. But because He was God, they set certain safeguards to be sure He would not use His divine powers to help himself.

- Let Him be born a Jew.
- Let the legitimacy of His birth be questioned.
- Let Him champion a cause so just, but so radical, that it brings down on him the hate, condemnation and destructive attacks of the political and religious authorities.
- Let Him be indicted on false charges, tried before a mob and sentenced by a cowardly ruler.
- Let Him experience what it is to be terribly alone and abandoned by his followers.
- Let Him be tortured and die a cruel and vicious death.
- Let His death be humiliating with scoffers jeering, mocking and spitting on him.
- Let his death take place alongside common criminals.

As each leader announced his portion of the sentence, loud shouts of approval went up from the great throng of people. As the last one had finished pronouncing his part of the sentence—there was a long silence. No one spoke or moved. **Suddenly all realized;** God had already served his sentence.

> For there is only One God and One Mediator between God and humanity, Christ Jesus, both human and divine, who gave himself as a ransom for all, revealing God's purpose at the appointed time.   1 Timothy 2:5-6 NIV®

Only One Way to Heaven isn't a new message. It's at the core of the entire New Testament of the Bible. Jesus said, "I am the way, the truth and the life and no person comes to the Father except through Me (John 14:6)." **There are no other options when approaching The True and Living God.**

Surprisingly, a significant percentage of those who say they are Christians don't find it palatable to agree with this non-negotiable spiritual parameter. Regardless, Jesus Christ is the Savior of the World whom God has sent to reconcile humankind. God's plan of providing Jesus Christ as our mediator will determine the eternal destiny of every person who dies. The critical questions will be, "Is our name recorded and written into the Lamb's Book of Life (Revelation 21:27)?" "Have we been reborn by the Spirit of the Living God, and has the Holy Spirit sent from the Lord Jesus Christ sealed us for eternity (Ephesians 4:30)?"

False hopes and wishful thinking are not going to help us, our family, friends, or those we love. One Way to God has and will remain controversial and unacceptable to those who are unable, or unwilling to accept God's means of rebirth to reinstate us into His eternal family.

The bending of a 'human will' to receive input from an Invisible God is the 'great battle of the soul.' We all want to make our own choices. On the other side of resisting, I favor yielding to the Creator of the Universe. His wisdom and greatness is above anything humans can fathom. The Omnipresent, All-Knowing, All-Seeing One's path is worthy of full exploration and consideration on His terms. I guarantee, anyone who turns to Him will be astonished by God's Wisdom and Glory! But, to follow God and His Son Jesus Christ and keep following is not without a cost.

> Jesus called the crowd together with His disciples, and said to them, "If anyone wishes to follow Me as My disciple, he must deny himself, setting aside selfish interests, and take up his cross, willingly enduring whatever may come, and follow Me, believing in Me, conforming to My example in living and, if need be, suffering or perhaps dying because of faith in Me."   Mark 8:34 Amp. Bible

Becoming a Christ follower by giving our life to God and obeying Jesus' command to take the Good News into the world, was front and center in our minds and hearts. The Lord gave us strength and determination to keep following and not turn back. In spiritual rebirth, God implants a number of core values which transform and give us faith and truth. Read-

ing the Gospel of Matthew, Mark, Luke or John all the way through, sealed the deal. We were called by the "Living God" and given something to do. 'Young and eager' we carried the news of 'Jesus being alive' to friends, family and everywhere we went, freely sharing the message of God's amazing love through Jesus Christ.

The results were mixed. We lacked wisdom and sensitivity, but our enthusiasm and God's presence in us was strong. One core value and truth that was embedded in our "rebirth" was: Jesus Christ is the Son of the Living God, the Messiah. Jesus Christ is the Savior who God sent to free mankind from the power of sin and death.

One Way to Heaven was central to what we knew to be true. Posters would eventually be made with one finger pointed heavenward, indicating Jesus is the Only Way to God.

> "For God so loved the world, that He gave His only begotten Son, so that whoever believes and trusts in Him as Savior will not perish, but have eternal life."   John 3:16 NIV®

When early Christians were being challenged or put on trial for miracles that happened as they spoke, lived and prayed in the Name of Jesus, they said:

> "If we are being put on trial today for a good deed done to a disabled man, as to how this man has been restored to health, let it be known and clearly understood by all of you, and by all the people of Israel, that in the Name of Jesus Christ the Nazarene, who you asked to be crucified

by the Romans, and who God raised from the dead; it is in His Name by the authority and power of Jesus, this man stands here before you in good health. This Jesus is the stone which was despised and rejected by you, the builders, but which became the chief Cornerstone. And there is salvation in no one else; for there is no other name under heaven that has been given among people by which we must be saved, for God has not provided any other alternative for salvation." Acts 4:10-12 Amp. Bible

Similar questions arose regarding those who were coming to faith in Jesus Christ as the Jesus Movement expanded. How did this person change so drastically? From being distant, defiant, angry, confused, depressed and completely unreliable; those who were coming to Jesus Christ were experiencing a heart and soul transformation that changed their behavior and character! Parents and family members shook their heads in astonishment! This doesn't look or sound like our son or daughter, brother or sister! Who is responsible for this miracle?

The reason this family members stands before you as a new person is because of the risen JESUS CHRIST!

It's not religion, the result of any drug, or anything else. It is through the power and authority of the Name and person of the Lord Jesus Christ and God's Holy Spirit infusing them with new life! The Bible describes the miracle in this way:

> Therefore if anyone is grafted into Christ, and joined to Him by faith, recognizing Jesus as the Savior and Messiah, they are a new creation, reborn and made alive by the Holy Spirit of God; the spiritual state of being dead to the things of God has changed and their previous moral condition is now under transformation by God's mighty power. All things are becoming new! An internal spiritual awakening ushered in by The True and Living God is producing new life.
> 2 Corinthians 5:17 Amp. Bible/Paraphrase

God's Time Table to Act

In God's sovereign plan, an unleashing of His Holy Spirit began occurring simultaneously in different parts of the USA. In the Haight we noticed a difference in how locals were responding, with more hunger and openness though our message hadn't changed.

Unbeknownst to us God was working supernaturally behind the scenes breathing His Spirit into a variety of individuals and places. Without human orchestration His Spirit was unleashed in harmony with His will and purposes. We were among those filled with power from on high.

We didn't realize it, but those who heard us did. Our words were charged with His fire. It was God's doing, much like Lancaster!

The Living Room & House of Acts

On a brisk afternoon I left Haight Street where I'd been engaged in lively dialogue with a variety of individuals about Jesus for several hours. I decided to walk a block north to Page Street which was less congested, to clear my head. Walking leisurely, I found a newly occupied storefront called the "Living Room" on the south side of the street. The door was locked, no one was present, but I saw a collection of magazines and Good News Bibles on some of the end tables. The storefront was decorated in a modest artsy way with old living room furniture, pictures and plants. In the back was a large table with enough seating for about eight people. I was curious.

Kent and I knew about another location in the Haight run by Dick Keys which was similar to a church. They did a good work, but were not geared to street people unless a convert was inclined to turn totally straight in appearance. I told Kent about my find and learned he'd recently become aware of this new mission through his ties with Evangelical Concerns. Pastor John McDonald from the Mill Valley Baptist Church and other EC pastors were helping pay the rent for this mission storefront.

Lonnie Frisbee

A few days later I popped by again and found the Living Room open. I met Danny Sands, Rick and Megan Sacks, and Lonnie Frisbee, who were each linked to a Christian commune located in Novato north of San Francisco called the 'House of Acts.' They helped with the day-to-day outreach of the Living Room. Lonnie had a beard, long hair—looking like he just stepped out of Biblical days. His demeanor was one of gentle intensity.

Danny was a mellow winsome guy with shoulder length thinning hair. He and his wife Sandy lived in Marin City. Rick had a huge smile, was direct and friendly, with a bushy afro and beard. His spouse Megan wore a long dress and had a gentle sweet spirit about her. They lived out of a truck he'd converted into a mobile living space. On this particular day the ladies from the House of Acts had prepared and sent in a large pot of soup and homemade bread to feed the team, or whoever wandered in. Coffee and tea was always available. The Living Room offered a quiet place to get away from the noisy, drug-infested streets. Anyone was welcome, questions about anything were OK and visitors often found it hard to resist the truth they were hearing. Free Bibles and literature were available and conversations seemed to lead naturally to the identity of Jesus Christ and His place in human history.

I liked the casual and comfortable feel of the Living Room and the conversational style of connecting with seekers who came by to check out what the place was about. Some popped by for food, or a warm place to be. This ministry was a significant encouragement to Kent and I. Getting to know the House of Acts group and having a place to bring or refer interested people on the west side of the Haight near Golden Gate Park was an answer to prayer. Anchor Rescue Mission was still a beneficial night-referral location for those in need of an evening meal, but the Living Room gave us a daytime place near the heart of the Haight to bring those interested in our message. The downside was the sporadic times the Living Room was open. This was understandable as all of the team lived in Marin County.

Ted & Liz Wise & 'The House of Acts'

I visited the House of Acts on a number of occasions and became friends with Ted and Liz Wise. Ted had bushy hair, a long mustache and was the jovial type with a nice laugh and friendly demeanor. Ted was gifted in leading Bible discussions, allowing ample room for dialogue. He had a keen wit, depth of understanding and exercised the ability to gracefully bring the conversation back to God and Jesus from some wild side-tracks. Ted was a sail-maker and artist dabbling in a variety of art forms. The graphic nearby is one of his pen and inks from these days.

On one of my visits, Ted told me he was friends with Pastor John McDonald of the Mill Valley Baptist Church who had helped reach out to he and his wife Liz. Liz had long brown hair and seemed like she had slipped right out of the pages of the Bible with her gentle and graceful manner.

Ted & Liz Wise

Others who lived at the 'House of Acts' were Jim and Judy Dopp and Steve and Sandi Heefner. Lonnie Frisbee and several single women lived there sporadically. I was interested in one of the single ladies which gave me reason to frequent Novato's House of Acts whenever possible. Lonnie's girlfriend Connie also stayed at the House of Acts when visiting from Southern California.

Creative Outreach

When I first came to the Haight in 1966 I stumbled on a free concert in Golden Gate Park, where The Steve Miller Blues Band played from the back of a flat-bed truck. Fast forward a couple of years and Kent and I, along with a group of novice musicians, attempted the same thing. We secured a permit, handed out flyers and set up on a flat-bed truck near an expanse of lawn on the north side of Golden Gate Park used for concerts. We were far from professional but we gave it a go! We had several guitars, bass, drums and a few of us sang. Our sound system was dinky compared to bigger bands.

I remember playing and singing one of the first Jesus People outreach tunes I'd learned from Don Matthews titled 'One Day Came.' Don was among the Lancaster group who'd received Christ and was part of the Way Inn Ranch in the early days. Here's his tune:

One Day Came - *Don Matthews*

1. One day came—when I looked around—and said to myself
Where is love?—that is to be found—from any-one else?
I realized—the false disguise—that there is none wise
Our hope it lies in Jesus Christ, a truthful Word in a—sinful life
Pull away from the darkness—and—strife!

2. Fear not child—the Lord has said—I'm not dead!
Hunger friend—for righteousness—and you'll be fed
Bring your life—and lay it before—the Son of God. Don't deny the need inside—in your hard heart His love can abide—He'll break down—the stones!

Bridge: Everybody says—what can you do?
Everybody's wondering—where is there truth?
Everybody's looking—where is there love?
You'll only find this—this from—above!

3. Lord, O Lord—I know You hear my plea—I bring it to Thee
Your will not mine—let my light shine—like the One that's divine
Soul and mind Holy Spirit—guide—throughout all time
Let me live—in the light of day—singing praises—to Your Name
With patience waiting for that blessed day—when He comes
Jesus the Son—when He comes—Jesus the Son—In that Name—I—adore!

KENT PHILPOTT

As hoped, some park goers came to see and hear what was going on, sat down to listen and hung around to dialogue afterwards. About fifty or seventy five people drifted into ear-shot of the concert and fifteen stayed. We didn't know what to expect and were glad to connect with those who were interested. We were sowing seeds of God's love. Whatever the outcome was fine with us. It was a beautiful day in Golden Gate Park and all was good!

This outing was a preface to many creative ventures to come, and motivated us to write more outreach tunes.

Kent was gradually beginning to look more like he belonged on the streets. Myself and others were seeking to solidify our understanding of spiritual truths revealed in the Bible and do a better job of communicating the life changing message of Jesus Christ.

The Sunny Side

It was a warm sunny morning in San Francisco when I jumped off the bus and walked up the hill to the small independent church I attended. My heart felt clean. It was such a relief to know I was being transformed into a new person in Jesus Christ. With a Bible held firmly in my hand I could hardly wait to be in the company of fellow Christians and sense the love and freedom we shared together that crossed racial and economic lines.

My feet felt light and I was full of excitement and anticipation of worship. I was eager to learn more about God's amazing love and Word! The church was comprised of mostly African-American believers with a smattering of other nationalities. There was something very special about how I felt among these brothers and sisters in Christ; a sense of acceptance and love, very different from my past. The people of this small San Fran church were special when it came to being inclusive, making everyone feel welcome!

The Breadth of God's Reach

Since becoming a Christian I'd had the opportunity to worship in a number of churches. In doing so, my perspective of who comprised God's church had broadened. I'd been in Black, Latino, White, Greek, Asian and racially-mixed churches; some conservative, traditional, quiet and reverent, others energetic and lively, each with their own organic spiritual uniqueness.

Considering the expanse of God's family throughout the world was mind boggling! I thought about it often. Amidst hundreds of languages and cultures, God is able to pour out His love, grace and presence into the lives of millions at the same time. A similar miracle happens when prayers are offered to the True and Living God throughout the globe and prayers are answered according to His plan and will. The reach of God's Spirit that fills the earth and universe is amazing!

Rules, Regulations and Traditions

Learning how to distinguish between what was of "Christ's Spirit" and what was "religion" that didn't free, but squeezed the life of Jesus out by requiring outward conformity to religious rules and traditions, was a new challenge.

In reading the Bible I found the majority of Jewish leaders and priests in Jesus' day were myopically zeroed in on rules, procedures and rituals of the Jewish faith, rather than showing God's love, mercy and compassion to those around them. The parable of the 'Good Samaritan' helped me understand God's perspective (Luke 10:25-37). In a similar way Matthew 23 opened my eyes to over-the-top adherence to religious rules, rituals and traditions which Jesus took issue with. Building on this, in Isaiah chapter 58, the prophet makes a case for what God's looking for when it comes to spiritual sacrifice and practice. Each of these Scripture passages helped me understand what God considers important.

Young Love

Romantic feelings for a lady resident at 'The House of Acts' about forty minutes north of San Francisco in the city of Novato had begun. Somehow my own issues and lack of any financial stability, didn't compute to my brain. With my biological clock of passion ticking I jumped the gun and encouraged my then girlfriend to move into San Fran. She stayed with a violin maker's family in the city rent-free, in exchange for baby-sitting. This gave us more together-time which resulted in our marrying. With minimal personal belongings, we made up for it with lots of life baggage to deal with.

Around this same time period, Kent graduated from Seminary and joined a small church in the Balboa Park area of San Francisco. Supportive of Kent's street ministry, church members caught a vision and opened a small mission to feed and accommodate street people.

SOUL INN - Kent Philpott's Recollections

Lincoln Park Baptist Church located at 4031 Balboa St. San Francisco CA was a store front church, pastored by Al Gossett. Dr. Francis DuBose, professor of Missions and Evangelism at Golden Gate Theological Seminary in Mill Valley, was a member and invited me to be part of the congregation after graduating seminary.

Early Residents, Staff & Friends
Soul Inn - Balboa St. SF, CA

I carefully considered the offer and decided to join the church. Dr. DuBose was a friend and had a significant role in supporting and encouraging me in my street ministry in the Haight. In time, as 'street ministry' needs continued to increase, I convinced the tiny congregation to host a Christian house commune within its facilities. We refitted three small Sunday school rooms with bunk beds, pillows, blankets and other items donated by the Salvation Army.

As the opening of Soul Inn neared, there was excitement as a sign was mounted on the outside of the building identifying this new phase of ministry. David Hoyt helped pick out a name and painted the sign we mounted. For days I visited the Haight Defense Committee that set up a table on the corner of Haight and Masonic that provided information about housing, medical attention, food, and emergency services.

At last Soul Inn was ready! On a rainy afternoon I proudly announced to the Haight Defense rep that Soul Inn was open to assist those in need.

A Food Multiplication Miracle

That evening, Paul Finn, Dave Palma and I had just finished off a quart can of pork and beans with about an inch left in the bottom of the pot. We were sitting around a 4' by 8' sheet of plywood, propped up by four metal folding chairs, when the front door of the Lincoln Park Baptist Church was flung open—and in walked 26 wet, tired, and hungry hippies. They had walked several miles, all the way from the Haight-Ashbury, and there they were—our first guests.

We invited them to have a seat in the 'church's sanctuary,' showed them where the single bathroom was, and disappeared back to the small make-shift kitchen in an adjoining room. We were numb with the unexpected number and seemed to go on autopilot. Paul, Dave, and I started filling up paper bowls with pork and beans. I ladled, Paul held the bowls, and Dave brought them out to our guests two at a time. We knew what was occurring, never said a word to each other, but kept on serving the food. If we'd thought about it, we would have probably said, "Sorry, no food." Instead, we marched to the kitchen, forgetting to pray, dipped into a pot with only one inch of pork and beans—and a miracle of food multiplication began. All 26 guests were served and there were still leftovers!

Paul and Dave were from two different parts of New York. After some time, they both went home and started Christian houses. Paul phoned me in 2006, and asked if I had received a CD he had sent on the 'Names of God.' After a little bit I asked him, "Paul, do you remember what happened the night we opened Soul Inn?" (I didn't want to alert him that I was curious if he remembered the miracle.)

Right away Paul said, "Oh yeah, wasn't that something!"

Miracles are mysterious, easy to doubt. This one was so incredible and unusual that it did not seem possible to have happened, but it had. It never occurred again, though I did see a continual run of the miraculous throughout the duration of the Jesus Movement, but never saw this type of miracle duplicated."

Waves of God's Spirit- D.E. Hoyt

With outreach continuing in the Haight, waves of something larger began. Street people we'd come to know were responding, asking Jesus into their lives. The initial miracle had begun, but many were still eking out an existence on the streets, scrounging for food and a place to crash. Most wanted to get out of the craziness of the city and begin to clear their heads. I recalled how I felt, and the importance of finding a quieter environment to process things and start a new life.

We needed ministry locations similar to the 'Way Inn Ranch,' 'The House of Acts' and 'Soul Inn.' With limited space, 'Soul Inn' had filled up quickly and was still in the city. Marin County seemed like the best place to look since it was out of the city and Kent and family lived there. Kent's familiarity with Marin and leads on potential paint jobs for us was an additional incentive for looking in this area.

ZION'S INN FOR GIRLS

Kent and his spouse Bobbie were looking for a spacious home to provide housing for the growing number of single women who had come to faith in Jesus. They located a two story home in the center of San Rafael at 128 Greenfield Avenue and rented it.

Kent invited us to join his family in establishing this new follow-up ministry and we accepted. I made arrangements to leave the mission and explained what our plan was. Sister Drayton and Yvonne understood. They'd

Early Ladies at Zion's Inn with Kent's Family - San Rafael, CA

graciously allowed my spouse and I to reside at the mission temporarily and our move was expected. Kent and I would both continue to be involved and help at Anchor Rescue Mission, but getting several Christian houses up and running in Marin County was a top priority.

We blinked our eyes and suddenly there were seven single girls living with us at Zion's Inn. God's timing was crazy good!

BERACHAH HOUSE

As hoped for, a discipleship house for guys was opened under the lead-

ership of Paul Bryant in nearby San Anselmo, not far from Zion's Inn. This enabled the two Christian houses to be in close enough proximity for joint meetings. With these start-ups, we were gaining momen-

"Berachah House" Early Brothers - San Anselmo, CA

tum and new believers were being added daily.

As we steadily grew, we found an increasingly small number of churches we could bring new Christians where they would be welcomed.

Some churches told us flat-out to leave. Most had doctrines of emphasis and tightly orchestrated worship with leader and congregation expectations for us to clean up our act and lose our hippie appearance. Visiting main-line churches was a stretch, as most were boring and too liberal. We had our own attitudes and perspectives on what church and worship should look like and were critical of what we didn't like. We wanted something more laid back, come as you are and Bible centered. When

Marin County - Berachah House Additions

unable to find a local match, we settled for our own worship gatherings with guitar music, some of our own songs, prayer and a good Bible study for the main course.

Change is a Comin and it's Gonna Do you Good!

While attending a teaching event in Oakland, my spouse and I ran into a Christian couple attending seminary in Berkeley who offered the use of their flat for a few weeks of privacy while they returned home to be with family over the holidays. This gave us our first taste of life in the East Bay and we liked it. It was Christmas and I busied myself painting a number of Scripture signs using Hebrews 13:8, which reads "Jesus Christ the same yesterday, today and forever."

During our stay in Berkeley, we learned of a small rental home in Pleasant Hill and made a deposit on it. The rent was a pittance and I agreed to do work on the home in exchange for a further rent reduction. We informed Kent and he gave us his blessing as we moved from Zion's Inn to a new beginning in the East Bay.

At last, a peaceful home setting to prepare for the birth of our first child. This move was just what we needed; a quieter setting, and less crowded living conditions and we felt at peace. Nearby was a strong Bible-centered Presbyterian church we visited, making a few new friends.

Another Krishna Devotee Receives Jesus

Pleasant Hill, Walnut Creek and Berkeley became my new focus of out-reach. With Pleasant Hill and Walnut Creek being more suburban, I made it a point to visit Berkeley a few times a week. On one excursion of sharing Christ and connecting with street people in Berkeley, I decided to visit a new Krishna Temple I'd heard about.

I arrived when a service was about to begin. Reluctantly, I bit the bullet and sat through the entire 'Kirtan' service, cringing in my spirit. Afterwards I engaged in conversation with a number of devotees, until pushed out of the building by several Krishna leaders in charge. One had recognized me from the San Francisco Temple and overheard me talking about Jesus Christ.

A solo devotee followed me outside to hear more about Christ— intrigued by the unfriendly and hostile response of his leaders. This young man was living in the temple in exchange for duties similar to my situation several years back. Learning I'd left Krishna Consciousness, he wanted to know why.

I shared what led up my encounter with God in the temple and how I was flooded with the presence of Jesus Christ. He asked me to help him do the same and we prayed on the spot. He had his own unique confirmation of God hearing his prayer and decided to leave the temple. Gathering up a few personal belongings to move out caused no small scene. The temple commander followed us out, threatening and cursing damnation on us. This response helped my new brother in Christ make a clean break with the Krishna Movement. That afternoon he returned with me to the tiny Pleasant Hill home. As indicated by the fuzzy picture, new converts from the Krishna temple had appearance issues that would gradually change over time.

New Brother in Christ
Out of Berkeley, CA Krishna Temple

HOME FOR HIS GLORY

Our Pleasant Hill-Lafayette home got its first live-in guest from the Berkeley, CA Krishna Temple. With 500 square feet of rental space we made do temporarily. Gradually other new converts and friends came to live with us. It was like the ancient fable of a family living in a shoe! Some came by way of street outreach in Berkeley and Oakland, a few migrated from Marin County because of roots in the East Bay, and others came from previous ministries who had a personal connection with us. In a short span of time our tiny house became Home For His Glory. Any semblance of privacy was gone.

With the dire need for more space an idea struck. What about the attic? Climbing up into it one day, it looked to be the most spacious place in the entire house. The pitched roof area wasn't the ideal height, but it could work. Conferring with our landlord, he agreed to help convert the attic into usable space. It was summer when our landlord, Oscar Anderson and I laid a tongue-and-groove wood floor which became the sleeping quarters for men. Drenched in sweat we used old boards and recycled nails he'd removed from other properties. Oscar was a frugal re-cycler, owning a number of rentals. If they weren't rented, they were filled with building materials he planned on using somewhere! Though eccentric he had a good heart and was a huge help to our growing ministry.

UPPER STREAMS

Oscar liked my willingness to work and improve things. Under the surface I think he had a soft spot for the Lord as well. Whatever the cause for favor, he agreed to rent us a second considerably larger home nearby in Walnut Creek at 2424 Olympic Blvd. The plan was for my spouse and I to move there along with several young ladies.

We named this second home Upper Streams. It had an expansive living room, perfect for group meetings and outreach. The presence of God's Spirit was strong at Upper Streams. In the early days, we'd throw a house-party every Friday or Saturday night. Prior to, we'd go out to the streets

"Upper Streams" Isaiah 44:3-4

and local strip where cars cruised and invite people to a party at Upper Streams. On average 20-40 visiting teens and young adults would cram into

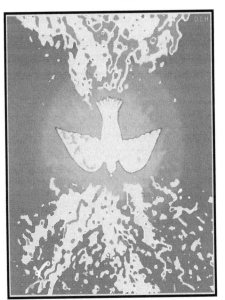

our living room on party night. We had plenty of refreshments on hand, played contemporary music in the background, or songs we'd written on guitar. Like Lancaster, every half-hour or so, someone would stand up and share why they believed in Jesus, sing an outreach song, or read a portion of the Bible, and God did the rest!

Sometimes God's presence was so thick our team couldn't speak. On these occasions, those visiting would be convinced by the presence of Jesus Christ and come to faith by a direct encounter with Him through the Holy Spirit. Some who came to Upper Streams with no faith in God told us as they approached the house they felt or saw the presence of God around this nondescript ranch home. What did they see? I never saw anything. Without understanding it, we were in the midst of a "God Visit." Many of those who received Christ would spread the word to all of their friends and they too would come to check out what was going on.

Placing ourselves in God's hands and receiving Jesus Christ into our hearts was the first step, but "continuing in the faith" when temptation, doubts and problems arose, required a personal commitment to persevere. *Following Jesus was entirely new for all of us.* Our former personality problems, sins, entanglement with anything satanic, ways of reacting, or attempts to avoid owning up to our short-comings, all resurfaced sooner or later.

Our "old nature" needed to die, but didn't want to! Our "new nature" in Jesus Christ was reinforced through prayer, regular study of the Scriptures, worship and outreach songs, receiving good preaching and teaching, and honest dialogue with our brothers and sisters in Christ. The miracle of "Christ in us" was authenticated by these things and when we shared the incredible message of Jesus with those who were in the world, without hope and without God (Ephesians 2:12).

We prayed often for strength to 'live the life' as Jesus' followers; for boldness to make Christ known, and wisdom to help others grow in their faith.

Christian houses in the Bay Area had a common vision for outreach. Anyone was welcome regardless of race, appearance, or social status. Food and emergency housing was given as normal hospitality. New worship and outreach songs were being written regularly. A typical gathering would include worship music and praise, prayer, personal sharing, Scripture reading and dialogue questions and answers. During the Bible reading portion, we might read a chapter or portion of Scripture, discuss what we read, share insights and talk about how to apply what we were studying. We clearly understood we were sinners being transformed!

In the early days of Upper Streams a young lady who was a college student began visiting our Bible studies. What unfolded in her life was the beginning of a series of miracles that would inspire all of us at Upper Streams.

'A Search' – by Anne Clowser O'Donnell

Anne's college professor gave the following introduction before she read her paper to the class:

"Anne was not sure if what had preoccupied her during most of the semester had been relevant to the class. It seems to me that the first stage of learning to understand others is to achieve peace of mind, which frees us to listen to others and love them. I encouraged her to share her experience with us."

[What follows are condensed excerpts from Anne's paper.]

"Before I knew Jesus, I didn't know what it was like to be happy. I felt hollow inside, barraged with disturbing thoughts, empty. Everyone is searching for something. I was searching for truth and happiness. I needed help—someone to show me what love is and how to discover happiness. I tried through a personal search, dabbling into Eastern religions, philosophies and self-discovery teachings that promised some type of break-through. Buddhism interested me but when summer break was over, nothing came of it.

When fall came, I found myself back in school in a psychology class asking more questions about life, happiness and love. The class talked about it, but I didn't find tangible answers. My anxiety and depression worsened. We played interactive interpersonal games in class, intended to draw out repressed feelings while getting to know each other. Feeling depleted and empty inside contributed to more emotional stress.

Playing these games seemed too close to real life which troubled me. To be someone's friend you had to play games. You had to say the right words, or you weren't accepted. I was in a friendship vacuum, leaving former friends in Oakland after our move to Danville, and the limited friends I met in high school had moved away. Making new friends now seemed impossible, requiring emotional strength I didn't have. Saying, "Hi, how are you?" Seemed like a monotonous, meaningless grouping of words. Words we're conditioned to say, without really caring, or wanting to hear the truth of what someone might be feeling or going through. I wanted to mean it, if I inquired, wanting it to be real! The same was true if someone asked me, "How are you?" I wanted to be able to be honest without them thinking I was a basket-case and walking away!

I started writing poetry to relieve inner turmoil. I'd sit in the entrance of the college campus watching faces as they passed, looking for some sign of happiness. I smiled at people who glanced my way hoping to observe someone who seemed to care. The faces seemed as empty as I felt and it scared me! I was searching, listening, reading and attempting to make sense of life with a measure of caution, not wanting to expose my fragile inner world to more hurt. At the same time, I didn't want to develop a hard shell, like one of my brothers. The alternative was no better, as I sank deeper into despair, fear and a dark depression. I was in the worst place I'd ever known emotionally, or mentally!

Out of the blue, some people in the Psychology class started talking about Jesus Christ. At first, I thought they were tripping, but listened anyway, desperate to find any morsel of truth. They talked about how Jesus could set you free of hang-ups and problems. Wow! They sounded crazy and their message too good to be true, but what did I have to lose? I'd tried finding peace and truth in reading books, drugs (once), why not this? They talked about God's love for us being poured out through Jesus, God's Son, and referred to Jesus in the present tense. They talked about Jesus as if he was alive. I knew from my Catholic upbringing that Jesus had died and risen from death, but I had no idea he could be here in the present!

These students radiated faith in Jesus and love for each other, saying they'd each had their own encounters with God. They were people like me with real feelings and problems, but seemed to have found the truth and now genuinely cared about each other. This was a strong indicator for me. Most people don't hug each other in public, but they did. They didn't seem to care what others might think. They did things for each other as well and lived communally; sharing life, problems and times of happiness together. Wow! I thought, if this is what Jesus can give—a chance to find the truth, drop facades and be real and be cared about, I wanted it!

I'm not sorry I turned to God. On the contrary, it's opened up a whole new world and changed much in my life. God did what no human could! He forgave me, put His Spirit inside me, accepted, loved and gave me hope again. It was a free gift I could not earn (Ephesians 2:8-10). Jesus put me on a new path. I'm not suggesting coming to God is easy. Releasing pride, sin, deep rooted selfishness, doubts, fears and the stuff that causes us pain and placing our trust in an invisible God is a step of faith. It takes having confidence that God will meet us. *He met me in a very dark place and breathed new life into my empty soul!* I'm moving forward as God's child, becoming more like Jesus, through the strength He gives me.

Those who think they are Christians without tangible signs of being set free from the baggage of sin and self, should examine themselves. Jesus Christ was sent to free us. He is able to do this, and is the only One we can depend on for this miracle! If anyone wants to experience firsthand what "true love and peace is", call out to God and you'll never be sorry. Ask! If you're sincere, you can count on an affirmative answer and a free gift from God, being set free, "So if the Son of God (Jesus) sets you free, you will be really free (John 8:36)!"

God isn't dead! The problem is, in our world there are so many things that offer false promises. We've turned away from God, thinking He is outdated. The Bible tells us that "Jesus Christ is the same yesterday, today and forever (Hebrews 13:8)."

This means what Jesus said and did, miracles included, still apply today! The invisible True God who created the world and everything in it is alive! God loves everyone on this planet, but He won't make any of us follow Him, if we stubbornly, or in ignorance don't want to. It's God who gave us free-will!"

The rippling effect of Anne's encounter with Jesus was just beginning.

Author's Note: Anne's additional comments and update can be found in Bio's 1 Chapter 27.

10

The San Fran East Bay Jesus People Movement

Somebody's Knocking at the Door
Vic Clowser

I was born in Oakland, California in 1954. I was the youngest of four kids for ten years until my two younger sisters were born. My oldest brother Steve, my sister Anne, my brother David, myself, our younger sisters, Valerie and Christina and our parents Ed and Maria, each entered into a personal relationship with God within a period of one year. The spark that lit the spiritual fire in our family was the result of one person standing up in a College Psychology class, sharing Jesus Christ had changed their life.

Our parents raised us Catholic. I attended Parochial school until the second grade when we moved to rural Danville in the East Bay Area in

1964. We attended the Catholic Church, but I continued my education in the public schools. We were raised to be respectful and develop a strong work ethic. My brothers and I each had paper routes at a young age followed by other employment. I remember being encouraged by my father to gather soda bottles and turn them in for pocket change; a result of him being raised in the Great Depression no doubt.

Poplar trees surrounded our home, which delivered a ton of leaves in the fall months that needed raking. I will forever remember Dad waking us up on every Saturday morning at 7:00 AM during this season with the declaration, "Boys, man your rakes!" Most likely, this was an outgrowth of his Navy training during WW2.

Our family was relatively normal, given the reflection of the times and social elements emerging in the 1960's. I remember my oldest brother was somewhat rebellious in his teen years and he and my father butted heads often, causing a strained relationship. My other siblings and I got along well and didn't give Mom and Dad too much grief.

My older sister Anne was attending Diablo Valley College in the fall of 1969 and was drawn to and intrigued by someone who had stood up in her psychology class and gave their testimony about "Jesus Christ being the way, the truth and the life" (John 14:6). Searching for truth and significance, she began attending a mid-week Bible study at 2424 Olympic Blvd in Walnut Creek at "Upper Streams" Christian house. Her melancholy depression began to fade as a result of attending these meetings and I was glad for her as she seemed genuinely happy for the first time in several years.

I was 15 years old at the time, a young teen, doing dumb stuff. One evening, my buddy Chris and I were up to no good, gallivanting through the neighborhood stealing Christmas lights off decorated outdoor trees. My mother called me back to the house and I thought I was busted. Instead, she asked me to go with my sister Anne to a Bible study, because she didn't want her traveling alone at night. I said good-bye to my friend, relieved I wasn't in trouble and was OK with tagging along with Anne.

Pulling into the driveway at Upper Streams, the first thing I saw was a Volkswagen van decoratively painted with the words "GOD IS LOVE." I recall thinking, "Looks like one of those hippie vans....that's cool!" We were welcomed by a guy who looked like he was from the Haight Ashbury District in San Francisco. He opened the door, greeted Anne warmly, then stepped onto the porch, put his arms around me gave me a big hug and said, "Welcome brother." This individual was David Hoyt. I later found out, he'd actually come to faith in Jesus Christ while living in the "Haight District."

I sensed there was acceptance and love in this greeting and from the others I met. I was intrigued. Worship songs prefaced the Bible Study, mostly written by those present, or friends they knew. Songs like, "One Day Came," "One in Christian Love" and others. Most of the songs were about Jesus making Himself known to those who were open and hungry for truth. During a time of prayer following the Bible Study, I remember kneeling down on the living room carpet. People were praying for different things. I was praying hard for Jesus to come into my life. I really wanted to receive him. Someone saw the strain on my face and put their arm around me to let me know I didn't have to try so hard. I relaxed and by faith asked Him to forgive my sins and come into my life.

I sensed and felt something wash over and inside me. En route home that evening, everything looked different; as if I was seeing through new eyes. This was a confirmation that I'd been made new in some way. One by one our whole family came to notice the change that God had begun in Anne's and my life. Within a year our entire family came to receive Jesus Christ as their Lord and Savior.

I witnessed a lot of people from different walks of life receive the Lord and transformation take place in their lives. The Bible was being opened, read and taught. Jesus became the focus of our lives. I remember coming home from school, grabbing my Bible and going into the back yard to read and digest anything out of the Word of God. I was hungry to learn more. I knew Jesus was alive and God was speaking to me through His Word and guiding me by His Spirit. I was learning things about God that I never knew, stuff you don't learn in high school—amazing truths! I was anxious to share Jesus and these things with others.

I remember having flyers printed up that said: "Come to a Party" at 2424 Olympic Boulevard." We passed these out on Friday nights in Walnut Creek at local hangouts where kids gathered and the local car strip. A handful always seemed to show up expecting to find a drug or alcohol party. What they received was the Good News of Jesus' love, truth and the message of His payment for our sin. Miraculously, God took over and individuals were nudged by God's presence to receive Jesus as Lord!

Upper Streams had a second Christian House for men called "Home for His Glory." This house was like a spiritual magnet as well. Many who were seeking truth, needing to be freed from drug or alcohol dependence, or their reliance on the occult, found the right place to experience deliverance and enter into a relationship with the True and Living God. The Bible says in Psalm 68 that "God sets the solitary (lonely) in families." This is what Christian Ministry Houses became for countless people; a place to be loved, mended, trained and sent into the community to share their faith and the Good News of what Jesus Christ had done for them. Christian houses peppered the Bay Area with relational friendship links. Whenever possible we visited each other to learn or worship together, or for joint outreaches.

These were times of significant growth and spiritual development; we were learning to follow the Lord, to study and interpret His Word correctly, about hearing God's voice, creative ways of sharing the gospel, about practicing God's love by our word, life and actions. Also, the importance of prayer and waiting on God's timing in life decisions and transitions. The use of Godly weapons when engaging in spiritual warfare against the forces of the Evil One, was a hot topic as well. We were for the most part unschooled spiritually. Those with organized church upbringings were also for the most part Bible illiterate.

Author's Note: Victor's full testimony with a life update can be found in Bio's 1 chapter 27

Vic's dad had his own story to tell.

A Beginning - Edward L. Clowser

I have wanted to share what the 'Good News' means to me and its effect on my family. I grew up in the small town of Onawa, Iowa during the 1930's in a difficult period in American history. Life was extremely hard for the average person due to the Great Depression.

Marie & Ed Clowser - San Fran Bay Area

My knowledge of religion and the church consisted of an awareness of various Protestant denominations and their attitude of suspicion and prejudice toward Catholics and Jews. I attended Sunday school at a Lutheran Church and also attended other Protestant services via the coaxing of my family from age 5 to 14. I thought worship was dull, repetitious and a waste of good play-time. The exception was the Christmas season which meant a huge Christmas tree, decorated lights, lots of candles and presents. No spiritual insights or breakthroughs occurred.

Moving to California in 1942 at the age of 17 was a significant adjustment, moving from a rural to urban environment. By 1943 I'd obtained several jobs and I moved away from home, living in boarding houses, eager to make my own choices, which weren't all good. As my eighteenth birthday approached, I had to make a major decision. I could wait and be drafted into the Army branch of the military, or I could enlist. I joined the Navy, graduated boot-camp and was assigned the Naval Construction Battalion and shipped into the WW II War theater in the Pacific.

The Navy and World War II

During the next two years of naval service I witnessed the release of man's fury toward his fellow humans. I understood the nature of war, but didn't accept war as the solution to mankind's problems. Behind the front lines in Okinawa, a truck full of Japanese prisoners of war passed who were being transported to a local POW camp. One of the prisoners looked over the side-rail of the truck and a Marine obliterated his face with the butt of his rifle, splattering blood on all of us. This unnecessary act of brutality filled me with revulsion toward the Marine and compassion for the Japanese POW.

The night before the invasion of Okinawa by US forces, I woke to a deafening roar and went topside on our ship to witness a vast armada of the US fleet bombarding the island. The sky lit up with each thunderous roar of naval guns. It was an eerie overwhelming feeling to witness such fire-power knowing it would result in direct confrontation with the enemy in combat. I recall praying to the God I didn't yet know, "Protect me from harms-way," a selfish and fear-filled prayer.

During the invasion assault landing, I was assigned as the pilot of a landing craft used to ferry troops, weapons, vehicles and supplies to the beachheads and between ships. There were constant air attacks, day and night, causing fear with Japan's use of Kamikaze suicide planes on our ships. During a daring Japanese daylight attack, the ship I was alongside, took a direct hit with 20mm ammo piercing our landing craft as well and ricocheting near my feet. I plunged overboard, calling out to an unknown God, "If you exist, save me!" I pulled two critically wounded men out of the water; one lived, returning from the hospital to tell me; the other died.

This would not be the last brush with death. Still enlisted, our naval landing craft was groping its way through a violent rain-squall, when a huge lightning-bolt struck our craft. A piece of the main bolt struck my deck-hand and me, knocking us down. Again I silently prayed, pleading for God to save us. Another close encounter happened as I was walking near enemy lines and two tall men dressed like native Okinawans nodded as they passed. Suddenly, a U.S. Marine patrol appeared asking if I'd seen two tall men. The two men I'd just encountered turned out to be Japanese Imperial Marines with sniper rifles hidden inside their clothing.

Memory of these events faded when World War II was over and I returned to school under the G. I. Bill. In university open-discussion was common-place regarding "life and how we should live it?" A wide variety of philosophies, political and religious groups were vying for people's loyalty. During numerous discussions, I began to distinguish a striking difference between Buddha, Mohammed, Confucius and Christianity. Religions were for the most part founded on individuals who were dead, with the exception of self-appointed gurus of the day. Christianity was different, because Jesus Christ was said to be the promised Messiah for the entire world and alive.

The teachings of the Bible claim Jesus is the Christ, foretold by the prophets, embodying God's nature and purpose for humankind that we should receive God's gift of Eternal Life. To accomplish this, Jesus the Messiah was crucified, died for human sin, was buried, was resurrected from death on the third day and was seen by hundreds of people. Christians say, "God pours out His Holy Spirit; the same Spirit that dwelt in Jesus into all who receive Jesus as Lord, as a confirmation that He is the authentic way to a genuine relationship with God; His Spirit bearing witness with ours."

I mentally understood these unique claims, but needed to investigate the different forms and expressions of Christianity. I decided on the Catholic model which embodied reverence, a liturgy and quieter worship. I respectfully argued with my priest about interpretation of Scripture and church doctrine. At this time I met my wife-to-be Maria, who was a devout Catholic and a spark that spurred my spiritual journey along.

In June of 1948 we married and started a family. Stephen was followed by Anne, David and Victor in close order. I obtained a middle management position supervising an Aircraft and Missile Repair Program for the Navy and the Air Force. Life was good with a suburban home in the country, two cars and a boat.

We sent our kids to Catholic schools, but as they entered their teenage years, religious education didn't prove any guarantee of moral living. We tried hard to be good Catholics and role models, but we fell short. Guilt was never eradicated in the confessional booth. Two more beautiful daughters were born during this period, Valerie and Christina.

It was now the turbulent 1960's, with unrest on a number of fronts; the Civil Rights Movement, the Vietnam War and the Cold War with Russia. Assassinations would follow. Many people were searching for an escape from these uncomfortable times. Adults medicated themselves with alcohol while "Flower Children" turned to mind altering drugs and hedonism. In 1965–66 the war in Vietnam was affecting millions of Americans and Vietnamese in the most painful ways possible. Body bags piled up on both sides of the conflict. I was not "pro war", having lived through it, seeing firsthand the horrors that unfold. I sympathized with a country that took to the streets to be heard, through "peace marches." I took part in a march in Golden Gate Park. Mark Twain voiced the balance our country was struggling to find, saying, "Support your country all of the time and your government only when they deserve it."

A Parental Mistake

Moving from Oakland to Danville California forced our children to change schools and make new friends. Our daughter Anne struggled with this move the most. After the dust had settled, we realized how we had contributed, without realizing it at the time. In our new city of Danville, we refused to let Anne attend a 'girls pajama party' with new kids and families we didn't know. This one event resulted in her being ostracized by a number of potential new friends who ended up rejecting her. Anne spiraled into a depression. Even then, we failed to acknowledge her severe emotional condition. Over time her depression affected the entire family. Sadly, Anne's downward spin resulted in years of unhappiness throughout the majority of her high school years.

Signs of Hope

In the fall of 1969 Anne entered Diablo Valley College. To our surprise, we noticed a profound change in her personality. She appeared to be much happier, joyful and more than willing to do her chores and beyond. Bewildered by this radical change in behavior, we wondered what had changed her hate to love, her debilitating depression to joy and her inner turmoil to peace; so we asked her.

She explained how she had met some students in her psychology class who told her about Jesus Christ being a personal friend and Savior and sent by God the Father. They told her if she believed that Jesus was God's Son and trusted Him to forgive her sins, He would change her life.

The change in Anne's behavior and outlook was undeniable! She was displaying love, joy, peace, kindness and other exemplary personality traits we hadn't seen since the innocence of her childhood. As Catholics, my wife and I were carefully processing this story and the radical change we were witnessing. Some of what we were hearing sounded foreign but at the same time familiar. Could God be this personal and real? We wondered.

Anne's brother Victor was 15 years old at the time and we asked him to attend the Christian meetings Anne was going to and spy-out the situation. We were skeptical, fearing there might be drugs involved since we learned young hippies were in abundance at these gatherings. Victor's report was not what we expected. He said, "I've been searching for something to fill an emptiness I've felt. I've tried a bunch of things—but they didn't work, or last, including drugs. I thought God would be the last place I'd look, since we've attended church as a family for years. But, I was wrong, God is real! I've entered into a personal relationship with Him and invited Him into my heart. Jesus said, 'I am the way, the truth and the life and no one can come to the Father, but through Me' (John 14:6)."

Victor's explanation and testimony was sincere. His attitude and behavior like Anne's was changing, but the real cause for this was still a mystery, which meant putting a pause on giving God all the credit.

In the spring of 1970 I attended a class on Mexican-American Psychology at Diablo Valley College with my daughter Anne. What an interesting experience! The class was sprinkled with radicals who were searching for a sensible reality in the world. This translated into experimenting with a wide range of drugs and philosophical schools of thought. As the class neared completion we were each assigned a final paper which was to embody "What the class had meant to us on a personal level."

My daughter Anne submitted a paper which confirmed some type of genuine transformation had occurred in her heart and soul, which became a reality. Hearing her share this article with the whole class and then reading it later astounded me. It forced a deeper level of reflection and critical thinking as the contents burned their way into my own heart and mind.

Into God's Hands

In January 1970, Anne and Victor had been sharing their spiritual experiences with their brother Dave. His response was they probably needed

Christ more than he did, because Victor had taken drugs and Anne had bouts with severe depression. Dave didn't sense any need. One night Victor came home excited after attending a Christian meeting in Berkeley because he'd seen people healed. He wanted to tell his brother Dave about it, but Dave pretended to be asleep.

Victor knew he wasn't asleep and he began telling him what had happened. Dave threw the covers off and blurted-out a number of personal problems and things that were troubling him. Dave knew that Victor loved him in a new way that he didn't understand. This had opened a door. That evening Dave prayed to find peace through Jesus Christ.

The following day Dave was scheduled to work at a hamburger drive-in but for some unknown reason didn't have to. Anne and Victor invited him to attend a Christian meeting and Dave decided to join them. In the course of the meeting someone quoted from the Bible Romans 10:9-10 "If you declare with your mouth, 'Jesus is Lord', and believe in your heart that God raised him from the dead, you will be saved. For it is with your heart that you believe and are made clean (justified) and it is with your mouth that you profess your faith and are saved."

Dave told me that at the very moment he heard these verses he believed that Jesus was the Messiah, the Christ of God. The confirmation that something significant had happened was glaringly obvious to the family by his outlook and changed attitude. He took a more positive approach to sharing work around the house, demonstrated generosity and stopped fighting with his siblings. He bought presents for his Mom and I with the money he earned at the drive-in. On many occasions, I'd find a new pair of pants, or money on my dresser. My own kids were buying gifts for me, instead of me buying for them. What a switcheroo! From a father's point of view I was delighted.

Anne, Dave and Victor continued to attend the Christian fellowship meetings at a Christian house called Upper Streams in Walnut Creek, CA. Sometimes they'd visit other similar ministries. In the beginning we'd drop them off and pick them up afterwards. Maria and I were invited to attend the meetings and one night did. It was quite an experience. Most of those in attendance were in there late teens and early twenties. They were the radical looking dudes, hippie types with beards and long hair.

They aroused my curiosity and skepticism simultaneously. I knew the reputation of radical groups of the day who were anything but harmless, like the Weathermen, Symbionese Liberation Army and others. As an outsider looking in, their outward hippie appearance stirred up a stereotype prejudice. My hyper concern would not last for long. Through interaction and dialogue, I found them to be entirely different than my preconceptions. They expressed a love for others that was real, not tainted with religious hypocrisy. I was impressed by their sincerity.

In the days that followed my wife Maria acted different, heavily preoccupied about something. Several days later, on returning from work, Maria, Dave and Vic had just returned from a Christian meeting and were talking about how Maria "got saved." This was Protestant jargon for someone accepting Jesus Christ as their Savior. I became livid with anger about all this. I asked her, "What is this nonsense about being 'saved?' Saved from what? Are you now some kind of religious fanatic?" I was furious with her, but to my surprise she didn't get angry in return. Instead, love seemed to flow from her. Her usual response was to react to my anger with anger of her own, but not this time. I was perplexed. The how and why of this change were beyond my human understanding. I could not find fault with her, only wonder and respect another family member's transformation.

Surrounded by new spiritual life softened me to attending Christian meetings with family members from time to time. On one of these occasions at a local church, a visiting lady evangelist was speaking and asked if any children wanted to come forward and give their hearts to Jesus. Much to our surprise our daughter Valerie who was seven at the time, went forward by herself. She was at the altar for about five minutes and I recall the woman evangelist bending gently over Valerie and praying for her. When Valerie returned to her seat, tears were streaming down her cheeks and I asked her what had happened. She told us, "God told me He loved me and would take care of me." I was impressed with the simplicity and profoundness of the moment; tucking it away in my memory for further thought concerning God.

My oldest son, Steve and I had something in common. Both of us were puzzled about what was going on in the family. The rest of the family all treated us with a respect we'd never experienced. Steve was rebellious about almost everything and extremely self-centered. He gravitated to any-thing that was enjoyable. He wasn't interested in anything that had hap-pened to his brothers and sisters, other than trying to taunt and provoke his brothers into a fight which he'd enjoyed doing in the past. When he tried doing so now and they didn't fall for his goading; he too was surprised.

Asked to attend another Christian meeting at a local church, I reluc-tantly agreed. Half-way into the meeting Steve came into the church and sat down in the front row. What was going on?! Later he stood up in front of total strangers, except for us, his family and repentantly denounced his way of life and behavior. Maria and I were shocked! We never expected anything like this in our wildest dreams. Our eldest son who had been so bitter, defi-ant and disillusioned with the world was being transformed into a different person. In the moment, I wondered, "Maybe God can be personal."

After witnessing the sudden but welcomed changes taking place in Steve's life, I found myself in a frustrated and confused position. I felt alien-ated from my family spiritually. I desired to be like them, to have what they had, but I didn't know how. The strife, arguments, and anger disappeared in our home. Instead, a peaceful, gentle, quiet new love seemed to flow out of them all. They reminded me of those I'd met at Christian meetings. I just couldn't figure it out, but knew it was real.

During this time-period I was occupied with several official business meetings for the Navy around the country, but recall my thoughts return-ing often to what was happening with my family. Away from home, I was experiencing a new type of loneliness that caused me to sit on my bed one night and begin weeping. I knew my family at home was in a different spiri-tual place than I was and I felt alienated and estranged from them. It wasn't because of them. I was on the outside, finding it difficult to open up fully to God.

One day, our other younger daughter Christina arrived home excited after a late afternoon bike ride. She couldn't wait to tell us about something she'd experienced. She started by describing the sun setting and illuminating the sky in hues of brilliant colors and went on to say, "Suddenly I felt God speaking to me, 'I want you to be a child in My kingdom.'" Christina our youngest, like each of our other children had opened her heart to God. All were convinced Jesus was real, for today, except me.

It was the beginning of summer and the family wanted to go on vacation together. This was highly unusual! Prior to this it was a difficult task trying to get all of the family to do anything together due to selfish interests. To my surprise this vacation turned out to be one of most pleasant we had spent together in a long time. The kids' attitudes were so different. All had helped set up camp before jumping in the nearby river. I pondered this, knowing God probably had something to do with making this trip so enjoyable.

The Last Hold Out

Shortly after, Maria won an all expenses paid vacation to a casino in Las Vegas. I was very excited since it was free! As the notion of a free vacation was settling in, Maria changed her mind asking me to take her to a Christian Conference instead. She said, Dr. Robert Frost, author of *Aglow with the Spirit* and other Christian speakers were going to be there and she would like to go and hear them. Furious, I told her she must be crazy to pass up a free vacation in Vegas in exchange for some dry religious lecture in the foothills! Her reaction to my outburst was one of love, understanding and willingness to yield to my wishes and go to Las Vegas without fighting, or arguing with me. This submissive calm response left me bewildered, so much so that I yielded to her wishes, taking her to the conference instead and paying for the accommodations without grumbling. "What was happening to me?"

On arrival at the Conference Center I detected the same love and warmth emanating from these straight looking people as I had felt among the hippie-types at Upper Streams. My training as an administrator and supervisor of personnel in the Navy aided me in discerning what was real, or a con (fake). The love and warmth I was encountering here was real. One of the first people we met at the conference was Dr. Robert C. Frost. Through dialogue we learned he too had a Catholic background and would be speaking as a Christian laymen and biochemistry teacher. From this initial introduction we felt a bond and listened carefully to his teaching sessions at the conference. As the first speaker on the conference roster, he was genuine, down to earth and impressed both Maria and I as he focused on how God drew him in and his personal encounter with God.

Next up was George Gillies, a former Wall-Street financier, ex-alco-holic, and previously ambassador to the United Nations. He gave a pow-erful testimony of how he came to meet and know God in a personal way. What I was hearing astounded me. Here was a guy who had amassed fame and fortune, but only found real peace through his acceptance of Jesus Christ. This man had achieved what I was still attempting to achieve along with millions of others in this world. Yet, in his talk he was adamant about not attaining anything of value until he met God personally at the age of sixty-nine. His wife had a simple testimony. One day she knelt down by her bed and asked God to take over her life. She said her life was a mess and God had transformed her.

I asked myself, "How could I have lived forty-three years with all that I'd been accumulating materially, raising a family, attending church, gaining knowledge and military training, and somehow missed connecting with the living and true God?" He seemed to be present in so many people's lives.

The Question

Late that evening, Maria and I ran into Dr. Frost in the dimly lit hotel lobby. As we were chatting, he asked if I knew Jesus. I said, "Sure, everybody knows who Jesus was."

"No, I mean do you know who Jesus is, and do you know him per-sonally as though he is another person?"

Gathering my thoughts I quietly responded, "Is it really possible to know Him in a personal way?"

Rapidly he put forth this question, "Would you like to?"

Considering, I paused and then said, "I believe I would."

We knelt down in the hotel lobby and I asked God to reveal Himself to me, if He was real. He did exactly that, as I surrendered my ego and whole self—asking Him to come into my life. In an unexplainable, spiritual and physiological way, my whole being was flooded with a love and warmth I'd never experienced. I was overwhelmed by what I now know to be God's forgiveness, mercy and grace. God was not dead as Nietzsche claimed, but very much alive! He truly had sent His Son Jesus to show us Himself, to give us a new birth and spiritual life as a new creation in the body of Christ.

After this experience I didn't know how I could share this occurrence with anyone, fearing some might think I too had become a religious fanatic. This epiphany about God was the turning point. Internally I knew nothing in life would ever be the same. I was in the early phases of being spiritually radicalized.

On returning home, with Jesus Christ on-board as my personal Savior and Lord, life was refreshingly different. I had a new perspective and view of almost everything. Reading the Bible, I found the portion where Jesus spoke to a religious leader named Nicodemus, teaching him about

Clowser Family

T - *David, Victor, Anne & Steve*
B - *Valerie, Ed, Marie & Christina*

spiritual rebirth, and how it was the only means by which anyone can enter the kingdom of God (John 3:1-17).

Reading this account helped me better understand what had happened within our entire family. In Acts chapter 9:1-22 of the Bible, I read another account about an enemy of Jesus Christ named Saul of Tarsus and his drastic and lasting conversion. It reminded me of how significantly God had changed our kids. This same life-changing phenomenon was what I heard from Dr. Robert Frost, George Gillies and witnessed at Upper

Streams, churches we'd visited and at the Christian Conference.

Desirous of being a good Dad, teaching my kids a strong work ethic, and being a good provider was important to me. I was blessed with a wonderful wife in Maria, and kids that ended up being instruments in God's hands, living examples of God's amazing and capable ability to change lives today! I was the hold-out, the last to yield, to be born of His Spirit, but God in His patience reached me!

The work of His Holy Spirit continues in our family to this day, thanks to God the Father and the Living and Risen Savior, Jesus Christ. God took a very fragmented family and put us back together again."

> "What good is it for someone to gain the
> whole world yet forfeit his (their) soul?"
> – Jesus   Mark 8:36 NIV®

Author's Note: Ed Clowser's full update and interaction with those who were part of the larger Jesus People Movement can be found in Bio's 1 chapter 27.

11

San Fran East Bay Jesus People Movement Part 2 & Beyond

Is Anybody Listening?
Berkeley, California

The streets of Berkeley California and UC Berkeley were churning with political, social and radical activism. The new kid on the block was the 'Christian World Liberation Front' (CWLF), bringing awareness of the need for a spiritual revolution.

UC Berkeley campus groups had championed huge protests when civil or free speech rights had been violated. Students for a Democratic Society (SDS) and The Free Speech Movement (FSM) were formidable in this fight. Heading up anti-Vietnam War demonstrations was the Student Nonviolent Coordinating Committee (SNCC). The New Feminist Movement (NFM) and The Berkeley Liberation Movement (BLM) was equally prominent. Ethnic and racial activist rallied huge support; the Third World Liberation Front TWLF and the Black Student Union (BSU) were determined to not be upstaged by other protest groups by staging one of the longest student strikes in American history.

Another player was the Black Panther Party (BPP) which had more recently emerged in Berkeley and Oakland with radical practices in reaction to police brutality and to promote Black Power. These and other activist and radical groups, including Socialist Communists, made Berkeley, California an intense place to be!

Holy Hubert No Compromise—Jesus is Lord!

Amidst this turbulent setting a street preacher named "Holy Hubert" had paved the way for the Christian World Liberation Front, aka, CWLF and other Jesus People who would follow. Hubert was scoffed, spit-on, beaten and hospitalized for his unwavering preaching about Jesus Christ. Most UC Berkeley campus students had either heard, seen, or knew about Hubert.

HOLY-HUBERT LINDSAY
Fearless Street Preacher

His voice was like the boom of a megaphone blasting through ideology, political and philosophical positions with a clear message, calling for repentance!

Hubert was a small slight man with a bit of a rattle in his voice, but there was nothing small about his ability to project his voice so that anyone within forty yards away could hear his words. His boldness, directness about sin, clarity in preaching the gospel of Jesus Christ, the offer of heaven or consequence of hell for those that reject God, reminded me of John the Baptist.

East Bay radicals didn't like 'Holy Hubert' because they didn't want to hear his convicting words. He interrupted issues of the day, asserting God had something to say! Those that didn't believe in God or whose conscience was pricked wanted to silence him. Hubert had lost most of his front teeth by now, by being hit by radical hecklers. He'd been hospitalized on a number of occasions with cuts, broken ribs and other injuries by attackers. In spite of it all, he continued to preach Jesus Christ as Savior and Lord, the only means of gaining entrance to heaven. One Way preaching!

What was coming wouldn't be much better for anti-Christian forces who hated the name of Jesus Christ. The Living God had called a number of his servants to go into the enemy's lair, to be additional voices of truth in the notoriously radical streets of Berkeley.

Christian World Liberation Front aka CWLF

The Christian World Liberation Front was established by a number of lead-ers from Campus Crusade for Christ with a vision. Jack Sparks and spouse, Pat and Karry Matrisci-ana, and a handful of others comprised the early team. Jack Sparks led this new endeavor with Pat Matrisciana at his side. These two are the ones we came to know.

Jack Sparks
Christian World Liberation Front

Disagreeing with the demands from Cam-pus Crusade for Christ headquarters to approve all published materials, CWLF became an inde-pendent entity soon after their newspaper began publishing. Their conviction was, "Jesus will create a soulful Christianity in Berkeley and contextualize the message to the university and local audience." Their newspaper, *Right On,* was one of the first Jesus People newspapers and the most respected.

The CWLF would remain on the front lines in the East Bay of San Francisco making Jesus Christ known to all who were open. Hubert contin-ued to preach between attacks and hospitalizations.

CWLF set up shop on Telegraph Avenue in the heart of Berkeley. They did so to counteract the strong overbearing presence of radical groups

NUMBER 10   PUBLISHED BY THE CHRISTIAN WORLD LIBERATION FRONT   1 FEBRUARY 1970

like the Berkeley Liberation Movement. The CWLF attracted a variety of people who joined their ranks along with new converts. CWLF provided housing and food for the homeless, counsel for drug users and began their own discipleship efforts. On the streets they employed street theater, one-on-one evangelism and distribution of the **Right On Newspaper.** In each venue of outreach they urged listeners or readers to consider Jesus Christ and His words, His death and resurrection.

The Upper Streams ministry team visited the weekly gatherings of CWLF on a number of occasions. One of their early members wrote, "I was with Jack Sparks and remember the Upper Streams team visiting CWLF meetings. Jack and our team members were impressed that everyone from Upper Streams was down on their knees with faces to the ground seeking the Lord during our prayer times. They brought us fresh songs of worship, helped us with outreach, and area-wide distribution of our Right On news-paper. Thank you." – Cheryl Heyman

A lot was going on in Berkeley and the world. In the USA large public demonstrations and marches were mounting in an attempt to force an end to the war in Viet Nam and bring American troops home. The Bay Area's trio of San Francisco, Oakland and Berkeley were geographical movement strongholds in this struggle. The campus at UC Berkeley was sizzling with activists and radicals.

'Sproul Hall Steps' on the campus was the location for the free-speech micro-phone. Rapidly CWLF made inroads and gained access to being on the microphone rotation roster.

CWLF & Upper Streams Make Jesus Known

God's Spirit gave us boldness in spite of the opposition. The example of Holy Hubert inspired us. Speaking from Sproul Steps, I recall the intensity of hecklers who'd yell at the top of their lungs, attempting to drown-out listeners from hearing the name of Jesus. This was a wild and crazy time!

Hecklers would taunt and threaten us, get in our face and do everything possible to intimidate, and make us stop speaking in Jesus' name. Some became so agitated, they'd throw things, spit, hiss, scream and wave their fists in our faces. It reminded me of what Paul the Apostle encountered, with riots breaking out in cities where he preached the gospel of Jesus Christ.

On one occasion, a number of our team from Upper Streams spoke at Sproul Steps at UC Berkeley. The hecklers were out in force, screaming at the top of their lungs, "Jesus is a lie! Screw your bigoted religion! God is dead! Take your fake religion back to the suburbs! F—you!"

Berkeley's radicals had an agenda of hating lots of things. At the top of their list was anything that resembled the government, establishment society, the organized church and the police. Veiled from the natural eye, there was a larger spiritual battle going on. The forces of light and darkness were at war. In the hyper-intensive atmosphere of Berkeley, good and evil stood out in stark contrast. The demons were enraged when hearing the name of Jesus Christ. They feared their coming doom and short-leash of time to deceive.

In the face of spiritual opposition, *God was raising up a growing number of Jesus People who weren't intimidated by radical threats.* We had our own history of defiant, aggressive, or passive resistance toward the establishment. Things were different now. We were being changed by the Creator of the universe! He was giving us a new perspective. We weren't pro-establishment or pro-radical left!

We'd been given awareness of an Eternal Kingdom. We were learning the acutely flawed government systems of this world could not rule righteously or fairly and did not have the wisdom or power to provide lasting Peace! The seductress of power, greed, hate and lust had deceived the nations and there was no remedy. The influence of sin had saturated the entire planet.

The alternative and positive news is through any number of means, God has the ability to reach anyone with a receptive heart and mind. We presented a Living God who was not like man! Not a liar, racist or corrupt! Not a puppet of any human government. Not a religion that uses God's name to promote a selfish or demonic agenda. As ambassadors of Jesus' Light and Truth we stood in stark contrast to the evils of the world caused by man's greed, hunger for power and exploitation of the weak and defenseless..

We encouraged anyone who would listen to consider God's gift of new life through His Son Jesus Christ. We saw our role as faithfully presenting the truth in the clearest, most sincere and urgent way possible. We implored people on God's behalf, to take a step toward God, to believe He is able to reveal Himself through His Son Jesus Christ! We knew some would consider our words; others would resist.

ALTAMONT ROCK FESTIVAL —Saturday Dec. 6th 1969

As was our growing practice, Upper Streams was willing to go into the dragon's lair to make Jesus Christ known. The chaos of a rock concert was not inviting, but it was an opportunity to let God's light shine amidst the darkness that engulfed these events.

Word was out; a huge Free Rock Festival had been moved during the last week of planning from Golden Gate Park to the dry rolling hills of the East Bay's Livermore region. The new site venue was Altamont, using the remote speedway nearby as the destination.

Since the change in event site put the concert in our area to the east we decided to go. In preparation, we put together a flyer-tract with a clear message of Jesus Christ and left it with the printer.

Interest in this concert was massive! A free concert was a huge draw and the line-up was impressive. Jefferson Airplane, Flying Burrito Brothers, Santana, Crosby Stills Nash and Young, the Grateful Dead and the Rolling Stones were on the billing.

Promoters hoped to recreate a Woodstock, NY atmosphere of

"peace and love" which had preceded this event by four months. Altamont was to be the West Coast counterpart.

When Saturday arrived our team loaded into vehicles, packed food and several boxes of handouts and headed out early in the morning hours, anticipating a long day. The Diablo Valley roads heading east were jammed, often to a near standstill as we neared the concert site several hours later. On arrival, we parked a quarter of a mile away from a huge natural bowl that was carved in the rolling hills where the concert stage was set up.

Seating was on the ground in the basin and along the natural rise of the hillside slopes. On the outside of the bowl, a limited number of

port-a-potties had been set up, each with long queues. The same long lines surrounded the food concessions, which in the course of the concert were unable to accommodate the massive crowds that came. Waves of concert-goers kept coming, cramming into the hillside areas of the bowl and outside on the perimeter forming a sea of humanity.

After several hours of distributing literature, I made my way into the bowl to check out the situation. It didn't look good. Near the stage, Hell's Angels had set up camp and the crowds had already swelled beyond capacity. With no designated seating and tempers flaring, a number of fights broke out. The patience of the crowd was growing thin with news of delays in the concert start-time. It looked like a fiasco in the making.

Altamont was a dry, dusty location, not a good choice for a huge concert. The lack of adequate practical resources began causing havoc early in the event. Limited water, food vendors, medical services, and port-a-potties were an inexcusable omission.

After leaving the bowl I rounded up our team and moved further back on the main road near to where we'd parked. We continued distributing literature for a few more hours till the wind and dust picked up and we decided to pack up and head home.

The following day we heard on the news that a Hell's Angels group member had killed someone who crossed their security line near the stage. Details of this and other tragic incidents surfaced over the next few days. The Stones' hiring of the Hell's Angels as their security force was at the top of the list of things that went wrong.

When the offer was first presented to the Hell's Angels, they didn't like it, as it put them in the role of playing law-enforcement. A new offer of $500 worth of beer to sit on the edge of the stage and party, making sure no one rushed the performers, got them to agree. As the concert progressed it became clear, "This was a disastrous idea!"

The Altamont Rock Festival Compiled News Reports

Over 300,000 fans made their way to Altamont hoping to hear a good concert and experience a feeling of "peace and love." Instead they encountered an organizational nightmare, a hostile crowd and an atmosphere of evil. The least of the problems was a 20 mile long traffic jam going and returning. The more serious news was four people actually died at the Altamont concert: one murdered, one drowned, and two run over. Fights were numerous with 185 injured, some severely. Many bad drug trips were also reported.

As the concert day wore on, Hell's Angels got riotously drunk and many fights broke out. One Hell's Angel smashed Jefferson Airplane singer Marty Balin in the head right on stage when Balin objected to the rough tactics the Angels were using on the crowd, knocking him unconscious. The Grateful Dead, scheduled to be the last act before the Rolling Stones, saw the anger, hostility and violence happening everywhere and refused to play. They quit the venue on the spot, packed-up and went home!

Instead of stepping in to fill the Grateful Dead's time slot, Jagger refused, insisting he would not take the stage until it got dark, as origi-

nally scheduled. With his wild makeup, costume and such frenzied songs as
"Sympathy for the Devil," Jagger wanted an edgy, demonic atmosphere for
the Stones' set. He got more than he bargained for. The long wait for the
Stones to take the stage worsened the crowd's mood and the Hell's Angels'
anger and multiple fights broke out. Finally it was dark enough to satisfy
Jagger, and the Stones took the stage. Just as they started their third song,
"Sympathy for the Devil", a wild fight broke out. The Stones' music stumbled to a halt; they pleaded with the crowd to "just be cool," then after a
long pause, nervously started playing again.

When they started their seventh song, "Under My Thumb", a young
man rushed the stage, was punched in the head by a Hell's Angel and thrown
back into the crowd. He returned with a gun and was fatally stabbed by a
Hell's Angel. As the young man lay dying on the ground several Hell's Angels
stomped on him with their heavy boots. The Stones could see a fracas
going on by the stage but didn't realize someone had just been killed right in

front of them. Fear-
ing a riot, they went
on to play eight more
songs, ending their
set and the violent
concert with "Street
Fighting Man."

The crowd left
behind a mountain of
garbage and litter. Out of 300,000 plus who attended, only 12 volunteers
stuck around and made an attempt to clean up the place. The whole experience of Altamont left most of the crowd and performers alike feeling sour,
frazzled and distressed. Writer Todd Gitlin penned, "The Altamont concert
marked 'the end of the Age of Aquarius!'"

Ironically the Altamont concert was being filmed for a documentary movie called *Gimme Shelter* which was released in 1970. There are two
seconds in the film that shows the fatal stabbing of the young man by
a Hell's Angel. Many believe the Altamont concert revealed the dark and
demonic side of the culture of the 1960s, bringing its lofty ideal of "love
and peace" to a sobering and final conclusion. Though many idolize the

Stones, they were puppets in the hands of the Evil One who unleashes death, hell and destruction.

Jesus People had already seen through the mystical mirage of drug-induced Peace and Love and Satanic counterfeits guised behind 'Rock Stars' who had no conscience about partnering with the devil and invoking him, like the Stones.

Prior to Altamont, evil was not recognized by many "peace and love" advocates. Hopeful idealism was so strong that it allowed many to set aside and ignore the bad stuff that was happening. Altamont, for all those who attended was a shocking wake-up call regarding the human limitations of living up to true Peace and Love.

Discipleship House Growth
A New Church Plant—Calvary Chapel

By now some of those who had received ministry at the House of Acts decided to head out and try their wings in ministry. Having residence roots in Southern Cal, Lonnie & Connie Frisbee headed south to the familiar beach area. With a love for evangelism and the model of community Frisbee had witnessed at the House of Acts, it wasn't surprising to hear that he and John Higgins were working together. John and Lonnie were both involved in a new ministry location called the House of Miracles on 19th Street in Costa Mesa.

Through a series of events Lonnie Frisbee met former Foursquare Gospel pastor (now independent), Chuck Smith, and local businessmen who Smith had gathered around him. Lonnie was asked to be the outreach point-person to the hippie population for a newly forming church, to be called Calvary Chapel.

Sensing the importance of this decision, Lonnie asked Danny Sands, Rick Rickets, Kent Philpott, Dale Alter and I, each from house ministries in the bay area, to travel south for a meeting with Smith's group to hear their proposal. Frisbee wanted us to listen-in, ask questions and give our honest opinion of the group and their intentions after meeting with them.

It was an uncomfortable gathering for me. Fifteen or so business-men surrounded us on chairs. We sat on the floor in the center of the

room. Pastor Smith and friends were straight. Listening to the dialogue left
me wondering if their intentions were to use Lonnie to build a mega church
for their own purposes. When the gathering was over Lonnie asked us for
our take on him being part of planting a hippie friendly church. I didn't
have a response.

As I recall, Kent encouraged Lonnie to set clear guidelines with
Smith and the elders, so they wouldn't be corralled into a "straight model,"
where outward conformity would be placed on new believers. Danny Sands
and Rick Ricketts urged Lonnie to guard the vision of allowing the Holy
Spirit a place of freedom in the ministry.

An Unlikely Merger is Forged

After prayerful consideration, Lonnie Frisbee and John Higgins joined
forces with independent pastor Chuck Smith's new church plant. An agreement was reached; the church would not require outward conformity or
attempt to control the Holy Spirit and Lonnie and John would both be free
to minister as they had been. Lonnie excelled in evangelism and John Higgins in establishing discipleship houses.

This ushered in the beginning of a southern California wave of new
Christians responding to God's Spirit. Frisbee focused the majority of his
energy in street and beach evangelism and preaching at the Wednesday night
gatherings at Calvary. Higgins continued teaching and mentoring new disciples and oversight of a rapidly expanding number of "House of Miracles."

Teens for Christ Coffee House

Nearby in Huntington Beach we decided to visit a former Teen Challenge Coffee House that had been taken over by the "Berg family." They
appeared to be a conservative evangelistic family ministry. The young adult
children did the music, singing and preaching with David & Eve Berg in the
background. Aaron was the main musician. Hosea did the preaching with
a voice that sounded like a frog and Linda & Faith would sing or speak as
needed. The Berg family seemed sincere in their faith and ministry to lift up
Jesus Christ as their Savior.

The father, David Berg, unbeknownst to his spouse and children
at the time, became susceptible to spiritual pride, bitterness and Scriptural
error.

Who could have possibly guessed this seemingly harmless family of six, could grow into one of the worst cults in American history? In the next few years they would mushroom into hundreds of followers and metamorphose into a destructive cult leaving a trail of heartbreak, broken families and moral deprivation that would affect every member, family and child within the group for multiple decades to come. Members and ex-members alike have experienced a fog of delusion and years of spiritual confusion as a result of what they were exposed to.

Linda & Faithy Berg - Teens for Christ
Huntington Beach, CA 1968

Since the group's earliest name, "Teens for Christ", the Berg family and all those who joined them have been known as "The Children of God," "The Family of Love," "The Family" and now "The Family International."

Hungry for power, control and more numbers to elevate the agenda of David Berg, this group would strike a devastating blow into the heart of the The Jesus Movement.

Author's Note: The details of these tragic events will be covered in upcoming chapters.

An Early Calvary Chapel Wednesday Night Gathering

On a warm Wednesday night, many months later, while visiting Lonnie and Connie, they invited me to attend a gathering at the new Calvary Chapel building. 400+ long-hair, hippie surfer types crammed into the pews; some sitting in the aisles, or outside near the open windows as the crowd swelled. From the beaches and streets they came, bringing family and friends. Some were regulars, seeking to grow in the faith and others were hearing about Jesus for the first time. The songs were fresh and the Holy Spirit was strong!

After a season of singing, Lonnie preached a short message, gave

an invitation for people to let Jesus into their hearts and be filled with the
Holy Spirit. From there, the Holy Spirit took over. A steady stream of
people moved to the front of the building to seek God's help and miracles
occurred. Salvation, Spirit-baptism, healing and deliverance from evil spirits
occurred simultaneously. God was present. There was no mistaking, this
was a God visit!

Lonnie told me he'd been taken under wing by Kathryn Kuhlman
who was an evangelist and faith healer. Following her model, Lonnie felt no
need to place his hands on people most of the time. He would ask God to
release his miracles and leave the rest in God's hands. Frisbee had the calling of an evangelist with gifts of miracles and faith. His protocol in ministry was to move out of the way and invite God's Holy Spirit to work freely.

Chuck Smith was in charge of the Sunday morning and evening
gatherings with expository line by line Bible teaching. Smith's gift of teaching, warmth and pastoral care complimented Frisbee's evangelism and Holy
Spirit ministry.

Back in the San Fran Bay Area

I received word my friend Gary Goodell from the Way Inn Ranch had come
to assist us with outreach in San Francisco and Oakland. Gary was a good
brother with a strong vision for reaching the lost and making disciples. He
and his wife Jane eventually settled in Oakland where Gary served as pastor
of a growing Foursquare Gospel church. About the same time I received
an unexpected financial gift from the brothers I'd known at the Way Inn
Ranch who were now students at Life Bible College in Los Angeles. I was
humbled to think they'd share out of their student poverty to support me
in ministry. I was thankful.

Upper Streams Was Humming!

Response to the message of Jesus Christ was steady at Upper Streams. We
did our small part and God did the big stuff! We sowed the seeds of his
kingdom, team members watered them, and God in His amazingly creative
way caused these seeds to grow (I Corinthians 3: 6-9). The words of the
prophet Jeremiah summed up our ongoing experience at Upper Streams.

> Blessed is the man who trusts in the Lord, whose confi-
> dence is in him. He will be like a tree planted by the water

that sends out roots by the stream. It does not fear when the heat comes; its leaves are always green. It has no worries of the year of drought and never fails to bear fruit. Jeremiah 17:7-8

The unexpected was a regular occurrence in our house ministries. One day a young man came to Upper Streams with our address scribbled on a small piece of paper.

Jack Fliehmann

I got saved on June 26th 1970. Leading up to that day, six months prior, I was taking any drug I could get my hands on; doctors told me I should expect to die soon.

I had moved into a commune in Berkeley where we lived in an old broken down Victorian with about 30 people; clothing optional, sex was always happening and witchcraft was the religion of the house.

I remember not sleeping or eating for a week at a time. LSD was my drug of choice. I would take 5 to 10 tabs a day just to see what would happen. On one trip I wandered the streets all night, ending up at the Campanile Tower (300 ft. tall) on the UC Berkeley campus. Out of character I climbed to the bell tower area and flipped out! Something broke in me that day. Previously, I'd been afraid of driving in a car and heights. I was being driven on a dangerous edge.

I had always enjoyed the revolts of the masses and had been involved in many. On the day my life would change, I threw a brick into a police car window. With police in hot pursuit, I flew through yards, jumped fences until the police finally gave up chase.

I got to a main road and hitched to Walnut Creek to a girlfriend's house. Her mother flipped out that I was at their home and threw me out. While leaving my friend passed me an address, saying anyone is welcome. On arrival at 2424 Olympia Blvd. (Upper Streams) I walked in hungry, tired, dirty and smelled badly.

Hippies were in the home playing guitars and singing songs about Jesus. A short talk about Jesus Christ and more singing followed. Then, I heard these words, "If anyone here wants to be forgiven for everything you have ever done wrong and let Jesus come live inside of you, raise your hand."

My hand shot up so fast, it was as if it was being lifted for me! I followed a group of about eight hippies like me who'd raised their hands to a back bedroom. A leader asked us to make it real and follow him in prayer to God. When the prayer ended, I was different, feeling like I'd had a hot shower on the inside.

I moved into a commune home of young men called "Home for His Glory" and lived there about 15 months. Healing of all kinds happened. This is where I started my real life. That was 46 years ago. Jesus continues to save me. Love, Jack, Walnut Creek, CA

Jack's decision to place himself in God's hands has taken him on a journey he could have never imagined. His love and faithfulness in following Jesus is strong. For the past fifteen years he's been traveling to Africa to help build an Orphanage School in the slums of Eldoret, Kenya with an African couple who direct the work, staff and teachers. This is a vibrant and growing ministry. See Missions Chapter 24 for a report. Jack's Bio update can be found in Chapter 27.

Music Ministry at Upper Streams

Music was a big part of outreach and worship at Upper Streams. New musicians and writers were springing up regularly. Learning the guitar was encouraged and team members were always willing to give free lessons to someone who wanted to learn. Occasionally we'd be the recipients of talented musicians who'd pop by.

On hearing Calvary Chapel's music group "Love Song" was visiting our area, we invited them to do a mini-concert at Upper Streams. One of the tunes they sang was "Welcome Back." What struck us about Love Song was their musicianship, harmonies and love for Jesus as Savior and Lord. The lead vocal of Love Song had been deep into drugs and eastern mysticism, finding no answers. He and the group were now followers of the True God and Jesus His Son. God had given them the ability to write and sing songs to welcome and encourage new believers. Love Song, by example encouraged us to give more attention to practicing guitar, harmonies and lyric writing.

Our Father's Family—Leadership Assistance

Unexpectedly, my friend Dan Pauly from southern CA popped in Upper Streams with a small group of Christians accompanying him. Their ministry in Pasadena, 'Our Father's Family' was in transition and they'd taken a trip north to see what was happening in our area. It was great to see Dan again, reminding me of our mutual mentor Mary Feister.

This visit would be a life-changer for both of us. Dan would meet his wife-to-be at Upper Streams, and we'd gain brother Philip Clore and sister Shelia Goudeau from Our Father's Family ministry to join our leadership team.

They arrived at the perfect time, providing encouragement and teaching to a steady stream of new believers. Dale Alter, Larry Gottlieb, Philip Clore and Shelia Goudeau stepped up to this task and gave me time for other ministry needs. These and many other faithful brothers and sisters were willing and faithful workers in the 'Upper Streams' and 'Home for His Glory' ministry. My trust in them was never misplaced. I've asked my good friend and brother

Dan Pauly & Dave Hoyt
Bibles in Hand
Both converted in 1967 and remain Life-time Friends

in Christ, Dale to share some of his recollections of coming to faith in Christ and what things were like in these early days.

> **Author's Note:** Dan's mission into Europe and Africa with Lonnie Frisbee is covered in the Missions Chapter 24 and his Bio update and personal comments can be found in Chapter 27.

Dale Alter

"Jesus is Who You're Looking For!"

Dale Alter

While roaming the Haight Ashbury, San Francisco in late 1967 I had a chance run in with Lonnie Frisbee. He quickly directed our conversation to the topic of Jesus Christ and began to explain that Jesus was God's Son. I was impressed by 'God's Love' that was strong in Lonnie. Thinking about my mind-expanding drug experiences to date, I said, "I think you need to take more LSD to open your mind back up."

He smiled saying, "I don't think so. *Jesus is who you're looking for!*" A seed was planted and there was something about that brief meeting that stuck with me.

In 1968, some nine months later, my psychedelic world came crashing in. It was on a Sunday night in August and I was with a good friend named Terry in a drug-altered condition trying to achieve higher consciousness through Yoga. I thought I was beginning to finally experience Samadhi (an experience of clear light and cosmic consciousness), when a voice I now know as the Holy Spirit asked me, "Where is the love?"

This question caused me to wonder; love hadn't been central to my experience in the psychedelic scene, or part of the teaching of the gurus I knew of. The most ego-centered selfish people I knew were boasting of ego-death. As I pondered the absence of love, I realized that I was deceived by Satan who masquerades himself as an angel of light (2 Corinthians 11:14).

In desperation I asked, "Where are you, God?"

He answered, "I am the Way, the Truth and the Life, no one comes to the Father but by Me." These words pierced through the haze of my drug world, into my heart. I saw idols inside of me knocked over like bowling pins. I, like many hippies, believed there were thousands of ways to God. I thought all teachers and Avatars were the same. The next thing I saw was a mental stream of my entire life with a running commentary of all my judgments on people who did the same things I did. I saw how I had dishonored my parents, treated women as objects, had lied and stolen. The running footage ended right where I had been earlier that day, telling people that "I and they were gods."

As I stood before the Creator of the universe, I felt very small, condemned by my own conscience for the selfish and careless life I had lived. I hung my head and waited for the gavel to come down. Instead I was taken in the spirit to the cross where I saw Jesus dying. He looked into my eyes and I realized that He knew me. I'd never realized that He'd died for my crimes and failures. I instantly grasped what sin was and saw the enormity of it. The blood of Jesus was washing me on the inside and a tremendous weight came off my soul. I was overwhelmingly drawn to the love I felt flowing from Jesus, and I asked God to forgive me!

I was transported into the arms of Christ, died with Him and then rose to life again in Him. This was the purest mystical experience I'd ever had in my young life. At the same time, I felt a foreign spirit being lifted from the back of my neck. The Holy Spirit came in and I knew that I was being reborn. In the days and months ahead my brain was miraculously healed of all the damage done by LSD and other psychedelics. At last, I felt happy, sane and alive!

Up to this point, drugs were the solution. Thankfully, Frisbee's witness to the reality of Jesus Christ prevailed! After receiving Jesus Christ, I tried to find Christians to have fellowship with. Visiting one church I asked, "What should I do, now that I'm a Christian?" Someone said, "Join the military and kill Commies for Christ."

Wow, I wasn't expecting that! I said, "What about Jesus' teaching in the Sermon on the Mount?"

"Peace is for the millennium (the 1,000 year reign of Christ on the earth)—not now!"

I learned this wasn't the typical view of most church people. After floundering for several months I decided to go to Marin County where some friends had a place named Berachah House. It was guided by two

'Babticostal' (Baptist/Pentecostal) students from Golden Gate Baptist Seminary, Kent Philpott and Paul Bryant. I lived at Berachah as one of the early house members and continued growing in my faith. During this time, I reconnected with Frisbee who lived in the House of Acts a few cities north in Novato.

At the time, life consisted of personal Bible study, prayer, group Bible studies and witnessing on the streets of Marin County and San Francisco. We saw lots of people come to faith in Christ. We also went to Berkeley and ministered on the university campus and baptized people in the fountain after they accepted Jesus.

One of the Christians I met in Marin County was David Hoyt. We ministered together on the streets of San Fran, Marin County, Berkeley and other East Bay cities speaking about Jesus Christ to any who would listen. We were also invited to speak in churches and coffee houses.

David decided to move to Walnut Creek to start another Jesus house in 1969. We started a brothers' house called Home for His Glory and a sisters' meeting house called Upper Streams. We had Friday and Saturday night meetings at Upper Streams, often filling the entire house with young people. It was not unusual for people to come in and suddenly be aware of the presence of God's Holy Spirit, overwhelming them with love. Hundreds of young men and women came to know Jesus in the months to come, with supernatural signs accompanying the testimony of Jesus.

Miracles of various types were tangible. I recall a brother named Vic Clowser in the living room of Upper Streams playing his guitar and singing in the Holy Spirit to the Lord in tongues. A Greek girl named Sylvia walked in and understood Victor's song as praise to God in her native tongue of Greek.

On another occasion our friend Mike Hash told us he was too sick to go to the meeting we had planned to attend, saying he had an upset stomach and fever. David and I said, "No way, be healed in Jesus' Name." He was instantly healed and accompanied us to that meeting.

When we shared testimonies of our conversion experience at Upper Streams, a church, or coffeehouse, the Holy Spirit would fill the place and people always received Jesus. When someone accepted Christ, we would baptize them in water as soon as water was available. We urged believers to totally surrender to God and receive the baptism of the Holy Spirit.

Most people spoke in tongues as we laid hands on them, but sometimes they would receive the Holy Spirit during worship and spontaneously begin singing in tongues (a heavenly language of worship). Corporate singing in the Spirit was a hallmark of our gatherings.

We saw people receive "supernatural dentistry" in the Lord's Presence with gold fillings and sometimes new teeth. The Lord lengthened short legs and healed a club foot of one young man. We saw God start cars with dead batteries and fill empty gas tanks. We were childlike in our faith and received financial support without telling people our needs. I don't remember many prayers for provision but God faithfully supplied rent and food money for each of our Christian houses.

Catholic Girl's High School Outreach

On one occasion we were asked to speak at a Catholic girl's high school. Our invitation was to address various classes at the same time and the morning Chapel service that followed. Our team from Upper Streams prayed intensely about this invitation, understanding the nuns who ran the school were placing faith in us to honor Jesus and hopefully stir the students to a more fervent faith in the Savior.

On arrival we were split up to share with various classes, as planned. When the class period concluded we gathered in the chapel for the morning worship service. Arriving a bit early, we heard a unison report from a number of students who had been in Kevin and Steve's class. The girls said, "We saw Kevin and Steve enveloped in a cloud of light as they spoke to us about Jesus." The girl's who told us this, were noticeably touched by God!

The norms of attending a Catholic school with exposure to doctrines and rituals had been suddenly infused with the presence of God! Many of these students were having a first-time spiritual experience of coming into contact with Jesus Christ! The chapel service was charged with God's presence. Toward the conclusion of chapel, Kevin prayed, 'Come Holy Spirit!' Instantly, many girls and nuns began speaking ecstatically in an unknown language and were filled with the Holy Spirit! These are just a few examples of how Jesus was at work opening hearts and revealing himself."

Author's Note: Dale's summary comments can be found in Bio's 2 Chapter 28.

Friendship with a Seasoned Open Bible Pastor Rev. & Mrs. Armand Ramseyer

Jesus People were open to, and needed, the friendships of seasoned Christians, especially those who had pure motives in offering help. All live-ins at 'Upper Streams' and 'Home for His Glory' were young Christians in need of Godly input, feeding, love and encouragement. Pastors Kent Philpott, Vinton Huffey, Goodell Sr., Gary Goodell, Sisters Yvonne and Drayton from Anchor Rescue Mission and Mary Feistier from the Monrovia Christian Bookstore had each given of their time and love in mentoring and encouraging me which was invaluable. I wanted this for our growing ministry team.

The key was to find edifying relationships that were healthy, minus a controlling agenda. We more than found this in Pastor Armand Ramseyer and his spouse from the Open Bible Church in Concord, California. Pastor Ramseyer had a heart of gold, untainted by religious ambition and the desire to control anything related to the Lord. On visiting our ministry at Upper Streams, he said, "This is like a dream come true, it reminds me of the early days of the revival that came out of Azusa Street in 1906 in Los Angeles, which helped launch Open Bible churches and many other ministries."

Witnessing the active work of God's Holy Spirit at Upper Streams, Pastor Ramseyer said he was willing to assist us in any way possible. He didn't ask us, but we chose to attend worship at Open Bible as often as able. We called on him for advice, prayer support and looked for opportunities to work together. Through this, a mutual and sincere friendship in Christ was formed.

Hiccups—A Price He was Willing to Pay

Unfortunately a sizable group of conservative attendees at his church left when we started visiting. The sight of long haired hippie types showing up for worship caused an exodus of these members. We felt terrible and responsible. Pastor Ramseyer wasn't worried about it. His stated view was

"God will help us!" This lessened our feelings of being bummed out.

Interestingly, it gave the church more freedom to embrace a new wave of God's Spirit at work. The loss of 'fossilized old-wood' conservatives was more than matched by the Lord. In the space of five months, the church tripled in size and kept growing as people were drawn to Christ and saved in almost every gathering. In time this ministry grew into a robust outreach ministry and founded a Christian school named Concord Christian Center.

Around this time-period, I learned of a ranch opened by Pat and Jerry Westfall they'd named Antioch Ranch. Their vision was to provide an atmosphere that allowed individuals to find refreshment with God in a nature setting. The ministry was open to all God brought to them, including hippies.

Antioch Ranch History—Told by Pat & Jerry Westfall

In the early 1960s a seed was planted in our hearts through a Christian retreat ministry in Southern California. This was a small country ministry that had found the value of hosting folks away from the business of their usual routine. God worked significantly in such a setting. Both of us were impacted by this fresh retreat approach to ministry. Together we realized that we were somehow destined to do something similar. As 'God's will'

Jerry & Pat Westfall - Founders of Antioc Ranch
Mendocino, CA

has a way of getting our attention, this is what happened.

In 1964, after Pat graduated from nursing school, and Jerry graduated from seminary, with two-week old Jane, we moved to Mendocino where a high school job was open. We immediately began looking for our "place in the country."

In the fall of 1965, after a year of searching for just the right place, God unquestionably led us to these 20 acres that we now call Antioch Ranch. Certainly there could be no place more beautiful than the Mendocino rugged coast and the majestic Redwoods of Northern California.

We purchased 20 acres with one fixer-upper, two bedroom, one bathroom house. The living room was once the garage for the homestead that we learned had burned down in the 1940s.

The Ranch had history, and a lush, overgrown orchard. It had some pasture land, hundreds of Redwoods, and was a nice distance from the fog belt. Jerry's folks helped with a modest down payment, and we "city-kids" did our best to bring some fresh order to this run down old place.

In 1967 Lori was born in a local hospital that is now Bed & Breakfast. From 1967 to 1969 we chafed over "nothing happening." Jerry continued teaching in Mendocino and we had become members of the local Presbyterian Church, a stretch for a couple of charismatic Baptists. Not exactly a match, but a lot of good came out of it that showed up later.

The year 1969 was a pivotal year for our family. Kathy was born in the now B & B!, Jerry's 11 year-old son came to live with us, and our Presbyterian pastor suggested we open our 20 acre "home" to the countless searching hippies flowing into Mendocino.

The idea nauseated us! But over the weeks that followed we couldn't shake this crazy idea. Yes, it was the Lord, so we jumped into what was later called the "Jesus Movement." For 11 years, thousands of wonderful and often weird young people journeyed through what we came to name Antioch Ranch. We used the name Antioch after the city in Syria where many of the early Christians found safety and spiritual nourishment. Was this God's retreat joke?

After 50 years Antioch Christian Ranch continues to provide respite with 5 spacious cabin rentals.: 707.937.5570 email: antioch@mcn.org.

Creative JP Expansion and Attributes

Discipleship Ranches, Centers, Coffeehouses and Christian Houses were multiplying rapidly in cities, suburbs and rural areas, meeting a practical need. Attending church for a few hours weekly was beneficial, but lacked the relational and discipleship ingredient that 'live in' ministries provided. At the time, "small groups and support groups" didn't exist in 95% of USA churches.

Ministry-based community groups and Christian houses jump-started and launched many young believers into a life-long commitment of service to God. By living in, or being attached to, an active Christian community, there was an accelerated opportunity to apply and develop natural and spiritual gifts. Bible study habits and spending time with God daily in prayer was encouraged. We did a lot together that strengthened relationships: work, chores, worship, music, eating, visiting, learning skills, studying, doing music and drama, teaching, witnessing and learning to serve, forgive and love each other. The bonds of friendship and love forged in these settings ran deep.

Jesus People ministries continued to spring up simultaneously. Hollywood, Santa Cruz, Oregon, Seattle, Canada, Milwaukee, Chicago and New York.

The Holy Spirit's fire fell on us with some ministry cross-pollination. The same fire descended on those with absolutely no interaction with other Jesus People. This phenomenon amazed us as most of these had the same core vision of making Jesus known through creative outreach, were endeavoring to provide discipleship training, and establishing Christian ministries that welcomed everyone!

Each JP ministry had their own unique story. All gave witness to Jesus Christ andtook Jesus' words of going into the world and making disciples seriously.

> Then Jesus came up and said to them, "All authority in heaven and on earth has been given to me. Therefore go and make disciples of all nations, baptizing them in the name of the Father and the Son and the Holy Spirit, teaching them to obey everything I have commanded you. And remember, I am with you always, to the end of the age."   Matthew 28:18-20 NET

Northwest Jesus People—Seattle, WA & Vancouver, B.C.
Jim Palosaari & Sue Cowper Intersect with Canadian Preacher Russ Griggs & Jesus People Army Leader, Linda Meissner

On the outskirts of Seattle Washington, in a rural town called Cathhart, Russ Griggs was preaching the gospel, conducting evangelistic tent meetings.

Traveling and low on funds, Jim Palosaari and Sue Cowper saw signs for free camping and followed them. On arrival they found the campsite was on land where a small tent revival meeting was being held. Camping nearby and invitations led to attending. Sue recalls, "As the only non-Christians, Russ was primarily preaching to us. In spite of intellectual battles, we were convinced by the Holy Spirit that Jesus Christ was God's Son and put our faith in Him." As the Scriptures teach, "Everyone who calls on the name of the Lord, will be saved (Acts 2:21)."

The miracle was genuine and spiritual life was unleashed. When the meetings were over, Russ and wife Rosie encouraged Jim and Sue to meet locals from the Jesus People Army in Seattle, led by friend, Linda Meissner. This introduction was beneficial, as Sue moved into "The House of Esther," a women's discipleship house, and Jim hooked up with a guy's house. Both Jim and Sue helped with the ministries of the Jesus People Army and their "Catacombs Coffee House."

As Jim and Sue became more committed in their faith and to each other, Russ Griggs was asked to officiate their wedding. With the passing of time and with God's prompting, Jim and Sue made a move to Milwaukee Wisconsin, not far from where Jim was raised in Oconomowoc. The birth of Jesus People Milwaukee was still in germination but not far off.

Meanwhile the Jesus People Army in Seattle and new outreaches in neighboring cities were going strong. Among these, a cluster of Christian house ministries, a coffeehouse and bakery were launched by Russ Griggs in Vancouver B.C., Canada.

Shiloh Youth Revival Centers—Oregon

In 1970, John Higgins, founder of the 'House of Miracles' ministry houses in Southern-Cal, headed north to Oregon with a handful of friends to start new Christian houses. Growing crops, purchasing land and securing labor contracts for members to adequately support the ministry were practical goals. The new name the group adopted was Shiloh. At the height of Shiloh's operation there were approximated 185 Shiloh houses or churches and the group had established a headquarters and Bible Training School on 92 acres, near Dexter, OR. *Unfortunately trouble was brewing for a number of JP ministries including Shiloh.*

At this writing John Higgins is Senior pastor at His Church Calvary Tri-City in Tempe, AZ where he has served for decades. John is a gifted Bible teacher who has faithfully followed Jesus Christ imparting God's Word for over 50+ years.

12

Mission Blood in our Veins

Into The South

Listening to Ollie Heath talk about the southern part of the USA was interesting. Ollie was the Christian house leader of Soul Inn in San Francisco and a student at a nearby seminary. I had met him though Kent and we'd developed a friendship conducting outreach together in San Fran. Ollie hailed from Mississippi and had used the term Bible Belt several times in describing where we would be heading on our USA mission trip.

Curious I asked, "So what exactly is the Bible Belt?"

"It's a geographical area in the southern USA, known for belief in God and the Bible", Ollie replied. "Three of the four states we plan to visit are part of this belt—Alabama, Georgia and Tennessee. We're also planning on going to Florida to speak on a university campus. The term Bible Belt is a general term. It's not accurate in describing what's going on spiritually. Believe me; the needs in this area are off the charts. A large percentage of the population in Bible Belt states don't believe in God, or have left the church. Others have just enough religion to keep them thinking they don't need to have a relationship with God. Many settle for a show of religion or minimal church attendance and throwing a few bucks in the offering plate at Christmas and Easter."

"Wow!" I replied. "It seemed strange to hear about being exposed to the truth and Jesus Christ and not being excited. I think its far out to be able to contact God directly and I'm thankful for that."

Our mission team was comprised of Paul Bryant, a seminary student and leader at Berachah House in San Anselmo, Ollie Heath, also a seminary student and leader at Soul Inn, Dale Alter from Home for His Glory in Pleasant Hill and I represented Upper Streams in Walnut Creek.

Paul's dad gave us use of a station wagon for the trip. We packed light. We were excited in anticipation of what we'd encounter. Ollie grew up in the south and arranged our itinerary. He'd contacted university campus groups to set speaking dates and lined up a couple of churches as well. In addition, our plan was to visit populated street areas and parks to connect with locals. We were especially interested in finding out what was happening in Atlanta, Georgia, a major hub in the south.

Bumps, Bruises and Need

A loud bang came from under the station wagon as it veered hard to the left into oncoming traffic. The front tire blowout came without warning! Gripping the wheel tightly I turned it to the right but it was too sharp and the wagon went out of control flying into the desert and rolling several times.

Two of our team had been asleep in the back bed of the wagon and a third was dozing, riding shotgun. When the wagon bounced its last time we were right side up. Looking around we were all in shock, but alive! My buddy Dale was the only one who was bleeding with a gash on the top of his head. He said he was OK. We were on the outskirts of Van Horn, Texas in the west desert flatlands. Fortunately, several passing cars stopped and someone reported the accident. Some twenty minutes later an emergency vehicle arrived. The squad took Dale to a nearby doctor and the rest of us were taxied into the small dusty town in a patrol car.

Early into our mission we were between a rock and a hard place. Should we go on, or turn back? Each of us had shattered glass skin issues, were sore and bruised. While Dale was getting his head stitched-up, we discussed our options. The first question to be sorted out was whether the wagon could be fixed. Paul's dad had loaned us the wheels and thankfully the vehicle was insured.

When the wagon was towed to town a few hours later we got the word from the local body shop mechanic that it was totaled. Rolling two or three times had destroyed too much to make a repair worthwhile. We were bummed by the news, but it helped eliminate this option. I felt bad about the accident as the driver. Apologizing to Paul, he replied, "Don't worry about it. It could have happened with anyone of us driving."

Despite this significant set-back, we agreed to continue on to our first stop in Mobile, Alabama. Ollie said he was positive we could obtain a replacement vehicle for the remainder of our journey once there.

Thankful to be alive, we decided to hitch-hike, splitting up in pairs to improve our chance of getting rides. The first day was a long one, with short rides. Minus cell phones we didn't know how the other two-some was doing. The aches and pains of the accident increased as the day dragged on. Hobbling down the road we felt tired and discouraged as the late afternoon sun baked the hot asphalt. We had money, but from what we'd been told, we weren't near a town with lodging.

Feeling at our lowest, we saw a huge travel coach cruising toward us. As it approached, it seemed to be slowing down but it was hard to tell with the sun in our eyes. "Oh, if they would only stop, I whispered under my breath! Please stop!" The next thing we knew the coach had pulled over in front of us and I could have sworn I saw Paul at the wheel!

"I might be hallucinating", I told Ollie, "but I think Paul is driving."

As we hobbled up to the open door, sure enough Paul was at the wheel with a huge ear-to-ear grin saying, "Come on board!"

This was amazing! The coach was a deluxe air-conditioned four-bunk travel motor home. Paul had more to tell us, "Guess what guys? The driver is transporting this coach to within a hundred miles of Mobile, Alabama!" This was unbelievable! Paul continued, "To top it off, he's glad to have help driving because he's been up for a day and a half. Right now he's asleep in one of the back bunks."

We could never have imagined this solution to our dismal car-wreck problem. With each of us weary and sore, having a place to rest and lay down was the best possible remedy for us physically and emotionally. The icing on the cake was this comfortable ride would bring us almost all the way to our first destination.

As the sun set across a big Texas horizon we were thankful and praised God for this amazing provision! Having driven for eight hours plus in the state we now knew the meaning of, "You can drive all day long and still be in Texas!"

When we reached Alabama, it was obvious we had longer hair than the locals and we got some strange looks. We were definitely in the south. Hitching the last lap went smoothly as Mobile was a direct shot south. Everywhere we looked was a lush green landscape of trees, lawns and a wide variety of southern plants. As a Californian, Mobile, Alabama is where I learned the meaning of "humidity." It was so moist, I had a hard time understanding how paint could adhere to the homes. On quick observation I noticed most of the newer homes were brick, but there was still wood trim to be painted.

As Ollie had assured us, his relatives were more than happy to provide us with a vehicle for the remainder of our trip. Ollie's home church was expecting us. Charles Simpson was the pastor of this Spirit-filled congregation of Southern Baptists. The hospitality of Ollie's family and church was amazing. We were cared for and treated like royalty. Everyone we met was friendly, welcoming and full of southern hospitality!

Ollie's family and church had been praying intensely for us on hearing of the tire blow-out and roll over. They too were encouraged by how we had been cared for by securing a long ride in a deluxe coach. After several days of respite in Mobile, we set out for university campuses in Alabama and Florida.

In both university venues we learned that student interest in Christian Campus Ministry was minimal. We spoke in open-air settings at both schools where students hung out. The crowds that gathered were in the 50-100 range, with only a handful hanging around afterwards to ask questions. Ollie and Paul were committed Christians, raised in the church and were both good speakers. Dale was a die-hard hippie, draft card burner, now Christian. I was the former troubled youth with a strong dose of world religions thrown in.

Our next stop was the Atlanta, Georgia area where we'd be addressing a large southern Baptist Church on Sunday and checking out the street scene in the meantime.

The Strip—Atlanta, Georgia

We'd heard of a migration of southern teens to an area near 14th and Peachtree Streets in Atlanta, called The Strip.

Teens, young adults and runaways had moved into the area to experiment with the hippie lifestyle. Visitors came to score drugs and check out the Peace and Love scene. We located the area, finding it was almost identical to the early days in the Haight-Ashbury. The strip was lined with young hippies and runaways from southern states. Drug dealers were out in force, taking advantage of novice hippies with suburban money.

We spent a good part of a day in the neighborhood talking with southern teens about Jesus and toward the end of the day located a Salvation Army Storefront Mission at the far end of the Strip. Their goal was to feed and clothe destitute street people. While visiting with them, they were noticeably concerned about being unable to serve the swelling number of teens that kept arriving. They also voiced frustration about their inability to provide anything in the way of spiritual ministry, or worship services to the population. The mission hadn't received the funding and leadership staff to do so. I pondered what I was hearing and seeing.

Like everywhere, street people live on the edge of survival and exploitation. Dealers are the top dogs, but usually blow their money on a reckless lifestyle of

Piedmont Park, Atlanta Georgia 1970

partying. Like in the Haight, those seeking to buy drugs were easy prey to price gouging, laced drugs, or bad trips. Most who don't get off the street end up disillusioned, spacey, depressed, hardened and desperate.

The lack of sexual restraint in the sixties came at a price. Sexual-related diseases and unwanted pregnancies caused many young ladies to wrestle with aborting the birth and the emotional trauma that followed. If a pregnancy went full term, huge questions loomed in the minds of those pregnant. How can I pay for this? Who is the dad? If I know who the dad is, will he step up and stay by my side? How will I take care of this baby? How will I feel if I put the baby up for adoption? If I have to go back home, how will I tell and face my parents? These were complicated decisions for most teens.

Visiting Atlanta's "Strip" touched something inside of me. There was a lot of need and no visible Christian witness. The night before we left Atlanta, we ate sandwiches at a nearby park and I slipped away to pray. I felt God was trying to tell me something but it wasn't clear. His presence was strong and I prayed with more intensity, listening carefully for the voice of the Holy Spirit, but nothing came. At this point Dale called me saying we needed to go. I knew there was unfinished spiritual business, but it would have to wait.

First Baptist Church
Decatur, Georgia

The next day was Sunday. We had an invite to speak at the First Baptist Church of Decatur, Georgia, thirty minutes north of Atlanta. On arrival Ollie learned the pastor would interview him briefly. We thought we'd each be given an opportunity to share something, but it wasn't in the works.

Regardless, Ollie did an excellent job conveying the need and response we were seeing in this new mission field. After the service a good number of people from this large established congregation made it a point to greet us and encourage us in the work the Lord had called us to. I didn't know it at the time, but this would not be the last encounter with this congregation. This church had over a hundred years of faithful ministry in this southern city with many members from the Atlanta metropolitan area.

Our Next Stop—Vanderbilt University
Nashville, Tennessee

Arriving at Vanderbilt University we were road weary. Grabbing a bite to eat was the first priority and then we'd check out the university. When we arrived on campus, I said "Wow, this reminds me of UC Berkeley, California."

Ollie disappeared into the student center and we started checking out the bulletin boards. On Ollie's return, his facial expression didn't look good. He'd found out the campus ministry he'd communicated with had let the ball drop; no one knew we were coming.

We quickly discerned that liberalism, world religions and anti-Christian sentiments were at an all-time high at the University. We decided to roam the campus and talk to students about Jesus. After several hours we reconnected and shared a similar report. Any mention of Jesus Christ was predominately met with intellectual indifference, or scorn. Ollie concluded that many of the Vanderbilt University students probably had religion and church shoved down their throats their whole lives and had cast it off, having never experienced a personal encounter with Jesus Christ.

Nashville was a let-down, but there was nothing we could do about it. It was what it was. This part of the Bible Belt was as Ollie had previously said, "filled with spiritual need."

As Vanderbilt was our last stop, we back-tracked south and chose a western route to get us back to the San Francisco Bay Area.

Remembering Atlanta in Prayer

A visual of Atlanta's Strip district remained. On returning home, Dale and I shared our impressions of the mission trip to all of our Upper Streams and Home for His Glory spiritual family. We highlighted the needs we'd seen in Atlanta's Strip area. I thought about when I'd prayed in the small Atlanta park, sensing something and the unfinished season of prayer. This nudged me to pray often for Atlanta. While doing so, I'd think about what we'd encountered there and the glaring need.

In the days and weeks ahead, we remembered the southern street people and universities during corporate prayer times. Philip and Shelia who'd joined our team from a ministry in southern California were especially interested, along with Alana a dear and faithful sister in our ministry, along with my wife and I. Each of us felt like God might be calling us to go to Atlanta to set up a new outreach house. We agreed to keep praying and wait for an answer.

A Surprising Offer

Over the next several weeks the possibility of a move to Atlanta came rapidly to a head when we received a letter passed on to us by Ollie Heath with an offer of sponsorship from the First Baptist Church in Decatur, Georgia. The impact of our brief visit to this sizable congregation was hard to read at the time, but it was now apparent they'd been listening to Ollie's words very carefully. The offer included places to live in private homes until they could help us find a home to occupy in Atlanta's Strip District to conduct outreach.

This offer, in conjunction with Atlanta being on the top of our prayer list, was so like God! This news pressed the five of us to pray in earnest about this offer. We decided to pray privately over a 24 hour time-period and come back together. When we met, the answer was a unified "Go."

Saying farewells, visiting family, and making arrangements with those who would move into leadership roles, came together without a hitch. To our amazement we were packed and ready to leave in few weeks.

The excitement of launching a new mission, with limitless possibilities of what God would do was exciting. The human side was more sober as we said our last good-byes to friends, gave away possessions we couldn't cart with us and left familiar places for the unknown. Picking up stakes and venturing out was scary to our flesh, but exhilarating in the Spirit!

We were young and riding a wave of adventure. Nothing seemed impossible! We were full of zeal for God and filled with compassion for those still trapped like we'd once been on drugs, living without restraints and deluded by weird philosophies and religions. This opportunity was one of following in Jesus' footsteps as disciples. We wouldn't be just talking about being Jesus' hands, feet, heart and voice, but were freshly making ourselves available to be just that.

Move to Atlanta, Georgia

From California we'd set out for Atlanta in a Volkswagen van packed to the gills. A simple message, "God is Love," was painted on each side of the van in bright colors. This was the motivation of our small team as we traveled east bound for Atlanta in the heart of the South. None of us had ever lived in this part of

the USA and wondered what it would be like. Our mission outing had given me a little exposure.

Suddenly the skies grew darker on the west Texas flatlands as a huge and powerful lightning and thunderstorm descended on us. The rain was too heavy to drive in, so we pulled off the road and waited it out. Lightning bolts danced around us, lighting the sky. Some struck ground followed by powerful booms of thunder shaking the earth around us. I don't know how our young daughter kept sleeping in the back of the van, oblivious to the storm. Little did we know, as intense and unpredictable as this storm was, so was our future.

When our small team from Living Streams finally arrived at the First Baptist Church of Decatur they were ready and waiting to direct us to private homes for food and rest. In the days ahead they assisted us in scouting out the neighborhoods near to the Strip for a house to rent. Within the first week we had narrowed our choice down to several large homes, but the one we liked best was condemned. It was a large eleven room home just one block off the Strip. The unknown was the cause of it being condemned, and what the requirements would be to bring it up to code? We needed to find out who owned it, and would the owner give us rental compensation for restoring the home. Within a week most of these questions had been answered.

The House of Judah—Atlanta, Georgia

The home needed complete water-line replacements, new copper, new sections of soil pipes, new toilets and fixtures. All the wiring and breaker boxes needed replacing and new electrical fixtures and outlets. The furnace needed to be replaced and some flues changed to heat the entire home evenly. The porch area needed structural reinforcement and a complete new floor installed due to rotting. Cosmetically, all the carpet had to go, the hardwood floors needed sanding and refinishing, the walls and ceilings needed texturing and repainting throughout. The exterior gutters on one side had to be replaced and the exterior of the home repainted. When I saw the list of code repairs required, I took a deep breath, wondering if securing this property would be possible.

After talking with several members of Decatur First Baptist they assured us that the code violations could be remedied. There was plenty of work ahead, but it was all doable. They also took on the task of negotiating a rent reduction with the owner of the property to offset all the repairs made. What impressed me about these Christian men and women was their faith and commitment to follow through on a project from beginning to end. They were doers, knew how to get things done and weren't afraid of tackling a challenge. Adding to their faithfulness was optimism and the promise to keep praying individually and as a congregation for the mission we'd be launching.

Before the work commenced a significant and ongoing rent reduction was negotiated with the owner of the property. With this in place the restoration work began. Each week brought significant progress, taking about eight weeks from beginning to end to make this older run-down home look incredible.

Contractors and members from Decatur First Baptist Church (DFBC) mapped out a plan. Plumbing, electrical, the furnace and structural stuff first, then on to redecorating. We showed up and did what we were asked to do, learning along the way. The church provided new sinks, toilets, and lighting fixtures and hired a painter-plasterer who textured all the ceilings and helped us paint the entire house inside and out.

DFBC also contracted with a professional who sanded and refinished all the downstairs wood floors and then carpeted the upstairs. At our request a prayer room was built in the front of the house with attached bench-seating surrounding the entire room.

The before and after renovation of the large Victorian home at 971 Piedmont Avenue, Atlanta, GA was amazing! When completely restored inside and out, it received the name, "House of Judah" after the Lion of the Tribe of Judah—Jesus Christ!

Refurbishing properties for God's work and purposes was becoming an inspiring and tangible way of occupying territory for God's kingdom. It always reminded me of what happens when we present ourselves before God. He heals and restores our mind, heart, soul and spirit. He makes us new and useful. We have a purpose and reason to get up in the morning!

There is no way we could thank all who came and worked putting their faith into action through sacrifice and practical service at our new mission house. When thinking about it I realized, "The team from Decatur Baptist was serving Jesus, doing whatever needed to be done with faith and excellence, keeping the mission in mind, helping establish another context for Jesus' light to shine! There was nothing in it for them, other than glorifying God with the gifts and talents He'd deposited in their lives."

In the coming days we were again amazed by a growing number of brothers and sisters from Decatur First Baptist Church who would team with us in a new and gutsy venture to enter demonic territory, in order to make Christ Jesus known.

Leap of Faith—DFBC & The House of Judah

Shortly after settling into the House of Judah we began spotting posters for a large Pop Festival to be held near to Atlanta with Jimi Hendrix and a slew of other bands on the billing. With the chaos and fiasco of Altamont fresh in our minds, we asked our new friends at Decatur First Baptist Church if they would consider joining us for an outreach at the event. Within 3 to 4 days we got word, "We're in!"

"That's great!" I replied.

"We can bring lots of other things; just let us know what you think we'll need," their spokesman replied.

Aware of the needs we'd seen at other large gatherings, I filled him in on what we could expect and a number of the practical needs we'd have.

This DFBC member had been our lead contact person throughout the remodel of the House of Judah and was quick to catch a vision for what I shared and other types of things we'd need.

I was psyched! DFBC would be helping us launch our first offensive outreach mission to the Atlanta Pop Festival. Knowing the DFBC group, they could be counted on and would be on top of things.

Day by day pieces to our preparation fell into place. I received a phone call from one of the church team letting us know they'd acquired two very large Army tents and a third near the same size. The end of that same week we learned a number of Christian doctors and nurses from the congregation, or friends of the congregation, had taken days off work and would be joining us for this mission. Each of them were busy gathering medical supplies and other necessary gear to insure we'd be as equipped as possible for the unexpected.

They were also working hard in a number of other areas, gathering a myriad of supplies we'd need including cots, blankets, sleeping bags, water, food, Coleman cooking stoves, large pots, utensils, large water and juice containers, coolers, dry ice, toiletries, camping lanterns, flashlights, several generators for electricity, lots of food and money to pay for the mission. The church would also be providing two large buses for transportation to and from, that would serve as a security safe-place for personal belongings that would be kept locked. We'd also be taking three or four large boxes of Bibles and outreach literature.

When the morning of departure to the Atlanta Pop Festival arrived, doctors, nurses, cooks, members from DFBC and our team gathered for prayer at the House of Judah. It was exciting to see the full team assembled and it felt good to be seeking the Lord's blessing together in one spot. After prayer we loaded up the two buses and a number of vans and were off. It was one of those memorable mornings with the sun burning off the early mist as we headed south of Atlanta.

An hour en route we noticed an increase of traffic and realized we were surrounded by other vehicles who were also heading to one of the largest rock festivals Atlanta had ever hosted. The radio was forecasting crowds of 350,000 and upward. I felt better about our team's preparation for this outreach than any other I'd taken part in.

The three-day event from July 3-5 had 30 artists or bands lined up. The festival billing included, Jimi Hendrix, The Allman Brothers, Mountain, Grand Funk Railroad, Gypsy, It's A Beautiful Day, Richie Havens, Jethro Tull, 10 Years After, B.B. King, Bob Seger, Procol Harum and a host of other

artists. The advertised Free-Camping for the concert event made it more affordable for many.

Our mission team was fortunate to have come early the first day, giving us our pick of the best site in the middle of the Free Camping Area. The larger festival center was a raceway where a large stage had been erected. The remainder of the festival site was recently-mowed weedy open land. The nearby small town of Byron, Georgia was no doubt in shock if they were listening to the radio, or watching the avalanche of vehicles descending upon their rural fields.

First on our agenda was the erecting of the army tents that had been loaned to us. When we unrolled the first, we were all shocked how big it was, and how much of a challenge it was to get it up. It had three very large center poles, with extensions, and numerous side poles 3-4 inches in diameter. Little by little we figured it out and got the first one erected and staked tautly. The second large and other smaller went together more easily. At the half-way point we broke for lunch. With everyone working together, by late afternoon we had all three tents raised. We used one tent for emergency and medical care, with cots and chairs. The second large tent we designated as our kitchen-eating area with a large serving line with stoves, food warmers, coolers, drink containers and tables and chairs for seating. We also used a corner for Bibles and outreach literature. The third tent was our team sleeping quarters full of cots. Our two buses were also available for rest spots.

Getting sleep the first night was sparse! We had so much to do and were figuring it out as we went. It's amazing when you get a bunch of doers together and somebody has to be in charge. We had several cooks who knew all about an efficient serving line, how to do food-prep and were excellent delegators. It was inspiring to see so many gifted people telling our House of Judah team what to do! We were assigned to food prep, the serving line and KP clean-up, witnessing and literature distribution, which was a good match! Several of our ladies assisted the Docs and RNs in the Medical Tent as well as our guys when intercession prayer for campers with terrifying bad drug trips was needed.

We quickly noticed the doctors and nurses had considerably more stamina than the rest of us. Pulling twelve hour shifts was the norm for most of them. We on the other hand were dragging, finally able to catch some sleep between 2-7 AM. Any loss of sleep

Altanta Pop Festival - July 3-5 1970
Byron, Georgia

however, was more than compensated by the working of God's Spirit helping campers in crisis. When I first saw the three tents up it seemed like a bit of over-kill until the masses descended.

Were We Needed There?

When we think our contribution or presence is no big deal, we need to think again. It was uncanny how needed our three tents were during this festival. We served multiple hundreds of meals, gave out clean water, hygiene supplies, blankets, and provided emergency medical assistance to several hundred campers. We also provided dialogue and prayer for many who came into our site seeking spiritual guidance, or those trying to come down from bad drug trips.

The most predominant medical emergencies we encountered were from glass cuts on the feet and ankles. Most required stitches and wound-care. More alarming and surprising were the amount of extreme emotional trauma incidents of teens flipping out from various drugs they'd taken. Almost non-stop, a number of cots were taken by kids who were trying to come down from a terrorizing drug trip. Potent or bad street drugs some-times mixed with alcohol and created crisis situations. Yelling, screaming with fear and terror, or convulsing with tremors was typical. We quickly turned to the power of prayer, grabbing a camp stool and parking ourselves beside the cot of a terrified, confused, or trembling camper providing on the spot intercessory prayer. When they regained stability, often hours later, we'd offer them a hot meal, a cool or hot drink, and share the message of God's love that is free to every person through Jesus Christ.

No one left our tents angry or upset! Many were nourished with food and water, helped medically, or prayed for through a bad drug trip with warmth and compassion. Practical needs were met. A safe place was provided as long as they needed it. Quickly, our cluster of tents and team gained a positive reputation among campers. Those who had been hurt, frightened by a bad drug trip, stolen from, or had spent all their money and were hungry and thirsty came to us for relief and help. They popped by for an occasional meal, to talk, or having heard from friends, just to check us out.

Our entire outreach team sensed God's peace and presence over our campsite as we went about our service calmly and prayerfully. In the midst of satanic confusion we were told by a growing number of festival campers among the hundreds who wandered into our site, that we were the only place of 'Light' at the festival. One visiting camper said, "I can see God's presence around your tents and in all of you!" This didn't surprise me as I too had seen a 'Light' around Christians at different times.

The divine appointments packed into these few days amazed us. We were at the right place at the right time, doing God's will, serving as Jesus would have, meeting real and tangible needs! Many came back to our tents day after day and brought others. *Needs were met, honest discussions about*

*God took place and some concert-goers were changed forever by opening
their minds and hearts to God and His Son, Jesus Christ.*

One evening as the sun set on the 1970 Atlanta Pop Festival skies, a small group of new Christians raised their hands and hearts heavenward in gratitude for God's amazing love and forgiveness that had enveloped them. Adding to this number and miracle, others joined them by the final day. A sizable group of those who had received Jesus Christ at the festival came back with us to Atlanta to be part of the House of Judah.

This was our first offensive mission in the south and it was an honor to jointly take part in this outing with a sacrificial group of Christian doctors, nurses and members of DFBC.

The leap of faith we'd taken, was supported by the Lord Himself. There was no need to ask, how did it go? We didn't do an evaluation, or fill out a survey! Changed and rescued lives before our eyes, gave us joy and confirmation of His work. Other seeds of truth and love were sown to God's glory that would sprout in His timing and way.

"HOUSE OF JUDAH" EARLY TEAM
971 PIEDMONT AVE. ATLANTA, GA

Being vessels of God's mercy, compassion and care, His hands, feet, words and prayers, gave us full assurance our resurrected Lord Jesus was with us! This outing was so much like Jesus' days on earth, an extension of His work continuing.

Life is Precious

Sad news came two months later in September of 1970. Jimi Hendrix died at the age of 27. A month later Janis Joplin, also age 27, died on October 4th. Regardless of what anyone may think about pop stars that die young, Jimi and Janis' life, like that of a young fallen soldier, cancer patient, or victim of some other tragedy resulting in death is a shock and heartbreaking. Life is here one moment and swept away so swiftly.

Since no man knows the future, who can tell him what
is to come? No man has power over the wind to contain
it; so no one has power over the day of his death.
Ecclesiastes 8:7-8a NIV®

This is a reminder of the precious gift of life we are given, with no guarantee of its length. What we do with our life is crucial. Placing our days and times in God's hands while we are in the land of the living, by receiving and following Jesus Christ is the only way to guarantee our eternal destiny.

For Jesus really has been raised from the dead. He is the
first of all those who will rise from death. The plague of
death came because of what Adam and Eve did. Rising
from the dead comes because of what Jesus, the Son of
God did. So because of Christ, all who are 'In-Him' will be
made alive. But here is the order of events. Christ is the
first of those who will rise from the dead. When He returns,
those who belong to Him will be raised to life.   -Paul
I Corinthians 15:20-24 (Paraphrased)

13

Crossroads

A Great Team

Sheila Goudeau and Alanna Lytle from Upper Streams and Pam Ballard from the Atlanta ministry took on the growing need and responsibility of discipling young women who were coming to faith in Christ. Philip Clore, Dan Matyi, Ron Baker and I did the same with the expanding group of young men. Within a short span of time the spacious House of Judah was filled.

Change didn't come easily. Many found it hard to believe they were worthy of being forgiven. Emotional wounds, drug habits, fear, anger and baggage from the past needed healing. This came instantaneously in some areas, but gradually in most.

Time and time again we saw God work in incredible ways, doing what only He could do! Ministry leaders and older Christians did their best to help those younger in the faith, but were unable to reach the deeper parts of the heart and soul. It was humbling and inspiring to see God do the inner-work of making an individual into a new person. *"Those who doubt God and His existence should consider the miracle of a changed life."* Each ministry I'd been part of was for the most part comprised of those who were experiencing this miracle and it was genuine!

Having a Prayer Room set aside solely for this purpose was extremely helpful at the House of Judah. It was a quiet place to study the Bible, pray and worship God without distractions. In the fish bowl of community housing, places to get away are important. We could always take a walk, but a prayer sanctuary within the house in colder months was a gift.

Revisiting the Spiritual Starting Line

Everyone who came to any of our Christian houses with minimal or no connection to God would make a choice. It would be personal, minus coercion. The invitation was to enter into a relationship with God and discover "new life." Unfortunately, most street people had already been burned by evil and were skeptical. Believing in something good had been snuffed out during hard times on the streets, or by other painful life experiences.

What needed to happen was a restart. The timing had to be right. Self-awareness of mistakes, bad attitudes, sins, needing help, hunger for truth, looking for answers like peace, love, or God were all a good preparation. Pride of self-sufficiency was often the last hold-out that needed to fall, before sincerely asking for God's help.

Each person has to step up to their own spiritual starting line. I know that God has deposited a measure of faith in everyone. They need to access this faith and shoot it upward to the Almighty who made them (Ephesians 2:8). Making this important choice to "open up to God and trust in His Son Jesus Christ" is the exercise of faith that is needed. It requires "openness of mind and heart," two areas of the self, reserved for what can be trusted. When the moment and timing is right, individuals let down their pride and survival security and offer a simple prayer, asking God to enter their life.

This simple act of faith, openness, asking and believing in God sets in motion the amazing working of God's Holy Spirit also known as the Spirit of Jesus Christ (Acts 16:17), resulting in a spiritual rebirth (John 3:3-8). The confirmation of this taking place is unique to each person. There may be some sign and immediate awareness, or a gradual one. "The Holy Spirit Himself testified with our spirit that we have been born into God's family" (Romans 8:16). The true test is, if we continue as Jesus' follower and obey His Words.

Some readers may have turned their backs on God and Jesus, trying to forget the truth they once held as precious. My suggestion is to prayerfully read Revelation chapters 1-3 and freshly hear God's Word and ask for His help where you need it. Don't continue on the path of being among those who fell away! It's a dead end.

> Jesus said, "If you continue in My Word, then you are truly My disciples and you will know the truth, and the truth will make you free."   John 8:31b-32 NASB

Love, Mercy & Forgiveness
Greater Than All My Sins!

A majority of people who come to God feel unworthy, too messed up to be forgiven, thinking they've committed too many heinous and disgusting sins, or hurt others in such terrible ways that no forgiveness is possible. They fear they've crossed the line—their history of sin and giving in to evil is too great for even God to forgive. The truth is, we are all unworthy and have done despicable things.

Thinking and feeling unworthy is not uncommon. This is especially true when a Christian knowingly turns away from the Living God and returns to the vomit of their former life of ongoing sin. It's not an easy way of life , but embarrassing with so much hiding going on. The problem is—no one can hide from God and sin is only pleasurable for a season (Hebrews 11:25).

For those of you who are coming to Jesus Christ for the first time, or if you're returning to the God of Truth, God's remedy is simple, Repent! Turn away from evil, your pet sins and resist the devil. Don't procrastinate. You eternal destiny is at stake. Allow God to restore you by humbly calling out to Him. Ask God for forgiveness and a new life in Jesus Christ.

God's Love, Mercy and Forgiveness extend far beyond what we can comprehend. God heals and forgives the absolute worst of sinners. Regularly He responds to the cry of desperate souls who call out to Him from places of terrible despair, evil, and darkness.

A powerful account of deliverance verifying this truth is recorded in Mark's Gospel chapter 5. An individual tormented by the devil is miraculously restored by Jesus Christ to his right mind. This is an amazing read (Mark 5 verses 1-18).

The Promises of God Reveal His Heart To Us

> For I will forgive their wickedness and will remember their sins no more.   Jeremiah 31:34b NIV®

The author of the New Testament book of Hebrews restates these gracious Words from God precisely in chapter 8:12 and later in Hebrews chapter 10:17. The promise is written in this way, *"Their sins and lawless acts I will remember no more."* Another prophet, Isaiah, speaking on God's behalf pens the same truth:

> "I, even I, am he who blots out your transgressions, for my own sake, and remembers your sins no more." Isaiah 43:25 NIV®

> The Psalmist David writes: "As far as the east is from the west, so far has he removed our transgressions from us."
> Psalm 103:12 NIV®

Amazing stuff, to be forgiven for all our bad behavior, thoughts and words. If there's anything foggy about believing God can forgive you, remember, Jesus Christ came to earth for this purpose. God the Father sent Him to reveal truth, die for human sin and be raised from the dead to conquer death. In doing this work, Jesus God's beloved son purchased the gift of eternal life for everyone who places their trust in the redemption he purchased on our behalf. This is the power of God to everyone who believes, but foolishness to all who reject God's offer.

We all reach a crossroad when we hear the Good News of what Jesus has done to redeem us. The sacrificial path He took to a crucifixion death to free us—was taken out of God's love for us. We can shrug it off, or look into Jesus' incredible work to rescue us spiritually and bring us into God's family.

A Transformation Process

Living in Christian community puts the spotlight on our flaws, much like living in a family, or when married. In community, your Christian brothers and sisters are your peers. Leaders in the community are like your older brothers and sisters, or life-coaches, mentors and teachers. In addition, the Holy Spirit, the Bible and prayer are your direct link to God for personal spiritual guidance.

Spiritually, every Christian is in the process of being transformed from the youngest Christian to the oldest. No one has arrived, or reached a sinless state! Anyone who says they have, is misleading themselves and others (1 John 1:10).

In a Christian church, small group or living in community we have an opportunity to rub shoulders with others and grow spiritually. It's a give and take process that requires openness and vulnerability. The Holy Spirit and those around us can help us face things we've been ignoring, or are simply oblivious to. Studying and applying what we learn from the Bible about being a Christ follower and the marks of discipleship aids us in the transformation process. Practicing listening prayer before God helps smooth out the rough spots when we're being pruned, or corrected by the Holy Spirit.

Christian House residents had a considerable amount of adjustments to make. Those who lived at the House of Judah were given chores for the **common good** of the overall ministry. This was a turning point for some who had the bad habit of avoiding work at all costs. A shared workload is essential in community. We encouraged good work habits, wise use of time, personal hygiene, use of personal strengths and discovery of new spiritual gifts.

We provided a relaxed schedule with meal and bed times, chores, work, outreach, worship, Bible study and prayer. A routine helped those who had lived on the streets. Though loosely structured, we respected and encouraged an individual's

TIME MAGAZINE

LEVITON - ATLANTA 1970

HOYT SHARING HIS FAITH IN JESUS
Footloose bearer of the Word

personal and free-time. Those who ran a given ministry house endeavored to be flexible and open to God's Spirit ,changing the schedule as needed. Unexpected events and circumstances arise daily in any outreach mission. For hyper controlling personalities this is unnerving. The facts stand. No two individuals or days are identical! Being flexible is wise and saves us from unneeded personal frustration.

Making Jesus Known

With the House of Judah located one block from the Atlanta's Strip, we connected with lots of street people. Our practice was to be out and about on the "Strip" daily, sharing the good news of Jesus Christ. Being visible and active on the streets brought attention to our mission and the word spread quickly. People came for meals, clothes, lodging, to find out what we were doing, to talk, inquire about God, or attend evening Bible studies.

The House of Judah was able to house 15-20 residents. We reserved these spots for those who had expressed a commitment to grow in their spiritual faith. We put overnight visitors on mattresses on the floor, or on the sizable covered porch for those who were used to sleeping out and a handful in what some called the "drunk tank" in our basement. The fumes emanating from over-night alcoholic guests gave this basement spot its name.

With our first home full, we found a second rental home that could accommodate seven ladies and turned the House of Judah into a guys' house. This relieved our immediate over-crowding, but more space would be needed soon. In the days and months ahead continual numeric and spiritual growth paved the way to open new Atlanta locations and branch out to other southern cities.

The Bread of Life Restaurant

Finding outside work for our resident team members was challenging. Many didn't have job skills, but were willing to learn and work. With a growing budget due to expansion, we prayed for this need throughout our ministry houses. Within two weeks, offers for work started coming in, which included an offer from a downtown restaurant owner wanting to employ 6-8 of our residents. It was perfect timing, putting a number of our people to work. As hoped, our ministry employees at the restaurant earned an excellent reputation for reliability and hard work in the first three months.

This translated into us being given the entire restaurant to manage under the supervision of our boss. With his permission we renamed it "Bread of Life," painted murals on the walls and spruced everything up from top to bottom. Stacie Gains was the amazing artist who painted the interior of the restaurant. The added responsibility of managing the restaurant put even more of our ministry residents to work. Wow! What could we say but, "Thank You Lord!"

Sensing God's blessing we went to work on the basement, remodeling it into a nightspot with a stage, tables, chairs and a sound system. A local newspaper reporter did a short article on our house ministries and the Bread of Life restaurant venue.

Lighting Candles—In Downtown Atlanta GA
George V.R. Smith Writes:

The Temple of Still Waters, The House of Judah and The Lighthouse are all located in Atlanta—supporting a downtown restaurant on Broad Street, close to Five Points.

The Bread of Life Restaurant, across from the First National Bank Building is not like other restaurants. Painted in bright colors are panoramic murals depicting the pastoral setting of the Holy Land.

"I like to come in here, because it's like coming into a different world," said one customer. Another clientele, John Brown, is an employee of a local art supply firm. He first learned about the religious eating place when he ran into several individuals from the restaurant's community who gave him an invite. "It's a pleasant change of pace from the business world and I've been back a number of times," said Brown, an artist at heart and a businessman out of necessity.

Bible excerpts are on top of the table napkin dispensers and along the wall nearby the menus. Another Bible verse is painted over the door—visible from the inside. Other Scripture verses are painted in the front window for perusal by passersby; including a sketch of George Washington on the front of a dollar bill—with the words, "Render unto Washington those things that belong to Washington and unto God those things that belong to God."

There is no evidence of evangelical arm-twisting. The staff is busy prepping and cooking, serving and waiting tables in a friendly manner. The restaurant is clean and well-maintained. Some staff on break may be seen reading their Bibles to themselves, to a companion—or anyone who has expressed an interest to learn more.

The young men and women in the Christian houses which staff the restaurant have turned away from the drug scene—now living by faith in Jesus Christ. All are willing to work. They work to support the community and their outreach missions. A handful work at the restaurant, or do carpentry, cleaning, plumbing, landscaping, arbor tree care and selling artwork.

The general overseer and leader of the group is evangelical Christian worker and ex-drug user David Hoyt. He has had a direct hand in opening and operations at the House of Judah on Piedmont Road and the spacious Temple of Still Waters on 14th Street—formerly a French Consulate. Prior to Hoyt and friends acquiring the old consulate to conduct ministry—a drug-related killing took place, which shocked the owner—and opened the way for the ministry team to rent and restore the property to its former stature. Hoyt and ministry friends have opened a number of other Christian renewal houses in California, Tennessee and Florida—utilizing community members to restore the properties.

A degree of the success of this broadening ministry seems to be traced to Hoyt and other community members' ability to speak to the hippie-culture and others interested, out of their own personal life stories of hard-time experiences. Hoyt spent 6 years in youth institutions and graduated to prison at age eighteen. Other Christian house residents had similar tales to tell of being lost and burned out on life until they had a spiritual encounter with Jesus Christ.

Hoyt recalls, "For the first time in my life I heard something from the Bible that literally blew my mind, 'For there is One God and One mediator between God and man, the man Christ Jesus (II Timothy 2:15).'

"I'd studied eastern religions trying to find the truth but came up empty! The truth wasn't found in Christ-Consciousness, Krishna Consciousness, Cosmic Consciousness, or Zen Buddhism's "Bodhi i.e. Enlightenment," or the Clear of Scientology. All are man-made paths of human striving to find self-realization—without God.

"The way to God is through Jesus Christ who lived a sacrificial life performing one miracle after another—died for human sin, was buried— and rose from death! God spoke to me twice in a Hindu temple, 'Call on me now.' When I called, Jesus Christ revealed himself in power—flooding my being with His Spirit and light. God's Spirit and the Bible made it crystal clear—all who are born of God's true Spirit must come through God's

Son—Jesus Christ—the true Messiah. I know this to be true because— Jesus Christ is making me into a new person! Trying to change on my own—didn't work."

Another Jesus follower, Ron Baker, who moves about on crutches and oversees the restaurant operation, talks of how the downtown facility was brought to their attention through prayer. With many brothers and sisters in need of outside jobs to keep the ministry afloat—prayer for work was offered. Within weeks a variety of job opportunities were offered— including managing a downtown restaurant and being given the freedom to make it representative of their mission. Baker said, "The types of jobs and the amount of them was an answer to prayer."

The sisters and brothers who comprise this new found spiritual family believe they have developed a drug-free urban life-style based on a faith that will last. They believe in the existence of evil, the devil, demons and their representatives. They believe God is directly responsible for rescuing them from destructive choices and the forces of evil.

Soon, they expect to open a downstairs coffeehouse at the restaurant to spread the word of Jesus in a nightclub entertainment atmosphere. "We call it a 'Light-Club' with the avowed purpose of lighting candles for Jesus Christ in the darkness."

These were creative days and God was blessing the work of our hands and the prayers of our hearts. People came to the restaurant to eat and the nightspot to hang out, listen to music and talk. Some came to see the novelty of what we were doing, others because they were hungry spiritually and had questions to ask. Many turned from casual inquirers and seekers, to believers in the Living God.

A Drug-House Transformed

On one of my witnessing endeavors in Atlanta I knocked on the door of an expansive property near the strip, now turned into apartments, notorious for being a center of drug dealing. As the door opened two people in the hallway were arguing over drugs, one pointing a gun and the other had a long sword/knife. In the next few minutes, one backed down retreating into an apartment. A couple of days later I learned that someone in this same building had been shot and killed over drugs.

With this information I set out to locate the owners of the building and began praying about securing this expansive property for our ministry. I learned the building and property had previously been a French Consulate. It was huge! On meeting the owners I assured them we would restore this property to its original state in exchange for the provision of all materials and a rent reduction. This arrangement was agreed on and our team went to work. We gave it the name "Temple of Still Waters." When the facility was fully restored we turned it into our worship center, office building and living quarters for married couples and later renamed it the Atlanta Discipleship Training Center.

Are Demons Real?

Two months earlier during an evening Bible Study while reading a passage of Scripture, a young lady in attendance began screaming and then thrashing-about in the center of the hardwood floor. Some 45 seconds later a loud blood-chilling high pitched shrilling came from her convulsing body for 1-2 minutes until a demon, or demons, finally whimpered and left her. A terrible stench lingered in the room. Now, lying limp on the floor in the middle of the Bible study group was a thin girl in a state of exhaustion.

The faces of those present said it all. Some mouths were gaping open. Others had eyes as wide saucers. A few had their hands over their mouth and noses. We were in unified shock! It had happened so quickly and unexpectedly and was so dark and evil, none of us knew how to react. What had occurred!?

We knew about demons, had made efforts to cast them out, but had never seen anything like this! 30 plus eye-witnesses at the Bible study were speechless! We didn't finish the Bible Study, but turned to prayer for the girl and ourselves.

Later that evening, the conclusion we arrived at was, on hearing the Word of God and the name of Jesus Christ, the demons become terrified and wanted to leave. At that moment, God put His finger on this young girl and carried out "a divine deliverance" to set her free.

How I wish all deliverances went as smoothly as with this young lady. Thankfully she made a resolved commitment to renounce all ties to the demonic. She received Jesus Christ as her Lord that evening and placed her faith and trust in God to protect her.

Darkness Strikes Again

We'd taken in a new lady disciple into one of our houses who began mani-festing unusual behavior after several days. She'd come to us on the referral of her boyfriend who was a resident in our house. In the days that followed she became bedridden, stopped eating, was screaming out, scratching her-self and demons were using her mouth to speak dark and vile things. It scared the ladies who were attending to her.

Her boyfriend said he knew she'd invited spirits to live in her pre-viously, but thought she'd stopped doing this. We concluded the demons were reacting to her being in a Christian environment. Unfortunately things got worse. We secured a hospital bed with rails, posted a 24/7 prayer vigil around her bed, had to wrap her wrists to prevent her from scratching herself. We were perplexed. We fasted and prayed and were able to cast some demons out of her, but on one occasions when the young lady was coherent, she said she didn't want the demons to leave and would invite them back.

Hearing this was alarming! Around the same time her boyfriend said he thought we should untie her wrists restraints, saying we were being too guarded with her. We gently told him this could be life-threatening because of what she'd already done to herself.

A day later, Philip came running up the stairs yelling, "David! We have a new problem!" Following Philip down the stairs to the prayer room, I saw for myself. The boyfriend of the lady resident with demons was stripped to his shorts, had pulled out one of the prayer benches, removed the cushions from the top, had positioned the bench so he could scrape 14 + inches down the center of his spinal column till it had been exposed to the bone. Bloody and writhing up and down on the corner of the bench the demons were present and speaking. The details are gruesome.

After 24 hours we managed to cast out all of the demons from this young man. He said he'd allowed them to come in out of sympathy for his girlfriend who was still in terrible shape. We urged him to close the door once and for all, to entertaining demons. He agreed, if we promised to get help for his girlfriend.

As we had been unable to keep the demons out of the girl we decided we'd bring her to a Bible Camp Meeting to be assessed by Derek Prince, an expert in demon activity and deliverance.

Jesus People Influenced by Church and Para-Church Ministries

JP ministries were influenced by Catholic & Protestant charismatic ministries, Baptists and Pentecostal groups, the Full Gospel Businessman, Youth with A Mission, Campus Crusade for Christ, Young Life, Youth for Christ, Billy Graham Evangelistic Association and a selection of gifted teachers, preachers and evangelists. JP respected and listened to: Billy Graham, Loren Cunningham (YWAM), Jay Kesler (Youth for Christ), George Verwer (Operation Mobilization), David Wilkerson (Teen Challenge) Winkey Pratney (author, evangelist), Robert Frost (author, speaker) Watchman Nee (writings), and Derek Prince, Bob Mumford, Charles Simpson, Don Basham, Ern Baxter and John Poole—(charismatic teachers). There were more.

We were excited to learn Charles Simpson and Derek Prince were going to be speaking at a Bible Camp near Atlanta. I'd met Charles Simpson, senior pastor of Ollie's church in Mobile Alabama and heard speaking tapes of Derek Prince, who was one of the top deliverance preachers of the day. With our current problem of a demon-possessed girl, we decided to take her to see Derek Prince for deliverance.

It was an incredibly difficult task transporting the girl to the Bible Camp with the demons still in control, but we did. When we met with Derek Prince privately and he saw the girl, he concluded she had invited too many demons and was unwilling to renounce them. He suggested we have her assessed by a mental facility for residential treatment. This didn't go over well with her boyfriend. What could we do? We left the conference early and headed back to Atlanta.

For close to a month our Christian house had seemed like a hospital of sorts on "demon alert." On returning to Atlanta we secured a residential mental-health treatment center for her and she was admitted. Her boyfriend left our ministry angry, ticked that we'd been unable to help her. We were sad. The optimum result couldn't be reached without her being willing to renounce the devil and his evil spirits.

Some may not believe in a literal hell, or demons. Based on what I and many others have seen firsthand in the trenches of mission and Christian house ministry, evil and demons do exist. Jesus taught:

> "When the unclean spirit goes out of a man, it passes through waterless places seeking rest, and not finding any, it says, 'I will return to my house from which I came.' And when it comes, it finds it swept and put in order. Then it goes and takes along seven other spirits more evil than itself, and they go in and live there; and the last state of that man (person) becomes worse than the first."   Luke 11:26 NIV®

Entertaining any form of evil is dangerous!

Arthur Blessitt
Man with the Cross

Touring the southern USA was young evangelist Arthur Blessitt carrying a

large cross the breadth of our country as a statement. We'd heard of his tour and wanted to be there to support him when he came through Georgia. A handful of our team from the Atlanta ministry houses made the drive to a large country church on a hill. I recall wondering if our vehicle could handle the climb, it was so steep.

Arthur Blessitt carrying a Cross, Georgia 1970

At the top of the hill stood a large southern style brick church structure with huge columns in the entry with a sanctuary that was long and narrow. The church was packed to overflowing on a warm southern night and the hand-fans were in motion. When Blessitt got up to speak you could feel the intensity of his conviction and vision. He preached with heart, with Jesus at the center. His feet had walked a long way since leaving Hollywood, California. Blessitt was a friendly, likeable guy with a vision tooled by God.

The walk and the cross were a platform to draw people's attention to following in Jesus' footsteps. With perspiration dripping down his face, the Gospel message of Jesus Christ was preached with clarity and power.

Southern Expansion

As the Atlanta ministries continued to blossom we received invitations to speak, sing and help set up similar outreaches in Nashville, Knoxville, and Chattanooga, Tennessee and Gainesville, Florida. In some of these cities a house or building had already been secured. In some settings we were asked to provide leadership. In other cities we'd be working as co-leaders and trainers of a local core-group who had a similar vision for outreach. Being open, we communicated these requests to our Atlanta team members, put the matter to prayer and asked God for direction.

Over the course of a month, team members began alerting us of their willingness to go to various cities. It was exciting for them. The downside was those who would be leaving were many of our day-to-day leadership in the houses or the restaurant. The expansion didn't involve a financial commitment as this was the responsibility of each of the sponsor cities, but it would affect the Atlanta ministry. Losing 6-8 reliable team leaders at one time was not ideal. Two of the outreach ventures became stable in a relatively short period of time with Bud Poston in Nashville and Dan Matyi in Gainesville, Florida.

In retrospect this expansion was premature. We knew transition and change was a part of ministry life, but we were already over our heads,

Worship Gathering at "Temple of Still Waters" - Atlanta, GA

unused to the financial pressure we were encountering to keep everything afloat.

Those who went to Chattanooga and Knoxville were experiencing difficulties that were not an easy fix. There were sponsor differences about how the ministry should be carried out, inconsistent funding for house supplies, staff allowances and outreach projects. Other issues were a lack of sponsor involvement, personality conflict, and the absence of local relational support for our team representatives. We addressed these issues with both parties in these locations, offered support and attempted to normalize the distress as able. I'm still amazed we were doing any of this at such young ages.

In the midst of these somewhat expected glitches, breakthroughs and good things were still happening in Atlanta and in the satellite missions. Young leaders and team members were becoming more reliable, old habits were falling away, emotional and spiritual healing was occurring, prayers were being answered and those who God put in our path were coming to faith in Jesus Christ.

Artistically our team was vibrant with fresh projects, writing new songs and staying creative at the restaurant and night spot. And, thankfully no one died at our restaurant because of our cooking!!

Our broader team was expressing God's love and grace through service, mercy and compassion and because of this, my heart was full of thanksgiving. Taking the message of Jesus Christ, which had opened our eyes and hearts back to the streets, where we had been reached was a privilege. We'd invite people home for a meal and many stayed. Somehow we found room. It was inspiring, yet tiring work, as the needs of those we came into contact with were complex. Exhaustion was normal, but OK. It was part of the package of being Jesus' follower.

The Dilemma

No one in our ministry had a background in accounting, administration, business, or strategic planning. This deficit became pronounced as significant growth continued. With a smattering of gifts in a variety of areas we'd been able to do well with start-up ministries, but things had changed. Lease agreements and utilities on a number of sizable properties, keeping a small fleet of vehicles up-and-running and managing a growing budget that included feeding and housing fifty ministry team members was increasingly demanding. Beyond these practical needs, all of our team members needed nurturing, encouragement and spiritual guidance.

On a warm southern night in Atlanta, Georgia a twenty-five year old young man walked the streets wondering where the solutions would come from. With the luxury of cash in his pockets he followed the sounds of country-rock playing in a huge bar and slipped in for a cold one. It was a Saturday night and the crowd of several hundred was raucous. A Jefferson Airplane tune was blasting which brought back old memories.

Walking to the far end of a huge bar he sought to blend in inconspicuously, check out the night life and forget about ministry problems. All was well, until some guy nearby said, "Aren't you the street preacher? Good to see you haven't forgotten about all of us who sin at night" and he walked away.

Taking a second swig of his beer, it wasn't as refreshing as he'd hoped; it was time to leave. Strange how being somewhere you don't belong, can turn sour so quickly. It wasn't so much the idea of a cold beer on a hot summer night, it was the disguise, attempting to blend in, escape the worries and think this would somehow relieve serious financial ministry problems.

Soul-searching, confession and praying for a way forward to find solutions followed. A young street-preacher was on the spot. This wouldn't be the first or last beer, or glass of wine the Holy Spirit put the brakes on, when it offered nothing but a temporal escape. A healthy diversion would have been a better alternative, along with a crash course in business and ministry financing.

What seemed insurmountable was the crunching of numbers, budgeting, hiring an accountant and having a stable fiscal plan in place for the whole of our Atlanta ministry. Our need was immediate and we'd already postponed what should have been in place a year earlier. Seeking out local help would have been ideal. We had managed to remain debt free, but faced a huge operating monthly budget. The bottom line—there was not enough income!

I contacted several friends from California ministries seeking financial management advice and expertise, but neither had the skills, or availability to drop everything and come to our aid. I would have contacted one of our original sponsors at First Baptist Church in Decatur, or Piedmont Baptist in Marietta, but was too embarrassed because we'd drifted out of contact and as a ministry we'd distanced ourselves from them. It was my fault for dropping the ball relationally and becoming overly wrapped up in our seeming success.

National TV Coverage

Earlier in the year NBC had visited Atlanta to film a documentary they were doing on the Jesus Movement. They spent a day visiting our ministry sites, restaurant and securing a few interviews. They said, "The country is trying to understand the growing phenomena of the Jesus People." When the airing date arrived we gathered around a small TV in the House of Judah to watch. Seeing our ministry on TV was exciting, but what caught my attention was another JP group calling themselves "The Children of God."

I was intrigued by their numbers ranging in the hundreds. I wondered how they kept their ministry running with food, housing, vehicles and the like. This was the hook that got me thinking about finding out what made this ministry tick. I wanted to see their administrative and organizational operations.

A Visit into Rural Texas

This was the backdrop for an unusual solo trip to Thurber, Texas, located 70 miles west of Fort Worth. I hoped to find solutions to help guide our ministry through the murky waters of a looming financial crisis.

My plan was to visit the group as a guest who'd heard about their ministry and wanted

to learn more. I would avoid sharing information about the Atlanta ministry, until I felt OK doing so. I flew into the area, took a bus, hitched and finally walked up a long dusty unpaved road to the Children of God desert camp. I felt apprehensive and nervous but it was too late now to turn back.

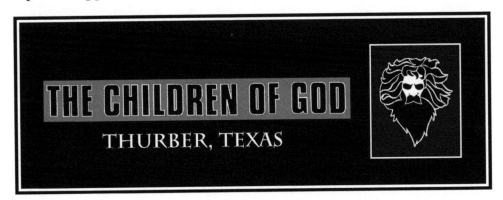

Desert Training Camp—Texas Soul Clinic

I'm not sure what I thought the ranch would look like, but when I approached the front gates, I was surprised to see armed guards at the entrance to the Texas Soul Clinic, and a large sign that read, "The Wicked shall be turned into Hell and all the Nations that Forget God." Psalm 9:17 followed by "NOT MUCH TIME LEFT!"

I asked the gate guards, "What's the reason for the guns?"

With a hint of sarcasm one guard spit back, "You know, the occasional jack rabbit." The other guard piped in saying "A deterrent. We only shoot to scare and warn drunk Red Necks who come near our camp shooting guns and making threats from their pick-up trucks."

I took this response at face value and temporarily put it out of my mind. One of the guards led me down a hill toward the main camp where I was interviewed by an older COG member and then taken further into camp. I was assigned a buddy. He briefed me on the rules and let me know he'd stay with me, show me the ropes and help me find the bunkhouse later. Within an hour I was swept up into the rigorous schedule of a Spiritual Boot Camp. Free time was for bathroom breaks in the outhouses and that was pretty much it! There was no let up in the schedule except for mealtimes and late at night. My buddy was always with me, except when I went into the outhouse and he'd wait outside. This took some getting used to. I learned this was their customary practice with every new person or visitor.

Five to six teaching sessions were given daily in an open-air covered pavilion, with several hundred young followers crammed closely together on benches, Bibles in hand. Each instructor taught in a similar high intensity fashion, weaving slogans into the teaching sessions that students would echo back shouting loudly in unison. I'd never seen anything like this before and wasn't sure what to think. COG teachers enlisted enthusiasm with the slogans, waking any who might be dozing and bringing wandering minds back to focus.

The slogans went like this, (Leader) "Jesus!" (Followers) "Revolution!" (Leader) "My family, my family!" (Followers) "Right or wrong my family!" The later slogan and the extreme implications were troubling.

Offsetting this, the group's love for one another, enthusiasm, commitment to Bible memory work, and focused attention during lengthy teaching sessions was impressive. A divergence from Bible teaching came when letters were read called, "Mo Letters." I didn't know what Mo meant. The content of these letters was practical advice on living, relationships, contrasting views between the group and the church, a radical call to discipleship and encouraged loyalty to the Children of God community.

The group incorporated a whole new range of driving worship songs and Jewish folk dances which was unique. Even the youngest converts seemed strong in their faith, sincere and loyal to God in ways beyond what I would have expected. As the days passed, I watched and listened carefully. Gradually, the positive dimensions of the COG outweighed some of my concerns.

At this point, I began asking questions about the financial structure of the group and how it could handle taking in so many new people. I was told the group had an aggressive philosophy about securing donations from companies, store chains and grocery stores. They had purchased a refrigerated truck for transporting these donated perishable items to the ranch in Thurber, Texas in the summertime heat. The same practice was used by their large Los Angeles colony.

Monetary income came mostly from new disciples. They urged all new members to turn over all their possessions, savings, and other capital to the Children of God movement as a sign of their dedication to God.

As my allotted visit time was drawing to a close I decided to reveal my identity in hopes of securing more information on how they sustained themselves organizationally and financially, beyond what I'd already learned.

VIP Treatment

I pulled aside one of their teaching leaders and made it known I represented an outreach Jesus People ministry in Atlanta, Georgia. This information was quickly relayed to COG leaders who introduced themselves and made a noticeable effort to be better hosts and win my support for their cause and work. Having shared the same TV special, they remembered our group.

I continued asking questions about how they handled expansion and financial crisis. The answer I heard was "Procurement Teams" for resources and financial support, and for new disciples to give all they owned in the way of savings, cars, lands, trusts, i.e. to "forsake all" when they joined the group. These resources were then absorbed into the COG's general fund.

I felt like there had to be other things we could incorporate in Atlanta, other than asking our team members to "forsake all." When I went down through the list of our team in my mind, almost all were dirt-poor. None that I knew of owned property, or had a savings account. Up to this point I was still only getting bits and pieces of the COG's organizational structure and wanted to know more about how they handled dispersion of leaders to different locations without hurting the home base. I also needed more information on how they went about making procurement contacts.

The COG leaders had their own agenda, as I had mine. As I fished for organization information, they purposed visiting our group to better understand our ministries needs. On the surface, COG leaders seemed genuinely interested in helping us with their offer to visit Atlanta to gain a better idea of what we were doing. They said they'd cover the costs.

The tentative plan was for us to have a joint worship celebration in Atlanta with a handful from their ministry. They would then tour our ministry houses and the restaurant and the next day we could have a problem-solving organizational discussion.

I told them I'd talk it over with our leaders and get back to them.

14

Bad Decision—Their Agenda

Author's Note: The recollections in Chapters 13-15 are subjective. Some may recall these events differently. Due to the emotional trauma many of us experienced, there may be omissions, but we've endeavored to retell what occurred accurately.

"I acknowledge my failures as a leader. I am deeply sorry for my part in what happened. I offer my sincere apology to each of you who were affected and wounded by the Children of God takeover and all that followed. These are difficult things to revisit."

– D.E. Hoyt

Returning to Atlanta I shared my experience and impressions of the Children of God with our young leaders, including cautions and strengths. After talking it through, our consensus was close to what I'd envisioned. *Our team agreed to invite a small group from the Children of God for a worship celebration, allow them tour our ministry and afterwards brainstorm on what could be done to strengthen our ministry's administrative and financial base.*

We communicated this to COG leaders and began the process of agreeing on a calendar time frame for a two day visit.

Shortly after making this decision, we began receiving phone calls from Christian friends on the West Coast, warning us about the COG. They told us the Children of God group was "out-there," probably a cult. Friends who had run-ins with them said they were aggressive and acted like robots. We weren't sure what to think.

One close friend was very angry and disappointed with us for even considering inviting them to visit. He said, "They're bad news, radical, on the border-line of being a cult from what I've heard. The Los Angeles COG group marches in 'sack-cloth' with yokes around their necks and huge staffs, in the style of Old Testament prophets. They're flat out weird! I've seen pictures of their vigils."

I listened, while thinking about my visit to Texas and what I'd seen for myself. I'd never seen a sackcloth vigil, but didn't doubt they conducted them. I told my buddy we'd consider his comments and pray about it.

THE CHILDREN OF GOD — On sackcloth protest vigil in Los Angeles, CA

I felt between a rock and a hard place. Our entire leadership team wanted to find a way to sustain our ministry on a solid footing. I communicated these new warnings to the Atlanta leaders and we continued to pray.

As events played out, we didn't call off the arranged visit with the Children of God. The absence of hard evidence of them being a cult was our reasoning. As the dates for the COG visit approached, the Atlanta team was excited, hopeful this might give us ideas and encouragement. Most of them had seen the NBC 'First Tuesday JP documentary' with footage of the group, which gave them an idea of what to expect.

COG Crash the Atlanta Ministry Center

Contrary to what we expected, on the COG arrival day, what occurred was beyond anything we imagined or anticipated!

The Atlanta Discipleship Training Center and Christian House ministries had about seventy live-in disciples and another 25-30 who were part of our community. In addition, we had satellite ministries scattered around several southern cities. Representatives from the satellite ministries and a majority from the Atlanta community would be present for the COG worship visit.

From everything we'd discussed with the COG to date, it sounded like they might bring a team of seven to ten group members tops, comprised of a handful of musicians and singers and one or two organizational leaders.

To our surprise, a large worship team was flown in from LA with several top leaders. Shortly after, two buses arrived from Cincinnati jam-packed with COG disciples followed by vehicles with leaders from the Thurber, Texas colony.

The large number of COG on our grounds was alarming! We hadn't agreed to this. COG leaders tried to assure us everything was all right, but we were a hard-sell at this point, nervous and leery.

CHILDREN OF GOD Bussed In

As their band was setting up, Atlanta leaders gathered in a back room to try and figure out what we should do. Before we could arrive at any decision, we received word our Atlanta people were freaking out! The high-powered and aggressive COG were in their faces.

In an attempt to lessen the fear we rejoined the swarm and mix of the two groups, attempting to assure as many of our Atlanta team as we could, that we'd be with them. A handful from Atlanta were so shaken, they left! The majority calmed down once worship began.

When the band was ready, I made a few introductions and turned it over to COG leaders to introduce their worship team and band. The band featured a prize COG convert, Jeremy Spencer from Fleetwood Mac, who played lead guitar. Their band was tight and the worship songs were strong and easy to learn.

Seated in the back of our worship area, I received a message that the police were outside and wanted to talk to someone in charge. I excused myself and went outside with several Atlanta leaders. A couple of COG leader's got wind of the situation and followed us.

The police said they'd received complaints from different sources. Some complaints were about vehicles parked everywhere, also about shouting and loud music. Other complaints came from our Atlanta people who'd left earlier. They'd called the police, saying something was wrong and they were afraid. One officer asked, "Is everything alright?"

COG leader Hosea Berg quickly responded, "Everything is alright. We just came to visit, and we'll be happy to move our vehicles, and turn down the volume of our worship band. We're sorry about the problems we've caused."

The officer nodded saying, "OK, but I don't want to have to come back."

When the police left and we turned to walk back to the house, several of our Atlanta team arrived in a car calling out to me. As I walked over toward them, Hosea followed. Our team members were frantic; "Don't you see what's happening? This group is nothing like us. There's something wrong. They're like zombies and Bible memory robots! David, please ask them to leave!"

With COG leader Hosea standing at my side, it was an awkward moment. I told them that nothing had occurred that was as bad as they feared. They continued pleading with me to do something.

Hosea leaned over to those in the car and said, "We just came for a music and worship celebration and I'm sorry some of our people scared you. I know some of our younger disciples are over-zealous and too intense. We're sorry. Why don't you try joining us for worship?"

The Atlanta brothers flatly refused and warned me again that something was wrong.

Hosea sent word to have their bus and van drivers move their vehicles to lessen the congestion around our ministry center. After giving them directions of where they could park, we headed back inside. Looking over my shoulder I saw several cars now parked on the street with Atlanta team members inside. They looked frightened and desperate. Walking back to the house I noticed the volume on the music had already been turned down considerably.

Talk about a strange night! I was uncertain what to think or do, hoping things would get better. I still couldn't believe we weren't told in advance about the large number of COG that had descended on our ministry. I turned to Hosea and queried, "Why did you bring all of your Cincinnati people down here?"

"We thought you're people would like to see how these young disciples were being trained. You don't have to worry about feeding them, we have food and stoves on our buses. We're all going to witness at a Rock Festival in Louisiana from here. Everybody's going, except a few who'll fly back to LA."

Hosea's words seemed reasonable for the first time. For a brief moment I felt a hopeful sense of relief.

Worship and singing was still going strong when we returned inside. When the COG worship team finished their set, Hosea stood up and explained why the Cincinnati colony had rendezvoused with them in Atlanta to caravan to the Louisiana Rock Festival together. Hosea was thin and small in stature, but his voice was deep and loud, uncharacteristic for his size. I would have thought he'd be six feet tall and several hundred pounds if I heard his voice alone.

I hoped the mention of them heading to the Louisiana Pop Festival calmed the concerns of our Atlanta group, as much as it did mine. Our worship team led the second phase of our celebration.

Having agreed there would be no teaching we transitioned to a short fifteen minute film the COG brought with them. It showed various ministry sites, demonstrations they'd led and outreach activities. This concluded our worship gathering and as hosts, we served sandwiches and drinks.

Pulling me aside, Hosea was eager to tell me about Joel, one of their main Bible teachers, he thought I should meet. Hosea said Joel had developed the discipleship curriculum the COG was using and he was an expert in end-time prophecy. While we were talking, an Atlanta leader whispered to me, "The police are here again because more complaints have been called in and they want to talk to somebody."

Overhearing this, Hosea leaned over to me and said, "Why don't you let me take care of it, it's probably about one of our vehicles. You shouldn't have to be bothered with this, I'll handle it."

"OK," I replied, "but if it's about something else let me know."

He disappeared with an Atlanta leader and came back in ten minutes saying it was just about moving one of their buses again.

By now the crowd at our headquarters had thinned. Hosea continued to encourage me to meet Joel, saying he was nearby. He reiterated that he thought Joel might be able to give me some specific insights into how to strengthen the training of disciples and our organization as a whole. I finally agreed.

With the go-ahead, Hosea, Joab and I set out by car to where Joel was staying. En route I learned that "nearby" was about 35 miles outside of Atlanta in a trailer park. When we arrived it was about 9:30 PM. Hosea introduced Joel as a significant player in the COG organizational structure. Joel had dark hair, was medium build and had a calm presence about him. All of us had refreshments and visited for an hour or so, sharing recent things that we were learning and how God was working.

Hosea said, "I'd like for you to spend at least a day with Joel and ask him anything you want. You can pick his brains. The teaching he's developed is the reason the level of commitment in our group is so high. It's why members and donors are willing to give so much financially, even properties to further our cause. He's also excellent at helping fine-tune organizational matters that could help you."

"We have a short wave and can be in touch if you want to leave for any reason. What do you say?" Hosea continued, "Our plan is, Joab and I will return to Atlanta to keep an eye on our

Hosea Berg

Joab COG General

Joel COG Teacher

group and make sure no more problems arise with the police."

Listening to Hosea explain things concisely was disarming. Without much thought I replied, "OK."

Immediately after Hosea and Joab left, it hit me, I needed to communicate with my spouse and Philip. Using the short-wave in the trailer I told Hosea I wanted him to tell my spouse and Philip where I was, the name of the trailer park and have them both call me on the short-wave in the morning.

The trailer was comfortable, capable of easily sleeping four. Emotionally tired, I decided to turn in for the night, settling into a lower bunk. I said goodnight to Joel and we agreed to talk in the morning. I needed sleep, but my mind was racing, revisiting the events of the day. I felt like I was in a twilight zone where illusions, agendas and motives couldn't be deciphered. Hosea was a smooth talker. I wondered what was true and what was COG orchestration and manipulation. Wading through the events and nuances of what had happened was confusing. Bewildered, I finally dozed off around 2 AM.

COG Leader on a Short Leash

Sharing breakfast with Joel was not what I expected. He was the most laid-back individual I'd met to date among the COG group. In casual dialogue I could see why he was the group's resident theologian and scholar. His specialty was prophecy and end-time events, but his breadth of Biblical knowledge in general was more than impressive. He maintained a humble attitude, as if some serious tragedy had recently occurred.

Around 11 AM, I spoke with my spouse and Philip by short-wave. They both sounded like everything was going fairly well. Philip said The COG was staying to themselves, on their own schedule and our people were not feeling as uneasy as the night before.

In the course of the first day of visiting with Joel, we talked about lots of subjects. He explained the reasoning behind the COG curriculum topics and why the group's emphasis on Bible memory work was effective. Later in the day we got into end-time prophecy. I listened to a number of new concepts, reserving judgment until I could process this information privately. The next area we dipped into was the organizational infrastructure of the COG and how they had built up a sizable financial base insuring their survival in leaner times. The combination of a strong multi-pronged procurement program, intentional fund-raising and requiring new recruits to sign over everything they own was what gave them physical stability up to this point.

Sensing a personal connection with Joel I introduced tougher questions, like "What are Mo letters? Who is Mo? Is there anything about the Children of God that you disagree with and don't like? How long have you been in the group and have you encountered any doubts about the direction of the group?"

One by one he answered these questions and confided in me about various problems he'd encountered. The brokenness I thought I'd seen in Joel, was real. He'd been disciplined for independent thinking, beliefs and questioning COG practices. David Berg, the main leader, had taken Joel out of circulation for a season for disciplinary reasons. He went on to explain that David Berg was the author of Mo letters. Berg's kids, Hosea, Faith, Aaron and Deborah were next in command. Something involving David Berg's wife, Eve, was an area that troubled him, but he felt it would be too disloyal to divulge more details.

Thankfully, Joel didn't attempt to indoctrinate me, which made our time more of a mutual learning experience. I'm sure Hosea would have been disappointed in Joel's less than Ra Ra COG posture, but he wasn't going to hear it from me.

It was morning of the second day at the trailer park. The time of dialogue with Joel had flown by. He was an interesting and talented disciple. I felt for him, realizing he was still on probation within the group and was in a battle with his conscience regarding hidden stuff he didn't agree with. His fate as a leader was up in the air.

My mind kept drifting to Atlanta. I was ready to return, to see my wife and the team and learn how everything was going. I short-waved Hosea informing him of this and that Joel and I had covered as much ground as I could process for the time being. He said he'd be at the trailer park in an hour or so and we could talk about everything then.

When Hosea arrived he was excited, "Guess what? Your Atlanta leaders and group want to join us witnessing at the Festival in Louisiana.

It's going to be an incredible time and I told them I'd talk with you and radio back your thoughts. Philip said he'd bring extra clothes for you. If it's agreeable with you, they can leave with our group in several hours and we can meet them down there. We're planning on leaving this evening when Faith joins us from Los Angeles and we can go down together in the RV."

It felt like I didn't have a choice. I didn't know what to say. Hosea seemed to read my mind, "You can talk to Philip if you're not sure, to get his feeling about things. We'll call him on the radio. I'm sure we can track him down."

Surprised by news of this turn of events I said, "OK." In about ten minutes Philip was on the radio but our connection was not the best. COG leaders were in close proximity on both ends of the short wave.

"Philip, what do you think? Is everyone in agreement about going to the festival?" How's my wife and the rest of the team with us doing this?"

In a static response "Yea, most of our group wants to go and it could be a good training time for our newer team members who've never done anything like this. I've talked with your wife and other team members who will be staying behind and they're OK with us going."

"So, you're saying it sounds good?"

"Yea, I'll bring a couple changes of clothes for you and see you there." His voice trailed off, and that was it.

I handed the radio back to Hosea saying, "It's a go."

"Great! You'll be glad. The LA band will be playing and we're going to reach lots of people." Hosea said he had stuff to do and would be picking up Faith at the airport later in the day and he was off.

I'd enjoyed the quiet of the trailer park and one-on-one time with Joel which continued throughout the day.

Early evening Hosea arrived at the trailer park with Faith Berg and other COG leaders in a number of vehicles who'd be caravaning to the pop festival. Hosea, Faith and a driver loaded their gear into the RV. Joel was assigned to another vehicle. Hosea was loud and hyper and Faith was a born extrovert, joyful and full of energy. Awkward and intimidating sums up how I felt. They were family and had tons to talk and laugh about. I asked Hosea about my wife and daughter and other families in our ministry. He said they were all fine. The fine answer was not reassuring, but all he offered.

En route to Louisiana, I tried not to worry, but did. Without a vehicle, or access to a phone, I was dependent on Hosea's agenda and control. In just two days, my choices had slipped away since the COG's arrival. I felt partially to blame. I wondered where all this was heading? Traveling through the night I dozed on and off and kept thinking about it.

1971 Celebration of Life Rock Festival McCrea, Louisiana

As planned, we met up at the Rock Festival. It was great to see the Atlanta team! Our younger team members were psyched to be at the festival, taking it all in and JP co-leader friends were engaged with COG counterparts, doing practical stuff that needed doing in setting up camp.

COG leaders kept a close eye on me, interrupting conversations, as soon as they began with anyone from Atlanta. Philip was kept so busy we

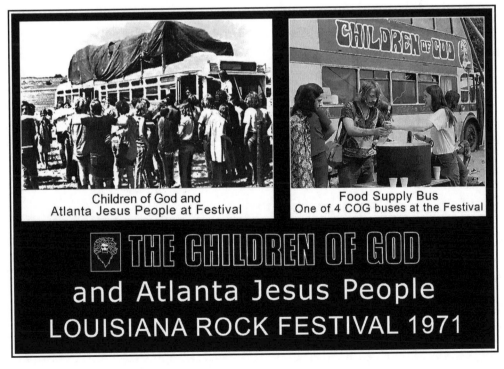

Children of God and
Atlanta Jesus People at Festival

Food Supply Bus
One of 4 COG buses at the Festival

THE CHILDREN OF GOD
and Atlanta Jesus People
LOUISIANA ROCK FESTIVAL 1971

hardly had any time to talk. When we finally had a few minutes, he said, "Some from our ministry want to visit the COG training center in Texas, your wife included. They have mid-wives who deliver babies regularly, at no cost. Getting close to her delivery time, she asked if you could meet her in Texas after the festival. She would bring your daughter and they will be in good hands."

What!? I thought. Before I could ask Philip to explain, we were interrupted by a COG leader asking for his assistance. The waters were getting murkier. This news seemed like one more calculated plan of the COG to keep moving us where they wanted to. It felt like we'd opened "Pandora's Box" and couldn't close it!

While at the festival, I tried to find out more about what had happened in Atlanta, but news was fuzzy. A few of our team had left after the COG's arrival, but most had stayed and were now "caught up in the COG spirit." They were impressed by the dedication and Bible knowledge of the COG members and Jeremy Spencer the lead guitarist from Fleetwood Mac. Many in our group were so recently out of the street scene that they were smitten by the LA band and Jeremy's guitar playing.

From my vantage point there wasn't anything positive about being at this festival. My inner turmoil was off the charts! The COG on the other hand were having a blast, using their band to gather listeners to witness to. The Atlanta team looked to be on-board with everything going on. While taking it all in, I noted COG leadership continued watching me like a hawk and had Atlanta leaders inundated with busy work. This was especially true of Philip who was my best friend and right hand leader. This never changed during the course of the festival. At times a sick feeling hit me in the pit of my belly, like what you feel when you've really blown-it, or someone dies.

Texas Soul Clinic Indoctrination

From the dirt and mud of the rock festival, new seekers joined both our groups and we packed into buses, vans, and cars, and headed back to the Children of God headquarters in Thurber, Texas. Instead of our Atlanta JP heading home, we'd been invited to the COG ranch in Texas. I was assigned to ride in one of the old school buses comprised of COG disciples and new people who'd joined the group at the festival. I remember bouncing down the Louisiana and Texas highways surrounded by radical COG disciples yelling slogans and singing at the top or their lungs. Cars passing by or near us looked shocked to hear the level of noise coming from the buses open windows in the heat of summer.

I'd learned from Hosea just before we left the festival site, my family and other wives from Atlanta had already arrived at the ranch. I assumed our larger Atlanta team would only be visiting for a few days, but didn't know about my family with the offer of mid-wife delivery services at the ranch. We had a doctor in Atlanta, but as uninsured, the full costs of the doctor and hospital delivery were going to be expensive. This factored into my wife favoring help from the COG midwives.

I replayed the events of the last week in my head during the hot bus ride back to The COG's main colony.

Life at Texas Soul Clinic was very different from our ministry in Atlanta. A non-stop schedule ran from 8 am—10 pm at night with zero free time. Those of us with children had limited access. The children were isolated in a Jewish-style kids Kibbutz. Mothers were allowed to visit daily, dads on occasion. Men with children felt frustrated about this rule. I wanted to see my daughter but COG leaders remained unmovable on this and other rules. COG female leaders kept my spouse and other wives from Atlanta busily occupied with one-on-one nurturing and special attention.

Intensive indoctrination of our Atlanta team and the new converts from the Louisiana Pop festival was the COG's focus. Little by little we learned from Hosea, that the majority of our team would be staying in Texas for training and the younger disciples were OK with this.

JP Leader Rendezvous

On a chance opportunity, after our assigned COG 'buddies' had left for the evening, I had a short five-minute opportunity to speak with three of our Atlanta leaders, Philip, Mark and Larry. Mark and Larry were fearful of COG indoctrination which was separating their wives from them emotionally. I voiced the same concern. Our wives' loyalty was noticeably shifting to the COG. Philip, still single, had seen enough indoctrination to be extremely concerned. We collectively agreed, we wanted to leave the Texas Soul Clinic but didn't know how to pull it off. We had no access to vehicles or money. If we had the means, Mark, Larry and I had a fear that even with the short amount of time that had past, our wives wouldn't want to leave. We ended our short visit when one of the spouses heard us talking near the RV where one of our leaders was staying. We didn't want her reporting this to COG women leaders.

Departure Plans on Hold

I could understand my spouse wanting to access the COG mid-wives in Texas. Since her arrival, a group of ladies had been working with her and she felt good about delivering at the ranch. Her approaching delivery time arrived and she gave birth to a healthy baby girl, our second child.

Living at the Children of God compound in Thurber, Texas was a positive experience for some, especially the ladies. Seasoned COG women had succeeded in gaining the loyalty of the wives and single young ladies from Atlanta. Single men had likewise adapted to the rigorous discipleship techniques of the COG.

Atlanta JP Leaders were going through the motions, but at odds with it all, feeling trapped and manipulated. We weren't able to meet again as we'd hoped and thus far had no departure plan. I'd been assigned work in the leather shop making sandals and yoke symbols that disciples wore around their necks. The work was a welcomed temporary distraction.

In contrast, the Biblical account and the yoke Jeremiah made and wore, cited in Jeremiah chapter 27, refers to God telling Judah, Israel and neighboring nations to submit to King Nebuchadnezzar of Babylon, saying it will go better for them if they do. The yokes the COG used in silent vigils and the message of destruction they warned of had nothing to do with what God told Jeremiah to use the yoke for.

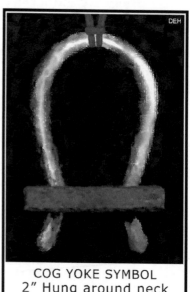

COG YOKE SYMBOL
2″ Hung around neck
with leather cord
[Idea from Jeremiah 27]

The larger versions of these yokes were worn during Silent Vigils accompanied by sackcloth attire and large wooden staffs. The image on the next page shows approximately one hundred COG members practicing for a silent vigil under the direction of Joab. Next to it is a COG member in full vigil attire. The COG's purpose for these vigils was to warn of a coming USA destruction!

THE CHILDREN OF GOD   Joab gives "Silent Vigil" Instructions

Journey to Nashville

There was a driving agenda and cloaked motives in the expansion efforts of the COG. Among the movers and shakers, Hosea Berg was at the top. In earlier conversations Hosea remembered my mention of a ministry we'd helped staff called the 23rd Psalm in Nashville, Tennessee and brought it up again. He said, "I'm planning a trip near Nashville and wanted to know if you'd like to join me? Maybe we could visit the ministry and I could provide them with information on how we disciple new followers. Just think about it."

Several days later he revisited the subject. "David, I plan to leave for Nashville this weekend and wanted to know if you wanted to come along." Reading my frustration level he continued, "I think this trip could be good for you. You'd see some of your old friends and get a break from thinking about your concerns here. I know this whole thing has been hard on you. We'll have some relaxed time on the road and you won't be expected to do anything. All I want to do is offer help to the 23rd Psalm Ministry. What do you say?"

Mentally and emotionally exhausted, I agreed; anything to get away from the non-stop schedule of the Texas Soul Clinic. After Hosea left I sighed and thought, O God, what's going on?

On the trip north to Nashville I felt like I'd been drugged. I kept thinking about Atlanta, wondering what had become of our ministry. When I'd ask Hosea, he'd say, "Everything is fine in Atlanta. The ministry houses and the restaurant are doing well. We've put some of our people in to fill the gaps. You don't have to worry about anything!"

His words didn't ease my concerns. When we finally arrived in Nashville, I was thankful for fresh air and familiar soil. Unfortunately, I quickly learned this was not a casual friendly visit to the 23rd Psalm Christian House ministry, but a high-powered sales pitch. Hosea had arranged to meet with all the leaders of the 23rd Psalm ministry including a handful of businessmen who were the financial backers of this work. The meeting was held in a large and somewhat ornate venue. I felt like a puppet on a string without any freedom unless Hosea was moving the strings.

The first person I saw was Bud Poston, a gifted leader from the House of Judah, who had moved to Nashville to help lead the 23rd Psalm House ministry.

On seeing me he approached and greeted me warmly. Seeing my dazed look, he put his hand on my shoulder and asked, "Are you OK, David?" I felt numb and couldn't answer. He could tell things weren't right. I could see he was concerned, but the meeting was ready to begin.

During a break, I connected with Bud and learned he and John Shugar had taken a scouting trip to Atlanta and found the COG people paranoid and unfriendly. This had occurred prior to Hosea's attempt to recruit the Nashville 23rd Psalm ministry. I was glad to hear they would have caution as they listened to Hosea's pitch.

Bud Poston
Atlanta & Nashville
Jesus People Leader

Whatever desired results Hosea had hope for, was not realized. My friend Bud Poston, Ken Pitts, Ron Klenk and Paul Campbell and other 23rd Psalm team leaders told Hosea, "Thanks, but no thanks!" They were very clear about taking a different approach to how they would conduct ministry in Nashville.

Soon Hosea and I were on the road heading south. The time away was OK, but it didn't change the distress I felt. Returning to Texas was depressing. My wife was more committed to the COG than ever and it was almost impossible for me to see either of our daughters. Lead women in the COG had considerable clout and they exercised it making husbands feel like they were unwanted when it came to them visiting their children in the "Kids Kibbutz."

> In an enemy camp
> Doubt is unacceptable
> Slogans scream at my being
> Right or wrong, my family—my family!
> COG control, manipulation and hidden agendas rule
> Troubling thoughts flood my mind   D.E.H.

Jesus People Ministries in COG Sights

Despite Hosea's failure to win over the 23rd Psalm House Ministry, the ambitions of the Berg Family were not deterred. In the weeks that followed I learned the COG had turned their focus to new potential Jesus People conquests. In passing, Hosea said other Jesus People ministries had contacted them asking for help. He thought the news would encourage me. I didn't respond.

Hosea was likable, but practiced a type of manipulation and orchestration, the likes of which I'd never encountered. It was frightening how smooth his words were while orchestrating people and maintaining an innocent demeanor at the same time. He didn't come across as outright evil, but I sensed darkness was nearby.

15

Over My Head

New Fish to Fry

Hosea's failure to spark interest among the 23rd Psalm Jesus People was but a momentary setback. The COG was driven by something, or someone at a hyper pace.

I later learned, around the same time Hosea was pitching the COG program to the Nashville JP ministry, two JP leaders from the Northwest had made contact with the COG and visited their Los Angeles operations separately.

Russ Griggs, JP leader in Vancouver BC, had heard about the COG through the media and also decided to go on an exploratory trip to see them. He visited the Los Angeles COG headquarters. As was the COG practice they showed him the best side of all they were doing. Organizationally the COG seemed to have it all together. While visiting, Griggs met some of the Berg family, Jethro and Deborah Berg (aka Linda Berg), Artie and Faith Berg.

JP leader Linda Meissner, from the Jesus People Army in Seattle, Washington, made an almost identical visit to check out the COG. Both JP groups were interested in all the COG was doing and their organizational abilities.

With new fish to fry, COG leaders turned their attention to Linda Meissner's Jesus People Army in Seattle, Washington and Russ Griggs' JP Ministry in Vancouver, British Colombia. Both had successful coffeehouses and a variety of Christian houses and were linked relationally. They would soon experience the strong lure and advance of COG leaders that would descend on Seattle, Washington and later Vancouver, BC. Hosea's plan was to have key COG leaders from Los Angeles and Texas join him for meetings with JP leaders from both Northwest groups.

Hosea's New Offer—an Escape Plan?

While sitting through an afternoon COG indoctrination session, Hosea tapped me on the shoulder and pulled me out. Any diversion was welcomed! As usual, Hosea's had some idea to sell. This one involved me traveling with him to the Northwest to meet with other Jesus People.

Seeing this as a possible doorway to escape, I agreed on the condition my spouse and two small children would accompany me. After a day or so of consideration and running it by other Berg family leaders, they agreed.

Hosea knew I wanted to leave the Texas compound and hoped this would give me a sense of purpose in the group and perhaps closeness with other Jesus People I could relate to. My hope was to leave the COG with my family if an opportunity arose. I wasn't a positive representative for the Children of God and they knew it. Outwardly I remained neutral, given my family situation.

As Hosea agreed, several days prior to the scheduled gathering in the Northwest, my family and I were flown to Seattle. A day later, my wife and two daughters were sent off to Bellingham, Washington to a remote conference site camp the COG had obtained the use of.

I voiced concerns to Hosea about separating my family again and reneging on our agreement. He said it was only temporary, because of limited housing in Seattle for other COG members would be arriving soon. What temporary meant was nebulous. He went on to say, "You are staying here so you can meet some northwest Jesus People.

Motive and Intentions

The COG had an aggressive mission to seize any opportunity that presented itself to further their cause. Their purpose in absorbing Jesus People Ministries who were floundering, was to garner any financial benefits and increase their member base.

The need among the Seattle and Vancouver ministries was identical to Atlanta; coping with rapid growth and the administrative challenge of meeting all the practical needs of food, housing, rents and utilities, while nurturing young Christians.

Young JP leaders often found themselves under high levels of pressure and stress to solve problems that were overwhelming and beyond their gifting. This was at the crux; the COG presented themselves as the remedy to organizational nightmares.

A meeting of northwest ministry leaders and the COG was set. Without delay Hosea Berg and spouse Esther, and other COG leaders began wooing Russ Griggs and Linda Meissner and other northwest leaders who were present.

The unanticipated fly in the ointment were JP leaders who flew into Seattle to attempt to dissuade Griggs and Meissner from joining. Jim Palosaari from Milwaukee was one of these. With Palosaari's relational ties to Griggs and Meissner, he urged them not to join. Several others did the same, to no avail.

COG leaders had the advantage of considerable alone time with Griggs and Meissner during their separate visits to COG headquarters in LA. Added to this was the VIP treatment and wooing of both by a collection of COG top leaders who had flown into Seattle. The COG was invested in orchestrating expansion!

When Hosea and other COG leaders were confident of having already influenced the JP leaders in a positive way, I was paraded into a large room to greet them. I don't remember saying much of anything. I recall shaking a few people's hands and being escorted out five minutes later. Hosea knew I was disgruntled. He was OK with showing me off as another JP leader who'd joined, with minimal expectations beyond this.

Seattle Jesus People Army & Vancouver JP— Join the COG

Over the next few days I learned the Seattle Jesus People Army and JP from Vancouver, BC had both joined the COG. I felt a tight-knot in my belly on hearing the news.

To appease my ongoing voiced frustration about being separated from my family, I was invited to go to Canada with Russ Griggs to see the ministry there. Hosea hoped I'd bond with Griggs and settle in with a new JP friend. Once in Canada I learned more about the Vancouver ministry. Over the course of a relatively short span of time, Russ Griggs had founded and provided leadership for four Christian house ministries, a bakery, a coffee house and a storefront for sales of a variety of items to support the BC ministry.

Griggs was a man on the move and gracious in his interaction with me. I liked him. He had a good heart and wasn't easily ruffled. I appreciated being able to talk to someone who didn't act like a COG robot with canned phrases.

There was considerable awkwardness among Russ' team when it came to adjusting to high-powered COG members seeking to disciple them. The Canadians were more laid back and it appeared to be an obvious mismatch when paired with aggressive COG members.

Still in a bit of a fog, I went about my days tagging along with Griggs. He ran a bakery as part of the coffee house and introduced me to rising early, making dough, kneading and shaping it for the ovens. When our bakery chores were completed mid-morning, Griggs checked in with the rest of the ministry leaders and facilities. En route to and from we talked about normal stuff. In time, he learned about my dilemma and frustration about being separated from my family. To remedy this, he arranged a ride for me to get to Bellingham to see my family.

Russ informed me he would be going to Texas for some COG training and wanted to get this done before leaving.

Bellingham Camp— North Coast of Washington State

Crossing over the Canadian border into Washington we headed to the COG Bellingham camp where I was dropped off.

On arrival in Bellingham, I was greeted with suspicion by a younger COG lady member who was stationed in a small building near the front of the camp. She eventually summoned a COG leader named Rachael just under the Berg family in leadership command. I'd encountered Rachael in Texas at their headquarters. She was a big-boned woman with dark hair and a frame like a man. The smile in the picture shown below was uncharacteristic of her; I never saw one.

She was a loyalist to the COG and leery of me. I asked if I could please see my wife and children. The answer was an unbendable, "No!" I pressed her, stating Hosea had promised unification with my family as the basis for coming to the Northwest. Without confirmation and an OK from Hosea she wasn't budging. This resulted in a fourteen hour wait in a bare room with COG members popping in and out. As nightfall settled in, torrents of rain descended on the remote camp-

Rachael - High Ranking COG Leader and One of Berg's Secret Wives

site with the sounds of thunder and lightning clapping in the background. I slept in a hard chair till morning.

The next day, I awaited word on my request to be united with my family. Finally, word came that Hosea had given permission for me to visit my wife, with Rachael present. I learned that Rachael was one of several who were paired with my spouse to keep her occupied and growing in loyalty to the COG. My wife was an Atlanta trophy. Her loyalty to the COG was an important example to the others from Atlanta who'd joined. I gradually discerned this as the reason she was treated so well and guarded carefully.

Visiting my spouse in Rachael's presence was useless, but I did so anyway. Nothing of substance was discussed. I asked about the children and she told me they were fine. Several times she restated how surprised she was I'd showed up out of the blue. Abruptly she said, "Because of camp rules the children won't be able to see you." It sounded like she just remembered a prompt fed to her by Rachael earlier. Our trio visit lasted about 10 minutes and Rachael escorted her out.

I hated the manipulation of the COG!

Part of the communication Rachael had passed along from Hosea was that he would be calling me on one of their short-wave radio phones and I was to stay put until then. I was tired of the 10x10 check-point room, but wasn't allowed to go anywhere else. They brought me food and drink and I had the use of a bathroom in the building.

While hanging out in this room, a handful of COG members popped in and out for communication and for check-point shift changes. In one conversation, I overheard a COG member tell another, "Hepatitis and something else had broken out at the camp due to lack of showers and possible food contamination."

The news was alarming, but carried with it a possible doorway to escape! I got word to Rachael that I needed to take my family and leave before they contracted hepatitis. She was surprised I knew anything about the outbreak. I didn't comment on how I knew. My request was followed by multiple short-wave negotiations with Hosea. I reminded him that the COG had absorbed over 10 quality vehicles from the Atlanta ministry and they owed me a running vehicle to help get my family away from the possibility of being infected by the virus spreading rapidly throughout the camp population. I remained insistent until Hosea finally gave in

My wife was hesitant to leave with me. As I was talking with her, COG women were counseling her to stay. She finally agreed at my urging to take some time aside, get away from the contagious environment at the camp for our children's sake. I hoped she'd re-evaluate her position and view of the COG.

An Unsettling Escape

Our drive from Bellingham, WA to California was full of confrontation, arguments and disagreement about the COG. She had found a home and felt a huge amount of support coming to her from the female network of leaders. They had showered her with VIP treatment, affirmation and friendship. They wanted her loyalty and had it!

The foggy coastal route to California was similar to the spiritual condition we were both in. We were in a tug a war about how we each felt about the COG. I was disillusioned and fed up. I was against their practices of manipulation, separation of families and the robot-type unthink-

ing disciples they were producing. She
felt the group provided stability, plenty
of female companionship, care for our
children and many other positive benefits.

The only thing we agreed on
was to go to Upper Streams in Walnut
Creek and ask if we could stay there
for a short period of time. Though we
had founded this ministry they'd heard
we'd joined a cult. This translated into
a respectful, but very cautious, acceptance of our request.

By now, most California JP
were suspicious of the COG and their
motives and rightly so. Regularly, Christian friends would show up at Upper

Steams to ask questions and warn me if I was still part of the COG. I told
them I didn't accept most of what the COG taught and that we were trying
to make a break. They in turn were concerned and fearful that the COG
had sent us to take over Upper Streams and other Bay Area JP ministries.
It was strange having former friends view us with distrust and fear. On the
other hand, I couldn't blame them.

A Ministry House—No Longer Safe

Ministry friends who lived at Upper Streams, though cautious, gave us the
use of the master bedroom. Within several days, COG leadership somehow
acquired the house's phone number and began calling. I had no idea how
they tracked us down, but it didn't go over well for those who had taken
us in. They were stressed to the max. To them, this posed a threat of their
ministry being taken over. Meanwhile the COG was busy apologizing by
phone for everything in the past, pleading with us to come back, which
appealed to my spouse.

Upper Streams leaders didn't know what to do. In desperation they
called a group of people I'd known from the area who were still attached to

the Upper Streams ministry, asking them to come and talk with me. They came and we talked in the front porch area. They wanted to know exactly what my intentions were. Being uncertain of what my spouse and I were going to do heightened their concern and alarm for the sake of the ministry. They told me that they thought we should try to find somewhere else to stay because of the stress and fear everyone felt. I agreed to try and they left.

The same day, several calls came in from COG top leaders. The idea they pitched was, to be part of a new team going to England for Christ-centered outreach, which they hoped would expand into Europe. They knew my heart was in outreach and baited the hook—emphasizing the wide open mission possibilities and spiritual need. They added, they had a plan to conduct ministry differently in Europe

The next day COG members arrived at Upper Streams which freaked-out the Upper Streams team. The JP locals at Upper Steams, who'd graciously allowed us to stay, became more fearful and didn't like the COG showing up on their doorstep! I was surprised as well. I asked them to please leave, which temporarily lowered the stress.

On two previous phone invites I'd turned down the COG's offer to go to England, though my wife wanted to go. Talking it out, I realized we were no longer trusted by our JP hosts and they wanted us to leave. We'd outstayed our welcome and our options had narrowed. This dilemma and the ongoing invitation by the COG nudged us to accept their offer to move to England and start over. Ugh!

Leaving from San Francisco we were flown to New York, where we stayed at a COG colony until flight arrangements could be made for us to go on to England. The NY COG house was over-crowded and the disciples were strange. The countryside was beautiful, but the intensity inside the colony was over-the-top with long teaching sessions, non-stop Scripture memorization and overly submissive residents to COG manipulation. The combination left me wanting to get out of there as quickly as possible. I picked up some type of hepatitis jaundice at this location that was going around and my complexion turned yellow.

Booked on a cheap charter flight with a stopover in Iceland for refueling, we were finally heading to England. Images of this flight are still vivid. The plane was packed to capacity, so much so, our family couldn't sit together. My spouse and two children were seated several isles in front of me until someone graciously gave up their seat so we could sit together. Both of our girls were now resting in our arms. It was a late night flight. Most on board were asleep with the exception of a few babies whimpering until nursed or given a bottle.

Didn't Want to Die in a Plane Crash!

Surrounded by dark clouds with wing lights in view, all seemed OK until our peaceful flight was abruptly caught in the middle of a severe thunder and lightning storm as we approached Iceland. In a short space of time all passengers were awakened by the shaking of the plane and the steward turning on the cabin lights, urging everyone to buckle up. Waves of heavy turbulence pounded the plane as passenger concern rose with every turbulent shake and bolt of lightning. Finally the captain's voice came on the intercom explaining that we couldn't land immediately because of a back-up of other flights that had been delayed by the same storm. In a holding pattern we began doing large laps over Iceland until cleared to land.

Knowing the purpose of landing in Iceland was for refueling, twenty to thirty minutes later, some passengers began voicing concern about running out of fuel. As this possible scenario was buzzing around the cabin, our left wing engine caught on fire! I took a deep breath and looked at my spouse as she started to wake. "What's going on?" She whispered.

"An engine fire on the left wing"

"Are we going to be OK?" She continued, gripping one of our girls more firmly.

"I hope so!"

Looking out the small left window we could both see the white and orange flames shooting sporadically from the engine. The rain and turbulence had increased with loud claps of thunder and lightning illuminating the sky, with the plane engine ablaze. We were praying, hoping others were too. The passenger adrenalin level was peaking. It was like a bad airplane movie with us in it. "Would we die? What would the captain do?" Unspoken questions we were afraid to ask. Looking around, the distress and concern on passenger and flight attendant faces said it all!

The captain had alerted the air traffic controllers on the ground of our engine fire emergency and obtained clearance to land. In the midst of the growing panic the captain came over the cabin intercom with the good

news, "Because of our emergency status we have been bumped into first place and we are readying to land."

Sighs of relief could be heard throughout the plane! "Phew!" I said. Making our decent to the runway caused an incredible sense of relief for passengers who clapped and cheered as we touched down. While exiting the plane the flight team told us we'd have at least a two hour layover. This changed when we heard over the terminal PA that mechanics had taken our plane out of service for an engine replacement. This news was followed by information on a replacement plane arriving in approximately four hours. The PA directive said all passenger luggage was being sent to baggage claim to be picked up in the interim. The long layover didn't seem to bother anyone; we were just glad to be alive! An alternative plane arrived some five hours later as promised and we boarded for our last lap to London, England.

Canadian Russ Griggs—A Humbling Realization

I thought about my new JP friend Russ Griggs from Vancouver BC and wondered how he was doing. My time with him in Canada had been the best respite since being coerced and manipulated into joining the COG.

> **Author's Note:** I would see Russ Griggs again in England and he gave me an update on what happened to the Northwest Jesus People ministry after the COG takeover.

COG leaders initiated a plan to send Griggs to Texas for 'Procurement' training. This would enable the COG to complete their seizure of the Vancouver ministry. During his absence almost all of the local JP who were part of the ministry were shipped out to undisclosed locations. This caused a huge stir of outrage in the BC community among those who had interactions with Griggs and the families and friends of the Jesus People who'd mysteriously disappeared.

As was the COG practice, the Vancouver JP was absorbed into the group and moved from place to place, to keep them disorientated. Any contact with family or friends was discouraged and phone use was not allowed.

In an attempt to put out the fires of protest in Vancouver, over what the COG had done and the spirit in which they had taken over, Griggs was sent back to Vancouver by the COG to smooth things over with the locals.

He told me later what tipped him off was the bitterness of the COG toward the "System," comprised of the church, families and former friends and the world in general, unless there was money or inheritances to be had.

All reports in circulation about the replacement COG members assigned to Vancouver were negative. There was uniformity in what locals outside the group were encountering. Those that spoke with Children of God members said, "COG members are aggressive, unfriendly, paranoid and manifest a bad attitude. In one-on-one interaction, they act like robots using canned phrases and have no conscience about lying. Their PR reps attempt to present themselves to the public, press and police as innocent of any wrongdoing—while damning the system, the church, parents and families behind closed doors."

This was similar to what Bud Poston reported regarding his fact-finding visit to the House of Judah and other Atlanta ministries.

When the lights went on for Griggs, the damage had already been done. All of his young leaders and ministry members had been scattered to unknown destinations, disappearing deep within the COG, similar to what happened to our Atlanta, GA team.

At this critical juncture, Griggs said enough is enough and severed ties with the COG. The news of this and the public outcry against the COG forced the evacuation of COG members from the area. Griggs' loss was devastating. It was a fiasco personally and within the Vancouver community at large.

Anger & Backlash Over COG Takeover
Blame Falls at Griggs' Doorstep

Parents, family members and friends of those who were swooped up into the COG and had been taken away were irate! All who had friendly contact with the Vancouver JP, along with the public who heard about it in the newspapers, were angry. Property owners of the JP rentals were furious. It was a mess! The full scrutiny and criticism from a variety of sources in Seattle, WA and Vancouver, BC were out in force.

At the same time, a fledgling group called "Free COG," who were against the COG, showed up. They wanted to help, but instead spewed out unwise critical comments to family members and the media. This did nothing but add fuel to the fire of an already tragic situation.

The media lapped it up, having a field day! As media stories go, this one wouldn't go away. It gained momentum, playing out over a number of months. It was a local, religious and social calamity that wouldn't go away! God's name and whatever good was done previously had been smeared by the actions of the COG.

An intense and continuing onslaught of blame and character attacks fell on the young Vancouver JP leader Russ Griggs. He faced the music and did his best to be honest, by admitting his error of inviting the COG into the area. He apologized and expressed his deep personal regret for having done so. He did not attempt to justify himself, but instead showed humility, integrity and understanding of those who attacked him fiercely with persistent verbal and written blows. He felt terrible about those who had been shipped out of the area by the cult.

Griggs' Seattle JP counterpart Linda Meissner, leader of the "Jesus People Army," was spared the embarrassment of public and media scorn and attacks. The COG sent her to Europe. She stayed in the COG as one of their ambassadors, glad to be free of her former ministry problems in Seattle. A similar scenario had unfolded for me. Atlanta was a blur. The leadership pressures and worries of the Atlanta ministry were in the past. I had no idea what had transpired after my departure. I was heading to England to start over and never faced the aftermath of public disapproval regarding the COG take over in Atlanta.

Griggs didn't get off so easily. He had to admit being wrong on multiple occasions, facing the fires of prolonged criticism. Many times he would have loved to run from this terrible situation but stayed, confessing his sins and making whatever amends were possible. Among the JP leaders who were deceived by the COG, Griggs was subjected to unrelenting criticism, anger and blame! The hard work of apologies and working through the penalties of breaking lease agreements (on now empty properties) to satisfy landlords was a financial burden. He accepted the blame from parents and the community.

Discouraged, Griggs hoped the next day would be better than the last. Fortunately, close friend Mel Davis, pastor of the Open Bible Chapel, helped Russ with housing, supportive counseling and encouraged him through these dark days.

◇

England—The UK

When we finally set down in England it felt good to be on solid ground. I made the decision to never fly on a cheap charter plane again! Being in a European country for the first time was an interesting cross-cultural experience. The dialect of the British customs officers and international passengers coming and going from all over the world was fascinating. Listening, I heard a variety of languages in the background as we navigated Heathrow Airport. European cars and buses, road signs, borough names and driving on the opposite side of the road was all new.

Unfortunately our cultural education was cut short once we met up with COG leadership who whisked us off to a large factory in a city called Bromley in Kent County.

Life in the COG commune was limiting, controlled, predictable and suffocating! After the first few days I cringed when the slogans were yelled out, "Revolution! For Jesus! My family, my family—right or wrong my family!" I hated the idea of undiscerning complete loyalty in this COG chant! *In my gut I knew the only thing that had changed was our geographical location.*

Over the next month my spouse was paired with prominent COG female leaders. I saw her and the children only for brief time frames. The kids were again isolated in the Kids Kibbutz. It was troubling. I was assigned work in the COG Bromley print shop, helping out wherever needed. I recall writing a prophetic letter warning American friends about a coming judgment on materialism, greed and idol worship. In spite of this display

of self-righteous agreement with the doctrine of coming judgment on the US, internal suspicion about COG core issues remained.

I didn't agree with the group's practice of separating married couples, limiting parental access to their children, and the dominant teaching on severing of ties with family and friends from the past. The COG "Mo Letters" and leader emphasis on viewing the church, family and friends with disdain behind closed doors was accompanied by a public relations policy of buttering up potential donors from the outside to gain financial and material support. It all smacked of hypocrisy and deception.

A lack of balance in teaching sessions in England was also becoming more noticeable. Mo Letters, in a short span of time were taking a more prominent role in being a near equal to the Bible. "Deeper Truth Mo Letters" were reserved for older disciples. Babes (aka younger disciples) were gradually introduced to varying levels of David Berg's writings. I wondered if anyone but the Berg family and a handful of top leaders knew what was really going on?

As these concerns converged, I received word that my spouse and I had been given our own room in the factory. With this development I turned my attention to reuniting with her and hopefully seeing our children. She seemed different, interested in being reconnected. After spending several days together I got the impression the COG wanted to use her to pull me back into a place of loyalty. It was apparent she'd arrived at a new level of dedication and was trying to be an example for me.

This reunification meant I could visit our two daughters. This was an emotional breakthrough. Keeping children away from their parents for lengthy periods of time, especially when they're toddlers, hurts the family. Some moms liked the freedom of the COG kibbutz, childcare and having a group of nannies. Moms could visit their children daily if they lived in close enough proximity to do so. Dads, on the other hand, might not be allowed to see their children for months at a time, even if in the same locality. It was obvious, loyalty of children was being shifted away from parents to the COG. I had no idea how destructive this would become in the COG's future.

New COG Direction—David Berg Appoints Himself 'The End-Time Prophet'

Working in the print shop I saw a new collection of Mo Letters that were being printed for higher ranking COG leaders. Without this level of clearance, I slipped the secret letters into my pocket to read later.

They were titled, "David," "The Psalm of David," and "The Key of David." In reading them carefully, David Berg introduced himself as being God's end-time prophet with special revelations. Self glorification was woven into each letter. This was the hardest evidence I had to date of where this group was headed.

I thought about my two day visit with Joel and the concerns he'd shared which had gotten him into trouble and put him in disfavor with David Berg. I reviewed the prominent COG characteristics that were out of sync with the Bible and mainstream Christianity. They were secrecy, control-manipulation, PR double standards, contempt toward the system, the

David Berg
aka Mo or Moses

church, family and friends of members, and varying levels of disclosure on beliefs. In addition to these were long indoctrination sessions, sleep deprivation, constant moving of people, group loyalty chants, rules and policies that keep members dependent and off-balance, no access to money or a phone, Mo Letters being elevated to near equal status with the Bible and separating husbands and wives and children. I knew there was more.

From the top, David Berg was steering the COG away from being truly God, Jesus Christ and Holy Spirit centered, to being led by him. The visibly bizarre aspects of the group were symptoms of more sinister core belief issues. The average follower had no idea what they'd gotten themselves into! It had all been cloaked up until now. Moses David Berg would no doubt gradually let the whole group in on his elevated status as God's special end-time prophet. I wondered what Joel would think about this?

It was distressing to realize my family and all of our team from Atlanta were part of a group which was becoming a full-blown cult. Unbelievable!

All Hell Breaks Loose!

What should I do? I decided to write David Berg a letter and voice my concern. I hand delivered the letter to a top leader at the Bromley, Kent factory without disclosing the contents. Several days later I was called before two of the local leaders. "You need to write a letter of apology to Moses" they barked.

Briefly stating my reason for raising concerns was not what they wanted to hear. They were unmoved by my concern saying they were loyal and in agreement with his writings. Agitated, one disciple yelled, "You're the one in the wrong! You need to repent and send a letter of apology to God's prophet!"

"I can't!" I replied firmly.

ANGRY COG

The Making of a Dangerous Cult

Suddenly, fear gripped me, when I thought about my wife, children and all of the Atlanta ministry friends under the COG influence. My refusal was one more act of insubordination. As they turned to leave I wondered, "What would come next?"

Who would have guessed one of the most dangerous cults in the last hundred years was being housed in an inconspicuous old factory in Bromley, Kent England. It was now jammed to capacity with Children of God from the USA and Britain.

On returning to the 7'x7' room we shared, my spouse knew something had just happened, and asked. She wasn't happy to hear I'd sent a letter to David Berg and had refused to recant whatever I'd said in it! She agreed there

Old Bromley Kent Factory UK, COG Headquarters

were things wrong with the COG, but was willing to overlook them. She reminded me of all the good they were doing! I listened, knowing she needed to voice her displeasure.

Married life had always been a challenge for us, but it was significantly more complicated with the COG in the middle. Whatever unity we'd been experiencing hadn't been going on long enough. I passed to her the Mo Letters that glorified David Berg as the new end-time prophet. She looked at them in a cursory way and then put them down. The content didn't faze her. "It doesn't matter! I like it here!"

I understood in part. She'd been taken in by COG women leaders and showered with VIP affirmation for eight months straight which gave her a strong sense of emotional belonging and acceptance. COG midwives had been by her side at the birthing of our second daughter and after-care. She'd been the recipient of extensive childcare for two toddlers and had made new friends in the group. I had underestimated how deeply this loyalty ran. I bit my lip, realizing she was in good standing with the COG and wasn't eager to ruin it!

Guards Posted

The following afternoon on returning to our room, my spouse's belongings were gone. The inside dead-bolt to the room had been removed. I was too disturbed to eat dinner and laid down. When I got up, I found two guards placed outside my door, visible from the small panel of vertical glass. Concern was growing. After several hours I fell into a light sleep until wakened by several COG leaders who were now in my room.

Startled, I sat up. They said they were giving me one last chance to recant my letter to David Berg. I listened, but said, "No."

Children of God Tribunal

On hearing this they left and returned an hour later, leading me to an upstairs meeting room. Eight COG leaders were present with Hosea in charge.

Several younger leaders harangued me about the misguided nerve I had, to send a letter full of doubts about David Berg, directly to him. "You need to repent! You've screwed up!"

Then, a door opened and my wife was escorted in and took a seat. She spoke up with confidence, "You have no right to say anything bad about the Children of God! They've been trying to help us. You're the one with problems! Our marriage has been falling apart for years. I believe them and not you!"

One of the leaders motioned to her and she exited the room.

Mo Letter Re: Demon Possession

After she left, Hosea pulled out a lengthy railing letter from David Berg full of rebukes and accusations of me being demonized. It took about ten minutes for Hosea to read it. The letter was titled, "Beelzebub Lord of the Flies." When he was through reading, he asked if I had a change of heart, or anything to say. It was clear I had no credibility after Berg had made a declaration of my demonized condition.

I paused and then said, "My loyalty is to God, Jesus Christ and the Word of God. I'm obeying the Holy Spirit and my conscience. I cannot put anything, or anyone, above God."

The leaders shrugged off my answer, noticeably unimpressed. They continued to mock me for being a fool to challenge Moses. Hosea concluded the meeting by picking a quote from his father's letter about my being demon-possessed.

I was surprised they didn't offer to exorcise my demons! Two guards led me back to my 7x7 office bedroom and one positioned himself outside the door.

I thought about the Berg Family and high ranking COG leaders, their requirements and intentions:

Don't disagree, or question—it's not allowed!
We'll tell you what to think and believe!
We'll post guards at your door if you screw up!
We'll take your family!
We'll accuse, humiliate and break you!

Ugh! With urgency I thought, "What will happen to my wife and children and what will they do with me? How will they deal with, or silence me?" Justifiably I was fearful. There had to be some way of getting out of this building!

16

Dark Night of the Soul

A Plan

The COG's ability to pit my spouse against me was devastating. I felt hurt and livid! Under COG influence, she was being reshaped into a different person.

The first thing I needed to do was get out of this factory! Who knew what the COG might do next. I'd heard rumors of Aaron Berg dying in a mountain climbing accident shortly after he'd disagreed with some of his father's (David Berg's) writings and replacing his mother Jane aka Eve permanently for his mistress-secretary, Maria.

I couldn't trust anyone in the COG movement. My Atlanta friends had been scattered to the winds and would soon read Mo's Letter "Beelzebub Lord of the Flies," describing me as a demon-possessed traitor who had dared to defy David Berg, challenging his authority as God's end-time prophet. Who knows what they will think?

With thoughts racing, I determined to stay awake. I gathered a few essentials and my passport, stuffing them into my pockets and laid down fully-dressed with my shoes on—placing a blanket over me. Lying still, I prayed to stay awake. I let a number of hours pass, hoping the guard outside my door would leave, or fall asleep. On occasion I'd hear shuffling, or a chair move and knew someone was still there.

Pre-Dawn Escape

Around 4 AM, I looked out the small window in the door and didn't see anyone. I gently opened the door a crack and no guard was present! Adrenalin flowing, I tip-toed down the cement corridor, then quietly down the metal

stairs and crossed the facility's transport area leading to a side-door at the opposite end of the factory. Hopeful, I turned the metal door latch and it wasn't locked. Phew, I needed this break!

An early morning thick fog lay over the Borough of Bromley which was ideal cover. The grey cobblestone streets were relatively empty with the exception of a few pedestrians and cyclists heading off to work early. Quickly, I made my way down a street not knowing where I was headed, having never been out of the factory since arriving in England. From Tweedy Road I turned down Sherman Road which led to High Street intersecting Church Road where I found a park behind a Parish Church. Finding a bench I sat down, grateful for the white wool scarf my spouse's mother had made me. It covered my neck and mouth lessening the damp and cold of the early hour, while waiting for daybreak.

The thought of my family and friends trapped inside the COG was unbearable. My emotions raced back and forth from relief to despair, from guilt for my own part in the fiasco, to fear of the COG finding me. The darkness of pre-dawn was my introduction to a Dark Night of the Soul.

Being captive in the COG was over. What had happened to my spouse, children, friends and ministry was not. COG deception had lured us in, removed freedom of movement and choice and we'd fallen prey. Jesus warned that Satan would come as a thief to steal, murder and destroy (John 8:44 and John 10:10) and he'd done just that.

Mid-morning I found a British police precinct and explained to the desk officer my predicament. I asked if he could have an officer accompany me to the COG factory to help me find my spouse and children. The police agreed to help. At the factory, two COG public relations representatives answered the door and told us that no one from my family lived there any longer.

We asked them to allow us access to the nursery, but they denied us entry, saying the children were napping and my children were not there. The Bobby (British Police) didn't know what to do at this point. Without search papers, all he could do was accompany me upstairs to retrieve my guitar and a few personal items and stay with me until we exited the building.

As the officer and I parted ways the reality of practical matters came to mind. I had no money, food or place to live. I lacked the resources of nearby family or friends and was in a foreign country without a work permit. It didn't look good, but just being physically free from COG control allowed me to put my dismal predicament to rest for the time being.

Good Samaritans—Still Practicing
Mr. Ken Burnett

Late afternoon I found a restaurant named "Quality Fare" in downtown Bromley and asked if I could work in exchange for food. Thankfully, the restaurant owner was present. He sent word to a waitress to serve me a meal and we'd talk about my situation afterwards. As I finished eating, Ken Burnett took a seat across the table, introduced himself and said, "Tell me what has happened." Emotionally exhausted I shared my predicament in a disjointed way. He listened carefully and patiently, recognizing I was distraught. When I'd finished, he said, "There's someone I want you to meet as soon as I can arrange it. In the meantime I will give you a place to stay."

With his hand, he motioned for me to follow him. Heading past the kitchen, we climbed a stairway to an upstairs floor and down a hallway to a well lit front room facing the street. "It's not much, but better than wandering the streets in the cold." There was a single bed, a small dresser and a wooden chair, and a bathroom down the hall.

"I'll pick up some sheets, blankets and a couple of towels at home and bring them here early evening. Remember, this is between us. With ordinances and such, I'm not supposed to let out this flat until renovations are complete. It used to be quarters for one of our employees years ago. I'll tell the cook and waitresses to feed you when come to the restaurant. Let me show you a side door you can come and go through. Will you be alright until then?"

"Sure."

"OK, here's a key. I'll be off and I will be praying!"

Mr. Ken Burnett was an on-the-go Brit, a man of compassion. My most urgent need of food and shelter had been provided. I was deeply grateful. After Ken left I wondered who he wanted me to meet. In the days ahead I learned Ken was a committed Christian, with many spiritual gifts and had founded a ministry called "Prayer for Israel."

He was a mirror of the "good Samaritan" in Jesus' parable (Luke 10:25-37), happy to provide food in his restaurant and gave me a small room above his business for a week or two until we could sort out what to do.

Several days passsed and Ken told me he had arranged a meeting with Mr. Kenneth Frampton the next morning. Ken said he was very interested in hearing about what had happened to me and my family.

Mr. Kenneth P. Frampton

Mr. Kenneth P. Frampton

Burnett accompanied me to Mr. Frampton's office a short distance from the restaurant. Mr. K.P. Frampton was an established business owner in property and land management, acquisitions and sales. He had a keen interest in hearing my story from beginning to end. At the same time, he had a previous commitment that only allowed him forty-five minutes for our first meeting. He listened intently. The forty-five minutes flew. We agreed to meet the next day to pick up where we left off.

For the second visit I walked to his property management offices and was directed by a secretary to take a seat in his private office. In short order Mr. Frampton entered with a warm greeting, shaking my hand and then took a seat on his office chair. With interest he asked if I would continue my story. Noticeably by body language and active listening, he was deeply concerned throughout the telling of the events I'd experienced. On finishing, he gave a deep sigh and said, "Oh my!"

A Huge Dilemma

It was an emotional relief to have Mr. Frampton carefully listen, but intuitively I knew there was something going on beneath the surface. It all became clear as Mr. Frampton succinctly told me his own dealings with the COG.

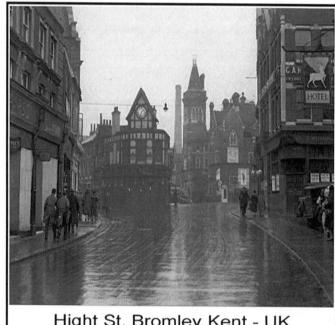

Hight St. Bromley, Kent - UK

He began, "I have two sons who have joined the Children of God here in England. They are very excited about being part of the COG, throwing in their lot with the group. On their request for help I've given them the use of the Bromley factory rent-free, where you lived and I'm supporting the group financially.

If the COG are indeed in error and have separated your family, have secret teachings, and an erroneous false and secret prophet leading them, I must do something. I only want to support those things and ministries that truly glorify Christ! If they are a cult, I need to sort out I can influence Keith and David to leave the group, without them viewing me as the enemy and turning against their mother and I."

Though highly invested with the COG, Mr. Frampton was a Christian of integrity, willing to research and secure the truth. He told me he believed my account, but needed to confirm my story with tangible evidence. He said, "Don't worry about being sustained physically. Ken Burnett and I will make sure you are OK. And I will do everything within my power to help you find your wife and children."

Mr. Frampton said he would stay in contact through Ken Burnett and let me know as soon as he had discovered anything. We bowed our heads in prayer, shook hands and I made my way out of the office and back down High Street.

Several days later I learned from Ken Burnett that Mr. Frampton had begun an investigation into the group's secret inner-world, beliefs and the like, with the intent of delving beyond their public relations image portrayed to outsiders. This news gave me hope. I had two advocates in Mr. Burnett and Mr. Frampton who believed me.

Failed Kidnap!

Preoccupied with eating a meal at Ken's restaurant, two men came to my booth and tried to physically drag me out of the restaurant! Both had small yokes around their necks identifying them as COG. Resisting and shoving one away drew attention and several employees who knew me came to my aid. Together we pushed them out of the restaurant and the cook told them emphatically, "Don't ever come back!" Afterward, he called the Bromley police precinct, reporting the incident.

This confirmed the concern I had for my well being in COG hands! I wondered, "What would they have done with me if I hadn't escaped the factory? Would I have ended up dead, like Aaron Berg, with the cause unknown other than a mysterious accident?" From then on I kept a careful lookout for COG members. If they were to kidnap me, it would be to keep my mouth shut and what would this look like?

Ken Burnett called Mr. Frampton and updated him on the attempted kidnap incident—verifying its accuracy through first-hand accounts of three of his restaurant employees. On hearing this, Mr. Frampton told Ken Burnett he would step-up his investigation. Mr. Frampton added, "Other unsettling stories like David's are beginning to surface."

Newspaper Reporter Goes Undercover

The lid of the COG public relations cover-up was blown off when a local newspaper placed a writer inside the Bromley COG factory as a new convert. He was in the compound long enough to see first-hand what the group's beliefs and practices were. After securing accurate information, he was able to leave the factory abruptly with the aid of other newspaper staff members.

Recounting his experience, he wrote a blistering article revealing the group's secretiveness, evasiveness, high security, deception to outsiders, and teaching on animosity toward the church, biological family members and former friends. In addition, he cited hatred toward the system, outside authority and the group's demand for total obedience to Children of God leaders, Mo Letters and David Berg as God's End Time Prophet. The gravity of this news when published got the attention of the public at large and was reported in the Bromley and Croydon newspapers.

Joint BBC & NBC Press Conference and Documentary

In short order, more damaging reports and voices of concern converged from those who had interactions with the COG. Among these were Mr. Kenneth Frampton, Ed Plowman a USA writer, Pastor Russ Griggs from Vancouver, BC, Mr. and Mrs. Moody from Manhasset, NY, representatives from Free COG, and investigative newspaper and television reporters from the US and Britain. Also weighing in were British pastors and para-church organizations that had talked with COG members and formerly involved individuals like myself. The combined witnesses and fact-finding efforts verified the COG's secretive, divisive and questionable practices.

Because of this, COG bases of operations in America, Canada and England were being investigated. With an escalation of family and community outcry and the COG's denial of these allegations, BBC of the UK and NBC of the US agreed to host a press conference, and film a documentary to hear both sides. NBC wanted to revisit their previous positive documentary on the COG which had aired on 'First Tuesday.'

COG leaders were invited to defend their claims of harmless Christian endeavors to help people and reach the lost, and they agreed. Former COG, family and friends of those still in the COG, Christian leaders, newspaper and media reporters who had substantial interaction with the COG, were also on the docket to be interviewed.

The press conference and a portion of the documentary filming were set to take place in London, England. With dates locked in, individuals from the USA and Canada made arrangements to fly to the UK.

BBC and NBC's goals were to provide a fair representation of both sides, let the facts stand, and allow the public to decide.

Issues of Concern

- Secretive, deceptive and divisive beliefs and cult-like practices.

- Regular use of public relation lies.

- The "Forsake All" doctrine and practice which requires members to turn over all belongings and financial holdings to the COG and asks members to sever all ties with their family and friends unless inheritance funds, property, or expensive belongings might be forthcoming.

- The disappearance of members within the group, i.e. sending new members to distant or secret locations and the refusal of COG leaders to advise outsiders of their whereabouts or how to make contact.

- Teachings that encourage contempt of the church and the system and creates fear and paranoia of the outside world.

- The absence of freedom of choice, movement, or to have any funds to be able to contact anyone outside of the group.

- The practice of assigning older member "buddies" who never let a new member out of their sight except when inside the bathroom (they wait outside).

- Teachings and slogan-chants that encourage 100% group loyalty at any cost, leaving no room for independent thinking, questioning, or discernment (I Corinthians 12:10)

- The use of brainwashing techniques of limited sleep, being moved from place to place secretly, no outside contact and a non-stop schedule that fills every waking hour from dawn to late-night.

- The elevation of Mo Letters to equal status as the Scriptures and sometimes surpassing.

- The latest development of David Berg claiming the status of being God's special end-time prophet.

Other questions and concerns surrounding David Berg pertained to his personal life. It was reported, but not yet proven that Berg had replaced his wife Eve with his secretary Maria. Another very troubling concern had to do with Aaron Berg's mysterious mountain climbing death which occurred shortly after he'd challenged his dad on numerous ethical issues and practices. The possibility of foul play carried out to keep Aaron silent was afloat during this news conference.

Public Consensus

When the press conference aired in England and the USA, the documentary was successful in verifying the COG was a dangerous cult!

The COG had arrived at the Press Conference with their public relations smiles and pitch about all the great things they were doing, bragging about their numbers and successes. The interviews with the COG Public Relations people present came across as over-rehearsed, canned PR soundbites. Hosea Berg and his team of COG representatives avoided giving direct answers to incriminating questions. When they slipped up and did, their answers were cover-up lies. They seemed oblivious about their deceptive PR being among the top reasons they were being investigated.

Interviews with former COG, family and friends who still had loved ones in the COG, and those who had negative interaction with the COG were clear and concise. In contrast, the COG members came across as deceptive.

NBC had serious concerns about their first filming of the COG that had aired on "First Tuesday" which had given the COG positive recognition. Since then, with the barrage of negative reports, they wanted to set the record straight if the group was in fact a cult.

BBC and NBC's news coverage, press conference and documentary made a strong impact in the US and UK. Hundreds of thousands of people became aware of what the COG really believed and practiced. This public warning averted many young Brits and Americans from joining the cult.

Across the USA and UK the COG was being exposed regularly and had to close up shop and leave. They claimed persecution to their followers, omitting the real reasons they were forced to leave.

Visit with Russ Griggs

I met up with Jesus People leader Pastor Russ Griggs at the BBC-NBC press conference. Up until a week prior, I didn't know Russ would be attending, or that he too had left the COG.

It was encouraging to see Russ and visit. We'd both been down a similar road of heartbreak and loss. Russ shared a cursory report on the aftermath he'd been dealing with since the Vancouver community drove the COG out of the area.

Author's Note: The details and aftermath of the Children of God gaining control over the Vancouver B.C. Jesus People ministries is located in Chapter 15.

The damage done in Atlanta, Seattle and Vancouver had been irreparable. Russ said the COG had been unable to fill the shoes of Vancouver JP because of their attitude and spirit. The locals picked up on the difference immediately. They were not going to support a bad-spirited group that lied all the time!

Russ gave me the highlights of the loss of the entire ministry, the anger in the community and prolonged newspaper coverage. He said the combination of public scorn and everything that had occurred with the COG had driven a wedge between he and his wife. It was sad. *We both shared the same error of unknowingly inviting a cult to visit.*

Griggs seemed to be OK but was shaken by the current issues surrounding his marital division. I was still an emotional mess. Attending the press conference was the first time of being around a larger group of people since leaving the COG. I still felt nervous and shell-shocked from all that had happened. Physically I was weak, anemic in appearance from not eating much. Some were concerned when they saw my appearance.

Seeing a handful of COG leaders from a distance at the conference was hard. Their coined phrases and mindless restating of COG public relations lies was almost too much to bear! Several recognized me and we gave each other dirty looks. As leaders they knew they were spewing out lies! I knew their days at Mr. Frampton's factory were numbered. Their PR stunt at the conference was probably just buying them a little more time until they found somewhere else on the continent to relocate.

Thank God Russ and I were both free from COG influence, but the fallout would continue for some time in both our lives. Not a day passed without me being grieved with guilt and concern for my spouse and children, the Atlanta JP team and all the others who had joined the COG thinking they had made a positive life-changing decision.

At the conference I met other British and USA families who'd lost loved ones into this cult. Each had their own tale of sorrow. Like Mr. Frampton and I, all of us were seeking the freedom of their family members still under the destructive influence of the COG.

Compassionate Care Givers

In England, I was the recipient of incredible kindness, mercy and love. It was extended to me by a number of Brits: Ken Burnett, Kenneth and Pauline Frampton, John and Greta Steare and children Christopher and Rachael, Clive and Gwyneth Frampton and Chris Frampton. Each played an important role in providing healing support and unconditional friendship.

Mr. Kenneth P. & Pauline Frampton

Kenneth and Pauline Frampton became surrogate parents and their son Chris became a brother for life.

My need of food, shelter and prayer support was first met by Ken Burnett who gave of this freely without reservation. Emotionally I was bolstered by John and Greta Steare and children.

In God's providence I met the Steare family in Bromley while living above Ken's restaurant. The Steare family accepted me in my wounded and fragile condition. Being with them in a family setting for meals and visits provided something healthy that was unexplainable. It was amazing they took a liking to me with all the pain I felt inside and emotional rawness still evident.

Christopher, Greta, John & Rachael Steare

The Steares were a committed Christian family with roots that sank deep in Christ. This was reflected in the love, acceptance and prayer support they graciously gave to this American. I learned a number of British traditions from them, but what I treasure most is that I was the recipient of God's compassion and unconditional love through them when I needed it most!

From the flat above Ken Burnett's restaurant I temporarily moved nearby to New Life Foundation, a drug rehab program facility with bunk beds and regular meals. This was a transition until Clive and Gwyneth Frampton could ready a room for me to live in at their home in Purley, Surrey.

While living at New Life I ran into a young Brit named Stephen who'd joined the COG, but was providentially too young to live at their commune at the time. When we met, he was still loosely connected to the COG in Bromley, but had his doubts about the "secret prophet" behind the Mo Letters. Our connection was beneficial for us both.

Stephen Spicer
A British COG Survivor—A Follower of Jesus

As a teen I associated myself with the COG when they established a colony in Bromley, Kent, England. As a newish Christian brought up in a stuffy church, they were a breath of fresh air. At the time they appeared fundamental and extreme at the same time.

I joined the COG but was too young to be accepted full-time. I attended their meetings on weekends and many weekday evenings with two girls from the neighborhood. We were referred to as examples of dedication to full-timers by COG leaders. I guess that's why around Easter that year, we were deemed advanced enough to know about the mysterious prophet and his "Mo Letters." I was given a new name by the COG, "Elijah" and one of the girls my age who I met there was given the name Beth.

The knowledge of a mysterious prophet had an effect on me adversely, contrary to what the COG may have hoped for. My parents were missionaries and while I wouldn't ever claim to be a theologian, this notion of a mysterious prophet began to jar my conscience. I had enough Christian DNA in me to begin to sauce-out (figure out) when stuff was not right. Knowledge of a secret prophet caused me to be more cautious and wary.

Around this time I received acceptance to university and became interested in a local church. I must admit, it was also the girls in the church that I fancied. I began taking a more objective view of COG. I still visited them, but less frequently.

In the summer of 1972 I got a voluntary job at the New Life Foundation in Bromley. NLF was a residential drug rehab place run by Vic Ramsey. Vic was neutral about the COG at the time but interested and impressed by my evangelical zeal. I was to be his graphic designer for the summer. Vic was partially sponsored by Kenneth Frampton who also sponsored the COG.

I hadn't been there for more than a few days when David Hoyt turned up, having recently left the COG, and was put up in one of the rooms on the top floor for several weeks. Ramsey tolerated David and me as bona-fide "Jesus Freaks." I recall David being in close communication with Mr. Frampton.

During these days Hoyt spent time with me in Bible studies, answering questions and addressing COG teachings he believed to be erroneous with Scriptural backing. This dialogue and input along with explaining how to put print and artwork together with limited resources was very helpful to me.

It was shortly after this time that the lid came off the COG in the UK. Up until now, the COG were thought to be an extreme part of the Jesus movement, but now the word was out that they were in fact a *'Cult'* in Christian disguise. David's insights and what the press revealed helped me to disassociate myself from COG.

Author's Note: Stephen's additional comments and biography update can be found in Bio chapter 28

The Stuff of Life That Touches the Soul

Clive and Gwyneth Frampton lived in the beautiful area of Purley, Surrey. They graciously gave me the use of their guest room making me feel welcome and comfortable. I knew this was temporary as Gwyneth was expecting their first child and the room I occupied would eventually be turned into a nursery. I lived with them for a number of months until the time drew close for their child to be born. During this time-frame, I visited Mr. and Mrs. Frampton and Chris on the weekends at Silver Grange in the same city.

The Frampton family and I shared a painful bond of still having loved ones within the COG. It hurt to think about it, but we did. We hoped for any news and shared updates as they came in. We debriefed and prayed together for family members, for the Atlanta group and for all COG members to have their eyes opened to see what was happening to them. We prayed in faith, hoping many would return to a pure and honorable faith in God, Jesus Christ and the Holy Spirit. We had no choice but to put this agonizing prayer request in the hands of the Almighty with fervor and constancy.

Hard Things to Do

Mr. & Mrs. Frampton had stopped supporting the COG financially and were weighing the timing of evicting them from their properties. Their two boys, Keith and David, were still in danger, as was my family. The properties the Frampton's had allowed the COG to use rent free were the last vestige of leverage the Frampton's had to secure a visit with their boys and hopefully for me to see my spouse and children. Both requests had been clearly presented to COG leadership. No affirmative response had yet been received.

The Framptons had been progressively taking decisive action to rein in their misguided support for the Children of God. The freezing of financial support was among the first steps. Involving the news media and encouraging investigative reporting on the COG was another decisive step which had raised public awareness regarding the cult-like practices of the group. They'd also spear-headed the push for BBC and NBC to do a press conference, helped fly Russ Griggs to and from Canada, invited other prominent Brits with knowledge of the COG to the press conference and had taken an unwavering personal stand against the COG and their practices at the press conference.

None of this had been easy on the Frampton family. Each move made, had potential negative repercussions when it came to how their two boys would respond and view them. I can attest to the Frampton's acting prayerfully out of love and obedience to God. They exemplified courage and Christian integrity with patience and mercy.

A Bond of Friendship

Distressed and guilt-ridden over the loss of my family and friends, being around people for any length of time caused anxiety. Understanding this, I found a true friend in Chris Frampton. He was my age and understood inner-anguish was not easily over-come.

Chris Frampton

Chris had endured suffering while hiking the Katmandu Trail. In his journeys of camping out and in remote hostels, he'd taken potent drugs, and had been robbed and beaten by fellow travelers more than once. Being a gentle soul, these events had caused inner pain and mental anguish. His robust love of life and trust in others had diminished. The upside was, these traumatic experiences had worked compassion into his soul.

Chris accepted my quiet suffering and confusion, playing his favorite music when I had nothing to say, which was most of the time. My poor decisions and personal loss of family and friends was all-consuming, overwhelming.

Bossington, Somerset - England

Rescuing me from isolation at the bed and breakfast where I now lived, Chris would pick me up in his MG and we'd head out on photo shoots, go horseback riding or take long drives into the rural countryside.

I enjoyed seeing roads lined with trees and quaint farms and the history of centuries gone by. Old established pubs were strategically placed for locals to access for a meal or lager. This is the England I grew to love. Tall hedges lining the roadsides and country lanes where thatched-roof cottages were nestled alongside narrow country roads.

Through the inner and outer clouds of grey, the sunshine of hope gently began to filter through with the passing of time.

Bed & Breakfast Digs

With the help of Mr. Frampton I'd secured digs in a B&B nearby. As months passed, my flat at Mrs. Woolsey's Bed and Breakfast in Purley, Surrey became a haven of rest; a place to study and begin to sort out all that had happened. My room was small and sparsely furnished with a bed, chair, small table and a half-wall of windows looking out on a few fruit trees with a landscape rising up a small hillside. Everything was green!

The home had three upstairs single room flats rented to men only. Mrs. Woolsey occupied the downstairs of the home. She was a slight, spunky, wiry lady in her late 50's who was unashamedly forthright with her opinions. She was not afraid to lay down the rules or put her tenants in their place when needed. Her language was as colorful as you might hear on a ship on the high seas. In contrast to her pirate cursing, she fancied classical music, which she'd play at full-volume most afternoons.

The home was clean and well cared for. Ms. Woolsey prepared breakfast, lunch and dinner each day as per the request of each tenant. Her cooking was far from gourmet, but the meals were hot and appreciated. If residents made arrangements in advance, the downstairs sitting room could be used for visitors.

My room was usually cold and damp, due to a half-wall of windows by my bed, but the secluded hillside view from the windows made up for whatever else was lacking. I felt safe here. I rarely saw the other tenants who were usually out in the day, other than the occasional coordinating of the common bathroom we shared.

When my room was so cold I couldn't concentrate, or when I took a bath, I would turn on a small electric heater for a few minutes to cut the edge. Mrs. Woolsey didn't like this American practice one bit. To her, it was a waste of electricity and her money!

To emphasize this, she'd slip into my room when I was in the bath and unplug the space heater. To my amazement, she carried this one step further. On returning to my flat one evening, I found a coin-operated box attached to the only electrical outlet in the room. We discussed this, but she wouldn't budge. "I'm not going to let you throw my rent money down the drain!"

This was a cultural lesson. "Ruddy Brits," rosy cheeks and the like were due to cooler in-home temperatures, exposure to crisp outside air, walking to market, the train or to the underground, playing soccer or rugby and frequent walks in the park. Any discomfort from a lack of warmth would need to be remedied by layers of clothes.

Beginning Stages of Debriefing

I studied the Bible to make sense of what God might be saying in light of all that had transpired, and debriefed by writing about what I'd seen and experienced. It was gut wrenching but helpful in sorting things out. For prayer purposes I wrote down the names of all the people in Atlanta who'd joined the COG and the new names given to each. This was important to do while I could remember. Looking at these names and thinking about each one led to prayer, remembering them, my family, the Frampton boys and others I'd heard about during the press conference.

Tears of sadness would well up during these times of intercession. Being free of the COG, while others remained trapped was bittersweet. I vowed to not forget any of our Atlanta team members.

Southern USA Ministry Friends Lost into the COG— Deciphering the Rise of Darkness

A compelling need to understand what had occurred to the COG became a driving passion in my soul. With family and friends still in, I needed insight. Providentially, a staff member at Deo Gloria Trust, a Christian ministry established by Mr. & Mrs. Frampton, loaned me Dr. Walter Martin's book, *The Kingdom of the Cults*.

Though thick and scholarly, I devoured and reread this book several times. I received counseling, insight and understanding by this read. There is a distinct spirit of delusion and fog attached to a cult.

Dr. Martins book exposes the deception and aids readers in severing cult ties if they're ready.

Though inspired, my heart was broken.

Birth Name aka COG Name	Birth Name aka COG Name
Shelia Goudeau aka Mara	Krig Newport aka I Judah
Philip Clore aka Kedar	Sue Rawlings aka Mercy
Dan Matyi aka Belteshazar	Thomas Rubner aka Mount of Olives
Larry Gottlieb aka Lo Ammi	Joan Taylor aka Hope
Cheryl Gottlieb aka Beca	Hugh Westberry aka Barnabas
V. S. Hoyt aka Victory	Karen Westberry aka Shalom
Mark Nyggard aka Zadoc	Pam Williams aka Pheobe
Francisco Patino aka Jordan	Pope Wilson aka Gideon
Pat Patino aka Elizabeth	P.D. Wehe aka Matthias
Stacie Gates aka Shebah	Ron Baker aka Reuben
Megan Jones aka Ruth	Edmond Ball aka Ed
Linda Waldrop aka Naomi	Sue Beatty aka Michal
Gloria Hammond aka Abigail	Michael Bedolfe aka Ben Hadad
Josie Brown aka Hannah	Billy Clark aka Aaron
Rita McKee aka Jockobed	Charles Dudley aka Jacob
Tracy Crow aka Tamar	Gary Cunningham aka Malachi III
Sally Dillard aka Sarah	Michael Davy aka Hesbon
Donna George aka Grace	Steve Cline aka Joel
Sharon Adams aka Leah	Marsha Crawford aka Rachael
Russ Drodge aka Lazarus	Jack Fargo aka Israel
Diane Drodge aka Tabitha	Dallas Gambill aka Watchman
Dennis Moore aka III Peter	Paul Hilgendorf aka Ephraim
Julia Jones aka Rejoice	Sidney Vail aka Teth
Alan Kamnin aka Joe	Burt Wheeler aka Andrew

All those listed above and below were part of our larger Jesus People
Ministry in Atlanta, Georgia or a satellite branch. We all had the misfortune

Birth Name aka COG Name	Birth Name aka COG Name
Billy Lindsey aka Jesse	Ed Dilworth aka Habakkuk
John Lyall aka Jake	William Doehler aka Timothy
Charles Pinson aka Adino	Steve Shelton aka Arah
Carol Potts aka Miriam	Tousy Wilson aka Amos
William Tomassi aka Hebrew	Stephen Lowe aka Jude
Roger Tucker aka Judah	Charles Leek aka Luke

Additional Southern Team - Birth Names

Carol Wheeler	Kay Nyggard
Stacie Gaines	Sandy Green
Allan Shaprio	Vickie Tassour
Phyllis Wayte	Regina Baker
John Elliott	Randy Stover
Anna Whitton	Greg Gustafson
Michael White	Rick Flowers
Jackie Blount	Mary Teressa
Glenda Grant	Dean Dulling
Rick Russel	Susan Twitty

of being caught up into the COG/FAMILY cult for various lengths of
time. Sincere prayer continues for these and all cult victims. [See Appendix
pg 709]

The Kingdom of the Cults book gave comparisons between cult
groups, and detailed the historical progression of deviations taken by
each one. The comparison sections highlight pivotal times when leaders
asked followers to accept their authority, teachings and revelations, though
contradictory to the teachings of the Bible.

The extent of error and deception unleashed could go any number
of ways. A revelation claim usually inferred no one outside a particular
group had a fresh revelation from God. This led to a cultist mind set, viewing outsiders as not being true Christians and caused members to view
them with suspicion, sometimes contempt, and always as lacking in understanding when it came to the 'REAL TRUTH!'

In some cases like the Mormon Church, a companion Book of Mormon was penned. The Book of Mormon claims Jesus Christ made a visit to the Americas to *a mysterious people that human history has no record of.* From small beginnings of special revelations, strange glasses, polygamy and ethically questionable practices of early leaders, they grew. The Mormons currently have prophets, a hierarchy that supersedes any other religious group and a labyrinth of rituals that make the Catholic Church's rituals look minimal.

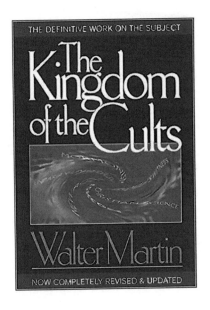

The Jehovah's Witnesses were another group Dr. Martin covers in his book. He explains how they reset End-of-the-World dates which have come and gone, and rewritten portions of the Bible inserting the name Jehovah wherever God is mentioned. The Mormons and Jehovah's Witnesses both embraced a monumental detour from contextual interpretation of the Bible.' Both groups purposely distanced themselves from mainstream Christianity, claiming to have a corner on divine truth for the last days and boast of a line of divinely appointed prophets. They teach their members Christians are misguided, void of truth and out of the loop when it comes to divine revelation and God's end time plan.

These and other insights were important to read about, study and understand. Dr. Martin's book helped me begin to grasp how spiritual error can infiltrate any group, even within a Christian context.

I prayed a lot during these days for family and friends. I'd try to picture each one in my mind, remembering their faces, smiles and laughter. This practice brought a hint of joy to my heart amidst the heart wrenching reality they'd been literally devoured by a dangerous cult. The range of emotions and thoughts when thinking about the Atlanta ministry takeover were all over the place. The most significant emotion was a profound sense of sadness—at the core of my being.

As months passed, the routine at Mrs. Woolsey's B&B became predictable. I was alone most of the time which was probably for the best. Sleep was a welcome healer. I was still unable to be around people for very long. The exception was connecting with my band of good Samaritans in a smaller context and popping by the Deo Gloria Trust offices from time to time.

The Arrangement

Prior to evicting the Children of God from the Bromley factory, Mr. Frampton put pressure on COG leaders to yield to his request to allow me to see my spouse. He'd provided them funds for this purpose, but nothing had come of it. After months of stalling and broken promises on their part, COG leaders finally gave in, fearing an imminent eviction from the Bromley factory if they didn't meet this request immediately. A follow-up request was for the Frampton's to have a visit with their two boys, Keith and David.

The arrangement Mr. Frampton had agreed on with COG leaders was for me to meet privately with my spouse. I was hopeful, but didn't know what I would say. The meeting place the COG insisted on was the Bromley factory. Neither Mr. Frampton nor I liked this, but we had no choice. For my safety, Mr. Frampton assigned a male staff member from Deo Gloria Trust to accompany me to the factory and remain in the background, out of earshot, when I met with my wife.

When we arrived at the factory we were met by a mid-level COG leader who led us inside the lower level and up a flight of metal stairs to a tier on the balcony. Four chairs were set out. I was instructed to take the chair that faced three across from me. The staff member from Deo Gloria stood 15 feet away as we waited. Looking around the factory it looked sparse, like the majority of COG supplies and vehicles had already been moved out.

Trying to be calm, I was startled when hearing an upstairs door open, and out walked my spouse accompanied by two high-ranking COG leaders. The threesome walked toward the three chairs and my spouse took the middle chair with leaders flanking her on both sides. If looks could kill I would be dead. All three appeared to be seething with anger. The COG had no intention of allowing me to speak privately with my wife. They had their own agenda, most likely to get me to shut-up and back-off.

Once again, I was witnessing the COG's manipulation and orchestration of circumstances to their advantage. My spouse was distant and cool with an uncharacteristic hard appearance. Both she and the cult leaders voiced anger toward me for things they'd heard I said about the group. At one point she announced, "I'm happy in the Children of God and the children are too. I want you to leave us alone! If you ever want to see your son or the girls again, you'd better stop attacking us!"

Following these words, they abruptly got up and left through the door they'd entered. The meeting was over in ten minutes tops.

I was stunned—not by their warnings, but by the news we had a son. I had no idea my spouse had been pregnant when I'd escaped by night from this same building. She must not have known at the time. With over nine months passing since then, it was all plausible.

Looking up, the Deo Gloria Trust staff member was at my side and the same COG leader that escorted us in was coming to see us out.

Debriefing

I relayed to Ken Burnett and Mr. Frampton the gist of what had happened and they felt as frustrated and discouraged as I did about the lies, false promises and ploys of the COG. Earlier in the same week Mr. & Mrs. Frampton had received difficult news when trying to negotiate a meeting with their boys. COG leaders informed them that both Keith and David had been sent to COG colonies outside of Europe and would not be returning to England any time soon. When the Frampton's asked for the locations, the COG refused to provide any details of the boys' whereabouts.

A Time for Firm Action

This turn of events regarding their sons and what I'd just encountered at the factory, along with all that was uncovered through the BBC and NBC press conference and documentary, sealed Mr. Frampton's resolve to evict the Children of God from all of his properties. The Frampton's had been patient and counted the cost. In addition, he wrote a public letter that was circulated in Christian circles and made available to the media.

Mr. Kenneth P. Frampton's Letter

"The Children of God, Family of Love, The Family, are the current names this group goes by. They are a revolutionary group of young people who are taught to forsake all and follow God, which means handing over all their goods to the group when joining the movement. All new converts must sign a document which promises this, allows mail censorship, and commands all followers to yield to strict obedience to COG leaders. All thought and action becomes centered on the cult.

New recruits are taught to read the Bible, memorize proof texts, and read letters published by their secret leader David Berg, alias Moses. These letters range from harmless to dangerous, depending on the intended audience. Much of the teaching is anti-social, rebellious, and anti-Christian in content. New recruits are gradually taught to accept these writings of David Berg as authoritative, as he claims these special revelations, visions, and prophecies are from God. Young followers are confused, because they have been helped and loved in this group.

David Berg claims he is the fulfillment of many Old Testament prophecies, an "anointed prophet." Followers are taught to obey him completely, even if he and other leaders under him are wrong. Followers are taught to sever family ties, and reject any old friends who stand in the way. The system of the world is hated. Lying is permitted when it is to your advantage, secrecy is OK. Scriptures can be bent in moral issues, and Moses' letters are on the same level as the Bible. Contrary to this, the Scriptures warn that false prophets are inwardly ravening wolves, and by their fruits we will know them (Matthew 7:15-16).

How distressing to realize this movement of the Children of God or Family of Love is nothing more than anti-Christian with a false prophet. I repent of having encouraged or helped this group which dishonors the name of Jesus Christ. I have tried to convince the COG leaders of their serious departure from the Scriptures without success.

Unfortunately, the lives of many have been marred and damaged by the poison of a false teacher and prophet. Satan was also tempted by pride and arrogance and fell into rebellion and perversion.

It is my hope and prayer, that many will be set free to serve God and His Son Jesus Christ, because we belong to God alone. Remember, "You were bought with a price; do not become servants of men (I Corinthians 7:23)." Therefore, "Stand fast in the liberty with which Christ has made us free, and do not be entangled again with the yoke of bondage (Galatians 5:1).

— K. P. Frampton

17

$$\text{\Large↚}$$

Spiritual Life Bursting Forth

Author's Note: The timetable for the start up of the Milwaukee Wisconsin Jesus People came prior to Linda Meissner and Russ Griggs' joining the COG.

Milwaukee Jesus People Beginnings
War Memorial Outreach

Inspired by what Jim and Sue Palosaari had seen on the west coast they stayed in touch with Linda Meissner, inviting her to speak at the War Memorial Stadium in Milwaukee. In preparation, Jim pulled together a new band called The Sheep. This was the beginning of Jim and Sue gathering a ministry team around them.

Jim and Sue knew the importance of reaching outward, including others and giving individuals a sense of belonging. They also knew the imperative of preaching the gospel and teaching the importance of putting faith into action. Being a follower of Jesus was not for the faint-hearted. There would be a cost! Most who became Christians in the Jesus People days experienced God's power, became witnesses to Jesus Christ's resurrection and sensed His amazing love and grace (Acts 4:33). Mike Damrow, one of the earliest to join up in Milwaukee, remembers these days well.

Mike Damrow
Songwriter & Early Sheep Band Member

"We formed a band with two weeks to prepare for the War Memorial outreach gig. We learned six songs. One of the girls wanted to name the band Inner Light but the name The Sheep prevailed when I shared a verse from Romans 8:36 about us being considered as sheep to be slaughtered until Christ rescued us. Our band was comprised of Rich Haas, Bonnie Spencer, Larry Barker (Mole), Dave Jawkowski (Bobo) and I. Bonnie was folksy, but we guys were more rock and rowdy.

The War Memorial Meetings were dynamic. The meetings were packed. Media coverage added interest. Lots of people came to Christ. Jim Palosaari and Linda Meissner worked together on this outreach with Linda taking the speaking lead. We went from 10 committed disciples to 30 overnight. Among those saved, were a bunch of students from Layton School of Art.

I was with Jim when we looked at a building on Brady Street as a possibility for a ministry coffee house. It had been a paint and hardware store and the rent was $325 a month, which seemed like a lot in 1971, and they wanted 3 months' rent in advance! When all the bills were paid from the War Memorial outreach we had $985. After paying the rent for the coffeehouse we had $10 left over.

Immediately we went to work on converting the rental property. It was located in the heart of Milwaukee's counterpart to the Haight-Ashbury. We named the coffeehouse, Jesus Christ Power House. New members from the art school painted murals from the life of Christ on the windows. Sue Palosaari utilized her writing skills, inviting these students to help put together a Jesus People newspaper we named *Street Level.* Both the coffeehouse and the newspaper gave us visibility and opportunity.

The Jesus People House was another stretch of faith. I moved into the house on Frederick Street, the first day we rented it, in February of that year. The place was in shambles with loose plaster, no heat, and was in need of massive work. That first day, Palosaari invited Channel 11 news to film our new Jesus People house! I think they were unimpressed by this dilapidated property.

I met my wife to be, Mary, in the summer of 1971 in Milwaukee. She lived next door to our Jesus People House. With our coffeehouse Jesus Christ Power House transformed into a functioning outreach location and the newspaper in circulation, the ministry was picking up steam, rapidly expanding as we shared the message of Jesus Christ being alive.

Jim had a strong sense of vision and utilized and affirmed ministry team talents, putting people to work! When it came to preaching and the whole of the ministry, the cross and the blood of Christ was at the core. Jim was sensitive to the pulse of the culture. With a theater background he knew the importance of being heard clearly, and everything related to projection and sound. Seeing gifts in others and nurturing them was a strong suit for Jim. Jim was interested in hearing about you, what you thought, what got your blood pumping, what inspired you. This was a gift. I was inspired to use my talents."

Author's Note: Mike's Testimony and Bio
update can be found in Testimonies chapter 25

Lynn Malmberg
A Milwaukee Jesus People Disciple

Larry Barker aka 'Mole', bass player and vocalist with The Sheep introduced his friend Lynn to Jesus Christ during this time period.

Lynn recalls: "The music was blaring. The TV was spitting out images that didn't fit the music but my tripping brain couldn't piece the two together anyway. I had taken a hit of acid an hour or two earlier, and now all I could do was sit in a frozen position reflecting on the past few months of my life.

In August of 1970, I was living in a hippie commune. Well, it was mostly a drug house and we prided ourselves on throwing great parties. How and why we never got busted was surprising. At any given time there were 10-15 people living at the house, but my closest friend, Mole aka Larry Barker, was the only one that I kept track of. Mole was a runaway follower of God, noticeably out of place and uncomfortable during our best parties.

He'd been living the *Hippie Life* for more years than I had, was tired, convicted and felt guilty about taking drugs. Whenever we'd get high together, he would get totally depressed. As soon as he came down, he'd start talking about Jesus. I had been raised Lutheran, so I wasn't sure what he meant when he told me that I needed to be Born Again.

Because he was my friend, I let him ramble on about that phrase and other things I'd never heard in church. I thought I was a Christian but he pointed out to me that my life was a mess. I believed everything I'd been taught in church, including that Jesus had gone to be with His Father 2,000 years ago, but since He was gone, how could He have anything to do with me now? When Larry would talk to me about Jesus I could see that he had found something different, some truth I really didn't understand.

Around this time, we were having one of our massive three day parties. I had just taken a hit of LSD and I looked up and saw my mother standing in the kitchen doorway. I said out loud, "Wow! I must really be wasted, that looks like my mother!" She and my father had decided to surprise me by taking me out to dinner and did that ever work! As you can imagine, dinnertime was not a relaxing social family time. On the way back, my Dad had to pull over to the side of the road because he was crying so much. Three months later he died of a massive heart attack on January 7, 1971. At the funeral, a number of relatives told me I'd put him there, and I believed it. What a burden to feel responsible for.

A few months later, a guy who lived upstairs from us got busted for possessing dynamite with the intention of blowing up some power plant in town. Where in the world did the "peace and love" go? Next, my dog got run over and Mole just up and left our communal house. This would have made a great country song if somebody had a pickup truck.

Meanwhile, back at the party the music was blaring and the TV was on. Suddenly, there was Mole on TV singing and playing guitar. He had blond hair and there was a spotlight on him that gave him a glowing effect. The word on the street was, a woman named Linda Meissner was in town and a band called The Sheep was performing with her. Apparently this was newsworthy, because it made the ten o'clock news.

Everyone at the party started talking about how crazy Mole looked. I was seeing something different. My friend appeared to have finally found the connection between the truth he was talking about and the peace he was looking for. Intuitively I understood that Jesus Christ was personally involved with him, something I'd never seen before.

The next day Mole came to get me and bring me to the Jesus People group he had joined. I argued with him and tried to get him to return to his life with me and our friends but he was adamant; he had begun a new life and he couldn't turn back now.

He told me the life I was living was satanic and that God wanted to deliver me from it. I thought he was nuts and sent him on his way. After he walked out the door, I looked around the house, and it was if God had taken the blinders off my eyes. We had marijuana and LSD stashed away in drawers and there was a poster on the wall showing various deviant sexual activities. The place was a mess and even the music began to give me messages that I knew were not right.

Okay, so he was right, and maybe I did have a few things to learn. I gave myself a week and then I found myself on a bus heading for Milwaukee. Mole and brother Dennis Knight picked me up at the bus station and the first thing I remember is that every time we got a green light instead of a red one, Dennis would start thanking the Lord. All I thought was "Oh brother what have I gotten myself into?!"

That night at dinner I sat between Mole and brother Rich Haas. Before we began, they asked if they could pray for me. "Sure", I said. Both of them put their hands on my head and started praying in a different language (tongues). I'd known Mole for over a year and never saw him doing anything this weird. To be honest, most of my stoned times were weirder. After dinner we headed off to visit a mutual friend called Crazy Paul.

As soon as we sat down, Mole started talking to Paul about Jesus and how he needed Him in his life. Listening to the conversation as a third person, I was able to let my guard down. No longer on the spot with the heat of Mole's fanaticism aimed at me, I could hear more clearly what he was saying. I had the eerie feeling that Mole had grown up and was leaving me behind and that was scary. When I looked at his face, I knew I needed and wanted whatever it was he had. It was soon obvious that Paul could care less about what he was hearing and Mole knew it, his words were for me.

A Question and a Prayer

With this turn of events, Mole redirected his attention to me, asking, "Would you like to know Jesus?" Before I could come up with an excuse I found myself saying, "Yes." Praying briefly in tongues, Mole then asked if I would repeat a prayer after him to invite Jesus to take over my life.

"I knew what a mess I'd made of things so far and how much I'd hurt my father before he died. My need for forgiveness for this and my reckless living and a chance to start over was on my mind just as Mole began praying. After our prayer, I didn't see fireworks, or feel any over-whelming emotions, but knew I was forgiven and loved and sensed things were going to change. It was March 29, 1971 at 11pm, when I became a child of the King. I would learn this transition to spiritual life is called being Birth by the Holy Spirit, or being Born Again. The Bible says: "For you have been born again, not of perishable seed, but of imperishable, through the living and enduring word of God. (I Peter 1:23)." JESUS was now my LORD and SAVIOR!

The Jesus People group Mole had joined was intense— significantly different from the hippie commune that I'd just left. There was no sex, no drugs, no smoking (of anything), no cursing and no dwelling on the sin that I had just left. When I considered these primary rules, I had no idea how I'd be able to live up to them. **While thinking about this, it hit me—I had nothing to go back to. This was a path of destruction. It was dark and lifeless. In contrast, Jesus has the words of eternal life (John 6:68)!**

On becoming part of the Milwaukee Jesus People I was around the fifteenth person to join up. We would gradually grow to about 150 people. But this morning I was a brand new Christian. The night before Mole had filled me with various Scriptures from Genesis to Revelation; all I could remember was that Jesus would one day return to take his disciples with Him.

When I woke up in the morning, to my surprise all three of my roommates were gone. I thought perhaps, they'd been taken to be in God's kingdom and I'd joined up too late! When going downstairs, to my relief brother Rich Haas met me with a big hug and a vacuum cleaner. He told me to vacuum the living room so I would feel part of the Jesus People family. I learned he got out of a lot chores with this approach. He was forgiven because he'd led most of the people in our house to the Lord.

After chores, Mole told me that we were going out to share our faith in Jesus. This was something I dreaded. I'd promised my old friends that I would not be like those crazy Jesus Freaks, going around preaching to everyone they saw. But Mole didn't ask me, he just said we were going! So we headed out to the University of Wisconsin Milwaukee Student Union to tell people about our new found faith. Mole got right into it and then turned to me and said that I should tell everyone what Jesus had done for me. Well, I had just gotten saved the night before so I really wasn't sure what to say. Other than telling them that Jesus loved them, I was at a loss. This would be the first of many outings of sharing my faith in Jesus and I actually got pretty good at it.

We lived in a big one family house on the east side called The Fredrick House and we also had a coffee house called, The Jesus Christ Power House. It was covered with great pictures depicting the life of Jesus and the walls were packed full of scriptures. We had a fairly large stage where the Sheep would entertain on Friday and Saturday nights to a mostly standing room only crowd. Jim Palosaari was our leader and he did the dynamic preaching that led many people to a walk with Jesus.

Every morning we would go the coffee house for Discipleship Training. We had teachers from the community which gave us in-depth Bible studies as well as lessons on apologetics. I especially remember Pastor Julius Malone who was such a dynamic and gifted Bible teacher. I had never heard anyone that excited about the Word of God. His love for God and the Bible was real. His Bible teaching was like opening an exciting novel, a page turner. In one of the first Bible studies, he taught out of the book of Acts on the story of Stephen and it came alive to me. We were all so impressed that it made us hurry to our own Bibles to find the same excitement he was finding, and find it we did. It was also a time for Scripture memorization. We did this by putting Scripture to song. I learned to sing many Psalms and various Scriptures from the New Testament.

When we outgrew our Fredrick Street House we eventually ended up in an old hospital where all 150 of us could be housed. This led to a decision to decentralize, sending out sizable teams to begin their own ministries. Thirty of us would accompany Jim & Sue on an airlift to Europe for a few weeks and then return to Milwaukee. With a love for kids, I was chosen as the babysitter. While in Europe, we embarked on an adventure that surprised us all."

Lynn may have seemed an unlikely choice, but became a faithful communication conduit in helping the Jesus Family England and Jesus People Milwaukee stay linked together communication wise in Christian love. She was also uniquely and unashamedly gifted in sharing her faith in Christ with anyone she encountered and was an exceptional Christian teacher to countless children. It is an honor for many of us to call her our friend.

Lynn's "life in Christ" was amazing! She went on to teach and led a wide variety of individuals and children to faith in Jesus and the Living God. We've just scratched the surface.

Lynn has passed from this life and is with the Lord.

If we live, we live for the Lord; and if we die, we die for the Lord. So, whether we live or die, we belong to the Lord. Romans 14:8 NIV®

Author's Note: God changed Lynn's life in wonderful ways, which would be passed on to hundreds of those she would meet over the course of her life. Lynn's continuing saga and complete story can be found in Bio's 2 chapter 28. I guarantee it will inspire you!

Milwaukee Ministry Teams Branching Out
Sue Palosaari Cowper

In the spring of 1972, we were offered an opportunity to fly to Europe. The invitation came from the Full Gospel Businessmen initiated by Milwaukee supporter Jay Dalton, who'd encouraged his association to include us on one of their two week evangelistic airlifts to Denmark and Sweden.

My husband Jim was developing a reputation throughout the Upper Midwest, employing a refreshing and compelling preaching style, with its dash of humor to sideswipe the undecided. Always one for the open road and new horizons, Jim didn't hesitate in accepting the offer to bring the Gospel to Europe. The deal struck, we'd be flying out in June.

Mission Team for Europe

Selecting only thirty of a well-honed group, many who'd been together over a year, was next to impossible. Some we loved must remain behind, but it would only be for a couple of weeks. We prayed, revised, worried over that list. It was posted, and then reposted again. We could feel the anticipation of wrenching apart, the reality of battle fatigue, the need for regeneration, yet dispersal was still looming. Who would we take to Europe?

Well, of course, we would include the band, The Sheep. Their music ministry had become the backbone of the Milwaukee group, their folk rock sound and songwriting by Mike Damrow, who would marry singer Mary, harmony by Rich Haas and Little Reed Midelsteadt, and "Mole" Larry Barker strumming bass. Lead guitarist Greg Nancarrow was married during the last week of festivities. Two were added for the short trip, drummer Jim Winn and Mark Schwabe.

Henry Huang, Jim's "right hand man," managed everything, with Dennis Knight as his helper. My friends on the *Street Level Newspaper,* Jenny Hanson, writer Arlene Czekalski, and Don Schendel my co-editor came along. Secretary Margie Kazmerik, as well as Kathy MacIntyre, Carol Durkin Trott, Linda Feltzer, and who could resist saying yes to Lynn Malmberg, who came along as "the babysitter."

Other Milwaukee Teams Sent

At the time of this offer to evangelize in Europe, the Milwaukee ministry had approximately 150 plus full-time disciples. Our base was a well-mopped hospital building, but we were rapidly running out of accommodation and infrastructure capabilities. Our enthusiasm for developing a discipleship training program had begun to wane. Delightful, inspired, inexhaustible, our disciples were also an unwieldy bunch, for who can govern the heart of a young Jesus Freak?

Only a few years older, Jim and I were sometimes overwhelmed, always tired, often making crucial decisions in the midst of some crises. This was not unusual in the overall Jesus movement, and a part of the reason it was eventually felled, but at this time we were unaware of the impossible parameters of our endeavors.

A bus-load of our group, now known as Jesus People USA (JPUSA) had earlier traveled south with John and Dawn Herrin and their children, including an emerging band then called Charity, later to become Rez Band, put together by Glenn Kaiser. Leaving town with great hurrahs, as we did each group we sent out, they returned to Milwaukee with leadership issues to air, and an intent to "form their own ministry" elsewhere. An uncomfortable few days of reconciliation meetings behind closed doors followed.

As the meetings dragged on, Jim had an idea; purposing we have a ceremony to send this part of our team out, bypassing all the drama! This idea grew of its own momentum, and soon we were planning a gala week of dispersal, including several marriages. Reconciled and somewhat mollified, John officiated the marriage of his daughter Wendi, to Glenn Kaiser and we prayed together and said our farewells.

Since the Milwaukee Jesus People was committed to the vision of carrying the Gospel of Jesus into new territories, another bold move was made at this same time. An opportunity arose to assist another outreach ministry in need of manpower and Christian workers. Sixty Milwaukee disciples were interested in taking this leap of faith to assist Bill Lowery's tent ministry, called Christ Is the Answer.

Bill and Sara Lowery's tent ministry was based in Davenport, Iowa.

Bill, was an ole' time fundamentalist preacher, saw the theatrical potential of rolling into town with hundreds of Jesus Freaks, jumping out of vehicles and onto the streets with newspapers and invitations to the night's preaching in the big tent. We'd worked with him earlier; it seemed a plausible opportunity for many young disciples. Bill's tent and trailer ministry, much like JPUSA, who'd eventually settle in Chicago, would become the start-up nucleus for an ever-enlarging vision that would one day expand and grow into many tent ministry teams in Europe.

As each Milwaukee team prepared to be sent it felt right. Most importantly it seemed pleasing to God as we prayed together and the teams were launched.

30 Member "Milwaukee Jesus People Team" Into Europe

With a thinned down ministry population in Milwaukee, our departure date in June was suddenly upon us. Those who would be going were excited about all the possibilities of venturing into the unknown, bringing the Gospel to those we'd encounter in Europe. Our thirty member team with Jim and I, would head out to Europe to evangelize in Sweden, Denmark, Finland, Germany, Holland and eventually the UK. At the time we thought we would be returning in several weeks to rejoin the remaining Jesus People who would be holding down the fort in Milwaukee. God had other plans in mind; filled with challenges, hardships and incredible opportunities.

When the Full Gospel Businessmen first proposed buying seats for 30 Jesus freaks, ostensibly for a two week run of testimonies (personal stories), music by The Sheep and Jim preaching to capacity crowds, they could not have foreseen our remarkable agility as Jesus freaks to reach out and find ways of relating to the younger culture. They'd expected us to take our place dutifully on stage alongside the boy who could remove his false eyeball to prove he could still "see" by God's miraculous power. Our 11th hour decision to "miss the plane and keep on going in Europe" would come as an afterthought just as we were about to return to the airport two weeks later.

Reality Check

My own anticipation was influenced by a lifetime of reading and obsession with foreign shores, and a previous rucksack summer hitchhiking through Europe. That I'd now be traveling with 30 other young Christians and an infant of six months did not deter me, as I envisioned myself able to overcome any hindrance. This romantic and inaccurate self-image would be replaced a few weeks out, when diapers needed laundering by hand and foreign church floors were no longer so appealing. But that came later. Photographs from those first two weeks show me in freshly ironed new clothes next to a van, laughing, in a field of flowers—probably relief after being cooped up for hours of driving at top speeds from one venue to the next through dense Swedish forests.

A sizable group would stay behind in Milwaukee with Frank Bass, a fellow we'd met during the month of Duluth revivals. As we would not return two weeks later, Bass must have felt like he'd been abandoned and the Milwaukee remnant gradually dispersed, some venturing off to start their own JP ministries in nearby cities.

In Sweden

In Sweden as guests of the Full Gospel Businessman's Association we conducted preaching and impromptu music concerts.

Among those who responded to hearing the message of Jesus Christ was a precious young Swedish girl who attended a Sheep Concert in Halsingborg, Sweden. Karin was 18 years old at the time.

Karin Gunnarsson Bienge

Behind Karin's contagious smile and kind heart, tragedy had struck more than once. When you look into her soft brown eyes, it's hard to imagine that at one time she was *driven by a need to rely on getting a fix to find any temporary peace.* Janis Joplin's legend in rock music, sad death, and her impact on young women who *idolized her, left a dark imprint.* Young women worldwide, like Karin, grew up putting dirty spikes into collapsing veins—paying a hefty price.

Karin grew up in Sweden, a beautiful country, unacquainted with massive slum districts, or environmental pollution. The landscape has a pristine purity and solitude about it. She seemed securely nestled in the comfort of middle class society.

Karin writes: "I was brought up in a good family, but was not happy. My friends and I would get drunk and sneak out at night. At 12 years old I was stealing and selling things at school. A girlfriend helped me, but got caught and gave me up. I was angry at her. My behavior at home was not good; my parents concluded I was uncontrollable and incorrigible.

I was assigned a court appointed overseer (similar to probation officer) who I grew to despise with a passion. Barraged with questions, I lied to her. Anger was moving toward hate. I became bitter, angry at school rules, the laws of society and even my own family. The courts wanted to put me away in a correctional school for girls, but I got lucky and was released into the custody of my mother."

At 14, Karin gravitated to the Super-Freaks of Halsingborg, who gathered around like tribes in Castle Park and smoked dope. "I watched and soon I was well into the drug scene. This world gradually became a second haven of identity. Strange doors open, using different drugs; sweet weed, hot smoke and sassafras. From Pot to Hash (hashish) and then Acid. Cheap thrills to feel good, trying to forget what I didn't like about life so far; too young to actually know. My fingers yellowing from nicotine, blowing smoke rings with chapped lips and a cotton mouth. My head would buzz with a cloudy forgetful high, tempered by paranoia of being watched by unseen eyes, or worse—the law. Spiraling into an acid trip, illusions would flow from reality to fantasy—indistinguishable, like in a Federico Fellini film.

I quickly graduated to the needle. My first fix of Speed made me feel powerful. I did an on and off run for five days, minus sleep and food. At 16, I met a foxy guy from Stockholm who had been on speed for 10 years. *We lived together and had drug experiences that grew dark, like living in or through hell.* Sometimes I'd start screaming in terror, or talking to people who weren't there.

I was experiencing what I'd heard in a number of Bob Dylan tunes, 'The people just get uglier and I have no sense of time.' In Ballad of a Thin Man, 'You know something is happening, but you don't know what it is.' For a lot of us, this led to risky living without much thought of where this might lead.

It's a sad twist of irony. You leave home to find love, because you feel misunderstood, because you can't do every crazy thing you want to do, to be free. *In a young mind you conclude, parental control and guidance is not love. In frustration you begin to despise your own family, situation at home and become intolerant of your parents.* In anger you run away, remembering the worst days of fighting; intentionally forgetting every good memory that may have happened. All of this is done to make leaving justifiable. *At last there are no restraints!*

Then you live with a man, make love, and yet there is a canyon of emptiness between you, never growing close to touching each other's soul. Two people living together, each alone. My boyfriend made speed his true love. In a defiance of sorts, I chose morphine as my drug of choice. He'd say, "It's better to use speed because it's dynamite, making you cool and aware."

I'd defend my friend Morphine saying, "Speed only makes you wired, paranoid and talk too much!" We disagreed and went to separate needles. He was haunted by paranoia. He'd suddenly jump up, run to the window muttering to himself—convinced the Drug Squad was watching our digs from behind the trees. Sometimes he'd grab a flashlight (torch) and run to the attic to catch them spying on us. It got on my nerves, interrupting my peaceful tripping.

Daily, I needed my fixes! I would steal alcohol and sell it to drunks, or get a supply of dope from Kobenhavn and sell it to support my habit. I saw Janis Joplin on television one night. I knew she was loaded on heroine. I went out that evening and hit some junk. For hours my body just screamed, it was horrific; death would have been a welcome relief. You never know how junk is cut and what it's mixed with; could be too pure. Two friends had died from overdoses; I kept thinking I'd be next.

During my drug days I went through varied wardrobe changes. I'd usually dress in black with a monkey on my back, or my favorite was a floor length cape, Dracula style for effect. I liked to go to horror movies and relate to the living dead vampires. Hiding behind my cape I'd sometimes parade around the streets like "queen morphine." In contrast, I might wear a see-through dress and saunter around like a mythical siren seeking attention or a lover.

With my boyfriend I felt like an object of sexual pleasure, a thing—less than human. On occasion he'd bring home sleazy homosexuals and I'd wake up to find one of them in bed. Sometimes he'd make me watch them which was disgusting. The darkness had grown blacker. Getting high was my only escape.

At 18, life was cold and bleak. I looked like death according to some. I attempted suicide, was thrown in jail, and my Mother had a nervous breakdown. The pendulum swung between choosing life or death. It could have gone either way.

Not much was happening in Halsingborg, Sweden at the time. It was finally spring after a long boring winter. Word got around that some Americans were putting on a concert and they were called Jesus People. I wanted to believe in Jesus, thinking he might be the only good thing left. Out of curiosity I went to one of their meetings and enjoyed it. I told my boyfriend that it was good. His response was, "Jesus People are only out to destroy people!"

On Saturday, we were out shopping and I noticed Jim Palosaari, the leader of the group at a kiosk, eating a hot dog. He came walking toward us, I felt like I should talk to him, but wasn't sure what to say. Instead he came over and began talking with us. Interested, we followed him to where 30 Jesus People were staying. The girls were camped out in one big room with all their sleeping bags laid out. They served us some tea, gave us something to eat and one of the guys played the guitar and sang a song for us. They were genuinely friendly. It was clear they had found a reason to live, something I would like.

Putting aside objections, my boyfriend joined me, attending the evening concert. As soon as we sat down I could sense something around me which I would later recognize as God's presence. I felt like this caused me to be more aware, and listened carefully.

Then, a lady singer in The Sheep band, Mary Damrow sang a solo. While she was singing the presence of God overwhelmed me and I began weeping, *broken and happy at the same time.* I knew God was doing something inside me. Right there in the middle of the concert my weeping turned to sobbing! I could feel the hate and ugliness leaving, the darkness being flushed out. After that a "peace" gently came over me. It wasn't anything like some chemically induced high. It was good and pure. Deep in my heart I knew that Jesus was alive and real! This was the night of my spiritual birth, when I invited Jesus Christ into my heart!

I threw my needle away and made a break with my boyfriend. Both were important steps in severing ties with my old life. I would soon learn this Scripture from the Bible:"

> Jesus said, "If you hold to my teaching, you are really my disciples. Then you will know the truth, and the truth will set you free."   John 8:31a-32 NIV®

Author's Note: Karin's Bio update of what God has done since this time and all He has brought her through can be found in Bio's 1 chapter 27.

Siv Algotsson, Irene Barker, Wilhelm Pinnow, Boise and Karin Gunnarsson all joined our team in Sweden.

Into Finland and Germany
Sue Palosaari Cowper

The next stop was Finland, Jim's country of ancestry. Finland was an important mission stop for the Jesus People team. Jim preached the gospel at several noted locations including Stone Church in Helsinki and The Sheep Christian band produced their first music album.

As we traveled into each country we visited, doors opened for concerts, preaching the gospel and interaction with the locals.

Prior to leaving the States we had to say no to Mike Drahfall, but

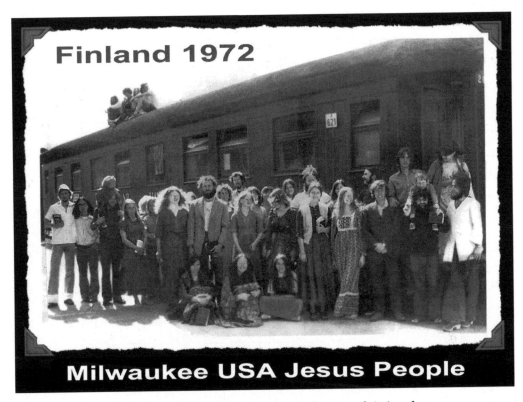

Finland 1972

Milwaukee USA Jesus People

that didn't deter him. He paid his own airfare and joined us on a street march in Helsinki, Finland.

It was a good thing that Mike had joined us as he helped us procure the vehicles to transport us, even when we were out of money. Owen also joined our team in Finland.

A few of our team would leave later that summer; Mike and Mary Damrow for medical needs with a baby on the way and some complications, Jim Winn for personal reasons, Mike and Michele Desvignes went to L'Abri, Paul Gardner to Lebanon, Dorrie M. and Nancy Ulman back to

The Sheep playing to crowd gathered

Milwaukee. Those remaining would become the backbone of our Europe ministry team with new additions on the way.

    The Sheep were also evolving amidst the change with new people stepping up to the plate, including Lisa Carothers as lead singer. Rehearsals were held in a God-for-saken former brothel front room, located in the desolate farm hamlet of Lautzenhausen, Germany. We gained another new team member when Sandy joined our ranks, in spite of the fact we were without funds to

Siv Algotsson & Lynn Nancarrow
Interview by budding reporter

Greg Nancarrow

support ourselves, dependent on a nearby air force base of kindly soldiers and their spouses who brought us food daily.

A young Henry Huang preaching in Europe

Jim Palosaari shares the Gospel
on the streets of Europe

Jim Palosaari & The Sheep
open-air Concert & Preaching

Jesus People singing & passing
out concert flyers in Europe

Holland

Still broke financially, and needing to move on, with only faith as our purse, we headed out in duct-taped vans once again. The first tinge of fall was in the air, with me again pregnant, Jed on my lap, and Jenny with a tiny infant, we headed over the border into Holland, most bearing valid passports.

> How are they to call on one they have not believed in? And how are they to believe in one they have not heard of? And how are they to hear without someone preaching to them? And how are they to preach unless they are sent? As it is written, How timely is the arrival of those who proclaim the good news.   Romans 10:14-15 NIV®

In spite of the hardships of sleeping on dingy pub floors, or sometimes in vehicles, team members did their best to keep their faith up and prayed with sincerity asking God to open doors for us to share our faith in Jesus with locals and to aid us in being able to continue in ministry in Europe.

The songs of the Jesus People were new and old. Old time choruses got a fresh wind of fire on long road trips, or in less than adequate temporary housing. I could sometimes hear our team singing "Sing till the power of the Lord comes down" with reverberations pulsing through the old building we were staying in till the wee hours of the morning.

It was here in Holland, on the day we'd only enough money left to buy a bag of Pom Frits (twice fried puffed potato type fries) with mayonnaise, that Jim received a telegram from Mr. Frampton in England, "Come immediately, money of no object."

Russell Griggs, now out of the COG and in London, had vetted us to Mr. Frampton. Our clothes in tatters, hope of civilization restored, Jim, Jed, and I boarded the next plane to London, England where our entire future took a new and exciting turn. The rest of our ministry team followed in vans to the border of England and then on to London.

Author's Note: Sue Palosaari's Bio capsule can be found in chapter 27 Sue's account of God's provision in a time of need is in chapter 25

The Real Jesus Revolution in England

With Russ Griggs in London to help with the press conference laid on by BBC & NBC News on the COG, he was able to explain to Mr. Frampton in detail all that had unfolded in the Northwest Jesus People merger with the COG and subsequent trail of sorrow. This reinforced all Mr. Frampton knew, but also brought to the surface how remiss Mr. Frampton felt about backing this group.

Distraught by the mistake of supporting the COG cult, Mr. KP Frampton wanted to counter this error. The whole episode of his misplaced trust in The Children of God weighed heavily on his heart, mind and soul. His dilemma of still having two of his sons, Keith and David, under COG influence remained unresolved.

Russ, aware of Jim and Sue's difficult circumstances in Holland, told Mr. Frampton about The Jesus People Milwaukee and their effective ministry in the US and in various European countries. Russ told Mr. Frampton, "This could be the antidote for the bad press and deceptive tactics of the COG. England needs real Jesus People!"

Mr. Frampton wanted assurances and made USA contacts immediately to verify Russ' reference and assurances that the Palosaari's had absolutely no connection to the Children of God. When confident this was true, Mr. Frampton moved immediately, sending a telegram to Jim Palosaari and began making arrangements to bring the team to England.

Russ' referral for Jim and Sue couldn't have come at a more perfect time! This was a huge answer to prayer on many levels that would spark the fresh fires of the Holy Spirit in England.

England—A Time for all Things Under Heaven
Sue Palosaari Cowper

We were now comfortably settled in SE London at the Queen's Hotel in the Crystal Palace, a ramshackled place where vagrants could still find shelter in the older non-remodeled sections. Quickly Mr. Frampton moved to secure a lease on a large spacious home nearby that was on the docket to possibly be torn down. The hotel in the meantime was more than adequate, a welcomed replacement for pub floors in Holland.

I remember the first time Jim and I saw David Hoyt in a restaurant in England, brought along by Mr. Frampton. I sat next to him. He looked like death, shell-shocked—in a cocoon of inner pain. We knew about the COG and their evils and heard snippets of his dash into the fire with his family. Mr. Frampton told us how they'd attempted to break him, like a victim of a Nazi inquisition, bringing his wife to testify against him, ruining her spirit by this act—sealing her alliance with a cloaked cult. I remember trying to get him to speak that evening and his words were few.

Now I know how horribly hurt and ashamed he felt over losing his family and for letting the Children of God come near a thriving southern ministry. Shame can paralyze a soul. I'm glad our Milwaukee Jesus People were all such ordinary caring people that we didn't miss a beat, taking him in and making a place for him to heal with us. We really had no sense of discrimination then. Our love was simple and pure, void of prejudice and a judgmental spirit. I sensed how horribly hurt and ashamed David felt over losing his family and for letting the Children of God come near a thriving southern ministry. Forming a new ministry in England together, we were a blessing to him as he too was to us, with the bonds of love running deep and enduring. Paul the apostle said it well.

> Praise be to the God and Father of our Lord Jesus Christ, the Father of compassion and the God of all comfort, who comforts us in all our troubles, so we can comfort those in any trouble with the comfort we ourselves have received from God. For just as the sufferings of Christ flow over into our lives, so also through Christ our comfort overflows. 2 Corinthians 1:3-5 NIV®

Hoyt and a few of our Milwaukee team were in charge of getting that drafty Edwardian home ready for occupancy—opening a wall in the downstairs to make one large room, patching, painting, getting the water and heat turned on and applying plastic coverings over all the windows to retain heat. We named the home 'Beulah Hill', based on Scriptures in Isaiah 62:4-5 that describes a land provided by God, a home of peace in a marriage with a new country, England. On our first night and all that were to follow at 56 Beulah Hill we were grateful and content with God's provision.

The England I Came to Love
D. E. Hoyt

Observing life in England was fascinating to me as an American. I'd already received the best gift of all via the incredible hospitality of being welcomed as a stranger into the homes and hearts of a number of families including the Milwaukee team and Jim and Sue (Matthew 25:35-40, Romans 12:13, Titus 1:8).

This gift of acceptance, love and kindness I will never forget. In addition to this, my eyes were opened to a culture of warmth, simplicity, dignity, seasoned by a long history reminiscent of all that's grand and noble, alongside historical flaws not worthy of repeating. Taking it all in, England was unlike anything I'd experienced. Not quick and rushed, but tidy, to be savored, much like a hot cup of tea in the winter.

In the early 1970's England had a distinct old world feel to it. Little things like milk on the doorstep with a froth of cream at the top and young children placed in carriages outside in a front garden to nap in the open air. Green rugby and soccer fields every-

CHRIS FRAMPTON

A Forested region in Surrey, England

where with kids not deterred to play in the cold, rain or fog. It was customary to visit specialized small shops that sold one thing or another. Seeing a full pig hanging in the butcher shop caused me to do a double-take more than once. Tea time in England—mid-morning and mid-afternoon—was a welcomed break; the undisputed right of every man, woman, and child. It was an allotted time for human toil to cease, an intentional pause in the day; often shared with others providing an opportunity to visit.

The pubs were a multipurpose place to gather for eating, drinking, darts and the like. The rich seemed to have old money and the everyday man or women who were employed, worked hard to make ends meet. People walked everywhere—to town for groceries, to bus stops, to catch trains and the underground. For the most part, the population was fit and healthier for it.

The transportation infrastructure was deeper than anything I'd ever seen. At every twist and turn in the road, and there were lots of them, there was a bus stop. Catching a bus could be exciting when it was already in motion by the time your feet landed on the back platform at the rear of its lower level. "Grab a bar and hang on!" To this day, I don't know how the bus cashiers kept up with all the people coming and going, collecting and servicing not just one, but two levels. The train system also spread out like a giant web winding its way outward to distant townships and villages. Some villages were so remote, once off the train and nearby roads; the rest was a dirt path walk to the village center.

The homes were substantial, varied, most often with splendid gardens, shrubbery and flowers in season. The larger city buildings, hotels, museums and the like were hundreds of years old. I thought about the artisans who'd worked without the luxury of modern equipment, or lifts, building mammoth structures of stone, most of which are still standing. The skyline of downtown London is filled with them, as is other larger cities in England and throughout the whole of Europe. Victoria Station in London amazed me as did the expanse of the underground.

While visiting York, England, I learned that in order to build a famous cathedral church there, the builders had to construct a ramp some five miles long to access and finish the upper sections. The quality of construction and architecture canceled any doubts about this country being primitive and backwards. Instead I saw first-hand a land with a long history of greatness. Visiting the outer parameter of Buckingham Palace in London was awe inspiring as was a visit to another palace in Scotland.

While in Edinburgh, Scotland I had an opportunity to visit Holyrood (Holy Cross) Palace. It is an example of incredible craftsmanship with longevity in mind. It was originally an Augustinian Abbey (church) built around 1100 AD some 900 years ago. In 1195, extensive monastic buildings were added, including cloisters, a chapter house, a refectory and guest houses. The enlarged abbey (church) prospered, and from an early date contained royal chambers for use by the Queen and other royal officials from England and Scotland.

The Palace of Holyrood has been home to royalty for over 500 years, and is still the official residence of the Queen while visiting Scotland for a week in late June to early July of each year. The three storey palace which includes a large attic has been renovated and updated over the centuries and welcomes the public for tours on a regular basis. The buildings have huge stone foundation blocks that are some 15 ft beneath the earth supporting this massive palace. It is set in a gorgeous area on the outskirts of Edinburgh.

Holyrood Palace Edinburgh, Scotland

England ◆ Scotland

The Queen's official residence in Edinburgh and home of Scottish royal History

The simple cultural dimensions of life in the UK refreshed my soul. I treasured non-hurried country walks; recalling one to a small village set back from the main road a mile or two. Blue and billowy clouds filled the sky, vegetable and flower gardens were in abundance, livestock and horses grazed in nearby lush green pastures. The history, the pristine freshness of the countryside, the English people and their hospitality—the whole package created a cultural friendship bond.

A few lyrics from a song set in England titled *'Tradin My Life,'* depicts memories and feelings from this period in time.

> *Tall hedges along the roadside, passing the centuries gone by*
> *Well, I been down to the country fair—riding high on a Ferris Wheel*
> *Well I'm at the age, and I want to know, I'm at the age and I'm growing old*
> *So I'm tradin my sorrows for a song in the morning*
> *Yes, I'm tradin my life, for a place next to You, Lord—yes I am*

18

$\not{+}$

The Power of God's Truth & Creativity

The London Krishna Temple

While walking in London, having a melancholy day, I stumbled on the ISKON Krishna Consciousness Temple. For years I'd made it a practice to dialogue with temple devotees in different cities about God and weave in the

message of His Son Jesus Christ explaining the purpose of Jesus' life, death and resurrection. I was always on the look-out for any devotee or guest who might give a listening ear. Today was no different, except

Radha Krishna Temple ISCON London UK

for the sobering reality of my family and friends still lost in the COG.

The Krishna Temple and grounds were buzzing with activity. A number of devotees were talking to guests on the long walkway leading up to the temple. I wasn't sure if a *Kirtan* (Hindu worship service) had just concluded, or was about to begin.

Hesitant, in a semi-depressed state, I snapped out of it by starting a conversation with a devotee. I asked about Wayne who had been my closest friend at the Krishna Temple in San Francisco. The devotee referred me to another who knew Wayne. On hearing I was an old friend of Wayne's and was genuinely concerned, he opened up to me. I learned Wayne had visited the temple for a number of months as a guest 'Sanyasan' teacher. The devotee pulled me aside off the walkway onto a patch of lawn continuing, "He suffered a nervous breakdown while with us. He stopped eating regularly and began identifying with the deity Radha (Krishna's female counterpart), to the point of losing all contact with reality. When he left here he was unable to speak and I don't know where he is now."

This was very sad news. As I only knew Wayne's first name in English I had no way to follow up. Stunned by this news, I succinctly shared my testimony of receiving Jesus Christ at the San Francisco ISCON Temple. When the devotee said he had to go, I ambled off the grounds with a sad heart thinking about and praying for Wayne.

On another outing in London, I met a seeker named Caroline Green with ties to the London Krishna Temple. When Caroline found out I'd previously been a devotee in the San Francisco temple her interest peaked.

As we talked, I learned Caroline was a part of the British music and theatrical arts community and had been influenced by George Harrison's release of "My Sweet Lord" which wove the Krishna mantra chant into his song This was one of the contributing factors that had drawn her to the London temple.

I urged her to pray directly to God and Jesus Christ His Son, explaining the purpose of Jesus' life, death, resurrection from the dead and promise of His Spirit. She listened intently. The following is a capsuled narrative of what preceded our meeting and what followed.

Caroline Green
As Told by Fiona Wilson, August 30th 1973

At age 22, Caroline Green aka (Linden) of Claygate, Surrey walked away from the hippie world of the rock musical *'Hair'* in an attempt to find meaning. She'd worked for two and a half years acting and singing in the lead role of Sheila. She was in the show in London and went on to tour Manchester, Birmingham, Bristol, Leeds, Newcastle and Nottingham. Over time, Caroline found the ideals and promised freedom of the 'Flower Children' had faded. *Hair* went through a metamorphic change with waning humor, cliché dialogue and less cast member appeal. Disillusioned, she left the show and traveled about England in quest of a purpose to life beyond "just existing." She visited friends, the countryside and churches finding them a peaceful place to pray.

Continuing to search for truth and meaning, she returned home and began visiting the Krishna Temple in London. Embracing the temple's

Hindu teaching she too was introduced to chanting the Krishna mantra. Caroline recalls an incident when she witnessed a girl get severely scalded with hot milk at the Krishna Temple. The temple devotees shrugged it off, showing no compassion or interest in caring for the girl's burns. This didn't seem right. Later that evening she took a walk, found a park bench and prayed. She said, "As I was praying God's Spirit descended on me. I didn't understand it, but believed my prayers were being heard." This was Caroline's first encounter with God.

Prior to this she'd encountered an American, David Hoyt on Oxford Street who had told her about Jesus Christ and encouraged her to pray directly to God and ask for the truth. Ironically, he'd formerly been a devotee at the Krishna Temple in San Francisco and knew a lot about Swami Baktivedanta's teachings and temple life. She was impressed by his convictions and missionary zeal and wondered about his emphasis on Jesus being

God's true Son and the means of discovering truth. Caroline told me, "If it were not for David's persistence and staying in touch, I may have never come to faith in Jesus Christ. Over the course of some nine months I gradually realized I'd been on the wrong path."

On David's invitation, Caroline visited the The Jesus Family Christian community he'd become a part of in the Upper Norwood, Crystal Palace in the southeast borough of London. Her visit to Beulah House and interaction with Jesus Family members resulted in a clear and unmistakable conversion encounter with Jesus Christ around January of 1973. Soon after she moved into the community to share in the life of the Jesus Family; a happy, service and outreach centered community of about 70 young Christians representing various countries. The vision of the Jesus Family community was to bring the light of the Gospel of Jesus Christ to England through music and song, writing, creative outreach and by practicing discipleship.

"I experienced a new life, filled with hope and truth and a community to aid me in putting this life into practice. As Jesus Christ had been raised from the dead, I too was being 'raised to new life' by God. Being reborn spiritually, freed me from a lot of spiritual confusion about God."

What other things changed personally?

"I came to know for myself that Jesus is the true door to heaven and this door is sprinkled with His own blood which covers my sin. His death on the cross was the great exchange, his life for mine. Jesus is the answer I was looking for! When Jesus Christ said, 'I am the way, the truth and the life and no one can come to the Father except through me (John 14:6),' His words pierced my heart. Life without Christ is like a boat with no rudder. There is no other answer. I have been saved by God's mercy and grace through Jesus' suffering on the cross, on my behalf! Understanding the Scriptures and what happened to me is part of the miracle. God gave me a renewed mind and a heart tuned to His voice and Word.

"As part of the Jesus Family in Upper Norwood we are learning how to love one another, be patient, be servant-minded and willingly do our share of work within the community. We eat together and supported each other spiritually. We study the Bible and pray corporately and on our own. We write and produce a Christian outreach newspaper, conduct Christian concerts and do our best to live as faithful followers of Jesus Christ. Single men and women have separate quarters with bunk beds and married couples are given their own rooms."

Caroline's participation and creative giftedness was beneficial to the entire Jesus Family community and the Lonesome Stone theatre team. Her humble and supportive ways were recognized and appreciated by all. By allowing the light of Jesus Christ to shine through her, she authenticated Jesus being alive to all who met and engaged with her. Thank you Caroline for the energy and heart of love you gave to so many!

D.E.Hoyt —

In spite of being distraught over family and friends still trapped in the COG, God was not hindered. Lifting up the name of Jesus Christ was a privilege, knowing God is always ready to translate Himself to any human heart by His Holy Spirit (Acts 10:34-48).

These truths were burned into my soul, "For there is one God and one mediator between God and men, the man Christ Jesus" (I Timothy 2:5). "It is by the name of Jesus Christ of Nazareth" that healing comes. And, "Salvation is found in no one else, for there is no other name under heaven, given among men by which we must be saved (Acts 4:10-12)."

The Jesus Family Ministry in England—Beginnings

Refurbishing Beulah Hill in Upper Norwood had gone well. With the practical work completed, heat and lights on, the team took occupancy.

Everyone was extremely thankful for a new home base. God's provision had come at just the right time.

Team members who'd come into England from Holland, road weary and in dire need of respite, considered these provisions tangible evidence of God's mercy, kindness and faithful care!

"This I recall to my mind, therefore have I hope. The Lord's loving kindnesses never cease, for His compassions never fail! They are new every morning: great is thy faithfulness. The Lord is my portion, says my soul, Therefore I have hope in Him.   Lamentations 3:21-24 NASB

God was amazingly present in this new beginning in England. I was warmly adopted into this new phase of ministry in the UK and made to feel welcome by all who came into England with Jim and Sue Palosaari.

Charlie Moorhouse put the finishing touches on the first floor meeting room by painting a large wall mural depicting Christ as the bridge for all humanity to gain access to that which is eternal. This artistic rendering was a spiritual conversation piece for visitors who may have never heard about God's provision of eternal life through His Son, Jesus Christ.

'Jesus Family' England

Early 'Jesus Family' - 56 Beulah Hill Rd. Upper Norwood, SE London

Team from:
Canada, Sweden, USA, England, Germany, Holland & Australia

Next on our agenda was the restoration of the two story office building that would be our new operations headquarters. With paint rollers and brushes in hand we soon had this modest but functional

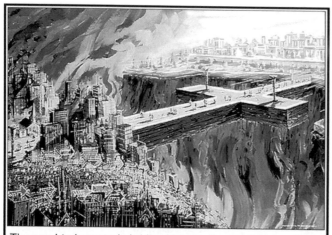

The road to heaven is bridged by the Cross of Jesus Christ
"The message about the cross is foolishness to those who are perishing but to us who are being saved, it is the power of God." I Corinthians 1:18

office space redecorated. The downstairs had a small room in the back I used for a bedroom. This allowed a more private living arrangement which I needed at this juncture in my healing. During the day there was considerable activity in the building which trailed off to quiet in the evenings.

During these down-times I'd think about my family and friends still trapped in the cult. This inner burden and low burning pain never left me. On the flip side, being part of the Jesus Family, sharing food and laughter and having work to do, helped get me back on my feet.

My friend Dennis kept a pet boa constrictor snake in an aquarium in the middle room of the office building downstairs. Curiosity seekers (especially ladies) always got an adrenalin rush when they saw heat lights on and decided to investigate. Oops!

In these early days, booking The Sheep into concert venues and telling others about Jesus Christ was our main focus. The Sheep band would play and the Good News of Jesus Christ would be shared usually via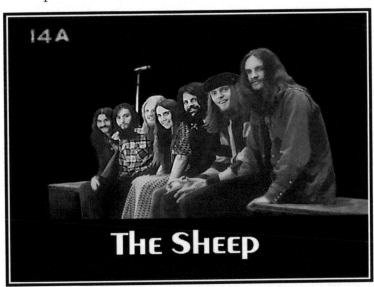

Jim Palosaari preaching a Gospel message. On occasion, we hooked up with Larry Norman, Randy Stonehill, The Mighty Flyers, or Capel House for joint concerts.

The UK Living Room Upper Norwood, SE. London

As a mission team, we wanted to reach locals from our area and decided to redecorate the downstairs of our office building. We made it into an after-hours spot. This attracted youth from Upper Norwood who came on Fridays and Saturdays for non-alcoholic drinks, snacks, and music. Older locals came after the pubs let out at 11 P.M. We called it the Living Room, borrowing the name from the Christian outreach storefront in San Francisco. Though small and intimate we connected with neighborhood young adults. At this venue a number of musicians shared Christ-centered tunes and testimonies. Each dimension of outreach seemed to lead to the next seamlessly.

Life was an adventure as a follower of Christ during the Jesus Movement. We took risks and were involved in amazing things because of God's grace (Acts 4:33). Our lives and many we reached were changed by Jesus Christ forever (II Corinthians 5:17-21). We began ministries by faith, often having very little money or resources. We believed anything was possible (Heb. 11:1). God provided properties and resources to open Christian houses, ranches, coffeehouses, restaurants, Christian book stores and small businesses which provided work and housing for those who were coming to faith in Christ. We started Christian music bands, outreach newspapers, developed theater teams and wrote songs and tracts about God.

On the heels of the Living Room was the writing and publication of a new UK Christian newspaper we called *Everyman.* Sue Palosaari was editor, Don Schendel Art and Layout editor, Arlene Czekalski Editorial Assistant, Lynn Malmberg, Margie Pinnow, Aram Outim, Carol Durkin and others assisted in a variety of ways. As a team we took the newspaper to the streets as a means of initiating dialogue and sharing our faith.

How the Jesus People Came Alive-Concerts
Sue Palosaari Cowper

Meanwhile Jim and the band were cooking-up and rehearsing a show that

would stun and stagger London audiences by its very verve, titled *How the Jesus People Came Alive.* This was to be our grand-slam approach; grab the audience with music and our hippie attire, and before they even realized what was coming, let-fly with the gospel, an approach that had worked before.

The idea was partially spawned by Mr. Frampton's desire to promote an alternative to the aggressive evangelism of the COG cult as they were now fanning out across Britain and onto the Continent. In earnest we all wanted to reverse the entrapment of young seekers who'd been mesmerized by Berg's god-awful cult. Mr. and Mrs. Frampton and David Hoyt had a deeper investment, desiring to draw out their own family members from the evil influences of this counterfeit.

We had a carte blanch open door to replace Berg's Children of God deception with The Truth! No hidden agenda, no secret prophet, just Jesus Christ! Already accomplished in road show ballyhoo, Jim and the band had no trouble developing a more sophisticated staging. Everyone knew their paces: Jesus freaks would get the word out on the streets during the day; audiences would come, the band would play, and by evening's end, more would be added to what we were now calling "The Jesus Family."

Fred Gartner was selected to give his meaty testimony. His imposing build and tangled beard gave him a brute presence on stage. His personal story was jaw-dropping, and Fred knew how to deliver it with impeccable timing. Jim would follow with the wrap up call to salvation. Altogether, it was something we'd done many times, and we'd developed a sense for the theatrics of performance, we were earnest, enthusiastic and believable.

From a trial venue we moved to the Greyhound Concert Hall and up a notch to Croydon's Fairfield Hall, following on the heels of The Carpenters, who'd been there a week earlier. With growing interest and decent audience response, things were looking up.

At one of these venues, Jim deviated from script, inviting any who were saved out of the audience to come up onto the stage. Across the house we arose, one by one, some carrying small

children, attending Christians, Jesus freaks, all moved towards the atrium, climbing the stairs to stand behind Jim, as we sang one of his favorites, "I have decided to follow Jesus." Talk about an electric moment! You could feel the zap in the air. Jim gave another invitation, this time for salvation. That night just about everyone raised their hands, bowed their heads, and offered a prayer.

While on stage, holding baby Jed in my arms, the Holy Spirit helped me visualize more of our team actively participating in a dramatic show. The story would unfold using authentically rescued street people from our team that God would transform on stage. I couldn't wait to tell Jim!

What unfolded through this rough germ idea was beyond anything I could have imagined."

Christian Multi-Media Theatrical Show England UK

When we returned home that evening I kept Jim up half the night spinning how we could develop everyone's testimonies into a full-blown show, no longer just a spoken testimony, but a living testimony through a variety of characters. I pitched the idea to use as many as possible, not just Fred and the Sheep, Siv & Irene and Dave, the standard threesome of music/tes-

timony and preaching, but the whole group. We'd need a plot, of course, and music; it would be a musical!

The story of the West Coast Jesus movement! We would come into a town with advance publicity, hire the largest venue, put up posters, hand out fliers, plug radio announcements, changing-up previous practices of evangelism. Our show would endeavor to reach a growing segment of British

Jim Palosaari - Milwalkee Jesus People, Jesus Family England
"I became a servant of this Gospel by the gift of God's grace given me by the working of His power." Ephesians 3:7

Society which had become unchurched, with less than 7% attending Christian places of worship. We'd invite the audience into the story, not just preach to, or at them. Wearied by my excited ramblings, Jim agreed to talk it over with Mr. Frampton, just to get some sleep.

A week later, Jim presented the idea to Mr. Frampton, and it was accepted! Not long afterwards, Jim, Dave Hoyt, Mike Damrow, Greg Nancarrow, Henry Huang and several others met in the upstairs Westow Street office building to share ideas for a script. I arrived late with the writing already underway. I was pregnant, had been ill all morning, Jed was cranky and needed to go home, so I returned to Beulah Hill.

I've regretted I didn't help write the script. My name wasn't even on the program, but an idea had been birthed in my heart when I saw the power of our ministry team on stage, at the end of what was then, "How the Jesus People Came Alive."

New Idea & Script Writing— D.E. Hoyt

Sue's idea was a good one! Jim had a strong theatrical background and knew the power of mixing things up with character parts to create interest and give the audience a variety of songs, characters and settings which were relatable.

This initial gathering to pick some characters and settle on a few scenes was an opportunity to be unified in the Spirit with a diversity of ideas flying around the room. This dynamic required good behavior and respect for one another, even if the ideas generated were not all used. What rose to the top, with group consensus, would be the ideas we'd use in the days ahead.

One of the team's songwriters, Mike Damrow had a cluster of ideas that were affirmed in our brainstorming session. From Mike's stay in Venice Beach, California a number of individuals he'd met while there were strong character ideas. We chose a character we would call "Bear" from a Venice Beach drug-dealer called Dancing Bear. Ironically San Francisco's main counter-culture drug maker and dealer, Owsley, had the nick-name of Bear. The vegetarian character was adopted from another Venice Beach resident who Mike had met, who was a die-hard vegetarian, who'd cut off his trigger-finger to avoid the draft. The transcendental meditation character was another local. The Old Lady was one of the people who'd witnessed to Mike in San Bernardino.

In our session I mentioned an event I'd witnessed at a peaceful anti-war protest on San Francisco's Haight Street when police and narcs descended on several hippie marchers with night-sticks beating them without cause. This idea was translated into the fight scene in the production. We also talked about northern and southern California beach baptisms and decided to film our own. Jim P. and others chimed-in and by the time we left the office building that day, we'd roughed out a plot and we'd soon settle on a name for the show.

The Heart and Soul of a New Rock Musical

We named the multi-media musical *Lonesome Stone*. Its precursor, *How the Jesus People Came Alive,* had undergone a metamorphosis. LS would add depth and characters, choreography, new song writing, the use of shorter thematic tunes, require a cast, support crews and involve many more participants. In essence Jim's original idea and Sue's expanded idea had merged into a new whole. The core story of a generation's search for meaning, reality and spiritual truth remained the same. We incorporated some music of the day to add relevance to the storyline. A crash course in theater was provided to the entire Jesus Family cast, followed by a rigorous rehearsal schedule in preparation of launching *Lonesome Stone.*

The setting for the show was San Francisco's Haight-Ashbury District, late 1967. The glory of the *Flower Power* era was rapidly spiraling downward when miraculously, new faces and voices of hope and truth came out of the dying embers and ashes of the hippie counter-culture. "Jesus People freaks" emerged carrying Bibles with the fire of the Holy Spirit on their lips and in their hearts.

The show would take the audience on a journey from the ideals of searching non-conformists, flower children and hippies, to unwelcome dark paths where they encountered evil, greed, bad drugs, violence, false teachers and disillusionment.

As the show progressed, the miracle of redemption would unfold as different cast members came to faith in Jesus Christ. A powerful ingredient in LS was the entire cast was comprised of actual Lonesome Stones who'd encountered these experiences or similar ones firsthand. We would offer an alternative to the "flower children dream" that had been crushed by Satan's counterfeits.

The production was sponsored by Deo Gloria Trust (a Christian benevolent trust) founded by Mr. & Mrs. K.P. Frampton in the early 1960's.

We were given the benefit of a professional range of equipment, lighting, choreography and directing. The show was a combination of drama, an ingenious light show with rear screen projection, contemporary music and new songs written especially for the show. The amount of sacrificial work, love, finances and heart put into this project was enormous.

The cast and majority of those helping were not paid with the exception of the choreographer and director who were professionals in the London theatrical community. On one occasion I made the mistake of teasingly asking Jim Palosaari, "How did we get all these individuals to volunteer their time?"

Jim quickly got me into a head-lock saying, "A little friendly persuasion, David."

Thankfully he was using the prop gun for the show! It deserves saying, in spite of Jim barking orders, he most often did so with an endearing sense of humor. Jim and I forged a bond of friendship that would last. *I am indebted to him as a friend who reached out and accepted me as a wounded Christian.*

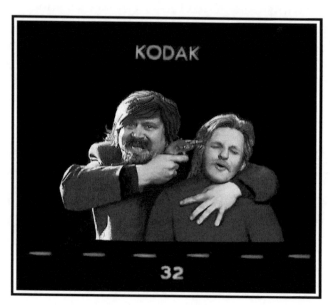

The work ahead seemed overwhelming in the beginning. We rented the Sundown Theatre in Brixton and began the rigors of rehearsals, choosing songs, distributing parts and lines. None of us had a clue about acting, or how a theatre production came together with the exception of Jim P and Caroline Green.

Our recently hired director Ian McDonald and choreographer Rufus helped us realize this in short order. As early rehearsals got underway our director and choreographer began the rigors of whipping us into shape. We were in shock! Our entire group was out of shape, flabby, slow of foot and uncoordinated when it came to movement on stage—a combined mess!

Though some ex-hippies have a lazy streak, not so when it came to the Milwaukee Jesus People, or the Europeans and Brits who joined the Jesus Family. Everyone dug deep and worked hard in rehearsals to get up to speed.

In the Studio

As the production's song choices fell into place we were off to a London studio to lay down tracks for our first Lonesome Stone cast album.

The recording sessions went well due to Greg and Mole's musical expertise. Other band members from The Sheep added their talents along with Mary Damrow, Siv Algotsson, Irene Barker, Fred Gartner, Caroline Green— all doing a great job. A few of us had difficulty with our takes, but finally caught on.

Greg Nancarrow & Larry Barker
in Recording Studio

Next steps were filming a beach baptism, decorating several double-decker buses, designing advertising posters, show programs and promotional material, working out glitches in the sound and lighting, tightening the show and training a team to manage in-house operations at the theatre prior to, during and after performances.

Baptism Outing & Filming

Finding a window of decent weather in England to film a baptism was dodgy. We hired a tour bus company to be on call and waited for good weather before finalizing the date. Our plan was to head south toward

Plymouth to the shoreline of the English Channel for a time of worship and singing, a baptism and then lunch. The baptism would be filmed for the purpose of showing this footage toward the finale of Lonesome Stone on a large screen above the rear of the stage.

Jim Palosaari officiated, with Jesus Family members assisting; baptizing in the Name of God the Father, Jesus Christ and the Holy Spirit. A number of new Christians were baptized, along with cast members who

Jim Palosaari teaching on baptism   Rich, Dave, Fred, Mary, Greg & Christian

were re-baptized for the filming.

Baptizing in ponds, rivers, lakes, the ocean, or swimming pools was common in Jesus People days. Most JP followed John and Jesus' example of baptism by immersion (Matthew 3:16-17). We did so during these bap-

Caroline Green's Baptism   Fred Gartner's Baptism

tisms.

The whole of this filming outing was an important pause from the intensity of demanding rehearsals and the considerable amount of work yet to be accomplished. It was fun to be on a tour bus relaxing, enjoying the scenery as we traveled to the coast. Spending time at the ocean, celebrating first-time baptisms and eating lunch in the sunshine at the beach was a welcome treat for us all! After eating we headed to Plymouth, for a brief tour of some of the older historic buildings and waterfront area.

It was hard to believe the launch of Lonesome Stone was just around the corner. We had to pinch ourselves that this was actually happening! Thankfully we were so busy with stuff to do we didn't have time to worry about it. Rehearsals had been moved from the older Brixton venue to the Rainbow Theatre where we were finalizing and tightening every aspect of the show.

Lonesome Stone's Launch at the Rainbow Theatre
232 Seven Sisters Rd. Finsbury Park, London UK

Booking the Rainbow Theatre for an extended time under normal circumstances would be near impossible. In the midst of a God Visit anything

could happen! Amazingly, a lease was signed for a two-month run which was a clear indicator we were in the center of God's plan.

The Rainbow Theatre, first a cinema, had been transformed into a famous Rock Theatre, a place for medium size London Concerts. The following groups or artists were either before or shortly after us: The Beach Boys, Pink Floyd, Queen, Genesis, Eric Clapton, Van Morrison, Kool & the Gang, Bob Marley & the Wailers, Paul McCartney's Wings, Steve Miller's Blues Band and a host of other well known acts.

Lonesome Stone's launch into the Rainbow venue, well known for artistic excellence, was a daunting but equally exciting opportunity. The vision to bring the Gospel into a context where the common person might come along, hear and experience God in a personal way, was a step beyond what the best of music concerts offered. Drenched in prayer and hard work, our Jesus People team moved forward.

Time, Look, Newsweek, US News and World Report, Rolling Stone

and a heap of other magazines and newspapers were attempting to wrap their heads around *'The Jesus Movement/Revolution.'*

The awakened spiritual interest had sparked the creation of both Godspell and Jesus Christ Superstar. Both musicals opened in NYC in 1971.

Godspell's infamous tune "Day by Day" was a huge hit. These shows

A Musical based on the
the Gospel according to St. Matthew

would probably never have seen the light of day without the Jesus Movement being a national and international ongoing phenomenon. In the mix *Lonesome Stone* would now give it a go.

Our premiere opening at the Rainbow in London was July 1st 1973. The uniqueness of *Lonesome Stone* was the cast; comprised of Jesus People whose lives were under reconstruction through the power of God's Spirit. Each cast member knew what it was like to be lost or trapped in a self-destructive lifestyle prior to placing their faith in Jesus Christ. This was the difference! The dialogue, songs and lives of the cast were steeped in communicating the Gospel of Jesus Christ and pointing those in attendance toward God. *Lonesome Stone* was the real deal!

No one had a clue how this new theatrical production would be received. The prep work had been massive. Months of rehearsals, tweaking and pouring our full attention and energy into this project had been all-consuming. Talents and abilities had been stretched and refined. Faith, prayer,

and trust had been exercised. Opening night was before us.

Early critics gave mixed reviews. Attendance was average, swelling on the weekends. It soon became apparent; the Rainbow run would be an opportunity to streamline the show.

The Rainbow was our boot-camp of sorts, equipping the team for fruitful ministry in the present and when the production would go on tour. The director and choreographer worked our butts off. The result was, the show tightened in all areas; acting, music, choreography, stage-crew duties, lighting, sound, rear-screen projection, theatre staffing responsibilities, along with skills in promotion and advertising.

A vital component and responsibility was representing God through our lives, words and character while interacting with audiences after the show. Jesus Family members and all nvolved in Lonesome Stone did so with those who stayed afterwards to ask questions, or chat about spiritual things.

To facilitate this, at the end of each show the audience was invited to visit with any of the cast, production or front house team. We listened, answered questions, discussed spiritual issues of concern and made ourselves available to pray with anyone who wanted us to do so for specific needs. Fielding questions about receiving Christ were always amazing opportunities to be 'In Christ' in the moment.

Being prayerful and in a good place in our own hearts was essential if we expected to point others to God in an honorable way. Sharing our faith wasn't new to us, but we needed to be sensitive to each person's unique needs and questions, responding as the Holy Spirit guided us. We understood each encounter was a one-of-a-kind 'Divine Appointment,' requiring more than a rehearsed religious spiel!

We were confident we were doing exactly what God had called us to do (Ephesians 2:10). People would be drawn to God by the Holy Spirit and transformed in the same way, in His way and timing.

Audiences were a mixture of seekers, believers, the curious and those who came along having no clue what the production was about. Lonesome Stone gave those in attendance an opportunity to be observers of how someone heard, thought through, responded and eventually decided to yield to God and release their faith in Jesus Christ.

Lonesome Stone was a Living Sermon comprised of humans who were being changed by God and adopted into His family.

> As you come to him, the Living Stone—(Jesus Christ), rejected by humans but chosen by God and precious to Him, you also, like living stones, are being built into a spiritual house to be a holy priesthood, offering spiritual sacrifices acceptable to God through Jesus Christ. I Peter 2:4-5 NIV®

The dialogue and songs in LS conveyed the paradoxes of the Flower Power Generation as they attempted to achieve big dreams amidst the forces of darkness. Dangerous drugs, unrestrained sex, greed, pagan and demonic religions, were thwarting the goals of Peace and Love. LS songs captured the inner-warfare cast members began to experience as their eyes were gradually opened to empty promises and misplaced trust. *When hope was in rare supply, tremors of spiritual life awakened by a outpouring of God's Spirit into an unlikely bunch of lost street people.*

Song Writers

Songs for the show were written by Mike Damrow, Greg Nancarrow, Rich Haas, Dave Hoyt, Joe Grier & David Eden, Randy Stonehill, Andrae Crouch, John Phillips, Gerry Goffin, Carole King and Buffalo Springfield.

The script for LS was a collaborative effort of Arlene Czekalski, Mike & Mary Damrow, D.E. Hoyt and Jim Palosaari. The script was refreshed from time to time, under the direction of Ian McDonald and Jim Palosaari.

The show instantly required a sizable number of Jesus Family team members to fill the many slots for the overall production. It was good to see so many step up with a commitment to excellence. What we didn't know how to do, we rapidly learned. In the first month of rehearsal we hadn't figured how to do the fight scene without actually exchanging blows. As I was in this scene and the one being wailed on, it was a welcome relief when someone came up with the novel idea of doing the fight scene in slow-motion, without inflicting physical harm on the character Stone. My body appreciated this timely suggestion!

19

Where Light Dispels Darkness

Lonesome Stone—A Multi-Media Rock Musical

Jim and Sue Palosaari cast the original vision. Jesus Family team members in collaboration added their creative input. Mr. K.P. Frampton and the Deo Gloria Trust supported this endeavor prayerfully and financially, with a clear goal to reach the lost

Lonesome Stone was an outreach vehicle ahead of its time, offering dialogue with cast members and an opportunity to enter into a relationship with the Living God! The unified goal of all involved was to make Jesus Christ known as the Risen and Living Savior, God's beloved Son!

The following is a brief tour of the theatrical production of *Lonesome Stone.* Images and the majority of song lyrics are included.

The production begins with the birth of war babies in the late 1940s through early 1950s. Artistically the babies are born on stage using clear plastic bags to simulate amniotic birth sacs. In the background, running movie footage of war planes in flight can be seen on large screens with the sounds of air-sirens blowing and bombs being dropped.

A haunting reminder of what had occurred in World War II. The song War Babies plays in the background. *War Babies* / Greg Nancarrow

The show quickly fast-forwards to a generation's search for Peace & Love rather than hate and war. The setting is San Francisco 1967. The tour guide is Greg Nancarrow, lead singer for the Sheep. Looking out on the horizon of the Haight District he catches a glimpse of a typical late teen on the streets.

"Lonesome Stone he's so proud and cold—but he's just nineteen years old! He's seen it all—done his most, Lonesome's just a walking ghost. He thinks he is a genius, mind as quick as grease—all he lacks is faith and love and a little peace . . . Oh what will he do with his life? Oh what will he do with his life?"
Lonesome Stone / Mike Damrow

Spinning off this gutsy tune we hear the pristine voice of Caroline Green. "If you're going to San Francisco be sure to wear some flowers in your hair, if you're going to San Francisco you're gonna meet some gentle people there. All across the nation, there's a strange vibration, people in motion, people in motion. There's a whole generation with a new explanation—people in motion." *San Francisco* / John Phillips

Caroline exudes the best of Flower Power idealism and draws us into a time when the dream was still alive.

Larry Barker (aka Mole) is the high energy vegetable lover. His pitch for artichokes, avocados, potatoes, tomatoes and asparagus carries effortlessly into song. "Slip me a carrot, daddy, or a squash if you're able. I don't want no hamburger patty—I got to have my vegetables.

I get high on peppers and eggplant, cauliflowers every hour – and do not let us forget the lettuce, organic grown will give you the power. O I gotta, gotta, gotta have my vegetables every day! Yes, I gotta, gotta, gotta have my vegetables everyday!" *Vegetables* / Randy Stonehill

Stone's in a dilemma and pessimistic. "Where do we go from here? I gotta know right now. Does it matter anyhow?" There's a thousand roads to take. Is there one that's meant for me? There's a thousand plans to make. Will they help me in eternity? Is there something in the stars? Is there someone in control? Do I have to go to Mars—to end this searching of my soul? Is there any right or any wrong? Is there any black or white? Or, is there only shades of gray? What would happen if I died tonight? Where do we go ?"

Where Do We Go From Here? / Greg Nancarrow & Larry Barker

Next up Queenie and Bear: Bear played by Fred Gartner and Queenie by Mary Damrow are two flamboyant characters larger than life. Queenie and Bear embody what's sour on the streets of San Francisco. They're the wheeling and dealing drug duo.

"If you want action baby, this is the place!" Bear and Queenie's fancy out-fits reveal the disparity between those they're exploiting and their flim-flam spiel that squeezes money out of their victims. "My business is dealing, my acid is strong. My dope is the best you can find in the Haight. I call her the Queen. You can see she's got class. We're partners in business, she handles the cash." *Bear Boogie* / Mike Damrow

There's something sinister and evil about life on the streets. You never know what will happen next. The good guys might be the bad guys. So-called friends might rip you off. The police might beat you without cause. Your street buddies might turn away and forget about you as you lie there in a pool of blood. Buffalo Springfield captured the scene accurately with this eerie tune.

"There's something happening here. What it is, ain't exactly clear. There's a man with a gun over there, tellin me—I got to beware. It's time we stop, children, what's that sound? Everybody look, what's going down. There's battle lines being drawn. Nobody's right if everybody's wrong. Young people speaking their minds—getting so much resistance, from behind. I think it's time we stop, hey, what's that sound? Everybody look what's going down. What a field day for the heat. A thousand people in the street. Singing songs and carry-

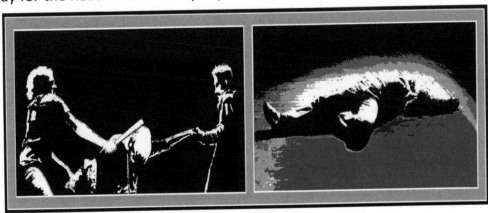

ing signs. Mostly saying—hooray for our side. Paranoia strikes deep. Into your life it will creep. It starts when you're always afraid. You step out of line—the man comes and takes you away. We better stop, hey, what's that sound—everybody look what's going down." *For What It's Worth* / Buffalo Springfield

Milwaukee Rich is finding the street people are getting weirder and crazier! Taunting him, they jeer and hiss, obsessed with freaking him out. He'd come here looking for "peace and love"—not some kind of freak show. As nighttime falls on the Haight District the demons come out to sport their wares. The hustle begins. What used to be safe is not. Sounds of gunshots split the air; blood splattered on the sidewalk is a chilling sign. People

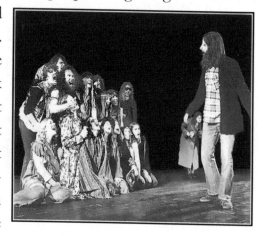

are getting ripped off left and right; young girls giving free-love are being cast-off and discarded, left to survive the harshness of street life.

When hope and truth are in short supply God shows up, transforming the worst of the lot. Who'd have guessed, the wild and outrageous drug dealer Bear would be the first to make a break with his old life; an unlikely candidate to become a friend of God.

His passion to share what he's discovered forces the question, "Is Bear the real-deal, or is Jesus just another scam in Bear's bag of tricks?"

Queenie and Stone, Milwaukee and Lisa are listening but not convinced. Bear isn't somebody you can trust! Still, they're thinking about the

change in Bear. He doesn't look as evil as he used to.

Stone turns his thoughts into song, "I went looking for love and a place to live, in a world—had nothing to give. And the streets have hurt me, and let me down, can't you see—well I'm a lonesome, lonesome—just a Stone."

Unimpressed with Bear—Slim responds, "San Francisco ain't the place for amazing Grace, Bear I think you're acting like a clown."

Strange how the past gets clouded when you're high most the time, doing your own thing. Later, while alone, Slim begins to remember what he'd walked away from.

"I think I'm going back, to the Lord I knew so well in my youth, I think I'm returning to the days when I was young enough to know the truth. Back when I knew God made all the flowers grow. The sun and sky were there, because He loved me so. His joy and peace could chase away the fear, and Jesus was a name I loved to hear. O I can recall when I wasn't afraid to reach out for His hand. When any sorrow came, only Jesus seemed to understand. So let other men debate their true realities, because I've found the truth back where it used to be.

It's the simple things He gives—I find I lack. So catch me if you can, I'm going back. Jesus loves me this I know, for the Bible tells me so. Little ones to Him belong. They are weak and He is strong. Yes, Jesus loves me, The Bible tells me so. It's the simple things you give, I find I lack. So catch me if you can, you know, I'm coming back." *Goin Back* / Gerry Goffin & Carole King / Rewrite Greg Nancarrow

God is Calling

There's an infusion of God's Holy Spirit descending on this group of Street People. Milwaukee Rich thinks about Bear who's become a follower of Jesus Christ.

"I remember when I last saw him on the road—and on his heart; he had such a heavy load. Now he don't seem that way anymore—since he's come on back, he's not like he was before. Looks like he's changed everything in his life—changed everything in his life. Things he's said, things he's done—he's now forsaken, to follow the Son. You can see the love on his face and the peace in his eyes. And he says it all comes from this man called Jesus Christ. And you can have all the same—if you don't deny. That He really is, the Way the Truth and the Life." John 14:6 *Changes* / Rich Haas

Stone's taking it all in—wondering. For some unexplainable reason—

Stone's heart is softening. Guitar in hand, a song of faith is born.

"Well I traveled down a long and lonely road, to places where it hurt for me to go. And everybody here—has been there too—and the song that I'm singing, it's for you. I'm not coming on with some religious trip. I'm talking about a man named Jesus Christ. You might not understand it—but I just can't hold it in. I've never been so happy in my life. Now I can see . . . Now I can see . . Now I can see . . .

For God so loved you and me—that he sent His son to die upon a tree. And He has carried all our sin and shame—and we can find forgiveness in His name. There's really something different about the Son of God—death could not hold him in the grave. He's reigning now in heaven and He holds the key to life—receive Him now, for He alone can save! He'll set you free—He'll set you free—He'll set you free!" *He'll Set You Free* / Dave Hoyt & Mike Damrow

Queenie has her own inner war to sort out.

"I have studied lives of men hoping to discover. What could be the greatest thing—young men should seek after. Some seek fortune, some seek fame—some men follow wisdom. What could be the greatest name, who has seen the vision? I have to know, before I die—I ask you why? There's something here—I realize—I see it shinning in their eyes." *Lives of Men* / Mike Damrow

Queenie Reaches Out in Abandonment

"Come Jesus, come—I'm ready. Come Jesus, come—and show me your way, your truth and life. So many years and seasons—so many tears and reasons—I turned away, from your gentle voice.

Foundations laid, on this world of sand—have all washed away to the sea and—there's nobody left here but me—and I'm not all—I thought I'd be. Patiently—you stood by—watching me with each try—that I made—to make it on my own. But now as I stand—amidst my shattered dream—somehow I think for the first time—yes, I think I really believe—I'm ready to receive your love. Lord, I know I've waited so long, but it's not—too late." *Come Jesus Come* / Greg Nancarrow

Feel as free as a bird in the sky—when I'm in the Spirit, I am so high. Different ways of receiving God's love, sometimes it's soft like the beauty of a white dove.

Free—hallelujah I am Free—Lord, just a prayer—and you know it's real. Hallelujah, I am free. It's good to know—it's good to know—it's good

Part of the Lonesome Stone cast on stage, with Baptisms shown on rear screen

to know. Ah ah ah ah, that you are free—and—you always will be. Ah ah ah ah it's good to know, that you are free—and you always will be!

I never knew what freedom could be—until my Lord Jesus came and touched me. And when the Son of God has set you free—the Holy Spirit manifests its beauty." *Free* / Mike Damrow

"Wake up, wake up—it's the break of day. Light is shining, showing you the way. Wake up to what Jesus has to say. All your life you've searched to find the truth. Try to realize—He's come for you. Don't you realize—He's come for you. Wake up little children and forsake your games. Your sins are forgiven you—for His Name's sake. For you, He has paid the price. For you, He was sacrificed. Rejoice—rejoice! Wake up old sleeping soul—your Father calls. For you can be reborn, washed clean and made new. God's love can change your life—by faith in Jesus Christ. Rejoice—rejoice!" *Rejoice* / Joe Grier & David Eden

The closing tune "Take A Little Time" is sung by all the cast sitting on the front of the stage. As Sue Palosaari envisioned, the cast and all those behind the scenes were using their gifts and gaining new ones. The cast alone was comprised of 25-30 Jesus Family members.

Take a Little Time - Andrae Crouch

Audience & Show Team Interaction

This tune is followed by an invitation for those in attendance to dialogue with any of the cast, stage, sound or house crew. We purposely avoided an orchestrated script. Instead, we sought to listen and engage in open and honest interaction. This was our one-on-one time to visit, answer questions and share in more depth what God accomplished through His Son, Jesus Christ. This naturally led to prayer, oftentimes to the acknowledgment of sin, need and the reception of God's gift of new life in Jesus Christ. Passing contact information to keep in touch was always important.

Early Cast Characters

Siv Algotsson – Bubbles
Larry Barker – Organo
Irene Barker – Tomato
Christian Beese – 2nd drunk
Gerd Bienge – meditator
Owen Brock – Yoyo
Gilbert Cailly – 3rd narc agent
Patricia Capelello – Venus
Odie Carter – revolutionary
Mary Damrow – Queenie
Carol Durkin – Rich's girl & Little old Lady
Fred Gartner – Bear
Caroline Green – Poppy

Rich Haas – Milwaukee Rich
D.E. Hoyt – Stone
Vincent Lobley – Zip (the speed freak)
John Marley – 2nd narc agent
Greg Nancarrow – Slim
Aram Outim – Guru
Wilhelm Pinnow – Wizard
Peter Smith – 1st narc agent
Matt Spranzy – Cosmic
Alan Turnell – 1st drunk
Susan Wilson – Bobby
Jim Palosaari - narrator

Music by "The Sheep"

Larry (Mole) Barker – lead & rhythm guitar + vocals
Lisa Carothers – vocals & organ
Rich Haas – vocals
Nick Malham – drums
Reed Mittelsteadt – vocals
Greg Nancarrow – lead & rhythm guitar + vocals
Wilhelm Pinnow – bass guitar

Musical & Vocal Artists

Ethel Krauss – flute
Matt Spransky – organ
Irene Barker – backup vocals
Siv Algotsson – backup vocals
Caroline Green – lead & backup vocals

Promotional Artist– Charlie Moorehouse
Costume Design – Karin Gunnarsson, Siv Algotsson, and Irene Barker

Support Crews

Stage, sound, light-show, house staff, advertising, secretarial and ticket sales, box office staff, transportation, food prep / catering and child-care were selflessly provided by the Jesus Family community and Christian volunteers who came along and pitched in.

Rebirth by God's Spirit

Regularly, those in attendance were struck by a song, scene, the transformation of cast members on stage, or something else that would touch them spiritually. In these instances God's Spirit could speak to an individual in an unmistakable way resulting in an invisible miracle of spiritual rebirth.

Sensing and being aware of God's love and truth through Jesus Christ's life, death and resurrection could be translated to a human heart and mind in a brief moment in time. When this occurred, it was a divine appointment. The purpose of Lonesome Stone was to present what was possible when someone opened their heart, mind and spirit to what is true and to the True Savior of this world, Jesus Christ..

Counterfeits didn't provide forgiveness of sin, or interaction with the Holy Spirit. Both are essential in genuine life-transformation! Be assured,

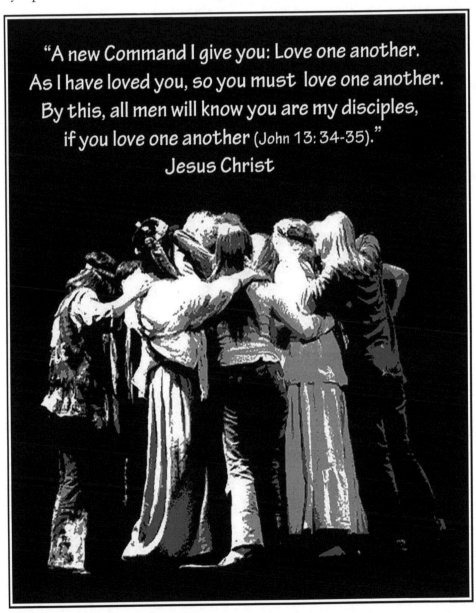

"A new Command I give you: Love one another.
As I have loved you, so you must love one another.
By this, all men will know you are my disciples,
if you love one another (John 13: 34-35)."
Jesus Christ

any and every miracle that took place related to *Lonesome Stone*, were not due to clever theatrical writing, smooth and polished acting or singing, but the creative working of The Living God!

The Jesus Family & Lonesome Stone Team & Cast by Country of Origin

Gerd Bienge – Germany
Caroline Green – England
Karin Gunnarsson – Sweden
Siv Algotsson – Sweden
Philippe LaFon – France
Danny Keating – Ireland
Margaret Keating – England
Larry Barker – USA
Irene Barker – Sweden
Christian Beese – Germany
Aram Outim – India
Dennis Knight – USA
Rich & Jenny Haas – USA
Lynn Malmberg – USA
Charlie Moorehouse – USA
Owen Brock – Canada
Sandy Brock – USA
Fred & Gail Gartner – USA
Matt Spransy – USA
Mike & Mary Damrow – USA
Henry Huang – USA
Dieter Gries – USA
Jim & Sue Palosaari – USA
D.E. Hoyt – USA
Carol Durkin – USA
Trevor Allen – England
Terry Moore - Wales

Margie Pinnow – USA
Wilhelm Pinnow – Germany
Linda Feltzer – USA
Odie Carter – USA
Arlene Czekalski – USA
Mike Drehfal – USA
Susan Wilson – USA
Greg & Lynn Nancarrow – USA
Reed Mittelstedt – USA
Don Schendel – USA
Lisa Carothers – USA
Nick Malham – England
Ian McDonald – England
Ethel Krauss – USA
Cris Barton
Vincent Lobley
John Marley – England
Peter Smith
Alan Turnell
Bill Wittala – USA
William N Smith
Ben Day – USA
Rosalind Day – England
Mike O'Neill – England
Gilbert Cailly
Mr. & Mrs. K P Frampton – England
Jurgen Kobs - Germanye

We were grateful for each person that plowed and reaped with us during these days and all the volunteers who came alongside to reach their communities for Christ. God helped us and lives were changed because He went with us. Deo Gloria – To God Be the Glory!

Among the many young Brits who attended Lonesome Stone, a young Andrew Whitman came and was significantly impacted. Andrew's dialogue with a cast member couldn't have come at a more perfect time. This interaction, combined with Andrew's open heart, activated and solidified a personal decision to ask Jesus Christ to be at the center of his life. This event would translate into a life-long relationship with the Lord, an intentional commitment to Godly service and the making of many disciples for Jesus Christ! Here is the first segment of his account.

Andrew Whitman

I was born in 1953 to parents who worked a mixed farm just inside the M25

motorway in Enfield, North London. They were nominally Christian in their moral values. During primary school I was packed off to Sunday school on Sunday afternoons for a couple of years, particularly enjoying "Draw Your Swords" (a game where you had to find a particular Bible verse speedily). Apart from this my only other exposure to the gospel was through a school-friend named Graham who dragged me along to Crusaders from time to time, a para-church group reaching children and young people.

In 1971 I went to Leeds University to study Economics, but actually ended up learning more about music, beer, dope and women. Like most people my age I was drawn into the hippie movement as a curious but cautious participant. I did the usual rounds of festivals, saw the Grateful Dead at Bickershaw and had my fair share of smoking cannabis with my housemates and friends. Many in my circle of friends were tripping on acid and taking speed, though for some reason I never ventured that far. University was a time of experimenting in lots of areas, but never quite finding what I was looking for.

As the oldest of three children, I was quite startled when my brother Richard and sister Claire claimed to have become Christians in 1972. This began with Claire being given a Gideon's Bible at her school. I distinctly remember giving them both a hard time for their new found faith!

Summer of 1973 was a formative season for me, while home from Leeds University before embarking on my final year of studies. Over the

August Bank Holiday weekend Richard and Claire invited me along to a
Christian rock musical called *Lonesome Stone* at the famous Rainbow Theatre in Finsbury Park, not far from my favorite football ground, where the
acclaimed Arsenal play!

Looking back I can see God was drawing me to go along, even
though I was not keen on it at first. I went two nights running, on the Friday and Saturday, and was mesmerized by the story of a hippie coming to
know Jesus. God particularly spoke to me through the song "Going back,"
which featured the lyrics, "I think I'm going back to the Lord I once knew
in my youth; I think I'm returning to the days when I was young enough to
know the truth."

Listening to these words reminded me
of the beautiful simplicity of Christ I'd encountered many years before in Sunday school. I've
often wondered since, when I was actually converted; perhaps back then, or at the Christian
musical *Lonesome Stone*?

On the first night of attending *Lonesome
Stone* I wandered around afterwards, genuinely
hoping one of the cast would approach me for a chat. When nothing happened I went up to Christian Beese, a German member of the Jesus Family
(who played the "second drunk" in the cast). He patiently listened to my
story and then prayed two separate prayers: first for God's peace to envelop
us and secondly, for Jesus to make himself known to me. I can't remember
praying any kind of "sinner's prayer," but knew I'd trusted Jesus, and felt a
profound sense of cleanness inside.

The cross especially captivated me, and positively "ruined" me for
anything else for the rest of my life. I returned to the show the next night,
which was the final Saturday of the two-month run at the Rainbow Theatre.
I remember linking up with Christian again, and also joining cast members
on the stage at the end of the performance.

A few days later I went out and bought a brown leather RSV Bible
and began to read it voraciously. It was utterly alive! I then started going
along to an Open Brethren church on Sunday mornings, even though culturally I felt like a "fish out of water." A retired missionary to Muslims,

Charles Marsh, took my family and I under his spiritual wing.

In late September, I made my way back to Leeds as "a new creation in Christ," somewhat dreading the final year of studies in Economics, as my earlier interest had seriously waned. In the first few weeks of returning to university the Christian Union unsuccessfully tried to recruit me, but I arrogantly refused point blank because they said I had to sign a doctrinal statement of belief!

Subsequently I got involved with the friendly Anglican Chaplaincy, and remain in touch with the Curate (assistant pastor) to this day. His colleague the Vicar (pastor) surprised me by agreeing to baptize me by full immersion in the local Baptist Church down the road, despite my having previously been "christened" in the Anglican Church as a baby!

Through my Chaplaincy friends I met two highly eccentric believers, Frank and Alan, the latter an ex-member of the Children of God cult. I recall intriguing conversations about Old Testament prophets and their relevance for today.

In early 1974, I discovered a team of two couples who had newly arrived to evangelize and disciple students through Campus Crusade for Christ, and was nurtured by one of them named Nigel Spencer. "Christian," from the Jesus Family in London also kept in touch regularly by letter and prayed for me. I recall Christian sending me literature warning me off the cults, stressing Jesus as the only way to God and encouraging me to receive the baptism in the Holy Spirit.

On Thursday 2nd May 1974, while completing my final year, I was instrumental in putting on a gig for *The Sheep* in the Union Refectory at Leeds University, alongside my spiritual mentor Nigel Spencer. This was a promotional gig for *Lonesome Stone* for the concert scheduled at St. George's Hall Bradford later that month from 6th–14th of May.

D.E.H.

I Cor. 15:10
"But by the grace of God I am what I am, and His grace to me was not without effect."

Shortly afterwards I visited the Jesus Family house at 56 Beulah Hill in Upper Norwood. I remember Phil Booth from Radio Worldwide leading an eye-opening Bible study on "Our Position in Christ" from Romans 6. This visit prompted new contact with the Deo Gloria Trust who sponsored the Jesus Family and Lonesome Stone outreach.

I continued to be magnetized by Jesus and his death for me. His grace was at work helping me yield to the Holy Spirit's promptings to allow God to be at the center of choices that would shape my life in the future.

Author's Note: More of Andrew Whitman's journey and personal update, highlighting decades of Christian ministry and service can be found in the Bio's 2 chapter 28.

Living Room Update

With the formation of the Lonesome Stone outreach involving so many team members from the Jesus Family, we made the decision to turn the Living Room outreach into a Christian Bookstore and leather shop which could easily be staffed by one or two residents from the Beulah Hill Christian house.

Deo Gloria Trust aided us in securing book racks and an initial inventory of Christian literature through contacts they referred us to. Leather was purchased by area vendors and fashioned into quality belts and other usable items for sale. The upstairs of the building remained an office for the Jesus Family and their broader ministry known as 'Outreach for Jesus.'

Contact for Christ

Meanwhile Mr. Frampton and Deo Gloria Trust were keen on establishing some type of follow-up ministry and began working with others Christian visionaries to accomplish this. What unfolded was "Contact for Christ" with the specific goal of helping people learn about Christ and the Christian life. Inquirers would be put in touch with those in their community who were available to chat with them, answer spiritual questions, introduce them to Christ and refer them to a welcoming Christ-centered church. The vision of Contact for Christ would also be to aid churches, evangelists and para-church ministries in their out-

reach efforts and follow-up. It's noteworthy to say Contact for Christ is in its 40th year and continues to facilitate thousands of contacts with inquirers and local Christian representatives. To God be the Glory, Deo Gloria!

Lonesome Stone on Tour

What will God do with this show? How will it be received in a country rich in theatrical heritage? What Christian footprint will remain in the UK and elsewhere?

In the coming chapters, we'll follow *Lonesome Stone* on tour in England, Scotland, Germany and the USA. What was it like being a cast member, living within the Jesus Family Community, visiting Beulah Hill, attending *Lonesome Stone*, or participating in this type of outreach mission work? What happened to Jesus Family participants with the passing of time?

We are excited to provide more eye-witness historical narratives and accounts of those who were active in the Jesus Movement living in the trenches. Collectively and individually we took steps of faith into the unknown. We witnessed God's presence assisting us amidst fierce spiritual warfare. Some of us faced great loss, tragedy and personal failings. In seasons of victory and joy, or in darkness and despair, God remained faithful. He never left us!

New Territory for a God Visit

Lonesome Stone's tour schedule took the team 200 miles north of London to one of England's largest cities, Manchester. In the early 1970's the greater Manchester area had a population of 2,730,000 people.

It's fair to say our theater production outreach of *Lonesome Stone* only scratched the surface of reaching this massive population. But, we were front-and-center and visible in the community, schools, on the streets, in the churches and covered by the media for a full month.

Spiritual discussions were popping up all over greater Manchester. "What do you know or think about this international theater team that claims through drama and song that Jesus Christ is not dead?"

Questioning and thinking was good. Interest was aroused. "Let's talk about it over tea." A new presence was in the city. As followers of Jesus we had a theatrical platform to get the message out. Early on, we could tell our presence was stirring things up.

We performed *Lonesome Stone* at the newly renovated Wythenshawe Forum Theatre; a 500-seat venue in the middle of what for many years was Europe's largest local authority housing project. The proximity of the venue to this expansive housing population was ideal. Sure enough, the crowds came and responded enthusiastically! We were surprised and thankful to witness God's hand of blessing on our fledgling theatre production and team. More importantly we praised God for the spiritual miracles that were occurring daily in the lives of those who attended the production. God's seeds were landing in good soil.

We were also fascinated to be in the Manchester area of England, learning and taking in the new sights and cultural differences of the north. We'd rented a large two story home in an older part of the

1970's Manchester, England skyline 10:10 AM

city and packed our theatre team into these new digs. It was a fun and adventurous time for most of us. In spite of cramped living conditions we knew we were in the center of God's plan. Cast members identified with, and got to know many of those who had received Christ as their personal Savior. Unfortunately, our digs were completely across town which limited after-hour interaction. To remedy this we started a Bible Study meeting once a week in Wythenshawe. Though money was tight for many of the locals, individuals would often return to LS again and again to keep up with fellowship and a point of contact with their new-found spiritual family. The cost for admission was minimal, intentionally lowered to make it more affordable for the large number of teens and lower income families in the community that wanted to come along.

The map of the districts of Manchester reflects the large expanse of the Wythenshawe district. If you're interested in the difference in UK names, check out the other districts on the map.

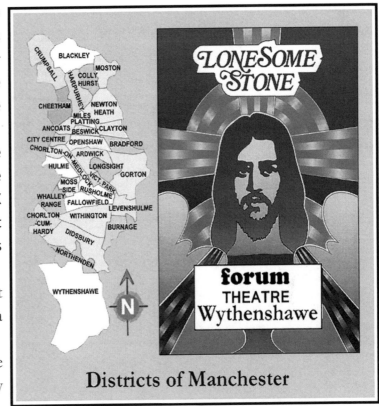

Districts of Manchester

The cast was housed in a neighborhood built in the late 1800's to early 1900's. The bricks and blocks were large and dark, with soot-stains from days gone by when burning coal was the main source of staying warm. By law, clean coal was now used, mainly for industrial purposes. Manchester was an old city going back to Roman occupation. It had now been divided into districts within Manchester proper. Some nearby neighborhoods were under demolition. The old British home we rented had a few interesting quirks with rooms tucked away in strange places. Our upstairs bath was one of these. The girls on our team had to go through a small guy's bedroom, that was similar in size to a large closet, to access the bathroom and routinely apologized for doing so. It didn't matter; we were on a mission following Jesus and making the best of things. With two bathrooms in the large home where 30-plus lived at any given time, we learned to speed up our bathroom time.

A solution was found when we stumbled on Bath House/Swimming Pool built in the early 1900's just a few blocks away from our digs. Earlier in the century, bath houses like this one were scattered across England. Manchester had around 10 strategically placed within its districts to accommodate working class people. They were a recreational center with a sizable pool in the center of each complex with public baths upstairs and an industrial laundry where people could bring their laundry for cleaning at a modest price. The cost for using the baths in the 1970's was about 35 pence (50 cents).

The first floor pool at the bath house was always in use during my visits. The center of the large pitched roof was made of glass panels to let natural light in during daylight hours. While bathers soaked in the luxury of a large tub they did so to the sound of swimmers laughing and playing in the water below. This bathhouse had about 15 upper bath stalls and was lined with changing stalls downstairs. This discovery met a huge practical need for our cast members who were crammed into an old Victorian home.

ENTRY   POOL   UPPER BATHS   LAUNDRY

As a special treat we were always on the hunt for some reasonably priced eating venues. We found one nearby that served a huge plate of noodles or rice with a conglomeration of beans, onions, vegetables and sometimes a smattering of some type of meat. It was run by Pakistanis who offered this special for 75 pence ($1.25) a plate. On special occasions we'd order some flat bread and chutney. A number of us enjoyed this type of food as a break from the community meals, or at off times when we had to fend for ourselves.

My buddy Chris Frampton came up from London several times to visit Manchester and see what we were up to. As an avid photographer he enjoyed taking photos of old England and the UK in transition. Nearby we had such a place where the old was coming down to make room for the new. Amidst the rubble of bricks and old beams he captured this image.

There wasn't any gold to be found at this demo site, but the show *Lonesome Stone was offering a spiritual treasure to attendees and they were finding it.* As the story goes, we were out and about doing part of the work and God was easily handling the

Manchester, England 1973
Photo / Chris Frampton

other 95% bringing about conversions and re-dedications of faith in Jesus Christ.

The people I'd met from the greater Manchester area were the salt of the earth type, a Northern England trait that seemed less stodgy and more open. I liked the area and began praying about what would happen to many of the new Christian teens that had received the gospel of Jesus with enthusiastic hearts. The Wythenshawe Projects reminded me of the brick reformatories I'd passed through as a young teen. It seemed God was growing a soft spot in my heart for the people of this area.

Going west from Manchester was Liverpool on the shoreline of the Irish Sea and nearby St. George's Channel. From there it was only a short boat or plane ride due west to Dublin, Ireland. We had one bloke on the LS team from Ireland, with the iconic name Danny.

I thought about Ireland from time to time, especially since a large Irish Dance Hall Club & Pub was on my walking route to our digs. It was housed in a large factory type building in a residential area with a large field next to it. During the week it was quiet, but on the weekends live-music could be heard from where we lived well past 2 AM. I wondered what it was like on the inside when the club was in full swing, but hadn't ventured in.

20

Teamwork

Irish Fighters

Following a *Lonesome Stone* evening performance and visiting with those who stayed to talk, it was late by the time a city bus let me off in my neighborhood. Tired and exhilarated by a good evening, I started my short walk of five blocks to our digs.

Immediately I could hear the blast of music, laughter and shouts coming from the Irish Dance Hall. The venue was spacious enough to easily accommodate 300 + and it was packed to the gills Friday, Saturday and Sunday evenings. Nearing the front of the club everything seemed normal with a handful of Irish blokes hanging about and the smell of smoke and beer wafting out the open front doors.

Turning the corner past the club, I stopped in my tracks. Directly in my path was a sizable fight scene taking place on a large block pad near the building. A crowd of about 75-100 had gathered cheering on the two fighters.

At first glance I thought of breaking the fight up, but quickly realized this was a bad idea. Doing so would probably get me killed! Something cultural was going down.

It was rainy and cold. An outside light mounted halfway up the

building was close enough to illuminate the silhouettes of the two going at it. Both appeared to have downed more than a pint or two. Their clothes were drenched from sweat and rain and their faces were bloodied and bruised. Male (Bloke) and female (Bird) onlookers were gawking, yelling, betting and cheering their mate. By the looks of things this fight could go on for

some time. Both were landing solid punches to the face and body as blood splattered on those closest to the fighters.

I put up my umbrella and walked to the other side where I had a better vantage point. After watching for five minutes or so, I realized these were two tough blokes hammering it out bare-fisted!

Seeing an opening, I stepped in closer when it appeared one fighter was losing momentum. Suddenly he had a resurgence of energy and landed a few hard punches. This turn of events evened the playing field, and the crowd cheered!

As the rain increased, I decided to pack it in and head home; leaving the blood, guts and the glory of victory or defeat to the crowd and fighters.

In the weeks that followed, when passing the club, I could still see the fight scene in my head. It was strange how it burned into my memory.

David and Barbara Clapham & Family

While in Manches-
ter, David and Barbara
Clapham and family
extended their kindness
and hospitality to a num-
ber of us from the *Lone-
some Stone* team.

They resided in the
outskirts of Manchester
in Woodford, Stockport,
Cheshire in a spacious
ranch home with three
young adult children; Phillipa, Debbie and Chris.

On their property was a large barn and grazing pasture land to
accommodate their horses. The countryside near their home was gorgeous;
a great place for country walks which I availed myself of whenever possible. For a number of us, the Claphams added a delightful bright spot of
human connection to our stay in Northern England and the Manchester
region. They were a host family to several of us and aided the Deo Gloria
Trust ministry in a variety of ways. David was a respected businessman and
community leader.

A Recording Venture

A number of us were writing new music which led to a musical camaraderie
between part of the The Mighty Flyers band, Phillipa Clapham (an accomplished pianist) and a handful of the musicians and singers from *Lonesome
Stone*. The Claphams opened their home for our rehearsals and fed us well.
We could see it was fun for David and Barbara to have their home bulging
with young musicians and creating new tunes with their daughter involved.

After a number of rehearsals we were off to a Manchester Recording Studio. The supportive teamwork was a breath of fresh air for me as the
group helped me lay down tracks for a number of songs that would later be
remixed at the famous Strawberry Studios.

This and other joint endeavors with The Mighty Flyers and the

Clapham family were musically and spiritually encouraging. Those who helped with these recording sessions were: Nick Stone-lead guitar, Evan Martin-hand drums, Nick Brotherwood-set drums (from The Mighty Flyers band), Phillipa Clapham-keyboards, Mike Damrow-bass, Ethel Krauss flute, Margaret Stiveson, Mary Damrow and Caroline Green-background vocals.

A Call to Follow-up

Toward the end of the booking of LS at the Forum Theatre, I felt less inclined to continue with the LS Production and more interested in the follow-up of new believers from the Wythenshawe area. Being a part of LS was exciting, and I appreciated this unusual opportunity, but something was happening spiritually in my inner world during prayer. This prompted careful listening to the Holy Spirit, knowing how important His guidance was.

Although our LS team had a good rapport with a number of area churches, there were none in close proximity to where the majority of recently converted adults and teens lived. It would have been ideal to find a local church where they would be accepted and assimilated, but we couldn't find one. Continuing to search for a local church I asked some of the Wythenshawe teens about the local Catholic Church. They said they'd visited but it was not a fit. This didn't surprise me. These were tougher kids, unpolished and probably couldn't sit through a mass without fidgeting or wanting to run out the back door!

The Wythenshawe projects in the early 1970s were known for alcoholism, drugs, gambling, crime, poverty, illiteracy and broken families. Some teens ran in packs, many without adequate home or educational support, regular meals or parental direction. Contributing to the above, the lack of parks and leisure facilities for teens, adults and families, or adequate nearby shopping was a glaring indictment on national and local government officials. Greater Manchester would eventually be forced to address these needs. In the present, Wythenshawe was considered a depressed area, part of 'Broken Britain' lacking in community spirit and pride.

This sounded like the kind of place and people God would be interested in visiting; an environment where the light of Jesus Christ could

make a difference and be appreciated! Ironically, the new Forum Theatre
in Wythenshawe was the venue where *Lonesome Stone* had been given a
month long run. Building the Forum Theatre was the city's attempt to bring
entertainment to this needy area as a first step of revitalization. What would
follow could be a long way off with other Manchester districts in the throes
of demolition and reconstruction.

With the need for follow-up ministry to the Wythenshawe group still
unresolved, I mentioned it to two couples from the Mighty Flyers, Nick
and Glennys Stone and Martin & Julia Evans. They lived side by side in a
duplex in Manchester and they agreed to pray about helping the Wythenshawe group.

Pondering this, I called Jim P. for his take on the possibly of my
leaving LS and staying on in Manchester to conduct follow-up ministry. As
Lonesome Stone was near and dear to his heart I wasn't sure what he'd
think. His response was supportive of me listening to the voice of the Holy
Spirit in this matter and he thought it was important to provide disciple-
ship for those who had responded in Wythenshawe. I checked in with Mr.
Frampton and his response was almost identical. This counsel was helpful.
I continued praying.

The next time I saw the Stone and Evans families, they said they
were up for providing Bible studies for the Wythenshawe group and I told
them I felt the same. Though being a part of *Lonesome Stone* was an
amazing lifetime experience, I was completely OK with transitioning out of
the show. Most decisions like this take time to be confident about, but not
so in this instance. Deciding in the affirmative to stay on in Manchester, I
called Jim to let him know.

Two Stones—The Passing of the Baton

Jim went to work immediately on securing my replacement. The plan
arrived at was agreeable to all and made for a seamless transition. The decision was for Rich Haas who played Milwaukee Rich in LS, to take on the
songs and dialogue and become the new *Stone* with an expanded role. Rich
was a gifted singer and musician and we all sensed this was a perfect match!
In addition, Rich had a heart for serving and evangelism and he excelled in

| Rich Haas | Two Stone's in Plymouth, England | D.E. Hoyt |

these new responsibilities, doing an awesome job!

The Old Rectory – Stockport

With my decision to stay on in Manchester solidified, I contacted David Clapham and presented the need for a location to conduct follow-up. A fortnight (two weeks) later, David Clapham called to say we could use an old rectory in the Stockport area. It was on the docket for demolition in 12-36 months, but in the meantime it was ours to use if we wanted it.

This was exciting! When I secured a ride to see the property, I was a bit shocked. Everything around the old rectory had been demolished. It was a strange sight on the horizon. There it stood—a lonely reminder from the past that once was surrounded by a thriving commu-

Outskirts of Manchester

nity of homes, churches, schools and shops. The entire neighborhood had become redundant as they say in England and had been torn down. All that remained was the old rectory. I wondered why they left its demolition till

last. As with many areas in Greater Manchester, old structures and neighborhoods were making way for the new, with better infrastructure, insula-
tion, more efficient use of space and more economical utilities.

When I passed the news of us obtaining the use of an old rectory
to the two families from the Mighty Flyers they were excited. Sight unseen
they thought the availability of the rectory for 12-36 months, rent free, was
an answer to prayer and they thanked God. With rectory keys in hand we
took a drive out to look the place over on the inside.

A quarter mile or so around the rectory in all directions the land
had been cleared to the ground. Dust and soot from the expansive demolition and a prolonged vacancy left the rectory in need of an extensive
deep-cleaning. Old coal soot was everywhere—greasy and not easy to come
off. We bought the best cleaners available and went to work with the help
of teens from Wythenshawe. It was messy work, but amusing, as we looked
like chimney sweeps at the end of each day.

The old building had a spacious kitchen and fairly large downstairs
meeting room. Cleaning the old stove and getting the electrics and gas
turned on was a top priority. Once the utilities were on and the cleaning
complete, we could move in. I was amazed the utilities still worked! Fortunately the power company had left the streets gas mains in place and a
line of telephone poles was still standing. In a timely manner the rectory
brightened with TLC and the addition of donated furniture.

What will the future hold for the old Stockport Rectory? Will anyone
want to come to such an isolated, dreary looking structure? It didn't take
long to find out. From cleaning, to move in day, to our first Bible Study
at the Rectory, the teens from the Wythenshawe projects let us know they
liked the old rectory. They thought it was cool! Others that came along to
meetings, to donate things or have tea, felt the same. Another obvious reason was right in front of our noses, "You couldn't get lost finding the only
structure that was standing for a quarter mile in every direction!"

Unleashing of Miracles in Greater Manchester

In short order, new believers were aglow with the presence of Christ, letting their joy and thanks spill out to family, friends, neighbors and anyone
who would listen. By believing in Jesus Christ, there was an unleashing of

the supernatural, otherworldly stuff we call miracles. There was deliverance from hardness, stubbornness, fear, hatred, bitterness, confusion and bondage vices. Those who experienced these changes and those around them who witnessed these transformations were in awe. This wasn't some magic trick, or human charade! What had, and was, occurring was consistent with centuries of divine interventions in human hearts since Jesus Christ was raised by God the Father from the dead. Spiritual rebirth and regeneration was taking place (Romans 10:13).

People queried, "Is God behind these life changes? Does He still

do this kind of stuff?" This sparked interest among skeptics and curiosity seekers. "Let's go down and check it out and have some fun scoffing!" Sometimes this backfired. A scoffer might wander too close to the presence of Jesus Christ. When this occurred, their conscience was activated by the Almighty, their spiritual eyes opened, and instantly they knew the truth for themselves; God is not dead! Jesus is alive!

Though we were relatively small in number, our impact in Manchester was felt. The newspapers were for the most part supportive and our theatre production reviews were affirming. We were on radio regularly and our bus could be seen on the streets during busy traffic times.

For those who came to faith in Christ, this outreach brought a new beginning, rippling out to families who had no compass of faith, many of whom had never darkened the doors of a church. Many of the hundreds of mid to late teens who attended *Lonesome Stone* would infuse their church youth groups, their schools, and part-time jobs with a spiritual spark of new life! New music would be written and voices that had never sung praises to God would do so. Faith, love and boldness to tell others about Jesus Christ as the Savior of the world would now guide these new Christians.

The *Lonesome Stone* team as a whole had occupied territory in Manchester for close to a month. Inherent in any traveling outreach ministry, it was time to move on. Those of us who stayed behind did so to retain the territory gained, to water and nurture spiritual seeds that were sprouting. To those without a church home, we became their spiritual family. We picked up younger teens and others with no means of transportation and met for Bible Studies, prayer, recreation, breaking bread and outreach. This was God's doing and we praised Him!

Servant Leaders at the Rectory

In answer to prayer Martin (Curly) and Julia Evans and Nick and Glennys Stone agreed to be the first to occupy the redundant old rectory with myself. The Evans and the Stones were well suited to this work. They were willing and excited to take on the follow-up ministry with the teens from Wythenshawe Housing Projects, Stockport and the surrounding Manchester area. Both couples had street smarts, compassion, humor and strong music gifts making them a perfect match for those they would minister to. The Wythenshawe Housing District was the largest in England at the time, a melting pot, teeming with need.

God's Faithful Care

God was the faithful provider when it came to the Rectory. Utility bills were paid by Deo Gloria Trust and local supporters. The day-to-day living expenses, supplies and acquiring food was a faith venture. Food and supplies came mostly from unexpected sources when they were needed most.

Living at the Rectory and other Jesus People houses reminded me of George Mueller of Bristol, England. Mueller's biography outlined his habit of praying in faith privately for specific needs to provide for a sizable group of orphans he cared for. The faithfulness of God to honor and answer these prayers was an ongoing series of one miracle after another. We could say "Amen" to what Mr. Mueller experienced! On occasion some team members had a regular income, but not enough to sustain the entire ministry. God could always be counted on to make up the difference when we prayed in faith and believed.

Cutting the Chill

Staying warm in England as a Southern Californian with less than optimal blood circulation was challenging and embarrassing. Under each of the chimneys in the rectory was a tiny fireplace for modest coal burning when winter temperatures dropped. I used paraffin and clean coal, but never figured out how to keep the fire burning for more than a few hours. Old coal, though dirty, burned better and longer, but was now outlawed for a variety of health and pollution reasons.

The rectory had two small wall mounted gas furnaces in the kitchen and bath tub area. There were no showers or central heat. I'd grown accustomed to taking baths and was getting better at not leaving soap in my hair. On freezing nights, I'd put on a pot of tea, turn on the other burners for a few minutes to cut the chill and hoped neither of the two couples at the rectory caught me in the act! Some Brits drink a nip of sherry to warm the belly, which works nicely prior to heading off to bed. When there was no sherry to be found, I used the stove burners!

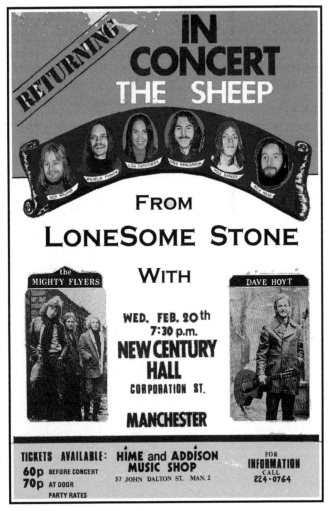

Martin (Curly) and Nick were humorous type blokes, with lots of patience. Julia and Glen-

nys provided a softer presence of grace, warmth, hospitality, the spice of
humor as well, and the gals could cook! All four were dedicated to growing
in their faith. The arrangement of these two couples living at the rectory
and conducting ministry was perfect!

Friendship with The Mighty Flyers band members grew as did our
continued outreach and joint endeavors. The Flyers adopted a handful of
us from the Jesus Family and we them. With the Flyers based mostly in
Manchester, we fanned the flames of energy and enthusiasm that *Lonesome Stone* had birthed. We even managed to get The Sheep back to Manchester from *Lonesome Stone* for a rare gig during a down-time from their
touring. The locals loved having them back in town!

The Mighty Flyers were a hard working UK band. David Reese, band
manager and lead singer was committed to musical excellence, which made
for focused rehearsals, giving ample time for newer tunes to be integrated
before introducing them in concert. England's history of successful bands
and musical heritage infused upcoming bands with the idea that in order to
be successful, short-cuts were out! Hard work and tight musicianship was
a requirement.

On the Lighter Side

Most Brits we came to know had a fun and wacky sense of humor. It spilled
out amidst work, tea
breaks and everyday
life. They also gave
themselves permission
without any guilt to go
on outings, play and go
on holiday.

It was rare for
the Jesus Family to
plan recreation as there
always seemed so much
to do, but The Mighty
Flyers were keen on
not letting any oppor-

ENGLAND 1973   "Manchester Rugby Squad"

tunity slip by! The Flyers and some of the Jesus Family gathered in a park in Manchester for a friendly game of rugby. As you'll notice, someone was always messing about.

Don't ask me where we managed to find a camera, but someone put one in my hand. Just getting the group in this semblance of order was a feat and it's turned out to be one of my favorite blurry photos from the day. They were a ruddy lot. Fitter for rugby, than a day at the pub!

Working Together

Jesus People in England were drawn by the Holy Spirit to work together for the purpose of lifting up Jesus Christ to the glory of the Father. With just 7% of England's population claiming any Christian spiritual affiliation, the work was enormous. The fields were white for harvest and the laborers were few (Luke 10:2). At the time there was only a handful of UK Christian bands out and about playing.

The Flyers represented the best of what would come in the days

ahead. They were more than willing to work together with other ministries, churches, or para-church ministries like the Jesus Family and Deo Gloria Trust, for the greater cause of reaching their Motherland with the Gospel of Christ.

David Reese, Nick Stone, Nick Brotherwood comprised the Flyers with Martin Evans helping with hand drums when called upon. The Flyers had no problem with not being top-billing for a concert and exemplified the role of putting others before themselves. They genuinely enjoyed the Jesus Family, The Sheep, and the *Lonesome Stone* theatre team.

THE MIGHTY FLYERS

DAVID REESE, NICK STONE,
NICK BROTHERWOOD

When *Lonesome Stone* moved on, The Mighty Flyers continued to maintain relationships with area pastors so as to be able to visit and encourage those who'd received Christ.

Area pastors who'd supported *Lonesome Stone* and *Mighty Flyers* concerts brought as many as they could from their churches. Many of these pastors were keen on outreach and had taken advantage of the momentum surrounding our citywide outreach, reaping the benefits. Participating together allowed the Holy Spirit room to work, resulting in an infusion of fresh energy, new life and a swelling in church attendance. This gave way to terrific opportunities for discipleship and ongoing outreach through creative endeavors they would come up with on their own; in harmony with their vision, location and member gifting. Infinite possibilities lie ahead! As the Scriptures say,

> No eye has ever seen, no ear has ever heard, nor has the human heart ever been capable of imagining, all the things God has prepared for those who love Him."
> Corinthians 2:9-10; Isaiah 64:4 NIV®

In the days ahead Mike Damrow, and Ben & Roslyn Day would assist the Mighty Flyers at the Rectory and other Christian Houses they would open.

Teamwork that Glorifies God
Pastor John & Kath Yates

Pastor John Yates and spouse Kath led their church in embracing continuing outreach in Manchester. A number from their church family had attended *Lonesome Stone* and Mighty Flyers concerts on a number of occasions. This interaction with Jesus People grew into a bond of friendship. Members from John and Kath's church family and their friends who'd received Christ or

taken a step of making a confession of faith, were thankful and appreciative for our ministry.

The Yates' church was located near greater Manchester in Dunkinfield, Cheshire. As the Mighty Flyers modeled the best among a handful of British Christian bands, the Yates did so as a church family through their relational openness with us.

Pastors can be notoriously controlling and overly protective of their congregation limiting and intentionally blocking any cross-pollination. Doing so hinders the body of Christ from functioning at its best through non-competitive cooperation and joint endeavors that glorify God.

I recall Pastor John inviting David Reese and I to participate in the baptism of young teens from his congregation including one of his daughters Alison, to be held at their home church in Dunkinfield. This request said volumes regarding John's open-heartedness and appreciation of our ministry contributions.

Being there was a lifetime memory, one David Reese and I would cherish. In outreach ministry, it isn't always possible to be brought into the inner circle of what happens after a concert or outreach event is over. Being present allowed us to witness the new life God had birthed by His Spirit, and the sincere commitment these teens had made to place their lives into God's hands and begin a new life in Jesus Christ.

The baptism would include around twelve new believers comprised of young ladies and men from the church family, or friends of the teens who'd recently received Christ at one of our outreach events. Pastor John took another step of maturity by asking David Reese and I to be in the baptismal with him, alternating in lead roles. Few pastors are secure enough to honor the contributing ministry of others in a public way.

Being actively involved was a positive witness to each teen of how the body of Christ is designed to work. A number of the teens said they hoped we'd be present. The result was, we were able to rejoice with those being baptized, the church family and some non-Christian parents who'd gathered. This was a spiritually healthy event.

Thankfully, someone was positioned behind a camera and took these pictures. Amazingly, I'm still in contact with several who were baptized in these photos. God is good, all the time! All the time, God is good!

The apostle Paul encouraged this type of teamwork.

> I planted, another waters, and God makes things grow. It's God who brings the increase. Neither is he who plants, or he who waters working alone. God is present, the One responsible for the growth. He who plants and the one who waters are working in harmony with God, who rewards each one according to their work.   I Corinthians 3:6-8 NIV®

Meanwhile at the Old Rectory

Spiritual life was blowing through and permeating every inch of this old building. What had been barren and quiet was alive with activity. Visitors and regulars were encountering acceptance, love, spiritual dialogue, truth and placing their trust in God's ability to be the rock of stability that had been missing.

Martin and Julie Evans and Nick and Glenna Stone were spiritual naturals for this work, full of grace and truth. Most who visited came with questions and needs. This prompted both couples to diligently search the Scriptures to honorably teach, lead and nurture. It was like watching the blossoming of a tree and witnessing the buds spring forth when these couples connected with those who came along for studies and activities.

Faltering

In the midst of blessings at the rectory, I began to experience anxiety and depression. Things weren't right in my inner world. The adrenalin rush surrounding being a part of the Jesus Family, *Lonesome Stone* and working with the Mighty Flyers, had held back emotional pain that was lying under the surface.

News came via Mr. Frampton stating the COG had taken a new moral nose dive into a number of evil practices. This compromised any and all integrity COG members may have been able to retain up to this point. From what I learned, all members from the youngest to the top leaders were being forced to set aside their conscience and the Bible in order to obey David Berg's new immoral doctrines and there were plenty of them.

Busyness had kept me occupied up to this point, but with this news, feelings of helplessness and irritability was back with a fury. My spouse's support of the COG and contempt toward me was a hard bullet to swallow. This turned over and over in my mind. How would I ever be able to wrench her and the children out of something so sinister, secretive and manipulative and now morally bankrupt, when she'd dug in her heels with the group and taken a stand against me? While mulling this over, a convergence of self-condemnation thoughts arose over my mistakes and bad choices that affected the whole of the Atlanta ministry.

How could I have been so stupid to have taken a solo trip to Thurber, Texas to visit the COG? And why would I invite them to Atlanta without fully vetting this group with a number of unbiased reliable sources? Ruminating over these and other discouraging scenarios wasn't good, but I couldn't stop the tapes from replaying! The repercussions were mental and emotional anguish and feelings of anger.

It surfaced in a Bible study, when suddenly out of the blue I became irritable and impatient with some of new Christian teens at the rectory, chewing them out for messing about. Wow! I could see the shock on their faces at my uncharacteristic behavior. Thankfully, no permanent damage was done, but all of those present felt awkward.

Martin and Julia gently confronted me after the study and I became defensive. I knew I'd blown it, but was still wound-up and rebuked Martin. I apologized later, but it was too late. A relational breach had occurred. It was not easy to overlook my behavior and I understood completely.

The last thing I wanted to do was let my pain and frustrations affect the ministry or the Wythenshawe teens adversely but I couldn't guarantee it wouldn't happen again. With this possibility, I realized I was no longer an asset at the rectory which sealed the decision to return to London and regroup.

Bouts of Depression

Returning to London wasn't much help. I was still in a funk. Reflecting on my last contact with my spouse and her defiant loyalty to the COG was disconcerting. Even if I knew where she was, it would most likely be impossible to extract her from the cult's grip. From what I'd heard the Children of God cult had become more evasive, closing up shop when exposed and relocating in another city or country. I resigned myself to prayer, believing somehow, someway my family and friends would eventually be free from this group's deceptive influence.

My emotional world was all over the place. Mood changes, depression and loneliness came and went. Sometimes I would wander into a pub for a lager and darts, or go for a long walk or to "the city" by train to catch a movie. I was legally married, in reality separated, but felt divorced. I was attracted to several women but couldn't consider anything serious.

In my heart I never stopped believing in trusting in God, but seemed thrown back to teenage days of being in between, not knowing what to do next. I was not without sin, drifting into confused days of pain and escape. Healing was very slow. In the mix were some good deeds, loyalty to God and an appreciation for His true family. I was confident God loved me, but deep down I felt useless and backslidden.

A Doctor Who Asked the Right Questions

Settling into my former one-room sleeping quarters in our ministry office building in London was less than optimal. My room only had a tiny door window to the outside and the entire building was damp and depressing. Breaking out in a hives-type rash from head to foot and feeling miserable pushed me to see a doctor.

This was the first time of seeking medical help since arriving in England. The doctor asked a lot of questions in a holistic fashion, which included my emotional world and things that had happened in the not too distant past. After listening carefully he concluded my body rash was probably caused by nerves and stress. He was sad to hear I'd lost my family and friends into a cult and thought I needed to consider making a significant change. He prescribed an ointment for the rash, but emphasized I needed to take better care of myself and give myself permission to do so. His input was appreciated.

For starters, I rented an upstairs flat near the crest of Crystal Palace with three large windows allowing plenty of natural light. This simple move lifted my spirit. Renting by the week was doable with the small Deo Gloria stipend I was receiving.

The thought of making a life change was interesting to ponder. Just thinking about possibly returning to the USA gave a resurgence of something to look forward to. Up to now, I hadn't thought much about what might be on the horizon with my family in the COG somewhere in Europe.

News of My Family

When it was needed most, I received a letter from my spouse's parents with pictures of our two girls and son. They had been to Denmark to visit other family members and had made arrangements with the COG to see their daughter and grandchildren. The important news they wanted to pass on to me was their daughter and grandchildren all looked healthy.

They also had an entirely new appreciation and understanding of the controlling tactics of the COG. They confirmed the group's secrecy and manipulation of everything to do with those in the group. These ploys had registered a big negative and they were no longer sympathetic toward the COG after this latest interaction with them, but very concerned about their daughter's involvement in this group.

In their letter they mentioned the runaround and deceptive maneuvers the COG had employed in making a private visit with their daughter and grandchildren almost impossible. Because my spouse's parents insisted, they overcame this obstacle through days of phone negotiations with COG leaders by agreeing to their demands. From what I gathered they had to pay for all expenses for the children to be brought into the country and miscellaneous other expenses. And the visit was under strict guidelines and conditions stipulated by the COG. These tactics were typical of the COG's manipulation of almost everything to do with their members. It was a rare occurrence for biological parents to be allowed to see their children. When the COG thought an inheritance might be forthcoming or something else significant to further their cause, they made exceptions.

From what my spouse's parents had gathered, their daughter and their grandchildren were brought in for the visit from unspecified secret locations. During the visit, their daughter said the children were living in a COG kibbutz in France and she was living on the outskirts of Copenhagen, Denmark. She'd volunteered this information, but it was still vague.

I was grateful for any news and the pictures! Their fate however of being trapped in the COG was a troubling reality.

A Common Bond

When I felt stronger emotionally, I'd visit the Jesus Family offices or the Beulah Hill house and reconnect with friends. What kept me away, was embarrassment about how *out-of-It* and depressed I felt. At the time I had no conception of how a significant life trauma can affect our stability for a period of time. I would later learn I qualified as a cult victim casualty with a hefty dose of PTS.

Reconnecting with the Jesus Family team in Upper Norwood and other friends was good for my soul. It's a gift to have those who know us on a deeper level and care about how we are doing. I was fortunate to have some of my best friends still living in the London area and I forced myself out of my cocoon to see them. They were Kenneth & Pauline Frampton, Chris Frampton, Clive & Gwyneth Frampton, and close Jesus Family friends based in London. Among this group was, Danny & Margaret

Keating, Gerd & Karin Bienge, Arlene Czekalski, Margie Pinnow, Jim & Sue Palosaari, Ben Day and Rosalind Palmer (soon to be married). Over the next several months I spent time with them in various settings and was encouraged by their friendship (2 Corinthians 1:3-7).

Our bond was, we were Christ-followers, imperfect, each struggling with our own issues while simultaneously engaged in spiritual warfare against the forces of darkness.

Amidst these battles, characteristics of compassion, mercy and grace grew stronger. The Greek word 'Koinonia' describes a type of Christian friendship I was receiving and am still deeply appreciative for. There are no guarantees we will experience Koinonia relationships, but it is possible.

A definition of **Koinonia** is: An honest, loyal, dependable friendship, centered in Christ. A safe confidential setting where we can bear our soul, confess our sins, share personal struggles and be completely honest without fear of being condemned, or damaging a valuable and trusted relationship.

A heart attitude of mutual humility is essential, usually born out of a clear understanding; without God's grace and mercy, no one can stand. We are all sinners, imperfect! Koinonia runs deep when it comes to compassion, mercy, forgiveness and understanding, but is balanced by pointing the one experiencing crisis to God, who is our greatest resource in times of trouble! Koinonia avoids condoning poor choices and bad behavior, or enabling the one in crisis by bailing them out of the consequences for habitual destructive practices. In discussion, words of truth and the Scriptures are honored as our guide for Christian behavior and practice.

I see this friendship existing without ulterior motives to control or use one another. It thrives when we respect each other **in-Christ** and do everything possible to aid each other in reaching our full potential. This bond is characterized by unconditional acceptance, practical assistance, on-going intercession in prayer and sacrificial service. It also includes grace-filled correction when needed, transformative listening and a willingness to think of our friend's needs as we would our own. *This type of friendship is an invaluable treasure to, respect and maintain— a gift which adds value and meaning to our entire life!*

Contrast this with a self-righteous individual who is aghast and cringes when a Christian friend takes a tumble, turning their back on them. This hurts and can easily destroy the relationship for good. The one who does this to a friend in trouble will sooner or later end up regretting having done so. This will occur when the table is turned and they have a severe crisis that leaves their world upside down.

Koinonia friends are not shocked by tragedy, failure or weaknesses in brothers or sisters in the faith. Life happens and the unexpected strikes the just and the unjust. We cannot and shouldn't attempt to draw firm conclusions about why individuals experience catastrophic events. It could be the accumulation of bad choices, the result of a spiritual attack, dead branches being cut off by the Almighty, or any number of natural, physical, or circumstantial tragedies that are common to everyone.

We may think we know why someone suffers, but our finite intellect doesn't conclusively understand it all. What we do know, is almost all of us will experience some type of tragedy and pain in this life. No one is exempt!

Doctor Check-Up

I continued checking in with the British doctor I was assigned and felt good about it and my rash began to subside. I was taking better care of myself, but was not my usual self confidence-wise. Wired to be a doer, it's strange when life circumstances force us into a pause mode.

Greenbelt Infrastructure

Sensing this, Jim P. gave me an assignment of meeting with James Holloway down in Suffolk County to view the proposed venue site for a Christian music festival. Jim asked me to brainstorm with James on behalf of the Jesus Family and Deo Gloria Trust on the myriad of practical details surrounding conducting a multi-day outdoor music celebration and teaching event.

Ideas had intersected with the practical realities of such a large undertaking. The Greenbelt of Suffolk County was decided on because of overall better weather, summer sunshine and the beautiful scenic setting. In our favor, James was well established in the community as a farmer, home owner, Christian musician and band member.

I remember the early morning train ride which turned into several hours each way with a number of connecting stops. James met me at the train station and carted me off to the purposed venue site for the festival.

First on our agenda was deciding on where the overhead power lines would be run above a relatively busy country road. The desired service location for the venue was hammered out, but would need to be confirmed and sorted out with the electric power company so new lines could be run and service turned on for the event.

Other logistics were discussed: What permits would be needed. What health and safety issues needed to be addressed and solved? Who would provide first aid? What types of food and vendors would service the event? How would running water, wash-up areas and showers be set-up? Who would provide rubbish removal and portable sanitation toilets? Our list grew. Action and delegation was incorporated into our discussion and note taking.

Many details needed to fall into place before the festival could become a reality. Representing Jim and Deo Gloria, this initial on-site meeting was a good beginning. Deo Gloria Trust had already made a commitment to help foot the bill and aid James Holloway and the other festival organizers in whatever way needed.

Mr. Frampton and Deo Gloria could be counted on to handle a variety of details which always amazed me. James and Jim were also men of action

DEO GLORIA PRODUCTIONS present:

GREENBELT

OPEN AIR MUSIC FESTIVAL + CAMPING

August Bank Holiday Weekend 23-26

1974

PARCHMENT·SHEEP with the Cast of LONESOME STONE
MALCOLM & ALWYN
ALEKSANDER JOHN
ALL THINGS NEW
GARTH HEWITT·KEVIN GOULD
AFTER THE FIRE
REGENERATION·JOHN & BRIAN·11:59·REALITY FOLK·NARNIA
MILLSTONE GRIT·BILLY MASON & FRIENDS·STEVE SCOTT
BRIGHT WINTER·MAL GROSCH·MIGHTY FLYERS·ASLAN
FATHER BROWN·LIVING STONES·STEVE TURNER
GENESIS RECONSTRUCTION·REVELATION and more....

On a beautiful farm in Charsfield, Suffolk

BIBLE TEACHING & WORKSHOPS

when it came to being movers and shakers. This threesome were the original visionaries behind Greenbelt. Each had plenty of contacts throughout England to get the word out and invite bands and speakers for this new music festival, outreach and discipling event. With a breadth of things to do they quickly brought in others to help manage the details.

What started back then, grew into the largest and longest running Christian music festival in the world, called *The Greenbelt Music Festival.* The Sheep and a growing number of Christian British Bands would play at the first festival with hundreds following them from many countries in the years ahead. God was most definitely at work!

Lonesome Stone continued touring with enthusiasm and dependence on the Holy Spirit to release new life in Jesus Christ wherever it went. The Jesus Family in London and its ministry properties continued to provide a home-base for cast and crew members needing respite.

On a regular basis the Jesus Family team headquarters in London and Greater Manchester's Jesus Family houses and Rectory House in Stockport focused on local outreach and follow up care. They offered Bible studies and a place for visitors to come along, ask questions and become actively involved in a life of faith.

Author's Note: Coming up in the next chapter are three eye witness accounts from this time-period by Trevor Allen and Ben & Rosalind Day.

21

Eyewitness Accounts
Trevor Allen & Ben & Rosalind Day

Trevor Allen of the UK
The Jesus Family England & Lonesome Stone

It was January 1973, at age 25 when I put things on pause and reflected on my spiritual trek. The journey had begun six years earlier with psychedelic drugs, systems of meditation, dropping out to travel to India and then to live in the wilds of Wales. Now, back in South London I had no idea this trek was nearing a climax. At the time, I thought I was in the city to gather money to travel to Africa, but wasn't sure why, or what I may find in this distant land.

A part of me thought I'd figured life out with a hotchpotch mixture of religious and philosophical beliefs. At the time, I had concluded there was some impersonal force behind everything, without absolutes and everything was relative. Still, in the deeper recesses of my being there was some elusive void to fill.

During this season of reflection I was arrested by a random thought that shook my confidence, **"What good was I, and would the world be any better, or worse off without me?"** Being honest, bad had more to do with me than good. This realization sent me into a mental spin exacerbated by recent stressful circumstances I'd experienced. I hadn't figured in "human purpose, or good and bad" which now contradicted my relativistic thinking.

These overlooked integral parts of human existence and any truths embedded in them had previously been missing in my calculations. For about a week I was at an all time low, fearful, anxious and lost in a spiritual state of emptiness. Mercifully, a measure of peace returned to me, but my preconceived notions about life had been dashed; I saw them for what they were, my haughty ideas limited in scope.

I was humbled and knew a greater truth outside of my brain existed but had no idea what it was. My peace was incomplete.

Unexpected Encounter

One afternoon, entering the flat I shared with friends, I found a hippie looking publication lying on a table, which I casually began browsing. I was surprised that it was talking about Jesus. What got my attention was the name, Jesus. I was reminded of different occasions when this name had some sort of impact on me; when reading, or somebody had spoken about him, or experiences which brought his name to the surface, all of which I had rejected.

Then, a stream of these occurrences began running through my mind and memory with my responses of rejection. It was sobering to be reminded of my negative and unreceptive attitude and heart to the name of Jesus.

While thinking about this, I was suddenly aware of a presence in the room, a stilling of things, something holy and foreign to my experience up till now. I then heard these words as an inaudible impression, *"I have tried to show you so many times that I love you, why are you running from me?"* I intuitively knew Jesus Christ was speaking to me.

I fell to my knees confessing I was sorry and that I wanted Him in my life. As I said this, I was showered with a sense of peace and love. I knew I was being changed in some mysterious way and without understanding much, **I was sure Jesus had died for me and was present; very much alive!**

Providentially Spared

God can use any means he wants to get through to people. In this case he used a paper produced by a group who were actually a cult. I went searching for them in Bromley, as I had a post office box number from this location but no other contact details. I looked high and low but found no trace of them.

Later, I realized I'd walked within yards of their door and then turned around; such is the grace of God that spared me from getting caught up in something evil. Instead I walked into a Christian bookshop asking for directions to find them. After a long conversation with the store clerk, I was made aware of the dubious nature of the Children of God. When I scanned the pamphlet again I could see the questionable content, even as a new Christian.

The storekeeper then redirected me to a group of Christians he knew of who could help me and allowed me to use the shop phone to contact them. A friendly American voice at the other end invited me to come over and meet up at their ministry house a few miles away in Crystal Palace. Within an hour I was there sobbing my story out to sympathetic ears.

This group was The Jesus Family, a commune of Jesus people with origins in Milwaukee, Wisconsin, USA. They had traveled through Europe with new members joining along the way and were now based in a large house on Beulah Hill, Upper Norwood.

Henry Huang, one of the leaders sat me down and explained how I could stay with them for a few days and see if we were mutually suited. I thought, "What's he talking about, I'm not going anywhere, I've come home", but just agreed.

Ironically, during the first day or so I had a relapse in my commitment and felt some kind of dark oppression come over me. It caused me to simply want to give up. Feeling distressed, I told Dave Hoyt, another JP leader, I was going to quit. After a long, virulent talk from him, which didn't convince me but had me dumbstruck, he simply said, "Let's pray." He and Dennis Knight laid hands on me and Dave prayed in tongues. As he did so I felt something dark and heavy literally lift from me and in its place something beautiful and fresh pour down and through my body as I was filled with the Holy Spirit. I felt as though I was walking on air and had to actually look down to see if my feet were on the ground.

Jesus Family Digs
56 Beulah Hill Rd.
Upper Norwood, SE London, UK

There were perhaps thirty of us, many from similar backgrounds to myself, a few married couples and children, but mostly young singles. The majority of our team were American but also Canadians and Europeans, Swedish, German and Dutch had been added and now Brits like myself. We were led by Jim Palosaari, a larger than life figure who wouldn't have looked out of place amongst Old Testament prophets.

I quickly became familiar with the ways of 56 Beulah Hill. Although there was not a strict pattern to the days, it quite often involved prayer meetings before communal breakfast, Bible studies, body meetings presided over by Jim, generally peanut butter and jelly sandwiches for lunch, street outreaches with our own Jesus newspapers, sometimes locally, sometimes into London's West End, practical chores and decorating, communal dinners and free time.

Sharing our faith in Jesus on the streets was an exciting experience, often resulting in deep conversations with people and sometimes with great joy when someone trusted in Jesus Christ to be their Savior.

Every Sunday afternoon we held a worship service which was often attended by people from the locality and was the forerunner of the "house church" that would be launched in the future. We also had contact with local churches and on occasion would visit their services and youth groups with the Jesus Family rock band 'The Sheep' playing. On one occasion we hired the larger Fairfield Halls in Croydon for a Sheep concert and the Gospel of Christ was preached by Jim.

Faith, Though Invisible Is Real

Faith in God was key to our ministry's survival. At one pre-breakfast prayer meeting we were informed that our finances were zilch and we had better pray if we wanted breakfast. Before our time of prayer had finished one team member came into the room saying, we should thank the Lord for answered prayer! "Someone has just left a large box of food on our doorstep!" In other instances, faith expressed may not yield an immediate answer. We pray in faith, hope, trust and ask God for His will to be done.

On another occasion, Jim took us on a "faith trip." There were about ten of us who were included in this outing, packed into a mini-bus. We headed out without finances to see where God would take us and what He would do through us. I reckon Jim had some plans arranged as we stayed at various places along the way without charge and had opportunity to share our faith (witness) and sell newspapers for a pittance. We ended up in Edinburgh, Scotland. While there and walking along Prince's Street I happened to stop a couple to witness. It turned out to be Jim's brother and wife who just happened to be visiting Scotland. They invited us all to come and stay overnight at their apartment. This seeming coincidence was orchestrated by the Lord and I knew it! My faith in God was again strengthened, but there is more to faith than arranging a divine appointment. I was learning to place what faith I'd been given in God's plan.

Through the Jesus Family outreach and events to be recounted next, many young people were drawn to the group and numbers swelled. It was probably breaking accommodation laws but we were crowded into rooms filled with bunk-beds, one against another. It was far from ideal but the sense of God's grace on our lives was such that made the less than ideal circumstances insignificant. Everyone got on and rejoiced in their new lives! Eventually, we were able to find additional housing and our numbers were thinned down in each residence.

An Adventure into Theatre

One momentous day Jim called a body meeting in which he informed a stunned group that we were going to create and perform an evangelistic, multi-media rock musical and furthermore that we would open at the renowned Rainbow Theatre, North London within a couple of month's time. This seemed like madness! Apart from Jim, who had a background in theatre the only other member who did was Caroline Green, who was in Hair.

In short order, a core of professional staff were hired; a director, a choreographer and a couple of lighting consultants. The cost of this was being borne by Mr. Kenneth Frampton, a Christian businessman who was the benefactor supporting the Jesus Family's outreach ministry in the UK.

Rehearsals began in an old empty theatre in Brixton about five miles down the road. I would drive our painted double-decker bus with the budding cast on board every morning and back again in the evening during the unusually warm early summer months. The weather was irrelevant as we were shut in to a dark auditorium all day and saw very little of the sunshine. Slowly and painfully it came together. I say slowly, but actually it was amazing how from a few ideas the musical was formed in a couple of months and found a name; *Lonesome Stone*.

It told the story of a young man seeking for meaning to his life, leaving a provincial smaller town and heading for San Francisco at the height of "flower power", only to find disillusionment. Amidst the chaos of dashed hope, his life was turned round along with the lives of many others when they encountered the reality of Jesus Christ. Some of the scenes portrayed in the production were actual experiences of members of the cast, or similar, conveying the real life emotions of being rescued out of darkness.

When we launched at the Rainbow Theatre, the show could have done with a bit more time to fine tune and polish things up, but everyone did their best. The reviews at the Rainbow were mixed and audiences small but it was the beginning of something special.

Lonesome Stone on Tour

From there the show headed for Manchester and the vast council estate of Wythenshawe. Here the response couldn't have been more different. Once word got around we played to a full house nearly every night for four weeks, attracting hundreds of young people, some returning again and again and many surrendering their lives to Jesus. It was a privilege even at the end of an exhausting day to minister to someone and lead them to Christ. Because of the overwhelming numbers becoming Christians it was felt that some should remain in Manchester to follow up. Dave Hoyt gave up his role in LS and united with two couples from the Mighty Flyers to establish a ministry in the Manchester area which locals could access for continued spiritual growth. This seemed good to all.

Meanwhile, *Lonesome Stone* rolled on down the road playing at Birmingham, Bradford, Sheffield, Stoke on Trent, Liverpool (twice), Edinburgh, Horsham,

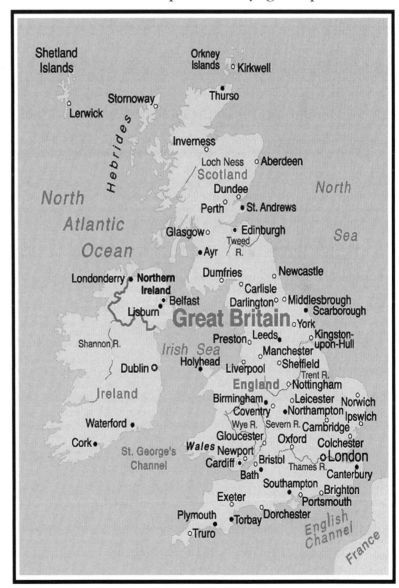

Cheltenham, the American Air Force base at Lakenheath, Suffolk plus those at Ramstein and Wiesbaden in Germany.

The anecdotes and experiences are too many to relate but I do remember speaking to two teenage school lads after one show and explaining the gospel briefly, using the Scriptures, and then asking if they wanted to commit their lives to Jesus. They both said yes and they followed me in a simple prayer for salvation. Neither showed any visible emotions. I advised them to get a Bible, begin reading and find a good church and we parted.

Sometime later, at one of the *Lonesome Stone* performances in a different city I met one of the two again after the show. Immediately I knew something deep had taken place. His whole countenance and manner had changed. I was talking to a born again Spirit filled believer, already showing signs of Christian maturity. It brought such joy to my heart and I thanked God that he had used me in part of the process.

There were short times in between the touring that we came back to base at Beulah Hill, well especially for me, driving back and forth with equipment and personnel. On one of these visits, I happened to be in the living room as Jim was talking to James Holloway and others. James was part of a Christian band in Suffolk whom we knew through another Suffolk band who had been incorporated into The Jesus Family called 'Capel House.' He also happened to be a farmer and the discussion was around putting on a Christian music festival, which James seemed up for, somewhere in the fields of Suffolk. "What are we going to call it?" Jim asked. As the conversation continued someone mentioned this general locale as being "greenbelt land" and immediately Jim said, "That's it, we'll call it The Greenbelt Music Festival."

The First Greenbelt & Beyond

In the summer of 1974 we camped in a Suffolk field, set up the stage and equipment and watched the people arrive. It had a cozy, pleasant and relaxed feel in the beautiful August weather and was enjoyed by all, with some 1,500 in attendance. We won't mention the infrastructure issues other to say they were very primitive!

Amazingly, Greenbelt has become an ongoing annual event which still happens to this day, although it has changed in content and venue a number of times. Its Christian roots remain and it attracts on average 20,000 campers and participants and many bands each year.

Lonesome Stone in the USA

The following month in September of 1974, the next phase of *Lonesome Stone* began. It was a return to the States for the original Milwaukee team and an exciting adventure for us Europeans. Landing in Toronto we soon made our way to our first stop, Toledo, Ohio, where I had the joy of leading a young man to Christ and with whom I'm still in contact. From late summer, through the fall and on into winter we traveled to Davenport, Iowa, Duluth, Minnesota, Sioux Falls, South Dakota, Kansas City, Missouri, and Lancaster, Pennsylvania. It was a punishing itinerary which had its unfortunate consequences. God had used LS with its intrinsic Gospel message to reach and save people at every destination venue, but the performance schedule, travel and pressures of non-stop activity had taken its toll.

Out of Character

People were tired, lacking motivation and frustrated. Relationships, including marriages suffered; there was a lack of pastoral care and a sense of unfairness. The fundamentals of prayer, Bible study and worship which had characterized The Jesus Family when I found it had virtually vanished.

I recall one instance in Kansas City when the temperatures had dropped and the first snow was falling. Some of us were surviving on a couple of sausages and some bread each day while others were using communal money to visit restaurants. This was typical of other problems that were uncharacteristic of us in the past. By the time Christmas rolled around and we ended up in Wisconsin, the original base from which the Jesus People Milwaukee had started, we were finished. *Lonesome Stone* had run its course and we knew it.

I'd seen it coming, yet dreaded this day. I knew the experience of being a part of LS among good friends, serving Christ through a theatrical outreach that impacted so many, was for a season in time; none the less it was bittersweet seeing this chapter close.

We all realized the reality of rejoining the secular world and finding work was inevitable and believed God would open the right doors. Thankfully, I was no longer floundering, seeking something intangible since Jesus had revealed himself to me.

I do admit, the thought of change and starting over on returning to the UK was scary, but all of us who'd been part of LS would be making the same transition back into the mainstream of society. By faith, we'd pray for one another as we stepped into the unknown asking for God's help in finding work and new places to live.

Extended Hospitality

For the time being the majority of the European contingent was housed with local Wisconsin families who showed such hospitality, generosity, care and patience towards us. We were welcomed into their homes at Christmas, stayed for the rest of the snowy winter and finally flew back to the UK in the spring.

Back in the UK

It was a blessed time of recuperation for which I will always be grateful. We went our separate ways and though I had not intended to make 56 Beulah Hill my home, when I visited the pull was too great and that's where I settled. The remnant that had remained was still being supported by Mr. Frampton and the little community was becoming a House Fellowship Church to the local community. Gradually, we weaned ourselves off the financial provision. I was one of the first to get a job, doing what I had been doing a lot of over the last two years; driving. Our attendance on Sundays grew and we became known as Beulah Hill Christian Fellowship.

BHCF became joined to a fledgling movement of churches, under the leadership of Terry Virgo, at the time known as Coastlands and later, New Frontiers International. I got back into artwork, which I had dropped years before, and began a career in graphics. I, and others, also moved out of the house to buy our own places but still met at Beulah Hill for worship and fellowship until the house needed to be sold.

Our temporary gathering location was squishing into the Bienge's flat for our meetings. Gerhard was from Germany and it was because of his German roots that I met my lovely wife Karin, who came to visit from

Stuttgart and we were married in 1980.

This same year we found a redundant looking church building down the hill in Thornton Heath that allowed us to use their hall for Sunday afternoon worship meetings. This church, Thornton Heath Baptist had only 12 members and no regular minister. We numbered around thirty with a full time pastor. Over time we became a blended congregation with the student pastor from nearby Spurgeon's Bible College who'd been providing ministry for the small Thornton Heath Baptist church. Our united congregation took on the name of Beulah Baptist Church.

Today the church is known as Beulah Family Church, with about 180 gathering for Sunday worship. It has been a privilege to serve on the leadership team since 1994. Over the years the faces and complexion of our church family changed and grew. It's a delight to see how the make-up of the local community is now reflected in the congregation with West Indians, Africans, Indians, Pakistanis, East Europeans as well as the indigenous British, oh yes, and German and American!

For a ten year period I was commissioned by the church as a freelance evangelist to the Asian community, reaching out to Muslims, Hindus, Sikhs and nominal Christians. In conjunction to this, I was asked to help lead an Asian Christian Fellowship that met in another church in neighboring Streatham.

The legacy of The Jesus Family's missionary journey to this part of South London is a vibrant local church where the gospel is preached, people are born again and nurtured to become ambassadors for Christ and many social action projects take place helping the poor and those with various support needs in their lives. To God be the glory! Deo Gloria!

Bio Update

Trevor & Karin Allen currently reside in Cambridge, England.
Children: James and Andrew (Both are strongly living for the Lord and married)
Grandchildren: Jonah, Lola-Faith, Pheobe and Micah
Vocation: Graphics; now retired)

Ministry: Elder, Beulah Family Church, Croydon & member of New Frontiers Church

Trevor and spouse moved to Cambridge to be nearer to close friends Phillip & Christine (from Jesus Family days) who were in ministry together for many years at Beulah Family Church

A special thanks to Trevor for his eye-witness narrative and providing an additional voice on the workings of God in his life and during this time period.

It's an honor to introduce Ben & Rosalind Day, dear life-time friends. We first met in the Jesus Family in the UK and have maintained our friendship through personal visits, mail, and by phone since.

Ben & Rosalind Palmer Day's Account
The Jesus Family London, Manchester and Pastoral Care USA

I first met both Ben and Rosalind in England. The first memories I have of Ben were, he had hair well below his waist and had the ability to speak Spanish fluently with a USA southern twang! The combination stood out to me as did his love for Jesus Christ and commitment to making Him known to others.

Ben is genuinely likable and friendly, with a fire in his soul to share Jesus Christ. Both he and his lovely wife Rosalind are examples of God's grace, lived-out over the long haul. God's birthing of the Jesus Movement intersected with both of them, bringing them together and aided them in spiritual formation. Their commitment to keep presenting themselves before God with humility and dependence has been their core strength. Ministry and service opportunities have resulted with fruitful results.

Ben's Family & Early Years

Ben Day was born in Baltimore, Maryland. His parents were from Harlan, Kentucky where his dad worked in the coal mines and later was an itinerant worker. He remembers his early upbringing in this way:

"My first memory is that of my mother singing 'Yes Jesus loves me,' but what I remember most is, 'Little ones to him belong, they are weak but he is strong.'" She lovingly explained that God was Spirit and that He was with me even though I could not see Him. God was present to watch over and protect me from harm and danger. I never had any childhood fears. Imagination is a wonderful thing and children have an inherent capability of understanding spiritual things. As our imagination is squelched with pragmatic things we can lose sight of this gift. This is why visionaries are fewer today; with cultural norms urging us toward safe choices inside the parameters of our particular societal cookie-cutter box.

I never felt like I fit into a fixed mold and disagreed with denominational doctrines I was exposed to while growing up. I wouldn't say I was rebellious, but I couldn't see myself as "A wretched old sinner saved by grace, in need of getting saved again weekly, or monthly, because of my backsliding ways." From my perspective, my salvation experience was more like a permanent adoption, flaws and all. I saw the world in its natural and spiritual dimension different than those around me and was OK with it.

My mother's spiritual background was holiness; Wesleyan, Armenian, Pentecostal. This is what she passed on to me, without knowing who or what they were; she had experienced the reality of conversion to Christ and the infilling of the Holy Spirit.

When did my experience move from believing God as protector and keeper to accepting Christ as Savior? I don't know. Not many babies remember coming down the birth canal, but they know they were born because they are alive and they have a birth certificate to authenticate this reality. My proof of salvation is the Word of God and the fruit that is manifested in and through my life.

A Call from God

I remember being called to go and preach. It was simple, not dramatic, I was 15 years old. I read in Mark 16:15 "Go into all the world and preach the Gospel to everyone." This verse and the Great Commission in Matthew 28:18-20 would change my life forever.

This call thrust me into mission work in Mexico, Central America,

Colombia, Haiti and a number of Caribbean Islands where I encountered Castro's communist influence and the evils of Spiritism. I worked with a larger Missions Team and was responsible for helping conduct youth meetings in places we went. During this time-frame I witnessed miracles parallel to those recorded in the Book of Acts and learned Spanish.

Back in the continental USA I continued with the same group with the same focus of conducting children's meetings and sharing the Gospel message. We ministered in Miami, Florida and in New York City. I was accused of being a Jesus freak, looking and talking the part. This was before I met anyone from the JP movement.

Mark 16:15

Jesus said, "Go into all the world and preach the gospel to every creature."

My first contact with JP was in Oklahoma City, Oklahoma when I met "Christ is the Answer" tent ministry led by Bill Lowery, with part of the team originating from the Milwaukee Jesus People. Ministering alongside them seemed a good spiritual fit, witnessing on the streets and returned to the tent at night with the people that we had invited to hear an evangelistic message given by Bill Lowery and his disciples. While among this JP group, they told me about Jim Palosaari and the newly established Jesus Family in England.

In Europe

I kept this in mind when my adventures of following Jesus eventually carried me to Europe. I was in West Berlin, Germany before the walls came down. My travels in Europe eventually brought me into England. I was single back then and very much a Jesus freak. I encountered the Jesus Family in London while sharing my faith on the streets, where they too were conducting outreach. I received a cordial invitation to work with them and did. My fondest memories are distributing copies of the Christian newspaper Everyman on the streets of London and sharing the Gospel of Christ. I was in my element. On occasions there were culture clashes, but on the whole the British people were very accepting of my ways and I tried to understand theirs.

My spiritual music exposure was churchy. I was pleasantly surprised with the music of The Sheep, Larry Norman, Don Francisco, Barry McGuire and others who brought freshness to worship and outreach music.

The production of *Lonesome Stone* seemed like a good outreach tool, but not relevant to me personally as I'd never been to San Francisco, or was into the kinds of things SF street people were into. Interacting with the Jesus Family cast members and hearing their testimonies, gave me a different perspective. It helped me understand and rejoice with them in their victory over the past and the miracle of coming to faith in Jesus Christ.

Marriage—a Gift from God

The Jesus Family was a very appropriate name. I met young men and women that I consider friends and family to this day. I also met my wife to be, Rosalind Palmer at the Jesus Family Beulah Hill house in Upper Norwood, London. I was engaged to her and we married in Watford, England in 1974. Shortly after we married, Rosalind and I returned to Ohio, USA for some nine months to spend time with my family.

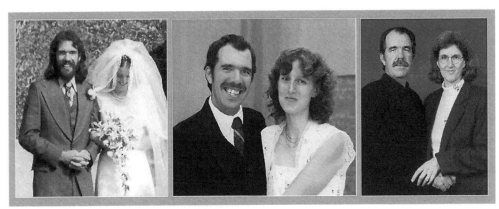

Ministry in Greater Manchester, UK

On invitation from the Mighty Flyers we returned to England to conduct ministry in the Manchester area. Rosalind and I worked in Stockport, England as house-father and mother to a group of young men and women whose lives were being changed through discipleship. Part of this ministry took place at an 'old rectory' provided for follow-up ministry for many youth who'd received Christ through the outreach of *Lonesome Stone* and the Mighty Flyers ministry. We also worked with David Reese leader of the Mighty Flyers band. I gladly served as their chauffeur, roadie, evangelist, or in whatever capacity they needed help.

Pastoral Ministry in the USA

Over time, Rosalind and I returned to the USA. I worked in the painting trade, studied for ministry, and applied myself to pastoral work, teaching and outreach. This calling has been ongoing for many years now. I was ordained as a minister in the Spanish Eastern District of the Assemblies of God. I accepted a number of pastorate and ministry positions over the years. Our family settled in McMinnville, Tennessee where our two boys were raised and we continue in ministry to this day. I currently pastor two churches in the United Methodist Church. One is English-speaking and the other is a Spanish-speaking congregation, each with unique challenges.

I'm thankful I learned and began speaking Spanish as a kid, incorporating it in Christian ministry and missions as I grew older. Becoming fluent in Spanish opened many doors and opportunities. Serving Spanish-speaking congregations has been a great privilege and met a need. Through a divine appointment I was invited to teach English and Spanish at the Tennessee Foreign Language Institute. I've also been able to assist a certified teacher at Motlow State College which required a master's degree. Thankfully, an exception was made (due to a high level of Spanish competency) and I was brought on-board; teaching and writing curriculum and tests for students.

My passion is to represent Christ and do so with integrity that flows out of a relationship with God. Those who know me understand my interest in ministry is not a religious performance to gain prestige, or pursue any status quo church agenda. I endeavor to be real and honest. I want to make a difference in the community, inside and outside the walls of the church. I endeavor to be a Barnabas type of encourager, assisting Christians in discovering and getting launched in their God-given calling.

Our Family

Rosalind and I have been married for 45 years now. We have two sons and five grandchildren. Our sons are Chris and Daniel. In High School our boys were called "Jesus Freaks"—a title both boys had in their high school yearbooks. Both of our sons have pastored in growing churches that began as church plants. Our oldest has now transitioned to becoming a plant for a large manufacturing company. Our grandchildren are: David, Ginny Ruth, Mikayla, Johnny and Eliana Grace.

Vision for the Future

God spoke to my heart a number of years ago and asked me to start over in ministry. Knowing what I know now, this is exciting! It causes me to believe I have many more years of ministry in my future. God's presence is at the center of my calling to live for Him. God's cyclical visits are essential for the life of His true church. The need for sacrificial and courageous disciple followers of The Father and His Son Jesus Christ continues.

> I heard the voice of the Lord. He said, "Who will I send? Who will go for us?" I said, "Here I am. Send me!"
> Isaiah 6:8 NIV®

Ben Day-Missions, EDU & Pastoral Ministry

20 yrs. Missions work with a variety of church-plant assists
Jesus Family, community discipleship ministry, Stockport, England UK
EDU: Undergrad: Mid-America Christian University / Oklahoma City, OK
Master of Divinity: United Theological Sem., United Brethren / Dayton, OH
Pastor, Nuevo Amanecer, McMinnville, Tenn. (Spanish) AOG
Pastor, Bethel, Smithville, Tenn. (Spanish) Dual charge
Pastor, Wesley Chapel UMC & Asbury UMC, Manchester, Tennessee
Pastor, Goose Pond UMC, McMinnville, Tennessee

Rosalind Day
Stockport House, Jesus Family

The sweet steadiness of ongoing faithful ministry in Jesus' wonderful

Name!

"After Ben and I married in June of 1974 we moved to Ohio for a season. While there we were invited by the Jesus Family in Manchester to return to England to live and work with them. We decided to do so and said "goodbye" to Ben's family in Ohio and returned to the UK. For the first few weeks we spent time with my family before heading north by train.

We arrived in Manchester in early 1975. At that time the Jesus Fam-
ily had three houses; one in Crumpsall, a second in Rochdale, and another in Stockport. We stayed for a few days at the house in Crumpsall before we were asked to help at the Rochdale house. The Elders of the Jesus Family ministry in Manchester were David Reese, Nick Stone, Nick Brotherwood and Martin Evans.

Nick and Glenny Stone were over the house in Rochdale and sev-
eral young people lived at this house. We helped with anything that needed doing. I recall, Nick worked closely with a local church and held Bible Studies at the church for new and young believers.

The Mighty Flyers band held concerts throughout the area and some of the people that came to live in the houses came to faith in Christ through their ministry. After a season at the Rochdale House we were asked to assist the JP Crumpsall house. We stayed in a small camper trailer parked in the front yard.

We took teams out on the streets of Manchester witnessing. We had a storefront where we prepared meals for everyone and met to pray for the teams going out.

From assisting at the Crumpsall house we were given the responsi-
bility of being house-parents at the Stockport ministry house. Most of the time there were seven young people living at the Old Rectory with various problems. One young girl who'd become pregnant previously, received the

Lord and she was moved to Stockport after delivering her baby. Most of the kids at the house worked day jobs. My husband Ben also secured work with the City of Manchester.

My job was taking care of the home, cleaning, shopping, cooking and doing the laundry. Gradually, our young residents absorbed the chore of doing their own laundry. Depending on the population and needs of the various JP houses, we did some shuffling of staff. It was decided that Nick and Glenny and their two children would join us at the Stockport Rectory ministry house. I was so glad to have another woman there to help.

Shortly after, I went to work at a Book Store the Jesus Family ran. In Stockport we held Bible studies with the kids and we traveled to Crumpsall house for Sunday morning worship services. We would stay the whole day; eat together, go for walks, watch football (soccer) and return home. The countryside in the North of England is so beautiful. I loved it there. Some of our resident kids had difficult problems, but it was an honor to be a light to them and a part of their discipling team.

Ephesians 2:18

"For through Him (Jesus) we have access to the Father by One Spirit."

I loved being part of the Jesus Family. It did have its challenges, but I loved the feeling of belonging and closeness of fellowship. After about a year in the Stockport ministry house we started thinking about returning to the USA. We spoke with the elders about it and they agreed that we could start looking for a flat, which we did. We lived in a tiny flat in Chorlton for about a year and saved money to return to the U.S.

We still participated in worship and activities of the Jesus Family and it was hard to leave the relationships we'd established. I was expecting our oldest son Chris at the time of our move. We made a pit-stop to see my family and flew on to the USA. It was the spring of 1978 when we settled in Tennessee and Chris was born in August of the same year.

All along the way, we've been on a continuing, exciting, never dull journey of following Jesus."

Rosalind Palmer Day
Bio Capsule

Rosalind attended Victoria Secondary School for Girls in Watford, England.

As a teenager into her early twenties she was employed in the workforce, including a clerical position in Manchester, England. After marrying she served with her husband as a counselor and house-parents for At-Risk Teens in the Jesus Family houses in greater Manchester, England. In the USA she was a stay-at-home Mom raising her two boys while assisting her husband in pastoral ministry. As the boys grew, Rosalind secured employment and a service opportunity at Lazarus House Hospice in Cookeville, Tennessee where she was actively involved for 15 years. She is the faithful helpmate for Ben as he continues to be active in Christian pastoral ministry.

A special thanks to Ben & Rosalind Day for sharing part of their journey during the Jesus People days and ongoing life of service to others in Jesus Christ's precious Name. Thank You Lord!

22

Battle Wounds
New Beginnings

Returning to the USA

After years of separation from my family still in the COG and experiencing varying levels of depression and stress, I grew homesick for the United States and was now seriously considering returning. Leaving good friends in England would be the hardest part. Countering this, the thought of change gave me something to look forward to and it grew on me.

Finally at peace about making this change, I talked it over with Mr. Frampton, explaining the rash and emotional roller coaster I'd been on. He and his family knew all too well, the stress and anguish of the cult ordeal and concurred with the doctor's recommendation to make a change. Mr. Frampton said his whole family would be sad to see me leave England, but understood. He was concerned for my well-being assuring me of his ongoing prayers. He also said he'd happily cover the airfare costs and write a letter of recommendation for me. In the meantime, he too would give thought and prayer to any contacts he might know of who could provide a new start for me stateside.

From the COG news conference we had both met a number of concerned families who had flown to the UK from the United States. One of the first families that came to both of us was Mr. & Mrs. Moody from New

York. When we contacted them and they learned I was looking to resettle in the USA, they had an idea. Their offer was for me to house-sit their Manhasset, Long Island NY home. At the press conference in London we'd shared meals together and had already struck up a supportive friendship of mutual empathy and prayer. Their daughter Melissa, like my family, was still lost somewhere within COG.

Through correspondence I learned they spent a majority of the year in Texas and a limited amount of time at their second home in NY since their kids were grown. My lodging at their NY home would be provided rent-free, in exchange for yard-work, home care and live-in security. I would be responsible for my personal expenses and food. Mulling it over, it sounded ideal. I enjoyed physical work and was excited to get back to work and have a quiet place to rebuild my life.

I wrote back and we agreed on a time for me to begin. I wasn't ready to return to California with all that had happened with the COG fiasco. I wasn't ready to face old friends in California yet. The fate of my family was a constant back-burner heartache. A lot was up in the air. It was going to take time.

Saying Goodbye

The Jesus Family had become my surrogate family along with the Framptons and the Steares in my darkest hours. It was hard to say goodbye because we'd shared our lives in many settings. So many held a special place in my heart; Gerd and Karin, Ben and Rosalind, Greg and Lynn, Mole and Irene, Rich and Jenny, Jim and Sue, Danny and Margaret, Lynn M., Henry, Dennis, Margie, Siv, Arlene, Caroline, Fred, Ethel and many more.

It was mid-1974 when I returned to the States and settled into the top floor attic at the Moody house on Long Island. The first thing on the agenda was securing work. Thankfully, I had some painting skills, ran a few ads and began working. The first few paychecks went towards buying paint tools, a couple of ladders and tarps. The Moody's gave me the use of an older car in the garage which was another blessing. The home was a two story with a finished attic and basement, nestled in a beautiful scenic neighborhood. The front yard was large, mostly grass and the back yard was forested with large trees.

It was an amazing provision from the Lord to be able to live here and I was grateful! I was also thankful to be working again with my hands and getting back into better physical shape. A number of the jobs I landed were strenuous high ladder work which trimmed my body fat quickly.

These were strange days of being in limbo emotionally. The house was empty and I spent a lot of time alone. Paint work, yard maintenance, playing guitar, writing and exploring Long Island filled my days. Spiritually, I felt like the Lord had given me this time to regroup in the quiet setting of Manhasset, Long Island. Respite from the battles of spiritual warfare was good for the soul as was hard physical work to send depression down the road! Defeat, self-condemnation and guilt over the Atlanta disaster would take years to work through. In the meantime, my prayers for my family and friends did not lessen. I couldn't secure their freedom—but I could pray in faith for their release!

There is a Time for Everything –Ecclesiastes 3:1-8 NIV®
And a season for every activity under the heavens:

A time to be born and a time to die,
A time to plant and a time to uproot,
A time to kill and a time to heal,
A time to tear down and a time to build,
A time to weep and a time to laugh,
A time to mourn and a time to dance,
A time to scatter stones and a time to gather them,
A time to embrace and a time to refrain from embracing,
A time to search and a time to give up,
A time to keep and a time to throw away,
A time to tear and a time to mend,
A time to be silent and a time to speak,
A time to love and a time to hate,
A time for war and a time for peace.

This portion of Scripture fit the ping-pong contrasting events which characterized the past number of years. *What occurs in this life is always changing.* Some of the harder parts of life cause pain and reactions which can't be avoided. I'd mourned and wept, been catapulted to the depths of despair, been stripped of family and friends, hated the COG for their deceptions and sought perspective. I'd been to war and now needed to mend and heal; to be silent before the Lord and find a place of peace. I didn't know how to be healed—but I knew God would help.

Under the silent snow
Brown, yellow and orange fallen leaves—
Lie still in the cold darkness of winter
Life beneath them is invisibly regenerating—germinating
Roots deepening, bulbs multiplying and seeds softening
With the thawing, all awaken, the earth trembles and stirs
As snow melts and spring rains irrigate
The Lord of Creation is nurturing
An annual Resurrection
May no footstep crush this new beginning
Or demons of hell smother this life
Quietly, out of human sight—miracles are once again underway!
Soon the sun will warm the soil
New and old sprouts will reach upward
That which seemed lifeless and dead, will rise
O Lord, do so for your servant
From the pangs of war, conflict and loss—
Raise up that which was near death
Intervene! Go deep to stimulate root growth
Replenish used-up nutrients from depleted soil
Let the living water and warmth
Of Your glorious Son Jesus restore
Cause resurrection life to rise again
To the glory of the Father
honor

A Letter that Stunned

Unexpectedly, I received a letter from my spouse in the COG. She'd obtained my address from her parents and felt OK writing since I was now back in the USA. Her mailing address was in France.

The purpose of her letter was to request a divorce. Her explanation was, she'd remarried someone in the cult and was having children by him. She said she had no plans of leaving the Children of God or returning to me. She asked me to agree to the divorce, because she wanted to be remarried legally for her new children's sake.

Though the request and news was stunning, it was what is was. I began thinking and praying about it and decided to comply with this request. It meant I would need to return to California, where we'd married, to establish residency, before filing for a divorce. With the passing of three years and into a fourth of being separated and waiting, the timing and circumstances behind the request seemed less alarming.

I felt less guilt associated with the dissolution of our marriage, because she'd initiated it, was living with and having children with someone she considered her husband. I was still angry at the Children of God and the role they'd played influence-wise in the destruction of our marriage and I remained deeply concerned for her and our children. From what I'd heard, the COG had unleashed new doctrines that had caused the break-up of hundreds of cult member marriages. Thoughts and feeling about everything related to the COG were troubling, knowing this was not a healthy environment for anyone!

NY Band of Friends

A growing interest in writing music had worked its way into my blood through Lonesome Stone and recording music in London and Manchester. Having a number of newer tunes ready to be polished for recording, I decided to run an ad for musicians and singers to help with a recording project. This ad and a few chance meetings brought together a number of musicians and singers who clicked relationally. Seven of us comprised our recording band; Les Steinweiss, Artie Lander, Camille Eskell, Linda Levine, Laura Barone, Rich Harris and I. Randy Weinstein was our flutist when recording and Les's spouse Marg and a handful of others were attached to us in other ways.

I had to pinch myself over how quickly we became fast and lasting

NY BAND of FRIENDS

Les, Joplin, Margie, Karen, Dave, Ginny, Artie, Camille, Laura, Linda, Rich

friends. Five were Jewish and the rest either Catholic or Protestant; the music we worked on was Christ centered. Out of love for music they willingly pooled their creative talents and ideas in arranging five songs for an upcoming recording session. Placing these recorded tunes with established artists was never realized, but what we gained through working together was of greater value.

The non-judgmental, accepting atmosphere that was present was exactly what each of us needed. At this time, I wouldn't have been able to handle rigid or legalistic religious relationships.

What God provided was a band of down-to-earth, giving and special NY friends. When we rehearsed, we easily incorporated each other's musical or vocal ideas which made our sessions uplifting. Socially we did all kinds of stuff together. Les and Marg took me on an amazing road trip into

PHOTOS / MARJIE STEINWEISS

Linda Levine   Dave & Ginny

Camille Eskell   Les Steinweiss

Vermont in the fall of the year during the leaves changing colors, the apple gathering and the making of maple syrup and apple cider. Little Joplin their daughter reminded me of my kids and was fun to be around.

Our small group supported each other's creative projects, shared meals and R&R together.

A New Relationship

Earlier in the year, while at a live-music venue with drummer friend, Rich—I encountered a beautiful young woman. The Camelot Inn in Mineola, Long Island was the setting. She had dark hair, brown eyes and a pleasant smile. We danced and seemed to hit it off. On the slower tunes, we both were trembling in each other's arms. Something was special about this meeting. Before she left with friends, I asked for her telephone number.

When I called, she seemed glad to hear from me and we began seeing each other. Ginny worked downtown in Manhattan in New York City in a government office as a pool secretary and lived in the Bronx. Seeking answers to some personal matters, she'd begun frequenting a prayer chapel on her lunch hour, asking God for help. She believed our meeting was an answer to these prayers. I felt the same way sensing God had allowed our paths to cross at just the right time. Ginny was a gentle soul with a good heart, raised in a Catholic family with 12 years of parochial schooling.

Early on I shared my spiritual journey, the Atlanta fiasco and what had happened since. She listened and seemed to understand the unusual nature of the crisis that had unfolded. I'd worried telling her might overwhelm her and cause her to back away. Instead, her feelings and our relationship grew stronger. It was a lot to take in, but she seemed to understand the complexity of what had occurred and was genuinely empathetic.

We went on long walks, visited parks and beaches, shared candlelight dinners, ate ice cream, and took in movies together. All of this was a personal emotional respite from carrying the weight of responsibility of past failures and the ongoing reality of family and friends still under COG influence.

My first impressions of Ginny were accurate. Her kind and sweet spirit was steady! Little by little, I felt a change come over me. I began to think about her all the time. Her warm personality was working its way into my lonely soul. She was like a rare and beautiful rose in bloom. I wrote letters and love poems to her when we weren't together and brought her plants and flowers.

Gradually, good thoughts and things to look forward to began to replace the pain of the past. In a relatively short period of time I began sensing Ginny and I were a good match. Her Catholic upbringing and my Protestant influences were not at war, but instead complemented each other as we found common spiritual ground. We knew it was important to keep God and Jesus Christ at the center of our relationship. Thankfully, she came from a stable Italian family. They accepted me even though I wasn't Italian, which was a good sign. And there was lots of family!

Meanwhile, plans were in the works for my return to California to establish residency and fulfill my agreement to file for divorce. As I began thinking about move dates, Artie, our conga player asked if he could come along. Artie was a reliable good friend and said we could take his vehicle. This instantly solved a number of logistical issues of transportation. Both of us had saved for this move, would share travel expenses and pool our money to rent an apartment on arrival in Marin County, California. By this time Artie was living in the basement apartment at the Moody home.

A Godly Visitor

A month or so prior leaving NY, Jack Wasson from "Christ for the Nations Bible College" in Dallas Texas called ahead and then paid us a visit in Manhasset, Long Island. He'd heard of me through the Moody family and was a concerned Christian who was connecting with and aiding former Children of God cult victims in their healing process and offering debriefing counseling.

Jack stayed with us for several days, offering dialogue opportunities as a means of helping me heal. Having already spent several years with the Jesus Family in England, post COG involvement, I wasn't a typical cult recovery candidate for debriefing. At the time I was benefiting most from quiet time before God and personal Bible reading. Getting it, Jack's ministry was redirected to my Jewish roommate Artie, showing him many Scriptures from the Bible and answering lots of questions. This resulted in Artie opening his heart to the Lord in wonderful ways.

Return to California

By the time we made our trip to California, Artie was a new Christian and beginning to read his Bible daily. Our plan was to camp across the United States. Hearing of this, my good friend Caroline Green, from the Jesus Family England asked if she could tag along for the adventure and we agreed.

Our trip was inspiring as we visited a number of national parks and saw some of the awesome beauty of God's creation from coast to coast. We camped in tents, cooked over the open fire, and hiked down the Grand Canyon to the Colorado River. Overall, this was an indelible life experience.

Moving to California was a big step. Artie and I felt it would all work out, once we got settled and working. San Diego was our first stop as my mom and Artie's parents lived there. A week after our arrival, Caroline flew back to the UK and Artie and I drove north to the San Francisco Bay Area. We'd decided to live in Marin County, where I would file for a divorce, and rented an apartment in the city of Novato. In short order, both Artie and I obtained work and began attending the Church of the Open Door in Novato. I wasn't sure how I felt about church involvement but my old friend, Kent Philpott was one of the pastors of the church in the city of San Rafael.

On reconnecting with Kent, he filled me in on why he became involved with this church. From what I gleaned, he and others from the Christian house ministries had joined forces with a few seminary pastors who were in the early stages of forming a church. With Kent's input and participation, the church welcomed street-people and anyone regardless of appearance, with a focus on discipleship. Recalling the problems we'd encountered when randomly taking new converts from Christian houses to local churches for worship, this seemed like a good step forward in providing healthy assimilation into a Christian family, minus the rejection we often encountered in past attempts when visiting some denominational churches.

Kent and friends would continue to operate Christian houses in concert with the Church of the Open Door. The church's larger goal was to expand their witness and influence for Christ in Marin County. When I arrived, the church had successfully opened a sizable Christian bookstore in

San Rafael which was running smoothly and was conducting ongoing Bible
Study outreaches in local colleges and area high schools.

Beginning Over & NY Wedding

As time has its own way of speedily slipping by, so it was with the filing for
and the finalization of my divorce. According to my ex-spouse's parents,
she and our three children continued to live in Europe under the Children
of God aka 'The Family International' influence and she'd delivered two
additional children by her cult husband.

Doing strenuous physical work in the painting trade left me too tired
to be as obsessed with this tragedy as in the past. As often as I thought of
the situation I prayed with intensity for their release from this influence.
For years, everything related to my now ex had been impossible to alter.
Prayer was the only weapon I knew of that could change what I could not,
so I continued to offer up prayers in faith for her and the children's release
from this group as well as my friends.

Meanwhile, Ginny and I continued to write and called as often as we
could afford to do so. The distance from New York to California seemed
to intensify our feelings toward each other. On a work break, Ginny flew
to San Diego and I traveled south to meet up at my Mom's for a few days.
During our visit we became engaged while touring the area of the Coro-
nado Hotel. After our brief rendezvous, Ginny flew back to NY and I
returned to San Fran. What followed was a long-distance engagement until
we decided to attend pre-marriage classes in California.

In anticipation of a wedding in December of 1976 Ginny secured
work with Fireman's Fund in San Francisco and moved to California. We
attended pre-marriage classes called Pre-Cana through the Catholic Church.
On completion of this program the local diocese helped us draft a letter
requesting we be accepted by Roman Catholic officials for marriage within
the Catholic Church due to the extenuating circumstances surrounding my
divorce.

We were hopeful our request would be accepted as this would mean
a lot to Ginny's family. In the fall of 76 as our wedding approached, we
learned our request had been denied. The head Monsignor of Holy Family
Parish in the Bronx was sorry to hear this and made arrangements with a

Lutheran pastor friend who agreed to conduct the ceremony at the Lutheran Church a half a block away from Holy Family. Ginny's family understood, knowing we'd done everything possible on our end to honor the family's spiritual heritage and wishes. All was good.

When our wedding day arrived, we gathered in the Bronx, New York, at Ginny's parents. The excitement of the day's events was in the air. A missing part of my attire was a pair of dress shoes which Ginny's father loaned me. In our penguin suits, Ginny's Dad, her brother Vinnie and I were finally ready. In another part of the house, Ginny was in the midst of final preparation. It felt good to be standing in the kitchen, knowing I'd been authentically accepted into Ginny's family.

The Lutheran church was a step down from the large sanctuary of Holy Family Parish, but better suited for our size of wedding. All of my NY band of friends and musicians were present along with Ginny's family and friends from near and far. My musician friends agreed to help with various readings and the Lutheran pastor handled the vows and other details of the service.

Ginny was a beautiful bride; cheeks flushed and eyes sparkling with joy. The covenant we made of dedicating ourselves to the Lord had been thought out and prayed over during our engagement year. We yielded our lives and future into God's hands to be used for His glory. We knew the importance of making a vow to God, knowing He would expect us to fulfill this promise.

The reception Ginny's parent's laid on was beautiful! We had an expansive high quality meal and traditional huge wedding cake, with a live band and dancing. An extra bonus was the surprise music set given by my NY band of friends I'd recorded with. As the evening progressed, I realized how many relatives there were on Ginny's side. It was a wonderful celebration. Our wedding song was, "I Need You", by America, appropriate to how we both felt.

Spiritual Commitments

On returning to California, we decided to affiliate with the Church of the Open Door in San Rafael and were asked to help the church expand its outreach ministry. In time we hosted a weekly Bible study, a Body Life group,

and helped pioneer several outreach teams into four local institutions where
teens and adults were incarcerated. God was supportive of these endeavors
and blessed them with success. During this time we had approximately 50
volunteers involved in these institutional outreaches.

Even though I was without formal seminary training, our home
church in San Rafael asked me to consider ordination to the ministry

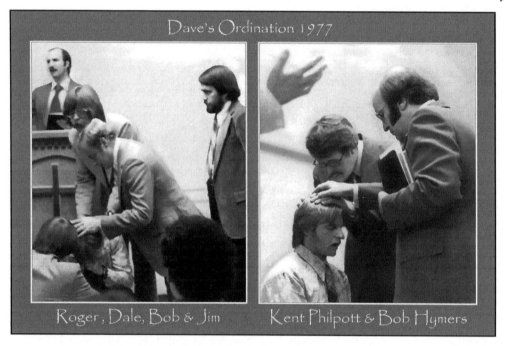

Dave's Ordination 1977

Roger, Dale, Bob & Jim   Kent Philpott & Bob Hymers

because of our outreach ministry and willingness to serve on a Foreign
Mission Team.

I agreed to this step and in 1977 was ordained to ministry in the
company of several hundred church friends. They came in support of two
of us who were being ordained and others who were being licensed. Ken
Sanders preached the charge to the church and Kent Philpott spoke to us
as candidates. A few of the Christian leaders and pastors present were: Jim
Smith, Mark Buckley, Bob Hymers, Roger Hoffman, Dale Alter and Bob
Gaulden.

Pastors and close friends prayed individually and earnestly for our
well-being and future ministry in representing Jesus Christ. This was an
overwhelmingly positive show of affirmation. I could not hold back the
tears.

Thinking of God's incredible grace which had rescued me from the pit of being hell-bound and probably facing a premature death, had burned gratitude into my soul. I felt unworthy, but "being in Christ", I knew He had made me acceptable to the Father. He had grafted me into His family. I viewed my ordination as a type of seal upon how I wanted to live my life on mission for Him. I was willingly choosing to follow, to go, to speak up for Jesus Christ and point others to Him. I was intent on using every gift and talent I possessed to glorify Him. I hope this book reflects this commitment.

Ginny Hoyt's Story
From Knowing about God—to Following Him

I was born in the Bronx, NY in a close-knit Italian family. I attended Catholic schools from grade 1-12 completing my studies at Saint Helena's, an all-girls high school in the Bronx.

Growing up, I can't remember a time when I did not know that Jesus Christ was my Savior. My faith was grounded in what I'd been taught in parochial schools and attending Holy Family Parish. Overall, believing in God and His Son was a very positive influence in my life. At the time, I didn't realize there was a difference between the faith I'd learned and having a relationship with God.

As a teenager, I had questions about the Catholic Church, but remained devoted. I learned about God, memorized a lot of catechism (spiritual EDU) questions and answers, but never made the connection of how this knowledge was to be applied to everyday life. I attended church on Sunday, but when Monday came—my activities and work took precedence. I said memorized prayers at night as a devotional practice.

Example and Spiritual Stirrings

I recall my Mom stopping her regular routine during the day, and going to the front room of our house to pray. I didn't think much about it at the time, but now understand her prayers and life was having a significant influence on me. She was a giver. She put others first by serving and taking care of them and praying for their needs. Her spiritual work and love became an important example to me.

Rough Sketch of First Album Cover

In my latter years in high school, one of our younger nuns brought in the cast album of the new Broadway musical, "Jesus Christ Superstar." She played it during class, and it got my attention. For me, it was a refreshing connection between God and real life—and I liked the music!

Around the same time, I heard about an evening co-ed "Bible study" to be led by a brother at the all-boys high school building on our campus. A group of girlfriends and I attended a number of studies. The initial draw was the excitement of being allowed into the boys building! What impressed me about these gatherings was students were getting together to study the Bible outside of church and the regular religious curriculum of the classroom.

In my senior year at St. Helena's one of our nuns gave me a job referral in Manhattan, NY. This resulted in a hire to work for a covert federal security agency in an undercover office after graduation. My work would entail being part of a secretarial short-hand and typing pool for field agents. For a number of years I was ordered by the agency not to reveal who I worked for, including my parents. The job paid well, was a good beginning and I agreed to and understood the security protocol.

A Divine Appointment

For work, I took the bus or subway to and from Manhattan five days a week. Coming home I'd sometimes take the subway to Flushing, Queens to go shopping and pick up the Q-44 bus home to the Bronx. Caching up on reading in route was a regular practice. On one occasion, while absorbed in reading a book called "Everybody's Lucifer" about the Rolling Stones, a guy sat down next to me.

He looked at me and spotted the cover of my book and said "I think God wants me to talk to you." My first thought was, this guy is looney and I began looking around for an escape plan to move seats. His next words were, "God is hearing your prayers and you should not give up!"

I was stunned as I had a specific situation I'd been praying about! How could he know I was a person who prayed? With prayer still being a mystery in many ways, to hear, "The God of the universe was actually listening to my prayers was astonishing." Tears formed as I contemplated God's interest in me. While absorbing this, the guy gave me a small pam-

phlet, titled Four Spiritual Laws. At this moment my stop came up, so I thanked him and got off the bus. Stepping onto sidewalk in my own neighborhood I was intrigued by this brief spiritual encounter

At home, I sat down and carefully read the pamphlet. It was a sum- mation of why Jesus came to earth, what He did, His death and resurrection, how to receive and then follow Him. Familiar with most of these facts in my upbringing, nothing clicked. What did captivate me was, "God was lis- tening to my prayers and I should not give up!"

In close proximity to this event, the musical "Godspell" came out as a new 'off Broadway' musical show in Manhattan. Working downtown had its advantages when it came to buying reasonably priced tickets and going to shows and musicals. My girlfriends and I wanted to see this particular musical because of a cute actor who was in it. We went, but spiritual impact of the show didn't get my attention at this first viewing.

My next exposure to 'Godspell' came through my brother's free ticket invite to see the premier of the movie in Manhattan. At that time my brother worked for the company who leased a tugboat for the filming of the movie, resulting in complimentary tickets to the company he was employed by. So, we went together to the premier showing. Seeing Godspell a second time in a film version had more of an effect on me.

Checking the Story Out for Myself

The idea that this play and movie was based on the Gospel of Matthew amazed me. I decided to dig out my New Testament from school and read Matthew for myself to see if the events and words from the musical were really in there. They were! It was not like I had never heard the Gospel previously; I'd heard it consistently in church and in school but the facts, details and nuances were often a blur.

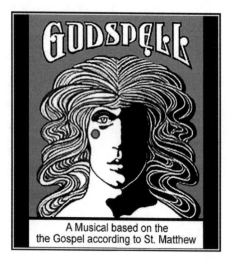

A Musical based on the the Gospel according to St. Matthew

This reading of the Gospel of Matthew was different! I read the whole story—from Jesus' birth, life, words, miracles, sacrificial death and astounding resurrection from the dead. All of what He said and did among the people, the persecution he received from religious Jews and the relationships He had with His Father and the disciples.

Jesus knew His disciples, what they thought, understood how they would react and was fully aware of their weaknesses. If God was this tuned in to individuals, He could easily know I'd been praying and what I was praying about. He wasn't as distant as I thought!

Growing up Catholic I had compartmentalized spiritual life to being centered in church life; attending mass, going to confession, honoring the sacraments, and adhering to the religious duties and responsibilities of a practicing Catholic. God and Jesus existed mainly within this parameter, with the exception of prayers offered, acts of mercy and good deeds performed outside of the church. A broader view of spiritual life was in its infancy, still forming.

I'm not sure how much time I gave to thinking this through, but I began to believe there was a lot more to spiritual life than I'd thus far experienced. I liked the idea that God was listening, so I began to pray more, asking Him to show me what to do. With all that happens at home and at work, I began going to a prayer chapel in Manhattan on occasion on my lunch hour to seek God's guidance.

A New Direction

One Friday night when I was out with some girlfriends, we went to the Camelot Inn in Mineola, Long Island on the recommendation that a live-band was playing. Dave and a friend were there to hear the band and for the night life. I met Dave when he asked me to dance. We visited and danced and I wrote my phone number on a match book cover before we went our separate ways.

Time passed and he finally called, resulting in a few dates. One night he asked, if I read the Bible. What? This was a first for me, not a topic that usually came up on a date! Fortunately, I could honestly say, "I had recently read the entire Gospel of Matthew." Whew!

This was the beginning of a new chapter in my life and an answer to a number of prayers. Spiritual things became a normal part of Dave and my conversations. Dave shared his life, victories and defeats, including the trauma filled events surrounding the COG cult and losing his family and friends into this group. He also shared the upside of a spiritual family in England and the theatre production of Lonesome Stone.

I too shared my life of growing up a Catholic and introduced Dave to my Mom, Dad and brother. This was good and they liked him!

At the time Dave had met a group of NY musicians who became friends and were in the midst of rehearsing regularly at the residence he cared for in Manhasset. The songs they were working on were for the most part Christ-centered which amazed me. I was welcomed into this group and we shared life, music, laughter and meals together. This was another dimension of a new beginning.

I was confident that God had led me to meet Dave and believed He would show me what I was to do and where He wanted me to go in the future. Back then, and even more so as time passed, I felt like God had picked me up out of my old life and put down into a new adventure!

Marriage & a New Church

As time went on, Dave and I were married and lived in Marin County, CA. We were part of a contemporary Christian church which was very new to me. I was so used to the traditional Catholic Mass that had become rote and routine. This church was alive and exciting! I looked forward to the worship services and Bible studies. The Holy Spirit began to work in me and I was eager to learn more about the Lord and His Word. My heart was changing.

I have heard many dramatic testimonies over the years where the Lord transformed a life radically, changing a person in very visible ways. My transformation was quieter, but still very real. I felt the Lord's hand in every aspect of my life, walking with me through every situation.

There is no longer a separation between God and living life. I have a relationship with God, the Living Lord, my Creator and Savor.

He has given me a new purpose. I am far from perfect, and have set-backs. The old nature surfaces from time to time. But the Lord knows my heart, and where I want to be. He graciously accepts me as I am and is always there for me during the rough spots. He knows me better than I know myself.

Psalm 51:10

"Create in me a pure heart, O God, and renew a loyal spirit within me."

My prayer life has changed. It's not "I promise I'll be good for the rest of my life if you would ......" I'm not bargaining anymore, or trying to make a deal. I'm talking to God, my friend and Father, the All-Powerful and All-Knowing God of the Universe, bringing my petitions to Him for myself and others. I know I'm not "bothering" Him. I've come to know He wants to be a part of every aspect of my life, and He's still listening, and always will be.

My desire is to maintain a heart that brings honor to God.

Create in me a pure heart, O God, and renew a loyal and committed spirit within me. Do not cast me from your presence or take your Holy Spirit from me. Restore to me the joy of your salvation and grant me a willing spirit, to sustain me.   Psalm 51:10–12 NIV®

Author's Note: See Ginny's update with inspiring Stories of Faith in Chapter 28, Bio's 2.

Val Skow Oliva's Journey to Faith in Christ
Jesus People Marin County, CA—and Beyond

My first encounter with the JP movement was in 1972 during a HS Social Studies class in Larkspur, California. Two young guys were invited to "share their faith." One had "Jesus Saves" stitched across the front panel of his overalls. My response to them was one of repulsion. I was incensed that someone let them in to speak to the class.

Even so, amidst a raging inner dialogue, some phrases like "the Peace of God, God's love for you and Inner Joy"— lodged in my mind. I thought "such liars, nobody has that." I was a cynical and depressed teenager. When the class ended, I couldn't get out of the room fast enough! I was stunned to see some students stay behind to engage in conversation with them. I remember thinking, it was as if aliens had appeared and kids were talking to them like nothing strange was going on.

Over the next 18 months my heart began to soften toward matters of faith and religion. Marin County in the '70's was a smörgåsbord of New Age, theosophical, and Eastern religious practices that beckoned involvement. It was "hip" to check out Ekankar, TM, Buddhism, and EST seminars. I checked out EST and finally agreed with the "let them eat EST" bumper stickers. It was obvious EST promoters were more interested in cashing in on people's interest monetarily rather than feeding the poor. A lot of hype surrounded alternative religions and philosophies of the day.

On the College of Marin campus in the fall of 1973, a "Christian" named Keith regularly engaged me in dialogue on topics of faith. I would counter with evolution and snippy not well thought-out cracks about Jesus Freaks and con-artists. He seemed ready for these responses. On one occasion he took me through a part of the Bible in the book of Romans that described God's plan and reason for sending His Son Jesus Christ to earth, to live, die and rise from the dead—so all who believe might be given the gift of eternal life. During his explanation I heard and understood for the first time the eternal consequences of rejecting God's Son. Seeing the truth from God's Word in the Bible with my own eyes was sobering (John 3:18, Roman 1:18-2:16, 3:9-18, 6:23, Proverbs 10:16). I'd talked to other Christians who'd emphasized God's love. Why wouldn't God love me?

The penalty for rejecting God and continuing in sin—in contrast to the full provision of forgiveness of sin and being brought into a relationship with God when inviting Christ to live inside me—made a hard case in God's favor—but I wasn't buying yet.

I erupted in expletives, stormed out of the place and drove off campus. Finding a place to stop, I exited the car, fell to my knees and cried out to God, "If you're real then I'm sorry for..." naming and repenting of every sin I could recall—pleading for God's mercy.

When prayed-out, a release came, followed by a peace flowing in my inner being; then a sense of joy's fullness—a witness to my spirit that God was REAL and Jesus Christ was Lord!

The radical transformation that was unfolding in my personal life and out-spoken witness of faith in Jesus Christ caused conflict and misunderstanding among my immediate family; not necessarily anyone's fault. From a cynical, depressed young adult to beaming with the light of Jesus on my face, was a lot to take in. The temporary break in family relationships hurt, but was understandable.

With several offers of a place to stay, God provided a job as a live-in babysitter with a Jewish family in Tiburon. I went from homeless to palatial living and a Datsun 240z to drive around. My needs were being more than adequately met and I saw God at work in the lives of the family as well.

Spiritual Home-Base—Church of the Open Door

The Jesus Movement was in full gear at this time. The leadership of The Open Door "discipled" me—explaining I didn't need to "get saved" after every "altar call." I grew in faith and zeal. With a dramatic heart change, spiritual life was real! The fledgling ministry of the Church of the Open Door met in the Boy Scout Hall in Mill Valley, CA under the leadership of Bob Hymers and two other Spirit-filled students and their spouses from the local Baptist Seminary, Roger and Ava Hoffman and Mike and Mona Riley.

With this team and a small group of believers, it provided a nurturing environment for personal discipleship, outreach and spiritual growth. On my days and evenings off I would join small groups for street evangelism. Sometimes we'd drive to Union Square in SF and Bob Hymers the senior pastor would preach from a small stand. The rest of us would engage the gathering crowd and speak openly of the resurrection of Jesus, salvation, and freedom from the penalty of sin. We were armed with prayer, pocket Bibles and leaflets.

When Kent Philpott's Christian House Ministries merged with The Church of the Open Door in 1974—it grew into an interesting and eclectic force in the community. This blending of ministries and a mini-revival at the Air Force Base on Mt. Tamalpais in Marin County—caused our numbers to explode with young airmen swelling our ranks.

We were blessed with two dynamic lead pastors—Bob Hymers and Kent Philpott. The Open Door moved out of the smaller Boy Scout Hall into the larger Carpenters Union Hall in San Rafael, CA. Worship services were exciting, as was outreach ministry taking place in a number of venues. Philpott and Hymers were strong leaders with different backgrounds and ideas about moving forward in discipleship and church ministry. This led to an impasse—and Hymers decided to make a move back to his home turf in LA, to begin a new ministry.

The Church of the Open Door in San Rafael gradually expanded with new church plants in Novato and Petaluma to accommodate House ministries and the growing community of believers. Smaller House Churches were also formed to give new leaders opportunities to teach and preach and to provide a smaller setting for discipleship and mid-week studies.

In impatience, I insisted on joining a team to plant a new outreach and possibly a church in San Francisco. I was discouraged by one of the pastors—but went anyway. I don't remember praying about it, or waiting on God's will for my life. I was willful, very impatient, and with the growth of the ministry there was less accountability. In haste I moved from Tiburon to "New Ephesus House" with five others, renting a flat on Noriega Street. We got jobs and gave 90% of our income to establish the work. This was my first experience living together with believers. I longed to grow and work closely with them but I was young, the least mature and the most-needy among the team members.

I stayed at New Ephesus for about eight months. The best fruit to come out of this work was Bob. We met Bob in North Beach where he gave his life to the Lord one Friday night. We invited him to come back to live at the house, but first asked him if he wanted to get "his things." He answered, "No, I have nothing to go back to."

Bob became a stellar house mate and grew as a believer. A few months later he asked me if I would accompany him down to the Ten-derloin district so that he could share his faith with a friend. I agreed and trusted God for our safety. Bob found his old friend and shared his faith so sweetly, and with humility explained why he hadn't been around. I often wondered why we targeted places like The Warf and Union Square to do street witnessing when the real ministry was deep in the bowels of the city. In retrospect, a brother should have gone along for that trip. But it's still a cherished memory and I'm glad that I witnessed it.

Mis-Step

Living in the SF Christian house was more routine and low key than I thought it would be. My expectations were not realistic. These were sea-soned believers, disciplined in the Word who maintained their own devotional life. With only two gatherings a week I spent a considerable amount of time alone, separated from those who knew me best in Marin. I felt bored and disappointed. Sadly, I didn't turn to the Lord to meet these needs, and my heart and mind began to wander. I wanted more action and activity.

During an evening of outreach at Fisherman's Wharf I had an encounter with a member of the "Children of God" group. We engaged in brisk discussion about the nature of being Sold-Out for Jesus. I was impressed with his zeal and the sharpness of his Scripture knowledge and attack. Receiving my first "Mo Letter" along with this interaction was the beginning of what turned into an intense interest in the COG group. I was secretive about this encounter to Open Door team members, having been previously warned by one of them. I didn't heed the warning—wanting to investigate myself.

Over the next few months my world destabilized as I continued to interact with the COG. A disconnect developed with the SF Open Door group. I didn't know who to talk to, or if I wanted to get their feed-back. Confused, I decided to leave the Christian house, entered into a period of questioning and reassessment and moved back to Marin County.

Not long after, I met up with the California Street colony of the COG in San Francisco and felt a strong compulsion to join. The decision was finalized when I traveled to Marin, gathered personal stuff, emptied my bank account and returned to the SF colony. It was a done deal—I'd dropped out of the system. I didn't realize at the time, but I'd been picked off by a 'counterfeit gospel and cult.'

I was guilty of being naive, gullible, impatient—but God still loved me. The Holy Spirit never left me during my short stay in the COG. He helped me begin to discern points of error within the COG which caused me to get out after several months. Taking it all in, I was devastated with the seriousness of my error. Grieved by my sin of willfulness, I repented with tears. I'd been side-tracked by a clever counterfeit. But even in this, God had never left me! "For you, LORD, have delivered me from death, my eyes from tears and my feet from stumbling (Psalm 116:8)."

I'd tried to circumvent God's path with a short-cut to find adventure, a sense of family and deeper relationships. There are no short cuts in God's plan for us. We can orchestrate away on our own, but God's path requires listening to His voice and patient submission to His will. I returned to Open Door Church—and started over from the point of where I left off. It was humbling. Some who knew me doubted I was ever saved. Thankfully, God was still in my corner. What others thought didn't matter, I was OK with it. I only wanted to please God.

Pastor Kent was the most understanding of my slip into the COG encounter and sent me to meet a friend of his in San Rafael. I was directed to a tiny storefront called "B Street in Motion" to meet Dave Hoyt. Meeting with Dave was a gift; a gracious and reassuring provision from the Lord. He was caring and accepting having lived through his own agony in joining the COG and finally escaping with wounds that would take years to heal. Dave and Ginny Hoyt opened their lives, home, and ministry to me. They provided a safe and authentic relationship that allowed me to come along side while sorting-out areas of spiritual confusion. To this day they hold a special place in my heart.

With a restorative personal healing underway—proclaiming the Good News of Jesus returned with renewed fervor. This led me to participating in a variety of mission outreaches. One is recorded in this book entitled "Mission into Mainland China."

Jesus People & Missions

One of the most striking differences between the time of the JP Movement and today is, an absence of outreach. Outreach was part of the package of being authentic caring believers. We didn't just gather together to enjoy great messages, fellowship and music—we took the mandate to go "preach the gospel and make disciples" to heart. It was understood, that speaking up for Jesus Christ was the main means hearers would learn about the way God had provided for salvation. Picking up a hitchhiker was an opportunity that could lead to someone receiving a clear witness about Jesus Christ and perhaps a life decision to receive Him—before being dropped off.

Another hallmark of strength among "Jesus People" ministries, churches and Christian houses in this time-period was honest, open, and accessible relationships. As our relationships with God was crucial—so was meaningful brother and sister in Christ relationships. The Apostle Paul said it well, "So we cared for you. Because we loved you so much, we were delighted to share with you not only the gospel of God—but our lives as well (1 Thessalonian s 2:8)." Life to life in the ups and downs, good-times and hard-times went a long way in helping us grow, knowing we had a genuine family in the faith, which yielded lifetime friendships.

After moving into another Christian House north of San Rafael the Lord blessed me with close friendships and new opportunities to serve. I was sent out by Open Door to work with a youth ministry called "Operation Mobilization" in the summer of 1976. Young believers were mobilized from concentrated areas of faith (US, Canada, and some European

Operation Mobilization (OM) Girls European Outreach Team 1976

Countries) to low areas of faith. This included countries like Turkey and Russia, but also immigrant neighborhoods in London and other European cities. We learned to work in small groups and form strategic outreach. We targeted neighborhoods with tracts and literature appropriate to the area. There was much preparation of the heart and language study.

One unforgettable moment occurred in Brussels Belgium when several small groups combined to meet up for a spontaneous "Open Air." We marched up a cobbled side street singing and praising God. Once arriving in the City Square, various participants began to give an account of their faith while others with language skills translated. The testimonies were as diverse as the participants, but all gave glory to God for his transformational work in their lives. A large crowd formed to listen. It was such a move of the Spirit that I had the sense of being connected to God's faithful witnesses through the ages. As suddenly as it started, it ended. It happened, I think, because we were focused and prepared for service to God.

On returning to Marin I found that I had been accepted into Nursing School. I worked in a Medical-Surgery Unit for several years, but still had a driving desire to live in Christian community and do outreach. I moved to a Community in Oregon, but it was not a match. Returning to Marin, doors opened to continue studying in the medical field. With the momentum of studying in higher education the Lord helped me to see that medical nursing was a life calling. The confirmation has been God's abiding presence surrounding me in this important work of providing comfort and care to countless patients over the years. The specific context of my work and spiritual ministry has been as a Cardiopulmonary nurse in a Critical Care Unit in a hospital in Oakland.

Opportunities to serve in short term outreach missions continued to open doors in Canada, Asia and China. These Mission trips opened my eyes to the vast love and Heart of God. Each time I've carried the gospel to others and seen the accomplishments He brings, I've understood more clearly than ever the need for willing vessels to represent Him. The fields are white and expansive, in need of harvest! Together with this greater realization I've seen the work He's done in my heart while on mission. This has far out-weighed any personal sacrifices I've made to be available.

God is great at multi-tasking! He will use us to bring the Living Word to others and minister to us simultaneously. Our job is be spiritually yielded vessels of integrity, soaked in prayer and diligent in giving God the glory. My most refining character changes have occurred when I thought that I was doing service for God. We are changed as the Holy Spirit works through us. The greatest gift to me in living and service in Jesus Name is His abiding presence.

> Jesus said, "I am the vine and you are the branches: He that abides in me, and I in him, the same brings forth much fruit: for without me you can do nothing."   John 15:5 NIV®

Reflecting

Looking back over the years, I find it hard to grasp just how unique the Jesus Movement generation was, and at the same time, how it was so like

God. It was as if heaven had opened wider for a brief season of time, to allow for a harvest of young people loosed from the grip of establishment constraints.

In other places of need I'm confident God continues to work today. He is not stagnant. As Jesus taught, "The wind blows wherever it pleases. You hear its sound, but you cannot tell where it comes from, or where it is going. So it is with everyone born of the Spirit (John 3:8)."

We see the touch of God on everything, all we do, everywhere we go. Our role is to walk in the Spirit (Galatians 5:16, Romans 8:4) and abide in Christ (John 15:1-10).

A Nurse's Prayer: Dear Lord, Come to Work with Me

For years, during my long commute (1.5 hrs. each way), I would pray and invite the Holy Spirit to come to work with me, asking God to take authority over my Unit at the Medical Center. Asking Jesus Christ to touch, heal, and minister as only he can, to those that I was about to be given charge over. When led by the Holy Spirit, I would reveal to a patient or staff member that I'd already been praying for them. My prayer was for God's comfort and personal touch in their lives and to meet their needs.

In my 35 years as a nurse I have seen many patients moved to tears, grateful and genuinely moved by this one act of faith on their behalf. Often this would open new doors for listening, dialogue and specific requests for prayer. The Lord is faithful. He can be trusted. His heart and love for us is beyond our ability to fully take in. Our steps with God are sure, when we walk in faith and stay in His Word. *Maranatha!* This prayer 'Maranatha' means "Come, Lord Jesus!" It's inspiration comes from Revelation 22:12-13 and 20.

Bio Snapshot

Valerie Skow Oliva was born and raised in San Francisco, CA
Education: Bachelors Degree Science / Nursing: BSN, CCRN
Val was not raised in a Christian home.

Val continues to work as a "Cardio-Vascular Nurse." In the last few years Val had a bout with cancer, underwent surgery, received treatment and is heading toward full remission.

"In recent years, the Lord has given me many happy road trips with my husband performing music and sharing with folks all around the US.

The Lord has also graciously provided family reconciliation and healing."

Author's Note: Val takes us on two fascinating and inspiring mission journeys into Mainland China in the Missions Chapter 24.

Coming Up

In the next chapter, 'Following in Jesus' Steps' we'll explore primary JP beliefs and practices. There were identifiable pros and cons of living in Christian Community. What were they? What is the 'Baptism of Fire' that infused the Jesus Movement with spiritual gifts, insights and abilities? How were so many without training able to speak with such conviction, power and boldness in Jesus Christ's Name?

The answers to these and many other questions are addressed in Chapter 23. They will include JP challenges and transferable principles which made Jesus People effective in reaching their generation.

23

FOLLOWING
IN JESUS' STEPS

Whoever claims to live in Him, must
walk as Jesus did. I John 2:6 NIV®

Living in Christian Community

Opening and maintaining a Christian discipleship house during the Jesus Movement era met numerous practical and spiritual needs simultaneously. A homeless and hungry street person could find a meal, clean clothes, a place to shower and a safe place to sleep. Missions the world over have been providing this type of humanitarian aid for centuries to those in need. The Biblical reason for doing so was penned by Jesus' brother James.

> What good is it, my brothers and sisters, if someone claims to have faith but has no deeds? Can such faith save them? Suppose a brother or a sister is without clothes and daily food. If one of you says to them, "Go in peace; keep warm and well fed," but does nothing about their physical needs, what good is it? In the same way, faith by itself, if it is not accompanied by action, is dead.   James 2:14-17 NIV®

At the time of the JP movement there was an anonymous poem inspired by the verses above. The words have a life of their own, changing from time to time while maintaining the spiritual principles James was addressing.

Go in Peace!

I was hungry and thirsty and you formed a group to discuss my need.
I was in tattered clothes, dirty and smelly, and you avoided getting too close.
I was sick and you asked yourself, "I wonder what sin caused this illness?"
I was hurt, lonely and confused; you saw me, but turned away.
I was imprisoned and you felt revulsion in your mind and heart.
I lost my job, business and savings in a financial slump--everything gone!
Then my spouse died, and before long I became homeless.
Depressed, I isolated myself; it was so painful I couldn't talk.
I never wanted to be a burden, emotionally troubled— an annoyance
I understand—no one knows what to do with me. I wonder myself.
It's very difficult to think and act correctly; am I too far gone—unredeemable?
I know I've sinned and made thousands of bad choices; I need forgiveness
Who am I? I'm all around you; I'm everywhere!

My face changes— as does my race, color and religion.
I need to live, eat and sleep and feel safe, but its hard on the streets.
I'm willing to work, can do some things, but have limitations.
I'm frightened by structure, confined spaces, critical and aggressive people.
Of course I want to become more normal—less confused and afraid;
To be loved, accepted and have friends, but feel stuck without a way out.
Some say God can heal the mind and heart and give forgiveness and peace
I believe in God, but don't know how to access his help.
Who am I? I'm all around you; I'm everywhere!

Do you recognize me?
You saw me when I was hungry and thirsty, dirty and smelly, sick and hurting.
I began hiding from everything and everyone and wanted to die.
I remember seeing you where religious people gather to sing and talk to God.
I'd been hoping to talk with to someone who might help me find God.
I desperately needed healing in my soul—a chance to start over.
You looked startled when you saw me standing there looking shabby.
I started to approach you, but you held up your hand and said,
"Go in Peace! Keep warm and may you find food and be blessed."
Then you quickly turned and walked away. I was stunned by this encounter.
I asked myself hundreds of times, why you spoke these words?
More confused than ever, I wondered, 'Is this what God is like?'

As JP we knew this poem was an indictment against those who claim to be God's followers—including us. To turn away from the needs of those we encounter is not like God. In Jesus' parable of the Good Samaritan, the Priest and the Levite ignored the man lying beaten on the side of the road. As religious leaders they knew this omission of failing to practice compassion would reflect badly on God (Luke 10:25-37, Isaiah 58). In contrast, an ostracized half-breed Samaritan stepped up, showing practical care, mercy and love to his fellow man in a time of urgent need!

Most JP identified with the Injured Man and the Samaritan. We knew what it was like to need help and we wanted to be like the Samaritan who showed mercy, grace and compassion. We knew Jesus was called to the poor, the prisoners, the blind, to set the oppressed free and to proclaim the year of the Lord's favor (Luke 4:16-21). We understood through direct experience, without God's grace and mercy we would have remained lost without hope or truth. With James' words and what Jesus modeled and taught, we could do nothing less than honor JESUS' command *to love God and our neighbor as if we were caring for ourselves* (Matthew 22:37–40).

Becoming a Disciple of Jesus

Most Christian missions the world over link their service and humanitarian provisions to encouraging those being helped to seek the true and Living God and His Son Jesus Christ for spiritual rebirth and entrance into God's kingdom. This conviction ran throughout JP Christian Houses.

Many came to our houses for a meal and to check us out. Sharing about God and spiritual life was always on the table, while keeping in mind the free will choice of a person to be interested, or not. Any affirmative spiritual response beyond this took place in 'Holy Ground' encounters between an individual and God.

We learned, what God does in a brief moment in time— is beyond anything we can ever do!

When God and a human heart connect, the opportunity is present for an individual to welcome God's love and salvation in Jesus Christ. When this occurs the mysterious and miraculous working of the Holy Spirit helps in the birthing process.

After Birth Care

Filled with New Life in the Spirit of God, we each began our journey in a different setting and way. We were all led to and gained access to the Scriptures of the Bible which confirmed our spiritual birth. In reading any of the Gospels of Matthew, Mark, Luke, or John, a window of understanding is opened about how Jesus called his disciples to follow him and asks us to do the same.

I cannot speak for others, but I knew following Jesus was for life. I needed Jesus Christ 'at the center of my life and choices!' The Holy Spirit works in harmony with the Word of God to create a clear conviction that a relationship of openness and obedience to God is essential. I would need to keep trusting and obeying!

In JP days we encouraged every Christian house member to be disciples of Jesus by their words and actions. We believed in Jesus' words in the 'Great Commission' when He sent out his followers into the world (Matthew 28:19-20) to introduce others to the true Light.

> Jesus said, "I am the light of the world. Whoever follows me
> will never walk in darkness, but will have the light of life."
>   John 8:12 NIV®

Today, an increasing number of USA city missions offer a 12-18 month residential program. Men's and women's programs are separate but similar. Men live in a dormitory together, working to break destructive habits and preparing for lives of wholeness and lasting productivity. This happens through:

- One-on-one and group counseling sessions with counselors who model Godly character

- Addiction recovery and family restoration curriculum

- An 'Education Center' offers one-on-one tutoring, remedial education and GED preparation, computer skills training, vocational training and job preparation

- Participation in the daily tasks of running the missions facility and programs teach responsibility, accountability, and joy of giving back

- Daily worship, prayer and Bible study puts men in touch with their Creator and God's purpose for their lives.

After 12 to 18 months in the program, most residents move to a re-entry phase in which they meet a basic criteria before graduation by:

1. Becoming connected to a local church community
2. Obtaining a job
3. Starting a savings account in a bank
4. Securing a place to live

In many instances Mission Donor Teams help furnish and equip graduate apartments. Other mission volunteers offer ongoing mentoring to graduates. Christian organizations like Teen Challenge Ministries and the Dream Center in Los Angeles have similar 12-18 month programs.

An Overview of Christian House Ministry

Christian Houses, though less structured, provided similar spiritual and practical training organically. This would always include study of the Bible and other spiritual literature, and the spiritual disciplines of prayer, fasting, service and evangelism. Receiving and giving forgiveness, confession of sin, unity, handling disagreements gracefully, being truthful, practicing restitution when needed were examples of how life in Jesus was changing us.

Other areas of discipleship involved the discovery and use of personal talents and gifts to glorify God within the community of faith and among those in need. Some of the gifts we saw flourish in community were traits of being encouraging, compassionate, showing love and mercy, being willing to help do whatever needed to be done, having faith for new ministry endeavors or the needs of others that arose, being reliable in carrying out tasks, welcoming new people, being hospitable, teachable and open to learning.

Our training in discipleship also included becoming a good listener to those who were struggling, being a peacemaker, loving God and those around you with a pure heart. *These and many more spiritual traits were the deeper stuff of being less self-centered and more like Jesus Christ.* Living in community accelerated the need to die to selfish ambitions and abide in Jesus Christ. Each step forward in becoming more like Jesus helped us live in harmony.

Practical opportunities to use gifts and talents were expansive in Christian Community. Some individuals excelled in using their hands to build or repair things, clean and organize. Others loved to cook and bake or learned to. Those artistically inclined liked to paint, write music, play instruments, sing or do drama, or operated sound and lighting equipment. Others learned a trade to support the ministry, obtained a license to drive larger vehicles, and took on the responsibility of facility or grounds maintenance. Some enjoyed studying, and teaching the Bible and doing research. Those with graphic or writing interests helped produce articles, newsletters, newspapers, outreach literature, posters or flyers for events, or answered community mail. Still others managed purchasing food and supplies, handling the financial records, secretarial duties or answering the phones for the community. Others helped visitors and new residents get settled, or provided child care and teaching for little ones. Those with mechanical gifts serviced and kept vehicles maintained and running. These and many more opportunities for service were an integral part of running and being an active participant in a Christian House community.

The positives of Christian Houses were many, but there were deficiencies. Living by faith from day to day, meant most JP leaders and their house residents were poor. We didn't think much beyond the present. It's no surprise, bank accounts, savings and money management skills were rare. JP ministries viewed amassing personal wealth, higher education and a life of self sufficiency with suspicion. Inner and spiritual conflict surrounded the use of money. Greed was everywhere, but didn't line up with following Jesus' life and teachings. JP who came from wealthy families resisted the selfishness that often accompanied this life. Learning how to manage money was for another time in the future when we'd be living on our own.

In the meantime, living in Christian community with brothers and sisters in the faith, provided a sense of family. Most JP hadn't been part of a structured family with God's love at the center.

JP houses provided live-in discipleship for those willing to learn, serve and commit themselves to following Jesus. These locations were usually rented/leased or donated for a period of time or permanently. We preferred having a guys' house for young men and a separate location for young women. Married couples lived in separate housing, or in one of the guys or girls locations.

The Purpose of JP Christian Houses

Christian houses during the Jesus Movement days met the practical need of rescuing many from a dangerous and temptation-ridden life on the streets. A Christian house was a safe place, providing temporary, or more permanent respite of body, mind and soul with supportive friendship opportunities.

There was nothing glamorous about starting or running a Christian House. Providing for the needs of those who visited or became more permanent residents while maintaining the day-to-day operations was exhausting work. It was similar to what the founders of orphanages and missions encountered; lots of emotional, physical, mental and spiritual needs. The house leaders I knew lived a simple life of sacrifice.

An Ongoing Occurrence

Imagine inviting a number of people for dinner that you don't know; each with problems, needs and life-baggage. *They come and enjoy the meal and company and decide they want to live with you!* This was typical of what occurred at our Christian houses. People came for a meal, or looking for some type of help and if they felt good about what they encountered, they'd ask to stay.

Another reason for having a Christian House in a community or city was to invite God's presence to impact the area for good. The leaders who led these houses were given the privilege of representing the Lord and meeting specific needs. We didn't expect people to know much about God's gift of new life in Jesus Christ, so we went out regularly into the surrounding community, engaged people in dialogue, shared literature and invited guests to our houses. Taking in a regular stream of people from different backgrounds created challenges we learned to accept as part of the package of following and representing God.

> JP would gradually learn Christian houses were not
> destined to be permanent, but for a time and season.

In the meantime, this model was extremely effective in discipleship training and missions work. Working together sacrificially with a focus on outreach, we were able to accomplish things with God's help that amazed us. Yielding our hearts to God willingly and then intentionally making ourselves available to carry out His work in making Jesus known was the key.

Our Hope for All Who Visited or Lived in a Christian House

Our goal, though not always realized, was for anyone who visited or lived at one of our Christian houses to encounter God's presence, love and truth. Intentionally we pointed everyone to God the Father and Jesus Christ as accessible and present. We believed God could reveal Himself to anyone we encountered and those who came to one of our Christian houses.

We wanted others to experience the type of acceptance, emotional healing, deliverance from evil and life-transformation we had. For this to happen we needed to walk in the Spirit and represent God well. This might occur by sharing food, lodging, listening, sharing our testimony, a few Bible verses, singing or praying with an individual.

We did our best to honor God by giving Him plenty of room to work in someone's heart, mind and spirit. Most of us had a fresh remembrance of what it was like being a seeker, or just plain lost, without a clue who God was, or how to access Him. A considerable number of those who visited encountered *the Presence of God* and wondered what this was. Any questions about God's presence provided a natural opportunity to explain the Good News of Jesus Christ.

What We Did

Most Christian houses conducted Bible Studies with an open-discussion format. We gathered for worship, singing, preaching and meals. We remembered Jesus' death by eating a small portion of bread which was symbolic of His broken body and then drank a small amount of grape juice, representing His spilt blood for us. Honoring God in Communion, we rededicated our lives as Jesus' disciples.

We gathered regularly for prayer lifting up missions around the world, local and ministry needs, for each other, our families and to be filled with God's Spirit and given the ability to represent Jesus honorably in what we did and said. We fasted individually. We intentionally went to places where people congregated to share the Gospel of God's Son. We worked with our hands, learning trades and life-skills. We humbled ourselves when we were wrong and asked for forgiveness from God and our brothers and sisters when needed.

We realized Missions like ours had been in existence throughout the centuries, long before the JP of the 1960's came along. Our Jesus People mission put us on the front lines of reaching and rescuing many without hope or any knowlege of God's love, or the new life offered through Jesus Christ. But would we lose site of this mission over time like some branches of the larger church had done over the centuries? This brings to mind a story some may have never heard.

Lifesaving Station—

"On a dangerous seacoast where shipwrecks often occurred, there was once a crude little lifesaving station and tiny lighthouse. The station was just a hut, and there was only one boat, but the few devoted locals kept a constant watch over the sea. With no thought for themselves, they went out persistently searching for survivors whose boats had hit the rocks.

Many among those rescued were pulled out of frigid and dangerous waters with injuries and massive personal needs. The small life-saving team provided essential medical care, food and housing, respite, transportation, and aided survivors in a variety of practical ways and assisted them in making contact with family or friends.

Hearing of the work of this small team, others in the larger community wanted to be associated with the station, and give

of their time and money and effort to support the work. New boats were bought and new crews trained. The little lifesaving station grew.

But, some of the newer members of the lifesaving station were unhappy about the site being so crude and poorly equipped. They felt that a more comfortable place should be provided as a first refuge for those rescued from the sea. They replaced the small old beds with newer ones, purchased new furniture and enlarged the building. This seemed good to all.

In a short span of time the Lifesaving Station became a popular gathering place for its members and they decorated it beautifully and furnished it exquisitely, because they'd decided to use it as a sort of club. Fewer members were now interested in going out on lifesaving missions, so they hired lifeboat crews to do the work. The life-saving motif remained on display in the club's main meeting room and there was an actual life boat in another room where club initiations were held.

About this time, a large ship was wrecked off the coast and the hired crews brought in boatloads of cold, wet, half-drowned people. They were dirty and sick. Many were of varied race and color origins. The beautiful new club was in chaos, so the property committee immediately had a shower house built outside the club where victims of shipwrecks could be cleaned up before coming inside.

At the next meeting, there was a split in the club membership. Most of the members wanted to stop the clubs life-saving activities because they were unpleasant and a hindrance to the normal social life of the club. Some members insisted that 'lifesaving' was their primary purpose and pointed out they were still called a Lifesaving Station.

Those who clung to the purpose of the station "saving the lost" were voted down and told if they wanted to save lives of all the various kinds of people who were shipwrecked in the regional waters, they could begin their own lifesaving station down the coast. They did.

As the years went by, the new station experienced the same changes that had occurred in the old. It evolved into a club, and yet another life saving station was founded and this cycle continued to repeat itself.

If you visit this seacoast today, you will find a number of exclusive clubs along the shore. Shipwrecks are still a frequent occurrence due to the large rocks, but most of the people drown."

Jesus said, "The Son of Man came to seek and to save the lost."
Luke 19:10

Who We Are—and What We Provide Through Him

I like to think of all Christ-followers as having an incredibly important purpose. Some use the analogy of us representing God by being 'His hands and feet, heart and voice of truth' in a harried and troubled world. God uses us to reveal Himself in tangible ways that others can see. When we show His love, speak His truth, emulate Jesus' character, show no partiality, forgive as He forgave us and practice ongoing deeds of kindness and mercy, giving glory to God—someone is watching! Nothing is wasted!

The everyday person is weary of the world's schemes—you know, the fiber optic storm of endless rhetoric, sales pitches, junk phone calls and emails, false news, inaccurate Internet information and pleas for money. We'd like to put on the brakes and say "stop!" The barrage of things coming at us is overwhelming and requires time consuming filtering. The unsolicited invasion of our privacy and greed-driven schemes is toxic to our well-being!

When sinking in the stormy waters of life a genuine lifeline is needed. *People are hungry for authentic help minus hidden agenda motives.* When looking for truth or wisdom we want the real deal! When seeking inner peace of heart and soul, we don't want to be sidetracked by anything false.

What we have to offer is not centered in us, but rather *God's presence of Light and Truth that's available in Jesus Christ.* This is the gift we have to share with a fragile and harried world.

We Are Christian

We are in the world, but not of it. We are foreigners in route to an eternal kingdom. God alone knows those who are attuned to him and we are part of His living church i.e. Body of Christ. Our central purpose is to bring glory to God by loving the Father, Son and Holy Spirit with all our heart, mind and strength, and our neighbor as ourselves.

By our words and deeds we are commissioned to point others to Jesus Christ (Colossians 3:17); compelling those without hope, direction or spiritual life to trust in the Living God and His Son. We have a lot to do in representing Him (Ephesians 1:9).

We are His hands, feet, heart
and voice of truth in this world

Who Did Jesus Die For?

If we attempted to list who Jesus died for, we could easily fill volumes describing every type of person, and every heart need and hope they represent. All are a match. All represent who God's Son died for. Boiled down, **Jesus died for everyone!**

His life, teachings, miracles and what He modeled was all for a purpose. His death and resurrection was the culmination of His mission on earth. This leads us to the 'Good News' aka the "Gospel of God's Son."

Picture yourself with no Bible nearby and someone asks you to explain the hope that lies within your heart (I Peter 3:15). You begin by sharing your story of coming to faith in God, but the person inquiring wants to hear the account of Jesus Christ's life on earth and why He is God's Son. Though we are imperfect, the Holy Spirit is able to translate our words and make them alive to a hearer's heart. But how will we unravel this amazing miracle of God breaking into human history?

What is The Gospel of God's Son, and why should anyone believe in Him? It *is in our best interest and that of others to be refreshed in the Biblical narrative of what has occurred and what is to come.*

Author's Note: A capsule rendering of The Gospel
of Jesus Christ can be found in chapter 32

Christian House Expansion and Leaders

During the JP movement-revolution there were hundreds of Christian houses, ranches and farms opened over a span of 10 years. House leaders were in the pressurized role of supervising everyday operational issues and welcoming all who entered the front door. A house leader might be the same age or younger than those who visited or lived in the house. They were responsible for maintaining house rules, monitoring chores, being peace-keepers and staying spiritually fit through prayer, Bible study and other spiritual disciplines.

When a resident or visitor was angry, it was a house leader's job to listen and resolve issues as gracefully as possible. Young leaders were often stretched to the limits when it came to the types of problems they encountered and the expenditure of emotional energy it took to appease unhappy campers and find solutions. On the plus side, their natural and spiritual gifts increased. All residents and visitors were accountable to one or more house leader.

There were no dress codes in the houses I was a part of, but personal hygiene was strongly encouraged, as well as maintaining a teachable and cooperative spirit. High on the list of house rules was showing respect and consideration for house residents.

Each Christian house had its own rules based on its location, target population and focus of ministry. A Christian house located in the inner city was entirely different than a rural ranch ministry. Reasonable rules and participation requirements in practical and spiritual areas was the norm.

The following highlights the "Jesus Family" in England and weaves in broader JP principles of faith and practice.

The Jesus Family England

The Jesus Family in England was a uniquely interesting and supportive community. Several things set it apart. A sincere love and acceptance of each other was strong along with an appreciation of the diversity of members and the countries they represented. The group was comprised of participants from USA, Canada, England, Ireland, Sweden, Germany, Holland, Australia and India.

With this mixture, world perspectives varied. Learning about each other's culture, language, and ways of doing things was fascinating and helped us work together in harmony. The highly desirable quality of appreciating, valuing and being open to learn from one another made us an inclusive, friendly community.

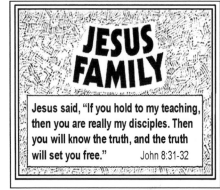

The absence of a rigid judgmental spirit was a refreshing characteristic, but this did not mean there was no substance or spiritual backbone in the overall ministry when it came to matters of faith and practice. The Father and Jesus Christ His Son and the Holy Spirit were firmly at the center with the Word of God as the source for defining faith and practice.

The open and kindred spirit of cooperation, love, compassion and inclusiveness bore good fruit which nurtured life-time friendships.

We were given the use of several large houses, nestled into boroughs in or close to London. One house was in Upper Norwood aka Crystal Palace in southeast London, called the 'Beulah Hill House.' Our office building was located nearby on the same road. The second house was in Bromley, Kent near London geographically.

The ministry schedule within the Jesus Family was turned upside down with the launch of the theatrical production *'Lonesome Stone.'* A flexible approach was employed to accommodate those involved in evening theatrical performances. Eating, sleeping, study, prayer and community gatherings were adjusted and creatively woven into everyone's schedule. The workload increased, for some overwhelmingly so. Theater production members had their own rigors to keep up with, as did those at the home base who provided childcare, meal prep, clean-up and ministry maintenance.

Different types of pressures arose for all, which were to be expected when living in a community with an outreach vision. Overall, the Jesus Family was amazingly grace-filled and resilient when it came to staying on top of the increased workload. This does not mean there were not troubling issues that arose for individuals and young families. Some of these problems were accentuated when a large contingency of the Jesus Family went on tour with *Lonesome Stone* while others stayed behind with young children to care for and more base operation responsibilities.

Living in a Christian community House was a mixture of pros and cons. The relational benefits of learning from one another, working and serving together was amazing. Having plenty of opportunities to develop and use spiritual and practical talents was another positive. On the flip side, being "I" centered and confident of 'always being right' required internal adjustments and a considerable amount of self-correcting.

Human Nature and Individualism

Formerly, many of us were willful and stubborn when it came to calling the shots. We liked being in control, freedom of movement and holding onto our pet sins. Since leaving home, we'd set our own schedule, went to bed and woke up when we wanted. Once we hit eighteen, we were adults! Maturity was lagging and would take time to catch up, but we didn't know this yet. **We were invincible, full of self and our own ideas about lots of things!**

Living in community was a wake-up call; a stark contrast to living on our own and doing our own thing. It was similar to living in a large biological family with a spiritual emphasis. We had to relearn receiving directions, being assigned chores, adhering to the house rules and being considerate of others. Living on our own, we called the shots, and thought we were right about almost everything. If someone challenged or disagreed with us, our survival skill was to become defensive. We weren't used to being told what to do, where to go, or confronted about faulty thinking or behavior.

Teachable Spirit

I wonder how many parents would give anything to encounter the rare trait of a teachable spirit in their teenager, or young adult child? JP were learning to seek God's guidance, maintain a teachable spirit and be an active participant in the work and goals of the community. Thankfully, the Bible (God's Word) and the Holy Spirit assisted us.

Walking in step with God's Spirit was the hardest thing we would ever do, and none of us were successful all of the time. The high calling of following Jesus requires sacrifice and perseverance. **Tenacious heart loyalty to God enabled us to stay pliable and yielded.** Serving and working in a Christian community was an incredible opportunity and life experience, which by nature mandated each participant keep their own personal relationship with God vibrant.

Discipleship, Sharing the Good News and Prayer

Every person's 'commitment to discipleship' was invaluable in a Christian community. It put us all on the same page, regardless of age, gender, or length of time being a Christian. *We were all sinners being transformed. Collectively we were an imperfect community with a perfect Lord and Savior who was our ultimate leader and model.* Working together in mission and service endeavors was a great way to learn how to work alongside others and accomplish far more than we could alone. It was on-the-job training with Jesus helping us to live out our faith in close proximity to others who were on the same intentionally committed journey.

Christian leaders acknowledge discipleship is the missing ingredient in most churches

Discipleship Core Essentials

What follows is a sampling of what we were learning in discipleship and endeavoring to put into practice during JP days. These principles and capsule teachings have their roots in Jesus' or the Apostles' teachings. Doing these things kept our hearts focused on God and our feet aimed in the right direction. God's Grace and our willing obedience to follow were a critical duo if we hoped to achieve these things.

Growing Up in Jesus

- Stay immersed in God's Word, absorbing, applying and obeying.
- Listen to and for God's voice in prayer and intercede for others persistently in faith.
- Learn to pray in harmony with God's Plan and Will and leave the results in His hands.
- Confess your sins regularly and forgive those who sin against you.
- Remain humble, teachable and yielded to God's Holy Spirit.
- Be faithful in the use of your abilities and spiritual gifts to glorify God.
- Speak up, pray, write and stand firmly against injustice.
- Accept and provide tangible help to those who've been wounded and abused by the world.

- Share boldly and freely what God has done in your heart; others need to hear and see.
- Practice random deeds of kindness. Bless others by showing God's Love whenever and wherever you can.
- Don't turn your eyes or heart away from those with genuine needs; be God's instrument of Mercy.
- Speak the truth in love, pointing others to God and His Son Jesus.
- Put on the full armor of God, resist the devil! Remain under the covering of Jesus Christ.
- Don't be ashamed of the Gospel of God's Son which is able to save all who believe! You may think God can't save someone, but He can.
- Ask for boldness in the Holy Spirit to make Jesus known.
- Be a person of compassion; exude kindness, goodness and mercy in Jesus' Name.
- Love your neighbors, your brothers and sisters in the faith and even your enemies.
- Honor the diversity in the body of Christ.
- Live sacrificially amidst a world of consumerism, and live within your means.
- Model your faith and convictions by your words and deeds.
- Train and disciple others as Jesus did. Lift someone up and help them grow in the faith.
- Do everything with excellence knowing you are working directly for the Lord!
- Continue following Jesus daily. Never give up!
- Give honor and glory to God in everything you do.

When we applied these and other Biblical principles, we'd often experience God's presence as a confirmation we were in step with Him.

A Desire to Glorify and Honor God

A desire to honor, please and obey God was embodied in the larger JP Movement. Our loyalty was not to religion, human leaders or a denomination, but to God the Father, Jesus Christ His Son and the Holy Spirit.

Students of the Word

Jesus People had a lot to learn. To satisfy this need, God planted a voracious appetite for the Word of God (II Timothy 2:15, Hebrews 4:12-13, Psalm 119). We wanted to know what God said ourselves, similar to the Samaritans who urged Jesus to stay with them for two additional days. The Samaritan account says, "And because of his (Jesus') words many more became believers. They said to the Samaritan woman, 'We no longer believe just because of what you said; now we have heard for ourselves, and we know that this man really is the Savior of the world (John 4:41-42).'"

Hearing and examining the Scriptures to verify what is true, strengthens faith and discernment. The Berean Jews in Paul's time of teaching and preaching did so. "They received the message (Gospel) with great eagerness and examined the Scriptures every day to see if what Paul said was true (Acts 17:11). They examined Old Testament Scriptures pertaining to the Messiah and core truths from God which had been diminished by Jewish tradition. The Apostle Peter confirms the power of God's Word saying, "For you have been born again, not of perishable seed, but of imperishable, through the living and enduring Word of God."

John's Gospel taught us the origins of God's Word. "In the beginning was the Word, and the Word was with God, and the Word was God. He was with God in the beginning. Through him all thing were made, without him nothing was made that has been made. In him was life, and that life was the light of men. The Word became flesh and made his dwelling among us. We have seen his glory, the glory of the One and only, who came from the Father, full of grace and truth. For the Law was given through Moses; grace and truth came through Jesus Christ (John 1:1-4, 14, 17)."

Without the compass of the Bible, we would be direction-less. We already knew what floundering was like and didn't want to return to the empty practice of 'doing our own thing' and 'pleasure seeking!'

We believed the Bible was God's Word, both Old and New Testaments, anointed by God and breathed upon by Him. We knew God carefully chose and guided each author found in the Bible to record the Truth so there would be an accurate record of God's work and activities among humans.

Faith & Trust

Many JP were endowed with a 'lack of fear' regarding calculated assurances of what tomorrow might bring. The way we approached living and ministry possibilities was similar to how Joshua did when God told him, "Have not I commanded you, be strong and courageous. Do not be terrified, do not be discouraged, for the Lord your God will be with you everywhere you go (Joshua 1:9)."

> Faith in the infinite possibilities God can initiate at any time of His choosing was in our DNA. We knew God as creative, active and present.

We were available and enthusiastic about representing Him in our world. At the same time our excitement was tempered by an internal awareness that attempting to serve God in our own steam, energy or ingenuity was futile. We didn't want to slip into the trend of some mainline churches that had become nominal in belief, neatly self-sufficient—but terribly lacking in exuding the life and power of Jesus Christ.

JP needed to be dependent on God's presence and guidance to help us to be effective and fruitful. We needed to learn how to pray and step out in faith, how to listen to the Holy Spirit and be God's instruments in the world.

Quirks and Faults

Life in community was fish-bowl living. For those who thrived and were energized by being around people it was exciting and invigorating. In contrast, those recharged by solitude found all the activity and noise a challenge. Exercise, ear plugs and leisure walks usually helped.

Being constantly around others could be emotionally exhausting, regardless! Personality types, personal baggage, differences, preferences and a lot of other stuff were squished together into the community melting pot.

> There were days when living and working in constant close proximity to others got on our last nerve! We'd feel like screaming, exiting the ministry; just running away!

Any number of stresses could unfold without warning and push someone into a place of anxiety, or a boiling point.

When this occurred, respite, a mini holiday, counseling, or coming up with something tangible to take the pressure off needed to be addressed immediately. Most ministries had resources to help facilitate this. A few days away often did wonders in restoring an individual's balance and sense of well being.

When this didn't work, it was time for a tired and exasperated team member to make a change. An individual's mental, emotional and spiritual health was crucial—along with the well-being of the community. If a person was unhappy, or felt like living in community was too stressful, it was important to recognize it and provide help for this individual.

The ideal protocol was to aid an individual in relocating when the funds were available to do so. *In healthy Jesus People ministries there was no guilt attached to a person leaving!* There were many circumstantial scenarios for a person needing to transition from living in a Christian house. While part of the Jesus Family in England, I lived in separate living accommodations while navigating emotional lows from the COG fiasco.

JP Spiritual Traditions

For the most part JP could be characterized as part of the low church of common people. There was very little in the way of rituals, candle or incense burning, cathedral type pomp, altars, or worship led by priests in robes. We didn't follow any liturgical calendar of Scripture readings or holy dates prescribed by High Church denominations. Two traditions which are found in the New Testament of the Bible were practiced by almost all Jesus People groups.

The Lord's Table of Communion

We remembered Jesus' death by reading the account of the last Passover meal Jesus shared with his disciples and partaking of the bread and cup of Communion. We honored Jesus' request to gather for this purpose; freshly remembering in our hearts the incredible sacrifice God made by sending His own Son to endure a cruel death in order to redeem and liberate all who would believe. Jesus' work of obeying His Father's plan by facing death on our behalf had ushered in a New Eternal Covenant that would birth millions into God's eternal family.

When we gathered, the Scriptures we read were Matthew 26:26-30, Mark 14:22-26, Luke 22:14-20, or Paul's rendering in I Corinthians 11:23-26. The Apostle Paul's warnings regarding steering clear of abuses were also cited in the I Corinthians passage.

Water Baptism

Water baptism was an important event among Jesus People. Jesus modeled it when he was baptized by John the Baptist. Our belief was in a Believers Baptism, which meant it was for those old enough to know what believing in and following Jesus Christ meant. It was a celebration of New Life in each person who had placed their trust in Jesus Christ. JP usually baptized by full immersion when water was available. Ideal locations were beaches, lakes, ponds and rivers. Secondary choices were church baptismals, swimming pools, hot-tubs etc. Baptism was a visual picture of putting off the old life and putting on a new life in Jesus Christ when rising out of the waters. If a person was unable to be baptized by immersion for any number of reasons, creative approaches were employed.

JP did not believe baptism or taking communion was a criteria for a person's salvation. Receiving Jesus Christ as one's personal Lord and Savior, i.e. being birthed by the Holy Spirit into God's family was the main event!

Easter—Resurrection Day from Pagan Origins?

The celebration of the resurrection of Jesus from death was practiced by most JP during the 'Easter' season, but not all.

Some Jesus People found scholarly Bible research that raised questions about the origins of Easter. It was noted in this research that the "Passover" season of the Jews took place during the spring of the year.

According to New Unger's Bible Dictionary and many Bible scholars there is evidence that 'Easter' was originally a pagan festival honoring various 'goddesses of spring' and the return of the sun. The Sumerian goddess 'Inanna' is among this group, known outside of Mesopotamia by her Babylonian name, 'Ishtar.' Followers of this supposed deity believed she was responsible for ushering in the spring season and more light from the sun.

The predominant goddess linking 'Easter' *to a pagan holiday by name is the Saxon goddess 'Eastra' whose followers offered sacrifices to her for bringing a return to Spring. The name 'Eastra' is rendered Easter in English.*

For this reason a strong case can be made that the church's early celebration of Easter has been adopted from pagan roots while keeping the goddess' name. In an attempt to correct this, the church of the 8th century made an official declaration that the spring holiday of Easter would henceforth be designated as the celebration day for the Resurrection of Jesus Christ.

Goddess of Spring 'Eastra'

Christians the world over weren't thrilled to learn both Catholic and Protestant church leaders introduced holidays with pagan roots and in this instance kept the name of the goddess. Take notice of the rabbit in this drawing. Where did the infamous bunny association with Easter come from?

Those who are privy to these things are equally shocked to learn the church invented and adopted numerous erroneous practices and doctrines over the centuries which had absolutely nothing to do with Jesus Christ, the Apostles' teachings, or any part of the Bible.

JP who learned of these things continued to stand firm on the reality of Jesus' resurrection from death. We knew His death and resurrection were the reason we had received New Life!

Since celebrating Jesus' resurrection was not recorded in the Bible, and a deluge of Easter bunny, egg and other cultural things had been added, we either celebrated the day of Jesus' resurrection or didn't, according to personal preference. Our overall practice was one of giving thanks daily for God's amazing gift of resurrection life that Jesus ushered in!

Most JP remained oblivious to church traditions and their origins and to erroneous doctrines and practices that were incorporated over the centuries.

Primary Jesus People House Rules

As within most families, reasonable behavior was required. Our added dimension was spiritual discipleship. In all JP houses, alcohol or drug use, premarital sex and LGBT relationships were not allowed. These practices, or violent or threatening behavior, stealing, lying and the like were considered unacceptable community behavior and could result in an individual being asked to leave. If a person decided they didn't want to accept community guidelines it was their choice. Most residents considered living in a

Christian house a privilege.

Basic JP House guidelines included carrying out house or grounds chores, participating in Bible studies and house meetings, abiding by a reasonable curfew and being considerate of other residents. Smoking was discouraged but tolerated if done outside. 'House Leaders' did their best to be reasonable and give opportunities to those who were not compliant with community rules to self-correct their behavior. If they did not want to comply, they were asked to leave.

Keeping a stash of drugs or alcohol was almost impossible without someone finding out. Most team members were committed to letting go of addictions and other destructive habits which had been their downfall in the past. Ongoing reminders to 'let destructive habits die' helped residents firm up their convictions about the new path they were on.

Turning away from former habits and learning to follow Jesus Christ was a topic emphasized and revisited regularly in all Christian houses.

Mortal Enemies

As disciples we are at war with five enemies, who continually attempt to seduce and create scenarios of temptation aimed at our downfall. The first three are embedded in our human nature and the world. They work like a magnet, luring us in with the aim of preoccupying us with the pursuit of worldly and fleshly appetites.

> "For all that is in the world—the lust and sensual craving of the flesh, the wandering and longing of the eyes and the boastful pride of life, i.e. pretentious confidence in one's resources or in the stability of earthly things—these do not come from the Father, but are from the world."
> John 2:16 Amp. Bible

The fourth and fifth enemies are the devil and his demons. Satan, the fallen angel formerly known as 'Lucifer' and his demon slaves hate everything to do with God, Jesus Christ and God's people. Long ago, he plotted a rebellion in the heavens in an attempt to overthrow God. Unsuccessful, he was punished by banishment to the earth. Enraged by being kicked out of heaven, he seeks to ruin everything God has created including us!

And the Evil One, the great dragon was thrown down, the

age-old serpent who is called the devil and Satan, who now continually seeks to deceive and seduce the entire inhabited world; he was thrown down to earth and his angels (demons) were thrown down with him.

Revelation 12:9 Amp. Bible

An unseen enemy of humans is constantly at work in the world, endeavoring to cause chaos and unleash evil wherever possible. *No one is immune from the temptations of our human nature, or this enemy who seeks to interfere with the amazing plan God has for each of us. Thankfully God is stronger!* The Bible urges us to place ourselves under the covering and protection of God and to put on spiritual armor, available to all who belong to Jesus Christ (Ephesians 6:1-20).

Some Christians and JP wrongly concluded they could reach a level of spirituality without satanic or fleshly attacks. At the last supper and in the 23rd Psalm we find the Enemy at the Table. In Job 1:6-7 Satan showed up with the angels and then before Job and God. Don't be fooled, the enemy we are at war with hates God and us! Facing temptation is part of living in a fallen world.

Health & Wealth Doctrine

A teaching of error affecting a segment of JP is still around today. It comes from teachers who promote what is called The Health and Wealth Gospel aka The Prosperity Gospel. *They falsely teach a guarantee of physical healing and monetary blessings if our Faith is strong enough.* 'Name It and Claim It' is one of the original catch phrases accompanying this teaching. The problem: If an adherent to this teaching does not receive what they ask for, they must be deficient in faith and spirituality. Discouragement and disillusionment follows. Some health and wealth teachers use this to their advantage, telling their followers a probable cause is tied to them not giving enough money. *And, of course, gifts of money to these teachers is always welcome so they can buy a newer and better jet!*

Those who have taught or currently teach this false doctrine are: E. W. Kenyon, Oral Roberts, A. A. Allen, Robert Tilton, T. L. Osborn, Joel Osteen, Creflo Dollar, Jesse Duplantis, Kenneth Copeland, Reverend Ike, and Kenneth Hagin.

The 'Wealth' aspect of this teaching, which tells people to claim money, lands, property is simply bad doctrine, not consistent with Jesus or the apostle's life and ministry as recorded in the Bible. Some JP fell for the lure, but most were not sucked in.

The promise of health and wealth is appealing, but not something we can wish or claim into reality. God asks us to pray in faith, for healing, but also to trust in His superior plan and purposes when a miracle does not occur. Numerous miracles of healing initiated by God happened before and during Jesus' ministry and since. We witnessed many in the JP movement, *but they didn't come because we willed them by our faith or power. God alone is the miracle worker!*

Each of us experience illness and aging. *To expect a promise of perfect health, or a 'Get Out of Death Card' when our allotted time on earth is up, is placing our hope in the wrong place.* As a former hospice chaplain, I know death is inevitable. For Jesus' followers, it is the doorway to eternal life. *When the angel's trumpet sounds at Jesus Christ's return we will rise!*

In the meantime, God does not give us the ability to be perfect, or escape the temptations of the flesh, or the devil. And we cannot guarantee a miracle for every person seeking some type of healing. In many instances God uses illness and life tragedies to get our attention and bring us closer to Him.

Mirror-Mirror on the Wall—Who's the Biggest Sinner of All?

The most troubling aspect of living in community was when our personal sins glared back at us so blatantly. *We were sure everyone in the entire ministry knew we were rotten to the core, a terrible despicable disciple.* With the weight of guilt on us for whatever we did, we might conclude all our secret sinful thoughts and actions were in plain view. Fortunately, this was not the case and most community members understood the reality of personal struggles, since all of us had our own shortcomings and guilt associated with these areas of weakness (Galatians 6:1-2).

The norm was confessing our weaknesses to those we were closest to, who in turn would be truthful and honest in counseling us. They in turn would pray with and for us with the absence of harsh judgment.

Sins are like weeds that need to be pulled over and over again until there are fewer of them. Transparency and openness was a beneficial aspect of living in community. Honest friendships where mutual compassion and mercy flowed back and forth allowed spiritual progress to flourish and Jesus' character to grow stronger in us.

Accountability

Answering to someone is all around us; in families, the workplace, school, sports, the military and throughout society. It's beneficial when we receive affirmation. It's equally valuable when we receive corrective input to help us improve and keep on track. What we learn from our mistakes is usually the most valuable.

Correction without hope is another matter, widely viewed as unhealthy and destructive. Unfortunately overbearing correction did occur in some JP Christian houses. In most cases it was curbed by the rest of the community. To crush someone for faults all of us have been guilty of in one form or another is blatant hypocrisy! Every person who does something wrong needs to be able to see a path to being forgiven and restored. Forgiveness and hope never get old and are primary core principles Jesus taught (Matthew 6:14-15)!

As Jesus People we were in the beginning stages of discipleship. The experience was beautiful and wonderful, as we reaped the rewards of peace, joy and a clean conscience. God's patience, forgiveness, grace and love, kept us going (Psalm 51, 30:5).

The central problem was, our sinful nature didn't want to die! Thankfully, we faced the good, bad and ugly in ourselves and others one day at a time. We learned to accept the principle of ongoing transformation into Jesus' likeness. God's mercy triumphed over the punishment we deserved!

Being rebuked by an elder in the community was not a fun experience. Who needs this type of humiliation?! When emotions flared, thinking about punching someone in the nose gave us some satisfaction, minus the actual deed. This is not to say there were never altercations in the larger JP movement.

God's Peace and Love

For the most part, God's peace surrounded JP houses and the Jesus Family community in England. We learned to share and hold lightly to material things, with the exception of our musical instruments! We learned heaps (Brit term) from each other. An enormous benefit was spending lots of

time together. As we grew in our faith side by side, a bond of love and appreciation was formed that continues.

> Jesus said, "I give you a new commandment, to love one another. Just as I have loved you—you also are to love one another. Everyone will know by this that you are my disciples if you have love for one another."   John 13:34–35

The need for and practice of loving one another is heightened when living in Christian community. People with softer, flexible and congenial personalities are better suited than those who are impatient, selfish, egotistical, uncompromising, inconsiderate, easily angered and confrontational. The latter have a rougher go when it comes to God's inevitable pruning (John 15:2). Clip, clip, clip—ouch!

> Therefore I exhort you, brothers and sisters, by the mercies of God, to present your bodies as a sacrifice—alive, holy, and pleasing to God—which is your reasonable service. Do not be conformed to this present world, but be transformed by the renewing of your mind, so that you may test and approve what is the will of God—what is good and well-pleasing and in harmony with the Truth."   Romans 12:1–2 NIV®

By studying the Word of God, our conscience was activated (Hebrews 4:12–13). We knew God wanted us to come clean about sin when it surfaced (Psalm 51). In numerous ways we were reminded that following Jesus was a call to live a sacrificial life (Luke 9:22). The Holy Spirit would guide us into truth and purge out what needed to go. Gradually godly character was being formed. Wisdom and understanding would be broadened over time (John 14:15–27, John 17, Titus 2:11–12, 3:1-8, I Peter 3:8–12, 2 Peter 1:3–10).

Truth Tellers

Thankfully God sent heralds of truth into the world; prophets of God, apostles, disciples; speaking the truth—all representing the True and Living God. Jesus' parting words to his disciples also applied to JP.

> All authority in heaven and on earth has been given to me. So you must go and make disciples of all nations. Baptize them in the name of the Father and of the Son and of the Holy Spirit. Teach them to obey everything I have commanded you. And you can be sure that I am always with you, to the very end. Matthew 28:18–20 NIV®

As Jesus' ministry was mostly among the common people, outside the confines of religious buildings and walls—the same applied to us. We gravitated to those who were out and about in public places. A high percentage were those that religious people wouldn't want to shake hands with, hug, or be around for any length of time. We connected with the unclean, smelly and rough. We were not so far removed from our previous life that we'd forgotten. This helped us avoid shrinking back from those who others might not be interested in. Like every human, people needed to experience God's acceptance, love, mercy and forgiveness.

In Awe & Counting the Cost

Who is willing, or worthy to follow in His steps? When John the Baptist was quizzed if he was the Christ, he answered: "I baptize you with water. But One more powerful than I will come, the thongs of whose sandals I am not worthy to untie. He will baptize you with the Holy Spirit and fire (Luke 3:16)."

Like John, we knew our limitations. Jesus is the one who saves and baptizes with the Holy Spirit. Following in Jesus' steps was, and still is a tall order. Jesus People were unworthy, but willing. Most were unpolished, without formal training, but knew how to read. By reading one Gospel, we understood there was a cost to following Jesus Christ.

Following God took Jesus to a Roman cross and death by crucifixion. Reading through Acts we learned Stephen was stoned to death. Saul who became Paul the apostle said, "I persecuted followers of this way to their death, arresting both men and women and throwing them in prison (Acts 22:4)." Paul went from being a persecutor to being persecuted for speaking and representing Jesus Christ.

Disciples of Jesus were not safe. They were despised, hated, persecuted and killed. History confirms widespread violent persecution throughout the centuries. Hatred and severe persecution of Christ followers continues today. It occurs in Communist and Muslim countries, in dictator-run regimes and among ethnic tribes or peoples who wish to carry out genocide on anyone with Christian or Jewish roots.

The Scriptures speak of persecution of God's people in the future (Revelation 12:17, 13:7, Daniel 11:33). There is a cost to being a follower of the True and Living God and His Son, Jesus Christ. A time will come when we will be considered an enemy of an anti-God one world government and the cost of following Jesus Christ and the Living God will increase. Many will fall away because of persecution.

Dying to Self

Self identity is primary to human existence. Unique fingerprints, DNA, and genes make us one of a kind. All the influences we've been exposed to and the environment in which we were raised all contribute to the person we are. When we come to faith in Jesus Christ, our personality is not obliterated, but God's presence is added. We become complete, a new creation (2 Corinthians 5:17) with God's Spirit now living in us.

Taking up our cross daily and following Jesus is the work of every Christian. Doing so requires dying to self and allowing our sinful nature to be subdued by the Holy Spirit. God wants our new nature in Christ to be at the center of our heart, mind and choices. When we are birthed by the Spirit of Jesus Christ, it's critical to keep listening to God's guidance. The Holy Spirit offers wisdom and character traits that come from Jesus Christ and enable us to become the person God created us to be. Dying to self and sin and rising with Jesus as a new creation is essential! It is a process of surrender from spiritual birth to physical death.

> Whoever wants to be my disciple must deny themselves and take up their cross daily and follow me.   Luke 9:23 NIV®

Intentional Resistance to God's Path

Life can be incredibly difficult when a person willfully decides to ignore the Spirit of God's influence. The depth of heartache, guilt, deprivation and anguish of soul can easily become bottomless for those who turn their back on God in defiant resistance. *To scorn God's offer of life is one of the biggest mistakes anyone can make!*

Without truth and a relationship with the Living God, we are susceptible to a meaningless existence of being consumed and driven to chase after the world's lusts, schemes, false gods and selfish ambitions. All are void of truth and real life! Cyclical bad choices ravage a person emotionally, physically and spiritually. A sad fate has overtaken many who started out as followers of Jesus, but chose to stop practicing their faith. Jesus' teaching on remaining faithful to the end, is reason for great concern for those who have turned back to their old life (Matthew 7:26; 25:10; 24:4-51; Mark 13:13; John 6:66; Revelation 14:12).

Urgent Need to be Under God's Protection

Receiving Jesus doesn't mean free-will or choice is removed. We can still be drawn into temptation. The Spirit of God inside us wants for us to do what's right and make good choices, but the lure of temptation is constantly tugging in the opposite direction. *We're usually attacked in areas where we're the weakest and most vulnerable.*

All Christ followers are in the same predicament. A destructive habit may have been conquered, but new and potentially crippling temptations can arise without warning. We are urged to choose God's way over and over again. I recently re-memorized Psalm 23 and the prayer Jesus taught the disciples sometimes called The Lord's Prayer in Matthew 6:9-14. I pray both of these portions of Scripture regularly to remind myself how desperately

I need to be centered and focused on walking in step with Jesus and the Father!

Choosing Between Life or Death (Deuteronomy 30:19)

Life: The True and Living One and His Son Jesus Christ offer every one who hears the Gospel of Jesus Christ an opportunity to be spiritually reborn and inherit eternal life. This second birth is accompanied by a portion of God's character of faith, courage, hope, truth, peace, kindness and love—deposited in our spirit to grow and flow out to others. These traits from God are the seal and confirmation of 'Christ' living in us through His Holy Spirit. Jesus calls this the abundant life (John 10:10 KJV), living in a relationship with God— with an ongoing transfusion of His nature, plus guidance and protection. .

Infinite possibilities and new directions are intrinsic to beginning a new life with God at the helm. He will give us wisdom in discerning who we were created to be, and ways we can utilize our natural talents and developing spiritual gifts to bless others with God's goodness, love and truth. We were created in God's image to honor Him with our lives; to value what is good and honest and enjoy work, family life and friends. God gave us eyes to enjoy the beauty, majesty and splendor of the natural world He created. His good plan for our lives is for us to find fulfillment and satisfaction in the work we do, be thankful and to have peace of mind, heart and spirit!

Death: In contrast, the god of this world, the devil and his demons are relentlessly attempting to draw humans away from God's goodness, truth, love and peace. Satan corrupts what is pure and good and turns it into *a greed driven mad pursuit of wealth, power, and lust on steroids!* The devil's aim is to derail the good plan God has for us—by tricking us into chasing after a twisted version of what God gives for free!

The devil revels in luring us in with deception and temptations that hook and bind the human soul. Obsessions, addictions, greed, and endless pleasure seeking doesn't fulfill the human heart, or make us healthy on the inside. These detours might numb and distract us or offer temporary enjoyment, but it doesn't last. God didn't create us to be manipulated into a frenzied life and a premature death caused by the Evil One. Jesus describes Satan in this way:

> "He was a murderer from the beginning, not holding to the truth, for there is no truth in him. When he lies, he speaks his native language, for he is a liar and the father of lies." John 8:44 NIV®)

We are wise to resist the devil's lies and promotion of the cravings of the eyes, the lusts of the flesh and pride that springs self sufficient arrogance.

God speaks to us through the Scriptures of the Bible about obeying Him and resisting the enemy (James 4:7, I John 2:16, Ephesians 6:10, Ephesians 2:10).

> Be on your guard; stand firm in the faith; be courageous; be strong.   1 Corinthians 16:13 NIV®

This spiritual advice is not only for us, but for those who will believe because we remain faithful to Jesus.

Evil is not retreating but shape-shifting in a myriad of disguises. This being true, up-to-date discernment between good and evil is critical. *Evil is always looking for ways to infiltrate and influence society to accept it, wanting to become the cultural norm.*

There will always be pressure to conform to the world's changing morals and expectations which are increasingly anti-God, anti-Christ, anti-Christian and anti-Jewish.

Consider the *Progressive, Liberal and Socialist agenda in America.* Most who promote these political and socialist views are aggressively intolerant, quick to malign, harass, lie, slander and in some instances physically attack those who do not agree with them.

Every follower of the True and Living God should be on *high alert.* We don't want to be like the frog in the kettle whose death was caused by a slow-boil. *Any society that allows evil to flourish and be protected will pay dearly. Evil wants acceptance, but hates those who resist its influence.*

Where did all the Good Come From?

Who is the author of order in the universe; the sun, moon, stars, planets in orbit, or the regeneration cycles (seasons) on the earth? Where did all the incredible resources on the earth come from? Who created the circuitry of the human brain, or the intricate details of bodily functions? Where does goodness, love and beauty come from? From the miracle of birth and new life to every wonder we see in nature's mountains, valleys, sunrises and sunsets, lakes, rivers, oceans, plants, flowers, trees and the vast variety of seeds that reproduce after their own kind. What is the source of these natural miracles? In amazement we see, or learn about the expansive variety of wildlife species in the sky, on land or in the waters of earth. Every species unique in coloring and design with instinctive abilities to find food and water to sustain life.

In quests for what lies beyond, we turn our gaze upward to the sun, moon planets and stars— wondering. For a good part of the 20th century, we did so thinking our immediate solar system was the extent of it.

Today, our understanding of the universe has monumentally expanded. The Hubble eXtreme Deep Field (XDF), an image made by combining 10 years of photographs from the Hubble Space Telescope, has now revealed our universe is comprised of at least 100 billion galaxies!

Given the unknowns on the earth and in the universe, researchers or scientists can easily spend their entire lives studying a focused area to find a cure for a disease like cancer, or to discover one piece of knowledge about the earth, a life species, or provide new information about our larger universe.

With this in mind, I hope you will consider the possibility of a Living and intelligent Creator who with incredible design and symmetry created order in the heavens and the earth—and deposited incredible natural resources to sustain life on planet earth.

What if the Earth was Unfriendly and Bland?

How depressing life would be if there were no colors. What if there were no birds in the sky, no animals on land, or amphibians in the sea? Or if we only had limited edible vegetables, grains and fruits? What if love, truth and kindness was no more, and killing, betrayal, lies, greed and hatred replaced them? What would life be like if there were no moderate temperatures—only scorching heat, or bitter cold below zero temperatures? This sounds like a world without God with the human race on the brink of self destruction.

Thankful or Scoffing?

Most of us enjoy the beauty or usefulness of what's at our disposal in nature, but may not think much about it. Splashing milk on our cereal in the morning doesn't mean we visualize the cow who gave the milk, or wonder how such useful creatures showed up on earth. Cows/cattle are among multiple thousands of animal resources that help sustain life on earth.

Another part of the earth's population scoff at the idea of any intelligent Creator. If you find yourself in this group, consider the millions of things we don't know about the world and universe. In a similar manner, you may not know much about spiritual life or God if you've never experienced it. All we ask is, keep reading with an open mind. .

Good and Evil

Viewing a newscast on TV or the Internet, or reading a newspaper, we cannot deny the reality of evil in the world. Some think evil is winning and there is more evil than good. Not so in nature! In expansive orchards throughout the world and in remote rain forests there are thousands of fruit-bearing trees. The vast majority of these trees and the fruits they produce are edible, delicious and nourishing for humans, or provide medicinal benefits in appropriate doses. Similarly in farming country and in gardens across the globe, edible crops are planted and harvested, and various livestock are raised for human consumption. But, not everything on the earth is safe, or suitable for consumption. What are some of the exceptions? Here's one:

The Tree of Death

The Manchineel Tree also called a 'Beach Apple', 'Poison Guava' or 'Tree of Death' is the most dangerous tree in the world to humans. Any skin contact with the bark, leaves or fruit can cause severe burn-like blisters. It is not safe to stand near the tree when it's raining as the raindrops carry diluted sap that can still severely burn the skin. All parts of this tree are extremely poisonous! The tree produces a small crabapple-type fruit which is toxic. Ingestion of any part of the tree can be lethal. The Manchineel tree is found in the tropical parts of southern North America, as well as Central

America, the Caribbean, and parts of northern South America.

The tree is so toxic, warning signs are posted at the base of its trunk, or the trunk is painted with a swatch of red paint to warn people to stay away.

Knowing human nature, we tend to ignore warning signs and enjoy dares. We don't like to be told we can't do something, but life saving warnings are different. As the Tree of Death is extremely dangerous and lethal, yielding to Satan exposes us to poison that could lead to our demise. Sin and deception always leave a trail of sorrow and pain.

The Scriptures teach us to be alert in the Spirit (I Peter 5:8)! Our job is to stay close to God in prayer, obey the Truth found in the Bible and keep placing ourselves and those we love under God's care and protection.

What Happens When We Fall, or Tragedy Strikes?

A non-Christian who sees a believer take a plunge into sin and keep following this destructive path will often be turned off to anything related to God.

The opposite occurs when a Christian remains faithful to the things of God and stays committed regardless of personal set-backs and failures. People understand making mistakes is part of life. Being sincerely sorry and asking for forgiveness is a sign of strength—not weakness, as is repenting to God.

A common denominator among everyone is tragedy, illness, accidents, or heartbreak. Again, when a Christ-follower remains prayerful, faithful and continues trusting in God in the midst of these types of trials, it speaks volumes.

Our legacy and testimony is a lot about how we handle problems and live our lives. You can be sure people are watching. As someone insightfully said, *"Our life is an easy book to read."* When we faithfully trust in God's goodness in spite of what happens, others see *'the Amazing Grace of God'* is active and available.

God's Helper and His Refining Fire

Seasoned disciples radiate their dependence on the grace, mercy and forgiveness of God. We've been to the depths of hell and back, fought and been wounded, fallen and been rescued; healed from near fatal blows and experienced God's mighty hand of deliverance. All of our armor bears the scars of battle and war. Like Peter, who denied knowing Jesus to remain safe, we've grieved over personal sins and sought forgiveness at the deepest part of our being.

In the trenches of pain, agony and defeat, triumph and joy, a cleansed heart and mind begins to emerge. Seeking titles, recognition or human applause is an embarrassing remembrance of self-righteousness and foolishness in light of all our sins.

The treasure of knowing God trumps everything this world offers. His friendship, presence and guidance is what gives us purpose. Growing in sensitivity to the Holy Spirit requires listening. *In solitude or on the go, God's Holy Spirit can speak to us.* The Holy Spirit is our 'Spiritual Coach and Counselor,' working in concert with God the Father, Jesus His Son and the Word of God in the entire Bible.

> Jesus said, "I will ask the Father, and he will give you a Counselor to help you and be with you forever— the Spirit of Truth. The world cannot accept him, because it neither sees him nor knows him. But you know Him, for He lives with you and will be in you. The Counselor, the Holy Spirit, whom the Father will send in My Name, will teach you all things and will remind you of everything I have said to you." John 14:16–17, 26 NIV®

The Holy Spirit's Work- aka God's 'Spirit of Truth'

- He is actively at work in the birth of every Christian, providing spiritual and practical counsel and strength.

- He draws a clear line between good and evil, providing instruction on what to take in and what to avoid through the Holy Scriptures of the Bible.

> When the Spirit of Truth comes, He will guide you into all the truth. - Jesus   John 16:13a ESV

- The Holy Spirit's attributes (fruit) are: love, joy, peace, forbearance, kindness, goodness, faithfulness, gentleness, self-control, truthful, the instrument of God's power and presence in miracles and the distributor of all 'Spiritual Gifts.'

- He speaks into our inner world and teaches us how to avoid giving into temptation and provides a way out (1 Corinthians 10:13).

- He allows a bad feeling in our gut, or troubles our conscience until we acknowledge we've done something wrong and He helps us repent, and return to fellowship with Him and others. (Ephesians 4:30).

- He is God's gardener in our inner being, pruning useless shoots, stems and dead branches so we might be healthy and bear much fruit (John 15:1-8).

- He comforts, refreshes and restores our soul. He guides us on the right path. He works alongside us as we carry out the work God gives us to do (Psalm 23:3; Ephesians 2:10).

- He increases our natural talents and spiritual gifts to bless and inspire others in the body of Christ and the lost, who are without hope and without God (Ephesians 2:10, I Peter 2:12).

- He reminds us of what God has asked us to do and nudges us to act.

- He is the spark of inspiration that gives us vision, motivating us to love God and carry Jesus' light and truth into the world through our words and good works.

- He is a perennial 'Prayer Warrior,' ready at anytime to lead us into God's presence to worship, give thanks and intercede for others and needs.

- He is the Spiritual Fire always burning, ready to be stoked to burn brighter, so Jesus' light might emanate from our earthen vessels, so others might see Jesus

- The apostle Paul told young Timothy to "Fan into flame the gift of God (the Holy Spirit) which is in you" (2 Timothy1:6).

   The Holy Spirit only brings Glory to God the Father and His Son Jesus Christ. The Holy Spirit always works in harmony with God's plan and will. The Father, Jesus Christ and the Holy Spirit are One.

Living Water, Wind and Fire

Living in an arid climate has taught me the importance of hydration. Staying hydrated is not an option. Humans, animals and plants become dangerously weak and die without regular hydration. Since the inception of life on planet Earth, water has always been at the center—sustaining, refreshing and contributing to the survival of the created world. Without water, life as we know it would not exist!

Jesus describes Himself as the giver of Living Water; water that is spiritually capable of quenching our thirst for truth, meaning and the knowledge of the eternal God (John 4:10-11, Rev.7:17). The water of the Holy Spirit is what nourishes us spiritually—bringing peace to our heart, mind and soul. It is what hydrates and rejuvenates us in the Spirit from day to day.

The Holy Spirit's presence is also described as 'wind or fire' (Acts 2:2),

Matthew 3:11, Luke 3:16). Water, Wind and Fire are powerful forces of nature that God has used to manifest His glory at various times in human history.

Each is an invaluable resource capable of benefiting our planet, or causing catastrophic destruction. Almost all of us have experienced or seen the power of these elements.

Wind is a respected, powerful force in nature that remains unpredictable. It makes sand dunes, changes shorelines, shifts sea-beds, drives storms and hurricanes—leaving even the best of meteorologists shaking their heads—wondering if the wind might change its course.

> In Jesus' words, "The wind blows where it wishes, and you hear the sound of it, but cannot tell where it comes from and where it goes."   John 3:8a NIV®

Fire is the third element used by God to reveal His glory and presence. In the human experience fire is incredibly useful and equally destructive. Fire can destroy a house and every possession in it in less than an hour. It can reduce an entire forest to a pile of ash and charred wood. It's also a terrifying weapon, with nearly unlimited destructive power. Fire kills more people every year than any other force of nature.

Yet, fire is extraordinarily helpful! It gave humans the first form of portable light and warmth. It gives us the ability to heat homes, cook food, fashion metal, strengthen pottery, harden bricks and drive power plants. There are few things that have done as much good as fire.

God's Presence in Fire

In Exodus, Moses sees a 'burning bush' that is not consumed. While viewing this phenomenon, God speaks to Moses, calling him to go back to Egypt and lead the Jewish people out of bondage. Once the Jewish people are out of Egypt, God sent a 'cloud by day' for shade and 'a pillar of fire' to light the way for Israel to travel by night (Exodus 13:21-22).

When Solomon was dedicating the temple in Jerusalem it is recorded, "As soon as Solomon finished his prayer, fire came down from heaven and consumed the burnt offering and the sacrifices, and the glory of the Lord filled the temple (2 Chronicles 7:1)."

Centuries later John the Baptist spoke of a baptism of fire from the Holy Spirit that the Messiah would give to his disciples, saying:

"I baptize you with water for repentance. But after me comes one who is more powerful than I, whose sandals I am not worthy to carry. He will baptize you with the Holy Spirit and fire.   (Matthew 3:11) NIV®

The Atmosphere in Jerusalem and Change in Jesus' Disciples

What was it like in the city of Jerusalem and the nearby region three days after the crucifixion of Jesus Christ? The long-standing plot by Jewish religious leaders to kill Jesus had been carried out by Roman executioners. It was like a bad dream; Judas' betrayal, the evil scheming of high ranking Jewish leaders, the angry mobs, the torture inflicted on Jesus by flogging and then by nailing Him to a cross. The finality of Jesus' death brought with it a cloud of gloom and despair for all who knew him, especially for his closest band of disciples. Sorrow, uncertainty and fear engulfed them in a cloud of shock. Those who had been in the garden when Jesus was arrested, felt guilt for abandoning him; Peter for denying him. What would happen now? The disciples weren't sure, but they were afraid.

Then, first person encounters with the risen Savior begin and they remember Jesus' words:

"The Son of Man is going to be delivered into the hands of men. They will kill him, and on the third day he will be raised to life."   Matthew 17:22-23a NIV®

The Promised Holy Spirit

After Jesus' resurrection, He appeared first to the women and then to the disciples. Seeing Jesus after he had risen from the dead was amazing, but mind-boggling. He could pass through walls (John 20:19-20) or appear anywhere, like the morning the disciples were returning in their boat from fishing all night, having caught nothing. From the shoreline Jesus called out to them; directing the disciples where to cast their nets one last time. Immediately they caught 153 large fish. On coming ashore they found Jesus had already cooked a breakfast of fish and bread on coals of fire in anticipation of their arrival (John chapter 21).

Hope was rekindled on each occasion they met with Jesus. On Jesus' last visit, He commanded them to go into all of the world with the Gospel message, to baptize in the name of the Father, the Son and the Holy

Spirit, and to make disciples (Matthew 18:19-20). At the conclusion of this encounter He gave them a specific directive before being taken up into heaven.

> "Return to Jerusalem and wait for the gift My Father prom-
> ised, which you have heard me speak about. For John
> baptized with water, but in a few days you will be baptized
> with the Holy Spirit and filled with power from on high."
> Acts 1:4; Luke 24:49 NIV®

The Bible describes the event in this way:

> "And suddenly there came a sound from heaven, as of a
> rushing mighty wind, and it filled the whole house where
> they were sitting. Then, there appeared to them divided
> tongues of fire, and these sat on each of them. And they
> were all filled with the Holy Spirit and began to speak with
> other tongues, as the Spirit gave them utterance."   Acts
> 2:2-4 NIV®

The Holy Spirit baptism was accompanied by a rushing mighty wind and spiritual tongues of fire. This outward manifestation of God's presence planted the Holy Spirit inside 120 of Jesus' disciples (Acts 1:15). The result was an immediate transformation of courage to speak and make Jesus known to those gathered and others who would come to listen. About three thousand believed in Jesus Christ and were baptized on this day (Acts 2:41).

What had unfolded defied human explanation. The Father's gift of the Holy Spirit was sent as Jesus promised and the disciples were filled with power from on high and became Jesus' witnesses in the world (Luke 24:39, Acts 1:4b, 1:8).

If you have never read one of the Gospels, or the Book of Acts, please do so and draw your own conclusions.

The disciples were no longer hiding in fear. Those who knew them saw the change as they spoke about Jesus boldly with authority. Hoping to be done with Jesus permanently, Jewish leaders were infuriated to learn Jesus' disciples were now out in public preaching in Jesus' Name and doing the same types of miracles among the people!

> With the social climate of Jerusalem still charged with anti-Jesus hatred, only God could embolden Jesus' shaky disciples, and He did.

As soon the Jewish leaders learned of this they brought Peter and John before them and commanded and threatened them to not speak of Jesus anymore. Notice how the early church prayed and what happened.

> Now, Lord, consider their threats and enable your servants to speak your word with great boldness. Stretch out your hand to heal and perform signs and wonders through the name of your holy servant Jesus. After they prayed, the place where they were meeting was shaken and they were all filled with the Holy Spirit and spoke the word of God boldly. Acts 4:29–32 NIV®

> When they (the religious Jews) saw the courage of Peter and John and realized that they were unschooled, ordinary men, they were astonished and they took note that these men had been with Jesus.   Acts 4:13 NIV®

The Jesus Movement's Baptism of Fire

In a similar way the public was trying to wrap their heads around a growing number of young and old in the Jesus Movement who were speaking with remarkable conviction about God. What was going on?

The how's and why's mystified family members, educators, the church and all those who encountered this bold new breed of Jesus follow-ers. It was obvious these were not 'suit and tie' Bible college or seminary students with religious training. These bold bearers of the Word of God claimed they'd received Jesus Christ in their hearts and they spoke and lived as if they had been miraculously rescued by God and couldn't help but tell others Jesus was alive!

We couldn't explain it ourselves! Jesus' Baptism of Fire was widespread in the JP movement, infusing us with boldness. Jesus' warning was taken to heart by all Jesus People I knew.

> If anyone is ashamed of me and my words, the Son of Man will be ashamed of him when he comes in his glory and in the glory of the Father and of the holy angels. Luke 9:26 NIV®

We chose to not be ashamed of God, Jesus Christ, the Holy Spirit, or the Gospel message (Romans 1:16–17). Why should we be? It was life-giving! We remembered how lost and trapped we'd been until God showed up (Psalm 126:5; James 2:12–13, James 5:11, 20, Ephesians 2:8–9).

The momentum in many Christian house ministries was similar to the early disciples trying to keep up with Jesus. On the adventurous side, God gave us the desires of our heart by allowing us to engage in meaningful, exciting and creative ministry. We were on the front lines, with clear visibility of the battle, witnessing and participating in both victories and defeats.

We made up for a large segment of the church's silence. **We knew Jesus Christ is always relevant and on the move.** His resurrection life had raised us up and put us to work!

The psalmist said it well:

"God makes His messengers like winds— His ministers a flaming fire."
Psalm 104:4 NIV®

24

Missions into China & Poland, East & West Germany, and Africa

- Val Skow Olivia – Into China
- Dan Pauly & Lonnie Frisbee – Into Europe & Africa
- Jack Fliehmann– Co-Founder of Orphanage & School Eldoret, Kenya – Africa

Mission into Mainland China
'Following God's Lead'
Val Skow Oliva

In the fall of 1984 I found myself sitting on top of my suitcase—secretly packed with Chinese Bibles. I had just stepped off a train at the busy Beijing station. The swarm of people departing trains created a momentum that carried me until I was deposited on the outskirts of the station plaza. In the bustling capital of China, I had no idea  how to find my hotel. Feeling disoriented, I stopped, sat on my luggage, and turned to God for help. In confidence I prayed, "I need Your help! I don't want to set out on my own. I trust You to send me help."

Lord, Use Me

A year earlier, a small group of like-minded friends from the "Church of the Open Door" in San Rafael, California made a pact together. We agreed to be accountable to one another, meet for prayer regularly, confess sin, and present ourselves before the Lord requesting He use our lives in a tangible way.

We sensed God leading us to set aside money for a mission's fund. We began to pray for countries and people groups as the Holy Spirit led us. I had a burden for the people of China and began meeting with a group of believers in the East Bay of San Francisco who were also praying for China.

During this time-period I received a post card from a friend who'd graduated from medical school and purchased an "around the world" ticket for both he and his wife. The card was from Chengdu, China. It simply stated, "Val, you have got to see this place. Will get in touch on our return."

Through prayer and this note, a seed was planted in my heart. I learned that believers in the Northern provinces above Beijing had little access to Bible Scriptures and were hand-copying sections for distribution to many who had no access. A Bible could be obtained from the official state-run "Three Self Church"—but few dared to sign their name on the official paperwork for fear of reprisals or personal monitoring by the government.

Bible Courier

Hearing of this need for the Scriptures, I learned of an organization looking for couriers to take trips into China to bring Bibles to designated Chinese Christian contacts within the country. I prayed intentionally with my church accountability group, asking for God's guidance. In conjunction, I made contact with the mission courier organization that worked in China to obtain more details. They filled me in on what they did, and joined with me in prayer—asking for confirmation if it was God's will for me to become a Bible courier.

In the months that followed, I began to ask God for tangible guidance and confirmation, if it was His plan for me to be a Bible courier to China. I considered the possibility of being jailed if caught smuggling Bibles into the country and began thinking through the ramifications this would have on my family and friends. I didn't want to attempt to cross the border into China without God's protection and the leading of the Holy Spirit.

The waiting and listening went on for months. Not knowing what to do was frustrating. The Lord was gracious and patient amidst my uncertainty, doubts and fears—mixed with faith. Weary of being unable to know what to do, I asked the Lord for a sign. I prayed, "Lord, if you want me to take Bibles into China, allow me run into a Chinese person from the mainland, today."

Prayer for Confirmation

My day began with anticipation, but as the day wore on, I forgot about this specific prayer. Later that evening I was invited up to the Oakland hills where a friend had moved to care for a gentleman suffering from MS. The invite was to join the whole family for dinner.

On arrival, offering to help, the wife asked me to mix the salad and take it into the dining room. Pushing through the swinging door I ran right into a tall Chinese woman who was entering the kitchen in the opposite direction. Recalling my earlier prayer, I immediately asked, "Where are you from?" She answered, "El Cerrito." Insistent, I asked again, "No, place of origin. Where are you from?" This time she answered "Beijing China." I almost dropped the salad bowl!

The woman's name was Jing. She was a nurse from China who had escaped through Hong Kong and come to America. Her mother, a University Professor, was killed during Mao Zedong's Cultural Revolution (1966-1976). She and her remaining family were sent to the "fields" to harvest straw and rice under a brutal quota system. Now a resident of the US, she too had been invited to dinner and was being interviewed as an additional caregiver for the family hosting us.

This confirmation of meeting a Chinese national concluded my vacillating on the subject of volunteering as a Bible courier. I began to prepare. I continued with language study, notified the courier organization, and was able to secure a month's leave from my job, which was an additional sign and answer to prayer. Things were falling into place and I felt "God's Peace."

Responses to Decision to Go

I told my pastor and immediate family my plans and absorbed their response. Almost everyone tried to talk me out of going. Too late! Saturation time in prayer and God's ongoing confirmation helped me be resolved to "obey His call." I wasn't asking for permission, or expecting they would fully understand. After my church's concerned interrogation failed to dissuade me, they pledged to support my mission to China in prayer and I was grateful.

Spiritual Hospitality

In October of 1984 I flew to Hong Kong. Thankfully, through a friends' contact I was able to secure a bunk in the women's dorm at the Youth With A Mission (YWAM) base. They graciously allowed me to stay five days before I made the journey into the mainland. Due to the nature of my mission, YWAM was not privy to any details, nor affiliated with the courier organization.

While in Hong Kong I met with a representative of the courier organization. I was given essential information, the phone number of my Mainland contact—and shown a map identifying the breadth of the "underground Chinese Christian church" scattered throughout China. This revelation and need for Bibles, fortified and validated my mission.

Prayer for Safe Passageway

The courier representative confirmed their promise to be praying during the time-period I would be going through customs. Their prayers for me would be simple and specific, "That the Bibles would not be discovered and that I would reach my contact person in Beijing without problems."

I boarded an overnight ferry to Guangzhou. From the stern I could see Hong Kong now aglow with neon lights and high-rise buildings blazing in the night sky. On the opposite side of the water, China lay ahead. No lights, just a faint glimmer of kerosene lamps speckled the hazy landscape. Excited, yet tired, I slept for a few hours until dawn.

Disembarking on the mainland, we were funneled into a building and cued up for custom inspections. As my luggage passed down a conveyor belt it went through an x-ray area. I noticed a young man crouch under the table behind the screen whose job was to scrutinize the contents of each bag. I felt compassion for this man and the health problems he'd most likely experience in the future from radiation exposure.

Now, second in line for inspection, the person ahead of me was being sharply questioned. The inspector used a demanding and authoritative tone with him. Speaking Cantonese he instructed the man to open his suitcase. He rifled through its contents asking him to unzip pockets and pull everything out.

In the intensity of the moment, I sensed my adrenalin peak and beads of sweat form. Urgent silent prayer realigned my mind and heart to turn to God's Word stored safely in my heart in Proverbs 3:5-6, "Trust in the Lord with all your heart. Lean not on your own understanding; in all your ways acknowledge Him, and He will make your paths straight."

It was now my turn. The customs agent asked me in English what I had to declare. I spoke slowly, made direct eye contact and responded, "Well, I have a Cannon Camera with two lenses, 20 rolls of film, an extra battery, some lens cleaner and a camera bag. I have a toothbrush, toothpaste, mosquito repellent, a jar of peanut butter, a box of tea bags…" As I droned on in this fashion, the inspector curtly waved his arm forward, as if annoyed, and said "Go."

Holding back my relief and elation, I dragged my unopened suitcase off the table and shuffled away—thankful and convinced of God's divine intervention! The Lord must have put blinders on the x-ray inspector. It was undeniable; the Holy Spirit was powerfully present during this customs inspection. Some might conclude this to be a chance customs oversight, but I knew different. God had answered the prayers offered by many in faith for my passing through customs—bearing a treasure for His church and protecting me from arrest.

Help from a Chinese Red Guard

Struggling to drag my heavy suitcase toward the train station, I met the gaze of a Chinese Red Guard officer who walked toward me, picked up my suitcase and boarded the train as I followed behind. He didn't speak but indicated my bag should go under the lowest of the three bunks. I said "xie xie" (thank you) and then climbed up to the third bunk, which became my quarters for the next three days. Ironically, the officer took the low bunk directly across from my suitcase, which was a concern.

Over the next few days, the people in the six bunks in our nook became friendly. Because of the many dialects and language differences in this vast country, not everyone can communicate with each other. My translation book with English, Pinion, and Chinese characters was passed around as we each took turns asking and answering questions. We shared our backgrounds and enjoyed visiting on different topics. After two days the soldier departed the train. I sighed with relief—unsure if he'd been officially following me, or not. A day later we arrived in Beijing.

The Lord had taken me safely through customs and now up to Beijing. I looked around and observed the bustling activity of this most political of China's cities. A great majority of people here wore the classic blue Mao jacket and hat with a red star. Mao had died 8 years earlier, but loyalty to him remained strong. There appeared to be more 'openness' though, under the current leader, Deng Xiaping.

Ha Lo! Bus or Bicycle?

In 1984 China, the bicycle was the predominant form of transportation. Buses and Mercedes Benz cabs shared the roadways as well. Amazingly, almost anything could be moved by bike; I saw bales of hay, lumber, and platforms with numerous cages full of animals.

Suddenly I heard a voice say "Ha lo" coming from a young college age youth who wanted to practice his English. Instantly I recognized he was an answer to prayer. After establishing rapport, I asked him where the Hotel Hwa was. He happily directed me to a bus stop where a crowd of people stood. He also informed me that I could rent a bicycle around the corner, and use it for as long as I was in the city. I opted for the bus.

When the bus arrived, it appeared to be packed full. Surprisingly, more people pushed on board and the bus moved on. I watched this scenario play out a few more times. As each bus arrived full, I couldn't imagine how even one person could squeeze on—but five or ten more people would press in and the bus would depart. In cartoon fashion the scene struck me as comical. I envisioned the metal bus frames bulging out further at each stop.

I never boarded a bus the entire week that I was in Beijing! Thinking about how I would manage to get off, once on and at the right stop dissuaded me from attempting.

Plan B was renting a bicycle. I bought a bungee cord and managed to load everything I had on the rear rack and I was off. I entered the traffic lane with hundreds of other bicycle commuters. Occasionally someone would ride up alongside and say, "Ha Lo." It was great fun—except for the intersections. They were scary as there were no clear rules of right-of-way, other than being at the right place to branch one direction or another. Amazingly, I managed. On finding my hotel, I parked my bike in a rack with 50 other identical black colored standard bikes. The key that unlocked my rental was the only differentiating factor. So as to later identify it, I tied a small blue thread on the handle bar and entered the hotel.

The hotel was an old building, simple and unadorned. It was used mainly for Chinese business travelers. After settling in, I called my contact and we set up a dinner date at a hotel across town. During my week in Beijing I learned several routes to the hotel where we were to meet. I practiced taking these routes at various times of day and evening so that it wouldn't seem unusual for me to be out and about on my bike.

Twice I took a cab to tourist destinations, spending a day on the "Great Wall" and another at the "Northern Palace." I was awestruck at these amazing remnants of the Chinese Empire. The rest of my time I walked, seeing the Forbidden City, and Tiananmen Square where I had leisure opportunity to visit and engage with Chinese youth.

Miracles of Mercy

On the request of a friend in my prayer group back in the USA I was asked to deliver a Bible to someone at Beijing University. On the day chosen to do so, I cued up with a long line of students required to show ID to enter a gate into the grounds of Beijing University. This famous University is where Chairman Mao first internalized and formed his Marxist-Leninist Revolutionary agenda. To attend Beijing University students had to be "card carrying" communists. In my shoulder bag was the name of a lady and a Chinese language Bible wrapped in brown paper to deliver. A university official was checking each ID carefully. When it was my turn, I had no ID to show. I had nothing to say. I was Caucasian. The official became confused, not knowing how to handle this unexpected situation, so I just walked through the gate like I belonged. I glanced back, as he put his head down and checked the next ID. As planned, I found the young lady, delivered her wrapped Bible package and quickly left the campus.

The Delivery

On a Thursday evening I bungee-corded the Bibles I'd carefully packed onto the rented bike and peddled through the now familiar but dark streets to the hotel across town to meet my contact. At dinner we made small talk, then went out to our bikes, made the exchange, and said goodbye. He would take the precious cargo northward to be distributed among underground churches. My part as a courier was now complete, with the exception of continued prayer for his safe travel and for the Bibles to find their way into the hands of believers trusting God to supply this need.

China an Expansive Country

The following two weeks were filled with travel adventures in China. Minus an agenda, I had freedom and time to explore. The Lord gave me favor in travel and a number of divine encounters. I traveled three days down the Yangtze River where I developed a few friendships that remain. I also traveled by plane, bus and boat through small villages to Guilin, and traveled

Rural Mainland China

down the Li Jiang River. So much prayer had gone into this trip that I felt like I was sometimes walking on air.

Return Visit—

I had opportunity to return to China in 1990. It was a changed country! What I'd experienced in 1984 was the last vestige of Old World China, before it exploded and modernized—with the exception of remote rural areas not yet affected.

On return I saw not only the fear and deep wounds of an older generation who had experienced the turmoil of Mao Zedong's (Mao Tsetung) cleansing campaigns, but also the fallout of the Tiananmen Square government crackdown. The innocence and idealism among youth and elder hopefuls was crushed in the spring of 1989 when the "Western Style" protests and take-over of the Square ended in a massacre as the entire world watched on television. The protestors had called for government accountability, freedom of the press and speech and made other human rights requests. I learned firsthand from Chinese friends of the tremendous effort made to launch this protest and the hope that filled the hearts of Chinese people during those first two weeks in Tiananmen Square. These dreams and aspirations met the non-yielding stance of China's communist government and now lay in ashes as another unpleasant memory of China's repressive history of near-absolute government control.

Today in China—Oppression & Persecution

The steady increase of followers of Jesus Christ in the People's Republic of China is evidence that Communism does not provide the type of meaning and fulfillment the human heart seeks.

Although officially atheistic, the People's Republic of China has adopted a Western veneer of materialism and surface progress that camouflages massive problems; unsafe working conditions, air pollution, human rights violations, repression of personal freedoms and attacks against any government opposition, including religious groups like Christianity.

It's dangerous to oppose the government, or be a Christian in China. The larger percentage of the nation's church is comprised of house-churches, forced to live in a survival mode underground. *Thousands of Christians have been jailed, imprisoned, tortured and killed for their faith in the past 70 years. Bibles, homes and properties have been confiscated. At any time, waves of persecution directed at any non-government group may occur—whenever the Chinese Republic wants to crack-down, or deems it necessary.*

After Chairman Mao's death in 1976, citizens began reassembling in church buildings which had been closed for many years. The new administration allowed assembly under the Government sanctioned "Three-Self (Patriotic) Church." These churches are the only legal gathering places for Protestant and Catholic believers. Those who identify with the government church may be questioned, shadowed, or become victims of reprisals for failing to disclose information on others they may know, who are non-registered believers. All government sanctioned worship services are monitored with closed circuit cameras. Pastors are required to attend a state sponsored seminary in Nanjing and official Bibles are heavily edited—with the intent of preserving the "Communist way of life and belief."

Not surprising, the majority of the 70 plus million believers meet in what has been described for years as the "Underground Church." Officials describe them as illegal and unlawful "House Churches"—unsanctioned, unpatriotic assemblies—deemed a threat to social stability. In spite of this, some house churches have purchased property or leased floors in high rise buildings to accommodate larger congregations with attendances in the 100's. Illegal assemblies are tolerated in some regions—while remaining susceptible to unannounced government punishment.

Larger more visible underground churches have recently been the target of a wave of crackdowns—resulting in property seizures, removal of crosses from architecture; and sudden disappearances of pastors, their wives, or key leaders. Smaller scale harassment is common with officials showing up at members' homes or place of work—attempting to persuade known house church members to join the "official church." Non-compliance can mean the loss of a job and additional retaliation.

Persecution of Christians or other groups is portrayed as maintaining law and order, or building code regulations. A property, or home where house church believers meet could be seized and the buildings demolished for illegal group gatherings, anti-government activity, or building code violations. The government has become more sophisticated in dealing with the Christian church in an attempt to avoid wide-scale clashes—yet showing force to curb expansion of non-government sanctioned gatherings.

The growth numbers within the Christian church in China remain undocumented and not publicized to protect the underground church. Chinese leaders are always concerned about how any religious or other group might shape China's political future, and its possible impact on the Communist Party's grip on power. Threats and punishment are the government's means of preventing anti-government groups, or any group including the underground churches, from meeting privately without government permission.

How Then Should We Pray for China?

If you were to ask a Christian in China how the West could pray for them, the answer might be shocking and humbling. We might assume they would want us to pray for more modernization, improved economic conditions, the ability to own things, more leisure time and more freedoms.

Instead Chinese believers are hesitant to seek, or make the same mistakes as the west, by being lulled into materialism, self-indulgence, or any lifestyle that would diminish their witness and loyalty to God and His Son, Jesus Christ.

Rampant political corruption and greed are two traits almost all Chinese citizens are repulsed by. Christians in China, would add their aversion to becoming lukewarm or mediocre in faith and practice.

Living under the thumb of an atheistic Chinese Republic, underground believers have learned to accept persecution. They draw courage from Jesus' words, "Remember these words that I said unto you. The servant is not greater than his Lord. If they have persecuted me, they will also persecute you (John 15:20)."

If you are led by God's Spirit to pray in earnest for Christians in China, or any other country where believers experience oppression, persecution, the absence of freedom, or threats of death—pray they will remain strong in their faith in all circumstances.

Ongoing prayers for all who love Him including ourselves are of great value. Praying through **Ephesians chapter 6:10-20** with persecuted Christians in mind and heart would be of great service to your brothers and sisters in the faith—who live under constant spiritual repression. Verses 19-20, if written in a plural context in an amplified manner might sound like this:

> **"Pray for us, that we might speak and live out the message of the Gospel with confidence, trusting in God's Word and Holy Spirit to make known the mysteries of God's love, redemption and plan of salvation through Jesus Christ. Though under persecution, with limited freedom—God's Word and Jesus' life is advancing! Pray that we might persevere in faithful obedience to Christ, and always represent The Father, Son and Holy Spirit with honor."**

What About Us –The Body of Christ in Free Countries?

Are we still in awe, amazed at God's love, mercy, forgiveness and gift of a New Life. Does thankfulness rise up in our inner being when we think about God's Goodness and Greatness? Amidst the muddied waters of liberalism and progressivism, are we still clear about right and wrong, good and evil? Do we see God, Jesus Christ and the Holy Spirit as they are; Holy, Righteous, True and One? Do we still hunger for and obey the Word of God to be our guide and compass in life? Is our First Love of knowing and following Jesus Christ, still Top Priority? Is our faith aligned with this truth; Jesus Christ has redeemed us from spiritual death? As the world changes for the worse, is our heart tuned to the Eternal Kingdom God has grafted us into?

Prayer: In season and out of season, teach us to fan the flame of the Holy Spirit. Strengthen our resolve to obey Your Word. Increase our faith, that we might stand firm in Your trustworthy promises. Protect those who belong to You from the evil one. Grant all of us courage in times of trials and persecution; Enable your church to glorify Your Holy Name in word and deed—that the glory of the Gospel of Jesus Christ might pierce the darkness, give hope to the weary and rescue the lost! So be it. Amen.

Acts 28:31; Revelation 2:4; 2 Timothy 1:6; Exodus 14:13; 1 Corinthians 16:13; 2 Corinthians 1:24; 2 Peter 1:4; Hebrews 8:6; Psalm 31:2; Colossians 1:13; Job 10:12; Psalm 104:3; John 14:15 &23; Matthew 28:18–20

Dan Pauly & Lonnie Frisbee
On Mission in Europe & Africa

In the fall of 1978 Dan Pauly & Lonnie Frisbee accompanied Dr. Charles Hardin of United Evangelical Churches on a mission trip to Europe and Africa. Our first stop was Poland, then on to West and East Germany— preaching the gospel everywhere we went. We spoke in Warsaw and in other Polish venues.

In the aftermath of Polish born Pope John Paul being installed, huge celebrations continued in Eastern Europe with openness to spiritual ministry. There was amazing reception to the words of Jesus Christ!

We then visited West Germany and then into Communist-controlled

East Germany. Inside of East Berlin near to what's known as "Check Point Charlie", our team had an opportunity to minister in an old 'state sanctioned' church. Dan recalls, "As we approached the church structure there was no sign—it appeared abandoned. Stepping inside, the interior was dark and drab; as if the Communist State wanted it this way. Some 250 believers were gathered. They looked tired and traumatized by the tyranny of an anti-God regime controlling, monitoring and limiting what they could or could not do."

Dan Pauly

Dan said, "When I looked out on the congregation from the front of the church, something stirred in me. When it was my turn to speak and I stood up, I felt like Jesus was viewing these believers through my eyes. I have never experienced anything like this since. It seemed like God was in the past and present remembering all the pain and oppression they had endured for years—while they remained faithful to the testimony of Jesus Christ. The words that came out of my mouth were, 'I see how much it has cost you to follow Jesus Christ. I see your pain and suffering.'

Suddenly, the congregation began weeping as God's love descended on us all. The believers gathered had heard God speaking to them, acknowledging their suffering, comforting them and now engulfing them with His holy presence of love. The darkness of the sanctuary was warmer and brighter."

"Praise be to the God and Father of our Lord Jesus Christ, the Father of compassion and the God of all comfort, who comforts us in all our troubles, so that we can comfort those in any trouble with the comfort we ourselves receive from God. For just as we share abundantly in the sufferings of Christ, so also our comfort abounds through Christ. If we are distressed, it is for your comfort and salvation; if we are comforted, it is for your comfort, which produces in you patient endurance of the same sufferings we suffer. And our hope for you is firm, because we know that just as you share in our sufferings, so also you share in our comfort."
2 Corinthians 1:3–7 NIV®

This experience was a vivid reminder of God's deep compassion for His suffering church. No preaching followed this outpouring which led naturally to prayer.

AFRICA

Africa is bigger than China, India, the contiguous U.S. and most of Europe—combined!

Kenya, Africa

From Europe, Hardin's mission team flew to Nairobi, Kenya. There they ministered in churches, villages and in the town square with hundreds com-

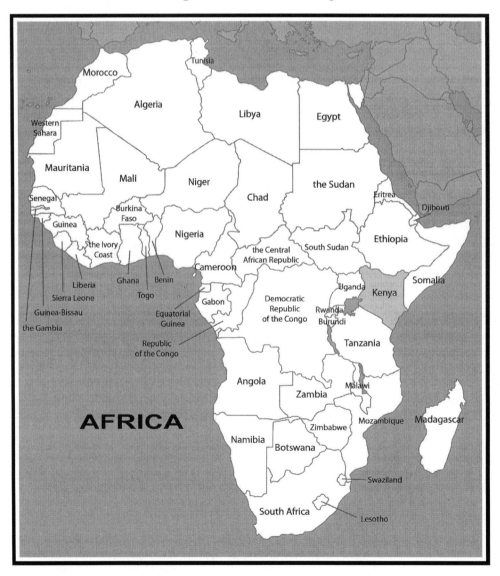

ing to faith in Christ. Dan had no idea how different the next stop would be.

Darkness Over Nigeria

From Kenya they flew to Lagos, the largest city in Nigeria. Exiting the plane, they were met by soldiers with machine guns pointed at them and it never got much better. They were quickly loaded into government vehicles and whisked off to be interrogated.

At the time, Lagos was the most dangerous place in the world to drive in. Bandits would stop vehicles, murder the passengers, steal their belongings and then strip anything of value. Locals would follow removing what was left, torch the vehicle and leave the charred remains lying on the road where the original crime took place. The streets were filthy with debris and the stench of open sewers filled the air. Poverty was massive. For security sake, the mission team's outreach ministry took place inside church structures.

From Lagos they traveled to Benin City, still within Nigeria. While there, Frisbee and Pauly wandered from the guarded compound where they were staying to check out a nearby street market. All seemed well until Frisbee began taking pictures of people on a disposable camera. When locals spotted him doing so, they sounded an alarm in their own language and soon Frisbee and Pauly were surrounded by 150 older boys and men. The men had huge swords tucked into their waist bands and in unison boys and men began making threatening noises and gestures.

Lonnie Frisbee

As danger escalated, Dan told Lonnie, "Put the camera away." Saying "They may think we're trying to steal their soul." Providentially, Lonnie had just run out of film. At this point, they were able to turn and quickly returned to the safety of the compound without mishap. They'd learned a lesson—indiscriminate picture taking of people in Nigeria could be dangerous to life and limb.

Reflecting on this event, Dan said, "They could have easily cut us into pieces and thrown our body parts into the bushes! We could see the anger and hostility in their eyes. We had crossed some kind of cultural line. There was a noticeable unfriendly, oppressive spirit of darkness over these people with the exception of the Christians we encountered in this predominantly Muslim populated country. Our team was only given liberty to conduct ministry inside of church structures. Local Christian leaders provided security as we traveled and for the church services. The entire time we were in Nigeria we saw no other white people."

Ghana, Africa

Their next stop was Accra, the capital and largest city in Ghana, founded by the "Ga" people of the Accra plains in the 1400's. It is located in what they call the gold coast on the Atlantic Ocean. In the late 1800's it became a British colony and has since gained its independence. English is the primary language in the region. The difference between Nigeria and Ghana was night and day. The people of Ghana were kind, warm, welcoming, gentle and loving, and very receptive to the Gospel of Christ.

In Nigeria, they found Muslim and military government resistance to anything Christian and an oppressive spirit over the land. Even so, Christ's light was alive in His believers. The church's work of sowing the 'gospel of truth' amidst this oppression was a testimony to the courage of Christians there.

Overall, the needs in Africa were enormous as was the spiritual hunger. In each location the mission team ministered, signs and wonders occurred. For Dan and others, faith grew as did an expanding view of the world.

The Good News Children's Centre
Orphanage and School— Eldoret, Kenya
Co-founded by Jack Fliehmann,
Jesus People — Walnut Creek, CA

For the past 14 years Jack has been helping build and staff an orphanage and school in the slums of Eldoret Kenya named the Good News Children's Centre (GNCC). Kenyan natives Wycliffe and Everlyne Khaemba co-founded the orphanage-school with Jack in 2004 and oversee the day-to-day operations. Wycliffe is a pastor and his wife Everlyne is the educator administrator. Both have devoted their lives to this mission which is strategically located in the center of the slums. They currently lease the property on which the Centre is located.

Jack has made the trek to Nairobi, Kenya and then on to Eldoret, two hundred miles away, twelve times. On each month-long visit he helps build and improve part of the orphanage-school infrastructure and encourages the dedicated African team of teachers that serve the GNCC and the children who are resident students.

Among the many improvements at the GNCC is a well with a four-stage filtration system which provides clean water for the Centre and the neighboring community. Camp and solar showers have been added to service the residents.

Eighty kids have been pulled out of homelessness, rescued from hunger, deplorable living conditions, and a potential future of sexual and physical exploitation. At the 'Good News Children's Centre' students receive regular meals, fresh water, showers, clean clothes, love and acceptance, education, a sense of family and a new beginning.

Daily life at the Centre is filled with learning, singing, dancing and spiritual nurturing. The GNCC has added five additional teachers to its team and is currently rated number one in quality education throughout the area. The school has six classroom areas and a designated church area for worship and gatherings. Out of the GNCC church, three satellite churches have been planted in nearby villages. Spiritual life of walking with God the Father and Jesus Christ His Son is an integral part of daily life at the Centre, as are the Scriptures of the Bible for nourishment and instruction. The children are learning to love God and praise Him for His kindness, mercy and love, and grow into young men and women of character with a heart to make a difference in the world as they grow into adulthood. .

Since the inception of the 'Good News Children's Centre', Jack and a few friends from the USA have sent monthly financial gifts to support the centre's practical needs and to provide a modest salary for the small staff and their families. More contributors are needed to help fund the GNCC orphanage-school. Christian workers are also needed to accompany Jack on his annual month long ministry visits which usually take place in August, December, or January. Round-trip airfare costs from the US are in the $1500 range. Accommodations for a month's stay with breakfast are an additional $ 700.

Jack writes: It is incredibly encouraging for the teachers and pastors in the slums to know they are not forgotten in their daily work of rescuing, educating and ministering to Eldoret orphans, widows and locals. When I am with them for a month, it seems like such a large task with many practical and spiritual things to do, but the work of touching these young lives, and staff families at the 'Good News Centre' is remarkable and praiseworthy!

Maxwell Simiyu's Story
A Child Found in the Slums of Eldoret
By Everlyne Achieng Khaemba

The first time we met Maxwell his life was miserable and full of hardship because his father died when he was very young and over time his mother was unable to care and provide him with basic needs since she was jobless. Maxwell felt the helplessness of his mother's plight and decided to run away to lessen her burden. In doing so he joined up with other street children who lived on their own in the slums of Eldoret.

He spent months on the streets sometimes without a single meal in a day. Street life for those who were young was hard, discouraging and a lonely existence with different ages of kids each struggling to survive. Maxwell felt hopeless, abandoned, without friends and love. He said, "No one on the streets showed love to me."

When things were at their worst for Maxwell, we met him. We encouraged him by showing a genuine interest in his situation and concern for his well being. We told him about God's love through Jesus Christ, explaining there's one person who loves him more than anyone else in the entire world and this person is Jesus Christ. We shared from the Word of God why God sent His Son into the world to be our friend and put His Spirit inside us to guide us. Maxwell responded by coming to his senses and accepting Jesus to be his own personal Savior.

We brought him to the Good News Children Centre to provide physical care and spiritual nurture. Through the 'love of Jesus' we helped Maxwell to feel welcome and genuinely loved. In this safe new environment Maxwell and other children like him thrive. They find and experience the Love of God, begin a new life spiritually, find a home and are able to pursue their education without the distraction of survival on the streets.

The Good News Children Centre has helped many orphans who live in the Eldoret slums through feeding programs, providing shelter and teaching about the love of God. We pray we will one day own our own property to accommodate more children and give them an opportunity to live a healthy and productive life, filled with good things with the Lord at the center.

Sincerely,
Your sister in Christ,
Everlyne Achieng Khaemba
Director of Good News Children's Centre

It is amazing for Jack to see the joy and enthusiasm present in the young lives of students at the GNCC who have been rescued from devastating circumstances of being orphaned; some cast off becoming street children in the slums of Eldoret without regular meals, love, education, and vulnerable to exploitation.

Looking For a Life-Giving Place to Support?

The "Good News Children's Centre" in Eldoret, Kenya is a good candidate. This fifteen year old orphanage-school in Kenya is carrying out the work of changing the lives of every student/resident. With Jesus Christ at the center, couple directors and each teacher are jointly providing a loving and nurturing education with life-skills and character building embedded. Many of these students will grow into Kenya's leaders of tomorrow and will never forget where they came from! They are receiving a spiritual and educational foundation that will give them many opportunities in life to become all God intended them to be and bless and encourage others throughout their lives.

100% of all financial gifts will be sent directly to the "Good News Children's Centre" in Eldoret, Kenya. Co-directors, Wycliffe and Everlyne Khaemba are diligent and responsible in providing a modest salary for teachers and food, clothing and supplies to the students of school and orphanage. Facility improvements are ongoing with the goal of someday purchasing their own property.

For more information write:

The "Good News Children's Centre"
Jack Fliehmann 2028 N. 6th Street
Concord, CA 94519

Author's Note: Jack's Testimony is located in Chapter 11 and His Bio update and more information on the Good News Centre can be found in Bio's 1 Chapter 27

25

Testimonies 1

- Mike Damrow
- Sue Palosaari Cowper – Faith Story
- Jenny Haas – Divine Appointments

Mike Damrow, Milwaukee Jesus People

"The future was wide open" –Tom Petty

I was born in San Bernardino California in September, 1950. My earliest memory is when I was four years old, riding in a truck. I was tucked up on a shelf behind the driver's seat. From there I could peer over my parents' shoulders and view the oncoming traffic heading west on Highway 66. My sisters Pat (ten) and Tracy (eight) were seated between my parents. My brother John (two) probably spent the whole trip in my mother's lap. We were heading east to Wisconsin.

My parents both grew up in Sheboygan, on the western shore of Lake Michigan. We had relatives in that area on both sides of the family. When we arrived there, my sisters stayed with "Auntie Ann." John and I stayed with "Uncle Teddy" and my parents stayed somewhere else.

I guess we were too poor to rent our own place for a while. My father was an artist of some talent. His specialty was oil paintings of the old West. He was also very good at wood carving and creating various artistic thing-a-ma-jigs. In his heart, he wished he could have been born 100 years earlier. I think he never outgrew his childhood dream of being a cowboy. His life was interrupted by World War II. He parachuted into France but never talked about it much. My mother said he came back from the army a changed man, but not changed for the better. He was a tough guy—old school.

He drank straight whiskey and wouldn't back down from a bar room fight. He could scare kids out of the yard with just a look. It's a good thing he was on our side instead of Germany's. We can thank my grandfather for that. He fought for the Kaiser in an earlier war. After the war my parents moved to southern California where my father got a job drawing cartoons for the Disney Company. According to him, it was a very tedious and monotonous job. He never accepted the 40 hour work week. He preferred doing freelance art as inspiration or whim moved him. He made enough from his oil paintings to support himself but not his whole family. My mother had some sort of breakdown and was committed to a mental hospital when I was six years old. When I was seven, my dad loaded up his car with paintings and headed west. He didn't return until I was fourteen years old.

In the meantime my siblings and I were placed in foster homes. My childhood was pretty rough by most standards but it got worse when my father returned. It may be a coincidence but the year I moved back in with him, my grades dropped from A's and B's to D's and F's.

"And the days went by like paper in the wind. Everything changed, then changed again." - Tom Petty

Teen Days

Around that time I started playing in a rock band with some friends from school. We called ourselves, "The Fugitives." We played vintage American Classic Rock. My sister Pat persuaded my dad to take me to the music store and buy a bass guitar. On the way home he said "you'll give that up in two weeks." (I'm still playing.) That summer he decided to move us to Milwaukee. During the course of my childhood, I had either moved or changed schools, an average of once a year. This made it hard for me to develop lasting friendships.

Most of my good friends have been musicians. My best friends have all been drummers. I dropped out of high school after my sophomore year deciding I may as well have some fun before I got shipped off to Viet Nam.

Before long, I was into the "hippie" counter-culture. My father and I didn't see eye to eye on much. When I was 16, he gave me a car he'd won in a poker game. It was a `57 Chevy, an American classic. He advised me to go far. I drove west on Route 66, along with my old friend Dennis, the drummer from "The "Fugitives." We headed for the West Coast to start another rock band. 'The future was wide open.'

I had been living in Southern California for a couple of years. I got a job in a boatyard and started attending classes at Venice Community Adult School. My main objective was to get a draft deferment but I was also working toward my high school diploma. One evening I got a call from my old friend Todd who had played guitar in the Fugitives. He was visiting relatives in the small town of Colton, located right next to San Bernardino. He invited me over for a visit so I went. When I realized how close I was to my home town I decided to go there for a look.

"Redemption comes to those who wait, forgiveness is the key." - Tom Petty

Arriving in downtown San Bernardino on a Saturday night, I met a bunch of teenage girls handing out gospel tracts. They were stationed in pairs at every street corner. After going several blocks, my pockets were stuffed with their paper invitations.

Finally, I met an elderly, white haired lady. I asked, "What are you doing out here so late at night?" She replied, "We're here because we love Jesus." I wondered why she would care about me, a total stranger, with hair down to my shoulders. If one more quasi religious space cadet had approached me, I would have told him to get lost. I was tired of the Krishna chanters, the Buddhist ranters and all the other fruits, flakes, and nuts. They didn't dub California "the granola belt" for nothing, but this lady was making sense to me. She was "speaking the truth in love." I prayed with her right then and there.

With my new found faith, and not much else, I decided to hitchhike to 'Big Sur' on the northern coast of California. I often went there when I wanted to get away from civilization, meditate and get back to nature. I had been influenced by the writings of Henry Thoreau and wanted to find my own Walden Pond. I hitchhiked north on Pacific Coast Hwy 1, got side-tracked by a pretty girl from San Diego and ended up in San Francisco's Haight-Ashbury, where my wallet was stolen. I had arrived too late to witness the "Summer of Love"

After a couple of days there, I was broke, with no identification, just a backpack and sleeping bag. My new friend from San Diego bought some granola, nuts and seeds for me as we parted company. I was determined to resume my quest as I headed back toward Big Sur. I hitchhiked south and was picked up by a girl in a red Volkswagen. She was headed to the same place as me. She drove up into the mountains and we set up camp together. We seemed compatible enough. We were both vegetarians and we both practiced transcendental meditation. As we were sitting by the campfire I pulled a Bible out of my backpack. "You're reading the Bible? That's a drag!!" She exclaimed.

"You're a drag" I replied. We parted company in the morning.

A Life or Death Incident

I began hiking west on what appeared to be a trail. As the day wore on the path gradually faded and finally disappeared. Before long I was totally lost. I could hear a river at the bottom of the canyon and I knew it flowed west to the ocean. I decided to head downhill to the river. The lower down the hill I got, the thicker the brush became and soon I was totally entangled. I saw a leafy tunnel ahead and slid down it. It was steeply sloped like a playground slide. Now I was making some progress.

Suddenly I found myself sliding on air. I had gone over the edge of a cliff. I grabbed onto to a small tree branch and hung on for dear life. The first thing I did was unhook my backpack, which was pretty heavy. It dropped straight down and bounced on the rocks below. When it hit the ground, it looked the size of a pea. I pictured myself bouncing the same way. Rid of that weight, I was able to hoist myself back up and consider my situation while perched at the cliff's edge. I was worn out from fighting my way through the thicket—while looking for a way down the mountain. Going back was not an option. The river below was inviting me to refresh myself in it's cool clean waters. Perhaps I could light a fire and be rescued, but could burn in it. Bad idea. I didn't have any matches anyway. Eventually I might doze off and fall to my death. I concluded that I was at the end of the line.

I prayed to God just to let Him know that I would probably be seeing Him soon. I didn't know about that old prayer that goes something like this: "God if You get me out of this, I will go to church every week and be a good person for the rest of my life, etc…" It didn't occur to me that God could rescue me off this cliff. Having finished my prayer, there was nothing else to do so I searched for a foothold below me, and then another and so on.

During the course of the next hour, I climbed down the face of that cliff. If you could see this cliff, you would know what a miracle this was because it was not angled but totally vertical. When I got to the bottom, I was so thirsty that I headed straight to the river. I never went back for my pack. It's probably still there. I was surprised to be alive. I had no money, no identification, no possessions except a few books and a guitar back at my apartment in Venice.

> Our God is a God who saves; from the Sovereign Lord comes escape from death.   Psalm 68:20 NIV®

I decided to head back to San Bernardino where perhaps I could find those Christians I'd met one week earlier. I hitchhiked back to Venice. It's around 60-70 miles from there to San Bernardino and its all freeway. It's against the law to hitchhike on the freeway. I was not in the mood for spending the day on LA on-ramps. I decided to pawn my guitar for bus fare. It was an early 60's Fender Stratocaster, an American Classic. I was currently jobless, clueless and without any earthly possessions. I had 64 dollars, and a bus ticket, and I was glad to be alive.

Arriving in downtown San Bernardino, I bought a newspaper and sat down on a park bench. I was there less than a minute when a red Volkswagen pulled up right in front of me. Out jumped two bearded longhairs carrying Bibles. They walked straight up to me and asked, "Have you met the Lord?" I replied, "Every time I come to this town, people talk to me about God. This never happens anywhere else." They invited me to dinner at their commune called 'The House of Miracles' in nearby Fontana.

By coincidence, Fontana is where my parents had lived when I was born. I thought "this must be a cosmic connection." This was in Feb. 1970. I don't remember exactly what I had prayed with that sweet elderly lady, but something was changed in me and I was on a new road. I had been cynical, critical and stuck in a downward spiral in my soul. I'd reached an impasse prior to San Bernardino.

I felt like the lyrics I'd later pen into a song. "Lonesome Stone he's so proud and cold, but he's just 19 years old. Seen it all, done his most, Lonesome's just a walking ghost."

Something new was happening in me. When I asked Jesus to forgive me and become Lord of my life, He began to lead me into His plan for me. A few years later, Lonesome Stone became the title song in a rock musical that premiered in London. My wife Mary and I flew to England to help with the production. The song Lonesome Stone was autobiographical. The producers used some of my ideas, a few songs and a team of us came up with the original script.

The play was about a number of residents who lived in the Haight District of San Francisco and a guy named 'Rich' who left his home in Milwaukee, Wisconsin and headed to California. Rich met various cosmic weirdos, hippies and an old lady screaming "Repent!" Among the cast of 'Street People" the drug dealer "Bear" came to faith in Jesus Christ first. All who knew him were shocked! This caused a stir on the streets and deep soul searching among his acquaintances. Is Bear's claim about following Jesus the real deal, or is this just another one scam?

What unfolds is a domino effect of 'Street People' facing their need and battling opening the door of their heart to Jesus. This was akin to what actually occurred in the San Francisco Bay Area in 1966-67.

"You belong somewhere you feel free" - Tom Petty

My wife Mary enjoyed playing the part of 'Queenie,' the female lead. She received some good reviews from the London theatre critics. Mike said, "I was offered the position of usher. I guarded the rear stage door entrance of the Rainbow Theatre. Every night, when the curtain rose, I felt like an outsider in my own life. I was the Phantom of the Rock Opera."

Cast member's take on the theatrical production of Lonesome Stone: "This was our own story; 'a cast with an amazing past.' The script was written and composed by a number of 'Jesus Family' members and the songs were a compilation of our team and other musical artist's of the day. This was a creative endeavor to tell a true story of a diverse group of 'Street People' coming to a saving faith in Jesus Christ and being delivered from the darkness of the times. *We wanted others to know 'Jesus was alive and could be known!"*

Mike continues: "Years later, in an adult Sunday School class we were asked to draw a picture representing ourselves and explain it. I drew a cross with a red dot on it. I explained that I am a carpenter and the vertical line is a plumb line. The horizontal line is a level line. "I'm on the level line, a bit left of center—by Sunday School standards."

> *"Running down a dream working on a mystery going wherever it leads." - Tom Petty*

Bio – Mike Damrow

These days, people call me an artist when they see my work. My dad was an artist. Michelangelo was an artist for the ages. I am a carpenter contractor. More importantly I am God's workmanship, an American classic; or in my wife's words, I'm a "piece of work."

Born: Sept. 1950
Born Again: Feb. 1970
Married: April, 1972 to Mary Pudlo
Children: Elizabeth 1974, Simon 1976, Jesse 1980, Molly 1982
Career: Boat builder apprentice 1968-69
Christian disciple, evangelist, musician 1970-1974
Carpenter since 1976
Carpenter Contractor since 1986 www.damrowstairs.com
Hobbies: Reading, songwriting, music www.bluecollartunes.com

Hardship and Provision
Sue Palosaari Cowper

"Jim and I were married at the Catacombs Coffee House in Seattle, Washington with Russ Griggs presiding. Russ introduced us to Linda Meissner a year earlier at her first coffeehouse, the 11th Hour in downtown Seattle. Our honeymoon hideaway was the tiny room at the top of the stairs above the choir loft of an old church. We and others lined up for the one and only bathroom shared with 50 enthusiastic Jesus People. Patience and grace was strong, helping us to accept things as they were.

I've always enjoyed honeymoon stories from those days. You'd think we all had been living during the 'Great Depression.' One couple, just married in the Milwaukee ministry, practiced sleeping on the floor in their new sleeping bags on their honeymoon night, preparing for our flight to evangelize in Europe the next day. Creature comforts were not the norm for Jesus People.

I remember till the day I die, the reoccurring days of oatmeal and other unusual meals accompanied by a simple prayer, and I hope with a great sense of humor! Oh, yes, oatmeal cooked with sprouted lentils. Then there were those tasty chicken gizzards and necks from the local mission because the homeless wouldn't eat them. We ate them, but avoided looking! Also on the list of delicacies were the donated homemade canned foods with questionable ingredients that could break a tooth; always an adventure in caution. And how about the nights we spent 'camping out' when lightning storms would suddenly break out? Those were the days—but not of wine and roses!

Only those who lived through events like this could find humor in such precarious predicaments. I have never laughed as much as I did back then! We were so extremely funny, much of the time; deliriously thankful and happy; hopeful and trusting.

I recall the miracles and what they stirred in us. Like a day, somewhere in Germany, Jim left with a small group to find better housing for our team. The rest of us stayed behind in upstairs donated rooms. **We had no food, money or phones** and no idea when Jim and those with him would return.

We got hungry, somewhere around noon. "Well, then," I said, hoping for something profound to come out of my mouth, "let's pray."

We were in the act of assembling on the floor, some already beginning to pray, when the door of our digs opened, and in walked a squad of soldiers from the nearby US Air Force Base, each carrying grocery bags filled with groceries, including porter house steaks!

Surprised and thankful, for sure! But other things were bouncing around inside each of us regarding an all seeing, knowing, caring and faithful God who saw our situation and need. *He came right to where we were and met that need.* In this instance, He used a part of a squad of US airmen. Faith and appreciation always grew, when out of a seemingly hopeless situation we were recipients of mercy and grace from above. Thank you Lord!

Jenny Haas – Milwaukee Jesus People
Telling the Whole Truth

Rich and I had dated in high school for about two years. I fell head over heels in love with him when I was 15. Six months later, he got into drugs. He called me his 'straight world', which I continued to be. I hated drugs and what it did to him. We eventually broke up. I had the same strong distaste for alcohol and what it did to people.

It was 1968 and my interests were art, nature and God. My group of friends were a mixture of jocks, nerds and hippies; I was mostly straight. The druggies would pass a joint and I'd say, "No thank you. I am already high on life. Ha!" Somehow they accepted this simple opt-out. Rich left the area right after graduation and I had no idea where he went.

I applied to "Layton School of Art & Design-Milwaukee" and was accepted. Early on I was told, "Unless you get high you're not going to fit in." This turned me off. School was OK and my love of art wasn't dashed by what anyone expected of me. I remained true to myself.

One day my old flame 'Milwaukee Rich' returned to the area and showed up on my doorstep. He told me he'd changed, recounting his story of hitchhiking to California and coming to faith in Jesus Christ through the invitation of a young Christian singer named Jamie Owens. He explained how her family had taken him in and helped him begin walking with Jesus. Nine months had passed and he'd come back to Milwaukee to share this with me, other friends, and anyone who'd listen. I saw a change in him and this got my attention!

Spiritual Roots & Spiritual Life

I'd been brought up Lutheran and had a fairly good understanding of the Bible. I knew what I'd learned was the truth, imparted by wonderful people who did their best to live out the Christian faith. At the same time, there was a disconnect between what I knew about God through the church and worship—and my daily life. I didn't know how to follow Jesus in practical ways, or anything about sharing my faith with others and a lot of other things.

When Rich talked to me about Christ being "alive," it seemed different. I knew plenty about the historical Jesus and I loved him, but Rich claimed to know the "living Jesus Christ" who had been raised from the dead. The change in Rich was undeniable, as was the light of Christ shinning in his eyes. This made me hungry for what he had. Something miraculous had occurred in him and from what he said, it was Jesus Christ's Holy Spirit living in him. These words were familiar to what I'd learned in church. From that point on I prayed that I too would be filled with the presence of Jesus and was!

Several months later, a small group of "Jesus People" landed in Milwaukee and Rich and I visited them. They were in the early stages of beginning a Christian community. It was exciting to meet other young Christians at a time when both Rich and I were hungry to learn about 'walking with Jesus.'

After this meeting, I felt a spiritual tug to quit art school and Rich and I joined the group. This new community was the real deal! Everyone who became a part of this new ministry were committed to following Jesus Christ, his teachings and applying it to their lives. We all had things we needed to let go of and a lot to learn. There were community rules to aid us in accomplishing this. No drugs, alcohol, demonic music or practices, no sex outside of marriage, the ladies were asked not expose themselves by dressing inappropriately, we all had assigned chores and everyone was asked to maintain a good attitude and teachable spirit.

Jim and Sue Palosaari were the community leaders. They believed God had called them to Milwaukee to bring the message of Jesus Christ to those who did not know Him and make disciples. We learned to study the Bible, tell others about God's love revealed in Jesus and share what we had with anyone in need. We also used our talents and abilities in the community. A number of us helped paint and decorate our new coffee house "Jesus Christ Power House" with murals and scripture verses.

In the early days of the community Linda Meissner was invited by Jim and Sue to aid us in outreach at a large stadium. She was gifted in outreach speaking and had helped Jim and Sue on the West Coast when they were getting started in their faith. She preached at the stadium meetings and our community did the follow-up of those who wanted to follow Jesus. Meissner was from Seattle, Washington, heading up a Christian community called "The Jesus People Army."

Following Jesus 'all out' was revolutionary and it took the mood of the times right to the top. It wasn't just about breaking with the negatives of society, the hippie or drug culture, or things in the church that seemed lifeless. It was a genuine endeavor to follow Jesus with our whole self; taking the Bible seriously and obeying what Jesus taught us to do. It was a relationship with God the Father, Jesus His Son and the Holy Spirit living in us and reaching out through us.

Living in the Milwaukee Christian community we learned the Bible in an accelerated way, reading regularly, discussing it and receiving teaching from Jim Palosaari and others who were gifted in this way. I felt like I was beginning to believe in God in a tangible way, taking hold of what I had learned about Him since a youth.

Though Rich and I were committed to the community, Rich had a hard time keeping his hands off me, which was a problem. Someone pointed out the Scripture to us, "It's better to marry than burn with lust (1 Corinthians 7:9)." Taking this to heart, as our relationship continued to blossom—we decided to get married.

I got pregnant a few months after our wedding and by then we were living in a large house with many others. As a married couple we were fortunate to have our own room and were thankful for this.

Super Spiritual & Spousal Isolation

The truth was, Rich was gifted at evangelism, but an absentee husband. He'd frequently go witnessing and be gone for ten to twelve hours. Or, he'd say, "I'm going down the hallway and I'll be right back", only to return five hours later! He'd say one thing and do the other and guise his lack of consideration as 'serving the Lord.' His running out the door to save the world left me feeling alone and it never got better!

When I got pregnant he didn't want to talk about it. We DIDN'T talk about it. I was devastated. It was nearly 6 months before he said, "Man, what are we going to do with a kid? Jesus is coming back any day and we need to preach the Gospel to everyone!"

Around this time, thirty members of our team were chosen to go to Europe on a tour and of course Rich was chosen. He was the 'super evangelist.' I was five and half months pregnant. We left on a three week trip that turned into 'a trip without any end.' When Rich and I left Milwaukee we shared an orange army surplus backpack. There was nothing in it for a baby! We thought we'd be back in the US in a few weeks.

While traveling through Finland I began to feel anxious as I was in my first pregnancy without doctor visits. I needed direction. Was I eating the right food, doing what I should be doing? I didn't know! Our cook, Paul J. was tuned in; sneaking me an extra egg or an orange whenever he could.

When I was uncomfortable riding in a vehicle for a lengthy period of time I'd ask if we could find a place to stop. At times I was made to feel like an inconvenience for asking. I'd sometimes think, if they could get away with it, they'd say, "OK, we'll stop the van. Get out have the baby in the field and get back in." That's how unimportant I felt, compared to the mission we were on. I resented being made to feel I was a burden and the absence of sensitivity to my being pregnant.

I survived with laughter that came from utter exhaustion; a strained chuckle that was a deep release for my anxiety. I didn't have the power or means to change anything! I thought it would be wrong to leave my husband, even though he was aloof most of the time, not present and didn't provide any emotional support, so I stayed in the relationship. The conviction of our group at this time was 'divorce' was not an option; it was against God's will and could only be considered on immoral grounds.

Emotional desertion wasn't on Jesus Peoples' radar at the time, but should have been! Ministries like ours used individuals who were effective, working them incredibly long hours and didn't compute how this affected their spouses and children.

Apparently, no one was aware or strong enough to rein in my husband and tell him he needed to give adequate time and personal support to me. The truth is, when we were together he could easily zone out and didn't seem to have it in him to give any emotional support, or engage in caring dialogue.

God's Sovereign Care

Amidst my real and ongoing pregnancy needs and quiet frustrations, I still saw God's hand on our group. In Europe while riding on a bus in the middle of nowhere, one of our tires' treads started to unravel. This urgent need forced us to pray that God would somehow put this tire back together till we passed through this desolate region, and He did. Seventy five miles later we reached our destination! This situation reminded us of how urgent needs were met like we'd read about in the Bible. Many times, when we had no food, we'd ask for God's help and through any number of people or sources we'd be cared for.

Nearing nine months pregnant, we had nowhere to live and I was stressed out! We prayed earnestly for help and God provided a married couple who wanted to take us in. We were in Germany now, looking for venues for our band, "Sheep" to play. Amazingly, our whole team found favor with a number of families stationed at the USA Air Force base in Lautzenhausen, Germany in the Rhineland-Palatinate that we'd met during Sheep concerts on the compound. The ladies at the base found housing for all of us!

They even threw me a "baby shower!" Up until that day I had absolutely nothing in the way of practical things for our baby which was due anytime. By the end of the party, I'd received everything I would need and the most beautiful handmade German quality baby clothes that my middle class family back home couldn't afford to buy. The clothing was exquisite and every gift perfect! The kindness and love shown by these US Air Force families has never been forgotten and warms my heart to this day.

Firstborn

I had what most would call a miracle birth of our first child. Someone gave us a weekend "anniversary gift" at a hotel in Bernkastel Kues, Germany. While there, I went into labor. I had left my 'Expectant Motherhood' book at the airbase so we drove back to retrieve it. I thought I was in labor, but unsure. I'd walked the cobblestone streets for hours in clogs earlier in the day and didn't know I was about to deliver my firstborn. After securing the 'Motherhood book' we decided it was better to be safe and headed out to the nearest hospital.

On arrival at the hospital in Traben-Traurback, Germany we were directed to the third story of the building where the delivery and maternity wards were located. The nurse spoke in German with limited English—conveying she didn't think I was far along enough in my pregnancy, or in labor. Already at the hospital we hoped she would make sure. Communication back and forth from English to German was difficult, but she agreed to put me on a bed and conduct a proper examination. As soon as she did, her eyes became as wide as saucers as she blurted out, "Baby, Ankommen" (to be born, arrive) and dashed out of the room to fetch a doctor.

As she left, I looked around; I was in a room with a large open window, with a view of a hillside with grape vines and distant castle ruins.

Watching small flies buzzing around the window in the morning light, I felt safe, with a huge sense of relief to be in a hospital receiving medical care. It was Sunday morning and the sounds of church bells were tolling, waking the day and calling parishioners to worship.

At this moment a familiar Psalm from the Bible went through my mind and being, "I lift up my eyes to the hills; where does my help come from? My help comes from the Lord the Maker of heaven and earth" (Psalm 121:1-2). God was reminding me He was in control, watching over me.

When the doctor and nurse returned I sensed I was ready. On their cue, I pushed three times and the baby came out! I had no pain. Praise the Lord, for His personal love and care, for He knew all about my need and the baby's! *24 hours earlier, I had no idea how delivering a baby would work out. God knew!*

On to Holland and Then England

After Germany we traveled to Holland. Times were hard in Holland—till one day we were miraculously invited to live in England. This invite came on the heels of many traveling and accommodation hardships. Through God's goodness we were given the use of a very large home in Upper Norwood, England. I spent most of my time mothering. Before long I was pregnant again, limiting my role in ministry outlets.

Instead of becoming part of the Lonesome Stone cast and team, I became part of the support team at our main ministry house. I'd take the pram (baby carriage) to town; buy groceries with others, for the growing numbers in the ministry. Returning home, I'd help cook dinner while watching my son Peter. When the theatre production was local the team would return later in the evening and there would be a hot meal waiting for them.

For me, it was a deeply lonely time, but rewarding to be caring for our son. I was usually in bed by the time Rich and our team arrived home from outreach activities. It was extremely difficult being married in our particular ministry. Rich and I were rarely together for quality time. *I was not a priority to him and he didn't want to be with me.* What he wanted mostly was to tell people about Christ, which he was very good at. Once in awhile I'd be able to accompany Rich and the team on witnessing outings. We'd head out to the downtown area of London and share with anyone we met about the love of God. Any type of outing was a blessing for me. Getting out helped me see the world a little differently and release some of my hidden depression. The bright side of being at the ministry base with a small support team was, I simply loved being a mother!

Spiritualizing

There was a time in our early ministry when team members were guilty of spiritualizing things by saying, "God is going to do this." Or, "God told me" Others claimed they'd received a spiritual insight, impression, a dream or wisdom from God about something. Most of these claims were hairbrained ideas; things an individual wanted to do, or have someone else do.

Growing up in the church gave me a measure of common sense when it came to stuff like this. This wasn't God, but immature Christians trying to sound spiritual or get their own way!

In spite of our many miss-steps and immaturity, this and other spurious practices were corrected.

Two Divine Appointments
Jenny Haas

Many years later, back in the USA I met someone who was tiling a bathroom in a new house while I was painting a mural in a different part of the home. We were both working as independent contractors. The tile contractor had been playing Christian music and came to see what I was doing, saying "Hi."

"I heard the music you were playing."

"Yes, I enjoy it."

On hearing his English accent we chatted about England. I told him I'd lived in Upper Norwood for a time—part of a Christian team that put on a rock musical. He was interested in hearing more, but had to get back to tiling. When lunchtime came he brought his lunch to where I was working and sat on the floor watching me paint.

Out of the blue he said, "I remember you! I used to look for your ministry's double-decker bus, and your team of 'Jesus Freaks.' I was an atheist and loved arguing with you all. I distinctly remember meeting four of you one night. I am convinced you were one of them. You had an outfit that was light blue denim with wide straps, straight across at the top; it was like a tunic and you had wide pants underneath. I remember when all of you walked away from our invigorating argument. Then you turned and came back to me, saying, "Whatever you think is OK, because no matter what, God loves you!"

When he first started talking, I didn't think he could possibly have met me. But when he described the pregnancy outfit my mom and I made without a pattern, tears filled my eyes. Turning around to look at him I knew his story was true.

His journey was a circuitous one, which he went on to explain. As an atheist with lots of opinions and arguments against God, he found himself paired up with a Canadian missionary in route to France sharing nearby seats. The missionary stayed up most of the night during their journey answering any and every question and doubt he had. On this journey, the tiling contractor had given his life to Christ and had joined a similar Christian ministry to the one we were in. He ended up marrying a girl from Milwaukee and years later moved to Wisconsin.

With the passing of decades, we'd met on a job-site as two independent contractors in the suburbs of Milwaukee after all these years. This was a fresh reminder that God is in control of all our efforts to be a light for Him. The results are always in His hands! In God's design He had allowed both meetings by 'divine appointment.'

In ways only God knew at the time, this second 'Divine Appointment' was an important confirmation. Earlier that morning I'd prayed to be encouraged in some way as I was having self-doubts about going on a mission trip. The Christian mission trip would be to the country of Africa and I'd be accompanying a group of teachers and nurses along with a handful of lay people like myself. Feeling inadequate, I'd questioned if I should be going.

My fears were settled by God in such a beautiful, creative and completely unexpected way by running into a Brit who remembered my witness to him which had contributed to his coming to faith in Christ. Praise the Lord, who does all things well! No one could have possibly encouraged me more than the Lord did this day!

A Few Lessons from Jenny's Account - Author Team

- Marrying based on physical attraction alone, without soul compatibility- can be disastrous.

- There are always repercussions in marriage when mutual nurturing is absent.

- Error: Using King James Version of Matthew 19:29 as a reason to leave spouse and children.

- Shirking spousal or family care by citing Christ's eminent return is a cop-out!

- Saying *"Thus saith the Lord"*, or *"the Lord told me"* to orchestrate or control situations and people, or elevate oneself as being more spiritually in tune, is fake spirituality! False prophets are notorious for using these types of pronouncements. When pride or manipulation of any kind is present, the claim of God speaking is usually not true.

- When a Christ follower sincerely believes God has spoken to them, an attitude of awe, humility and obedience should be reflected. It's likewise a good idea to hold the Lords council close to ones heart and listen for a confirmation.

Bio Capsule— Jenny Haas

Jenny and her first husband divorced many years ago. As a single mom she raised three beautiful children mostly on her own. Peter, Ben and JoHanna (Hansi). Jenny has maintained her walk with Christ through many ups and downs. She is an excellent mother, prayer warrior, servant and example to her family. In recent years she completed university and obtained her teaching degree. She remarried and has a younger daughter named Brecken. She resides in Wisconsin, USA.

26

Testimonies 2

- Larry (Mole) Barker
- Paul Jones
- Dan Scalf
- Michael Clark – Road Trip
- Jo Sappenfield

Larry Barker
Milwaukee Jesus People

My name is Larry Barker. In 1971, I was known as "Mole" and played guitar and sang in the Milwaukee band "The Sheep."

I asked Jesus into my life in Tucson, Arizona in December 1969. At the time I was waiting for a discharge from the army.

A man who was attending what was then called "The Lighthouse Church" came to the park where some hippies were hanging out and taking

dope. His mission was to talk to us about Jesus, even though most simply mocked him.

One day my friend and I sat down and talked with him. We were both high on LSD and not confrontational at the time. He proceeded to tell us how we needed to admit we were sinners and ask Jesus into our heart. He explained that God would then take up residence in us and we'd receive salvation and a personal relationship with Him.

I didn't see what harm that would do so I prayed and asked Jesus Christ into my heart. I looked around and even though I was "peaking" on LSD, I became instantly "straight" (came down off the drugs). This was amazing to me as I was expecting a three to four hour 'trip.'

From that time on I went to The Lighthouse Church every weekend and started learning about Jesus and what had happened to me. I knew something was different and the Bible started coming alive.

When I returned to Milwaukee, Wisconsin, I thought I would get back to "normal" with my friends there, but found every time I tried to get stoned I always became depressed. I felt God was pursuing me! But I was afraid that whatever God wanted me to do I would fail at it. It seemed like a cosmic joke. This was my pattern for the whole next year. Life became so miserable that I finally told God I would do whatever He wanted. By this time I was living outside of Whitewater, Wisconsin with some friends.

I lost my job, moved back to Milwaukee, and a friend told me about the crazy 'Jesus People' that would even pray for the muffler on their car. I wanted to meet these people and was so encouraged and inspired, that I moved in with them. This is what God wanted me to do.

At this time we were a group of about seven people living in a vintage house on the east side of Milwaukee. We were led by Jim Palosaari and his wife, Sue. Our days were spent praying, learning the Bible, and going to the streets witnessing about Jesus. We formed a band called "The Sheep," did Jesus Rallies and started a coffeehouse called "The Jesus Christ Powerhouse." Mike Damrow was one of the "Original 7" in the Milwaukee group and wrote most of the songs for 'The Sheep,' and was in the band in the early days. People began coming from everywhere and God added to our numbers daily (Acts 2:42-47).

The next year we grew to 150 people and took part in a 40 day revival in Duluth, Minnesota, tent meetings in Davenport, Iowa, and then a group of us flew to Copenhagen, Denmark to talk and sing about Jesus there. We had originally planned to be there for a few weeks which turned into a two year adventure of outreach in various parts of Europe.

Our Travels in Europe

We traveled to Sweden, Finland, Germany, Holland, Scotland, and were based in London for a time, playing in places like the Rainbow Theatre and The Cavern in Liverpool where the Beatles first played. We also played in many other concert venues throughout England and Scotland.

"The Sheep" recorded four albums and provided the music for "Lonesome Stone." LS was a multimedia rock musical named and based on a song Mike Damrow had written and part of his personal journey and encounter with Jesus Christ.

Lonesome Stone came to the US in 1974 to tour new venues stateside. With team members road-weary and funds diminishing the production ran its course in the first year. Since that time my family and I have lived in many parts of the United States and then moved to Sweden, where after eight years I went through the heartache of a divorce.

Restoration

Returning again to the States, I was welcomed with open arms by my Jesus People friends. I've experienced God's restoration and renovation and now know God's love in a much deeper way than ever before. Since 1997 I have been serving God as a worship leader and I will always keep praising Him for never leaving or giving up on me.

Bio Update

Since then Larry has worked in the trades for a livelihood, while serving as worship leader at a local church. He and other Jesus People from early days in Milwaukee have continued in supportive fellowship one to another. A group of them including Larry have been ministering together, providing worship and ministry to inmates in a local prison for a number of years.

Recently Larry was remarried to Shereen, an early member of the original Milwaukee Jesus People. Larry is a grace-filled Christian with a servant heart. He is a hard worker, gifted guitarist, singer and loyal friend to many.

My Experience of the Jesus Revolution
Paul Jones – A Follower of Jesus

I joined 'the Green Berets of the Jesus Revolution,' as they were called by the UK's *Buzz Magazine*, a couple of days after my 18th birthday, in 1971.

I had become a Christian at a Billy Graham crusade in London when I was 12. Following Billy's advice, I joined 'a Bible-believing church' and was baptized. I read the Bible and prayed daily, enjoyed learning a lot, and shared my experience with anyone who would listen. God had given me a new life, and I wanted everyone else to receive it too!

But when I turned 16, I got into trouble. I started closely reading the Sermon on the Mount, and hit problems when I tried to live up to just one of the stringent demands Jesus made of his followers—telling the absolute truth. I couldn't do it.

I was also struggling to synthesize the apparently irreconcilable doctrines of predestination and free will, both of which I found in the Scriptures. When I mustered up courage to talk with a church elder about this, he said, "Paul, stop trying to understand this stuff; just believe!" This response concerned me. Was he insinuating that being a Christian meant we needed to switch off our minds? Fortunately, I later realized Jesus has something to say about this... For the following 18 months, I stopped saying I was a Christian, though I still believed in God and that I had become his child: I just felt I wasn't living up to be called one yet.

Then my best friend, the Head Boy and leader of the Christian Union, whose weekly meetings were normally attended by about 6-12 boys, invited a group of radical Christians who had set up home in our town to come and speak one Wednesday lunchtime.

The meeting in the art department was crammed out by about 100-120 boys attracted by the visit of three long-haired 'Jesus Freaks' to our conservative grammar school (and maybe by the fact that one was an attractive girl).

They shared their stories, sang a song and challenged us to follow Jesus. Afterwards, when we should have been playing football during our games period, six of my friends and I subjected them to the third degree on every objection to Christian faith we could think of. There was myself, my friend and another member of the school magazine editorial committee; and then three members of the alternative magazine I had founded. These might have been more sympathetic to our visitors, as they were members of a student rock group, and some had experimented with drugs.

But we spent the next two hours aggressively seeking to demolish them intellectually. While one was clearly rattled and angry, and the girl was upset, the third just calmly picked at his guitar, and from time to time made a thoughtful comment.

This calmness under pressure impressed me, although I felt that they had come off worse during the exchange. So that evening I visited their community in Bromley, and spent about three hours going over some of the things we had discussed with 'Zohar', who was someone better able to give good answers to such questions.

I revisited the following evening, and didn't go home. I had joined the 'Children of God' (COG).

Initially, the experience was a discipleship 'boot camp.' Two meals a day of admittedly generous portions of low-grade food, long sessions listening to readings of letters from the founder of the group, David Brandt Berg, known as 'Moses David,' memorizing two verses of scripture each day, and spending three or four hours on the streets witnessing to people mainly our sort of age, were all a shock to the system. But it was not the highly regimented daily routine, or the high-intensity sessions and atmosphere that most struck me: it was the idea that at last, I had joined a group really committed to being disciples of Jesus.

Each of us had 'forsaken all,' as Jesus calls his followers to do. For me, that meant my family, my education, and my future. But what we gained was a spiritual family of precious brothers and sisters equally engaged in bringing the true message of new life that can be found in Christ alone.

We slept in two derelict houses in Grove Park (girls in one, guys in another) and went to a disused factory in nearby Bromley for our breakfast, teaching sessions, and preparation for witnessing forays to London or local streets. We had a double-decker bus which was an ideal way to get a team to wherever there were young people, as well as providing a place for con-versation, and a way to get

them back to base, if they looked like possible converts. The properties and bus had been made available by Kenneth Frampton, a Christian busi-nessman whose sons Keith and David also joined the group.

Our tracts were printed in the Bromley factory, and in Grove Park. 'Eman Artist' designed the tracts and the "New Improved Truth" news-papers we distributed on the streets. It was only after I left that I realized that David Berg had been living just a couple of hundred meters down the road from the factory: his identity and location were always closely-guarded secrets, even from the members. We never saw him, though we certainly saw his daughter, Faith (the only member, to my knowledge, allowed to use a birth name), son 'Hosea' (Jonathan), and (briefly), his other daughter, 'Deborah' (Linda).

In those early days, we handed out gospels of John to people inter-ested in our message, and invited people back to the commune each day for an evening meal and further talk.

We had been love-bombed: hugs, passionate songs, conversations and expectations were the order of the day, and we aimed to love-bomb others into the kingdom of God.

I started as a 'babe,' went on a two-week intensive leadership train-ing course in a village hall in Horsmonden, Kent, and returned to become 'a provisioner'—someone who got up at four AM to ask for donations of crates of unsold goods at the early morning London food markets.

There were no radios, TVs, papers or books in any of these properties; the daily routine was highly regimented; and the atmosphere was extremely high-intensity. It was only later that I realized that combined with a low-quality diet and sleep deprivation, these are classic factors of alienation and brainwashing techniques.

Amsterdam

From Bromley I was sent to 'colonies,' as the communes were called, in Brussels, Antwerp and finally Amsterdam. I became a 'welcomer' (someone who deals with outsiders) and a trainee colony leader. At midnight, when most of the others got into their sleeping bags on mattresses on the floor, guys on the first floor, girls on the second, I would go up to the leaders' quarters on the third floor to hear 'Peter Amsterdam' (Stephen Kelly) read restricted circulation 'Mo letters.' I would get to my sleeping bag at about 4.00am, then get up at 8.00am at the start of the next day's routine. The leaders were not usually seen at that time, though…

In Amsterdam, we were within walking distance of Dam Square and Vondel Park, the Dutch equivalents of Trafalgar Square and St James Park in London. Here we met hundreds of American and European hippies who like us had 'dropped out' seeking truth, or perhaps a lifestyle of drugs, sex and rock and roll.

It was wonderful to spend four hours in the summer afternoons connecting with people, telling our stories and the message of Jesus, and then being able to invite them back to the colony for a meal and further talk, sometimes late into the night. We were a colony of about 60, and during the summer months often entertained about 100 guests in the evenings.

At that time, our doctrines and practices were standard evangelical stuff. So it came as a surprise to discover during a late-night reading of, I think, *Old Church – New Church,* that David Berg had separated from his wife, Jane, known as 'Mother Eve', and was now in an ongoing sexual relationship with his secretary, 'Maria' (Karen Zerby).

It would have been one thing to discover that he had committed adultery, but repented of it. It was another thing to be presented with this as a revelation of the license granted to 'God's End-Time Prophet' whose teachings and revelations were to supersede those of the Bible.

Each night I would adopt a Muslim prayer position on my sleeping bag, and pray for a very brief time before sleep overwhelmed me. I knew that what David Berg was doing was not right, according to the Bible, but I struggled with the conviction that I had to leave the group.

I am ashamed to say I even bargained with God, thinking that the story of 'Gideon's fleece' endorsed this. I was giving my life to share the good news with young people; I deeply loved my fellow-members; I had forsaken all. Didn't God understand that? Couldn't I continue to do all this good stuff even if the leader was practicing a sinful lifestyle?

And there was a major barrier to leaving for every member of the group: the leaders, held our passports, and none of us apart from the leaders had any cash at all.

So I told God, 'If you send one of Moses David's own children to Amsterdam to tell me to return to the UK, then I'll know that this conviction comes from you, and I'll leave.'

Three days later, that happened. 'Hosea' came to Amsterdam and two or three days afterwards asked me to take some materials back to Bromley. I took my passport, some cash for the ferry, made the delivery, and returned to my parents' home. Not knowing what else to do, I picked up my education, with a view to going to university.

From Bad to Rotten

David Hoyt, a more important member, having been a leader in a US Jesus People group which merged with the COG, also left at about the same time. Somehow I came across a 'Mo' letter that referred to him and me as Judases who were not to be readmitted, and in fact were effectively excommunicated.

I learned of the death in Switzerland of Berg's older son, 'Aaron' (Paul) who had fallen from a mountain. I had seen him once; accompanied by people I was told were his bodyguards because he was so 'spacey.' He certainly looked it: maybe he had mental health problems.

I wondered: unlike his brother and sisters, did he have no role and prominence in the group because he disagreed with or was rejected by his father? Did he commit suicide? Was he even pushed? All that was pure speculation, but when I read in a paper that two members of the group had apparently committed suicide on the same day by jumping from church towers in Belgium in towns about 60 miles apart, I thought the coincidence was too great.

This may seem paranoid, but I later discovered in Deborah Davis's (Linda Berg's) book, The Children of God, that some members of the wider Berg family consider both possible, and Deborah confirmed that his father had rejected him.

I also met other former members who showed me 'Mo' letters that advocated Flirty-Fishing (essentially, religious prostitution), promiscuity among members, whether or not they were already married, 'spirit guides,' and even sexual relationships with children. I remember a line from one letter that said: 'Jesus calls you to lay down your life for your brother. Would you lay down your *wife* for your brother, if he has the need?' Anyone not prepared to follow this teaching was deemed an 'old wineskin,' not worthy to be part of the The Children of God.

Survival

I was occasionally tempted to return to the group, despite all this. The churches I visited seemed so lukewarm, worldly and middle-class. They were not engaged in reaching out to people with the gospel they said they believed. Their Christianity did not seem to cost much beyond a couple of hours on Sundays. After all, I wouldn't need to take part in immorality, I reasoned… and I had successfully resisted leaders' pressure to marry one of the members who was romantically interested in me.

But God in his continuing grace let me discover other expressions of the Jesus Revolution that were radical and counter-cultural, but without the heretical teachings and cult practices. I became aware of Jesus People USA's *Cornerstone magazine*, the Christian World Liberation Front's *Radix Magazine*, Keith Green's *Last Days Ministries Newsletter*, Calvary Chapel's *The Truth newspaper*, and some papers produced by Australian Jesus People groups. These showed that there were groups seeking to live out radical Christian discipleship, and that Christians could present the Good News in a culturally relevant and exciting way, energetically engaging with the intellectual, social and political issues of the day. Subscriptions to *Cornerstone and Radix* were my life-savers.

I started a Christian magazine called Apocalypse. There were articles by writers I admired, cartoons and youth-oriented illustrations by friends. Mr. Frampton saw it and invited me to work for him in a new charity named Deo Gloria Trust (Deo Gloria means 'to God be the glory'). I withdrew my university application, and went to work at Deo Gloria Trust.

Deo Gloria sponsored the Jesus Family, led by Jim and Sue Palosaari, which put on Lonesome Stone, an evangelistic rock musical which told the story of how many young people at that time found true peace and love in returning to Jesus Christ, despite having sought it in drugs, sex, music, meditation or Eastern religions.

Meeting the Jesus Family was great. *Lonesome Stone* was excellently done, involving a rock band, a good storyline, and emotive imagery projected onto screens at the back of the stage—an innovation at the time, although a standard feature now. Like the COG, they were committed to sharing the Good News, and lived in community. But unlike the COG, they were not heretical.

I got to know some of the cast and technicians as friends, and interviewed band members for their magazine, Everyman. This helped me to realize one of the things I enjoy doing: writing and working on magazines, which I had played with at secondary (high) school.

I ended up as a self-employed graphic designer, writing and designing on magazines and literature mainly for Christian charities and mission agencies.

Reflections

Was the Jesus Revolution a good thing or just a flash in the pan? I think it was a wonderful movement that offered new life to hippies and young people generally, and also the churches willing to open their doors and hearts to them.

The Children of God became a cult later known as the Family International, or just the Family, which has wrecked thousands of lives. I thank God that he got me out of it before the teaching and practices became completely immoral. Had I stayed, or married a fellow-member, it would have become much harder to leave.

The true Jesus Revolution produced some things that lasted, and others that didn't. A few of the ongoing results: 'Jesus Music' which became the Contemporary Christian Music movement; Jesus People USA intentional community; and the UK's Greenbelt Festival. But most important are the individuals who met the risen Jesus through members of the Revolution, and who are still following him today.   - Paul Jones

Addendum from Paul Jones

I no longer call myself a Christian, but a follower of Jesus. I find this is more helpful in opening conversations with non-Christians. To me, 'becoming a Christian' may be misunderstood as entering a static state, like 'becoming a Communist.' But Jesus called people to follow him, rather than to 'become a Christian,' 'let Him into their hearts,' 'give their lives to Him,' or other phrases which are not found in the Bible. It's an ongoing relationship of learning, obedience and transformation. Crucially, I have had to learn to hear the voice of Jesus leading me away from religion's false teachers and into truth and freedom.

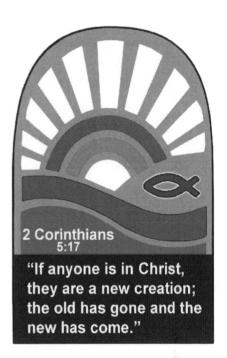

2 Corinthians
5:17

"If anyone is in Christ, they are a new creation; the old has gone and the new has come."

Dan Scalf—East Coast Jesus People
Mary Held-News Service, with D. E. Hoyt
Living Simply— So Others Can Simply Live

Dan Scalf is an international missionary who has journeyed to numerous nations and a variety USA states preaching the gospel of Jesus Christ. In the eyes of man, this young teenager was the least likely to ever have such a testimony. But he was not the least likely in the eyes of God. He was the perfect candidate for the job.

It all began in September 1971 at the age of 16 when he awoke with a severe headache. Diagnosed with a terminal brain tumor, he spent four months in the hospital undergoing various kinds of therapy. During this time he became addicted to morphine and codeine. Addicted to pain medication with a life-threatening brain tumor was a bad combination. Life looked hopeless.

That is, until he received a call from a fellow schoolmate Kathryn Knapp (now Kathy Sprague) who brought him this simple message of hope: "She told me Jesus loved me, but I just laughed at her," said Scalf. That was January 1972. Knapp told him to pray, but he didn't know how. Later when recalling this invitation to pray, Scalf finally said, "God if you're real, reveal yourself to me and I'll give you my life."

God began to reveal himself to Scalf in more ways than one. He was in the hospital for only five more days after praying this prayer. Incredibly, the doctors were unable to find any sign of the tumor in further tests and he was also delivered from his dependence on pain reducing drugs.

After recovering, Dan returned to high school, where he led a number of his classmates to faith in Christ.

Several months later in March of 1972, Jim Palosaari and the Milwaukee Jesus Movement came to the Quad Cities of Davenport and Bettendorf in Iowa, and Rock Island, Moline and East Moline in Illinois for three-days of gospel meetings. The unexpected occurred when these meetings turned into several months of evangelistic gatherings because of an avalanche of spiritual response.

In one of these meetings Palosaari preached on the "Call to Discipleship" and a young Dan Scalf knew God was speaking directly to him about committing his life to be an ambassador of Jesus Christ to carry the 'Gospel' into all the world. In the same meeting Scalf's brother received Christ. The work of God's Spirit was strong in these meetings yielding an abundance of changed lives.

Dan recalls, "In May I quit high school to go into the ministry full-time. I hitchhiked to Decatur, IL and joined 'Christ is the Answer Crusade' under the leadership of Bill Lowery." This ministry group traveled throughout the United States, pitching a large tent for evangelistic meetings and living in tents. This is where Scalf learned to trust God for his daily needs. He told the Lord he would gladly live simply, so that others could simply live. This conviction would become the core of his life's work and mission.

At age 17 Scalf was invited to be a part of a Full Gospel Businessman's airlift to Scandinavian countries to conduct outreach missions. Inspired by what he saw firsthand, Scalf was hooked! In1973 he and fellow Christian Frank Seekins traveled to Halifax, Nova Scotia where they landed a job on a freighter headed to Europe. "We arrived in Hamburg, Germany ten days later with limited funds in our pockets and no local contacts."

Seekins stayed in Germany to share his faith, but Scalf hitchhiked into Sweden hoping to share the Gospel there. On arrival, Scalf learned Sweden had adopted religious instruction as part of its government sponsored educational curriculum. With this information, he saw an opportunity. The next step was to find local educational authorities. On doing so, he requested permission to share his account of coming to faith in Christ in city schools. Education officials were intrigued by a young American fired up spiritually and convinced of his faith.

Because of this, Scalf was allowed to share his testimony in a number of middle and high schools. During the first several weeks of addressing classes and assemblies, several hundred students responded to the message of Jesus Christ with eagerness and faith. This reception of the "Good News" inspired Scalf as he thought about Jesus' words,

> "The harvest is plentiful, but the workers are few. Ask the Lord of the harvest, therefore, to send out workers into his harvest field."   Luke 10:2 NIV®

Thankful to be a worker in God's fields, Scalf knew it is the Lord Almighty who creates spiritual hunger and releases *New Life in open hearts who welcome Him in.*

While still in Sweden, Scalf decided to preach the gospel in one of the city parks hoping someone within earshot would understand English. While doing so, a woman began translating for him as he presented the Gospel of Christ. Afterwards, she invited Scalf and others to her home for Bible study and asked Dan if he would share his testimony. Three days later, a half-page article with his testimony went out to multiple thousands of people in Sweden through a large newspaper with an expansive distribution.

Asking around, Dan learned, the lady who had provided the translation in the park and invited Dan to a Bible study in her home was a well-established newspaper reporter named Ylva Eggehorn. She is now among Sweden's most famous contemporary Christian writers. This is just one of many divine appointments Dan would encounter.

Scalf made his first trip to Russia a few months later, linking up with the Slaviska Missionen aka Slavic Mission. In 1974 he was asked to assist Brother Andrew and his Open Doors International Ministry with the mission of smuggling Bibles into Russia. In 1976 young Scalf turned 21 years old while preaching in Leningrad, now called St. Petersburg, Russia. These were faith-filled exciting days of being available to God!

Scalf's evangelistic journeys were conducted in a similar way that early Christians would have traveled; without marketing teams, a published itinerary and no demographic analysis of the regions he was entering. These were Holy Spirit led ventures filled with the unexpected.

Returning to the US as a young adult Scalf continued to minister to youth locally and secured a job with a Pro-Life, Pro-Family political campaign group from 1977-1990. Though meeting the practical need of steady work, his tenure of working for a good cause ran its course as the Lord began speaking to Scalf's heart about his original vision and calling to carry the 'Gospel' into the world.

Scalf knew God could do amazing things when someone said, "Yes I'll go!" With this in mind and heart in the 1990's, Dan returned to Europe and was given an opportunity to assist in establishing new churches in war-torn Soviet Georgia which was in the midst of a civil war. In this troubled region he and other European-based ministries successfully planted a number of churches in various cities. In the chaos of war, many believed and received Jesus Christ as their Lord. Sadly, the war claimed the lives of many young Christians while others were imprisoned because of their faith in Christ.

Through those Dan had worked with in Soviet Georgia and newer European ministry contacts, Scalf was offered an opportunity to aid Russian Jews fleeing communism by driving them to safety across the border into 'Free Europe' by bus. These crossings were often a 'life or death' situation for those fleeing Russian oppression and persecution. Over time, buses were added to the expanding ministry. This work and exposure increased Scalf's vision regarding the needs of persecuted Jews and Christians in various parts of Europe and Asia.

From these early days, other places of need became evident and contacts were established. This brought Dan Scalf into direct contact with a goodly number of Christian leaders and pastors in Asia who were experiencing severe and life-threatening persecution in Muslim countries. Due to the dire needs of believers in these regions, Scalf established a Humanitarian Aid Ministry which has served and met many practical needs of those living under constant persecution. Most of those who have been helped are Christian nationals who have been targeted by extremist Muslim groups who have an agenda of eradicating any Christian presence within their country.

Scalf's home base is Atlanta, Illinois USA. He continues to preach the Gospel wherever doors open. His main focus in recent years has been assisting persecuted Christians in Communist and Muslim countries by making their needs known and by providing emergency assistance as funds permit.

More recently Dan Scalf's health has taken a turn for the worse after experiencing a stroke in June of 2017. Please remember Dan in prayer. He has been a faithful evangelist to those who sit in darkness bringing truth, hope and the Gospel of Jesus Christ. He's also been an advocate for those with great need by providing practical assistance to brothers and sisters in Christ who suffer for their faith in distant lands.

"It's all about Jesus Christ. I live simply, so others may simply live."

Northwest Jesus People Road Trip
Michael Clark

In 1971 part of our Spokane Jesus People team were stranded when our old Trail-ways diesel bus broke down. We were along the Columbia River in Oregon about five miles from the nearest town. Several of our team took off hiking into town for help.

While waiting, an older sister in the Lord pulled up behind us and was having trouble with her VW camper bus. I was able to fix it and she gave us two arm-loads of food, pots to warm it up in, and it was more than enough for lunch for our team of twelve.

Ironically a team member had just finished asking our leader if we had missed God—because he'd been told we'd never miss a meal. This isn't a Biblical promise, but he'd assumed it to be so, when taught about the Lord's provisions—as long as we followed and obeyed God.

The team leader responded, "It's not noon yet. We'll just have to wait and see."

A few minutes later I walked on board the bus carrying the bags of food we'd been given and a birthday cake. The lady who gave this gift of food said, "It must be somebody's birthday on your bus."

I asked our team if anybody had a birthday—with no response. Then the hitchhiker we'd picked up in Spokane said, "It's my birthday!" The guest hitchhiker was blown away as we sang 'Happy Birthday' realizing no one knew it was his birthday and everybody got a taste of his birthday cake! This insignificant event awakened him to realize that God knew him and loved him. It increased our faith as well.

It's good to recall how often God faithfully showed up, providing for us and those we were endeavoring to minister to. A broken-down bus was a little hiccup in our day in the big picture of things. In hundreds of circumstances beyond this, opportunities arose for God to work and teach us something. We witnessed gas tanks that didn't run dry, a kettle of soup that never emptied all day when serving the hungry, rain storms and squalls that went around us, donations that were not appealed for but came in, miraculous healings, hundreds of salvations through people hearing and responding in faith to the 'Good News of Jesus Christ.'

God's ongoing love and constant care brought about a humbling of our souls. To think, the 'True God' of the universe had chosen us and included us in His plan was staggering. He not only rescued us from death but gave us the gift of eternal life because of all Jesus had done on our behalf. Words fall short of describing what we sensed, when we thought about Jesus' sacrifice of enduring an excruciating death, so we could be saved.

We were deeply grateful! Amazed! And we wanted to share this 'new life' that was available in our Risen Savior Jesus!

Jo Sappenfield
Northwest Jesus People

"My spiritual journey took shape at the age of 16 when someone by the name of God encountered me as I was shooting up a hit of acid with my boyfriend on the Oregon Coast. I knew God was real—having opted for the insurance policy that would keep me out of hell—saying the sinner's

prayer when I was nine years old. I was God's child, my prayer had been received, but the reality of "Christ living in me" had not been the path I'd chosen, or wanted up until now.

How dare I think that in spite of waking up early in the mornings to the daily intercession of my father to his heavenly Father on my behalf, that my life could continue uninterrupted? Wasn't I free to pursue my secret, unaccountable and dangerous

actions? I should have known better than to try and run from God in the opposite direction. God's children know His voice, and He called my name just as I was about to go into the Under Realm of Darkness. There was no doubt in my mind where the voice was coming from. God may sit on a Throne—but He's not immobile! His Holy Spirit showed up at just the right moment.

This encounter produced repentance—a turning from secret activities and self-destructive choices. I was given permission from my earthly father to leave the public high school where I attended and transfer to an accredited correspondence school until I graduated. I then joined the Jesus People Army and moved into their ladies house called the House of Esther on Dayton Street in the U-District of Seattle, Washington. My intentions were clear and focused. I wanted to walk in the light and follow in Jesus Christ's footsteps.

It was here that I became part of God's army; He has one, you know. This branch of His army was founded by Christian visionaries who took the call to share their lives and faith in Jesus Christ as a mandate to be followed. I have many war stories of struggles, set-backs and victories.

The same types of personal and spiritual battles and discipleship victories are recorded in the Bible. They attest to the reality of God's army of disciples and ongoing enlistment program. God is very interested in the recruitment of those who are serious about doing His will and representing Him on this earth!

God's work and calling on my life was not in vain. It was a career decision! Although the scenery and the faces of those I encounter or minister to change, God has put it in my heart to ask Him regularly to use my life to encourage others to approach Him. When I wake each day, I do so asking for fresh marching orders from my Savior and Lord, Jesus Christ.

Jo –Walking with Jesus

At 66 in earthly years as of June 2019—I'm as committed to Jesus Christ as ever. In heavenly time, I'm an eternal being. I've been quickened and made alive by the same Life-Giving Spirit of God which raised Christ from the dead (Romans 8:11).

I see my life on earth as a gift, an opportunity to be a light for the Father, Son and Holy Spirit. My spiritual life began as a young teen and there is no end in sight since I'm in His family and part of an Eternal Kingdom (John 3:16; 2 Peter 1:11; Daniel 4:3; Revelation 22:1–5).

My hope in God's promises and Word is firm. "Your Word, Lord, is eternal; it stands firm in the heavens (Psalm 119:89)."

> No longer will there be any curse. The throne of God and the
> Lamb will be in the city, and his servants will serve him.

They will see his face, and his name will be on their foreheads. There will be no more night. They will not need the
light of a lamp or the light of the sun, for the Lord God will
give them light. And they will reign forever and ever. Revelation 22:3–5 NIV®

27

Bio's 1
Updates & Contributor Comments

- Lynn Malmberg – Milwaukee & UK JP
- Karin Gunnarsson Bienge – Sweden, JP UK
- Victor Clowser – Upper Streams CA JP
- Sue Palosaari Cowper – Milwaukee, UK & NW JP
- Ann Clowser O'Donnell – Upper Streams CA JP
- Jack Fliehmann – Home for His Glory, CA JP
- Ed Clowser – San Fran East Bay JP

Lynn Malmberg
Life Witness and Faith in God

Lynn received Jesus Christ in Milwaukee, Wisconsin and never turned back! She traveled to Europe with Jim and Sue Palosaari's team from the Milwaukee Jesus People. Her life-long ministry with children began in the Beulah Hill House in London, England where the 'Jesus Family' ministry began.

In addition to her gift with kids, which reached and inspired hundreds of children, her passion, ability and boldness in sharing

Jesus Christ blossomed.

After Lonesome Stone Lynn lived and ministered at Beulah Hill House, aiding those returning from LS and others in need of ministry for one year, as a new form of Christian community was developed

In 1975 she returned to the USA to re-establish a relationship with her Mom. After considerable work, they became best of friends. Her Mom had a life-changing spiritual experience while in the hospital. Lynn commented, "I saw an unusual look on Mom's face and asked her what was going on." Her Mom said, "I was just with Jesus. Jesus and I were walking on the beach together with his arm around me as the sun set. Jesus was with me." This experience opened the door for her Mom to invite Jesus to be her Lord and Savior. When Lynn's Mom passed in 2002, Lynn was surrounded by her Jesus Family friends. Mike, Mary and Shereen sang, and Rich and Mole were by her side.

Back to 1975, Lynn was living with Jesus Family friends in Sheboygan, WI; Mike and Mary Damrow, Reed Mittelsteadt, Lisa Carothers and Odie and Sue Carter.

In 1977 she moved back to Milwaukee and took a job in an inner city daycare. The daycare had many problems organizationally, but she fell in love with the predominantly black children the center served. These children made an indelible imprint on Lynn's heart. Unfortunately, as an Anglo, navigating to and from the center was not without incident. After a number of threats and near disastrous run-ins with people from the hood, Lynn sadly had to leave this job.

About this time, 'Living Stone Fellowship' and Pastor Van helped pay for Lynn to return to school and she enrolled at the University of Wisconsin, Milwaukee. She was taught and mentored by Bessy Gray an instructor at UWM. Lynn graduated UWM on the Dean's honor roll with a degree in Community Education / majoring in Child Care.

She was then hired to work with Bessie Gray's Daycare in inner city Milwaukee. This working environment was challenging but equally rewarding. Bessie was an incredible mentor. Lynn worked with her for several years.

Shepherd's Corner Day Care

This led to Lynn launching her own daycare center called "Shepherd's Corner Day Care" on 52nd and Lisbon which Lynn directed for three years. The daycare was licensed to serve 19 children and she had six part to full time teachers. The funding for this location was complex with vouchers, partial stipends and income-based payment for childcare. It was complicated to meet salaries with uncertain and changing state and federal funding, but they managed to stay afloat during this period.

United Methodist Children's Services Childcare

The next door that swung open was at the United Methodist Children's Services Childcare where Lynn worked for many years in a leadership role. They served 60 children with a staff of 12 teachers. At the time Lynn was the only white person on staff, but was warmly accepted. This was an excellent fit for Lynn and she thrived in this setting with a larger team and adequate funding. Recognizing Lynn's giftedness with kids, she was asked to teach childcare related classes at Milwaukee Technical College for the next 5 years and taken on as a new board member of the 'Wisconsin Early Childhood Association.' These opportunities were fulfilling affirmations.

During these years and beyond, Lynn would continue to expand her musical ministry with children, writing and teaching fun and spiritual songs for them. For 15 years she was actively involved in leading and bringing in others to aid her in providing workshops for kids, parents and preschool teachers. In the process she completed several collections of children's songs. Concordia Lutheran Publishing purchased one of her songs to be included in the "Little Ones Sing" songbook. The tune is called "Happy Birthday Jesus" and is still in circulation throughout the USA and other countries.

In 2000 Lynn retired from her position at UM Children's Services Childcare. She views this season as her Waterloo—a time of great testing. After two knee surgeries, many encounters with hostile parents, working in a very dangerous neighborhood fraught with guns, knives and violence, Lynn decided it was time to make a change. Theresa Turifoy, who Lynn had mentored, stepped up and has continued as director at UM Childcare since.

Taycheedah Women's Prison

The next door that swung open came via her years of childcare. A child who was 'difficult to calm' fell into the arms of Lynn and that was it. A relationship of friendship developed with the mother Gail Barwis who served as a Chaplain of Taycheedah Women's Prison in Wisconsin. Sensing Lynn would be an excellent representative of the Lord, Lynn was invited to be a part of an ongoing rotation of guest speakers and worship leaders for the prison's Sunday worship services.

This invitation was expanded to include Mike and Mary Damrow, Larry Barker, Mike Drehfal and a number of others from the Milwaukee Jesus People and Lonesome Stone days. Women prisoners expressed regularly that they related to the team members' honesty and vulnerability in sharing matters of faith, personal struggle and life in Jesus Christ. The women inmates didn't feel preached at—but rather encouraged in knowing and beginning to believe that God was capable of transforming and rebuilding their lives.

Milwaukee Ethiopian Church

An enduring highlight of Lynn's life of ministry has been the last 10 years of Christian Ed teaching and music ministry with the children of the Milwaukee Ethiopian Church. An enduring bond of love formed. Younger children, then mid to late teens felt they had learned to love God and be His followers. The life of Jesus had been revealed in hundreds of ways through Lynn's life and their own lives of faith began expressing spiritual vitality. This legacy blessed Lynn beyond words. These same kids prayed and continued to stay in regular touch despite Lynn's many physical battles.

As with each of us, family, friends, co-workers and the special people God puts in our lives gave meaning, reason to hope and courage, strength to carry on—and keep shining for Jesus. In tangible ways Lynn sensed her Father's care through a community from the Jesus People Milwaukee and Lonesome Stone days who remained in close friendship with Lynn. The church may be weak and sometimes appear dead—but God's people are not! He has His own scattered around, who at the just the right time and place show up!

Lynn has been a faithful friend, who stayed in touch with more Jesus

People friends than most. Her life was not been without flaws, mistakes, problems and heartache—but every one of us could always count on Lynn to be real!

Delicate Surgery

Early in 2015 God brought Lynn through a 4.5 hour surgery with over four feet of incisions. She was surrounded by many longtime Jesus People friends with over 40 years of history together. More recent friends also gathered along with Ethiopian Christian friends and children, all praying intensely for this delicate surgery, and Lynn's well-being. This prayer gathering occurred the night before surgery in a hotel near the hospital. A lead pastor from the

Ethiopian church prayed this, "You O Lord, be the knife and the scissors! You O Lord guide every movement of the surgeon's hands. You O Lord be glorified in what you will do."

The next morning Lynn repeated this prayer, praying it in the presence of the attending doctors and nurses directly prior to going into surgery. She asked them to hold hands before she prayed. A number of the professional staff gathered said they were touched, appreciating this genuine prayer of faith, and let Lynn know it. Lynn's surgery was of the nature that she was told in advance, she could die. To her, it was all about God's will, and placing herself in the Lord's hands through trust and surrender.

Post surgery, a visiting African pastor was brought along to the hospital from the airport in the company of many friends from the Ethiopian church. While they were all gathered around thanking God for bringing Lynn successfully through surgery, the visiting pastor was asked to lead in a prayer for Lynn. Poised to pray, he paused with an unusual look on his face. Others standing next to him asked what was wrong. He replied, "All I see is wings everywhere surrounding our sister Lynn." In a brief moment in time God had opened his eyes to catch a glimpse of what was happening in the spirit world. Lynn was later told by friends in the Ethiopian congregation that this was completely out of the ordinary for this respected visiting pastor and leader. He'd commented that he'd never seen anything like this previously.

Lynn was a gifted one-on-one evangelist. Her heart beat with joy to see others find her incredible Savior, Jesus Christ, who has been her loyal friend and companion and 'King of Kings and Lord of Lords, God's Son!'

In the last year of Lynn's life she was able to lead her caregiver Joslyn to faith in God. Joslyn's brother is Tony Romo, a NFL Texas Cowboys quarterback. Joslyn and Lynn continued to connect spiritually in one-on-one discipleship mentoring. Lynn encountered so many people in her lifetime who quickly learned who was at the center of her life by her faithful and compelling witness of Jesus her Lord.

May we be as bold as she was to let our light as a witness of the True Savior who is the only remedy for this tired and conflict ridden world.

Education and Ministry

University of Wisconsin, Milwaukee, WI

Community Education, Child Care Degree

40 years of Ministry in Christian Education and Music Ministry with Children

Uniquely gifted one-on-one Evangelist

Lynn passed from this life into eternity in 2016

Bio—Karin Gunnarsson Bienge

Karin grew up in Sweden. At the age of 18 at a Sheep Concert in Halsingborg—she received Jesus Christ as her Savior. She recalls, "Mary Damrow was singing and God's presence overwhelmed me. I was sobbing, broken and happy at the same time. I knew God was doing something inside of me." Karin joined the JP outreach team and journeyed through Europe into England where she has lived since. In her words, "I love England."

Karin was an invaluable asset in the Jesus Family. Her gentle and friendly manner, hard work and dedication to Jesus made her invaluable among the larger team.

Karin married Gerd Bienge and they have three children together; Hannah, Peter and Kristina, and two grandchildren, Harlen and Rudi-Mae. While her husband was serving in a church leadership role a crisis occurred, due to unfaithfulness on his part. A divorce, a broken heart and confusion for the children was the aftermath.

In Karin's Own Words

"I couldn't attend my home church because of the scandal—which went public. I went away from the Lord for seven years. It was me that went away. I didn't want church people feeling sorry for me. Perhaps it was my pride. I needed someone to have tea with—a friend.

I didn't need or want a lot of questions about the fiasco. It was too painful to revisit. It was in my head anyway. It was so easy to be reminded of—by anything. I was in shock with a broken heart. What could anyone say? Words fall short.

What I needed was time, to let things settle—a friend's support, a background person to accept me as I was, or a Christian to be present and to pray for me. I worked as many extra hours as possible to raise the three children alone. God's Grace helped me to gradually trust again. Trust Him!"

Karin attends Christ Central Church, Penge, London. She works at Burrellmead Residential Home as a Senior Caregiver and Shift Leader. She has 20 years on the job supervising personnel, doctor contacts, handling deaths, emergencies and all related paperwork. She enjoys interacting with her kids and grandkids, walking and bicycling. She remains a committed Christian, always thankful that God is her Rock in the midst of a shaky world.

Bio—Victor Clowser

"I have been a sheet metal worker for the last 37 years and am currently operating as an estimator and project manager for a Mechanical Contractor in Santa Cruz, CA doing heating, air conditioning and plumbing work. Now retired, I'm catching up and assisting at our local church.

My wife Stephanie and I have been married for 37 years and have three children and two grandchildren. They are spread across the globe from Nashville, TN to Perth, Australia with Santa Cruz in between.

We have been attending the Coastlands Foursquare Church in Aptos for the last 29 years and have served in various capacities of Worship Leader, Children's Ministry, Home Group Leader, overseeing home groups, Vacation Bible School, Ushering, Church Council, Missions Council and I am currently serving as the Men's Ministries Leader.

Every story of faith has God at the center—expressing uniquely the great work He has done—and is still doing in our lives! From the bottom of my heart, I am thankful that He called us and continues to rescue us from darkness and bring us into His marvelous light (I Peter 2:9).

> "How then shall they call on Him in whom they have not believed? And how shall they believe in Him of whom they have not heard? And how shall they hear without a preacher? As it is written: How beautiful are the feet of those who preach the gospel of peace, who bring glad tidings of good things!"   Romans 10:14–15 NIV®

Bio—Susan Palosaari Cowper

I was born in 1943 in a suburb of Los Angeles, California and graduated from South Pasadena High School in 1961.

Education

BA, English major/Art minor, SF State; Teaching credential, Language Arts, Southern Oregon University AA
My father was head of LA County and City Health Dept (he was an MD), my mother an Ethno Botanist, teacher, and artist.

My children are:

Jedidiah, married to Che (Rachael) – Jed is now living in the Philippines

Cody, married to Gabby. He is a Shipping Manager for an LA firm.

Sophia, Advancement Coordinator at St Mary's High School in Medford, OR.

My blessed son Seth is deceased.

Bio Update

In recent years I've been teaching English and Elementary Art at Amicitia American School in Morocco.

Lifetime Vocational Work: Teaching, Costumer, Artist and Writer.

We live in the mountains of Idylewild, CA; I've been married to Larry Medinger for 20 years; previously married to Jim Palosaari.

Bio—Anne Clowser O'Donnell
San Fran East Bay Area JP

Anne was born in Oakland, CA. She grew up in Oakland and Danville, CA, graduating from Danville High School. She studied at Diablo Community College and was a live-in participant at "Upper Streams" Christian House in Walnut Creek, CA and part of the Jesus Movement.

Family: Anne is married to Shawn O'Donnell. They have two adult children and seven grandchildren. Their daughter, Heather Margo and husband James, have three children: Fox, Sophia and Max. Their son, Devin and wife Allison, have four children: Emersen, Erileigh, London, Caedmon.

Vocational Work: Teacher's aide in Santa Cruz and Capitola public schools in the 1980's (Two years full-time, numerous years part-time). Secretary for Santa Cruz Bible Church from 1989-2010.

Ministries Involved In: Upper Streams, Open Bible Church, Mission Street Fellowship, Bible Study Fellowship (five years) BSF Children's ministry (two years), Santa Cruz Bible Church. Caraway Street (children's outreach and high school ministry). Missions work in Mexico; building houses in the colonials in border towns of Tijuana. Presently attend Free Methodist Church in Corralitos, CA—and host and facilitate a 'Women's Home Bible Study' (past seven years).

Anne Speaks to the Impact of the Jesus Movement

God gave me relief from crushing depression. He let me know through His Word the Bible that He loved me, and my life had value and purpose.

When I was trying to decide whether to follow Christ or become a Buddhist, Dale Altar (JP disciple) shared with me from the Bible Jesus' Words, "I am the way, the truth, and the life, no one comes to the Father except through Me (John 14:6)." After hearing this direct claim from Jesus, His words stuck in my mind and heart, and I knew what He said was true!

After becoming a Christian, I attended Bible studies at "Upper Streams" which helped fortify my heart and mind as the healing process from depression took hold. The Word of God helped me to forgive those who I thought or felt had wounded me.

In time, I was given leadership responsibilities at Upper Streams. Though in the midst of becoming established spiritually, and feeling inadequate—God used my life and struggles to encourage younger Christian ladies who were just getting started in their faith walk. As with many things I've learned since, on-the-job training can stretch us in unique ways beyond what we thought was possible.

In my opinion the Jesus Movement was a true work of God's Holy Spirit, drawing many young people who were searching for truth to the true Messiah, Jesus Christ. I was added to the number.

I've experienced God's faithfulness, healing in my emotions and marriage, and His amazing love that continues to pursue me and each one of us! The Scriptures have been my rock. Here is one of my favorites that describes God's mercy and grace that 'lifts us out of dark places.'

> God is faithful to comfort and come alongside those who are
> troubled and grieve in Zion. He provides a 'crown of beauty'
> instead of the ashes of hopelessness. He gives the 'oil of joy'
> instead of the spirit of heaviness and 'a garment of praise'
> instead of despair. His chosen will be called 'Oaks of Righ-
> teousness,' a planting of the LORD, for the display of His splen-
> dor and glory.   Isaiah 61:2b-3 Paraphrase

Bio—Jack Fliehmann
Jesus People Walnut Creek, CA
Home for His Glory

Jack was born in California and came to faith in Christ at a gathering at 'Upper Streams' Christian house in Walnut Creek. He would later marry Debra Hines who also received Jesus Christ as her Savior at 'Upper Streams' a few years later.

Jack & Debra Fliehmann have three children and four grandkids. They are a close-knit family, with several kids and grandkids living with them. Debra is a writer and Jack currently works in a hospital cafeteria. They remain faithful servants of Jesus Christ, full of His love.

For many years Jack gathered with remnants from the JP for fellowship and mutual encouragement. Jack and spouse Debra have both remained active in Christian outreach, house church ministry and with the organized church.

Their love and nurturing in Christ extends beyond their own family and local community to the "Good News Children's Centre" orphanage-school located in the slums of Eldoret, Kenya, which Jack has been deeply involved with since its infancy. Below is a capsule overview; a full inspiring report can be found in the Missions chapter.

The Good News Children's Centre Orphanage & School

The "Good News Children's Centre" is a fifteen year old orphanage-school located in the slums of Eldoret, Kenya. It serves the children who live at the orphanage in wonderful ways through providing food, water, showers, clean clothes, a bed, school supplies, hygiene products and very importantly a loving, welcoming and safe place to be.

The African husband and wife who direct the orphanage-school and the small group of Christian teachers on staff, love the children and feel God has called them to this work. They, teach, mentor, guide, coach and endeavor to encourage and inspire each student to love and serve God and His Son Jesus Christ.

The educational level of the school is the highest in the immediate region. In addition to normal studies, the teachers and staff help lead fun activities through games, song and dance, worship and praise.

Students are also guided in developing personal character traits of responsibility, courage, compassion, honesty, initiative, faithfulness, optimism, perseverance, respect, and service.

All students are expected to care for their personal belongings, and are assigned chores in cleaning and maintaining their living quarters, the school, the chapel, the grounds and the dining area. Some older students assist the staff in food preparation and clean-up after meals.

Mid to older teens are also taught life skills in building and repairing things and given 'leadership' opportunities.

GN students are thankful for every bit of kindness and mercy that has been shown to them. At just the right time Jesus Christ sent someone to help them get connected with the GN Centre. Many of these students will grow into Kenya's leaders of tomorrow and will never forget where they came from!

Author's Note: More information on The Good News Children's Centre and its life-changing ministry can be found in Chapter 24.

Mentoring Buddies – Jack Fliehmann & Kevin Sherfey

While living at 'Home for His Glory' (the men's counterpart of 'Upper Streams'). Jack struck up a friendship with an alcoholic named Kevin Sherfey who was visiting. Kevin became an alcoholic at a very young age and wasn't sure if he could ever change and be worthy of being accepted by God. While on a walk together, Jack prayed with Kevin to receive Christ and be filled with the Holy Spirit. On returning from the walk both life changing miracles had occurred in Kevin and he was filled with joy!

From this beginning a life-long friendship of mentoring one another developed between Jack and Kevin. In the early days they went out to the streets in the area sharing their faith in Jesus Christ and helping anyone they ran across with practical needs while imparting spiritual life and truth. At one point the two and their families moved to the same city to minister together.

Kevin Sherfey now lives in Washington State, has planted a house church and helped connect twelve area house churches for joint events and gatherings.

Bio—Edward L. Clowser

I was born in Onawa, Iowa in 1926 during the "Great Depression." Life was hard, jobs were scarce, the economy was in shambles and social welfare was non-existent. People walked a lot. Cars shared the road with horse-drawn wagons in the rural farm country. Television had not been invented. I went to rural school from age 5-16 in Iowa.

We attended Sunday School at a Lutheran Church and other Protestant services via the coaxing of my family.

Church seemed dull, repetitious and a waste of good play-time. I learned Protestant groups had an attitude of suspicion and prejudice toward Catholics and Jews. Catholics felt the same toward Protestants and Jews. Jews stayed mostly to themselves. Holy-roller Pentecostals were viewed with suspicion by Protestants and Catholics. I wasn't sure what to think. I was just a kid and religion was confusing.

In 1942 our family moved to California from rural to urban living. At seventeen I went out on my own, working and living independently until I joined the Navy and entered WW II in the Pacific taking part in battles in Saipan and Okinawa. As a pilot of a landing craft tied to a larger ship, a suicide Kamikaze plane dove at us. I prayed to an unknown God for help and jumped into the sea. I helped two men out of the ocean. One was terribly burned and the other did not survive. Many were killed. Later on land, two Japanese Imperial Marine snipers in disguise passed us on a trail. In a storm I was struck by a lightning bolt while piloting a landing craft. In total I had five close calls in harm's way with death.

After the war I finished high school, attended Heald Engineering College and secured an electrical job at the Naval Air Station in Alameda, California. I was granted security clearance to work on military aircraft. In time, the Navy sent me to U.C. Berkley for additional classes in "Supervisory Development" and "Executive Training." I earned an adult teaching credential in Spanish, Electricity and Personnel Training and Management. I was eventually selected to manage the Air Launched Missile Repair Program for the Navy and Air Force. Vocationally, life was good.

In 1946 I met my wife-to-be Maria Neri who worked for Marchant Calculating Machine Company. We married in 1948. Our children in order of birth are Steven, Anne, David, Victor, Valerie and Christina. We lived in Oakland and then Danville, CA during the turbulent years of social unrest in the late 1960's and early 1970's. Though our family attended Catholic Church, we experienced severe problems in our home that were beyond our ability to solve. In God's mercy He intervened.

The "Jesus Revolution Awakening", destined to bring spiritual reality and peace to thousands, interacted with our family directly. We were lost in a quagmire of religion and disbelief that God could possibly be personally capable of affecting our everyday lives. Thank God we were wrong!

Near to our home were two Christian houses that sprung up out of this awakening. One was called "Upper Streams" in Walnut Creek, CA and the second, "Home for His Glory" in Lafayette, CA both founded by a friend, David Hoyt. In the years ahead our family along with Dale Alter, would open another area Christian house called, "The House of the Prince of Peace" in San Ramon, CA.

My wife and I shared a variety of roles at the "Prince of Peace" Christian house. Maria cooked and shopped for groceries. I helped lease the property, build bunk beds, gather and provide a variety of resources. Both Maria and I welcomed a steady flow of visitors who came seeking spiritual and practical help. Some were traveling through, needing a meal, place to stay overnight and others became live-in residents. Most needed encouragement and basic life-counseling. All heard the message of Jesus' gift of salvation and offer of new life. We, like other Christian houses, conducted Bible studies, worship and outreach into the community.

As we taught, preached the Gospel, encountered evil, prayed for the sick and shared life together in Christian community—God was teaching and instructing us. Jesus' Word was planted in us, alive and being refreshed in our hearts and minds as we represented Him. In John 14:26 Jesus said, "But the Advocate, the Holy Spirit, whom the Father will send in my name, will teach you all things and will remind you of everything I have said to you." This is exactly what we experienced first-hand!

We visited most of the Christian houses in the Bay Area and the "House of Judah" in Atlanta, Georgia, which Hoyt and a group from Upper Streams had pioneered. We observed that Peachtree Street in Atlanta was similar to Haight-Ashbury in San Francisco. In a non-conventional way God was using Christian Houses to be a safe place for young people to visit, share a meal, learn about God, learn how to work and be reliable, be discipled, do outreach together, provide open Bible Studies and be a light in the community where they were located. The need was growing as the promise of "Peace and Love" was rapidly disintegrating.

Who started this movement? The movement called the Jesus Movement, or Jesus Revolution from 1967–77 was a phenomenon that baffled many. Questions about the simultaneous outbreak of God's Spirit in multiple locations around the same time period, minus human orchestration, left many shaking their heads. And why would God use hippie-types who lacked formal training, who were for the most part viewed with suspicion by the straight elements of society? Where did they get the courage to speak fearlessly and publicly in Jesus' Name? And, why was their simple message resounding in the hearts of their hearers with such undeniable life-changing results? Many questions were asked and conclusions drawn in an attempt to explain the unexplainable work of God's Holy Spirit. Good luck!

Interestingly, those living during the time of Jesus' ministry from A.D. 30 and onward were equally amazed when they heard Jesus Christ's disciples speak boldly in Jesus' Name. In Acts 4:13 it's recorded, "When they saw the courage of Peter and John and realized that they were unschooled, ordinary men, they were astonished and they took note that these men had been with Jesus."

"Had been with Jesus!" In the Jesus Movement, God spoke through hundreds of ordinary men and women who had a personal encounter with Jesus—who took the "Good News" of salvation and the promise of new life everywhere they went. Jesus was front and center, "the true leader." There were hundreds of sub-leaders, raised up by God who did their small part in this movement with the aim of glorifying God and pointing others to Jesus Christ.

The sub-leaders and Jesus Revolution participants I met were Dale Alter, Mike Hash and David Hoyt when he and a small team started Home for His Glory and Upper Streams. I also met pastor A.O. Ramseyer of the Open Bible Fellowship, Howard Rose, Ted Wise, Chris Pike and Kent Philpott who officiated our daughter Anne's wedding. I also met Lonnie Frisbee in Santa Cruz at the Mission Street Fellowship where I served as an elder, and later attended his funeral in 1993 at the Crystal Cathedral in Garden Grove, California. Each of these sub-leaders were flawed instruments of clay. They received Jesus as Lord, obeyed God's call, took risks and spread the 'Good News' of Jesus far and wide.

Maria and I have come to appreciate the value of what Jesus told the Samaritan woman, "The Father is looking for those who will worship Him in Spirit and Truth" (John 4:23-24). The Jews of Jesus' day worshiped in the temple, the Samaritans on a mountain, but God is looking for worship in "Spirit and Truth!" Each of us must determine if we are worshiping and following God in Spirit and Truth, or if our worship and following has been eroded by religion.

Marrying my wife Maria and surrendering my life to Christ are the greatest decisions I've made in this life; alongside, the unique gift of each of our six children who have given us 12 grandchildren and 12 great-grand-children!

There is evil in the world. No critical thinking person can deny this. More importantly, in this troubled world—there is a Savior, and His name is Jesus Christ.

What good is it for someone to gain the whole world, yet forfeit their soul? – Jesus
Mark 8:36 NIV®

28

Bio's 2
Updates & Author Comments

- Ginny Hoyt – USA, 'Two God Stories'
- Andrew Whitman – UK JP
- Dale Alter – Upper Streams CA JP
- Stephen Spicer, UK JP
- Dan Pauly – Our Fathers Family – Southern CA JP
- D.E. Hoyt – SF Bay Area, Atlanta & England JP
- Kent Philpott – SF and Marin County CA JP

Ginny Hoyt's Bio Journey
Work History

Covert federal security agency NYC – 4 yrs.
Fireman's Fund, San Francisco, CA – 4 yrs.
Missionary Board, Ashland, OH – 22 yrs.
Professional Security Consultants –12 yrs.
Albuquerque, New Mexico USA

Growing up Italian in NYC & Family

Dave and Ginny have two adult children together: Marianne & Susie. Dave
& I have been married for 40+ years. He

always says, "It's a miracle!"

I have one brother, Vinnie, a year younger than me. Growing up our family lived in a three-story attached brick house in the Bronx, NY. When we were younger, my mother's parents and her brother and sister also lived there. My parents each had five siblings, so you can imagine our home was always filled with aunts, uncles and cousins! Being Italian, pasta was often on the menu and always on Sundays after church. We had a very close-knit neighborhood, with neighbors being more like family, always watching out and taking care of each other. After supper in the warmer weather, parents were outside on lawn chairs, or sitting on the front 'stoop' (stairs) visiting while groups of neighborhood kids played together. Our family names on both sides were Palombo and Antonelli.

Ministry Participation & Outreach

> I always felt that my gifts were behind the scenes in a supportive capacity doing whatever needed to be done; praying, serving—and being actively engaged as well.

In California, we were part of a Juvenile Hall and Honor Farm outreach ministry. I was way out of my comfort zone, but wanted the Lord to use me. I would mingle and try to engage teens or honor farm residents in dialogue. Some younger teens were withdrawn, but most of the honor farm residents were open to talking. I was glad to provide a listening ear and weave in spiritual things. These interactions gave the opportunity to point to God as the source of giving peace and direction in life. This was important for inmates who'd be facing a new start on probation or parole.

While living in Marin County I worked in San Francisco for Fireman's Fund Insurance Company, where the Lord gave me opportunities to share my faith. Co-workers would come up to me and say "something's different about you" or out of the blue ask "do you know anything about God or the Holy Spirit?" Great conversation starters! I used these opportunities to point others to Jesus who is the source of real life.

Catholic Youth Group

Years later we lived in Glen Cove, Long Island, where both of our daughters were born. Somehow we met members from St. Patrick's Catholic Church and they reached out to us. We attended Bible Studies they hosted, and eventually were asked to lead their High School Youth Group. I'll never forget having the teens over to our apartment for a spaghetti dinner the night I went into labor with our first child! The teens were very interested in trying to see who could pick the actual hour of the birth!

This high school youth group would take on an incredible project of hosting a city-wide "Talent Show" with a multi-denominational worship team and a ribboned and judged "Art Show" for the entire city of Glen Cove, NY. This was very much a God thing!

Nursing Home Ministry

In Glen Cove, NY we also began a Nursing Home ministry in two facilities. We went weekly on Sunday afternoons. Dave would bring a devotional and his guitar, and we would sing the older hymns the residents wanted to hear. Wonderful things happened.

Seminary & Missions

From NY we moved to Ohio for Dave to go to seminary, and I began working in the office of the Brethren Church Missionary Board and was with them for 22 years. At the time we had missionaries in nine countries and numerous "home missionaries" starting churches around the U.S. I was happy to be part of this ministry doing the 'behind the scenes' things that helped them 'be on the front lines for Christ'.

As Dave had not yet learned to type, I was an honorary seminary student typing all his papers. Thankfully Dave went to night school and took Typing 1 & 2. Praise God! Miraculously he did graduate Seminary with a high grade in 1986! Before and after graduation we served in a student pastorate and two other pastoral positions. In both settings we helped establish outreach into local Juvenile Halls.

Ashland, OH - Jr. & Sr. High Discipleship Ministry

In one church, we helped develop a mentoring and discipleship ministry for Jr. & Sr. High teens. Many of these students went on to be Christian leaders in various capacities including pastors and university campus ministers.

Mentoring a High School Student

I was fortunate to be a part of the mentoring ministry, where I was paired with one high school teenage girl. We got together and talked about life and struggles, prayed and looked up Scriptures together with the aim of learning how to let God and faith fit into our daily life.

The student I mentored was Lena. She'd been raised Catholic and wanted to give something back to teens like her who would benefit by knowing God could be a part of their daily life. To achieve this, in her Jr. and Sr. years of high school and early college, she began working at a Catholic summer camp as a volunteer counselor.

Fast forward: Lena was killed in a head-on car accident on a rural country road in her early college years.

Death & Life

At her funeral, hundreds of Catholic teens and young adults showed up that she had influenced for Christ. All present were sad and shocked by Lena's sudden death. We too were numb. Many students spoke of how her faith and life in Jesus had impacted and changed them.

No investment of our time of 'being in Christ' to help or guide someone is ever wasted! In the midst of this tragedy, God's light and love was still shinning and would live on through those Lena's life had touched.

Ashland Detention Center

Our 8+ years of ministry to Ashland Detention Center kids was amazing! We taught them Christian contemporary songs, which they loved, bought a good guitar for the center, did art and photography projects with them, taught them from the Bible and witnessed some of the toughest, most bitter and angry teens soften and receive Christ. A number of these teens learned a trade working with Dave doing painting work on homes after being released.

The Funny Side of a Miracle– At the Restaurant

On one occasion when we were eating out with our two daughters, then in high school, a lady sitting nearby with her family, came over to our table saying, "Richard will be joining us soon and he will really want to see you Dave!"

As high school girls are, ours were inquisitive and one of them blurted out, "Who's Richard?" When Dave mentioned Richard's last name they were both aghast with looks of shock and disbelief on their faces.

Here's the Scoop: Richard was the most notorious hood in Ashland, Ohio, a city of approximately 20,000. His reputation was one of fighting with cops and beating up on anyone who got in his way. His juvenile rap-sheet looked like that of a career criminal.

Suicide Attempt

Dave got to know Richard in the Detention center. He sat in on a couple of Bible Studies, usually more disruptive than receptive, but he liked Dave. One evening we got a call from the detention center, saying Richard had hung himself in his cell and they hadn't found him immediately. He had been life-flighted to a larger Hospital in a neighboring city and he was on life-support in a coma.

Dave went straightway to the hospital and spent most of the night with the family. This was the beginning of several weeks of regular hospital visits and intense prayer.

To everyone's surprise Richard came out of the coma a month later! It was truly a miracle! Doctors hadn't given his family much hope knowing his odds of recovery without brain damage were slim because of the length of time he'd been hanging and the prolonged period in a coma. *The outcome of Richard resurfacing without permanent brain damage was incredible.* Doctors, nurses and the family attributed Richard's pulling through a miracle! Some added, "From God!"

Richard's family told him about Dave's regular hospital presence which opened a door for Dave and Richard to meet up again. Everything that had occurred had changed Richard's demeanor. In the past he'd been a crazed person always doing bizarre and dangerous things, talking loud and scaring people. Richard was calmer now and more receptive to dialogue, listening and discussing spiritual things.

One day Dave got a call from Richard, "I made the decision to give my life to God and have asked Jesus into my heart." This was incredibly positive news to hear! Richard went on to say, "I made the prayer on my own, wanting this to be real and honest before God. I confessed my terrible behavior and the reckless life I've been leading hurting people. I asked God to forgive me and I believe He heard me."

Dave got together with Richard after this for one lengthy visit, but almost immediately Richard moved to the nearby city of Mansfield to break ties with former negative relationships and we lost touch with him.

Back at the Restaurant

We waited as long as possible, but Richard didn't arrive. Since it was a school night and our girls needed to get home, we told his family we needed to go and headed to the register to pay our bill.

Just then, Richard popped in the front door. He rushed over to Dave, gave him a big hug and said, "You'll never guess what's happening to me. I passed my GED and have started college part time. I'm working and I found a good church where I fit in. It's amazing! Jesus' life is for real! Thank you for not giving up and praying for me!" As you can imagine our teenage girls had stepped as far back from the hug and interaction as possible and were in awe! Richard had gone from near death to new life in Jesus Christ; from being a notoriously dangerous hood, to a changed person! To God be the glory!

These two true stories show the power of the Risen Christ! They also reveal the importance of the human side of our contribution when we're 'in Christ' in word, life and presence.

> Stories like these occur daily around the globe. Some may have touched your family, friends or acquaintances. For all who are immediately involved in witnessing a miracle, a transformation, or what rises from the ashes of tragedy—there's a unison conviction, 'God is very much alive!'

New Mexico

Moving to New Mexico in 2006 has been like a breath of fresh air for both Dave and I. We love the 300 sunny days per year, the spectacular view of the Sandia Mountains from our backyard and the incredible 'big sky' vistas and cloud formations.

Culturally, our area is diverse with a near equal Spanish, Mexican, Native American and Gringo population. Since being here our main focus of ministry has been in our neighborhood of 47 family units on our street. We've been part of a neighborhood leadership team that serves these neighbors in a variety of ways. We know almost all of our neighbors and their kids and host a lot of events at our home.

We also have been involved in serving and outreach to the homeless population and I've served as a hospice volunteer to patients and families. Dave and I also have a 'Prayer Intercession Ministry' we take part in weekly at a local prayer chapel. In addition, we've been blessed with new friendships in NM, while we treasure and try to keep in touch with older friends. Our newest joy is having one of our daughters, her husband and two boys move to NM.

Andrew Whitman's Journey
"I Continue to be Awed by Jesus and His Death For Me!"

God's ongoing grace helps me yield to the Holy Spirit's promptings; giving Jesus His rightful place at the center of my life and decisions.

Since coming to an 'active faith in Christ' after a 'Lonesome Stone' show when brother Christian prayed with me, I've been on an amazing journey.

Following graduation from university I became lead vocalist in a Christian rock band 'Sirius.' Other band members were Nick Young (keyboards), Jules Hardwick (guitar), Deluxe Bunyar (bass) and Brian Morris (drums). Our original plan was to go on the road with the message of Jesus. Due to personal and spiritual immaturity, these plans were axed.

Interested in aligning myself with Christian outreach, I ran into members of 'Campus Crusade for Christ' which led to training and service with them.

Concurrently 'Lonesome Stone' was touring and new Christian bands and Jesus People were emerging in different parts of the UK. The Holy Spirit inspired vision and unified message was, 'Jesus Christ is alive and can be known!'

The excitement and 'Breath of God' through the 'Jesus People Movement' was now taking hold in the UK. God was reaching the lost and simultaneously invigorating church teens who heard about it. Visiting USA Jesus People singer Larry Norman and preacher Arthur Blessitt contributed to the stirrings that were birthing a new generation of Jesus followers. Other JP musicians and speakers would follow.

The Jesus Movement was combating the UK's secular ousting of God wherever possible. At the time only 7% of the population was religiously active. Jesus People sought to let the light of Jesus Christ shine brightly and give every person interested the opportunity to ask God for themselves if Jesus Christ was the Savior.

With a growing response among the younger generation, a handful of Christian visionaries began discussing and praying about introducing an Outdoor Christian Music Festival as a means of inspiration, outreach and providing essential Bible teaching. The name chosen was "Greenbelt."

Greenbelt was a collaborative Christian endeavor which began in 1974. 'Jesus Family' leader Jim Palosaari and James Holloway of the band "All Things New," "Capel House" musician Steve Shaw, and Deo Gloria Trust founder Mr. K.P. Frampton worked together to host the first festival at 'Prospect Farm' in Woodbridge Suffolk, England.

I attended 'Greenbelt Christian Music Festival' during these early years meeting new people, getting reacquainted with older friends and reconnecting with Jesus Family members. During the early years of Greenbelt I'd entered into service with 'Campus Crusade for Christ.'

Early Ministry

My first steps forward in serving Christ came about when I entered full-time student ministry with 'Campus Crusade for Christ' for a period of seven years. I received training in London and was then assigned to Edinburgh, Scotland for one year. From there I was asked to pioneer a new team in Newcastle-Upon-Tyne. I was later called upon to assist in training new 'Campus Crusade for Christ' staff members in London and Birmingham.

In the early 1970's every Christian in the UK and many other nations had the scourge of cults to deal with. Seekers looking for answers were bombarded with lies and deception coming from gurus and cults who attempted to sway people toward them and away from the true gospel of Jesus Christ.

These cults muddied the waters and left people confused. I was able to help a few cult victims achieve freedom from both Rev. Moon's "Moonies" and the "Children of God" who chose to shake off the influence of these destructive groups and teachings.

Always indebted to the ministry of Lonesome Stone and the Jesus Family I learned Mr. Frampton and Deo Gloria Trust sponsored these ministries. Thankfully, I was able to meet Mr. Frampton in person and thank him for his many charitable endeavors to further the cause of Christ in the UK. I told him how I too had been reached at a 'Lonesome Stone' show at the Rainbow Theatre in London, which had forever set my heart and feet on a course of Christian service. In his gracious way, he affirmed me and was happy to learn of my ongoing service for Christ.

Sadly, I lost touch with my German friend Christian a year or so after coming to faith in Jesus. Happily, I would rediscover him years later through Facebook. This renewal of friendship led to being invited by him to officiate his daughter Maris' wedding in Hamburg, Germany in July of 2015. The joy of this in person reunion at such a special time for his family brought full circle the reminder of the Lord's mercies who brings about lifetime relationships that would otherwise be unlikely. It's been amazing to link up again, express my gratitude to Christian, and together, give God the glory!

The same reconnection occurred with the late Jim Palosaari before Jim's death in 2011. I'll always have a soft spot in my heart for the 'Jesus Family' and 'Lonesome Stone' theatre team who pointed me to Christ and inspired me to commit my life to Him. After serving with 'Campus Crusade for Christ' it was clear I would spend the rest of my life on mission and in service to The Father and to His Son Jesus Christ.

Higher Education

Theology Degree 3 years, London Bible College now London School of Theology

Master in Ministry 2012, Homiletics/Preaching: Spurgeon's College, London UK

* Currently conducting research for a Ph.D. with the Open University— Looking at the impact of the Jesus People Movement in Britain.

Pastoral Ministry

I've been privileged to serve in pastoral positions for four churches

Senior Pastor, Godmanchester Baptist Church (near Cambridge) 1985-1996
Team Pastor, Kingsgate Community Church, Norwich 1997-2000
Equipping Pastor, Bournemouth Community Church from 2000-2014
Small Group Pastor, Godfirst Church in Christchurch from 2015-17

Teaching Ministry

Moorlands Bible College - Sopley, near Christchurch, Dorset
Lecturer in Preaching Skills from 2001-2014
Lecturer in both Hermeneutics and the Doctrine of God from 2015
Tutor to Placement-Based students

Author

"Free to Hope", a commentary on 1 Peter in the Baker Bible Guide series, published as a Crossway Bible Guide in Britain.

Christianity Magazine, The Jesus People Revolution: the 60's hippies who changed the world, September 2017 publication

Children - now Adults

Philip Whitman (b.1983)
Thomas Whitman (b.1986)

Spouse

Rosie Whitman (nee Chittick)
Married 25th June 1980
Rosie is Northern Irish
Vocation - Occupational Therapist

Current

Freelance preaching, teaching and training (especially with an emphasis on the centrality of Scripture connected to the power of the Holy Spirit).

I'm celebrating 44 years on the Christian road, and have had quite an attack of nostalgia, connecting with some Jesus Family members via Facebook, reading a number of books about the Jesus people movement, and reflecting on my spiritual roots. I firmly believe, despite the naivety, this era of the Jesus People was one of genuine 'spiritual awakening.'

The unchurched were reached for Jesus, largely outside, but sometimes alongside the more established church. The lack of written documentation of the impact of this revival in the UK has caused me to begin research and writing on this subject. My first article with UK's Christianity Magazine was an initial overview of the JP that I hope to expand.

Reflections on a Forty+ Year Journey

- A clear passion for the person of Jesus and the reality of following Him in relationship.

- The beauty and importance of authentic Christian community.

- The evangelistic importance of culturally meeting people where they are.

- A sense that the JP has not been fully recognized for its many contributions.

- Gratitude to God for keeping me through many ups and downs on the road with Him.

I Cor. 15:10
"But by the grace of God I am what I am, and His grace to me was not without effect."

Amidst Andrew's writing and editing of his testimony and Bio update he was diagnosed with cancer. Following this he underwent chemotherapy treatments. Praise God he is currently in remission!

A special thanks to Andrew Whitman for taking part in this project and his ongoing ministry.

Dale Alter Writes

I received Jesus Christ as Savior and Lord of my heart, mind and soul, over 40 years ago. I have gone through many joys and triumphs as well as a lot of sad and painful experiences.

Jesus has been the best friend I have ever known. His patient and unfailing love has been the core of my existence. I have experienced the presence of the Lord thousands of times and endeavor to abide in

Him. I have seen Jesus liberate people from addiction, depression, demons and heal people. I've seen the deaf receive hearing, the blind their sight, and those without mobility to walk!

I'm happiest worshiping the Lord with friends, or waiting before the Lord in quietness. God has given me Peace that is present—even in difficult times. The love of Jesus and Papa God poured out in my heart is all I need.

If you want to know Jesus, pray a simple prayer: "God I want to know You. Forgive me for my sins. I forgive everyone who has hurt me. Come into my heart Lord Jesus and fill me with Your Holy Spirit, in Jesus Name."

Everyone who calls on the name of the Lord will be saved.
Romans 10:13 NIV®

Bio—Stephen Spicer UK

God sorted me out and I stopped being embarrassed about being a Christian. My encounter with the COG was curtailed by the Grace of God. Loving God and my neighbor has been my life focus.

Not long after I met Dave Hoyt in Bromley, Kent. He went to be part of a Christian team that would establish itself in Upper Norwood, London soon to be called 'The Jesus Family.' I visited this group of Christians from time to time.

That September I went to Art School and the Jesus Family went on to produce the rock musical "Lonesome Stone." I volunteered as part of the front of the house team at the Rainbow Theatre as my schedule permitted. The last time I saw David was the final night of Lonesome Stone at the Rainbow.

He teaches graphic design & multimedia at Bath College in the North East Somerset District, England

What God Did in My Life During the Jesus Movement

He took me out of the soul destroying, spiritually bankrupt, authoritarian, judgmental and joyless Plymouth Brethren to discovering what I could be as a Christian. If this hadn't happened, I may have given up on God.

By studying basic theology I gained a more sound understanding of the Scriptures and uncovered the tools to evaluate doctrines and teachings. I learned how to be active in evangelism. I gained discernment to be able to distinguish between man-made religious rules and the essentials of what God actually teaches in the Bible. I gained confidence in being a Christian.

My favorite Scripture verses are woven into these comments

> Do not judge so that you will not be judged. For by the standard you judge you will be judged, and the measure you use will be the measure you receive. Why are you so quick to point out the speck in your brother's eye, but fail to see the beam of wood in your own? – Jesus   Matthew 7:1-3 NET Bible

My View of the Jesus Movement

It was a pivotal time. God enabled faith to grow and gave us clarity about Jesus

Christ's role of being the One True Savior. As God's Spirit moved over Jesus People we were changed and filled with the dynamite of His Holy Spirit! When human leaders usurped authority or espoused what was false, error occurred, like what happened in the COG. This was confusing, but God's truth prevailed.

The Jesus People shook the Western World and the religious establishment for a number of years, infusing it with new life. Attempting to recreate these times would be futile. God is still moving today in His own mysterious way to break into human history with a fresh outpouring of His Spirit. This is His sovereign work.

Our work is to become all things to all men, so that we may reach our generation and save some (I Corinthians 9:22b). The challenge before the church and seasoned believers is to not condemn what God does in releasing His Spirit into the world, the people He chooses to use, and the way or means by which this outpouring occurs.

Ministry Involvement

I have always been associated with a local church, using my dominant gifts as needed. I avoid Bible studies where challenging traditional thinking does not play well. Sadly, back and forth dialogue that expresses differing perspectives is often misunderstood in many Christian settings. The following are fruitful ministries I've been a part of over the years.

Greenbelt Festival

I participated up through the ranks to Programme & Visual Arts Manager.

Christian Motorcycle Association

Founding member of God's Squad CMC, UK, serving as vice-president for a number of years. We were an off-shoot of God's Squad CMC, Australia. God's Squad was founded by John Smith, who was a light in the Jesus Movement in the early 1970's. His book "On the Side of the Angels" is a good read.

Life Witness

Involvement with local Art Community /Bath, England 7 years. Personal ministry to ailing spouse with multiple needs.

Stephen was born in Chelsea and raised south London. He is married with 3 adult children. He attended Chelsea School of Art / graduated with a London Certificate in Art and Design. He is a freelance Graphic Designer and lives in Bath, England

Spiritual Insights

No one has all the truth!

> For now we see only a reflection as in a mirror; then we shall see face to face. Now I know in part; then I shall know fully, even as I am fully known.   Corinthians 13:12 NIV®

Love God with all of your being and your neighbor as yourself. These are the two greatest commandments. Loving God will enable us to love our neighbor. Cultural traditions and differences are everywhere. God's command is to love. Should we expect someone to change their culture to ours and become like us? No!

Love the Lord your God with all your heart and with all your soul and with all your mind and with all your strength. The second is this: 'Love your neighbor as yourself.' There is no commandment greater than these. – Jesus (Mark 12:30–31 NIV®)

Jesus prayed that Christians would be united or one in John 17:11, 21-26. In practice the church has ignored this. Doctrines and practices have separated us. We have failed to put aside differences in order to 'be one' in Christ. There is but one Head, Jesus Christ to an extremely diverse church culturally.

Sadly, we have an even greater separation among the Body of Christ (Christians the world over) caused by human emphasis on pet doctrines, the adoption of false doctrines, group distinctives and church rituals that each group considers sacred.

What should be sacred is living by the greatest commandments!

Dan Pauly—Bio and Comments
Neptune Beach, Florida Ministry & Beyond

From Bethel Union Church and being part of 'Our Fathers Family' Christian House ministries in Southern California, Dan's connections with friends from these days continued.

With the passing of time Dan and friends would open a Christian House and Community in Neptune Beach, Florida. Some from 'Our Father's Family' Christian houses moved to Florida to help start this ministry. To support himself, Dan opened and operated a 'Leather Shop' in neighboring Jacksonville Beach, Florida. He and several dozen friends enjoyed a number of years of living in community and reaching out to those in the area.

Dan eventually moved back to Southern California and was active in several outgrowths of the JPM until lured in by the 'Shepherding Movement.' Well known Charismatic leaders/teachers of the day founded it, but it was destined to fall apart due to legalistic and leadership control abuses. After this experience a convergence of negative heart-attitudes and events collided.

Dan attributes bitterness toward God and specific people as core reasons his life began to fall apart. A divorce, alcoholism and an automobile accident would follow. Depressed, bitter and angry, he took a nosedive into his old life, until warned by God, "If you continue to live like this, you won't live much longer." This sobering word from the Almighty would lead Dan on a circuitous route until he repented. Thankfully, Dan was restored by the Mercy and Grace of God and he is daily grateful for God's amazing love that rescued him from this dark place.

Looking Back

The waves of God's Spirit during the Jesus People Movement were like a Tsunami reaching sand and soil that had never seen water before. We thought it was the norm. The finger of God touched us in amazing ways—awakening us to Jesus Christ. God was active and moving in power! There were amazing testimonies that no one could possibly fabricate. We were open to moving spontaneously with God and accepting people as they were.

Though I am free and belong to no one, I make myself a slave to everyone, to win as many as possible. To the weak I became weak, to win the weak: I have become all things to all men so that by all possible means I might save some.

1 Corinthians 9:19, 22 NIV®

Being available to God and open to the needs of people wherever we went opened doors for Divine Appointments to be the norm. Knowing we were valued, loved and forgiven by God—fired us up and made us want to share the amazing gift of a relationship with God through Jesus Christ His Son!

Dan's Mentors

Dr. Luther Meyer – A seasoned and anointed teacher, professor and pastor
Costa Dier – A Third-world "Evangelist and Church Planter"

Bob Mumford – A Christian teaching mentor with an emphasis on sanctification
Kathryn Kulhman –A Christian faith healer, who in humility relied on the Holy Spirit

Some of Dan's Christian Buddies

Paul Dancheck, Max Rappaport, Andre Crouch, D.E. Hoyt, Lonnie Frisbee, John Wimber, Our Father's House community ministries and others—too numerous to name.

Dan's World Today

Dan married Rebecca in 1995 and they live on a rural ranch in New Mexico. For their livelihood, Dan and his wife run an antique business. In 2011, Dan's son Sam was shot and killed. This tragedy has rocked them to the core. Dan chose to forgive everyone involved. With the help of family and close friends and the Christian community at Christ Church in Santa Fe they are healing and remain steadfast in the faith.

In the past, Dan and Rebecca were part of Calvary Chapel in Santa Fe for close to 10 years. They tried persistently to establish friendships but encountered a relationally barren church.

As a way of combating Christian isolationism and legalism, Dan and Rebecca began attending Christ Church in Santa Fe and made a renewed commitment to practice hospitality to a wide variety of individuals who are attracted by their friendship and acceptance.

Though their home is only 1400 square feet, they have sizable gatherings on their property with a relational emphasis. "We host people for meals and social gatherings from diverse backgrounds and beliefs. In the midst of seeming chaos, amazing things take place. People enjoy non-structured opportunities to dialogue in a welcoming and friendly setting. Our hope is, each guest will be able to sample the kindness, love and acceptance of Christ flowing through us—and like after tasting a good pie, will want the recipe, i.e. the truth and a relationship with God."

Dan and Rebecca are not bashful about their faith in Jesus Christ and have been blessed with many new and lasting friendships as well as opportunities to lead others to Christ by hosting these gatherings which include weddings and pond baptisms.

These days, Dan & his wife Rebecca have no desire for recognition. We are happy to be among God's unknown vessels that help others find Him. Being in the background, available and ready to be God's instruments to aid others in finding hope and freedom is something we see as a calling. Part of the reasoning for this came through a spiritual vision Dan had some time back.

Dan Explains the Vision

"I saw Jesus take a medium size knife from beneath a blue sash that was near his mid-section. I then saw the hands and wrists of a man bound by tight cords. Jesus took the knife, cut the cords freeing the man and quickly tucked the knife back beneath the sash.

Immediately, the thought came, "You will be like this knife. I'm going to keep you tucked away in a safe place, and when I need you I'll take you out and use you to set captives free." Dan knew that in Isaiah 61:1 and in Luke 4:18, both Isaiah and Jesus said setting captives free was on God's heart.

> The Spirit of the Lord God is upon me, because the Lord has anointed and commissioned me to bring 'Good News' to the humble and afflicted; He has sent me to bind up the wounds of the brokenhearted, to proclaim release from confinement and condemnation to captives and freedom to prisoners.
> Isaiah 61:1 Amplified Bible

This vision was clear and understandable. In response, Dan seeks to be sensitive to the Holy Spirit and available to God for His use. "The Lord revealed the benefit of being one who bears a small holy knife that cuts the cords of bondage for another through Jesus' strength and power without public attention and then becomes invisible, safely tucked close to Him.

I'm not always aware of every divine appointment, but am available for as many as the Lord helps me to be alert to. My batting average isn't perfect, but whose is? I'm of some value to the Lord and He's confirmed this by His ongoing Mercy and Grace in my life and ongoing opportunities to help others find freedom in Jesus Christ."

One of Dan's Sayings

"Some say God is Jewish. We know He's beyond ethnicity—but He chose the Jewish People and placed His Son Jesus into a Jewish family. As a typical Jewish Father, He wants a good return on His investment!"

In spite of our mis-steps, God wants us to be fruitful for His glory— not to fade into obscurity out of shame, or attempt to run from God, or adopt a selfish lifestyle. He wants a good return on His investment. He wants us to continue to bear good fruit in Jesus Christ and give the glory to God! He wants us to make it to the finish line!

Life Bible Verses

Just as in His love He chose us in Christ, selected us for Himself as His own, before the foundation of the world, so that we would be holy, set apart for Him, and blameless in His sight. In love He predestined and lovingly planned for us to be adopted to Himself as His own children through Jesus Christ, in accordance with the kind intention and good pleasure of His will. Ephesians 1:4–5 Amplified Bible

In Him we have received an inheritance and destiny—we were claimed by God as His own when having been pre-destined (chosen, appointed beforehand) according to the purpose of Him who works everything in agreement with the counsel and design of His will.   Ephesians 1:11 Amplified Bible

For it is by grace you have been saved, through faith—and this is not from yourselves, it is the gift of God— not by works, so that no one can boast. For we are God's handi-work, created in Christ Jesus to do good works, which God prepared in advance for us to do.   Ephesians 2:8-10 NIV®

Bio Snapshot—D.E. Hoyt

David was born in Los Angeles, California. His childhood and early adult life was extremely turbulent. He was incarcerated in nine juvenile justice and correctional institutions from ages nine through twenty-one.

At 18 while incarcerated, an honest search for God began, culminating in the Haight Ashbury District of San Francisco in early 1967. On a cool morning, about 7:15 AM, in the middle of a worship service at the Radha Krishna Temple on Frederick Street, a fire and panic broke out.

Those in attendance fled. David and a few others who lived at the temple stayed behind. Venturing down the stairs to the basement where the fire was, David heard a voice say the same words twice, "Call on me now." Frozen on the stairs a silent prayer was offered, "God, if Jesus Christ is Your Son, please reveal it to me." (Jeremiah 33:3)

David recalls, "Immediately I was flooded with a powerful presence of light that seemed to permeate every part of my mind, body and spirit. Intuitively I knew this was God. He was accepting and forgiving me and Jesus Christ's Spirit was revealing this. Jesus Christ was the true Son of God and he had been raised from the dead (John 1:12-18, Hebrews 9:11-15, Jeremiah. 17:14). Jesus' presence was unmistakable!

This was the beginning of a new life. What followed was an amazing journey of following Jesus Christ in ways similar to what I read about in the book of Acts.

The adventure was going well, until I invited the Children of God to visit our Atlanta Ministry and they ended up taking over most of our Jesus People houses in the Southern part of the USA. My spouse remarried in the Children of God and we divorced. She and our three children and her new family eventually exited the cult with her new husband. The fiasco was huge, a back-burner issue for years of ongoing prayer.

Mentors & Friends

I was mentored by Pastor Kent Philpott, Pastor Vinton Huffey, Mary Feister, Sisters Yvonne and Drayton of Anchor Rescue Mission, Pastor Armand Ramseyer and Kenneth P. Frampton. Each taught and modeled unique dimensions of vision, service, integrity, trust, prayer and faith, and how to love and obey God.

My best memories spring from times with these mentors and other seasoned Christ followers whom God would send. As my younger years were lived mostly in isolation, it was a new experience to be accepted, cared about, encouraged and prayed for.

In a response of gratefulness I endeavored to be teachable and take in the wisdom of those who had walked before me. I treasure each mentor who intentionally gave their time and love while always pointing me to be in fellowship with the Father and Jesus Christ His Son.

A secondary incredible gift was Christian friendship among peers. The things I've learned from both mentors and close friends have stayed with me. *I still think of their words, what we did together, what I learned watching them, when praying together, sharing the Gospel and the mutual love we shared.*

The locations where many of these peer friendships originated were 'Upper Streams' - Walnut Creek, CA / 'House of Judah' - Atlanta, GA / Jesus Family - London, UK, Lonesome Stone Theatre Team, UK / NY band of friends Manhasset, NY / and Church of the Open Door - San Fran Bay Area.

Jesus People, Church & Outreach Ministry

Excelsior Baptist Church - Byron CA
Assembly of God Church - Monrovia, CA
Foursquare Gospel Church - Lancaster, CA
JP The Way Inn Ranch - Lancaster, CA
Anchor Rescue Mission - Filmore District, San Francisco, CA
JP Zion's Inn - San Rafael, CA
JP Home For His Glory - Pleasant Hill, CA
JP Upper Streams - Walnut Creek, CA
JP House of Judah - Atlanta, GA
JP Temple of Still Waters - Atlanta GA
JP The Bread of Life Restaurant - Atlanta, GA
JP Jesus Family - London, England

JP The Living Room - London, England
JP Lonesome Stone Theatre Team Outreach - London & Manchester, England
JP The Rectory Outreach - Manchester, England
Church of the Open Door Outreach to Juvenile, Jails, Honor Farm - San Rafael, CA
St. Patrick's Catholic Church - Glen Cove, NY - HS Min + Community Outreach
Glengariff Health Care Center & Forest Manor Nursing Homes- Glen Cove, NY
First Presbyterian Church - Crestline, OH - Student Pastor
Mansfield Psych Hospital Outreach - Mansfield, OH, Chaplain
Walcrest Brethren Church - Pastor Mansfield, OH
Licking Memorial Hospital Chaplaincy - Newark, OH - Chaplain Intern
Park Street Brethren Church, Pastor of Youth Discipleship - Ashland, OH
Tri-County Detention School, Ashland County - guest speaker, Ashland, OH
Ashland & Mansfield OH Detention Centers - Chaplain
Paradise Hills United Methodist Church – Albuquerque, NM
Hospice Chaplain - Albuquerque, New Mexico.

Family

In December of 1976 Dave married Ginny. They have remained active in ongoing ministry over the years. They currently reside in Albuquerque, New Mexico. In addition to Dave's three older children, Dave and Ginny have two daughters, Marianne and Susie.

Education & Ordination

Ashland University: Undergrad Equivalency, English and Correctional Counseling
Ashland Theological Seminary - Ashland, Ohio
Master of Divinity / Pastoral Care / Counseling / Chaplaincy
Ordained with: 'Church of the Open Door', CA and 'The Brethren Church', OH
45+ years Christian Service in missions, theatre, pastorates / correctional, geriatric, and hospice chaplaincies

Bio—Kent A. Philpott
JP San Fran & Marin County, CA
1960s-70s Haight Ashbury Outreach
Pastor & JP House Leader- Trainer

As a young pastor and seminary student Kent carved out time to visit the 'Haight District' of San Francisco in early 1967. His aim was to pursue building relationships, and share the 'good news' of Jesus Christ with those interested. This outreach continued for years, ushering in effective ministry to the counter-culture 'Peace and Love' generation and street people of San Fran Bay Area.

Driving down the road and hearing a new release of "San Fran-

cisco" was the spark that got Kent thinking
and praying about visiting the Haight Ashbury District of San Fran. John Phillips of
the Mamas and the Papas penned the tune
and Scott McKenzie sang it. It was a hit in
the USA and # 1 in England. For many listeners this was the air-wave invitation that
would inform counter-culture hopefuls of
the coming 1967 Summer of Love.

In retrospect, it was interesting how
the Holy Spirit used this song on the car
radio to prompt Kent to take the time to
visit the Haight. On one of Kent's outings in the Haight-Ashbury he ran
into and made friends with a young man who was aligned with the Radha
Krishna Hindu Temple, led by Swami A.C. Bhaktivedanta. Spiritual dialogue and studies of the Christian Bible followed. This culminated in the
conversion of Krishna devotee David Hoyt who encountered Jesus Christ
through an unusual series of events.

Afterwards, Hoyt was invited to live with Kent and his family in
seminary housing. The seminary would forbid these types of guests in the
future, but in the meantime Kent was committed to aiding Hoyt with housing, spiritual training and encouragement. This led to working together in
outreach and staying connected.

For Philpott, this initial exposure to the needs represented in the
Haight Ashbury would translate into years of ongoing ministry. Philpott
connected with hundreds of hippies, street people, truth seekers, high
school and college students who found new life in Jesus Christ. This led
to the formation of Christian houses and bookstores in the San Fran Bay
Area. The houses provided a safe environment for young Christians seeking
to leave the craziness of street-life, drugs and other bad stuff.

Christian bookstores offered an alternative to the rapidly growing occult literature that was flooding mainstream book outlets. Christian
bookstores also provided employment for some house residents. In addition to Christian bookstores, a myriad of other companies were started by
those who lived in these Christian houses. Business start-ups like: plumb-

ing, carpentry, painting, fencing, building, landscaping, masonry, graphics, cosmetology and others were launched. Employment with one of these companies helped Christian house residents learn work ethics, life-skills and a viable trade to help pay the rents, utility and food bills where they lived. Those who ran these companies took on even more responsibility and grew in a variety of ways.

Over the course of some 15 years Kent was instrumental in starting, assisting, or providing leadership guidance for many Christian houses and young churches. They were located in: San Rafael, San Anselmo, Novato, Petaluma, Point Reyes, Kentfield, Mill Valley, Woodacre, Redwood City, Sausalito, Sonoma, Santa Rosa, San Jose and San Francisco. Some locations opened Christian bookstores and had more than one house in operation. Each house conducted Bible studies and local outreach.

In 1972 Kent Philpott and fellow pastors Bob Hymers, Roger Hoffman, Jim Smith and Mike Riley planted a church in San Rafael called Church of the Open Door. The church was integral in helping staff and support many of the expansion ministries mentioned above. Emerging young pastors from these ministries were, Mark Buckley, Kenny Sanders, Frank Worthen, Bob Burns, Bob Gaulden, Jeff Silliman and many more.

Some of the names of these Christian Houses were: Soul Inn, Zion's Inn, Berachah House & Farm, Thyatira Farm, Solid Rock and Glory House.

Soul Inn

At the urging of Dr. Francis DuBose, professor of missions and evangelism at Golden Gate Baptist Theological Seminary, Philpott became a member of Lincoln Park Baptist Church, pastored by Al Gossett. From there Philpott started the first of the House Ministries Christian houses, Soul Inn, on Balboa Street, between 41st and 42nd Avenues in San Francisco's Richmond District. Working then with David Hoyt, former devotee of the Hare Krishna Temple on Frederick Street in San Francisco, Soul Inn was the first of many Christian houses to be established, from San Jose to Santa Rosa, California.

Evangelical Concerns

Evangelical Concerns was formed by a handful of San Francisco area pastors who responded to the absence of any Christian outreach to hippies in the San Fran Bay area. John MacDonald of First Baptist Church in Mill Valley was the catalyst. He'd seen the spiritual breakthrough Ted and Liz Wise had experienced who were now attending his church. Though Ted was young in the faith, MacDonald sensed God could use both he and Liz to make Christ known to the mushrooming hippie population in the SF Bay Area. This led MacDonald to contact pastor and laymen friends who he knew, or thought might be supportive of this type of outreach.

Those that joined MacDonald in founding this non-profit outreach ministry to hippies were: Pastor John Streater of First Baptist Church of San Francisco; Streater's assistant pastor, Howard Day; Ed Plowman, pastor of Presidio Baptist Church, San Francisco, Pastor John McDonald, pastor of First Baptist Church of Mill Valley and a small group of laymen.

The first person Evangelical Concerns would support was Ted Wise who opened the House of Acts in Novato, CA and the Living Room store-front in the Haight-Ashbury. Wise accomplished this with the help of people he knew and new friends who had also come to faith in Christ. Some of the early residents at the House of Acts and workers at the Living Room were: Ted & Liz Wise, Danny Sands, Rick & Megan Sacks, Steve Heafner, Jim Dopp, Lonnie & Connie Frisbee.

Over time Philpott and others would be asked to participate in the work and ministry of Evangelical Concerns.

USA Road-Trip

In 1969, Philpott made an extended trip across the country handing out literature, mostly Right On, published by Christian World Liberation Front. They went to colleges and universities from California to Alabama, along U.S. Highway10, also visiting churches. The Jesus People Movement was spreading.

Joyful Noise

Philpott played in a Christian folk band, made up of members of the Marin County Bible Studies and Christian House Ministry. Joyful Noise played at high schools, colleges, churches, and other venues for over three years, traveling as far as Atlanta, Georgia, with stops in between. Philpott would say it was the most significant ministry he ever engaged in. In 1969 Joyful Noise, over a three week period, presented concerts at every high school in Atlanta, Georgia, all arranged by Cora Vance of that city.

Bible Studies at High Schools and Colleges

Bible studies at high schools and colleges was a focus of Philpott's work in the late 1960s and early 1970s, along with an evening service at both the Lucas Valley Community Church in San Rafael and the Christian Church of Marin, also in San Rafael.

Christian General Store

The first of many Christian bookstores was established in 1970 on 4th Street in San Rafael, CA, run by Betty Kenner. Later a counseling branch would be added called the Marin Christian Counseling Center with Philpott providing counseling ministry as an additional outreach into the community.

Book – Two Brothers in Haight

Throughout the street ministry in the Haight-Ashbury Philpott kept a journal, as did D.E. Hoyt. Philpott turned the journal into a book titled, *Two Brothers in Haight* and Zondervan Publishing House of Grand Rapids, Michigan, was interested. Bob DeVries of Zondervan met with Hoyt and Philpott and decided to publish the book. Ed Plowman was hired by Zondervan to rewrite the book. During the rewrite, Hoyt and ministry teams in the southern US were seduced by the Children of God cult. Philpott requested the book be canceled. Hoyt escaped the COG in London, England nine months later. Unfortunately, his wife and children were whisked away by cult leaders, shipped out of country and disappeared deep within the cult. The aftermath of these events was so horrific, the book project was abandoned.

Love in Action

In 1972, a group of men and women who were self-proclaimed Christians and homosexuals or lesbians met with Philpott and formed a support group. Kent had met a number of these individuals through his counseling ministry. Each in the group were seeking a way out of the gay lifestyle. One of the women came up with a name for the group, based on verses in 1 John 3, Love in Action.

After some time, the group decided to publish what they were doing for the sake of others who also wanted to leave the gay life behind and Philpott was asked to write a book which was called, The Third Sex? Logos International of Plainfield, New Jersey, published the book in 1975. A sequel, The Gay Theology was published in 1977. These books attracted wide attention to Love in Action, and the ministry, under Frank Worthen, grew dramatically. Philpott left active work with Love in Action in 1978 to pursue work in a doctoral program.

Feet of Clay

As Philpott acknowledges, his leadership within the Jesus People Movement during his early pastoral ministry, was no stranger to conflict. His autocratic style, accompanied by moral missteps, led to a crisis affecting a thriving cluster of Open Door churches in Northern California. A number of these churches were led by Jesus People. The fallout was painful for all.

San Quentin Prison Ministry

Due to the influence of Dr. Francis Dubose, Philpott began volunteering at the Protestant Garden Chapel at San Quentin State Prison, CA in 1969. He taught New Testament for the chapel's School of Theology and then conducted a fellowship group for Yoke Fellows Ministry. This ended with the "George Jackson shootout" in 1971. In 1985, due to the urging of Harry Howard,

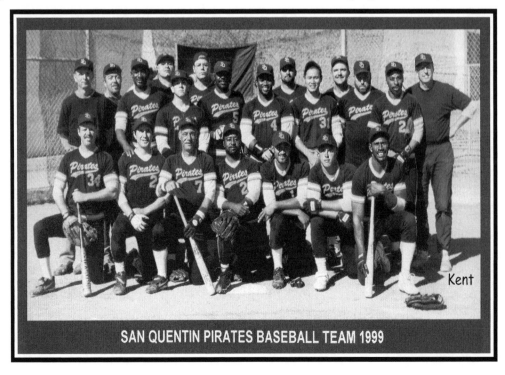

SAN QUENTIN PIRATES BASEBALL TEAM 1999

former chaplain at the prison, Philpott again began volunteering out of the Protestant Chapel under the leadership of Chaplain Earl Smith, doing cell to cell visitation with the Man to Man ministry led by Carl Gleeman.

In 1997, Philpott was asked by Chaplain Earl Smith to work with the newly formed San Quentin baseball team, and he continued in this capacity for 15 years until 2012. During that time he also developed a slow-pitch softball program and an eight-man flag football team.

High School Baseball Coaching and Managing

Kent has just completed his eleventh season as a high school baseball coach. He began at Tamalpais High School, then at Terra Linda High School, and is presently back at Tam High in Mill Valley, CA.

Snapshot of Christian Beginnings

Kent became a Christian in 1963 through the preaching of Pastor Robert D. Lewis at the First Baptist Church of Fairfield, California, a Southern Baptist Church, which licensed him to the Gospel Ministry in 1965 and recommended him for seminary that year. Kent attended Golden Gate Baptist Seminary in Mill Valley, CA.

Ordination & Pastorates

October 2, 1966, Kent was ordained by the Excelsior Baptist Church in Byron, California, with Pastor Robert D. Lewis preaching the ordination sermon. A seminary student at the time, Philpott remained as pastor at Byron until 1968. His next pastorate was with the Church of the Open Door, followed by an American Baptist Church. Kent's longest pastorate began in 1984 to the present at Miller Avenue Baptist in Mill Valley, CA.

Family

Married to Roberta (Bobbie) Philpott in 1961, three children – Dawn Doreen (Dory), Grace Marie, and Vernon Robert. By Dory and James LaRue, four grandchildren – Suzanne, Michelle, Jackie, and will. By Grace and Bill Reed, four grandchildren – Holly, Emily, Kelly, and Billy. Married Lisa Maree Silverman in 1982, two children – Laura Elizabeth and Jenna Maree. Married Katie Leslie Coddaire in 2009.

EDU

Glendale & Napa Community colleges - AA degree
Sacramento State - BA degree, psychology major 1965
Golden Gate Baptist Seminary - M.Div. Degree 1965-1968
San Francisco Theological Seminary - D.Min. Degree 1976-1980

Remembering

- Lonnie Frisbee
- Jim Palosaari
- Vinton E. Huffey

Lonnie Frisbee
D.E. Hoyt with Sue Palosaari Cowper & Dan Pauly

Lonnie Frisbee was among a cluster of early voices that spoke boldly in Jesus Christ's Name in the San Fran Bay area in the beginning of the Jesus People Movement. The year was 1967.

Around this time the saying, 'God is Dead' penned by German writer Heinrich Heine (a mentor of Nietzsche) had been publicized and was afloat in Europe and the Americas. Interestingly, God had a response in the works to Heine's intellectual thesis; one which would surprise most all who encountered it.

Amidst the 1960s climate of social upheavals and a timid organized church under attack for widespread liberalism and minimal spiritual substance—a God visit began. It took place predominantly among unchurched youth. Their origins were not what society would have expected as God chose an unlikely group from the youth culture; surfers, hippies, those who had been incarcerated, street people and those searching for truth. Some who learned of this outpouring of the Holy Spirit and conversions to Jesus Christ thought God had made a mistake.

Does God know what He is doing? Surely He must know these teens and young adults are sinners, unreliable, undisciplined, without cultural moorings, lacking education and are without adequate religious training.

Jesus and the Father must have grinned in unison at the age old self-righteous conclusion of those who just don't get it! The Lord of heaven and earth can call and transform anyone He chooses!

Jesus' disciples were not picked because of their social pedigree or elevated educational and religious training. They were normal everyday people—sinners. In a similar way, when Jesus chose us, we too were sinners, imperfect and in need of ongoing forgiveness.

Did Frisbee have scars and sins to overcome? Affirmative! Lonnie had a dark home life. He was raped at age eight, frequently ran away from home due to abuse, was absent from school so often that he barely learned to read or write. At age fifteen he joined a gay underground art community and disappeared into the drug culture.

Thankfully, Frisbee's story didn't end there. In 1967 at age 18 Lonnie came to faith in Jesus Christ while on a LSD trip. He had a lot of wild ideas prior to and after. They would be tempered as he learned to read and study the Bible and became friends with other Christians from his generation and older believers as well.

As a young Christian Lonnie aligned himself with the 'House of Acts' Christian community house in Novato, CA and their outreach ministry 'The Living Room' in San Fran's Haight District.

Shared Ministry in the Haight District

I'd been converted while living in the 'Haight' a year or so earlier, had been to Monrovia and Lancaster and returned to San Fran on Kent's invite. The House of Acts Christians and Kent and I were now active in the Haight District during the same time period sharing the message of Jesus Christ.

Resistance to Jesus Christ was still strong on the streets, but we learned to move around the hecklers on the lookout for those who were receptive. As Jesus was lifted up, we began to see a growing openness and curiosity among street people. Little by little individuals began coming to faith in Jesus Christ and turning away from strange religions, demonic practices, drugs and anti-Christ beliefs. The response among street people was minimal, but it was not unusual for us to be speaking in Jesus' Name and visually see a person overwhelmed by 'God's presence' which usually led to them opening their heart and mind to Jesus Christ.

Frisbee, with Southern Cal roots, decided to team up with John Higgins and head south. Together they opened the first 'House of Miracles' on 19th Street in Costa Mesa, CA which became their base of operations for outreach and discipleship. A group of Jesus People from the San Fran Bay area traveled south and visited Lonnie at the House of Miracles on his request as he and Higgins had some big decisions to make about aligning themselves with a church.

Prior to our visit, Frisbee and Higgins met up with Pastor Chuck Smith and his immediate family and a relationship developed. This evolved into both Frisbee and Higgins being asked to consider joining ranks with Smith and Calvary Chapel during it's infancy. We sat in on a discussion with conservative Calvary Chapel board members and Smith as merger ideas were discussed with Higgins and Frisbee. Lonnie wanted his San Fran Jesus People friends' opinion on Smith's church group and this possible merger.

What followed is well documented, though not always accurately. What is factual is Calvary Chapel expanded by leaps and bounds with thousands of teens and adults responding to Jesus Christ with Frisbee and Smith working side by side. John Higgins was behind the scenes diligently establishing and overseeing discipleship houses which grew to nineteen.

Frisbee was anointed and gifted by God with a heart for sharing and preaching freely about Jesus Christ, one-on-one, at a beach as a crowd gathered, or at the Wednesday night Calvary Chapel gathering of young people overflowing beyond capacity. Looking back, Frisbee was one of the most effective evangelists that emerged during the Jesus People Movement.

He and Higgins influenced Calvary Chapel in monumental ways by inviting hippies, surfers and street kids to come as they were. Jesus Christ was lifted up, many who heard the gospel of Jesus received Him and new converts were introduced to the Bible and the power of the Holy Spirit. Leading the 'House of Miracles' discipleship ministry, Higgins grew into an extremely Christ honoring, effective and understandable Bible teacher. Smith's verse by verse expository preaching and teaching in Calvary Chapel's worship services aided new converts in becoming students of the Word.

Meanwhile, Frisbee's enthusiasm, openness to God and dependence on the Holy Spirit continued to be a huge drawing point for those who poured through the doors of Calvary Chapel.

Fast Forward to 1976–77

John Wimber begins a home fellowship group. They meet primarily to seek the Lord in prayer and have honest dialogue. In the spring of 1977 the home group has outgrown meeting in homes and decides to rent a gymnasium to launch a church in Yorba Linda and affiliate with Calvary Chapel.

In a similar time-frame pastor Kenn Gulliksen is sent out from Calvary to plant a church in West LA calling it 'Vineyard.' The church is characterized by being more receptive to the ministry of the Holy Spirit. On hearing this, a small cluster of Calvary church plants relate to this emphasis and take on the Vineyard name as well.

Back in Yorba Linda, Wimber's wife Carol begins her own journey of seeking to better understand the working of the Holy Spirit, joining a charismatic prayer group inspired by the popular book, "Aglow with the Spirit" by Dr. Robert Frost. John Wimber is also investigating through his contacts at Fuller Theological Seminary. This keeps both John and Carol in the loop of seeking to understand and be receptive to the workings of the Holy Spirit.

At a Calvary conference Pastor John Wimber and Pastor Kenn Gulliksen connect sharing mutual interests and become friends. Both are intent on being open to the ministry of the Holy Spirit. They also share a similar vision for aiding the needy of this world through acts of mercy. They agree, the church is called to be the hands, feet and heart of Jesus among those who sit in darkness without food, clothes, hope, love or God.

> Speak up for those who cannot speak for themselves, for the rights of all who are destitute. Speak up and judge fairly; defend the rights of the poor and needy.
> Proverbs 31:8–9 NIV®

Gulliksen and Wimber inspire and influence each other. In response, Yorba Linda Calvary leans intentionally into a posture of prayer, listening and seeking God's presence in worship and its outreaches of compassion to the poor.

1980

On Mother's Day 1980 Wimber invites "Jesus People" evangelist Lonnie Frisbee to speak at the Sunday evening worship gathering at Calvary Yorba Linda.

By this time Frisbee has been let go and ostracized from Costa Mesa's Calvary Chapel for homosexual activity. This is Lonnie's nemesis sin from his old life.

John Wimber, privy to Frisbee's battle with lapses into this sin, believes God is not done with Lonnie. He recognizes God's calling and anointing on Lonnie's life and wants to see him find a path forward through repentance and restoration. Meeting privately with Frisbee, Wimber affirms a commitment to help Lonnie through a supportive spiritual friendship. This is at the heart of why he invites Lonnie to speak at his church, believing his involvement in ministry will aid Lonnie in recovery and standing against temptation.

At the end of Frisbee's sermon at Yorba Linda, Lonnie explained how the Holy Spirit has been grieved by the church's resistance and wants to be invited in. Frisbee then asks those under 25 to come forward and raise their hands and hearts to the Lord and requests the adults to raise their hands toward the youth gathered in the front of the church. Lonnie then invites and asks both youth and adults to join him in a spirit of expectation and worship and invite the Holy Spirit to come. *To everyone's surprise the Holy Spirit honors this request and descends!*

Wimber was shocked along with all who were present. Adults and teens that had been leery or hesitant regarding the Holy Spirit are flooded with His presence. There was nothing normal about this Sunday evening service which did not end on time!

Wimber acknowledges he wrestled with understanding this 'visitation' all night long, pouring over historical writings that described similar events occurring during the Whitfield and Wesley revivals and other Holy Spirit outpourings over the centuries. The next morning he receives a call from a pastor friend who listens to Wimber's explanation of what happened and then confirms this phenomenon to be from God. According to Wimber, this was his first encounter with the supernatural power of God.

This initial event thrust Wimber's church into a steady flow of Holy Spirit-filled gatherings. News of Jesus Christ's strong presence at Yorba Linda Calvary spread rapidly. The youth of the church were on fire, sharing Jesus Christ all over the city. Lonnie was in the thick of this outpouring, ministering predominately in the Afterglow Prayer Room. A lot of people came to faith in Christ, were filled with the Holy Spirit and there were approximately 700 baptisms in the first three months. Church attendance swelled into the thousands as Jesus was honored and glorified.

Meanwhile, Wimber's relational connection with Pastor Ken Gulliksen and his cluster of Vineyard Churches deepens. In light of the powerful ongoing visitations of the Holy Spirit, Wimber begins to feel more commonality with the Vineyard grouping of churches.

Calvary and Vineyard Churches at a Crossroad

Word is out about 'big doings' and unusual 'church growth' at Yorba Linda. Reports of Lonnie Frisbee's ministry at the church and close ties with Wimber have also surfaced. The growing bond between Gulliksen and Yorba Linda has also been noted.

Both friend and foes from Calvary Chapels have been out to see Wimber and visit the churches worship services to scope out what is going on. The reports vary.

There is concern among Calvary Chapel leadership and Chuck Smith that Wimber, Gulliksen and Vineyard churches are moving away from

Word-centered ministry to seeking the Holy Spirit in an unbalanced way.

In a cursory snapshot, the controversy comes to a head and Smith offers Calvary pastors who know John Wimber, Kenn Gulliksen and other Vineyard pastors the opportunity to join the Vineyard group, or remain with Calvary Chapel. Some take Smith up on his offer and convert their churches to Vineyard, others remain with Calvary. Though tense with some hard feelings, the separation was handled as gracefully as possible. *This results in a formal parting of ways between Calvary and Vineyard churches.*

Wimber's church was renamed 'Vineyard Christian Fellowship.' Gulliksen, Wimber and pastor friends who aligned with Vineyard go on to establish more Holy Spirit friendly churches and over the course of the next few years Wimber is given the lead role within Vineyard's expansion and mission endeavors.

The Aftermath

Both Calvary and Vineyard Churches continue to embrace their intentional evangelism roots that can be traced back to Lonnie Frisbee, John Higgins and the larger 'Jesus People Movement.' Calvary and Vineyard have remained separate entities planting new churches throughout the USA, Canada, Europe and across the globe.

Vineyard has remained Holy Spirit friendly, with questionable excesses reported that may be human or possibly demonic counterfeits. Calvary Chapel churches vary, but most have intentionally shut down any openness to the Holy Spirit's ministry. Their commitment to verse by verse expository teaching and preaching is admirable, but some think Calvary has gone too far in reaction to their parting of the ways with Vineyard.

> While visiting a large Calvary Chapel Church worshippers were told by ushers not to raise or wave their hands during worship. Visiting another sizable Calvary church, the pastor in his sermon mocked by name Charismatic and Pentecostal Christians who spoke in tongues.   D.E. Hoyt

These two occurrences surprised and saddened me. Many independent church plants and mainstream denominational churches now have considerably more freedom in worship and practice in embracing the Holy Spirit than Calvary Chapel churches.

The time may be here for the pendulum to swing back to 'a centered balance' in both Calvary and Vineyard Churches if they desire to be healthy in the future.

Wimber & Frisbee on Mission

Wimber's relationship with Lonnie Frisbee led them to jointly lead a missions team to South Africa and Europe where explosive outpourings of the Holy Spirit occurred.

Hundreds came to faith in Jesus Christ. The blind, lame and those with serious illnesses were healed when the Holy Spirit came upon them. In Carol Wimber's book, "John Wimber: The Way it Was" Carol describes amazing stories from this and other mission trips and tells how important Lonnie Frisbee was in aiding Vineyard churches and their outreach missions. John Wimber also documents the significant contribution Lonnie made in impacting he and Carol personally, and the larger expansion and vision of Vineyard Churches, in his book 'Power Evangelism.'

A Leper Among Us

Some leaders in the Calvary Church movement have tried to erase Lonnie Frisbee from their memory by writing him out of their early history. They obviously have decided he is an embarrassment and might tarnish Calvary Chapel's reputation.

Many of us say, "Shame on you! Who is without sin?"

Some forget that Pastor Chuck Smith who was a strong proponent of Rapture Theology was obsessed with speculating on possible time frames for Christ's return to take the church out of this world.

Although Smith never gave a specific date, he said Jesus would return by May 1981. When this month came and went, he updated Christ's return to sometime before Dec 31, 1981. Lots of people were with Chuck at Costa Mesa Calvary Chapel Church on that final midnight New Year's Eve at the end of 1981. They went home disappointed and disillusioned. Many left Calvary Chapel Church and some left the faith.

In Matthew 24:36 Jesus succinctly says, **No one but the Father knows the day or hour of his return; no man, no angel and not even the Son of God!** As a student of the Scriptures, one would think Smith would have taken

Jesus' words to heart and not entertain any notion of time-frame predictions.

Instead, Chuck Smith had an unbalanced obsession for the Rapture to arrive. With the Rapture being a central distinctive doctrine in Calvary Chapel Churches—was Chuck so wrapped up in his own hopes, dreams and theological position that he couldn't resist choosing a time frame? Since a Rapture never occurred by the end of 1981 was Chuck Smith a false prophet?

Or, was this his sin, his life-long obsession, revealing Smith's humanity and weakness?

If you check out Calvary's church history you won't find any mention of Chuck Smith's inaccurate rapture predictions, or the incredible contribution Lonnie Frisbee made as the primary instrument God used to draw thousands of young adults to faith in Jesus Christ who became a part of Calvary Chapel. Those of us who were part of the Jesus Movement know there would have been no need for a massive tent if Frisbee had not been a part of Calvary's beginnings.

God does not erase us when we falter or sin. If that were the case, heaven would be empty! Bible authors anointed by the Holy Spirit recorded events as they were, warts and all! The facts, mistakes, and sins of God's people and how they came to a place of repentance, gives us hope and serves as a warning.

> If you, Lord, kept a record of sins, Lord, who could stand?
> Psalm 130:3 NIV®

Jesus made it clear what our attitude should be toward others who sin, since we too are sinners, saying "The one who is without sin, you cast the first stone" (John 8:7b). In teaching his disciples how to pray he encourages us to intentionally pray to the Father "Forgive us our sins, as we forgive others" (Luke 11:4).

Lonnie was a recipient of God's mercy, grace and forgiveness. God rescued him out of a life where he'd been sexually abused as a child. He lived with confusion, fear and isolation with minimal educational opportunities and limited friendships. God saw his internal anguish and watched him as he gravitated into a gay arts community and then into bizarre hallucinogenic drug trips. It was during one of these trips that Jesus Christ revealed Himself to Lonnie.

Among honest followers of Jesus Christ there is an understanding, we are all sinners. Most can take it one step further and say I'm among the worst of sinners. Paul the Apostle said so of himself (I Timothy 1:15-16). When backed up against a wall by religious condemnation Lonnie said, "To know me is to hate me."

Why? He knew like Johnny Cash, "I'll disappoint you, let you down, hurt you." Lonnie realized he was so far from perfect, people would hate him if they were privy to all his sins. Keep in mind, many highly regarded Christians have passed through their own 'dark night of the soul.' These Christians know what repeated failures and sins are—because they too, as believers have been overtaken by their nemeses. Who but God knows the depths of darkness that sinner-saint warriors pass through.

I've interacted with many wounded Christians who have suffered, failed, fallen from grace, lost their family, felt overwhelming guilt, been judged so harshly by the community of faith they could barely raise their heads.

I've seen and heard church leaders say and do things that are the total opposite of God when it comes to justice, truth and mercy; and do so with self-righteous pride—void of any humility.

All believers are sinners! As long as we are in the flesh we are vulnerable and susceptible to fleshly temptation and the devil's lure. If anyone reading this is thinking, "Not me!" God disagrees with you.

> Indeed, there is no one on earth who is righteous, no one who does what is right and never sins.   Ecclesiastes 7:20 NIV®

> There is no one righteous, not even one.   Romans 3:10 NIV®

Shortly after receiving Christ, Lonnie began using the gifts God gave him by stepping into the unknown and faithfully proclaiming Jesus Christ. **Thousands were swept into the Kingdom of God during the Jesus People Movement where he and others ministered.**

Beyond the Jesus Movement, Lonnie was given the opportunity to travel to many countries throughout the world sharing the Good News of Jesus Christ and walking in the power of the Holy Spirit. Miracles accompanied his mission work.

The Name of God the Father, Jesus Christ and the Holy Spirit were on his lips. The Word of God was precious to him. He died young, a fallen warrior. The self-righteous despised him. Those of us who were his friends knew all too well, there but for the grace of God we too would have died prematurely because of our sins.

Thank you, Lonnie, for the great energy you gave to further the kingdom of God among your generation of hippies and truth seekers, and later in locations across the globe that desperately needed the Light of Jesus Christ to shine!

My Brother & Friend Jim Palosaari
D.E. Hoyt

Jim was called and appointed by God as an important voice in the Jesus People Movement. He was a sinner, received into God's family by the grace and mercy of Jesus Christ and His work on the cross. Jim was refreshingly not religious! He was anointed by God with a vision beyond his ability to accomplish alone.

Jim and Sue Palosaari began their ministry endeavors in Milwaukee, WI, establishing a coffee house named 'Jesus Christ Power House' and a discipleship house for new Christians. The next decisive step was renting the War Memorial Stadium in Milwaukee for a large outreach. In preparation, a new band was formed 'The Sheep' who provided the music while Linda Meissner of the Jesus People Army preached the event on Jim's invite. This resulted in new Christians being added to their number.

Jim came into his stride, taking his Jesus People team to conduct city-wide revivals in Duluth, Minnesota and in Davenport, Iowa. Both yielded surprising results. The Davenport outreach scheduled for three days, went on for several months with several thousand receiving Christ. In Milwaukee, Jim & Sue gained access to an old hospital naming it 'The Discipleship Training Center' and soon it was at capacity with several hundred young Christians living there.

From this early Milwaukee group, independent teams were sent out which would become Jesus People USA (JPUSA) and "Resurrection Band" in Chicago and "Christ is the Answer" which would expand into Europe. Jim and Sue would go on to help found the Jesus Family England and Lonesome Stone theatrical team.

Thankfully, God placed a wide variety of committed, dedicated and gifted Christians around Jim who helped bring vision into reality with help from above. Others were grafted into this outreach vision as the ministry expanded beyond what any would have imagined.

We created, worked, shared, dreamed and walked together as lifetime friends. When I was a shell of a man, broken by the loss of my first family into the Children of God cult, I met Jim. He knew about my stateside ministry prior to this fiasco and was deeply concerned.

Stranded and wounded in England, Jim and Sue, along with others who became the 'Jesus Family London' reached out to me. Jim called me the 'ghost that walked', making reference to our first meeting when I was pale, in shock and still grief-stricken by the cult ordeal.

Jim understood what pain was about; welcoming, accepting and leaving room for God to bring healing. I felt no pressure, was afforded ample space, was offered opportunities to use my gifts as able and experienced the warmth of something real, 'centered in Jesus.' This dynamic bonded me into a spiritual family that cared and loved each other. For this display of tangible human compassion, I'm still thankful after many decades!

Kenneth and Pauline Frampton were my friends, my 'Good Samaritans.' Jim & Sue and the Milwaukee team were like the 'Inn Keeper' who cared for me and others that entered this new British ministry.

God did things in England that amazed us; carrying us on the wave of His Spirit, opening a wide door of ministry as 'Deo Gloria Trust' partnered with our vision to share Jesus through creative outreach that was before its time.

By phone, personal visits in San Francisco, Southern California, Nashville, Huntington Beach, New Mexico and Wisconsin we connected on a heart level. Our dialogue was always honest and open. No facade or delusions of personal importance. We talked about our desire to keep doing better with God's help and impact our world. Jim and I confided together,

Jim Palossari and his faithful dog Sam

repented of sins, acknowledged failures, discussed overcoming habits and shared back and forth on a variety current and eternal topics.

Like each of us, Jim had faults. He didn't eat right, exercise, or take care of himself as he should have. He was impatient and demanding at times, but he was warm, generous and loved people genuinely. He had a personality and heart as huge as life, loved a good laugh and enjoyed the simple things of life like a meal and a quality visit with a friend. He was good-hearted and loyal as the day was long, honoring long-term friendships.

His favorite food was a plain hamburger, no seasoning and nothing but the burger and the buns. I can hear Jim ordering this as if he were beside me now, "No mayo, ketchup, onions, lettuce, pickles, or seasoning—just plain!"

Jim, like Jesus, saw potential and giftedness in people and he encouraged them to use their abilities and talents in God's kingdom work. He remained unattached to material possessions, caring more about relationships.

Over the years, Jim experienced devastating grief over the untimely death of his son Seth, a divorce, the death of a spouse and the death of his companion dog, 'Sam.'

As the years pass, I say, "Give me something that's genuine!" I'm not impressed by spiritual terminology, fabricated or exaggerated spiritual conquests, miracle counterfeits, self-righteous legalism, attendance or church plant numbers, harsh and unforgiving judgments that omit the accuser's sins.

I want the truth, mixed with mercy, forgiveness, compassion and grace. If there is no ongoing grace, it's not the true Gospel of Jesus Christ! Who could stand if all our sins were brought out of the shadows into daylight? No one!

I'm thankful that two sinners like Jim and I met, shared in ministry and life's battles, remained lifetime friends and continued in loyalty to our Savior Jesus Christ.

On Resurrection Day with My Buddy

Jim and I will walk together as friends with a swifter and healthier stride and talk about new things in the Kingdom of God. If God allows us to be part of the First Resurrection (Revelation 20:4-6) we may be fitted with eternal armor, riding the clouds into battle on kingdom steeds, or given some small post of responsibility to reign with Christ for 1000 years.

If part of the Second Resurrection, we will be equally thankful! In awe, we'll realize more clearly than ever the greatness of God, the vastness of His Kingdom and His Mercy and Grace that rescued us. In reverence we'll look to the Father and the King of Kings and the Lord of Lords, Jesus Christ who shed His blood for us that we might be forgiven, born of the Spirit and inherit eternal life.

We'll have put on that which is eternal and be truly alive! Together with full hearts we'll say, "Praise Be To Lamb of God Jesus Christ and to the Father, forever and ever! Amen."

If Jim says, "Just give me a hamburger plain", I will definitely smack him!

Rev. Vinton E. Huffey
A Godly Mentor–D.E. Hoyt

Pastor Huffey had a mid-sized Assembly of God congregation to care for when we met. Thankfully, he was happy to carve out time to disciple and mentor several of us and was enthusiastic about it. We were a breath of fresh air to him because we were excited to grow and share the Good News of Jesus in the larger community.

Rev. Vinton E. Huffey
July 7,1915 -Feb.25, 2008

While under his spiritual care for most of a year, he modeled a Godly life of faithfulness to Jesus Christ, the Bible and dependence on the Holy Spirit. His spiritual gifts and wisdom were noticeably a result of time spent with God in prayer and he taught all in the congregation to embrace this same priority. From Pastor Huffey, we learned:

Developing a relationship with God is the greatest thing we can do for ourselves and others!

This relationship enables us to talk and listen to God, helps us learn His wisdom and perspective, how to live in this world and gives us strength and guidance to carry out His will. And, spending time in God's presence, His nature and character is grafted into ours.

Through fellowship with God, we know when we need to confess and turn from known sins and when He wants us to forgive someone. It is also where we find courage and perseverance to endure all types of hardships and tragedies. When our heart is wounded or broken, our health diminished, or the death of a friend or loved one occurs, it is the Lord who knows how to comfort us. Our relationship with God is the most valuable resource we have in this life. *Things change and change again thousands of times, but God is the rock that is firm and reliable.* Pastor Huffey was an inspiring Bible preacher who instilled these types of truths in us.

To aid those new in the faith, he taught us a Christ–centered Foundations Class over the course of twelve weeks. The class included: God's Nature and Plan, The Supremacy of Christ, The Word of God, The Holy Spirit, The Body of Christ, Prayer, Sharing Christ, The Gifts of the Holy Spirit, I Corinthians 13 on Love is the Greatest, the Books of the Bible, How to Study the Bible, How to use a Concordance & Memorize Scripture, the Purpose of Baptism and Communion, Discipleship Disciplines, Service in Jesus' Name with humility and authority. These studies gave each of us an important foundation of tools to draw from in the years to come.

As a new Christian, I was a blank slate, absorbing Bible teaching without fear of being misled, because pastor Huffey was very careful to rightly divide the Word of God in an honorable way.

On one occasion I recall him teaching, "The Holy Spirit only glorifies God the Father and Jesus Christ His Son. God will never share His glory with sinful men or women. *Beware of anyone who attempts to take the place of God, or His Son Jesus Christ. They may claim some elevated spiritual status to get people to follow them, but they are false prophets, deluded by pride and error.*" The Bible text he used for this teaching was Matthew 24:4–5, 23–31 where Jesus is speaking in the first person with strong warnings about impostors, false teachers false prophets, or some who would claim to be Christ (The Messiah).

Several years later, I would remember this warning when Children of God leader, David Berg announced he was God's special End-Time Prophet. Recalling the Scriptures of warning in Matthew 24 provided Biblical discernment to resist Berg's claim and exit this cult.

In addition to Bible teaching, Pastor Huffey gave me extra work for pay doing landscaping projects at his home. He also took me with him when he'd visit the sick, or take communion to shut-ins and accompanied me to public places where we would dialogue with people about Jesus Christ.

> As a seasoned Christian Pastor, he included me, we walked together in Christ and I learned as we went. It was practical on the job training.

Huffey pastored the First Assembly of God Church in Monrovia, CA for 20 years before retiring to establish a program to bring churches back to America's inner cities. His small book titled 'Born on the Seventh Day' highlights this journey and vision.

Pastor Huffey loved fixing things. Afternoons often found him with a nail and hammer—doing repairs, something he said helped him come up with sermons. Vinton was a man of faith and optimism, and he liked the long shot. His great pleasure was people. They energized him.

Whether he was attending an inner-city church or staging a garage sale as an excuse to sit in the sun and talk to neighbors—he was always ready to listen and look for any opportunity to introduce the center of his life, the Lord Jesus Christ. He'd often develop conversations with strangers by saying *"There's a lot of bad news in the world today. Would you like to hear some good news?"*

As the perennial optimist Vinton saw each day as a gift. Between ages 90-92, when asked how he was doing, he'd always reply, *"Oh, I'm having a great day!"*

Pastor Huffey died at home peacefully on Feb. 25, 2008 at age 92.

30

EPILOGUE

A Summing Up
Telling it Like it Was and Is!

Why Did God Birth the Jesus People Movement?

The Jesus Movement was God's spark of light, truth and love woven into the larger Peace & Love Movement. The hope for a counter-culture Utopian society rapidly faded over the course of a few short years.

The Jesus Movement was God's way of redeeming part of a generation. The lure of psychedelic rock, strange drugs, free love, pagan religions, the occult and witchcraft, alongside bizarre practices and fetishes was destroying the hippie dream. *Satan had disguised himself as the guru of Peace and Love, with a goal to destroy our lives and future.*

But, God the Father and Jesus Christ His Son were on a mission to cut through the darkness of the evil one's deception. God delivered thousands of us from a binge of casting off all restraints and being pawns in the hands of the Prince of Darkness! And, because of His intervention:

Jesus People would carry the 'Good News' of Jesus Christ to many parts of the world reaching the unchurched and lost. Simultaneously we set an example to the established church of the need for outreach. In time we would infuse the church with new life, music, worship and discipleship wherever it was welcome.

The JP movement revitalized the church across the globe in unseen ways which may never be known. We were carried by the wind of God's Holy Spirit letting the presence of Jesus Christ permeate our comings and goings.

We were still human, made mistakes, sinned and had a lot to learn about following Jesus. The miracle was, He'd rescued and chosen us— and we were unanimously in awe!

Unfortunately, there were counterfeits that arose that caused great harm. These cults will be identified later in this chapter and in-depth in the Appendix.

Why God's Choice of Jesus People Worked

Jesus People were young, available, unattached to material things and financial security. We believed God had something for us to do. We lived simply, had only a few sets of clothes and were willing to share what we had (Acts

4:32). We picked up hitch-hikers, took in strangers (Luke 10:25-37), went without food when needed (Acts 13:3), were persecuted verbally and physically for representing and speaking in Jesus Christ's name and were OK with it (Matthew 5:11-12, Luke 21:12-15, II Timothy 3:12).

We put our personal goals on hold to follow in Jesus' steps. We presented every talent and gift we had to serve God. We were open to learning new things and interested in other cultures. We were inspired by God's love and acceptance of us. *We believed with all our heart and soul that the message of Jesus Christ was and is the spiritual doorway to eternal life.* God planted a conviction in our hearts that carrying the Gospel of Jesus into the all the world was exactly what He wanted us to do!

Where Did We Come From?

Some Jesus People were relatively unscathed from negative life influences, but the majority had baggage! Those with early life and teen problems usually came from fragmented or abusive families. Extreme discipline, rejection, and the absence of tangible love, left emotional and mental scars. A lack of support in education and learning how to do things contributed. Absentee parents who failed to provide adequate supervision invited other problems.

Other 1960s social and cultural issues factored into kids running away, getting high, hooking up with a 'cause', or joining the 'Peace and Love' movement. A growing number within USA society were disillusioned with war, materialism, mindless conformity and being force-fed what to think and believe.

Unbeknownst to Love and Peace followers, thinkers, authors, artists, poets and movers and shakers, they were being beguiled by a false promise of 'Peace.' This promise couldn't be attained with a foundation of drugs, illicit sex, psychedelic rock, satanic influences or pagan religions. The same elusive goal of securing lasting 'Peace' was not being attained in mainstream society eitherl.

Those who sought to live in harmony with nature and each other, or have more access to drugs and sex, moved to communal houses, farms, or ranch communes.

Street People

For many without much money, hanging out on the streets and crashing in local parks was the cheapest alternative if they wanted to stay in San Fran or any other city. Those who lived on the streets for even a short time absorbed the practices of lying, stealing, poor hygiene, substance abuse, association with the occult and trading sex for food or housing. Some escaped, but for many this became the reality.

Street people survival skills included running, intense anger reactions (to scare people away), isolation, and any number of drugs or alcohol to numb confusion, anger or tormenting evil spirits. A slew of 'bad memories and choices' equaled a *'troubled heart and spirit',* susceptible to further manipulation by Satan.

If a street person needed medication to treat anxiety, depression, paranoia, suicidal thoughts and actions—most couldn't afford the meds, or simply refused to take them. Mental and social interaction problems plagued many street people

We took in those who wanted help and were willing to make some adjustments in their lifestyle, to make it doable for both them and us. Sadly some career street people have an incredibly difficult time handling any structure. They would rather sleep outside in cold weather than be inside if there were any rules or if they felt confined. When anyone seeking help didn't have these types of social problems we were thankful. It enabled our offer of practical and spiritual help less drama and more reception.

We Aided Others as God Had Helped Us

Regardless, we all had quirks, short-comings, a history of mistakes and bad choices. Most needed to learn how to redirect themselves away from self-destructive behavior. Christian house leaders were tuned-in to the universal need to be loved, accepted, forgiven and enter into a relationship with the Father, Son and Holy Spirit.

For most of us, God's intervention of connecting with us was beyond anything we knew about, or thought possible. This was the amazing part of representing Him to those who entered through our doors. God was offering the opportunity to each person, to start over at living life with His help!'

When we were overwhelmed by sins; You forgave our transgressions.   Psalm 65:3 NIV®

Interested in the fate of a generation on the brink of disaster, God reached deep into the 1960s demon's lair of darkness. He pulled multiple thousands out of this pit of destruction by revealing His Son Jesus Christ to all who received Him.

The Jesus Movement unfolded at a perfect junction, gathering in a harvest of young and old, straight and hippies. God's rescue was in harmony with His nature of "Compassion." The whole of Psalms 103 and 107 describe God's heart of mercy which rescues and saves when nothing else can.

> It is the Almighty who redeems our life from the pit and crowns us with love and compassion.   Psalm 103:4 NIV®

The public, media and parents were baffled. What's going on? How did this happen? Understanding this sudden surge of Spiritual Life unfolding remained a mystery as the multiplication of Jesus People continued. Some wondered, *"Will this Jesus fad eventually fade into obscurity?"*

Some Christians had been praying for decades for an awakening. 'The Jesus Movement' was an answer to the prayers of thousands. For prayer warriors, there was reason for great joy and thanksgiving for what God was doing to save part of a generation which could have been entirely lost. Jesus said it best:

> In the same way, I tell you, there is rejoicing in the presence of the angels of God over one sinner who repents.   Luke 15:10 NIV®

The Naysayers and Religious Pharisees

Naysayers don't readily believe stuff and by nature are pessimistic. This is not all bad. It's good to be cautious with all the impostors and scam artists out there. A naysayer without 'spiritual understanding,' could draw any number of conclusions about Jesus People and they did.

The religious Pharisee was a different breed. Jesus' description of these religious leaders should cause us all to be cautious and do everything we can to avoid becoming self righteous, proud, scornful and filled with loathing *toward spiritual life that blooms outside our sphere of control.* In Matthew chapter 23 Jesus gives an extensive rebuke and scathing warning to this group of religious elite.

It's crazy how every generation has its ultra critical religious leaders who conclude *only they know how to follow the correct way of doing things and think they've been commissioned to save the church from corruption and heresy.*

In becoming self appointed as righteous, they walk in pristine religious halls where they are honored as wise and respected. Some of them preach to large throngs, write books and have their teachings streaming out all over the world. In time they think they are qualified to speak for God on things that **'God reserves as His territory alone!'**

I've heard a prominent Christian teacher state that the entire Charismatic 'Spirit-filled' branch of Christ's Body, including the Jesus People Movement, were and are part of the devil's Strange Fire.

Aren't you glad those who believe this aren't God!? When I consider Jesus' words about 'blasphemy of the Holy Spirit being unforgivable,' and know this means attributing the work of God's Spirit to Satan—it's a dangerous and possibly irreversible stance John MacArthur and his group of followers have taken. I recall the Pharisees said the same types of things about Jesus, his ministry and his miraculous works.

MacArthur and those who line up with him and those who espouse these condemnations of Christians should be very worried indeed. Good luck explaining these accusations to God, since **half a billion believers (one fourth of all Christians) consider themselves to be spirit-filled and are the fastest growing branch in all of Christianity.**

MacArthur's reckless and dangerous teaching is simply false! Those who've been given influence in the body of Christ and lead others into possibly blaspheming the Holy Spirit. Anyone we speaks like this should consider the repercussions of erroneous 'fire talk' that could earn them a place in the real "Lake of Fire!" What if Jesus were to say to MacArthur at the end of his life, "You should have know better, you blasphemed the Holy Spirit and mocked my church! Who do you think you are!? "

There are counterfeit manifestations of the Holy Spirit in Spirit-filled groups and churches. The same applies to there being counterfeit Christians, sexual predators and erroneous teachers in groups and churches that don't believe the Miraculous Gifts of the Holy Spirit exist in the present.

Counterfeits, false doctrines and excesses are meant to be dealt with on a case-by-case basis. The question that naturally arises: *Does the church acknowledge, respect and utilize the spiritual gift of Discernment, aka Distinguishing between spirits (I Corinthians 12:10)?*

The purpose of the gift of Discernment is to help Christians identify evil and error, disguised behind a spiritual front. Jesus taught:

> For false messiahs and false prophets will appear and perform great signs and wonders to deceive, if possible, even the elect.   Matthew 24:24 NIV®

If the elect, God's people could be misled, why would God remove any gifts of the Holy Spirit from the church when evil is steadily increasing? Fast forward to a time when worldwide persecution of Christians is launched against those who resist a 'One World Government.' With a greater deluge of deception flooding the world, shouldn't the church be adequately equipped with every gift of the Holy Spirit to aid them in being a light and standing firm in the Faith and Truth? The Scriptures speak clearly of the severity of persecution, during the seven year reign of the Anti-Christ (See chapter 32 'That Which is to Come' - for a preview and Bible references).

The most significant argument against the miraculous or any of the gifts of the Holy Spirit being taken back by God is: Jesus and the Apostles never taught the Holy Spirit and spiritual gifts poured into God's church would no longer be needed and removed! If this were true, we'd have ample collaborating support in the Scriptures to alert the church.

Circling back to the judgments of John MacArthur and friends who teach all Spirit-filled groups are being guided by Demonic Strange Fire from the devil. MacArthur teaches, all Pentecostal and Charismatics worldwide are a false church, as dangerous as any cult or heresy that has ever assaulted Christianity. His conclusion and condemnation is based on I Corinthians 13:8.

Alarmed by MacArthur's wide-sweeping rant of blaspheming the Holy Spirit, Bible scholars representing the Body of Christ and hailing from a wide variety of denominations, unanimously disagreed with MacArthur's faulty and poor exegesis of the Scriptures. He and others who take this outrageous stand are no longer standing on holy, but dangerous ground!

Jesus People, like myself learned the hard way about the nuances of spiritual error, false teachers and false prophets. A concise JP teaching on this topic evolved called: The Holy Spirit and Parallel Counterfeits JP 101. It is found in this chapter on page 655.

How Did JP Change?

Being loved by God blew our minds and softened our hearts. Experiencing God's love, forgiveness and acceptance was the best gift we'd ever received! *This invisible yet tangible gift of God's Holy Spirit taking up residence in us was beyond anything we could ever have hoped for.* We knew this was the result of Jesus' death as a payment for our sin. We were recipients of God-directed Holy Spirit surgery.

> I will give you a new heart and put a new spirit in you; I will remove from you your heart of stone and give you a heart of flesh.   Ezekiel 36:26 NIV®

The reality of having our heart and mind touched by the Almighty left many of us in a state of euphoria for days, sometimes weeks, or months. The change in our attitude, way of seeing things, thinking and behaving was a miracle. We had passed from being troubled, lost and dead inside to suddenly having true spiritual life! The light of God's presence was all over us, awakening good things we never knew existed.

The invisible emotional world of fear and despair was replaced by invisible hope and love. When you experience this replacement for yourself—it takes your breath away! In the best type of awe possible, you feel it from the top of your head to the tip of your toes. We were in the process of becoming a new people!

**Being accepted and loved by God— blew
our minds and softened our hearts**

> Therefore if anyone is in Christ, grafted in, joined to Him by faith, he or she is a new creature; reborn by the Holy Spirit. The old way of living and previous self-centered, immoral behavior begins dying immediately, the state of being spiritually lost has past away. All things are becoming new because God has ushered in New Life in our heart and soul.
> 2 Corinthians 5:17 AMP/Paraphrased

Starting Over as Jesus Followers

Few Jesus People had higher education degrees, social standing, or an established work history. The majority of us were just starting out in life, trying to find our way. If anything we were on the lower rung socially. We were similar to Jesus' first disciples, everyday common people.

Paul, formerly known as Saul, was a persecutor of Jesus' followers until he encountered Jesus Christ and believed (Acts 9). His life was forever altered and he started over. On receiving Jesus Christ, a reboot on life had occurred for us too. When we stumbled on this portion of Scripture we were encouraged.

> Brothers and sisters, think of what you were when you were called. Not many of you were wise by human standards; not many were influential; not many were of noble birth. But God chose the foolish things of the world to shame the wise; God chose the weak things of the world to shame the strong. God chose the lowly things of this world and the despised things—and the things that are not—to nullify the things that are, so that no one may boast before him. It is because of Him that you are in Christ Jesus, who has become for us wisdom from God—that is, our righteousness, holiness and redemption. Therefore, as it is written: "Let the one who boasts, boast in the Lord."   I Corinthians 1: 26–31 NIV®

Battle Within + Family and Peers

JP had internal adjustments to make and a New Life to process. We wondered what family and friends would think about us. Will they think I'm hyper-religious, over the top? Will I lose my friends? What will my parents or siblings say? Will they conclude I'm trying to escape responsibilities? How will following Jesus Christ affect my education, work, finances and my future? Not all JP had to worry about this when they came right off the streets, but a lot of JP who had regular contact with their family and friends, had jobs or went to school did.

Some families were extremely thankful for the changes they saw in their kids—minus the spiritual part. Other parents were aghast their kid had turned to Jesus. I have a friend who was deeply troubled mentally, on meds and placed in mental hospitals when growing up. When he received Jesus Christ, he began acting normal and happy. His parents went ballistic when they heard God and Jesus were responsible and they put him back into a mental hospital. He was eventually released after a considerable period of time and a lot of leg work from Christian friend advocates.

A lot of JP lost their circle of friends when they began following

Jesus. Some JP were taken 'out of the family will' and ridiculed at family gatherings. Other parents flat-out rejected their kids because they'd received Christ as their Savior and wanted to live for Him. A spiritual choice with Jesus at the center clashed with everything this type of family was into.

Thankfully, many families were softer to the amazing transformations that Jesus Christ brought into the lives of their children. The Clowser family, whose story is embedded in this book, experienced one miracle after another until the whole family entered into a vibrant relationship with Jesus Christ. *Their response is an important example of what God can do when He is given room to work.*

Internal Choices

Jesus People who had placed their faith in God, now had priorities to sort through. With God at the center we needed to evaluate what we were learning in the Bible and compare it to social norms. Materialism, extreme patriotism, idolizing music or sports, family life, a career, or adhering to the expectations of family and friends needed to be thought through and prayed about. We realized loyalty to God needed to be the top priority along with what He wanted us to be about. Toward the end of the Jesus People Movement, Dr. Francis A. Schaeffer developed a film and a study curriculum on the question, "How Should We Then Live?" This question was at the core of what JP were endeavoring to discover.

"What Now?" Said a New Christian

When a street person came to believe in Jesus Christ, they needed to get off the streets and become established in the faith. Most street converts didn't have a job, or place to live. If they had a place to live it was usually a drug infested flat or building filled with demonic activity.

This need led us to establish discipleship houses by faith (Hebrews 11:1). With very little money or resources we rented or leased houses, storefronts, farms and small ranches, believing we'd somehow be able to pay the bills. We also opened coffee houses, restaurants, book stores and started a variety of small businesses which provided work for a growing number of young Christians who needed jobs. The creative expansion included Christian music groups/bands, newspapers, theater teams and a slew of new songs and tracts about God.

The notion of not caring about people who were in need of help was unacceptable to Jesus People (Matthew 25:34-46, James 2:14- 24). We sent out teams to carry the gospel of Jesus to venues throughout the USA, Europe and into other parts of the world (Matthew 28:18-20). These outreach missions were accompanied by meeting both practical and spiritual needs.

Traditional Church Leaders & Jesus People

Some pastors, teachers and leaders interacted with the JP with an agenda. Many wanted us to conform to a straight model by cutting our hair and wearing different clothes to authenticate our conversion to Christ. Their desire was to make us presentable to their traditional churches. Some JP fell prey to this offer, for the trade-off of being mentored by a pastor or teacher they respected.

Other Pastors, Teachers and Evangelists *used new converts from the JP movement to advertise or promote their name or ministries.* Still others wanted JP to submit to denominational beliefs and practices in order to be accepted, with a promise of a position, funding, or some form of licensing for ministry.

Jesus People and the Mainstream Church

Most JP were uninformed, naive and unsure what to make of mainstream churches and denominations. Since coming to believe in Jesus Christ, most of us felt it wasn't our place to be too critical of the church, since we'd been miraculously grafted into it by God's grace and mercy. At the same time we didn't know where we fit.

Some JP had religious upbringings; others were out of the loop completely when it came to church. A percentage of JP had participated in Sunday School, Catechism, Vacation Bible School, youth groups and worship services while they were growing up.

Exposure to any of the above was either positive or negative. *The majority of Jesus People I spoke to who attended church as a kid, said it hadn't connected with them on a heart level.* This is not to say that the input and love shown by sincere Christian leaders and teacher's and the spiritual seeds sown, were not of value!

Some JP had negative child or youth experiences when attending rigid, manipulating or abusive expressions of the church. Other JP who had positive experiences in church when younger, said this influence had more or less fallen by the wayside when they hit their teen and young adult years.

A significant number of Jesus People with church backgrounds were surprised to learn many church rituals, rules, doctrine beliefs and practices were not in the Bible. This was confusing, leaving unanswered questions for later on.

The Culture of the Church—Positive or Negative?

Many of the churches we visited didn't have prayer gatherings; group Bible studies, training in how to share Jesus Christ with others, outreach into the community, or opportunities or programs that equipped individuals in the development and use of their talents and spiritual gifts. This baffled us.

What we usually encountered were pastors, staff, elders or deacons who tightly controlled every aspect of the church's life and services. A secondary unspoken emphasis was on **passive attendance and cultural conformity**, with expectations for everyone to look conservatively straight. We also learned the protocol in most churches for newcomers was to attend regularly, tithe faithfully and after a year or two of participation, a low-level area of serving in the church might be made available. This seemed like a prolonged, discouraging way of integrating new Christians and quenching their fire.

For the most part Jesus People didn't fit into churches we tried to assimilate into. The primary reasons were: Limited JP opportunities for personal growth and participation, conformity requirements, traditional and denominational emphasis, liberal or legalistic church practices and doctrines. These along with unfriendliness made it obvious, we were not welcome.

Being honest, the church didn't look or feel anything like what we read about in the New Testament

The church we encountered was well organized, with unbendable religious procedures in place. Some places of worship were simple; others were ominous, massive structures with opulent decorations. A glaring absence in most was **Jesus' nature of love, truth, open-fellowship and welcoming.** *It seemed like religious order, traditions and all the trappings had literally squeezed the Life of God and Jesus' nature out of the church.*

Factoring in 2000 years of religious leaders being in charge; the church seemed to have evolved into something that Jesus Christ and God the Father wouldn't recognize. This was disturbing to think about.

Jesus People Leaders and Flaws

JP had plenty of their own problems! We had less structure and religious baggage but were not immune to our own mistakes and omissions. Group members who elevated leaders for any reason as being infallible was a huge mistake! JP leaders were average, doing their best, with the abilities and spiritual giftings they'd been given. The majority of the houses I knew of, or was part of had flaws. *The most significant problem I witnessed in myself and others was leaders overstepping their authority.* A strong personality leader could easily dominate; become overbearing, demanding, manipulative and unreasonable while mandating obedience from ministry participants (I Peter 5:3). Some leaders exploited those under them by working them non-stop without adequate personal or rest time to accomplish their own goals.

Many Jesus People put their trust in movement leaders without actively practicing discernment, or challenging them when they were out of line. Unchecked JP leaders did hurt people by using their authority in a manner not fitting of the gospel of Jesus Christ. Other JP leaders were unbalanced in promoting their pet doctrines, or unbending and legalistic when structuring ministry rules.

JP leaders who were willing to repent when needed and take responsibility for their sins, helped ministry participants evaluate their involvement in a group, and recognize the humanness of this leader. Stubborn leaders who refused to repent were a cancer to their group and for some strange reason came to believe they owned the ministry. Some were given the boot! A handful, through intimidation and other manipulative practices weathered the storms, got rid of the opposition and continued to abuse ministry participants.

In contrast, JP leaders who set a godly example by their words and actions set the tone for a healthy ministry. For this to occur leaders needed to be reverent before a Holy God, always mindful of the moral and ethical responsibility of guiding others in the faith. The characteristic needed are: truthfulness, sound doctrine, love, compassion, humility, faithfulness and an intentional goal of directiing all praise and glory to God the Father and His Son Jesus Christ. The standard is high, but reasonable for anyone to seeks to represent God and guide others spiritually.

Ministry Before Family?

Jenny Haas' honest account gives insight into a common problem Jesus People faced with the absence of adequate attention given to marriages and families (Chapter 25 beginning at page 549). What caused this omission?

In the early days, most JP were single which simplified a wide range of logistical, relational and housing needs. As JP married new challenges arose. Unfortunately, other than providing private space or rooms for married couples—we continued to conduct ministry without thinking through the needs of couples and their growing families.

When living in Christian community, ministry goals and accomplishing them was usually given top priority—above marriage, raising children and family life. *Our understanding of the Bible played into this non-intentional error.*

Matthew 19:29 is a classic example of how JP looked at the 'Good News Mission.' We were taught, or came to believe on our own, that the work of spreading the 'Gospel of Jesus' was the royal road. We understood this to be a higher path than our personal, married, and family needs. This understanding came from the 'King James Version' rendering of Jesus' words:

> "And every one that hath forsaken houses, or brethren, or sisters, or father, or mother, or wife, or children, or lands, for my name's sake, shall receive a hundredfold, and shall inherit everlasting life."   Matthew 19:29 KJV

What needed to be parsed out was Jesus' intent in this passage. Each of us knew highly committed Christians who had not left their homes, spouses, children, families, businesses and were serving Christ faithfully where they lived, surrounded by their immediate family and sometime extended family that supported them.

Even so, JP took this passage literally and it was reinforced by our predominant use of 'King James Version' Bibles. This gave some spouses (male and female) a built in theological excuse to not give adequate love and attention to their marriage and children.

At the time we didn't know the vast majority of Bible translations didn't include the word "wife." Surprise!

Many believe the intent of this passage is not so much about parting with material things or relationships, or gaining a hundred times what we originally had, or even gaining everlasting life—as much as it is, *not allowing anything to stand in competition with our love of God.*

Out of immaturity and ignorance we didn't know how to strike a balance in putting Jesus' words into practice. It was admirable to place a high priority on carrying the Gospel of Jesus Christ into the world. *But it was an error to conclude this outreach to the world, lessened our equally high priority of providing spiritual care and love for our spouse and children!*

In JP days, *wives were already sacrificing in incredible ways,* participating in the day to day activities of ministry, using their gifts to support us personally and to help the ministry be successful.

This is a small sampling of problems JP encountered. When the dust settled and the outpouring of the Holy Spirit subsided, some JP turned back to their old life and ungodly habits and denied the Lord that bought them. Other JP disappeared into obscurity and left the life of discipleship in exchange for pleasures of the world and the flesh. Some settled into lukewarm, comfortable religion, going through the motions—minus any fire in their soul to obey God, tell others about Christ, or be intentional in following in Jesus' steps.

Thank God many pressed on in faithful service to Jesus Christ having made a lifelong commitment to follow the Lord in spite of hardships, setbacks and the many trials of this life. All who did so should keep asking, *"Am I doing what Jesus gave me to do in representing Him in this world?"* If not, our religion, beliefs, and self righteous convictions mean nothing! Jesus said, "Follow Me" (Matthew 4:19, 8:22, 9:9, 16:24, 19:21)!

Those reading who are 'sitting on your hands' doing nothing to bring glory to God where you live, work or among those you interact with, should be very concerned.

You may 'say and think' you are a Christ follower, but to obey God is always the test of being authentic. If we are abiding in the Vine of Christ, God will guide us to serve, love, speak and help others *because of His life living in us. Jesus put it this way:*

"Let your light shine before others, that they may see your good deeds and glorify your Father in heaven." Matthew 5:16b NIV®

The Holy Spirit and Parallel Counterfeits JP 101

Counterfeits were attracted to the JP Movement like a magnet, poised to infiltrate at any opening. Like today, the devil is on the prowl, seeking anyone he may devour (I Peter 5:8).

The Holy Spirit benefits Christians in astonishing seen and unseen ways, teaching and leading us on God's good path. At the same time the devil and his demons seek to ruin what God is doing.

Jesus taught, "But while everyone was sleeping, his enemy came and sowed weeds among the wheat, and went away." Matthew 13:25 NIV®

The enemy is brazen—wanting to deceive God's own people by introducing a 'look, and sound alike' of God's Spirit. With this occurring regularly among followers of Jesus Christ in different settings, it's an important topic to shed light on. The backdrop is warfare against 'spirits of divination' posing as the Holy Spirit. They are counterfeit evil spirits that mimic God's work.

The Gifts and Offices the Father and Jesus Christ His Son provide for believers and the church are activated by the Holy Spirit in accordance with God's will. They are given to strengthen Jesus' followers, the church body, and to be a witness of God's goodness and truth to those who have not yet been reborn by God's Spirit.

Gifts of The Holy Spirit

Wisdom, Knowledge, Faith, Healing, Miraculous Powers, Prophecy, Distinguishing between spirits, the ability to speak in different kinds of tongues and the ability to interpret unknown tongues (found in I Corinthians 12:7–10.) Serving, helping, guiding, teaching, encouraging, giving, leading, showing mercy and hospitality (I Corinthians 12:28).

Offices

Apostles, Prophets, Evangelists, Pastors and Teachers (Ephesians 4:11). A parallel term for apostle is missionary, or church planter.

Counterfeit Characteristics and Behavior

Paul the Apostle refers to those who claim their own apostleship as 'Super-Apostles' in II Corinthians 11:5, 12:11. He adds this discernment:

> For such people are 'false apostles,' deceitful workers, masquerading as apostles of Christ. And no wonder, for Satan himself masquerades as an angel of light. I Corinthians 11:13–14 NIV®

Jeremiah lived during a resurgence of false religious prophets.

> "The prophets are prophesying lies in My name. I have not sent them, appointed them, or spoken to them. They are prophesying false visions, divinations (the practice of trying to foretell future events or discover hidden knowledge by using occult, evil and demonic spirits) idolatries and delusions of their own minds."   Jeremiah 14:14 NIV®

This is a timely warning given current day self-proclaimed prophets are accessing the spirit realm claiming their words are from God, but are instead from the spirit world of darkness and the delusions of their own hearts and minds.

Be On the Lookout For . . .

Those who claim to have had: Special impressions, dreams, visions, angel visits, out of body experiences, voice guides, anointings, revelations, prophecies, bizarre manifestations and noises, supposed trips to heaven, tongues and interpretations that occur privately, or are non-Biblical.

A common false prophet's ploy is to claim God said or did something in order to manipulate people or circumstances.

The same applies to the use of the 'name of Jesus.' Many counterfeit cults use the name of Jesus, but their ideas and beliefs about the name of Jesus have nothing to do with the Jesus Christ of the Bible. The apostle Peter urges us to be on the alert (I Peter 5:8).

Testing Supernatural Claims (I John 4:1)

- *Is God, Jesus Christ and the Holy Spirit being glorified?*

- *Is a person, persons, or group claiming supernatural miracles or special revelations introducing any transference of loyalty away from God the*

Father, Jesus Christ His Son and the Holy Spirit?

- Are the Scriptures of the Bible being rightly divided (II Timothy 2:15), or are new prophetic words, teachings and doctrines being introduced to replace or update God's Word in the Bible, for this present time?

- Is there any contact with the spirit-world (deceased spirits from the dead), or immoral sexual or deviant behavior being practiced secretly or openly?

- Are there additions to the Gospel message of God sending His Son Jesus Christ into the world to forgive sin and give eternal life to all who believe in Him?

- Does this new group and its leader or leaders claim to be special apostles, prophets, teachers, or the Messiah? Does their teaching contain: "We represent the new end-time era of truth for human history?" Are they suggesting any changes or additions to the New Covenant as recorded in the Bible?

Cult Infiltrators

Cults of the time period saw the Jesus People Movement as an opportunity to recruit from to boost their following. The Children of God and The Way International were two of the most aggressive in doing so. The Shepherding Movement was also guilty of wounding and confusing many young JP.

The Way International

"The Way International" re-emerged during the JP movement. Its origins date back several decades to 1942. Its founder, Pastor Victor Peter Wierwille started out with a radio program promoting his private revelations which were contrary to Biblical Christianity. In 1955 he named his group 'The Way', now known as 'The Way International.' The group adopted and promoted beliefs that progressively got worse. The Way morphed into denying the deity of Jesus Christ, licensed sexual immorality, mimicked speaking in tongues, taught good works would earn a place in heaven and worked at recruiting JP into their fold.

The Shepherding Movement

Toward the end of the JP Movement another devastating blow was leveled at Jesus People and associated ministries. It was ushered in through what was called "The Ft. Lauderdale Five" composed of five charismatic leader teachers who were respected by many Jesus People. The leaders were Bob Mumford, Derek Prince, Charles Simpson, Don Basham and Ern Baxter. John Poole was later added to this leadership group. The group became known as The Shepherding Movement.

These charismatic leaders devised a plan to bring under their wing significant numbers of individuals and families, many of whom had been in the JP Movement, with the intended goal of providing a "Spiritual Covering" for them. To accomplish this a pyramid structure of small groups were set up with tiers of leaders above each group.

The under-shepherds would answer to and receive counsel from the top Shepherding Leaders. What evolved was movement-wide prophetic leadership directives that ended up abusing by way of employing extreme control over individuals and families.

Marriages and families were broken apart and a significant amount of disillusionment occurred. Some of the top Shepherding leaders repented before they died, for all the spiritual harm they caused to thousands who had put their trust and confidence in their leadership.

The Children of God aka The Family - Synopsis

In 1968 David Brandt Berg, spouse Jane and four children Aaron, Hosea, Linda and Faith were given an opportunity to run a coffee house in Huntington Beach, California called the 'Light Club.' Their ministry focus was making sandwiches for hungry locals at the beach and inviting them to the coffee house for music, a gospel message and more food. Over time new converts and others joined the group. At first glance they seemed and sounded Christian, but a number of Christians who interacted with them said something was off.

When the coffee house ministry ran its course the Berg family took to the road with those who had joined their ranks traveling in caravan fashion. During this time frame David Berg took a mistress from the ranks of the young women who'd joined and he claimed to have received special revelations from God about himself and the young woman Maria Zerby who would co-lead a new nation. Shortly after, the group's name was changed to 'The Children of God.'

Gradually, Berg's radical doctrines and practices increased and were disseminated through 'Mo Letters' to be read to members at the Texas Soul Clinic in Thurber, Texas and the COG West Coast counterpart in

Los Angeles. As the group grew the same practice was adopted in all new locations.

Unbeknownst to most COG members in 1971-72

- David Berg was interacting with a 'departed Gypsy King spirit-guide.'
- He claimed to be God's specially anointed End-Time prophet.'
- Using prophesy he manipulated top leaders into 100% loyalty to him..
- Desiring total sexual freedom he acquired a handful of wives.
- Brainwashing indoctrination methods were being used on all members..
- By teaching and practice Berg was intentionally creating a 'closed group.'
- He wanted his words to supersede the teachings of the Bible.

Hating the social 'System' and its laws and despising the 'Church' at large for its outdated morality and hypocrisy— Berg railed on both regularly in his 'Mo Letters.' These targets, accompanied by teaching members to distrust family and friends on the outside played a significant role in the creation of a 'closed religious group'— isolated from any outside influence intentionally.

An in-depth detailed history on the COG-FAMILY with new documentation, firsthand accounts and numerous blurb comments from members who lived in this group during all of its eras has been carefully compiled, bringing us up to fall of 2019. This report can be found in the Appendix section of this book.

Appendix Preview—The Complexity of Cults and Recovery

Tragedy, heartbreak, abuse and death are a part of a larger trail of sorrows cults leave behind in their wake. Most cults fall into the following categories: Radical, Political, Religious, Terrorist, Hate, Occult, Racist, Supremacy, Family or Societal

In the past fifty years six religious cults have been in the 'public eye' for good reason. They are:

- 'Heaven's Gate' Community
- 'The Branch Davidians' of Waco, Texas

- 'Jim Jones' People's Temple USA & Jonestown, Guyana'
- 'Scientology'
- 'The Unification Church' Rev. Sun Moon
- 'The Children of God' aka 'Family of Love' aka 'The Family' and now called 'The Family International' founded by David Brandt Berg

The Unification Church and The Children of God aka The Family are the focus of an in-depth investigative research project to discern the truth about each group. In a more cursory manner, the salient facts surrounding the tragedy that unfolded with the 'Heaven's Gate' community, the 'Branch Davidians' of Waco, Texas and Jim Jones' People's Temple, provides a sober warning about the control cult leaders can wield over their followers leading to mass-deaths. The other cult on our list is 'Scientology.' It's rightly nicknamed 'The Cult of Greed'. It thrives on the pursuit of money and power in high places in hopes of one day controlling the entire world. Their lofty goal and bizarre alien belief system is out of a Si-Fi script, in fitting with their founder, Ron Hubbard, a science fiction writer. The findings on each group are synthesized in the Appendix.

Cult Recovery Preview

Having personally traversed cult recovery—I recall the individual nature of what I experienced and its lingering impact on my thinking, emotions, spiritual life and what I could do, or not do. Since we're all wired with one-of-a-kind inner constitutions, your stress and rebounding skills will be different than any other cult survivor.

With this in mind we've carefully compiled more general suggestions we found helpful in advancing our recovery. The act of leaving and starting over is a huge step. We applaud each cult survivor who has done so and want you to know we are praying for you

We know a restart encompasses a myriad of practical adjustments amidst emotional upheaval. With transparency we recall these days of starting over from scratch and some of the troubling memories, flash-backs and nightmares that hounded us. We share recovery ideas which could help reduce these.

The time it took for us to feel up to rejoining the workforce, or return to school, feel hope or sense some semblance of inner peace was different for each of us, but we remember being OK with 'one day at a time.'

Finding the inner strength to forgive ourselves, God, or other cult members would take time. An immediate need was, dislodging all cult doctrines, beliefs and practices from our mind and heart and renouncing every form of evil that had been entertained while in any cult.

This brings us to the troubling reality that religious cults can twist and ruin our view of God, Jesus Christ, the Holy Spirit, or the Truth found in God's Word the Holy Bible. I waged this battle and armed myself with the truth of the Scriptures alongside a comprehensive study on the 'Origins and Progression of Cults.' This information accompanied by other topics and resources for cult survivors, friends and immediate family members can be found in the Appendix.

Speaking from experience, spiritual restoration is 100% available, but requires attention and openness on our part to do the inner work needed and seek out help when we get stuck. Realigning ourselves with the True and Living God and asking for help is essential in finding healing of heart, soul and mind.

Peter, who denied Jesus Christ three times following his arrest and tortuous flogging, gives us this advice, "Humble yourself under the mighty hand of God and He will faithfully lift you up and restore you" (I Peter 5:6 Para).

A Lack of Godly Mentors in the Jesus People Movement

A significant weakness in the Jesus People Movement was the absence of seasoned Christian pastors, teachers and mentors who could have modeled Biblical integrity, character, purity, wisdom and prayer. A handful of these types of mentors, teachers and pastors did come along, but not nearly enough! The ones who were helpful and used greatly didn't seek to control or quench the fire of God's Holy Spirit and our commitment to discipleship and sharing the Good News.

JP During Times of Testing, Trials and Failures

Following Jesus doesn't eliminate problems, pain or set-backs. The idea of throwing in the towel never seemed like a good idea to most of us. Peter summed it up well, "Lord, to whom shall we go? You have the words of eternal life; and we have believed, and have come to know, that you are the Holy One of God—the Christ of God" (John 6:68-69). Our personal shortcomings and everything 'that was and is' troubling in the world or church didn't make God's pathway wrong!

> "So, how did everything go on your journey as Jesus People?" Ans. "Being most honest, there were days and months and even years that were extremely difficult. Following Jesus does not eliminate troubles!"

Had we known the unexpected tragedies that would strike, and fall-out from our bad decisions or immaturity, we might have bailed; some did.

I'm personally grateful for the supernatural amount of grace that God gave to help many of us navigate extremely dark times. Some troubles had nothing to do with our behavior while others were caused by it.

These severe personal trials, hitting our head against the wall and finding ourselves in the vomit of our own sin, placed us in a vulnerable position. With precise aim the enemy of our soul, the devil, could point to our sin and issue a fierce condemnation and be 100% accurate. What could we say? Guilt-ridden and depressed, we'd have to agree, we were a disgrace to God.

Walking in this type of darkness, entombed in hours, days or weeks of despair, anger, or inner turmoil, with the shadow of death lurking, and condemning thoughts accusing, we hopefully will call out for God's help. The Psalmist said it well,

> I am poor and needy, may the Lord think of me. You are my help and my deliverer; You are my God, do not delay!   Psalm 40:17 NIV®

This is what God's Altar is for. The Father and the Son call us to bring our depression and despair, guilt, hopelessness and the burdens we can't possibly carry on our own, and request help from The One True God.

We are not superhuman, or super-spiritual to the point of being able to carry the full weight of difficulties found in this life in the flesh. Think about it. We can't love, forgive or deal with violence or catastrophes without God's assistance. In the same way we can't follow and trust in God without His help!

> Approaching God's throne of grace is always the best first choice, but human nature pushes it into

last place until all other options fail.

Finally in desperation we get it right and offer the simplest of prayers. "Dear Lord, I need Your Help!"

Forgiven and Reinstated

God sees our situation and hears our heart's cry! He will not turn away from us when our heart is contrite and humble (James 4:10, I Peter 5:5b). Returning to the Lord is an amazing two-step process of repentance and coming back under God's grace, mercy and protection (Isaiah 44:22, 55:7). In a way only God is capable of, a miraculous outpouring of undeserved love and forgiveness enters our being. Sin is blotted out. The distress of failure, or the darkness of despair and hopelessness lifts!

This is God's grace working through the Holy Spirit, touching our mind, heart and soul. In an invisible yet tangible way 'God's Peace' returns. As Jesus is referred to as the 'Prince of Peace,' this is a perfect description of what occurs when we are restored (Isaiah 9:6).

> Jesus said, "Peace I leave with you; my peace I give you."   John 14:27a NIV®

As with Peter, who denied the Lord Jesus three times, *God stands ready to reinstate us.* Though we are guilty, this guilt of sin is once again washed away by the power of the blood of Jesus Christ who continues as our eternal high priest—forgiving, healing and restoring (Hebrews 4:14-16). This is why the hymn "Amazing Grace" is so cherished among believers.

> The Grace and mercy that was present at our
> Salvation—continues throughout our lives!

When praying the prayer (Our Father) that Jesus gave, it succinctly answers any and all questions about our ongoing battle with the flesh, the world and the evil one. Our need is significant because we are human, live in a fallen world and the enemy of our soul is at war with God (Matthew 6:9-13). For this reason we are urged to commit the keeping of our souls to our faithful Creator (I Peter 4:19).

Who is This God, Who Carries on With a Sinner Like Me?

The Christian band the News Boys sang a tune "Great is Your Faithfulness" with the lyrics, "Great is Your faithfulness—to carry on with a sinner like me." These words cause thankfulness to rise in my spirit. This senti-ment of gratefulness resonated with Jesus People who were continuously appreciative of God reaching as far and deep as He had, rescuing us. To be forgiven and accepted with the additional promise of everlasting life in God's household is incredible!

> God's continued care, interaction and love for us in spite
> of our sin nature screw-ups, verifies God's Amazing Grace!

Jesus People: Agape Love/Koinonia Fellowship

In the Jesus People Movement important things were woven into the fabric of what God did among us. There was creative freedom, time for honest life sharing, for teaching one another how to do things like playing a musi-cal instrument, singing, drawing and painting, or learning a new skill or trade. We were given opportunities to pass on to each other lots of new things related to reaching our world for Christ and faithfulness in present-ing ourselves before the Lord.

In most 'Christian Houses' and JP ministries we felt loved and cared about, part of a family, listened to, a person of value, safe and protected. We were taught how to intercede for others and specific needs in prayer, and how to release our faith and wait for God's answers. We received guidance in fasting from food and using our abilities and spiritual gifts to glorify God. We learned how to study the Bible, use Bible helps, listen to the Holy Spirit for specific guidance, worship God from the heart, sacrifice our time, energy and money, serve and put others needs before our own and be less selfish. We benefited by being able to ask questions and learn from our peers and leaders.

We were constantly reminded of the plight and questions of those outside of Christ by interacting with them. *We intentionally set aside time to go and be among the lost and invite them to where we lived for meals and more visiting.* We learned to share the gospel in a clear manner and actively listen.

We asked for God's forgiveness when we sinned and forgiveness from others when we said or did something hurtful. And we forgave oth-ers when they offended us. We also learned how to mentor and disciple someone younger than us in the faith, how to preach a sermon, lead a Bible study, a prayer gathering, or a discussion group; and the list goes on.

Adequate time for relational interaction occurred because we were not always being herded and controlled. In an atmosphere of being open, vulnerable, truthful and non-judgmental, we learned to love our brothers and sisters in the faith. Friendship roots had time to be watered and fed. In an atmosphere of mercy, grace and compassion as fellow sinners in route to heaven—we agreed to speak truth into each other's lives and pray for one another.

The Greatest of All Challenges

The greatest commandment Jesus taught caused us to bow our heads and hearts knowing this was beyond anything we'd ever attempted.

> Love the Lord your God with all your heart, with all your soul, with all your strength, with all your mind and Love your neighbor as yourself.   Luke 10:27 NIV®

We didn't have a clue how to love God, or our neighbor! The first step was learning about God, who He is, what He likes (Deuteronomy 10:12, Luke 10:27) and what God hates (Proverbs 6:16-19, Deuteronomy 12:31, Deuteronomy 18:9-13). A fuller understanding of these things would come by rightly dividing God's Word (the Bible, 2 Timothy 2:15) which would also reveal what loving our neighbor looked like (Isaiah 58:6-7, Luke 10:25-37).

Reading the Bible gave us an initial understanding of God's nature and His interaction with humans since the beginning of time. It provided many examples of how God's servants loved and obeyed Him. We also read about those who rejected and ignored God and how they harmed or exploited their neighbors.

We each had a choice to make. I chose to love God by listening to and obeying His guidance. All JP made a similar choice. We loved God by obeying Him. We loved others by putting their needs before our own. *We were on the steepest learning curve of our lives.* Loving God and those around us was contrary to our human nature. In the little things of daily living, God helped us to be more considerate and put our love into action beyond lip service (James 2:14-22).

Jesus People—Going Out In Jesus Name

God gave us boldness in sharing the Good News, carrying our Bibles, handing out tracts and engaging people in dialogue at parks, beaches, high schools, colleges, universities, juvenile halls, city jails, honor farms, prisons and on the streets. As we went, miracles took place on a regular basis. The most frequent miracle was people opening their heart to Jesus Christ; often accompanied by coming down from a drug they'd taken, deliverance from a demonic spirit, physical healing, or mental confusion being lifted (Luke 9:1-6, Acts 8:4-8).

We prayed in advance of going, while among those in need, and after every outing (Joshua 1:9). We asked God to speak through us and guide our steps to those we were intended to speak with. *We realized the big stuff that needed to happen would be God's doing!* He took the truth we presented to individuals and applied it to their need. If what they heard was mixed with faith and openness of heart, a mysterious in-breaking from God would occur (Acts 8:26-40).

It was in our spiritual DNA to share our faith. We were not ashamed of God our Father, Jesus Christ His Son, the Holy Spirit, the Bible or the gospel message (Romans 1:16).

Going out to tell others about God and His Son Jesus Christ was sometimes challenging. **Some people would yell, spit, curse, or attempt to hit us** (see John 15:18-19). We encountered evil and the devil regularly. We stood our ground in the authority of Jesus Christ. Demons would get roused when hearing the name of Jesus Christ and cause a scene. Shop owners would get upset because of all the commotion in front of their stores. Anything could happen (Mark 5:1-20, Acts 19:23-34)! The Lord went with us, consistently backing up our words, allowing us to bear spiritual fruit (John 15:14-17). We rarely ran into church people sharing their faith in these venues.

> "My food," said Jesus, "is to do the will of him who sent me and to finish his work. Do you not say four months more and then the harvest? I tell you, open your eyes and look at the fields! They are ripe for harvest. Even now the reaper draws his wages; even now he harvests the crop for eternal life, so the sower and the reaper may be glad together."   John 4:34–36 NIV®

JP and Biblical Judgment—Hell

Having been recipients of mercy and forgiveness, most JP didn't use the terminology "Turn or Burn" when conducting outreach. This didn't mean the subject of hell and judgment was off limits. Because judgment of the wicked and evil is prominent in the Bible, we came to accept this as God's wise choice. Who would want to spend eternity with a hideous demon cackling in your ear? Having seen and smelled the evil, vile stench of demons up close in Atlanta, Georgia and having been attacked by the devil on numerous occasions I agreed with God 100%!

At the Beulah Hill Christian House in Upper Norwood, England we had a large mural painting on a wall in our downstairs gathering room. The image was of heaven and the earth with a huge canyon between. A strong stone bridge spanned from one side of the canyon to the other in the shape of a cross. At the bottom of the canyon were flames arising from a lake of fire. This image sparked conversations between our team and seekers or visitors.

Both Old and New Testaments of the Bible speak of a punishment site. The names used in the Scriptures are Sheol, Hell, Hades, Gehenna, Abyss and Lake of Fire. Scientific research into earth's inner layers have uncovered astounding parallels between Biblical descriptions of hell and a gigantic 'ocean of fire' that surrounds the core of the earth (Revelation 20:7-15). God told us about this long before it was confirmed by the scientific community!

Embers and Praise

I give thanks to God for every person who took up their cross to follow in Jesus' steps during the Jesus People Movement. The amount of sacrifice and love given by Jesus People was massive.

When the Holy Spirit fires of the Jesus Movement died down to embers ten years or so after its birth, participants had many adjustments to make. We made a valiant effort, against all odds, and turned part of our world upside down with the Good News of Jesus Christ. Because we listened and followed Jesus, the entire 'Peace and Love Generation' was not lost, but many came to a saving faith and knowledge of Jesus Christ.

> We stepped up and did what God asked of us. We walked into the unknown in faith and confronted the enemy of truth and God on his territory. God counted us worthy in spite of our weaknesses. Willing to "Go", we put our

personal goals and desires on hold to obey God and He accompanied us!

God moved in supernatural power—thrusting us out into His "whitened fields of harvest." Our words were infused with the power of 'His Words' which drew listeners to Him. We co-labored with the Almighty. We saw hundreds of lives including our own transformed. God considered us worthy, by both using and increasing our giftedness. We willingly made do with very little personal money and belongings, learning to live by faith and were OK with it. By following Jesus in unchartered territory we witnessed miracles of all kinds.

We were in awe when ministries arose from nothing. We saw the creative hand of God at work and His Holy Spirit poured out in multiple ways. We witnessed doors open beyond our wildest dreams and provisions provided supernaturally. Obeying the Great Commission to 'Go' out in Jesus' Name was not a chore, but a privilege. Mercy and Love lifted and sent us!

> **Most participants in the Jesus People Movement didn't realize we were a part of a God initiated Holy Spirit in-breaking in human history to rescue a sizable portion of the 1960's-70's generation. The majority of us were unchurched; all of us were lost. God did the seeming impossible by revealing His risen Son, Jesus Christ in power, love and truth. In awe, we received the Gift of new life!**

When our mission endeavors ended, some Jesus People were relieved to no longer be living in a Christian ministry house, ranch or similar setting. Other JP missed the close proximity of friends to connect with regularly. In the trenches of outreach, serving and giving—honest and genuine lifetime friendships in the faith had been forged.

Some Jesus People now had young families and needed to establish their family unit, but remained in touch with their JP friends. Some shared in ministry together when living in the same geographical area.

For JP who'd put their education and work goals aside, it was time to return to school, or develop new skills to provide a livelihood for themselves or their family. Other JP would transition naturally into continuing educational training for ministry, outreach or missions work, or serve within a church or Para-Church Ministry group.

Post JP Days and Hooking Up With a Church

Those with established roots in a church body made the adjustment seamlessly when already involved in some form of music, outreach, teaching, discipling, prayer, or serving ministry in a church.

Other Jesus People who had been part of an outreach mission (community) for a number of years, without any connection to a church or denomination, needed to find a faith community match..

Background: Most JP had served in ministries where their gifts and talents found wide-birth of expression. We were students of the Word, committed to prayer and discipleship disciplines. We enjoyed honest back and forth dialogue with Christian friends. Sharing the Gospel of Jesus Christ and meeting practical needs in the community was in our DNA. Without realizing it, Christian Houses were a para-church ministry with a focus on outreach and discipleship to our own generation.

Transitioning from being part to full-time in JP ministry to a 'church attendance model' was strange. We were not used to sitting on the sidelines and or the sometimes expansive deep-structure of church government, leadership and congregational protocol.

Locating a healthy church doctrinally, relationally, and with core values of prayer, discipleship and outreach—with opportunities for new people to become active within a reasonable amount of time, was not easy to find.

Post JP days, with 25 years pastoral and chaplaincy service—I've visited over two hundred churches while serving in a handful of pastorates and chaplaincy positions. The reason for these numerous church visits, was to be able to make good referrals. These recommendations were for young Christians, a family looking for a good church, or family members of hospice patients who needed and wanted to secure Christ-centered spiritual help and link up with church home.

To my surprise the majority of approximately 200 churches were dysfunctional, unfriendly, ingrown, significantly denominationally focused, relationally barren, had autocratic leaders, strange doctrines, or some other negative quirk. The exceptions were under 10%.

This is what post JP ran into when searching for a Faith Community to be a part of. Some persevered visiting until they found a match, others gave up.

Ex-cult members found it substantially more difficult to consider visiting a Christian church. Their spiritual life had been tumbled upside down by deception and anti-church teaching. Almost everything associated with religion was painful and embarrassing. The negative humiliation of being deceived, caused many former cult members to shut-down spiritually.

The Jesus Family England, Church of the Open Door in California and a half Jewish-half Gentile congregation in Glen Cove, New York helped me regain my spiritual balance.

Wanting to understand how the church should work, to correct personal flaws and deepen my spiritual roots I returned to school. Some university and three years of Seminary followed. Heady education was less than inspiring, but I grew while attending. Thankfully, I was accepted into a 400 hour hospital chaplaincy internship as part of my studies which helped keep me grounded in outreach ministry.

On completing a Masters of Divinity' degree I aligned with a 200 year old denomination for 18 years. Authentically Christians? Yes. Good people? Yes. Focused on their identity and distinctions as a denomination? Yes. Limited in outreach vision? Yes. How widespread and prevalent are other denominational groups like this? Pervasive.

Meaningful Relationships in the Church?
Many Church-goers Don't Want Relationships

Being unable to develop meaningful relationships in a church is discouraging for those seeking Christ-centered friends. *A close to barren relational church seems strange, but it is becoming more predominant*

My wife recently reminded me, *many church attendees are not interested in developing relationships.* They attend faithfully, put their kids in Sunday School, drop something in the offering, enjoy the music and sermon and go home. That's it!

Different Expectations

Views on church attendance run the spectrum; "I'm here to worship God, and hear God's Word." In agreement another adds, "I like the music, our band and our preacher; they're all very entertaining!" Someone listening agrees, piping in, "We like the free food and drinks and church socials too!"

An entirely different group in the same church is interested in the worship, preaching and teaching and learning how to apply the Bible to everyday life. This group wants to grow in their relationship with God and be connected with fellow Christians who are on this same journey. Their goal is to become fruit-bearing followers of Jesus Christ, equipped to encourage fellow Christians but also reach those outside the faith and beyond the grounds of the church. A former JP would probably fit best in this latter group.

The Way It Was and the Way It Is

Some in our immediate neighborhood of 47 families say they feel they live in a time capsule Neighborhood from the Past. Neighbors know each other on a first name basis, share meals together, watch each other's property, take in packages for each other and get to know the kids on the block. We provide an email and phone list for new incoming neighbors of all residents. We schedule annual events and do various things together.

Today's world is very different. Those who never locked their doors in the past have to, including us. We also use clubs on our cars that are parked outside. With the rise of crime we're forced to become security conscious. Our comings and goings are more guarded and it seems this social caution has spilled into the church with more guardedness and less interest in building relationships. Adding to this problem is the busyness of the world and society as a whole.

In today's harried world, people are rushing about trying to get ahead, raise a family and make 'their own dreams come true.' Young and old are absorbed with what they already have going on. Thankfully there are exceptions, but this is the millennial reality. *The only way to combat this encroaching lifestyle is to intentionally listen to the Lord regarding what you can personally do to offer an inclusive alternative to those around you.*

Relational Hurdles in the Church

Strike 1. The 'meet and greet' handshakes while coming in the front doors, or during a sliver of time after announcements is limited.

Strike 2. Study groups and Sunday School classes make attempts to help people connect, but class agenda, curriculum and time restraints work against this.

Strike 3. Church potlucks and barbecues are designed to give members and visitors leisure time, but time spent in line can easily interfere with getting to a table before others are near done and ready to leave. In addition, if you're not one of the regulars you may end up sitting alone.

Strike 4. On occasion a few established church members will give a social or home invite to a new person that is more or less a 'welcome to the church'—not intended to offer much more. These individuals are often over-extended in church life without much time left to invest in new people.

Insightful Unspoken Questions

Large numbers of those who attend church do so because of personal needs, or a willingness to give. They arrive at church hopeful and return home with a smattering of spiritual food, but wonder, "Does anybody really care about me, my journey, joys and the hard times I've passed through? *Am I destined for the same empty relational void after each service?* Am I just another attendance number?

Is anybody interested in my struggles; want to know about me, what type of work I do, what my talents and interests are? I wish someone would ask me what areas of ministry or service I'd like to contribute my time and energy into. I'm willing to give money and my presence in worship, but I wish I could find a sense of fulfillment in serving God in some meaningful way in the church and also in the community. I need help getting started."

The needs, hopes and dreams of faithful attenders are routinely ignored by church leaders who are mostly consumed with their own agenda. Many churches follow their leader's example of emphasizing worship attendance and church programs minus any emphasis on 'Body Life' friendships in Christ. Is this the new norm we should accept? I hope not!

Wouldn't it be great if churches would give adequate time and priority to facilitating an environment where Jesus Christ's Words would have a chance at becoming reality?

"By this everyone will know that you are my disciples, if you love one another."   John 13:35 NIV®

A Gritty Friendship

In the movie "Tombstone" there's a scene that resonates with me about friendship. Doc Holiday is lying in a small western hospital dying of a lung disease. His friend Wyatt Earp comes to see him, taking a seat bedside. Doc's eyes open to a squint and he sees Wyatt. Wyatt slowly reaches in his pocket and pulls out a deck of cards and says, "Let's play."

Doc, feeling too ill to hold the cards and resigned to dying, doesn't seem up to it. This doesn't deter Wyatt as he calls "Five Card Stud" and proceeds to deal both hands. As Doc looks on with a small grin, Wyatt plays both hands calling out each card.

As a hospice chaplain and being bedside with those who were dying, this scene of friendship engagement and presence speaks volumes.

Integration Differences between the Church & JP

New people and visitors are not much more than a novelty in many churches. They boost attendance, give money, help the church feel they're doing something right but relational interest in these people can be minimal. Other than saying 'hi,' or 'welcome,' the average church member doesn't know what else to do. They feel awkward.

I've thought a lot about the current church dynamic of how difficult it can be to make 'fast friends' (in less than a year or two) in a church and how it was during the Jesus People Movement. As I recall we made new friends regularly. We were excited to meet new people and many of these friendships remained.

> Jesus People were young and open. We were excited about our faith, happy to have new friends to serve God with. There were no rules about making a person wait to get involved. We welcomed and made a place for newcomers. We were enthusiastic about helping them feel accepted, appreciated and loved. We invited them to do lots of stuff with us and encouraged them to use their natural and spiritual talents to glorify God and His Son Jesus Christ.   D.E.H.

If someone was newer in the faith than us, we took them under our wing and taught them from the Bible what we had learned thus far. We shared meals together regularly and discussed questions we had about God and how to apply our faith. We prayed together often. We saw ourselves as a team of friends under Jesus our Savior. As all of us were saved and rescued; nobody was better than the other, or less of a sinner.

We were all part of 'God's Living Church' comprised of 'Living Stones' who'd been purchased by Jesus' sacrificial death for mankind.

(I Peter 2:5, 1:18-19).Our faith was activated in a miraculous yet simple organic way by the Holy Spirit. *We didn't need permission to help a person receive Christ, pray out loud, or be ordained to baptize a new Christian.* We were not attached to material things, human traditions, religious non-essential rules, or physical structures designated for worship.

In Jesus' day the Jews worshiped in synagogues or in the temple in Jerusalem, the Samaritans worshiped on a mountain, but Jesus said:

> "A time is coming and has now come when the true wor-
> shipers will worship the Father in the 'Spirit and in truth,'
> for they are the kind of worshipers the Father seeks. God is
> spirit, and his worshipers must worship in the Spirit and in
> truth."   John 4:23-24 NIV®

This was a distinct difference between the organized church and JP. *We liked the open air, connecting with people out and about and we saw the value of what Jesus modeled as God's way of reaching our generation.*

The organized church of today is often hidden in the confines of buildings, with minimal interaction with the lost of this world. Is this God's plan?

Religious Schizophrenia— Anonymous

"Mega Church, Medium Mega, Autocratically Controlled, Limited Partic-ipation, One Head Talking, Men Leaders only, Women & Men Leader-ship, Homegrown, Ingrown, Spirit Led, Word Led, Denominational Blues, Agenda-Agenda-Agenda, Overfed, Underfed, Convicted, Ostracized, Crit-icized, Over-Worked, Under-Worked, Needed, Not Needed, Numb, Stag-nant, Comfortable, Lethargic, Have Pain-No Doctor, Need Prayer, Church Doesn't Pray Much, Want to Learn, Force Fed, Told What to Believe and Think, Ideas Squelched, Board says No!, Choir Leader is Mean, Deacon Tom is Mad at Me Again, Church Needs Cleaners, Church Needs More $, I Want to Help Reach the Lost, but I'm needed in my introverted schizo-phrenic church!"

What Church?

Street people would sometimes ask Jesus People, "So what church are you a part of?"

We had a difficult time with this question. I'd sometimes blurt out,

"My church is with God the Father, Jesus Christ and the Holy Spirit", while scratching my head trying to figure out what to add. We wanted to point people directly to God and not have them turned off by naming a specific church or denomination. The person asking this question usually had a perplexed look on their face after hearing The Father, Son and Holy Spirit. If possible we'd follow this up immediately with an explanation about the importance of going directly to God and Jesus Christ for truth and answers.

'Tell It Like It Is!' – Anonymous

My spiritual leaders listen mostly to themselves. If they heard me saying what I'm telling you—I'd be excommunicated! They don't say it all the time, but all of us in the church know; they believe they're the vision casters, closer to the Almighty than the rest of us. They more or less use us; tell us what to do and what to believe. It's more of a religious thing, than being loved, listened to, or valued as fellow followers of Jesus.

The only time we're praised or encouraged by them is for regular attendance, giving money and accomplishing the ideas they come up with.

The pastors, elders and deacons are really good at micro-managing everything, but sometimes go overboard. I used my talents in the church faithfully for ten years, but grew discouraged by being corrected so often. The leaders detailed exactly how they wanted everything done. Our church's leaders are what you would call "obsessive compulsive, control freaks!"

They know the Scriptures extremely well, but seem obsessed with introducing new catch-phrases and transitions to make them sound 'cool' like TV, news, or conference speakers. For the most part, doctrine stuff is OK, other than their pet doctrines, which are off. If they heard me saying this stuff, I'd be crucified!

My greatest concern, besides the leaders thinking they're always right is, the way they control every aspect of worship down to the minute. There's absolutely no time for member or attendee participation other than the worship team or choir director. Sunday is their grand performance! They think they're moving us ahead as a congregation, but we're being held back. *We are their spiritual experiment, at creating more spiritual life in us and growing the church.*

God Himself could not penetrate our worship order of service! If Jesus Christ were to stand in our midst, the leaders are so full of themselves, they wouldn't listen to Him. I'm 99% sure they'd motion the ushers or deacons to have Jesus thrown out the front door!

Another huge frustration I've struggled with for years is securing friends in the church. It's almost impossible! I've tried for twelve years. The only thing I found was a 'Coffee and Donut Men's Group' that mainly meets to shoot the breeze.

I've been a loyal member but just can't do this anymore. I'm going to walk away from this church. Yep, I'm done!

> "We thrive when we feel valued, listened to, respected, loved,
> able to contribute our abilities, ideas and vision. We long for
> meaningful relationships in Christ that are genuine."   —honor

New Wine & Old Wineskins

Some Jesus People were poured into 500+ year old wineskins, others into 100+ year old skins, and still others into recent Church Plant wineskins.

Denominational churches and some newer churches required JP align with doctrinal positions and embrace the group's historical roots in order to be fully accepted and fit in.

Jesus spoke about new wine and old wineskins in Luke's Gospel saying:

> "And no one pours new wine into old skins. If he does, the
> new wine will burst the skins, the wine will run out and the
> old wineskins will be ruined. No, new wine must be poured
> into new wineskins. And no one after drinking old wine
> wants the new, for he says, 'The old is better.'"   Luke
> 5:37–39 NIV®

The old wine is smoother, settled, palatable and safe for consumption according to a wine connoisseur, but the old skins are fragile. In contrast, the newer wine is not fully seasoned but still good and the new skins are strong!

How does Jesus' word apply to the Jesus Movement, or any outpouring of God's Spirit?

A wine-maker makes a new batch of wine that is uniquely robust, but not fully seasoned. To the common person who cannot afford well-aged wine, or has never tasted wine before, this new wine is excellent!

Happy with this new wine, the wine-maker decides to make a *large batch and distribute it for free!* He sends it out to distributors who dispense it freely so more people can taste the new wine and learn about the maker.

The Jesus Movement was the 'New Wine' God poured into new wine-skins. It was useful and effective when introduced to the common person—tasting extremely good to a generation who had no idea of the Lord's plan for them. *It more than satisfied a lost person's taste and was free!* The Father, Son and Holy Spirit were behind this generous offer of Truth, Love and Redemption.

The distribution of New Wine in places where the lost congregated, gave those who were receptive the opportunity to meet the Wine Maker and His Son. Consider how often God works outside the temple, synagogue or church, while continuing His amazing work in the church when welcome.

Both the old and new wine is valuable in the hands of the the Almighty aka the 'Wise Winemaker' who looks for vessels who are willing to be emptied and refilled again and again.

Always Transferable

Most Christians would agree fervent Love of God and one's neighbor still rules as the Greatest Commandment in the New Testament (Matt. 22:37-40).

How good and pleasing it would be if churches would elevate 'God the Father, Jesus His Son, the Holy Spirit and the Word of God', and place a focus on love of one's neighbor and the lost. If this was practiced, *an outpouring of God's presence wouldn't be a historical notion of the past.*

I Believe in God - Inspired by a song sung by Joan Baez

I Believe in God—and God's not us!
I believe He is, was—and will always be
Wise, Just, Loving and Fair—Eternal, Living and Knowable
I believe in God—and God's not me!
He is unboxable, unlimited, creative—unstoppable
Flowing through, around and past human barriers
I believe in God—and God's not you!
I know, God is sad—by the atrocities humans are responsible for.
The scourge of greed and hate—war, terror, fear, misery and more—grieve Him
I believe in God—and God's not this!

We were created to love God, Justice and Mercy
Instilled to hate what is cruel and evil
How can we know this True and Living God?
Turn away from Idols and everything false
Seek the Almighty with your whole heart
I believe in Jesus who is God's Son
Who lived, died, rose from death
And lives to bring us back to The Father
I believe in God—who calls us to listen and follow Him.   – honor

Questions for Followers of Jesus Christ

In what way does God want to use me to reach my world? Is there an area of need God has been talking to me about? What are my strongest personal abilities and spiritual gifts? How can I use these abilities to meet an area of need locally or somewhere in the world? What research needs to be done? Is there someone involved in this type of ministry I should contact? What specific practical and spiritual steps should I take in moving forward to avoid procrastinating? What time and money am I willing to freely give? When will I begin making myself available?

> We are God's workmanship, created in Christ Jesus, born of the Spirit and available. God has gifted and prepared us; prearranging opportunities for us to serve, speak and live— representing Jesus Christ.   Ephesians 2:10 Paraphrased

What Does the Future Hold?

In other places on planet earth, in the past, now and in the future— the work of the Almighty continues. At this very moment God is answering millions of prayers, healing and comforting, extending His love and presence into hearts and places of need globally. No doubt He is embarking on yet another visit or rescue mission somewhere on earth.

> *"My Father is always at His work to this very day, and I too am working."* – Jesus the Christ   *John 5:17 NIV®*

Think Big—God is!

31

THEN & NOW SNAPSHOTS

Martin Luther King Jr. and Civil Rights
Team praying before a March

James Baldwin, Joan Baez & James Forman
1965 march for Voting Rights from Montogomery
to Selma Alabama (54 miles).

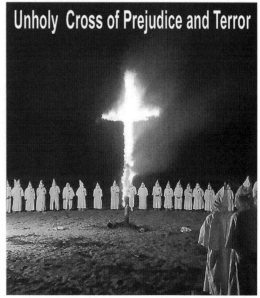

Four Young African American Girls Die in Church Bombing

On Sunday September 15, 1963 a bomb killed four young girls and seriously injured 20 other church members. Klu Klux Klan members planted 10-15 sticks of dynamite with a timer under the front steps of the 16th Street Baptist Church in Birmingham, Alabama.

When the bomb exploded it made a gaping hole in a restroom wall, creating a crater over two-feet deep in the basement and spraying debris all over the building. The blast was so powerful, that it blew a motorist from his car, destroyed vehicles parked outside and shattered windows blocks away. The young girls pictured below died in this bombing.

| Addie Mae Collins | Carol Robertson | Denise McNair | Cynthia Wesley |
| 14 yrs. | 14 yrs. | 11 yrs. | 14 yrs. |

Tragically, 50 other racially motivated bombings took place in Birmingham, AL alongside other violent acts toward African Americans that resulted in 100's of innocent deaths and injuries.

Fact: God created all humans in His own image (Genesis 1:27). God does not prefer one color of skin above another. Racial prejudice springs from spiritual ignorance.

1957

PLEASE STAND BY

PHOTO / CHRIS KJOBECH

Mario Savio (front row 2nd in from right) leads student protestors
at UC Berkeley Campus on Nov. 20, 1964

Mario, an Italian Catholic attended University of Manhattan and Queens College NY.
In 1963 he spent the summer improving sanitary problems by building facilities in
the slums of Taxco, Mexico. In 1964 he joined the 'Freedom Summer Project' in
Mississippi helping African Americans register to vote and teaching at the Freedom
School for Black children in McComb, Mississippi. Savio and another Civil Rights
worker were violently attacked by 2 men that summer. In the fall of 1964, Savio enrolled at UC Berkeley. He and others led protests at a San Francisco hotel that
refused to serve African Americans. At UC Berkeley all political activism was
banned. This fired up Savio and others who began student protests in the fall of 1964.

Peaceful Protest March in Washington DC 1963 for Equal Rights: for Jobs, Voting, Housing, Integrated Schools & Freedom for All

This Strike-March took place in Memphis, Tennessee. 700 African American Sanitation Workers took part because of dangerous working conditions that killed workers in garbage compactors. Racial discrimination and unfair wages were additional reasons for this protest from February 12th - April 16th, 1968.

San Francisco Nov 15.1969
Moratorium on Vietnam War

Women Protest Vietnam War with Arms locked
at Fort Dix Army Base, New Jersey 1969

AGENT ORANGE
THE LEGACY OF MISERY

U.S. aircraft sprayed approximately 20 million gallons of herbicides over Vietnam, Cambodia and Laos from 1961 to 1971 to destroy leaves and food crops. **AGENT ORANGE** containing the poisonous chemical 'Dioxin' was the most commonly used. An estimated 2.8 million U.S. vets were exposed to this deadly chemical and 3.5 million Vietnamese people.

The U.S. Department of Veteran Affairs has identified 13 deadly diseases and many cancers associated with exposure to Agent Orange. In addition, tens of thousands of individuals have suffered serious birth defects including missing and deformed limbs, cerebral palsy, spinal deterioration, and physical and mental disabilities. The debilitating effects of Agent Orange are now being passed to the third and fourth generation.

The wide use of Agent Orange over a ten year period has affected 4.5 million acres in 30 provinces. The soil and river pollution continues to poison the food chain and thwart vegetation growth. Nearly 50 percent of the country's mangroves, which protect the shoreline from typhoons and tsunamis were destroyed. The legacy of environmental devastation, deaths, suffering and birth deformities due to Agent Orange continues.

4 Killed 9 Wounded at Kent State,Ohio US National Guard Shoot Peaceful Student Protestors at Anti-War Rally

May 18, 1970

Newsweek

Protesters remember those killed in Vietnam in one week in a demonstration at the Nebraska State Capitol Building.

WHEN THE POWER OF LOVE OVERCOMES THE LOVE OF POWER, THE WORLD WILL KNOW PEACE

"Precious in the sight of the Lord is the death of His faithful servants."   Psalm 116:15

Evil people fear the righteous and hate their work of promoting MERCY, EQUALITY, JUSTICE and TRUTH. In opposition they promote lies, fear and greed, while ignoring corruption, immorality and violence.

God-haters in places of power do the bidding of their father the devil, a liar and deceiver from the beginning. He offers them power, wealth and prominence, if they will spew out his lies and resist all who serve the Living God and His Son Jesus Christ. The seductive goal they embrace, is to invite the *spirit of the ANTI-CHRIST to occupy greater places of authority in every sector of regional and national governing.*

Be on guard, stand firm in the faith. Don't be deceived by leaders who dispise God, Jews and Christians. They are engulfed in a *satanic spirit of strong DELUSION.*

Honor God. Speak the Truth. Be a light to all who need to escape the enemy's spell. Lift up Jesus Christ who lives! May the God of Peace be with us.

THE JESUS MOVEMENT SWEEPS ACROSS THE USA AND BEYOND 1967-79

The pictures in this section focus on Jesus People who are integral to this book in some way. The photos are time-period, thru the years, personal visits and a reunion.

Many lifetime friendships were forged in the Jesus Movement that remain. Amidst triumphs and joy, set-backs, or heartbreaking loss, mutual prayer and caring support continues. Jesus saved us and gave us a nurturing treasure of Koinonia friendships in Him.

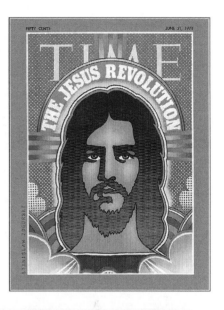

Carol Durkin Trott
Europe
Faithfully sharing her faith in Christ

ONE WAY TO HEAVEN

Arthur Blessitt, known as the Preacher on the 'Sunset Strip' left Hollywood CA in late 1969 to carry a 12 ft. wood cross to Washington DC. In 1970 he reached the Capitol where he fasted for 40 days in front of the Washington Monument.

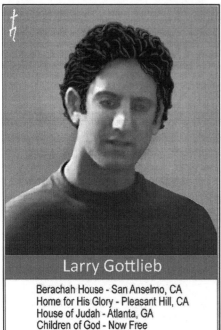

Larry Gottlieb

Berachah House - San Anselmo, CA
Home for His Glory - Pleasant Hill, CA
House of Judah - Atlanta, GA
Children of God - Now Free

(Left) Jack Sparks - Christian World Liberation Front
(Right) Duane Peterson - Hollywood Free Paper

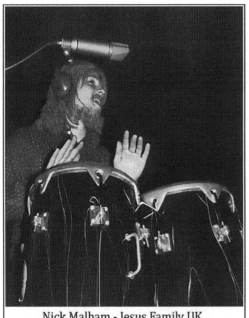

Nick Malham - Jesus Family UK
LONESOME STONE MUSICAL TEAM

D.E. Hoyt   Kent Philpott
SAN FRANCISCO, CALIFORNIA 1968

Margaret Keating Stiverson- Jesus Family UK
"Looking to Jesus the author and perfector of my faith."
Hebrews 12:2

Ethal Krauss Moore
Jesus Family UK & Lonesome Stone Theater Team

Caroline Green as 'Poppy'
in Lonesome Stone Theatre Show

D.E. HOYT - BEHIND DIGS
IN MANCHESTER, ENGLAND

Carol B.C. - Jesus Family UK
Lonesome Stone Promotion
Deo Gloria Trust

Karin Günnarsson Bienge
Jesus Family UK 1970's

Karin Günnarsson premarried in front of
The Living Room located at 41 Westow St.
Upper Norwood, London England UK

The Jesus Family's outreach in the UK began with their band The
Sheep performing concerts with testimonies woven in, followed by
Jim Palosarri preaching a clear Gospel message. The borough of
Watford, just northwest of London proper, was one of the early
sites chosen. This was a precursor to the Jesus Family launching
the multi-media rock musical 'Lonesome Stone.'

JUNE 30 1972

LIFE

The Great Jesus Rally in Dallas

Explo 72 was a 6 Day Rally and Training Event sponsored by Campus Crusade for Christ. *It ended up being one of the largest gatherings within the era of the 1970s Jesus Movement. Close to a million people participated from 72 different countries.*

This venue was intentionally inclusive, welcoming all who were curious about God, seekers and non religious alike. Street-people, hippies, straight, or those with Protestant or Catholic backgrounds and Jesus People made the trek. Most traveling distances took part in all the training sessions and evening worship.

The focus was on reaching out to high school and university age students with the Good News of Jesus Christ and providing personal training in various types of evangelism.

Day activites and training sessions were

attended by about 80,000 with nightly events soaring to around 100,000. The larger events were held in the Dallas Cotton Bown Stadium with Billy Graham preaching for six of the Bowl gatherings.

On Saturday, an 8 hour Music Concert was given to an audience of 200,000. The headliners of the concert were: Love Song, Larry Norman, Randy Matthews, The Archers, Children of the Day, Johnny Cash and Kris Kristofferson.

The response to the offer to receive Jesus Christ and live for God was massive, as was the desire to be trained in personal evangelism.

A university student who attended, researched what happened to those from the USA who had enrolled in all the training offered. He found a high percentage were now engaged in Christian ministry or service. Many had enrolled in Bible College or Seminary becoming pastors, teachers and chaplains. Others joined a Campus Ministry, a US Mission, or became missionaries abroad.

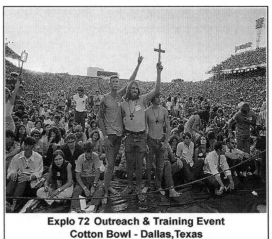

**Explo 72 Outreach & Training Event
Cotton Bowl - Dallas, Texas**

Siv Algotsson Spransy
Cast: LoneSome Stone Musical
Jesus Family UK

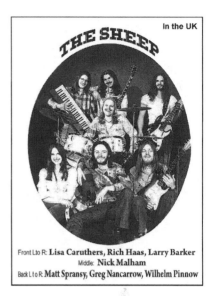

Front L to R: **Lisa Caruthers, Rich Haas, Larry Barker**
Middle: **Nick Malham**
Back L to R: **Matt Spransy, Greg Nancarrow, Wilhelm Pinnow**

Duane Peterson, editor of the (Christian) Hollywood Free Paper assisted in organizing and hosting this event. Worship and Praise was led by the bands listed around the image of The Palladium venue on Sunset Boulevard in Hollywood, California.

Iona Jones & Alison Yates
Greater Manchester, England
Baptized during early stages of the Jesus People in the UK
[See Chapter 20]

ARTHUR BLESSIT

Though raised in a church environment, Larry's life was turned upside down when he was 21 through a reconversion encounter with Jesus Christ. The year was 1968.

LARRY NORMAN

1947-2007

His band "People!" had been recording with Capitol Records since 1966 and had been on various tours for 3 years, opening for The Doors, The Who, Janis Joplin and Jimi Hendrix. During this time 'People!' had covered the tune 'I Love You' by The Zombies and scored a Billboard hit.

Now home they'd recorded their first album. To everyone's surprise, Larry quit the band on the day People!'s debut album was released. Larry's head and heart was now moving in a new direction.

Through his contacts with Capitol he was retained to write musicals for them. On his own he began writing Christ-centered tunes, incorporating his love for the blues, rock n roll, meaty lyrics and drawing inspiration from Elvis Presley and his African American home church.

The rest of his leisure time was spent on the streets of Hollywood telling people about Jesus. While out and about he was confronted by the needs he saw. In response, Norman gave most of his meager wages and royalty money to start a halfway house and buy food and clothes for new Christians.

In 1969 Larry released his first solo album 'Upon This Rock', followed by 'Street Level', 'Bootleg' and 'Only Visiting This Planet.' The rest is a long history of over a hundred albums. Some ot the songs that put him on the map were: *The Great American Novel, Why Should the Devil Have all the Good Music, The Outlaw, Jesus is the Rock that Doesn't Roll, I Wish We'd all Been Ready, and Why Don't You Look Into Jesus, He's Got the Answers.*

Larry performed at the White House twice and in Moscow at the 80,000 seat Olympic Stadium. He headlined venues like The Hollywood Bowl, The Sidney Opera House, The Palladium and London's prestigious Albert Hall which was sold out six times, two times on the same day!

Larry Norman had feet of clay and his life was not without missteps, heartache and pain. Someone else can do the judging and they did. His music was banned from almost all Christian Radio and many Christian Bookstores for most of his career. His lyrics and his music were considered too radical, political and socially disturbing! It rubbed too hard against 'staunch religious bigotry.' Larry was in good company, Joan Baez and Bob Dylan were banned for similar reasons.

Inspite of it all, Larry remained true to being a follower of Jesus Christ. He repented when he sinned and asked for forgiveness when he needed to. His gifts from God were used well. His life did make a difference! His place in heaven is secure.

In 2001 Larry Norman was inducted into the Gospel Music Hall of Fame alongside Elvis Presley

D.E. HOYT & RUSS GRIGGS

Ginny Hoyt & Sue Palosarri Cowper

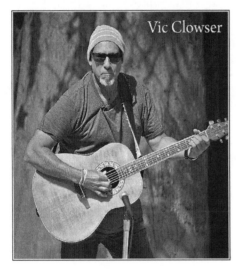

CHRIS FRAMPTON & D.E. HOYT

DAN PAULY & D.E. HOYT

Dave Maylon received Christ on the streets of London, England in the early 1970's. With but a few Bible verses scribbled on a small piece of paper by D.E.H., he began faithfully following Jesus. Fifty + amazing years have past filled with one-on-one evangelism, open air preaching and radio ministry. Dave and his wife Marie have three boys: Michael, Andrew and Simon and live in Bradford, West Yorkshire, Northern England - UK.

Jesus is Lord!

T. Lynn Nancarrow, Mary Damrow, Jenny Haas, Shereen Barker, Carol Trott
B. Lynn Malmberg & Ginny Hoyt

Fixing our eyes on Jesus, the author and perfecter of our faith. Hebrews 12:2 a

Russ Griggs Jim Palosaari Becky Griggs Ginny & D.E. Hoyt

GREG NANCARROW LARRY BARKER
ORIGINAL MEMBERS OF 'THE SHEEP'
2010 JP REUNION IN WISCONSIN

Caroline Wager Green
Jesus Family UK

Mary Damrow - JP Milwaukee 2011
"I will praise God's name in song and
and glorify Him with thanksgiving."
Psalm 69:30

Tucson AZ 2008

B. Bill Lowery & D.E.H.
F. Jed Palosaari, Vinnie Palombo, Jim Palosaari
Water-B&W

Camp Verde , AZ

FRED GARTNER & D.E. HOYT

South Coast of England · near Plymouth UK

Jesus the Christ

"My prayer is not that you take them out of the world, but that You would protect them from the evil one. They are not of the world, even as I am not of it.

Sanctify them by the Truth; Your Word is truth. As You sent me into the world, I have sent them into the world. For them I sanctify myself, that they too may be truly sanctified.

My prayer is not for them alone. I pray also for those who will believe in me through their message, that all of them may be One Father, just as You are in me and I am in You. May they also be in us so that the world may believe that You have sent me."

John 17:15-21

32

THE GOOD NEWS
The Gospel of God's Son, Jesus Christ

God sent His Son Jesus Christ into the world to reveal the Father and purchase eternal life for all who believe, receive and follow Him (John 3:16). God the Father, Jesus Christ and the Holy Spirit are One in all things, accomplishing and revealing God's eternal plan (John 10:30).

Birth of the Messiah

"God sent the angel Gabriel to Mary saying, 'Greetings, you who are highly favored! The Lord is with you.' Mary was shaken at his words and wondered what kind of greeting this might be. But the angel said to her, "Do not be afraid, Mary; you have found favor with God. You will conceive and give birth to a son, and you are to call him Jesus. He will be great and will be called the Son of the Most High. The Lord God will give him the throne of his father David, and he will reign over Jacob's descendants forever; his kingdom will never end."

"How will this be," Mary asked the angel, "since I am a virgin?"

The angel answered, "The Holy Spirit will come upon you, and the power of the Most High will overshadow you. So the Holy One to be born will be called the "Son of God." Even Elizabeth your relative is going to have a child in her old age, and she who was said to be unable to conceive is in her sixth month. For no word from God will ever fail; nothing is impossible with God! (Luke 1:28-37)"

God also spoke to Joseph, betrothed to Mary, through an angel in a dream saying, "Joseph son of David, do not be afraid to take Mary home as your wife, because what is conceived in her is from the Holy Spirit. She will give birth to a son, and you are to give him the name Jesus, because he will save his people from their sins (Matthew 1:20-21)."

Meanwhile, Zechariah and spouse Elizabeth in the hill country of Judea gave birth to a baby God instructed them to call John. Zechariah the father said, "And you, my child, will be a prophet of the Most High; for you will go on before the Lord to prepare the way for him, to give his people the knowledge of salvation through the forgiveness of their sins, because of the tender mercy of our God, by which the rising sun will come to us from heaven to shine on those living in darkness and in the shadow of death, to guide our feet into the path of peace" (Luke 1:76-79).

Simultaneously God directed wise men from the east to follow a star to worship the new king of the Jews to be born (Matthew 2:1-2). On the night of Jesus' birth, "There were shepherds living out in the fields nearby, keeping watch over their flocks at night. An angel of the Lord appeared to them, and the glory of the Lord shone around them, and they were terrified. But the angel said to them, "Do not be afraid. I bring you good news that will cause great joy for all the people. Today in the town of David a Savior has been born to you; he is the Messiah, the Lord. This will be a sign to you: You will find a baby wrapped in cloths and lying in a manger."

> "Suddenly a great company of the heavenly host appeared with the angel, praising God and saying, 'Glory to God in the highest heaven, and on earth peace to those on whom his favor rests.'"   Luke 2:8-14.'" NIV®

Bearing Witness: Jesus the Messiah

In accordance with Jewish law, Mary and Joseph took Jesus to the temple in Jerusalem to be dedicated to the Lord. In the temple courts they encountered God's servant Simeon. "He was waiting for the consolation of Israel, and the Holy Spirit was on him. It had been revealed to him by the Holy Spirit that he would not die before he had seen the Lord's Messiah. Moved by the Spirit, he went into the temple courts. When the parents brought in the child Jesus to do for him what the custom of the Law required, Simeon took him in his arms and praised God, saying: 'Sovereign Lord, as you have promised, you may now dismiss your servant in peace.

For my eyes have seen your salvation, which you have prepared in the sight of all nations: a light for revelation to the Gentiles, and the glory of your people Israel.'"

Then Simeon blessed them and said to Mary, his mother: "This child is destined to cause the falling and rising of many in Israel, and to be a sign that will be spoken against, so that the thoughts of many hearts will be revealed. And a sword will pierce your own soul too."

There was also a prophet, Anna, the daughter of Penuel, of the tribe of Asher. She was very old; she had lived with her husband seven years after her marriage, and then was a widow until she was eighty-four. She never left the temple but worshiped night and day, fasting and praying. Coming up to them at that very moment, she gave thanks to God and spoke about the child to all who were looking forward to the redemption of Jerusalem.

When Joseph and Mary had done everything required by the Law of the Lord, they returned to Galilee to their own town of Nazareth. And the child grew and became strong; he was filled with wisdom, and the grace of God was on him." (Luke 2:25b-40)

At Jesus' baptism, the Scriptures record this about what occurred, "Just as Jesus was coming up out of the water; he (John the Baptist) saw heaven being torn open and the Holy Spirit descending on him like a dove. At this same moment a voice from heaven spoke, "This is My Son, whom I love; with Him I am well pleased." (Matthew 3:16-17)

The Temptation of Jesus

Jesus was then led by the Holy Spirit into the wilderness to be tempted by the devil. He fasted for forty days and nights. At the end of this time He faced Satan, overcoming the tempter without sinning. Jesus faithfully honored His Father in all He said and did, resisting the devil (Matthew 4:1-11).

The Heart of the Good News

Jesus calls us to repent of evil doing and believe God sent Him into the world as Savior/Messiah for all of mankind. When we believe in Jesus Christ we are born of the Spirit of God and we receive the gift of eternal life (John 3:1-21). God confirms Jesus is the Savior of the world by speaking Words of Truth from the Father, by many miraculous signs and wonders. Through healing, raising the dead, feeding thousands, controlling the elements and nature and by casting out demons Jesus demonstrated He is God's Son, Lord of heaven and earth, King of kings and the Lord of Lords (Luke 4:36, 5:17, 9:1, 24:19, 24:30, John 10:38, Acts 10:38, Romans 5:6, I Corinthians 15:20-28).

> It is by God's mercy and grace that we have been saved, not because of anything good we have done (Ephesians 2:8, Romans 11:16). "All of us are unclean and sinful; all our righteous acts are like filthy rags (rotten garbage) (Isaiah 64:6a)." NIV®

Jesus taught us to seek the kingdom of heaven first and represent His kingdom here on earth (Matthew 6:33). He commissions us follow Him, to take up our cross daily (Matthew 4:19, Mark 8:34), to stay alert and ready (Matthew 25:1-13, Mark 13:33, I Peter 4:7), filled with the Holy Spirit (Acts 1:1-11), to follow his example by rescuing the lost (Luke 15:4-7) and to make disciples (Matthew 28:19, John 15:1-17).

The Death of Jesus the Christ

Jesus gave up His life voluntarily in obedience to the Father (John 10:14-18). He was crucified, died and was buried, sealing the New Covenant with His broken body and shed blood to free all who receive and believe Him (Matthew 26:28-29, I Corinthians 15:1-8). On the day of Jesus' death the curtain in the temple was torn in two, from top to bottom, the earth shook and the rocks split. Tombs of many holy people who had died broke open and they were raised to life. The Roman centurion and guards at the crucifixion site exclaimed, "Surely he was the Son of God!" (Matthew 27:50-54).

The Resurrection of Jesus Christ

Death was swallowed up in Victory! On the third day after Jesus' death, there was a violent earthquake. An angel of God rolled back the gravestone to reveal Jesus had risen, conquering death, and told the women disciples who had come to the tomb exactly what had happened (Matthew 28:2-4). Jesus appeared first to Mary Magdalene, out of whom he had driven seven demons (Mark 16:9). He then appeared to other women disciples saying "Do not be afraid. Go tell my brothers to go to Galilee, there they will see me" (Matthew 28:2-10).

The apostle Paul revisits the Resurrection of Jesus. "For what I received I passed on to you as of first importance: that Christ died for our sins according to the Scriptures, that he was buried, that he was raised on the third day and that he appeared to Peter (Cephas), and then to the Twelve. After that, He appeared to more than five hundred of the brothers and sisters at the same time, most of whom are still living, though some have fallen asleep. Then he appeared to James, then to all the apostles, and last of all he appeared to me also, as to one abnormally born" (I Corinthians 15:3-8). Jesus now sits at the right hand of the Majesty on High forever making intercession for His own (Hebrew 1:1-3, John 17:20-26).

God's amazing work of providing salvation for all who believe in Him includes our reception and diligence to walk in the Truth and Light of Jesus Christ.

Standing Firm

God the Father, His Son Jesus Christ and the Holy Spirit are One. They teach us to resist the devil and his demons and every deception we encounter in Jesus' Name (I Peter 5:8, Revelation 12:10-11, Ephesians 6:10-19), James 4:7, Acts 16:18. Again,

> "Be on your guard; stand firm in the faith; be courageous; be strong."   I Corinthians 16:13 NIV®

WHAT IS TO COME

THE RISE OF THE ANTI-CHRIST

"All people, great and small, rich and poor, free and slave, were forced to receive a mark on their right hands or on their foreheads, so that they could not buy or sell, unless they had the mark, which is the name of the beast or the number of its name. This calls for wisdom. Let the person who has insight calculate the number of the beast, for it is the number of a man. That number is 666."   Revelation 13:16-18

Jesus warns: "For false messiahs and false prophets will appear and perform great signs and wonders to deceive, if possible, even the elect. See, I have told you ahead of time. "So if anyone tells you, 'There he is, out in the wilderness,' do not go out; or, 'Here he is, in the inner rooms,' do not believe it."   Matthew 24:24-26 NIV®

THE BEASTS AND THEIR FALSE PROPHET

BEAST OUT OF THE SEA

"The dragon stood on the shore of the sea. And I saw a beast coming out of the sea. It had ten horns and seven heads, with ten crowns on its horns, and on each head a blasphemous name. The beast I saw resembled a leopard, but had feet like those of a bear and a mouth like that of a lion. The dragon gave the beast his power and his throne and great authority. One of the heads of the beast seemed to have had a fatal wound, but the fatal wound had been healed. The whole world was filled with wonder and followed the beast. People worshiped the dragon because he had given authority to the beast, and they also worshiped the beast and asked, 'Who is like the beast? Who can wage war against it?'"

The beast was given a mouth to utter proud words and blasphemies and to exercise its authority for forty-two months. It opened its mouth to blaspheme God, and to slander his name and his dwelling place and those who live in heaven. It was given power to wage war against God's holy people and to conquer them. And it was given authority over every tribe, people, language and nation. All inhabitants of the earth will worship the beast—all whose names have not been written in the Lamb's book of life, the Lamb who was slain from the creation of the world (Revelation 20:1-9).

BEAST OUT OF THE EARTH

"Then I saw a second beast, coming out of the earth. It had two horns like a lamb, but it spoke like a dragon. It exercised all the authority of the first beast on its behalf, and made the earth and its inhabitants worship the first beast, whose fatal wound had been healed. And it performed great signs, even causing fire to come down from heaven to the earth in full view of the people.

Because of the signs it was given power to perform on behalf of the first beast, it deceived the inhabitants of the earth. It ordered them to set up an image in honor of the beast who was wounded by the sword and yet lived. The second beast was given power to give breath to the image of the first beast, so that the image could speak and cause all who refused to worship the image to be killed. It also forced all people, great and small, rich and poor, free and slave, to receive a mark on their right hands or on their foreheads, so that they could not buy or sell unless they had the mark, which is the name of the beast or the number of its name.

This calls for wisdom. Let the person who has insight calculate the number of the beast, for it is the number of a man. That number is 666 (Revelation 13:11-18)."

Jesus said, "You will be hated by everyone because of me, but the one who stands firm to the end will be saved." Matthew 10:22 NIV®

The Return of Jesus Christ the Messiah

"Then will appear the sign of the Son of Man in heaven. And then all the peoples of the earth will mourn when they see the Son of Man coming on the clouds of heaven, with power and great glory. And he will send his angels with a loud trumpet call, and they will gather his elect from the four winds, from one end of the heavens to the other (Matthew 24:30-31)."

God's prophet Daniel said, "In my vision at night I looked, and there before me was one like a Son of Man, coming with the clouds of heaven. He approached the Ancient of Days and was led into his presence. He was given authority, glory and sovereign power; all nations and peoples of every language worshiped him. His dominion is an everlasting dominion that will not pass away, and his kingdom is one that will never be destroyed (Daniel 7:13-14)."

It is God who will vanquish darkness and evil! Satan was defeated when Jesus died. Phase two of his doom will begin when he is bound during Jesus Christ's thousand year reign on earth (Revelation 20:1-3). In heaven a new song was sung to honor Jesus the Lion of the tribe of Judah, who has triumphed, "You are worthy to take the scroll and to open its seals, because you were slain, and with your blood you purchased for God persons from every tribe and language and people and nation. You have made them to be a kingdom and priests to serve our God, and they will reign on the earth (Revelation 5:9-10)."

"I saw thrones on which were seated those who had been given authority to judge. And I saw the souls of those who had been beheaded because of their testimony about Jesus and because of the Word of God. They had not worshiped the beast or its image and had not received its mark on their foreheads or their hands. They came to life and reigned with Christ a thousand years (The rest of the dead did not come to life until the thousand years were ended). This is the first resurrection. Blessed and holy are those who share in the first resurrection. The second death has no power over them, but they will be priests of God and of Christ and will reign with him for a thousand years (Revelation 20:4-6)."

SATAN'S FINAL DOOM

When the thousand years are over, Satan will be released from his prison and go out to deceive the nations.

He will make war against God, His people and the city He loves. Satan's last attempt to lead an army against the Almighty God and His Son Jesus, will fail and he will meet his final doom (Revelation 20:7-9). "And the devil which deceived them was thrown into the lake of burning sulfur, where the beast and the false prophet had been thrown. They will be tormented day and night forever and ever.(Revelation 20:10)."

Final Things

This calls for patient endurance on the part of the people of God who keep his commands and remain faithful to Jesus (Revelation 14:12). A new heaven and earth will follow (Revelation chapters 21-22). "Beyond all question, the mystery from which true godliness springs is great: He (Jesus) appeared in the flesh, was vindicated by the Spirit, was seen by angels, was preached among the nations, was believed on in the world, was taken up in glory (I Timothy 3:16)."

"Look, I am coming soon! My reward is with me, and I will give to each person according to what they have done. I am the Alpha and the Omega, the First and the Last, the Beginning and the End.

Blessed are those who wash their robes, that they may have the right to the tree of life and may go through the gates into the city. Outside are the dogs, those who practice magic arts, the sexually immoral, the murderers, the idolaters and everyone who loves and practices falsehood.

I, Jesus, have sent my angel to give you this testimony for the churches. I am the Root and the Offspring of David, and the bright Morning Star."   Revelation 22:12-16 NIV®

"I am the Alpha and the Omega," says the Lord God, "who is, and who was, and who is to come, the Almighty."

Revelation 1:8

APPENDIX

The Complexity of Cults and Recovery

Author's Note: This portion of the book is not for underage readers or adults who would be traumatized by exposure to accounts of severe abuse of children, teens and adults by cult leaders and members.

We hope to help readers identify what cults are by citing some overarching types and giving specific examples of recent or active cults on the world stage. Some readers may still be involved in a group that you're unsure about. What follows should be insightful to help you make an intelligent decision about distancing yourself from any group who makes outrageous claims about their special leader or leaders, their uniqueness above every other group in the world, or seeks to manipulate and use you, exploit you financially and in extreme cults, remove freedom of movement and almost all personal choices. When we hear or read news coverage about a bizarre event surrounding a cult, a common question arises: "Why would anyone join this group!?"

The Invite

There are numerous contributing factors which make individuals susceptible to a cult's invite and subsequent joining. Affluent cults target professionals, highly educated individuals, well known personalities and those with influence and money. The majority of cults recruit from any spectrum of society. Almost all cults have multi-pronged luring points: secrecy and intrigue, promotion of being able to go deeper into special revelations (which may include rituals and secret rites), a sensual or marriage draw, overwhelming love and acceptance shown to new members (love bombing), lodging, food and friendships, the offer of a Cause and Special Mission to pour one's life and energy into. Others delineate the unique spiritual benefits of being under God's special End-Time leader or leaders, and the honor of being a recipient of updated divine guidance when part of this Specially Chosen Group.

Cult Variations

Using a broad brush-stroke, cults span a wide spectrum, each unique. In spite of differences, a common denominator is the control which they have, and seek to maintain over their followers. It may be mental, emotional, sexual, financial, physical, social, spiritual or demonic. Most cults embody a combination of these.

Cults are clever at finding connecting points with potential followers. In addition to whatever this may be, an unseen force is at work that can blindside even smart level headed individuals. It is the presence of evil spirits who cloak themselves and dispense a spell of deception. The Bible describes it in this way

> "Now the Holy Spirit speaks clearly; in the last days, some will leave the faith and be swept up into listening to and following 'seducing spirits and doctrines of devils."
>
> I Timothy 4:1 NIV®

This warning is directed to Christ-followers, but applies to everyone. *It's important to understand, evil spirits covertly control every cult, past, present and future.* They indoctrinate with intensity and seek to seduce anyone who will buy into their lies.

Some cults isolate members from the outside world for a period of time; others require permanent separation from the world. All cults expect 100% loyalty, no questioning of authority, full allegiance to the cause, teachings and doctrines. The largest disadvantage for new recruits is—*they don't have a full picture of what they're getting into.* Cults are notorious for weaving in doses of deception until the loyalty of new recruits is achieved. Loyalty and support is what cults want. Once a member is firmly entrenched, no one knows the direction a cult may take in the future.

To stay in the group, new members have no choice but to yield to certain requirements immediately, or leave if able. Submitting to a cult's protocol demands is non-negotiable. Underage children and teens whose parents join are innocent victims; entering a bizarre world of darkness. Most are subjected to an onslaught of indoctrination.

Big Cults with Social Status

In the past two centuries, hundreds of cults have surfaced on the world stage. Some religious cults have gained social acceptance by cloaking their bizarre beliefs and practices. Mormons, Jehovah's Witnesses and Scientology are among these. Insiders in these groups acknowledge there is plenty of secrecy about their true beliefs and practices which are intentionally kept from the public. These three cults allow freedom of movement within society and use social and financial assets to strengthen and promote the group's cause and expansion. This does not make them less dangerous! It means society has let its guard down. These cults do everything possible to avoid attention, while still holding to their secret rites, practices and beliefs which are diametrically opposed to mainstream society and Christianity.

Both Mormons and Jehovah's Witnesses departed from their Christian roots and replaced the truth in the Bible with a twist of interpretation or revelations that set both groups apart as *the new end-time holders of divine truth.* The Mormons make this distinction in their name, calling themselves Latter Day Saints. When interacting with either of these two groups, or their teachings, *a distinct difference of beliefs separate them from mainstream Christianity and each other.* In carefully reading the Book of Mormon I found numerous passages that specifically attacked Christians and put them in a bad light. The same *anti-Christian spirit is pervasive in other religious cults*. It might not be in written form as it is in the Book of Mormon, but the same sentiment of, *'We have the latest and most accurate truths from our leaders and God and Christians are out of the loop.'*

Radical Cults

Extreme and radical cults draw more scrutiny because of social outcry, media coverage, and criminal indictments and convictions. Sadly, many dangerous religious cults elude detection and move about under the radar until numerous complaints force local law enforcement authorities or government agencies to investigate. At this late stage, cult followers may be thoroughly indoctrinated, be defensive of the group's beliefs, or have accepted that any questioning by authorities from the outside is 'persecution.'

Cult members who have been forced to compromise themselves sexually, or conscience-wise, may be so deeply entrenched they are unable to acknowledge they've been led astray by bad teachings and practices. Any number of things can create 'a closed mindset' to outside intervention.

Cults that come under social and criminal scrutiny are usually quick to relocate if there's opportunity to do so. Many cult leaders have resorted to 'life on the run' to avoid criminal prosecution and being sentenced to prison.

Political, Religious, Terrorist and Hate-Cults

The rise of political, religious, terrorist and hate-cults in the 21st century is a sobering reality. Al Qaeda, the Taliban, Isis, Boko Haram, Lashkar-E-Taiba, Al-shabaab, Hamas, Hezbollah and similar groups are fueled by hate. They recruit and train members to torture, mutilate, kill, be human-shields or suicide-bombers, dispense chemical weapons, or by any means possible, incite terror by murdering and maiming their perceived enemies and the innocent.

Child programming recruitment is a viable tool used by these cults. Taliban controlled elementary schools called 'Madrassas' have the highest potential for students being radicalized and recruited by terrorist organizations. They perpetuate an exclusionary world view within Islamic sects and loathing toward the western world and other religious Faiths. Though smaller in number than public schools, their radical ideals continue to have a strong influence in various regions of Pakistan and Afghanistan.

The pendulum swings in many of these schools from moderate to radical indoctrination. Some teach bomb-making and encourage students to consider becoming suicide bombers. Adult influence of this type from sunrise to sunset does terrible things to minds and hearts of young recipients. Destructive indoctrination or abuse of children during formative years can cripple, twist, or make monsters out of them and this is exactly what happens in radical Jihadist settings.

Taliban, Al Qaeda, Isis and other radically controlled education facilities that exist in some Arab countries teach an ideology of destroying all enemies, including fellow Muslims and annihilating "western infidels." Most of these radical schools are deficient in standard curriculum and teaching resources.

This is an example of terrorist-cult practices of indoctrination that brainwash the minds of young and older children to perpetuate a Jihadist mentality and further the cause of terrorism.

The Occult

Satan worship, Santeria, Spiritism, Voodoo, Shaman practices, Witch-craft/Wicca, New Age and Mystical religions lead followers knowingly, or unknowingly, into contact with the devil and his demons. New agers may not realize what lies beneath the surface, but it's not God or truth!

Racist, Religious Supremacy, Family or Societal Cults

Racist or religious supremacy groups that promote ethnic or religious cleansing are akin to terrorist cults who kill their opponents. Communal, sexual, survivalist, ancestral worship or family controlled groups, or extreme personality, philosophical and self-help groups run the gamut from being unsafe to extremely dangerous.

Religious Cults

Religious cults are usually centered on a leader, idols of worship and/or beliefs and teachings. Man-made religions date back to the earliest records of human history. Multiple thousands of pagan gods, statues and idols have been fashioned and worshiped.

> *Worship of a man-made idol is a poor substitute for contact with the Invisible God who created everything in the universe.*

Elevating, or attributing superior status to a human being who is flawed and sinful is always misplaced trust. There is only One Holy God who alone is worthy of praise and adoration.

Because someone "claims to be" a seer, a prophet, the messiah, or some type of end-time revelator with insights no one else has, does not make it true! God followers and seekers can be misled by the appearance of light, wisdom and crumbs of spiritual truth that are often borrowed or twisted to promote a religion, or a religious leader's purposes and agenda.

The Seeker's Dilemma

A universal problem is discerning what is true, by sifting through a myriad of religious choices. Stone's song, Where Do We Go From Here? pinpoints the predicament.

> "There's a thousand roads to take. Is there one that's meant for me? There's a thousand plans to make. Will they help me in eternity? Is there something in the stars? Is there someone in control? Do I have to go to Mars—to end this searching of my soul?"

Our souls are hungry for meaning and truth, which launches an ensuing search. Where to look is the next hurdle to jump. Many religions and cults have pagan or man-made origins. Some have evolved from seekers like Gautama Buddha into an expansive religion he would not support or recognize. Man-made religions and cults exist in contrast to "a personal relationship with the True and Living God, who desires to be worshiped in Spirit and in Truth."

Counterfeits of God are routinely mysterious and secretive when it comes to revealing all they believe, or the numerous rituals their followers must eventually adhere to in order to be accepted by God, become a god, or to maintain good standing within a group.

Deceptive religious cults lead their followers into serious and long-lasting spiritual error, fleece them of their money, exploit them sexually and use them as 'work slaves' from sunrise to sunset. Routinely this involves recruiting and promoting and selling items the cult has produced. In worst case scenarios leaders coerce or force followers into mass-suicide deaths. Cults are dangerous!

Preview of What's to Come

It's extremely difficult to fully understanding what former cult members have experienced, seen, participated in, or been threatened and forced to do. The specific types of things cult victims are subjected to, the bizarre nature and horrors of these practices and the harm caused will be covered in the pages ahead with statements from cult members and survivors.

Gaining physical freedom from a radical controlling cult may or may not be possible. Dislodging harmful indoctrination is another hurdle. The hardest thing any cult survivor will do is "come to terms with the unhealthy things they've learned, supported and practiced." *Getting bad stuff out of your head and heart is a cleansing process that takes time.* What ex-cult members face when they leave a group is basically pushing the restart button on life—with memories still in place, often torturous haunting ones—which include toxic doctrines and practices still influencing and lingering.

What does cult recovery look like and how does it happen? This delicate subject will be explored.

Due to the wide range of cult groups and levels of involvement, each person who's been in one will have a different experience. Some cults that span decades have had leader, doctrine and practice changes which have made it better for some members and worse for others. For those who are still involved in a questionable group relationally, emotionally, or spiritually, I hope the substance of this chapter will cause caution to rise up in you and enlist strength to do whatever is necessary to free yourself from any destructive and manipulative influence.

A Personal Word

If you're currently in a cult, or a cult survivor, my heart goes out to you. I can't begin to convey the compassion and love in Christ I feel and send to you! I've been praying for you to have strength, discernment, clearness of thinking, courage to do the right thing and to not give up on Jesus Christ. I know it's possible to return to an honest uncomplicated relationship with God. I know His love and grace is greater than all of our sins and missteps. **Listen carefully to what the Lord might be saying and read with an open mind and heart.**

Six Cults

Tragedy, heartbreak, abuse and death are a part of a larger trail of sorrows cults leave behind in their wake. In the past fifty years six cults have been in the 'public eye' for good reason. They are:

- 'Heaven's Gate' Community
- 'The Branch Davidians' of Waco, Texas
- 'Jim Jones' People's Temple USA & Jonestown, Guyana'
- 'Scientology'
- 'The Unification Church' Rev. Sun Moon
- 'The Children of God' aka 'Family of Love' aka, 'The Family'—now called , 'The Family International'

Scientology, The Unification Church and The Family International are still active in numerous countries under a cloak of respectability and affluence. The Family International falsely promotes themselves as Christian.

Heaven's Gate Community—aka 'The Space Cult'

In the 1970s, Marshall Applewhite and Bonnie Nettles came to believe that they were the two witnesses referenced in chapter 11 of the Book of Revelation. They used apocalyptic prophecies to persuade followers that salvation would come in the form of a spaceship. People who wandered into their nomadic monastery located in an expansive mansion in San Diego County had to cut themselves off from their families and their previous lives. There were rules that controlled what people wore and ate, not to mention what they believed.

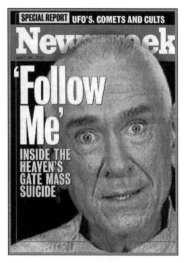

The group's beliefs shifted over the years after the death of Nettles. The group's hope of being taken bodily in a spaceship did not occur. They'd hoped to be kept in such a ship in a cocoon state, until a full transformation into heaven. *In March 1997, all 39 members were found dead from apparent suicide in preparation for their transition to heaven.* It was surmised they settled for their souls being transported to the spaceship.

Branch Davidians—Waco, Texas

"HIS NAME WAS DEATH AND HELL FOLLOWED WITH HIM." Revelation 6:8

David Koresh, expelled from the Seventh Day Adventist church, joined the Branch Davidians. In time he became the leader of this 20th century cult—which would meet a violent and controversial end in Waco, Texas. Among Koresh's controversial teachings was his New Light doctrine. This teaching declared all women in the group were his rightful spiritual wives, including under-age girls and women already married. Cult members overlooked his sexual exploits, accepting this to be part of his calling.

He declared himself to be the messiah and taught the apocalypse was imminent. To prepare, Koresh amassed a large firearms arsenal for self-defense. After a 51 day stand-off with US Federal ATF officers, the ATF battered the walls of the cult's compound and sent in tear gas in February of 1993 on illegal weapons charges.

Unfortunately, a fire broke out inside the compound and 80 cult members died. Sixty adults including Koresh, and twenty children, were killed in this tragedy. The cause of the fire remains inconclusive.

A Cult Survivor's Take on this Confrontation:

"The absence of a number of creative ideas to engage David Koresh in dialogue from 'supposed cult experts' heightened this growing crisis. There should have been multiple attempts at negotiating with Koresh and the exploration of a variety of solutions to avoid a confrontation. With ATF officers, cult counselors, and other government officials all privy to the Branch Davidians having a stockpile of weapons and beliefs in an imminent apocalypse— *the only positive option was to defuse the situation.*

Understandably, ATF and other government officials grew weary and impatient as this stand-off dragged on for days, then weeks and neared two months. What were these cult experts doing? Were they brainstorming creatively on communication tactics and compromises with Koresh? Were they building relational bridges, or at a standstill? Had the government and ATF officials shut-down taking any advice from cult counselors? We do not know; but we do know when practical options other than confrontation grew scarce, a tragedy loomed.

When ATF sent in tanks to ram the compound and used tear-gas to control those inside, all of us who've been in a cult knew immediately this was not going to end well for Koresh and his followers. Confrontation with this type of cult will never work. *It didn't have to end this way!*"

BRANCH DAVIDIANS COMPOUND
80 Cult members died in this tragedy - 60 adults & 20 children

Jim Jones' People's Temple

Jim Jones was a Pentecostal preacher. Although white, Jones attracted a diverse ethnic representation in his congregations by his expressed beliefs in integration and racial equality.

Jones began the People's Temple in the 1950s. The group moved from Indianapolis, Indiana to Ukiah, California in 1965. The next step was planting a church in San Francisco and another in Los Angeles. Both thrived with diverse ethnic representation. In the early 1970's Jones began building a commune called 'Jonestown' named after himself in Guyana, South America, when authorities began looking into allegations of fraud and abuse. His paranoia was justified as investigations intensified in the coming years.

Then, in 1977 Jones learned of an upcoming scathing exposé on the life of 'People's Temple.' His church was accused by the media of financial fraud, physical abuse of its members and mistreatment of children. Fearful and paranoid of what might unfold in this investigation, he and his loyal congregation made the decision to speed up the building of Jonestown in Guyana, South America with the aim of fleeing the USA as soon as possible. Some 500 members of Jones' People's Temple had already traveled to Jonestown to help build a 'Socialist Utopia' on a tract of land surrounded by jungle

With numerous reports of "cult abuse" by former members—combined with human rights violations filtering back to relatives of members—US Congressman of California, Leo Ryan, agreed to investigate.

Jonestown—Far from Paradise!

For those who had given their sweat and life's energy to constructing Jonestown, it was not turning out to be the paradise their leader had promised. Temple members who were able, worked 10 hour days and were subjected to various punishments if they questioned Jones' authority. Their passports were confiscated, their letters home were censored and members were encouraged to inform on one another. By this time Jones was teaching a form of communist socialism he'd imported from North Korea,

China and Russia and required members to attend evening indoctrination sessions and watch films on socialist doctrines and practices. Exhaustion was setting in.

Those closest to Jones said he was declining mentally and had become addicted to drugs. The ongoing duress of the government and media investigations had made him extremely paranoid and irrational. Jones was convinced the U.S. government and others were out to destroy him. Around this time Jones instituted the "White Nights rehearsals" which entailed a mass-suicide vote and a mock suicide drill where all present drank from a cup of grape cool-aid.

Jonestown had become a confusing, troubling and potentially unsafe place to live. Some Temple members were calm, fully indoctrinated, armed with weapons and ready for anything. Many were alarmed, without the resources or means to leave.

In November of 1978 US Congressman from California Leo Ryan decided to visit Guyana for himself, accompanied by a delegation of 18 others which included reporters and cameramen. After arriving in Guyana, Ryan negotiated with Jones to conduct interviews at Jonestown with cult members to substantiate, or disprove negative reports.

Jones finally agreed. After two days of interviews, group members began asking Ryan to help them escape. At this same time, cult leaders learned that at least '14 Temple members wanted to escape.' Shortly after, Ryan was attacked by a cult member wielding a knife. At this point, Congressman Ryan and his team knew their lives were in jeopardy. In haste, Ryan's group made their way to the nearby airstrip where two planes were standing by.

On Nov. 18, 1978, while preparing to leave, Jones' followers ambushed and opened fire on Ryan's party at the airstrip. Congressman Leo Ryan, three

journalists, and one cult member seeking to escape, died of gunshot wounds. Several others were wounded but survived.

Later that day, *Jones convinced his congregation to kill themselves by ingesting a poison (cyanide) laced punch. It's believed, those wanting to leave with Ryan and many other cult members who were unwilling to participate in the mass suicide, were forced to drink the poisonous punch at gun-point.* This hypothesis was surmised by the large amount of guns confiscated at the mass suicide site.

Amazingly, a small handful of cult members ran into the nearby jungle and escaped being detected. In all, more than 918 people died, including 283 children. The death total includes cult members at Jonestown, a small contingency of Jones' followers at Georgetown, and California Congressman Leo Ryan and part of his delegation.

Scientology

Science fiction writer L. Ron Hubbard founded the Church of Scientology in 1952. For years Ron Hubbard's book, 'Dianetics' was advertised and sold on television. It promised to unlock the keys to personal well being, but in reality, it was a come-on introduction to one of the more High Powered cults of today.

The goal of this group is to recruit the wealthy and powerful, high profile celebrity personalities, worldwide government officials—and one day take over the world via the ORG aka the Organization. Time magazine named Scientology "The Cult of Greed." 'The Church of Scientology' has become a reflection of the wealth it possesses, decorating its facilities with opulence and luxury in harmony with mostly affluent members.

Scientology teaching is based on "Alien Mythology" and high intensity one-on-one recorded auditing in closed-door sessions. The stated goal of the audit process is to aid members in achieving a Clear status from damaging life, or previous life memories. Auditors listen, akin to therapy counseling, for the purpose of assisting participants in debriefing from past pain.

In the formation days of Scientology, the group rented office spaces and handed out flyers on the streets, offering free personality tests to lure in possible recruits. I visited one of their operations in Southern California many years ago. After completing the personality test, a staff member reviewed it with me. Next, came a sales pitch encouraging the study of

Scientology and being audited. As I recall the audit fees were substantial, considerably beyond my means.

Today, with an abundance of money in its coffers, Scientology's previous recruitment tactics have long since been replaced by refinement and the formation of approximately 1,100 churches. Unorthodox Worship Services are one of Scientology's means of introducing their beliefs and gaining new members.

Bizarre Alien Beliefs

One of the main beliefs of the Church of Scientology is a teaching stating everyone's soul has been damaged. Souls are damaged because the souls of **3.5 trillion aliens were banished to earth by a Warlord named Xenu.** The aliens, called Thetans, were put into volcanoes and then destroyed by nuclear bombs. Scientology's role is to help people now occupied by Thetans shed these and other harmful memories through being audited.

Scientology has developed a very sophisticated system of teaching which encompasses many levels and advanced steps beyond these. The median price for navigating through the group's entire curriculum runs about $380,000. Most Scientology participants don't realize this—paying for and studying one level at a time.

Scientology, like most cults is growing rapidly, endeavoring to establish legitimacy in societies around the globe. It fiercely goes after those who oppose them. Defectors are viewed as enemies. Many have lost their families into the cult. *There have been at least 10 suspicious deaths* associated with those who have either left Scientology, or have exposed the evils and control manipulation of the cult. Are Scientology beliefs strange? Is this cult dangerous? What do you think?

The Reverend Sun Myung Moon & Hak Ja Han True Father, True Mother—The Messiah [Case Study]

Moon's family converted to Christianity when he was age 10 and joined the Presbyterian Church. Moon's early vocational interest was studying electrical engineering in Tokyo, Japan.

During these years and beyond he was a social activist against North Korean communism. In 1947 he was sentenced to five years imprisonment in North Korea for spying for South Korea, but was liberated by the US troops three years into his sentence during the Korean War.

In 1954 Moon founded the Unification Church in Seoul, Korea. His teachings viewed the Cold War between democracy and communism as the final conflict between God and Satan. At his new church he preached a conservative family-orientated value system and his own interpretation of the Bible. He taught adamantly against communism which would be a lifetime passion.

Messiah Status & Doctrine

Moon claimed that at the age of 15, Jesus anointed him to carry out his unfinished work by becoming "A Parent" to all of humanity aka "True

Father." *Moon and an early disciple wrote a book called "Divine Principle" which gained the status of scripture within the Unification Church.* Moon incorporated some of the teachings of older Korean minister Kim Baek-moon who said Jesus had also given him a mission. Kim Baek's

was to establish the 'new Israel' on earth. Sun Moon considered Kim to be a John the Baptist figure who preceded him, paving the way for Moon as the 'Messiah.'

Moon married his second wife Hak Ja Han in 1960 just after her

17th birthday. Moon called her the "True Mother" and she and Moon were referred to as the "True Parents." Moon taught Jesus was divine, but not God. Moon was the second Adam Messiah, who would create the perfect family that would lead to humanity's liberation. The task of physically redeeming mankind was left to the "True Parents." Moon and Han would link married couples and their families to God. Han would give birth to 14 children who were to be called "True Children."

The Divine Principle says about Moon: "With the fullness of time, God has sent one person to this earth to resolve the fundamental problems of human life and the universe. His name is Sun Myung Moon. *For several decades he wandered through the spirit world so vast as to be beyond imagining.* He trod a bloody path of suffering in search of the truth, passing through tribulations that God alone remembers. Since he understood that no one can find the ultimate truth to save humanity without first passing through the bitterest of trials, he fought alone against millions of devils, both in the spiritual and physical worlds, and triumphed over them all. Through intimate spiritual communion with God and by meeting with Jesus and many saints in Paradise, he brought to light all the secrets of Heaven."

Moon's central goal was to establish the Kingdom of Heaven on earth. 'In Jin,' one of Moon's daughters says, "What Jesus told my father back then is, 'I did not come to die. I came to find my perfect bride, and we would create this thing called the 'True Family,' and we would encourage all of humanity to graft onto that true family through this thing called holy blessing."

James Beverley, a professor at Tyndale Seminary in Toronto and an expert on Moon, says "Moon believed he was the Messiah, that he was sinless and that he was the true father of mankind. He believed he was the true representative of God on Earth, and that he has liberated the universe. He taught in one of his sermons that the 'Hallelujah' chorus is really about him, and people will eventually in heaven sing praises to Rev. Moon."

In 1975, Moon sent out missionaries to 120 countries. The Unification Church followed up by making large financial investments in civic organizations and business projects in these countries. In the same year he founded the Unification Theological Seminary in Barrytown, New York which is still running.

Political, Social & Economic Influence of Moon

Sun Myung Moon was a political, social and economic force to be reckoned with. He had presidential and political contacts all over the globe and business holdings in numerous countries. He fought to save Nixon during Watergate and was chummy with numerous right-wing USA presidents and political figures that he funded.

Moon founded News World Communications aka News Media Corporation in 1976. It owns United Press International with newspapers in Latin America, South Korea, Japan, South Africa, Egypt and the USA. Moon co-owned the Washington Times for many years promoting right-wing politics and causes. On 2 November 2010, Moon and a group of former Times editors purchased the entire holdings of the Washington Times from News World. Moon also founded the Tongil Group which is involved in production, tourism, publishing, pharmaceuticals and a Korean ballet troupe.

Other Moon business enterprises include the New Yorker Hotel in Manhattan, Bridgeport University in Connecticut, Pyongwha Automobile Company, Varadero Tsako Shipyard of Uruguay, Saeilo Machinery Company of Japan, and United Trade Industries of the Netherlands. Moon also owns hotels, resorts, sports teams, restaurants, seafood supply chains and many other companies including an arms factory in the USA. It's believed that Moon's empire of diversified business holdings are in the multi-billions of dollars. Moon traveled the world with his family in his private jets. One jet purchase was $40 million with $10 million in upgrades. He also owned large helicopters to visit his Geomun Island Palace.

'Moon World Headquarters' is located in New York, while the source of its financing remains shrouded in mystery. Because of its religious status, its secrecy and its tendency to deal in cash, no one has been able to offer a definitive account of all of the sources of Moon's funding.

An investigation by the Washington Post in 1984 concluded that tens of millions of dollars per year were coming from door-to-door sales programs conducted by church members in the US, Japan, Korea and all the countries where Moon had sent missionaries. One glaringly deceptive practice was fraudulently soliciting large sums from gullible old people in Japan to remove heredity sins of ancestors and bring peace in the present. Moonie fund-raisers called this 'Heavenly Deception' as they posed as Buddhists.

Moon's Social, Cultural and Religious Imprint

The Moon organization operates a maze of foundations, social and cultural groups, campus groups, religious groups, advocacy associations and other NGO organizations (non-governmental organization: an organization that tries to achieve social or political aims but is not controlled by a government). A recent list includes the names of over 1,000 different non-profit organizations under the Moon umbrella. Most of these groups have benign and hard-to-remember titles such as the Collegiate Association for the Research of Principles (CARP), the major Moon group for organizing college and university students. Key groups include the Family Federation for World Peace and Unification, the Women's Federation for World Peace, the World Culture and Sports Festival, the Inter-religious and International Federation for World Peace, and the Youth Federation for World Peace. Other groups include the World Media Conference, the Professors' World Peace Academy, the Assembly of the World's Religions, and the International Leadership Seminars.

Secretive Indoctrination

A come-on ploy used in the USA was to invite people to a free dinner sponsored by the "Creative Community Project." One attendee recalls, "At the dinner, I was invited to a weekend on a farm in northern California, near the town of Boonville. Although they told me there would be discussions about their ideals, as well as games and recreation, my hosts made no mention of the Unification Church or Moon. (In fact, as I later learned, they went out of their way to conceal this connection.) I agreed to go to Boonville, where I ended up staying for four eventful weeks, during which time I was lectured to relentlessly on the basic ideas of the 'Divine Principle.' At last, near the end of my stay, my hosts revealed the name of their founder, Rev. Sun Myung Moon and said the Bay Area group was in fact part of a worldwide movement called the Unification Church." The cat was out of the bag!

Stephen Hassan said, "I didn't know about Moon himself until several weeks into my indoctrination. This was a typical practice used by the Moonies of the day."

Fundraising

For many years Moon's growing army of street soldiers called 'Moonies' raised money by hawking flowers, pictures and candles in airports and on street corners. Those who lived during these times remember the barrage of Moonies on the streets and airports selling and taking donations in the USA. Those selling these items made a pittance while the majority of monies went into various bank accounts of the Unification Church. Between 1970 and 1976 the U.S. Unification Church was raking in 8-15 million dollars a year from flower and candle sales alone. Funds raised for the UC beyond this, far exceeded these amounts when members give their life savings and holdings to the church.

Stephen Hassan explained his USA Unification Church fundraising experience, "I was with the Moonies for two-and-a-half years. I worked, studied, or prayed 16-20 hours per day—seven days a week. My work began as strictly a fund-raiser. In time my responsibilities grew to recruiting, training others, and community PR. Everyone on my team was told they had to raise a minimum of $100 a day. If they weren't able to, they were not allowed to sleep. Individual team member failures to reach quotas affected the group to which they were attached. As a leader I often denied myself sleep in support of them. Many fund-raisers burned out due to physical exhaustion. We knew Moon and his family lived a lavish lifestyle but tried to not think about this since we thought they were "The Royal Family of the Universe."

Moonies did extensive fundraising in the 120 countries where he'd sent out missionaries. His faithful used a variety of means they thought would be effective within that particular society under Moon's supervision. In all of these instances, Moonie followers worked from sunrise to sunset with very limited free-time and as a result suffered from exhaustion, physical illness and mental break-downs.

Japan Fleeced by Moon

At the time the scam began, the Unification Church had a terrible reputation in Japan affecting Moonie fundraising. As Japan was primarily a Buddhist-believing country, UC members were asked by Moon to disguise themselves as members of a Buddhist sect who had a remedy plan to ease current family and health crises by addressing ancestral sins. *Backdrop:*

When Japanese people are unhappy or meet difficulty and misfortune, the cause is believed to be evil acts committed by deceased family members. The remedy to change this cycle is for family members to do 'good deeds' in the present.

Moon's plan involved the production of quality marble vases, statues of a modern Buddha and Buddhist temple pagodas in varying sizes—made in Korea. The purchase of one of these objects by a Japanese follower of Buddha would fulfill doing a 'good-deed' by supporting the Buddhist cause in the world. Moon's sales team claimed this would instataneously resolve any and all evil deeds of deceased family members and bring peace to the family.

The larger, or more intricately artistic the item was, the more could be asked in the way of a price or donation. If an item cost $100-200 to produce, it could bring a sale price or donation of $1,000 to 3,000 or more. Japanese elderly were targeted for this Unification Church sales pitch, along with anyone who believed a current 'good work' could cover past ancestral sins and make life better. Moon claimed he knew nothing about this practice. Japanese historians have documented this fraud perpetrated on the

Japanese people with Moon as the brains behind 'the Scam' of UC members posing as members of a Buddhist sect.

Moon personally extracted over $500 MILLION from Japanese women (aka sisters who followed Moon) in the fall of 1993. He demanded that 50,000 Japanese women attend his workshops on Cheju Island and each had to pay a fee of

$10,000. Approximately 51,800 attended. This was one of a number of training events held on this island to secure the loyalty of Japanese women to the Unification Church. The groups of sisters came in staggered waves over a three-month time period. Moon participated part- time and was aided by a number of church keynote speakers and teachers for the majority of the workshops. Previously and during this time-frame Rev. Sun Myung Moon was not allowed in Japan due to the public revelations of deceptions carried out by his followers on the Japanese people..

Bizarre Coronation & UN Request

Years later on March 23, 2004 Moon was involved in a bizarre coronation at the Dirksen Senate Office Building in Washington, D.C., which was attended by congressmen, senators, and other dignitaries. At the end of an awards ceremony, a bejeweled crown was placed on Moon's head and he was proclaimed the "King of Peace, (aka) Emperor and Savior of the Universe."

Influential at the United Nations, he pushed to have himself named United Nations Secretary General 'In Perpetuity.' In spite of his considerable influence on the world stage of knowing the rich and powerful and walking among an international array of Presidents and dignitaries, Rev. Moon fell short in persuading the entire world that he was the Messiah and that he should be offered the mantle of # 1 in world and universe leadership!

It should be noted Moon was friends with US Presidents Nixon, Reagan and George H.W. Bush. Each supported various Moon endeavors and causes.

Speaking Tours and Mass Weddings

Rev. Sun Myung Moon & spouse Han also raised huge amounts of money by speaking tours. They encouraged the faithful to give beyond what they could afford to further the cause of establishing 'World Peace' through "True Families." Moon's mass-weddings bankrolled the movement with staggering costs to grooms, brides and their families. Many individuals and families had to go into significant debt to be able to pay the fees required to be a part of a Unification Church mass-wedding. The charges were kept secret as there was a huge disparity between what individuals had to pay from various countries. Japan was charged the highest rates. It's been reported on numerous occasions, that Moon never forgave Japan for its past aggressions against Korea. Payback came by way of fleecing and over-charging the Japanese.

Mass-Weddings

The controversial practice of organizing and hosting mass-weddings in the USA and in Korea got the attention of lots of people. The unusual part of this phenomena was most of whom were being joined had never met before. There were exceptions, like those already engaged and others who reaffirmed their wedding vows. The overwhelming majority however were first-time weddings, matched by Moon. In time, Han and trusted spiritual leaders helped. For the most part couples were matched from photographs and brief bio information. The concept in UC mass-weddings was to match couples from different countries, ethnicity and religions, believing inter-national and inter-cultural weddings would speed up World Peace. Many couples married did not share a common language. Most were expected to have a 40 day abstinence from sex and at the end of this, spend 3 days in UC prescribed sexual activity.

Mass-Wedding Time Line

1960 –4 couples on April 11 in South Korea

1961 –33 couples on May 15 in South Korea

1962 –72 couples on June 4 in South Korea

1963 –124 couples on July 24 in South Korea

1968 –430 couples on Feb. 22 in South Korea

1969 –43 couples on different dates in England, USA and Japan

1970 –777 couples on Oct. 21 with Japanese, US and Western participants

1975 –1,800 couples on Feb. 8 with Japanese and Western participants

1977 –74 couples on Feb. 21 at the "World Mission Center', NY)

1978 –118 couples on May 21 in London, England UK

1982 –2,075 couples on July 01 at 'Madison Square Garden', NY USA

1982 –6,000 couples on Oct.14 in Seoul, Korea

1988 –6,500 couples on Oct. 30: Korean, Japanese & Misc. Asian participants

1989 –1,275 couples on Jan. 12 with 87 countries representative participants

1992 –32,000 couples on Aug. 25 Multi-Country at 'Olympic Stadium', South Korea

1995 – 360,000 couples on Aug. 25 (Satellite + ceremony in Seoul, S. Korea)

1997 –28,000 couples on Oct. 14 at 'RFK Stadium' in Washington, D.C. USA

2009 –10,000 couples at 'Sun Moon Univ.' Tangjung Crystal Valley, central S. Korea

2012—Sept.2 'Sun Myung Moon' dies

2013 –3,500 couples on Feb. 17 in Gapyeong, South Korea

2017 –44,000 couples in Sept. (20,000 remotely by Internet) Gapyeong, S.Korea.

The latest 2017 event was called *"A Cosmic Blessing Ceremony"* remembering the 5th year since Rev. Sun Myung Moon's death. It was presided over by "True Mother" in Cheongshim Peace World Center arena in Gapyeong, South Korea.

The Dark Side of the Moon Royal Family

The entire premise of the Unification Church is one of promoting conservative family values, i.e. creating True Families and worshiping True Father Sun Myung Moon as the Messiah and True Mother Hak Ja Han.

Young Girls Become Moon's Objects of Sexual Exploits

Early Unification Church member Annie Choi confesses this was not what she experienced in the formation of the church and beyond. She should know since she was coerced into a sexual relationship with Sun Myung Moon for a number of years beginning at the age of 16 and she would give birth to one of his sons, "Park," while Moon was in his 2nd marriage to Han.

Choi joined Moon's church along with her mother and sister in the early 1950s. At the time, the family lived in the southern Korean city of Pusan. Moon had fled there after being freed by American troops from a communist labor camp in North Korea.

Initially, Moon had only a few dozen followers, who met in a two-room house on the outskirts of town. The group was taught they were to sacrifice everything for the church. For young female members, this included their virginity. Choi says the initiation rites for early female disciples involved having sex with Moon three times. She also alleges that Moon kept a stable of a half-dozen concubines, known as the 'Six Marys,' and inducted her into the group when she was 17. Sometimes, she adds, he would assemble them all in a circle and require them to perform sex acts with him. Choi's account is consistent with the testimony of other early followers, who claim that Moon's Unification Church began as an erotic cult, with Moon "purifying" female followers through sexual rites.

Ironically, around this time, Moon began preaching sex outside of marriage was one of the worst sins. Choi and other insiders allege that Moon's philandering continued long after his 2nd marriage to Han in 1960. Choi says because Moon favored her, she kept having sex with him regularly until 1964, when she moved to the United States to attend Georgetown University, in Washington, DC. Prior to her departure, Choi claims, she and Moon were married in a secret ceremony.

The following year, Moon made his first trip to the United States and stayed for several months with his deputy, Bo Hi Pak, near the nation's capital. During the trip, he spent a good deal of time with Choi. Before long, in 1965 Choi was carrying Moon's child. The intrigue of how Moon tried to cover-up his 'love child' involves drama and deception. It's believed Park was not the only extramarital child that Moon sired. Other reports are still being researched for accuracy.

Trouble in Paradise

Moon's 14 legitimate children were for the most part raised by faithful Moon followers acting as surrogate parents and nannies. Fearful of overstepping their roles and displeasing "True Parents" and their offspring "True Children", those caring for the children were afraid to give corrective guidance. What resulted were defiant, spoiled and unruly children. Most had access to significant sums of money, beyond their maturity level of handling. The oldest son Steve became a cocaine addict with a fascination for high-caliber guns and had a propensity for violence. He caused no small amount of havoc for the entire family, blowing through hundreds of thousands of dollars of the church's money. He had been given oversight of the USA's music ministry based in NYC. In an attempt to rein Steve in, Moon & Han arranged for Steve to wed a naive 15-year-old Korean girl named Nansook Hong aka Grace in 1982. According to her she was beaten and bloodied on a regular basis when Steve slipped into fits of rage.

Moon's forth child In Jin (daughter) was given leadership over the USA Unification Church. She too was married via an arranged marriage. The groom Moon picked was James, the son of Moon's main USA leader Bo Hi Pak. In Jin was not attracted to her nerdy and shy husband but went along with things for the time being.

In 1984-85 Moon was convicted of and sentenced to 18 months in jail for US tax evasion. The Unification Church launched a 30 million dollar campaign to overturn this conviction and rallied an impressive collection of politicians and right-wing religious figures. Moon's daughter In Jin was chosen to be the spokesperson for this effort which turned out to be successful in gaining Moon his release.

Later, while governing the church, In Jin entered into an extramarital affair resulting in an illegitimate child and she went into seclusion after this came to light. She ended up divorcing James and remarried her new lover. In the aftermath, In Jin fell out of favor with the Moon family and was removed from her leadership role with the US church.

In 1994, Heung Jin aka Richard age 17, Moon's 2nd oldest son, died in a tragic car accident on an icy road in New York, colliding with a semi-truck.

A year later in 1995, Grace had enough of Steve's regular violence after he'd hit her in the face and licked the blood of his hand in mockery. In fear for the children and herself she packed her five children into the back of a cargo van and fled their East Garden estate. She later filed for divorce and published a devastating exposé of life inside the compound, "*In the Shadow of the Moons.*"

In 1998, Grace and Moon's daughter In Jin both claimed they were victims of husband abuse and went on "60 Minutes", unleashing a flurry of allegations about sex, drugs, and violence inside Moon's ideal family. Moon was still reeling from this bombshell when, the following year, his second-youngest son, Phillip, who was also trapped in an unhappy arranged marriage, hurled himself from the seventeenth floor of a Harrah's casino in Nevada and died.

Moon's Illegitimate Son "Park"
Recalling What Finally Happened to Him

Park says "Suddenly, the blinders came off. I could see how strange life inside the movement was—the things we did, the way we thought. When you begin to break free from that kind of brainwashing, it's almost like an out-of-body experience." Park had witnessed firsthand the contradictions, lies, deceptions and cover-ups carried out to keep up the appearance of the Moon family being a model "Pure Family."

Those who take the time through research and sincere prayer will find the answers to hard questions. Most who have left the Unification Church grew weary of contrived intellectual somersaults and spiritual rationalizing in order to shut down their conscience. Some things are just not right and there are lots of these in Moon's Unification Church in history, doctrine/beliefs, practice and motives.

Update on 'The Unification Church'

The Unification church is still recruiting and running its empire of businesses, churches, seminaries, colleges, hotels, resorts, sports teams, ballet institutes and social and political organizations. Whenever possible Moon's legitimate children are in charge, overseeing operations. Lying and misleading is still the norm and Moon still holds the role of 'King of the Universe.' Faithful followers continue to support and don't ask questions. The majority of those who engage in mass-weddings do so out of loneliness in hopes of finding a life's partner and to promote the noble goal of good families and World Peace. The lure of this cult is multifaceted.

The lead author is confident, 'True Family' and 'True Children' are human and not divine! The Bible speaks to these types of religious impersonations. Remember, Sun Myung Moon is in a grave. Jesus Christ was raised by God the True Father!

> Jesus replied to them: "Watch out that no one deceives you. For many will come in my name, saying, 'I am the Messiah,' and they will deceive many."   Matthew 24:4-5

Speaking for God, the prophet Jeremiah describes
what happens in almost all religious cults.

> The prophets are prophesying lies in My name. I have not sent them, appointed them, or spoken to them. They are prophesying false vision, divinations (the practice of trying to foretell future events or discover hidden knowledge by using occult, i.e. evil and demonic spirits) idolatries and delusions of their own minds.   Jeremiah 14:14 NIV®

Research Resources:

New Republic Magazine	First Things First Journal
How Well Do You Know Your	"Waning Moon" K. Gordon Neufeld
Moon?	Huffington Post News
Mother Jones	AOL News
Institute on Religion & Public Life	Rationalwiki.org
Buzz-feed News	NPR News
The Telegraph UK	Celebrity Net Worth
BBC News	New World Encyclopedia
The Daily Mail UK	NY Times
The Guardian US Edition	Let Us Reason.com
World History	Daily Beast.com
The Mirror World News	Wikipedia

The Children of God, aka The Family of Love, The Family, now **The Family International**

The leader of this movement was David Brandt Berg aka Moses David, Moses, King David, Father David. Was he who he claimed to be, the End-Time Prophet sent by God?

The woman who became his co-leader is Maria Zerby Fontaine aka Mama Maria, Queen Maria. To avoid legal prosecution she changed her name to Katherine Rianna Smith.

TFI is the most widely covered group in this book. My tenure of being in this group, then called the COG, was strained—beginning in mid 1971 to mid 1972, approximately eleven months. I left after being the central figure in a COG Tribunal. After the event guards were posted outside my door until around the 4 AM hour. When I realized they were gone, I left the factory under the cover of a deep fog shortly afterward. The next morning accompanied by the British police we asked to see my wife and children. A COG leader said she and the children no longer lived there.

THE CHILDREN OF GOD

They were undoubtedly lying as only five hours had past, but there was nothing we could do, lacking a search warrant. I later learned my spouse had been sent to an undisclosed location in Denmark and the children had been placed in a COG Kibbutz in France. I remained in England for several years attempting to locate them without success. I finally returned to the USA in late 1974.

I've kept abreast of the COG / The Family with my immediate family and many friends still in the group. An important means of staying in the loop has been by direct interaction with those who have contacted me from the group, their family members and those who've left. I've secured and read 'Family' literature extensively and kept abreast of their website since its inception, reading dozens of articles. I've also accessed and read numerous articles on the X-Family website and viewed other resources and videos that have chronicled *The Family's history and changes over the years.*

With a spirit of compassion and truthfulness I've endeavored to synthesize these findings into digestible sections. We'll view the prominent historical progression of the group, the way they've handled themselves or been received in various countries, their controversial teachings and practices, cover member and X-member comments and experiences, and consider the practical and spiritual dimensions of Recovery.

Early 'Children of God' History and Beyond

This history begins in 1967 when David Brandt Berg was a Missionary

Alliance pastor without a church to pastor. Those who knew Berg said the reason he was church-less was due to his erratic behavior and spurious beliefs. Berg's mother, a perennial advocate of her son, learned of a Teen Challenge coffee house in Huntington Beach that was closing and let Berg know about it.

Disillusioned with the organized church Berg jumped at the opportunity to run a coffee house. In 1968 he and his spouse Jane and four children took the helm and renamed the coffeehouse the Light Club. At the time, Berg's family were called Teens for Christ. Area hippies began frequenting the club for music and peanut butter sandwiches. I visited the club during this time frame and it appeared to be sparsely attended with Berg's kids Aaron, Hosea, Linda and Faith conducting the majority of singing and preaching to those who wandered in. Over time new converts began joining their work. On the surface the ministry seemed a bit odd, but Christian.

In 1969 Berg said he received a Revelation from God that a disastrous earthquake was about to hit California, and cause part of the state to slide into the ocean. He led the group out of Huntington Beach to wander throughout the southwest for eight months. The earthquake never materialized as Berg prophesied, but the possibility of it happening in the future remained.

While on the road preaching and witnessing intermittently, Berg's group grew to around fifty and decided to split up into several teams. David Berg took a small team to Laurentide, Canada in his motor home.

Sensing the need to have a home base, Berg struck a deal with Fred Jordon who owned an abandoned ranch in Thurber, Texas formerly known as The Texas Soul Clinic. Jordon was the founder of the 'Soul Clinic' mission in LA's skid-row district. He also had a TV program to update his supporters on his mission endeavors. With the promise of helping Jordon navigate out of a financial slump, Berg pitched the idea of Jordon filming some of his new converts on Jordon's television show. With details still to be worked out, Berg's group was given the use of the abandoned Texas ranch, based on this promise.

The Birth of a New Nation

In the interim, while waiting to take occupancy of the Texas Soul Clinic,

David Berg arranged for the Teens for Christ teams which had been on the road, to rendezvous in Vienna, Virginia for training sessions at a country farm.

One evening Berg called a special meeting for his children and their spouses (the group's top leadership) which ended up being an all-nighter. Throughout the night Berg alluded to special revelations he'd received in Canada without spelling out what exactly these were, but saying they would usher in monumental changes and thrust the group forward.

Those present said the whole family got involved in prophesying back and forth. As the session continued, family members urged Berg to reveal the content of the prophecies he'd received in Canada. Near dawn Berg finally revealed what he called 'The Prophet of a New Nation' which included taking his then secretary Maria Zerby as his new wife. Berg said Maria represented the new church.

Berg went on to explain how he and Maria Zerby had jointly received these prophecies in Laurentide, Canada while alone in Berg's motor home. According to Berg, Maria would speak in tongues and he would give the interpretation.

The reaction among family members to these prophecies was shock! Up to this point, family members and the entire group had been 'puritanical' in regard to moral conduct. This event caused the first major "Conscience Crossroads" for Berg family members and their spouses.

Anticipating this, Berg went on to give lengthy prophecies warning family members of being rejected by God if they chose to dismiss and not heed the word of God's prophet.

The focus of these prophecies called for complete loyalty to this new thing God was doing. Somehow, Berg pulled this off. He demanded loyalty and pressed everyone in the family to verbally express their loyalty to him which included his wife Eve's willing acceptance of Maria's role as his new wife. Berg utilized fear of being rejected by God and missing out on what God was doing to persuade his top leader family members. These New Nation doctrine and teaching sessions taught by David Berg went on for several weeks.

The Vienna, Virginia experience marked the establishment of a unique spiritual Nation to be led by God's new end-time prophet David Berg. By a supposed divine appointment he told his followers he had been granted rights beyond the limitations of traditional Scriptural morality. According to Berg, and the prophecies he'd received in Laurentide, God had blessed his taking Maria Zerby to be his queen and made all things pure.

As Berg family members and their spouses were still reeling with this new arrangement of their dad now having two wives and dubbed as 'The end-time Prophet,' other morally compromising directives were on the way.

Shortly following Vienna, Berg and family took occupancy of the "Texas Soul Clinic" in Thurber, Texas and the group chose a new name, "The Children of God."

Owner Fred Jordon gave the use of this former missionary unoccupied training ranch to the Berg family along with another warehouse facility in Los Angeles in exchange for filming new COG convert's testimonies on his TV show to raise money. Both Jordon and Berg were happily using each other.

During this time frame, Berg directed the newly named 'Children of God' to act out his prophecy about California's coming doom by conducting Silent Vigils dressed in sackcloth, with staves, yokes around their necks and scroll signs. These vigils drew considerable attention to the group; some wanted and in other instances unwanted.

Departed Gypsy King—Spirit Guide

While in Texas David Berg visited a Gypsy camp in the Houston area and reported he met with the leader king of this band of Gypsies. Fast forward several months and Berg claimed he received the ability to speak in another language while lying in bed naked with his new wife Maria and another COG lady disciple named Martha.

Berg later concluded the new tongue was the spirit of 'Abrahim' a departed Gypsy King from several centuries in the past speaking through him. Abrahim became Berg's personal spirit guide and directed him in almost all of the prophecies and letters that would eventually become the COG Bible. Berg said Abrahim told him he'd been the guiding spirit for the Gypsy band in Houston, but had decided to leave them and live with Berg as his personal spirit guide and counselor.

The way 'Abrahim' spoke to Berg and Maria was by Berg speaking in tongues and Maria interpreting. According to Berg, Maria was the only one who had the gift of interpreting Abrahim's messages.

COG Growth & NBC Filming

Meanwhile, the Children of God were in the midst of a significant growth spurt with full-time recruits growing from 75 to 300 members, split between the Texas ranch and the LA factory.

Simultaneously, the Jesus People Movement was gaining momentum in various cities across the USA. On hearing of the rise of young 'Jesus Followers' NBC went looking for Jesus Movement ministries to film and interview for its 'First Tuesday' documentary show. The Atlanta, Georgia ministry then based in the 'House of Judah' was one of the first groups they chose to film. Unknowingly, NBC also filmed the 'Children of God' group in Thurber, Texas thinking they too were 'Jesus People.'

When the show aired on national TV, the Atlanta Jesus People were surprised to learn of the group called 'Children of God.' When NBC filmed the COG, no mention was made of it being a New Nation with a End Time Prophet. From what NBC saw at the time, the COG were just another expression of the Jesus People Movement.

Conscience Breakdown

Just following the NBC filming, *Berg introduced the 'All Things Lawful and Pure' doctrine of sexual partner swapping between his immediate family members and shortly afterwards, between all COG leaders and their spouses directly under them.* Berg was intent on breaking with the 'old church' biblical traditions and introducing radical new doctrines that would liberate and set his new nation apart!

Berg accomplished this by inviting his immediate family and spouses to Dallas, Texas for training sessions where he taught the "All Things Pure doctrine." Deborah and others said he did this in a way that left no options for resistance. *Unquestioning loyalty was a requirement under God's end-time prophet.* After these sessions all present were required to engage in sexual partner swapping to prove their loyalty to Berg's new directives. All but one or two family members participated. Those who didn't fell out of favor with Berg. The next level down in COG leadership from the Texas Soul Clinic were then invited and Berg gave the same teaching, requiring them to participate in spouse swapping as a means of breaking ties with the Old Church.

> "A Revolution is a total break with the traditions of man and his churches and his preconceived ideas about God and misconceptions of morality. We have turned completely around and are going a different direction, no longer man's way but God's way, and we are free to enjoy to the full the beauties and wonders of His Creation with all of its pleasures which He Himself created for our enjoyment." - David Berg

COG leaders who succumbed to Berg's directives became part of *a secret inner circle*—comprised of those who had broken with the old stale church. By the time Berg left the Texas Soul Clinic and headed to Oklahoma, Berg had taken two more wives, Martha and Rachael in addition to Maria and Eve. In Berg's mind he was redefining Scriptural morality within his New Nation. *Berg believed the Scriptures were outdated and puritanical nonsense!* He would mock Bible verses similar to the one below.

> "The acts of the sinful nature are obvious: sexual immorality, impurity and debauchery; idolatry and witchcraft; drunkenness, orgies and the like. Those who live like this shall not inherit the kingdom of God." Galatians 5:20 NIV®

Why Did People Join Up?

In the early days of the Children of God many joined because the group appeared to be on the front lines of going into all the world to preach the Gospel of Jesus. The COG thought of themselves as Sold-Out disciples and used this uniqueness to recruit new members.

The foundational doctrine in the COG was 'Forsake All' based on Luke 14:33. In practice this meant forsaking family, friends, school and personal goals. In addition, this meant forsaking all bank accounts, savings, bonds, trusts, land, property, inheritances, vehicles and possessions which were to be turned over to the COG. Everything of value needed to be given to further the ministry. New recruits were taught to be enthusiastic about making this type of all-out commitment.

The COG nurtured the idea of being special in God's eyes for this radical commitment! Other seeds were planted during the indoctrination period, including: hatred toward the system of government, all authorities, society as a whole, the organized church and parental rules and values.

Family and friends were viewed with suspicion. They were considered enemies who regularly fought against the group's vision. This ploy was used by David Berg to separate followers from the outside world and solidify their commitment to his closed New Nation. The radical nature of 'forsaking all' also played into the social rebellion of the times. Another tactic employed by the COG to help new members sever ties with their former life, was to give every incoming member a new name. In the early 1970's it was a Biblical name. This made it very difficult for outsiders to track down a family member, which became even harder when the COG sent new members all over the globe to distant unknown locations.

The Lure

Regardless of how people came to find themselves within the COG, the practice of indoctrinating first, prior to revealing higher levels of leadership beliefs and practices was the protocol during the early 1970's.

I recall the lure of the COG as being multi-pronged. Some liked the high energy songs and guitar music, Jewish folk dancing, the religious zeal of 'sold out' disciples, or the adventure of traveling the world. Some were 'star struck' when Jeremy Spencer of Fleetwood Mac joined the group in Los Angeles around 1970. Many were drawn by giving their life to a worthy cause and being part of an 'end time revolution' that could change the world for Jesus.

Plenty of new followers were hungry for relationships; psyched by the idea of having lots of brothers and sisters in the faith with the potential of being hooked up with a compatible spouse one day. Moms and dads were excited by the idea of someone else doing the majority of the demanding day-to-day work of raising babies, toddlers, tweens and teenagers in COG children kibbutz's. A practical incentive for couples expecting was the availability of midwives to deliver babies for free, minus the hassle of securing a doctor, scheduling regular visits and coming up with money to pay doctor and hospital bills.

The organizational ability of the COG was also attractive. It relieved disciples of the worry of paying bills, rents, buying food and other mundane responsibilities they may have dreaded, or felt unprepared for. The trade-off was no income and dwindling personal choices plus over 50 hours per week of assigned work to grow the revolution.

Higher and mid levels of leadership were intrigued by the notion of being *The Chosen Group* with *'The' End-Time Prophet of God.* Individually, and as a group, this was special and elevated the movements sense of importance in the world. *They alone had a Prophet who regularly receives detailed messages from God?*

New members were oblivious to cloaked internal COG beliefs that lower level members were not allowed to know about or see. This put all new recruits at a disadvantage.

As a member of 'The Atlanta Jesus People,' we were oblivious to the COG's hidden teachings and agenda. In what we thought was a simple visit to aid us in solving organizational and financial problems, we entered into a Twilight Zone experience. COG leaders intentionally misled us at every turn, manipulating circumstances until we no longer had choices. These maneuvers set the stage for a planned ministry takeover. In just a few short weeks all of our ministry properties and restaurant were under COG control.

Children of God growth and expansion had picked up steam with the absorption of our Atlanta Jesus People and satellite locations scattered in several neighboring states and the merger with the Northwest Jesus People.

Outwardly these numeric additions looked to be successful for the COG, but their manipulative and deceptive characteristics were beginning to backfire and draw negative attention.

Top COG Leaders Flee the USA

The media in the US brought public awareness of the dangers of the COG which has helped law enforcement to follow through on reports of abuse, excessive control of members, brainwashing, financial manipulation, and embezzlement.

With authorities closing in on colony leaders who were practicing these abuses and additional inquiries about those who ran the COG were gaining momentum— *David Berg and family along with top leaders decide to leave the USA to avoid criminal prosecution and relocate in England.*

In the UK, the group was given the use of a spacious factory in Bromley Kent, capable of housing a sizable number of disciples. In short order a new British colony is up and running with a Print Shop and Kids Kibbutz. Branching out into Europe is also underway with Faithy Berg launching the offensive. The COG now claim around 1,500 full-time recruits.

A Prophet with Special Words from God

David Berg and his mistress Maria Zerby directed the COG from the safety of a private residence in a London suburb. Their exact whereabouts is kept a secret with the exception of immediate family and a handful of top COG leaders. Berg's means of directing the growing movement is through 'Mo (Moses) Letters' which had been previously used in a sporadic manner. With spirit-guide 'Abrahim' now talking to Berg regularly, an accelerated amount of Mo Letters are being written, printed and distributed to all the COG groups (colonies).

The majority of the COG are still in the dark about Berg's relationship with Maria and his self-appointment as God's End-Time Prophet. His legal wife Jane Berg, also known as Mother Eve, was replaced by Maria and other unofficial wives and concubines.

Working in the Bromley COG print shop part-time, I saw a batch of three new 'Mo Letters' that had just come off the press. At the time they were designated for higher leadership reading only. Curious, I took copies of each and placed them inside my shirt when I left the shop.

Later, I read them carefully when alone. The titles of these letters were, "David" "The Key of David" and "The Psalm of David." In these letters Berg introduces the claim of being God's chosen End Time Prophet with the ability to hear God's voice and lead the Children of God forward in a mighty spiritual revolution. This was the first I'd heard of this. He used Scriptures throughout taking them mostly out of context.

From what I learned later, up until now only the 'top leaders' in the COG were privy to Berg's claim of being an 'The End Time Prophet.' Distribution of these letters to all 'colony leaders' and possibly 'secondary leaders' under them would usher in a wider awareness of Berg's declaration of being God's special prophet. This would cause a movement-wide shift in how the COG saw themselves. It would usher in the belief they were *'the special people of God on earth with a 'End Time Prophet.'*

In response I wrote a personal letter to David Berg, challenging his self-appointment as God's End Time Prophet and misuse of the Scriptures to support this claim. Placing the letter in an envelope and sealing it, I passed it to a leader at the Bromley Colony. With God's help based on my understanding of the Bible, I had rejected these self-glorifying revelations, but would pay for the audacity of doing so.

All hell hit the fan when Berg read my letter! This led to insistent demands from Bromley leaders to recant my comments and repent. Declining, I was brought before a 'Tribunal' of COG leaders. Berg had penned a response letter for the event, stating I was Beelzebub, i.e. the devil, and my doubts of his authority were evidence of having 'A Lying Spirit' and being demon possessed. (Details of these events are recorded in Chapters 15-16) The tribunal raised concern about what they might do to me next. This catapulted me out of the COG through a middle of the night escape.

Berg's self-glorification letters were a turning point for the COG. This paved the way for Berg to elevate his 'Mo Letters' as being equal to or superseding the Bible in the days to come, with hundreds of letters sent out claiming his divine status.

Berg's Sexual World & Fund-Raising Idea

By 1972 David Berg had multiple wives and visiting concubines. Upper and lower level leadership partner swapping continued and sexual sharing between singles had begun. With growing pains and the need for more operating money, Berg and Maria began devising a new plan.

Unbeknownst to even top leaders, Berg had an idea up his sleeve. He and Maria were piloting a fundraising technique with Maria Zerby having sex with men for money, favors, or sizable gifts. Considering the implications of what could happen with a population explosion with new group babies and a lot more money to work with, Berg and Maria felt the time was right to prime the pump.

In the Mo Letter 'Priestess of Love' Berg introduces the concept of 'Flirty-Fishing' to members. He explains, "Maria has had 40 sex partners she's loved with Jesus' love and only got pregnant once!" The letter is a sales pitch to encourage all the ladies to consider the great value of reaching lonely men with the love of Jesus. The punch line is: Help Maria, help us reach the lost and help us to grow our finances. The seed was planted with the aim of revisiting this topic soon. In the interim Berg and Maria continue to consider how this new ministry will serve a number of purposes simultaneously.

They review how their new doctrines have been received by members. They feel good about securing group loyalty to Berg as God's End Time Prophet and being successful in introducing Spirit Guides. They also sense they've taken a strong stand in emphasizing unquestioning loyalty through 'Mo Letters' including the 'Beelzebub Lord of the Flies' *which warn about trouble makers, doubters and dissenters.* Berg's Mo Letters have reinforced the warning multiple times, *"It's a sin to doubt God's appointed leader, prophet and his word!"*

Berg's and Maria's consensus is, with this groundwork in place, members should be cautious about resisting this new outreach fund-raiser. In the fall of 1972 Berg and Maria take the decisive step and introduce 'Flirty-Fishing' It catches many married couples and single women in the movement by surprise. The fund-raiser is not mandated, but strongly encouraged. This is a hard pill for members to swallow and many leave. In the background Flirty-Fishing continues to catch on with Berg's Mo Letters spurring on this lucrative money maker.

Mo Letters Become the Word of God With Greater Authority than the Bible

In 1973 Berg proclaims 'Mo Letters' are the 'Word of God,' with greater authority than the Bible. This has been in the making for some time with Bergs' elevated status growing in his mind and heart. Another reason for this announcement was directly related to the types of things he and Maria were now asking of Family disciples.

Christians in the group knew Berg's flood of new doctrines and practices were in complete contradiction to what the Bible taught. Sensing this struggle of conscience, Berg realized the time had come to address this problem and secure control. He did so by saying the Bible was outdated and his words and authority superseded it. This was not entirely new as Berg had primed the pump with many special revelations and teachings saying God's New Nation was being guided in a new and fresh direction.

To help members make this transition mentally, Berg had his Mo Letters compiled into Scripture form to elevate there physical appearance, increase reading and remind members these letters came directly from God's End-Time prophet.

These were troubling times for those who had joined the group in good faith believing the COG/Family wanted to reach the world for Jesus Christ and do good things.

The above are different volumes of "Mo Letters" bound in Bible form

Instead, what was coming would be an avalanche of doctrines and practices that would devastate and irreparably harm thousands of members.

The Family Sexual Revolution

In late 1973 into 1974 there was a soaring increase of Mo Letters on sex. Among them were "Revolutionary Sex," "Revolutionary Women," "Revolutionary Marriage," "One Wife," and "Mountain Maid." These and other letters encouraged a break with traditional marriage and Godly morals. They were aimed to burst the bubble of puritanical religious restraints.

Mo's new grouping of Sex Letters facilitated the dissolving of hundreds of existing marriages and encouraged members to take new partners, or just randomly enjoy sex when desired. Women were instructed to freely share. This practice swept through the groups increasing numbers.

In addition to these Mo Letters was another series titled 'Goddesses' where *Berg states he is now having spirit-sex with departed sex goddesses.* Unbelievably, Berg still refers to God as being the inspiration behind all of these teachings. The Bible disagrees.

> "If anyone comes and preaches another Jesus, whom we have not preached, or you encounter another spirit, which you have not received, or another gospel, which is different than what you've accepted, beware!

For such are false apostles, deceitful workers, transforming themselves into the apostles of Christ (or prophets of God). Don't be surprised; for Satan is capable of transforming himself into an angel of light. Therefore it is no great thing if his ministers are also transformed to appear as ministers of righteousness; whose end shall be according to their deeds." 2 Corinthians 10:4, 13-15 NIV®

Spirit Guides

Berg's relationship with deceased Gypsy King Abrahim continues, but in addition, he's made contact with other powerful spirits. He's had *Spirit Sex* with deceased goddesses from the spirit world and engaged in spirit meetings with a deceased medium called Madame-M. These and other spirit guides are mentioned in Mo Letters, with the prompt for members to contact their own spirit guides along with the spirits listed below which Berg says are fighting for The Family.

Abrahim - a deceased Bulgarian Gypsy King

Arcothon - aka *Arcros* a conduit for god's power

Brunheld - fights for TFI

Ellya - draws members to use the keys of the kingdom.

Contact with spirit guides spread like wildfire among adult and underage members. According to most who lived in TF during this time period:

The entire COG-Family became a hive of
sensual, unclean, lying and demonic spirits.

COG Characteristics

By 1974 New York and other US state investigations were underway through various Attorney General offices. Charity fraud and widespread member abuse were at the center of these probes. The group's deceptive tactics of lying to the public, press and families, and shipping new recruits out of the area, or country with no forwarding contact information and excessive control over members were among the alarming practices of this group. Literally hundreds of new recruits had been carted off and then disappeared without any trace. Local COG leaders were directed by Berg to be as evasive as possible and not give any information to families, friends, or legal authorities.

This and other questionable COG doctrines and practices causes a red flag to go up. Families and friends of COG recruits fear for their safety and well-being. In growing numbers, they've contacted law enforcement and the press, seeking assistance in locating their loved ones.

With the majority of COG colonies still in the USA, under careful scrutiny by the law, Berg goes on the offensive in his Mo Letters by railing against the enemies of God who are persecuting them. He reiterates their devilish goal is to try to disrupt the work of God in the USA.

As public awareness of COG abuses and investigations increase, Berg tires of *An Evil Land, God Will Judge!* Amidst his Mo Letter confrontation with America for troubling his colonies, Berg pens a Mo Letter stating he's received a prophecy about the destruction of America.

Comet Kohoutek Heralds Doomsday

In 1974 Berg claims to have received a prophecy from God telling him the comet Kohoutek will hit and destroy all life in the USA. This is followed by directives for all USA colonies to organized for a *Great Escape.* The goal is to leave the USA and send out teams to various countries in Europe, South America, Asia and Australia and let America reap the consequences for harassing God's prophet and people! The Great Escape exodus of COG members from America is carried out and members are scattered to the winds over land and sea. [Fact: The comet never hit or destroyed America]

'Family of Love' Embrace Fund-Raiser

In 1978 the COG adopt a new name, **The Family of Love** *and Flirty-Fishing is accepted movement-wide as a fund-raiser and outreach tool.* With David

Berg firmly in control of 'The Family of Love' and Maria Zerby at his side as 'Queen Maria' aka Mama Maria, Berg unleashes dozens of new 'Mo Letters' introducing a variety of deviant sexual practices which he and Maria were already practicing. These horrendous and damaging practices became the new norm within TFI.

During this era Flirty-Fishing was TF's most profitable fund-raiser. All young women, 18 or older were expected to Flirty-Fish from two to five nights a week. Seventeen year olds also took part in everything but fornication.

Anguish of conscience accompanied this new doctrine for COG women and if married, their husbands. Sexual prostitution was not what anyone would have expected to be mandated. A significant number of married couples and single women felt helplessly trapped. If they wanted to stay in the now **Family of Love** and not be left behind they had to comply, or leave. Many chose to leave. Those who stayed in the group became sex slaves, defiled their conscience and paid a severe price by having a self proclaimed prophet as their sex pimp.

Underage Victims

The new sexual freedoms given to adult members offered increased loosening of parental responsibility. Berg taught, "The children belong to God, and he will take care of them." *Berg's intention was to eliminate marital and family bonds. He wanted everyone in 'The Family' from adult to child, loyal to him as the commander-in-chief, prophet of God.*

For parents, this meant very limited time with their natural children. Many ladies ended up giving birth to 8-12 children who they rarely saw and a growing number of Family kids had no idea who their parents were. Berg knew movement-wide sexual freedom would yield a large new population of members who would be raised looking to him as God's Prophet.

Sexual Child Abuse and Exploitation

Berg's next barrage of sexual letters zeroed in on the children. He wrote a letter called 'Holy Holes' followed by numerous Mo Letters unleashing and encouraging sex between children, adult to child sex, parent to child sex (incest), lesbianism and other sexual molestation practices.

The smiles in the picture above were soon to change when physical, emotional, spiritual and legal woes began plaguing the 'Family of Love.'

Indoctrination of children from ages five to seventeen via sex literature and videos was TFI's main curriculum alongside Mo Letters for

DAVID BERG'S 'CHILDREN OF GOD' BROTHEL OF EARLY 'FLIRTY FISH'
1977 Island of Tenerife in Canary Islands of Spain
_____

Bottom Row - Center 3
Rachael   David Berg aka Moses   Maria Zerby aka Queen

at least 14 years. Berg also encouraged the filming and photographing of underage children in sexually stimulating behavior or sex acts. Berg and Maria and other leaders under their guidance made numerous sex videos to be reproduced and shown throughout the entire movement. One ex-Family member who was in the group for over 20 years told me, "David Berg was a sex maniac and could not get enough in the way of perversions."

Telling David Berg 'Mo Letter' Quotes

- Incest is OK, because there's no better place for a young man to learn about doing it, than from his own mother.

- Eleven and twelve year-olds are capable of becoming pregnant, so why shouldn't they be having sex?

- F—ing your parents and grandparents is awesome.

- Everybody is married to everybody else.

- Pictures of naked congregation members, referred to as 'Nudie-Cuties,' make good bookmarks for the Bible.

- Men should not be gay, but it is hot when women are gay.

- It is OK to lie to nonbelievers in order to protect God's work.

> "Is there a limit? One can see from this progression occurring in less than a decade in a closed society (cult), that immorality doesn't stand still. Nor does it satisfy or bring lasting pleasure. It grows and steadily becomes more perverse and wicked. Sex, most certainly contains within it a moral code and a self-destruct principle. What form of sensual pleasure lies beyond what the TFI are now doing? What form of perversion lies beyond incest, sodomy, and child abuse? I do not care to put that answer in print."
>
> -Deborah (Linda Berg) Davis

Many of these sexual perversions and practices were aimed at underage children with adults participating or encouraging. These illegal practices paired with Berg's Flirty-Fishing Prostitution Ring brought TFI into the public spotlight for good reason.

> Wherever TFI went, investigations would ensue. Many adult 'Family' members were arrested in various countries and underage children were taken into custody for various lengths of time. TFI was banned from a number of countries because of their sexual abuse of minors and illegal prostitution practices.

From 1974 to1994, some twenty years, legal and law enforcement woes for The Family were continuous. *Sexual abuse and harsh physical and emotional abuse of minors along with excessive control of all members were the predominant reasons for these investigations and arrests.*

From 1987 to 1994 a third name change was introduced; 'The Family' the group's new moniker. Most agree this name change was due to the bad reputation, negative press coverage and legal battles the group was engaged in.

Numerous raids on COG houses found children between the ages of 2-17 living in cramped quarters, many underfed and poorly clothed. Retrieval of sexually graphic literature promoting sex between adults and children was confiscated in every instance. Evidence of incest, sexual abuse and molestation of minors was pervasive. Police found a videotape showing a father having sex with his daughter, titled "Virtual State of Servitude."Other literature was also secured verifying **The Family** was using prostitution as a means of fund-raising.

Raids on The Family's group houses were conducted based on local complaints and reports of child abuse. There was no indication that these raids had been coordinated between various countries. Some prosecutions stuck, others never materialized.

International Investigations 1971-2000

Beginning in America, then England investigations into the alarming practices of the Children of God/The Family under its various name changes commenced. These investigations spread quickly to Europe, Australia, India and Asia. Concerns for the well being of members and new recruits were about:

1. The disappearance of young adults with no way to locate or contact them.
2. Unashamed secrecy, deception and lying about new members whereabouts.
3. Use of brainwashing techniques of limited sleep and lengthy indoctrination.
4. Severe sexual, physical and mental and excessive discipline abuses.
5. Teaching parent members to engage in incest with their children
6. Forcing adult women into Flirty-Fishing Prostitution to support TFI.
7. Separating children from their biological parents with limited, or no access.
8. Separating Family-units by shipping them to different unknown locations.
9. Teaching married members to find new sex partners, and destroying marriages.
10. Bullying by fear: Telling members they will be damned by God if they leave
11. Manipulating members so they have no money, phone access, or passports
12. Non-stop 24/7 monitoring of members and removal of personal choice

13. Requiring new members to turn over everything they own.

14. Censoring all incoming and outgoing mail

15. Forbidding children and teens to attend school

16. A closed community that damns the entire outside world.

17. Mandatory obedience to David Berg and TF.

Discipline, Confinement and 24/7 Surveillance

TFI's practice of excessive discipline and confinement of members has been well documented by a variety of sources. Ex-members, underage advocacy agencies, the courts and various law enforcement and government agencies have all confirmed the dangerous and abusive treatment of child and adult members.

These unbridled abuses of adult, teen and child members took place over decades. To hide these practices members were confined, under 24/7 surveillance. The majority had no contact with anyone outside the group. If trusted members did interact with the outside world, they were taught to lie. 'Media Houses' were set up to coach all members what to say to the police, child welfare agency representatives or reporters when TF was under investigation.

'The Family' became notorious human rights violations. They confiscated member's passports, withheld mail and money, separated marriages and isolated children in kibbutz's, limiting or cutting off any parental access. Unfortunately, the depth of abuse

Because of this, TF were regularly under investigation for various types of human rights violations. They confiscated member's passports, withheld mail and money, separated marriages and isolated children in kibbutz's, limiting or cutting off parental access.

The severity of abuse was extreme. Underage children and teens were subjected to harsh and regular spankings for minor infractions of hundreds of rules via a demerit system. When placed on Silence Restriction, the person being punished had to wear a sign around their neck indicating no one is to talk to them. Other disciplines included: withholding food, sleep deprivation, isolation in a locked room or closet, forced sexual acts in front of peers to humiliate, hard labor, discontinuing of education, not being given clean clothes, not allowed fresh air or sunshine, made to sleep on the floor without a mattress or blanket, or increased indoctrination sessions.

> Hundreds of underage members have been mentally, physically, emotionally and spiritually damaged by these abuses. Eleven suicide deaths related to these abuses have been documented.

- In Buenos Aires, Argentina 268 children were taken into protective custody.
- In Barcelona, Spain, 22 children were placed in protective custody.
- In Sydney & Melbourne, Australia, 140 kids were taken into protective custody.
- In Condrieu, France 40 children were taken into protective custody.

To date 33 + legal cases have been filed against TFI for child abuse and excessive control of members. The diverse nations where these legal cases were filed affirm the abusive practices were entrenched throughout the TFI. Arrests and legal cases against TFI under its various name changes took place in Argentina, Australia, Brazil, France, Italy, Japan, Norway, Peru, Spain, Sweden, the UK, the USA, Mexico and Venezuela.

The Family + Mo & Maria on the Run!

> With law enforcement chasing Berg and Maria for sexual abuse of children and their Flirty-Fishing prostitution operation—both leaders are on the run. Berg claims, "We're being persecuted!"

Investigations, indictments and law suits follow them everywhere they go. In 1985 with the heat escalating Berg and Maria finally called off the practice of adult to child sex—making it punishable by excommunication. This is ironic since both Berg and Maria were the initiators of all of these adult to child sex practices they taught by example and then spread throughout 'The Family.' Other abuses of adult and underage teens and kids continued.

Merry Berg—Daughter of Aaron Berg.

"I was upset with my family when I was 13 years old. I came to realize grandfather was a hypocrite who made too many rules for people. He would write one thing one day, the opposite the next, because he said God was changing. He was very contradictory. He was a chronic alcoholic. It was very confusing. When he was sick he would drink and call different women in for sexual relations or sexual comfort. It was very difficult to respect this man when he was so drunk. I now look back at his writings as the ravings of a drunken madman. I was losing my faith in the group and in the prophet."

At age 14, I divulged my doubts to my grandfather and others. After they gave me a good talking to and my doubts didn't leave, I was punished with physical beatings, followed be several forceful attempts at exorcising demons from me. As they kept saying I had demons, I thought I began to see them. At night I would wake in terror. Several times I was stripped naked and spanked in front of my family.

When nothing worked I was banished to the Portuguese Island of Macao (Macau) near Hong Kong for three years and placed under my uncle Hosea's supervision. While there, I was subjected to isolation for close to six months, put on silence restrictions, forced to do incredibly hard physical work, physically beaten, sexually abused and had my head banged against the wall. I was under 24 hour surveillance, was bombarded by intense psychological questioning and placed in a reprogramming regiment to reintroduce 'Family' doctrines. I pretended to become compliant, but knew the whole thing was terribly wrong.

During this time I prayed intensely to Jesus Christ and He comforted me. Other teens were sent to Macau who also had been rebellious and they too were subjected to similar reprogramming tactics, to bring them back into 'Family' loyalty. When I empathized with them and it was discovered—I was put in a mental hospital and heavily sedated.

When I got better, being in the hospital had opened a door for me to escape and be sent to live with my grandma Jane (Eve) in the States. Eventually I would move to live with my aunt Linda (Deborah) Berg Davis and reunite with a number of my immediate family who were already out of 'The Family.'

Regaining an understanding of all that happened and beginning life over has been gradual but steady. I've gone back to school and am hopeful.

Merry's Words to Encourage

I have been greatly abused in many ways. Many times I was tempted to get bitter and blame God for it because I thought it was coming from His hand. There were times I doubted His existence. But in the times of my deepest crisis, I had no other refuge to flee to but Him. He was the One who worked things out. This Scripture came alive to me while living in Macau, "There is a friend who sticks closer than a brother (Proverbs 18:24)." So I prayed earnestly many times, "Lord, help me not to get bitter against You or harden my heart. Give me a solid, strong faith that cannot be shaken no matter what."

I rejoice to tell you that He did just that. It is obvious that only His supernatural grace could have brought me through these horrendous experiences and turnout "normal" and without being super-cynical.

My faith is stronger than ever, and no one can tell me that God isn't real and just and still working today. The sovereignty of God is displayed clearly in the supernatural way in which He delivered me out of each bad situation. I now look towards the future with excitement and anticipation.

The following passage describes my testimony:

"I waited patiently for the Lord; and he inclined unto me, and heard my cry. He brought me up also out of a horrible pit, out of the miry clay, and set my feet upon a rock, and established my goings. He hath put a new song in my mouth, even praise unto our God: many shall see it, and fear, and shall trust in the Lord."   Psalm 40:1-3 NIV®

"I want to encourage everyone to dedicate their lives fully to Jesus Christ and to always put their trust in God."
- Merry Berg

Discipline Camps

Macao aka Macau Island was the first 'Family' experiment with bringing an epidemic of rebellion among teens under control. Merry Berg was the first to experience these horrors. With some degree of success and applause from David Berg, his son Jonathan Berg aka (Hosea) expanded his work with rebellious teens, calling the program 'The Macao Detention Center.' It was similar to a 'hard labor camp' in any 'Communist regime.' The teens at Macao were made to work seven days a week, breaking up cement or old sidewalks and doing other hard labor. Each teen was on permanent 'silence restriction' and required to write confessions of their doubts or criticisms of leadership and report their disloyalty on a daily basis. Many were subjected to beatings and lengthy indoctrination sessions daily.

The retraining of disillusioned and rebellious teenagers led to the creation of more locations similar to Macao called 'Teen Training Camps' in Mexico, Peru and Japan. These camps grew into more permanent camps called 'Teen-Combos' aka 'Combos' where hundreds of incorrigible 'Family' teens were exposed to a wide variety of disciplines as at Macao, to 'break the rebellious spirit.'

'Combo Camps' were established in Chaclacayo, **Peru** / Pilar (Buenos Aires) **Argentina** / Bangkok, **Thailand** / Obuda, Budapest **Hungary** / Vienna, **Austria** / and Monterrey, **Mexico**. In time this led to the creation of 'Victor Camps' where teens were kept until broken, i.e. 'they got the victory' over rebellion. These camps were located in remote and isolated areas where there was minimal likelihood of escape. The largest Victor Camp was in *San Paulo, Brazil*. All of these camps beginning at Macao *'conducted brutal abuse of rebellious or doubting 'Family' teens.*

A significant number of teens who passed through these camps ended up compliant, but deeply wounded, withdrawn, disabled emotionally and unable to socialize. Teens who managed to retain their identity and 'resist being broken' grew intensely angry with hate toward their abusers and the lie of The Family being a nurturing healthy spiritual environment that represented God.

A Large Population of Child & Teen Victims

With TFI population numbers ranging as high as 20,000 at one time, and 13,000 of these being underage, the amount of sexual, mental and physical abuse-punishment was expansive.

Ravaged

Except for the very youngest, most of these children and teens were drawn into Berg and Maria's sexual world of experimentation. *Literally thousands of children were exploited and ravaged sexually over a 14 year period.* Children 2-7 were molested, children 8-17 were exploited as objects of sexual pleasure by adults, parents and peers. Female teens age 17 were allowed to join the Flirty-Fishing campaigns and engage in most sexually luring practices.

Litnessing

Berg was always coming up with new fund-raisers for his growing band of disciples to carry out. With Flirty-Fishing coming under fire from the authorities and increased venereal diseases, he revved up printing and selling Mo Letters with quotas to be met. The undertaking was massive, but not as lucrative as FF. Many concluded the strangeness of Berg's letters about spirit-guides, pornographic content and spewing out random tiraids didn't help sales.

Standing up for The Victims

A huge number of people have passed through or been raised in 'The Family.' Many former members have disappeared into obscurity in a cocoon of pain and regret and their voices will never be heard. Those who have shared their capsule comments in this chapter do so to make sure the truth is told for this present generation and those to come. We've reduced the number, but provide enough to give an accurate overview of the kinds of abuses members experienced.

X-COG, The Family of Love, The Family, The Family International and Parents Speak Out:

General:

Leaders kept our passports and didn't give us money so we couldn't just leave.

We were not allowed to contact outside family or friends or make phone calls.

I was kept busy 12 to16 hours a day and assigned a partner if new or doubting.

I was not allowed to go to school and didn't learn how to read until I was nine.

The majority of kibbutz nannies were overworked, cruel and abusive.

As a kid I didn't have clean clothes most the time and rarely had shoes to wear.

We hardly ever got to go outside and play because we were a closed community.

I and other kids who were my friends went to sleep crying for years over the abuses.

Many of us had no clue who our parents were and grew to hate our life in the family.

I was told I'd be a traitor and die if I left the Family and everyone would hate me.

As punishment my head was shaved like Hitler's mandate to Jews— to humble me.

I had to sever my emotional ties with Family members to be strong enough to leave.

I didn't know right from wrong, or truth from a lie after absorbing Berg's teachings.

We were tightly controlled as kids when underage kids began to outnumber the adults.

To curb rebellion, 12 yr. olds and up had to write daily reports on our thought life.

The regiment inside TF was rigid & manipulating with almost no free time.

We were kept off balance by *The Family* moving us often and minimal sleep.

For decades we heard, "To leave the Family, meant we would be cursed by God!"

I was *'Used-Up'* by TFI and exited an abused and broken person, with no faith.

We were taught, The Family was the only people on earth following God.

I felt like an abused prisoner in TF, with no choices or way to leave.

I had a nervous breakdown over what happened in TF and the abuse I witnessed.

My kids were raised in a Family kibbutz and severely abused— today they hate me.

I've had to block out almost all memories of life in this *cult* in order to function.

Berg's 2 big prophecies of Jesus' return and the USA being destroyed never happened!

Maria's big prophecy about her son Ricky becoming a great prince never materialized.

Mo & Maria manipulated everything and micro managed all leaders and members.

TFI's roots are rebellion; Berg hated the church, government & families.

In a few short years, Berg put his revelations above the Bible to gain complete control.

Having a secret prophet in hiding made us feel important and kept everyone guessing.

Kids we were asked to spy on each other and got a reward when we reported someone.

Mo's teachings split up our marriage and removed any contact with our children.

We used Christian words to *Outsider Christian Systemites,* but inwardly despised them.

Kids were taught to never talk to outsiders, the police or reporters unless trained.

During TFL era a huge number of Family members didn't know their parents.

I had no idea where my parents or siblings were and had no way of finding them.

I spent 15 years in TF which ruined my life. TF fed us demonic lies and I fell for it.

I had mental breaking points over what TF became and the perversions we accepted.

Maria & Peter, the groups leaders have tried to erase TF's sordid and evil history.

Admitting I'd been deceived was hard to acknowledge, but freed me to move forward.

A fear-driven numbing of conscience enabled this cult to deceive and flourish.

My spouse was intentionally turned against me and I had no access to our children.

Moses David Berg and Maria used their prophecies to control and manipulate us.

I had to make a quota selling Mo's sex Letters that people didn't want.

Berg dissolved marriages and promoted multiple partners—resulting in lots of kids.

Kids were the property of The Family. Hundreds of us didn't know our parents.

We were indoctrinated daily in lengthy sessions to promote loyalty to Berg and TF.

Mo got angry often; in fits of rage and fury he would demote leaders for any reason.

I'm convinced— David Berg was a schizophrenic, ego & sex driven false prophet!

TFI's Website Scrubbing is a another example of how they try to trick outsiders.

Many *Family* kids who didn't know their parents, became disturbed and angry.

Out of TF for 10 years, God is gradually restoring me through studying the Bible.

Sexual Perversions and Abuse:

Mo's obsession with sex polluted the entire Family; hundreds were severely abused.

Mo and Maria were fixated on Sex and Spiritism which they disseminated to us.

Mo said God was tired of marriage; we could abandon it and have sex with anyone.

At age 12 I was forced to watch sex videos to learn how to perform sexual acts.

The aftermath of sexual abuse left *Family* kids unhappy, depressed and wounded.

My mom dressed up pretty to go Flirty-Fishing, but had to get drunk before she went.

All colony books and videos were about sex. Sex drove everything in *The Family*.

At ages 6-11 we were encouraged to fondle, masterbate and give oral sex to others.

From age 12 and up I had to *'share'* by giving sex to teens & adults who wanted it.

I wasn't allowed to wear panties at night in case an adult wanted sex.

From ages11-16 I was taught to dance nude for videos because I was pretty.

Berg and Maria wrote lots of letters and books and made sex videos for us to watch.

At 12 years old I was taught giving sex to peers, adults and even parents was OK.

One of my nannies raped and molested me on a number of occasions.

Molesting and sibling-to-sibling sex was rampant for many years.

I rarely saw my parents. In the kibbutz I was beaten & sexually molested regularly.

At age 14, as the only girl in our house, I had to *share sex* with a number of the boys.

I was forced to Flirty-Fish at age 18 and hated it— FF ruined my concept of sex.

Once Flirty-Fishing began, we should have all left! Many ladies burnt out quickly.

Even with herpes & venereal diseases we had to keep on Flirty-Fishing.

By 1978 we were a worldwide prostitution ring with The Family coffers rapidly filling.

I had at least 75 sex partners during *The Family of Love* era. I'm now totally ashamed!

Taking communion and then having group sex was another one of Berg's sick ideas.

Moses David said he owned all the women and girls for his pleasure and reveled in it.

Berg said God would care for all the babies; some colonies had over 50 underage kids!

All money received from Flirty-Fishing was turned over to local family leaders.

My wife is still scarred emotionally from Flirty-Fishing and turned off to God.

TFI's current leader Maria, began the practice of incest in the group and promoted it.

Nothing was off limits in Mo & Maria's sex bag; Berg seduced his own grandchildren.

Berg was sex-crazed, turning members into sex slaves for profit.

Mo poisoned us with sex perversions and sent sex videos for 12-17 year olds to watch.

Beginning at age 12 through 17 years old we were forced to watch sex videos regularly.

When the police shut down Flirty-Fishing, I was told to join an escort service.

I was with 100 other kids in Australia. All of us were all physically and sexually abused.

I purposely got pregnant to escape Flirty-Fishing; it was so wrong and degrading.

I never rode a bike, watched TV, or saw a movie, only *sex video tapes.*

At 17, I was urged to prove my loyalty to Berg and TF by *'Sharing'* (sex) where I lived.

Most early parents agonized when their kids were placed in *'kid's kibbutz sex hives.'*

My mom literally went *'crazy'* with guilt because of all the sex she participated in.

I will never get married or have kids! Being sexually abused for years—turned me off.

Spiritism:

When Berg and Maria let the Occult and Spiritism into TF, demons overtook us.

Berg continually spewed out depraved teachings—inspired by *'unclean spirits.'*

Having spirit guides led to sex with spirits and tormenting dreams.

Enticed by the spirits in David Berg, we waited anxiously for every new Mo-letter.

By inviting evil spirits in, I changed. Lying and immoral behavior became the norm.

My mother became extremely mean and uncaring after evil spirits entered her

Mo's said *'holy ghosts' were spirits from the dead* we were to welcome in.

Inviting evil spirits as spiritual guides was stupid! It devastated the entire Family.

A spirit of strong delusion had, and still has a grip on TFI. What they teach is a lie!

The spirit guides I met through TF were evil and disgusting—wanting to control me.

Mo's partner Mama Maria loves the occult and enjoys promoting spiritism.

Punishment, Physical and Emotional Abuse:

As a kid I was beaten regularly and had bruises on different parts of my body.

When punished I had to wear a sign, 'Silence Restriction' around my neck.

I was accused of being the devil by Mo and sent far away to be punished.

Teen, Victor and Combo Camps were remote teen discipline/indoctrination sites.

All leaders lived in fear of being punished, demoted or sent to some remote spot.

Any questioning or failure to obey Berg's directives was disloyalty and punishable.

As a kid, I was severely punished and put into isolation often for 1-3 days

Life in The Family was a hell-hole of abuse—especially for kids who got it the worst.

I was starved and isolated in a closet to break me and stop my questioning.

All colony leaders dreaded being rebuked or excommunicated over minor mistakes.

I was locked in a small room for several days with only water—to humble me.

Life in the Family was like a bad dream, *full of evil occurrences you couldn't stop.*

Family leaders tried to expel my demons of doubt many times—unsuccessfully.

Family leaders have no remorse about the terrible abuses they put the group through.

Several of my Family nannies found pleasure in abusing and hurting me.

I was locked inside a small room for 5 days with limited food and water.

My punishment was isolation and being required to write an apology 100's of times.

To doubt Mo's authority, if found out, meant sever punishment for lengthy periods.

I had young friends who went crazy and committed suicide because of being abused.

Life was so bleak for tweens and teens I tried to commit suicide a number of times.

I had no privacy except on the toilet and I couldn't trust anyone in TF.

I had to submit to TF's teachings and practices, or be placed in isolation.

Aftermath for X Family

I may never dislodge some memories of abuse that haunt my thoughts and dreams.

10 years out, I'm still leery and suspicious of people and spiritual things.

I waited too long to leave, fearing I'd be hated by my friends and family inside.

My view of God and Jesus Christ is all screwed up and I've been out for 15 years.

I know this doesn't sound good, but if heaven is like TFI, I don't want to go.

At first I just wanted to hide. I never tell people what happened— it was so evil.

Since leaving TFI, I've been in a Twilight Zone of inner turmoil.

I escaped on foot with no money in a foreign land. *It was 100% the right thing to do!*

Once out of TF, it took 2 years before I could bring myself to pray.

Since leaving I've been in a fog; I feel anger, disgust, guilt, fear and confusion.

Remembering all the bad stuff done to us as kids— all I can think about is revenge.

I'm afraid to tell others what happened to us in TF; who could possibly understand?!

Working through the terrible experiences I had in TF seems impossible, but I'm trying.

My outside family helped my children and I escape with airfare and loving support.

Since out, I've found a Cult Support Group which has helped a lot. They get it!

I've had to reset all my beliefs through carefully restudying what Jesus Christ taught.

TFI's website has been scrubbed clean to hide all of its *Abusive Crimes!*

No matter what TFI appears to be, beware of their hidden agenda and deceptions!

We were not allowed to think for ourselves or make decisions. Leaders did that for us.

The Family International is among the most secretive, manipulative, abusive and deceptive cults in recent history.

A Damaged Prince Who Dies Too Young

Maria got pregnant on one of her 'Flirty-Fishing' outings and later gave birth to a son named Ricky Rodriquez while living in Spain. He was given the name 'Davidito' by Berg, who took him in as a stepson but never legally adopted him. Berg and Maria gave him the title of 'Prince' within the Family which he never attained to.

Ricky's Experience

Living in the 'Royal Family' was not all it was cracked up to be, according to Ricky. He was raised in a strict regimented setting, with high expectations placed on him. No TV and little free time to just be a kid. *His mother and several nannies engaged him in various sexual activities over the years, beginning when he was a toddler.* This created a deep level of confusion and pent up anger. In time he was encouraged to be sexually active with his siblings. It took a toll on his mind and heart. These and other perverted sexual mandates converged with TF's secrecy, lying and physical punishment of his friends. He felt others got things a lot worse than he did. In his words, "They treated us like crap! They were sick perverts! We were their sex slaves!"

Ricky referred to 'Teen Camp' as a place where pre-teens and teens were exposed to some very sick sex stuff including sex with animals. Older girls were taught to have sex with boys as young as 5 years old. This was going on alongside heavy indoctrination. Everyone was required to read Mo's 'Teen Sex' letter and other sex letters which went into great detail. "My perverted mother along with Moses pushed all kinds of sex stuff on all of us. They wanted all of the younger kids who couldn't get pregnant to have as much sex as possible before puberty. They wanted us to masturbate as if we were 'making love with Jesus.' None of it computed. It was sick and messed up!"

A Very Sad Ending

When 'adult sexual abuse of minors' was discontinued in the late 1980's in TF, *Berg and Maria decided to have a psychological evaluation conducted on Ricky to prove that childhood abuse had no lasting effect on underage children, teens, or young adults.*

Sometime around 1990 Psychologist Dr. Lawrence Lilliston was hired by Maria to perform a psychological test on Ricky to confirm there was not any permanent damage caused by his being exposed to and experiencing some child abuse. The 'test report' findings indicated "Ricky was fine!"

With a sigh of relief, Berg and Maria concluded TF was off the hook! Without haste they made use of this report to inform all Family leaders and adults that all was good, "the kids will get over their emotional issues!" TF was hopeful this would be the case to lessen their legal and financial woes over underage sexual and physical abuse that had been in the court cases around the world for over 14 years.

But were these findings reliable? *What psychologist could conclude kids who were severely abused sexually, physically and psychologically for years, could grow into happy and well-adjusted adults without any emotional or mental trauma surfacing?* One has to wonder whether Ricky's psychological evaluation was performed with an expectation communicated to Dr. Lilliston in advance?

Fast forward to 2001; Ricky is now in his mid-twenties, engaged to be married and he and his fiancée both decide to leave TF. Ricky's anger and frustration has peaked. 20 years of continual indoctrination and sexual, physical and emotional abuse accompanied by unrelenting control of his movements had to stop!

On leaving he tells his mom, (Maria now leader of TF) *"We cannot continue to condone or be party to what we feel is an abusive, manipulative organization that teaches false doctrine. You have devoured God's sheep, ruining people's lives by propagating false doctrines and advocating harmful practices in the name of God, and as far as I can see, show no regret or remorse."*

Leaving was the first step, but dislodging bad stuff from his inner world was not possible. By 2004 Ricky and spouse had settled in Washington State, trying to start over. Unfortunately, *Ricky couldn't get all the terrible memories of Life in TF out of his head. They flooded his waking hours and tormented him at night.* Revisiting sick, unspeakable events of abuse and perversions stirred up intense anger and thoughts of revenge.

Fixated on the abuse perpetrated on thousands of kids in TF, he becomes determined to do something about it. He was livid with anger that no one has been held accountable! TF has never confessed to all of the horrific things they taught and promoted in the name of God. Instead, his mom and other Family leadership had brushed it aside by erasing all the atrocities committed against kids as a *non-alarming common mistake.* They've rewritten their history and purposely removed thousands of Mo and Maria Letters that verify the abuse. In Ricky's own words, "We were methodically molested, tortured, raped, and many were murdered—by being driven to suicide."

As a prolonged culmination of years of abuse, Ricky concludes someone must pay and revenge seems the only just and righteous solution. He feels, at least the world will be reminded of what all the kids like him suffered at the hands of Family perverts! X-Family members will know their pain has been acknowledged.

With Berg dead, Ricky knows his mom, *Maria, is the ongoing source of evil along with 'Peter' Amsterdam aka Steven Kelly* (now Christopher Smith) running TF. She and Peter continue to propel TFI forward glossing over the severe abuse perpetrated against thousands of members.

In October of 2004 Ricky moves to Tucson, Arizona and obtains work as an electrician. According to accounts by friends and relatives, he moved there because he heard his mother had visited Angela Smith who lives there. Ricky thinks Maria will return to Tucson and he wants to find her. After being in Tucson several months he learns his mom will most likely not be returning anytime soon.

In December of 2004 Ricky begins devising a plan of carrying out revenge on his mom's good friend, Angela Smith who he associates with his early childhood sexual abuse.

According to Ricky and others, Angela lived with Berg and Maria in their home for a number of years and was involved in his abuse, or by omission said and did nothing while the abuse was occurring when Ricky was a young boy. Ricky is also aware that Angela was among the first Flirty-Fish prostitutes to join his mom on outings during the time-frame when he was conceived through these sex outings. In short, Angela was deeply involved and complicit in many of the sexual and other perversions TF adopted.

Resigned to settle for revenge on Angela Smith, Ricky makes a video as a means of explaining to anyone who might view it, what he's thinking and what he plans to do. Having personally viewed this video, the contents suggest Ricky feels he's run out of options and he's resigned to make some-one who was in on the perversions in TFI, pay. He feels it's his responsibil-ity, since TFI has failed to admit their guilt.

In January 2005, Ricky met with Angela Smith for dinner and afterwards she returned to his apartment where he stabbed her to death. He then drove to Blythe, California where he shot himself in the head.

In advance he'd made plans for the videotape he'd made to be distributed to friends, family and former members explaining his actions. In this video, Rick says he saw himself as a vigilante avenging children like him and his sisters who'd been subject to rapes and beatings and made into sex slaves. "There's this need that I have," he said. "It's not a want. It's a need for revenge. It's a need for jus-tice, because I can't go on like this."

Angela Smith's birth name was Susan Joy Kauten. The names Angela was known by in TF were: Joy, Sue, Cedar, Trust and Hope. She like many other **higher ups in TF** changed their last name to Smith to avoid being found, or prosecuted for crimes perpetrated in the past.

Ricky Rodriguez's birth name was David Moses Zerby (nicknamed Davidito or Pete) and later legally changed his name to Richard Peter Smith. He was 30 years old when he took his life.

Two more deaths were now added to a number that keeps growing because of the massive abuses The Family International perpetrated.

Aftermath of Horror

Anguish of heart, tears of regret and guilt has been the pervasive experi-ence for those who've left the COG aka 'The Family'. My first family finally left in the late 1970's. Many friends from Atlanta also left at different times and began their lives over. Continuing ramifications have been felt regard-ing various doctrines that were taught, accepted and practiced. Innocent children were swept up into it all.

Consider the disillusionment, embarrassment, confusion and terrible memories that live on among those abused and ravaged by this cult. When the name of God is used next to such horrendous evil—the entire concept of spiritual things can easily become repulsive.

This is why religious cult victims who survive and manage to free themselves are often wounded so deeply—they cannot bring themselves to open their heart to anything or anyone including God. Memories and flashbacks of pain and abuse, guilt and hate are extremely hard to dislodge. We don't want to revisit them. What we'd like most is to block them out forever!

Legacy of Terror and Abuse

The Berg family: David Berg and son Paul aka Aaron Berg are deceased. Daughter Faithy and other son Hosea are believed to still be active in TFI. Deborah Linda Berg escaped with her children in the late 1980's.

The fourteen year practice of sexually abusing children including incest and female members being required to prostitute for money or donations was abandoned in 1987—mostly due to venereal disease, public outcry, legal prosecution and expensive law suits filed against 'The Family.'

Other abusive practices continued among members as did Mo Letter directives that kept members perversely entertained and leaders fearing punishment and demotions. An innumerable number of families were dissolved and a myriad left TFI disillusioned, used up, broken and deeply wounded. Many thousands of underage kids during 14 years of severe abuse were physically, sexually, emotionally and mentally terrorized, traumatized and suffer from long-lasting emotional scars. The history of the "Family" during this time-frame is heartbreaking. Over 11 suicide deaths have been documented as a result of members being abused.

Berg's Reprobate Mentality
Deborah(Linda Berg) Davis

> "There are so many examples of my dad's depraved mind, and how he treats both adults and children like objects on a game board, to be moved around, used, abused, and exploited for the sake of his personal pleasure and cause.'

My father is arrogant, continually inventing new ways to commit evil. He is heartless, having lost all natural affection. He no longer loves those he should. He is motivated by a lust for power and sensual pleasure; to him, love is lust. He states, "God is sex!" He thinks nothing of taking wives from their husbands, or sending fathers away from their children, never to see them again. He has proudly proclaimed, "I don't like that word 'married' anymore either!" People in the movement are now 'mated' for convenience sake. When one tires of the other, they move on. And as for the children, my dad's teaching that "God will take care of them" with all the abuse that has occurred, is further proof he doesn't care. I am shocked at what my father has become."

David Berg and Maria Zerby Fontaine (now Katherine Rianna Smith), jointly modeled and then released an avalanche of non-Biblical teachings, doctrines and practices that ravaged their members. To justify this behavior which was the opposite of Scripture, they elevated 'Mo Letters' above the Bible claiming God had given them new freedoms. The bad fruit that fell because of these claims is one of the most heartbreaking accounts of religious deception and abuse of its members in modern times.

What's "The Family International" Morphing into Today with Queen Maria—The New Leader?

Before David Berg died he passed the mantle of leadership to Maria saying she would carry on the work as the great prophetess. After Berg's death in 1994 Maria Zerby Fontaine entered the writing fray with her own *'Spiritism and sexual letters' with obscene artwork accompanying.* She claimed she pre-existed and was among Jesus' favorite lovers in heaven before she came to earth. She had a 'Family' artist draw a picture of Jesus caressing one of her breasts on the cover of one of her letters.

In prophecies published for her followers, she claims Jesus told her, "You are Maria of the End, the prophetess, the un-locker of the mysteries of heaven (Heavenly Birthdays -Maria Letter 3193, Para.87)." *She also claims her birth was a turning point in the history of life on earth, and that she was sent to earth so 'Family members' may partake of her beauty and purity.* It is also claimed that she has the power to heal by supernatural means.

She has solidified her role as "Queen" through multiple letters, child story books, video interviews and other communications to Family International followers.

Queen Maria's current husband is Steven Kelly aka 'Peter Amsterdam' aka King Peter, who in recent years has legally changed his name to Christopher Smith.

1995 Reorganization

In 1995 TFI reorganized itself, adopting a membership charter which codified the beliefs, rights, and responsibilities of full-time Family members. Family members and communities would now operate according to their own decisions and initiative within the framework of The Family Internationals Charter. *Fifteen years of strange doctrines and practices continued until the next change.*

2010 TFI Reboot

In 2010, after a two-year process of evaluation, The Family made a change in their structure, doctrine, and practices. The longstanding practice of living in 'communal housing' aka 'colonies' was discontinued. *This reorganization resulted in the adoption of a new organizational model and the closure of the majority of TFI's previous communal centers.* TFI says this change was made in order to better achieve their purpose of reaching the world with the gospel message, and to allow for greater diversity.

Currently, *TFI is organized as an Online community.* To reflect the organization's restructuring and its aims of empowering individuals to operate independently, the Family's governing charter was streamlined and modified.

TF went from hyper micro-managing everything in their member's lives to becoming an 'Online Community' according to TFI public relations communications. Some believe they still operate strategic communal compounds and training centers in remote places.

The new image of TFI is a Christian Fellowship. Peter Amsterdam and Maria Fontaine now appear conservative in their photos. *TFI website appears shockingly Christian, but is not!*

New members are oblivious to TFI's horrendous history as one of the worst sex-cults in modern times. Those who join will probably never be allowed to read the near 3000 Mo Letters that reveal the sinister and perverse foundation upon which this group was founded. *Children born or raised in this group from 1973-1994 were victims of the worst types of child abuse reported among any religious cult recorded in modern history.*

Scrubbing Down 'The Family's (TFI) Crime Scene

The group is still active in some 80 countries doing outreach and recruiting. TFI's 2018-19 website articles and literature appear Bible-based and traditionally Christian. *TFI has carefully removed thousands of Mo letters claiming his "Super Prophet" status, and hundreds of additional Mo letters that coerced female members into prostitution, encouraged sex abuse of children, molestation of minors, lesbian practices and incest etc.*

Maria's self-glorification status as Queen, 'Sex and Spiritism letters' 'Sex and Masturbation with Jesus Letters' have likewise been removed from public view. TFI's website has retained a few tame Mo letters for viewing which are heavily sanitized. On their site-map I found several more, but they too had all of Berg's ranting and ravings removed.

At this writing I have read many of the articles posted on TFI website. These include doctrinal positions, beliefs on different topics, TFI's statement of faith, devotional literature, leader articles, member articles and magazine articles. I've also explored and read over their theological teaching on topics of faith. Most of these writing are now using Bible references.

TFI's magazine *"Activated"* has a sizable number of articles. Many use Bible and deceased Christian author quotes. *"Viewpoints"* contains articles written by members and friends. Another website archival link is called *"Anchor"* which contains an index of not too distant past teachings. Nearby is the *"Director's Corner"* featuring a variety of articles written by current leaders Maria Fontaine & Peter Amsterdam. All articles come across as polished and Christian. Peter Amsterdam has emerged as the theologian, Bible teacher and main writer for TFI when it comes to doctrine. He is busily amassing a new resource library for Online members. At least 300 of Peter's and 100 of Maria's articles are posted as of May of 2018. All articles have been sanitized from previously recognizable cult literature.

TFI is currently based in Neugasse, Switzerland. They have a company called Aurora Production. Aurora sells TFI literature, teaching materials, books, greeting cards, music and other resources—all appearing and sounding Christian. They no doubt will be attempting to place their literature with Christian publishers and distributors all over the world.

Hidden Agenda

Anything controversial is for members only. Several years ago I found a 'Deeper Truths' tab on their website that led to letters from Mo and Maria on topics of 'Sex and Spiritism' and a few other radical themes. This site-map tab is no longer available to the public.

Also on their website is their Statement of Faith. It says, *"Our fundamental beliefs are generally in accordance with those held by Christians the world over; we also embrace some untraditional doctrines."*

In another location on their web page I read, *"It is our belief that heterosexual relations, when practiced as God ordained and intended between consenting adults, are a pure and natural wonder of God's creation, and permissible according to Scripture."*

TFI's Core Non-Christian Practices

1) Open-sex between 18 years and older adults members.

2) Inviting personal Spirit-Guides for direction, protection and to receive a spirit-tongue.

3) Secrecy, deception i.e. lying to new members and outsiders.

4) Use of different personal, or Group Front-Names to hide their identity.

TFI's Current Status

➢ David Berg, aka Mo, David, Moses David, Father David, is still acknowledged as TFI founder. TFI history portrayal of Berg is one who was kind, gentle, caring, loving and wise i.e. Father David. Most who've followed his 'Mo' Letter directives through the group's sordid history do not agree!

➢ Maria Zerby aka Fontaine (new legal name Katherine Rianna Smith taken in 1997) aka Queen Maria, co-directs TFI with her

- husband, Steven Kelley aka Peter Amsterdam.

- TFI still boasts Flirty-Fishing Sex has won 100,000 souls to Christ.

- Open Sex Sharing among members is still practiced but not mentioned to outsiders.

- Inviting Spirit-Guide Partners is active. These spirits are called ministering spirits, personal angels or holy spirits (in plural). The spirits, or spiritual beings TFI claims are available to members are:

  Abrahim a deceased Bulgarian Gypsy King
  Arcothon aka *Arcros* a conduit for god's power
  Brunheld – fights for TFI
  Ellya – draws members to use the keys of the kingdom. This refers to one of the groups mysterious doctrines.

Since David Berg's death, Maria has increased her dependence in the Spirit World and accelerated teaching on this subject encouraging Spirit Sex and Channeling. Some think this is partially due to her becoming clinically blind. The reality is, there are numerous Spirits controlling and deeply embedded in TFI that don't want to leave!

- TFI has rewritten their history and entirely erased their horrifying member abuse history including the 'Family of Love' years from 1978-86

- TFI has removed over 3000+ Mo Letters from David Berg and several hundred Maria Zerby Letters from public view that reveal their core beliefs and practices throughout their history.

- The longstanding practice of deceiving the public and younger members continues. Lying is permissible when hiding the beliefs, practices, doctrines, intentions, or anything related to TFI so it might maintain an advantage over members and outsiders who might be 'used.' Example: Peter Amsterdam will happily meet with any Christian leader who might be sympathetic to TFI. Using conservative Christian jargon, he happily points to the group's website that appears Christian to undiscerning viewers. Flying under the name Aurora Publishing, a massive literature publishing and distribution campaign has been underway in recent years. I choked when I read their new motto of 'timeless values!'

➢ Recently while reading their Online articles I ran across Jesus' prophesying in the first person and in other instances, God talking in the first person. These types of long quotes were TFI member authors' words—not found in the Bible. I also found mention of spirit-guides referred to as personal angels. The initials DBB are at the end of various quotes. These refer to David Brant Berg who Maria and Peter have purposely assigned a lower profile to for good reason.

➢ TFI continues its practice of extreme secrecy surrounding leadership and finances. World Services (WS), the central administrative wing of 'The Family International', continues to operate in complete secrecy, with very few members of The Family actually knowing their whereabouts or the identities of the members in those offices. All higher ups operate under pseudonyms instead of their more commonly known Bible names. Many leader members or former leaders have legally changed their names several times as in Maria Zerby's case to avoid prosecution in child and members abuse cases. The last name chosen by most is Smith.

Is Deliverance From TFI Deception Possible?

The answer is a resounding YES! God's grace, mercy, love and pardoning ability is greater than all our sins and mis-steps!

Multiple thousands were swept up into the zeal and growth of TFI who appeared to be wholeheartedly committed to God. In the early days, only a few top leaders knew of David Berg's alliance with the Spirit-world and taking multiple wives. Soon he used his authority and teachings to pressure his own family and other young leaders into sexual partner swapping.

Eventually the entire group was swept up into these types non-Biblical directives. One X-Family confessed:

"We drank the poison, fell prey to the doctrines of demons, gave into group pressure, or out of fear were paralyzed into silence. Our conscience was seared and became numb. One perversion and spiritual error after another was unleashed through Mo Letter directives. We gave in, lost our way and no longer knew what the Truth was!"

Is there spiritual hope for a person who turns 100% away from a cult and its teachings? Yes, there's always hope if a person is willing to do an about-face and resist all that is evil and call out to the True and Living God in humility, asking for His help.

Can an individual cling to part of a cult's teachings and still be a Christian? No human can authoritatively answer this question, but there is a strong case to be made for making a clean break with the teachings and practices of any cult. Religious cults twist and manipulate truth weaving in their own doctrines. If a cult uses the Bible, their interpretations and special teachings are fused into a collection of toxic and polluted doctrines. The Holy Scriptures give us this directive:

> Come out from among them and be separate, says the
> Lord. Do not touch, cling or hold onto what is evil and
> unclean—and I will receive you.   2 Corinthians 6:17

Since religious cults are under the guidance and have been infiltrated by a host of evil, unclean, lying and divination spirits (satanic religious), posing to represent God—a widespread *'strong delusion'* is present. This delusion is what lures people in and keeps them under a cult's influence. *If we were to see through the eyes of the 'Holy Spirit' when looking at a cult or a pagan religion, we would be shocked to see demons controlling and manipulating everything!*

Using the name of God or Jesus Christ by a cult is nothing more than a front to appear Christian, while cloaking what they really believe. They are preaching another Jesus.

Jesus Christ said: "Watch out that you are not deceived. For many will come in my name, claiming, 'I am he,' and, 'The time is near.' Do not follow them" (Luke 21:8).

Ingesting or holding onto teachings from any known or suspected cult is opening the door for evil to enter, or reenter. *When a person is diagnosed with cancer, the way forward is clear; remove all of the cancer with surgery, or begin some combative treatment plan to kill all the cancer cells!* The same applies to a cult's teaching and practices—we need 'a complete cleanse' from the 'spirit of error and delusion' that is embedded in all cults. Renounce it all!

For decades TFI has claimed to represent God and Jesus Christ. It's a LIE of gargantuan proportions! The way forward for anyone who wants to be cleansed is—

Ask God the True Father and Jesus Christ His Son for forgiveness of every sin committed while in this cult; for discernment and courage to renounce every evil spirit and all deceptive teachings taken in. In humility, ask God to cleanse your soul. Place yourself under the covering of Almighty God and ask Him to guard your heart, mind and soul. Make this earnest petition in the authority and power of the Name of Jesus Christ.

Have TFI Leader's Repented?

As noted, TFI's website now looks and sounds Christian. *In the past, all image and public relations attempts by the group failed when examined carefully.* With TFI's long history of hiding its inner beliefs and intentions from outsiders, it's almost impossible to know with accuracy what evils are still being taught and practiced in secret.

Those who've viewed TFI's general letter of apology about some children being abused doesn't acknowledge the massive 'sexual, mental and physical atrocities' perpetrated on underage and adult members spanning 25 + years. During and beyond this time frame, the 'harsh and abusive discipline' of member's continued. TFI's generic and cursory apology skirts any mention of the kinds and seriousness of these abuses because they were all illegal!

X-Family view of TFI's token apology letter

"While the TFI eventually disavowed its most abusive sexual, physical, emotional and discipline practices, they have done nothing to bring abusers to justice, or acknowledge their leadership role in promoting these mandated doctrines that unleashed horrific abuse. The absence of acknowledging the specific abuses TFI was responsible for, is because *they were all illegal!* "

In addition to skirting any detailed admission of guilt, those responsible have changed their last names to *Smith* to avoid legal prosecution for numerous crimes. Thousands of 'Family Members' were severely abused. One X-Family member says, "Our well-being was never a priority to leaders!"

Have TFI's leaders repented? Is there any sense of sorrow on their part for thrusting thousands of female members into sex-trafficking under the guise of being on a spiritual mission of evangelism? Have Family leaders communicated a contrite heart before God, their members and X-Members for all the sexual perversions they taught and mandated members to participate in— including incest?

TFI's current website and X-Family members agree there is an absence of true repentance for all the abuses carried out. One X-Family members writes, "The Family is like a Chameleon lizard changing colors to survive. Very little has changed. At their core, they are dependent on demon spirit guides, now disguising themselves as holy spirits."

No Christ-centered Christian group under the guidance of the Father and Jesus Christ His Son, and the Holy Spirit would pride themselves in claiming to have won 100,000 souls to Christ through Flirty-Sex-Fishing. As Maria Zerby was the originator of this sexual practice of prostitution, she must find it hard to let go of these lofty statistics that both she and cohort David Brant Berg loved to brag about.

Female members who were *forced into sexual prostitution* disagree strongly with TFI's version of Flirty-Fishing. They say, *"Leading men to God through giving them sex, almost never happened! We were urged to obtain money for sex and move on to the next prospect, with individual fund-raising quotas we had to meet before returning to where we lived."*

> Historically, sacred prostitution, temple prostitution, cult prostitution, and religious prostitution all have roots of alliance with heathen and pagan people groups, inspired by demons of lust.

X-Family members from the 'Flirty-Fishing' era confirm this practice was the main money maker that sustained The Family of Love until authorities across the globe discovered TFI's Prostitution Ring. Legal woes and prosecution for prostitution and a variety of underage abuses including adult to child sex and incest, forced the shutdown of Flirty-Fishing and some child-sexual abuse practices.

A fund-raiser adopted which ran parallel to FF was called 'Litnessing' which entailed selling Mo Letters and other literature on the streets. Both men and women were required to do this and given quotas to meet. Though not as lucrative as Flirty-Fishing, it was legal.

In the present, TFI has attempted to erase decades of their history and thousands of radical, spiritism and sexually perverse 'Mo and Maria Letters' and teachings. In 2018 I found a few on TFI's website which were heavily redacted and scrubbed down to hide the crimes of TFI. They were under the subheading 'Deeper Truths.'

These teachings are not new, but an old demonic ploy of Satan. God warned followers of Jesus Christ in the city of Thyatira about a false prophetess named Jezebel who was leading some believers into sexual immorality and idol worship. Note the similarity of supposed 'Deep Secrets' she was disseminating and the warning given to the church.

> "I say to the rest of you in Thyatira, do not hold to her teachings. Don't be seduced by Satan's so-called 'deep secrets." Revelation 2:24 NIV®

-The Apostle John

TFI's 2018-19 Website

On TFI's website there is no acknowledgment of wrongdoing and decades of severe abuse of members. Instead they tally and brag about phenomenal successes and accomplishments.

TFI's website quote: "The Family International has been characterized by its missionary and humanitarian activities around the globe. As of 2014, members had shared the gospel message with nearly 310 million people and prayed with nearly 35 million people to receive God's gift of salvation. Since The Family Internationals inception in 1968, members have produced and distributed over 1.1 billion pieces of gospel literature in 61 languages, and over 16.6 million audio tapes /CD's and DVD's in 20 languages." In another location on TFI's current website it says, 100,000 souls have been won to Christ through 'Flirty-Fishing.'

The claim that 100,000 have come to faith in Christ through sexual prostitution and their new propaganda subheading below of 'Timeless Values' makes me want to puke!

AURORA PRODUCTION AG
SWITZERLAND
TIMELESS VALUES IN A CHANGING WORLD

AURORA PRODUCTIONS AG is The Family International's newest online (front) store. *Book buyers and distribution outlets should steer clear of this counterfeit Christian publishing company.*

Considering the widespread physical, emotional and sexual abuse of members and destructive doctrines taught and practiced, it's surprising TFI would be proud of their exaggerated statistics. Especially since The content of what was distributed in literature, audio tapes, or by one on one encounters was not representative of God, but filled with sexually deviant and spiritism teachings.

Berg, Zerby and Kelly Attack Their Enemies

A longstanding practice of now deceased David Berg was to demonize anyone who challenged or disagreed with him. It didn't matter who it was. His own family members were not exempt. His most loyal followers' heads could be on the chopping block over any real or imagined minor failure, mistake or omission. Berg hated being detoured from the mission and any-one who stood in the way had better look out! He maintained 'The Voice of Authority from God" and was not afraid to use it!

On June 12th of 1972 Berg wrote a scathing Mo Letter 'Baalzebub— Lord of the Flies' aka Beelzebub, about Jesus People leader D. E. Hoyt and ended the letter with specific directions to all colonies about dealing with anyone who might be a demon-possessed doubter regarding Berg's role as 'God's Voice and Prophet for the End-Times.'

In point five of this 'Mo Letter,' Berg highlights the reason he was angered and disgusted with this Jesus People leader: Vs. 5. "HE REALLY LET THE DEVIL IN THIS TIME, denouncing leadership as false prophets and the Children of God as a false cult. He not only listened to the Devil's lies him-self, but he passed them on to others. In one prophecy alone, written in his own hand, which I have here, *he utters a false prophecy which contains exactly 40 lies about us all.*" (Quote from David Berg's Mo Letter about David E. Hoyt from the Atlanta Jesus People)

In this Mo Letter Berg says D. E. Hoyt has a 'Lying Spirit', is a trouble maker and has let demons in. This letter accomplished Berg's goal of removing any credibility Hoyt had with around 80 who had previously been part of the Atlanta Jesus People Ministries. As noted earlier, Hoyt was responding to a new 'Mo Letter Series' called 'David' that glorifies Berg as 'God's special end-time prophet who claims he speaking for God.'

Dealing with Those who Challenge

Long before the days of the Texas Soul Clinic, Berg's immediate family knew their dad didn't like having his authority questioned. In fact he hated it! He hated a lot of things; he hated the world system, the church, parents and friends of members outside the group and societal rules that limited his freedom and desires!

As early as 1968 Berg grew to hate the sanctity of marriage and the archaic nature of the Scriptures. He also hated law enforcement officials, government investigative bodies, child protection agencies and the courts who wanted the truth regarding sexual, physical and emotional child abuse and excessive member control. *Berg wanted freedom without any parameters!*

Why should The COG / The Family be accountable to anyone! *Berg wanted to be above the laws of the land in countries where he and other members lived and operated.* As God's End-time Prophet, why should he have to submit to the authorities of man or archaic puritanical spiritual teachings from the Bible? How dare any of them challenge God's prophet!

Labels Used For 'Family' Enemies

Berg, Zerby and Kelly have each used a variety of names to describe those they consider enemies of The Family. *Each have written and published letters defending TFI and damning those who criticized them. Berg led this rebuttal battle for years, always up for a fight with words to discredit anyone he considered to be a foe.*

The names and labels used by TF to describe their adversaries are: Systemites, Self Righteous Hypocrites, Traitors, Apostates, Detractors, Demon Possessed, Vicious Enemies, Defectors, Puritanical Old Bottles, The Devil, Anti-God and Judas.

When Family leaders are challenged or critiqued, this opposition is viewed as: Lies from the Apostates, Lying devils, Delusions of the enemy,

Vicious liars, Promoters of a Smear Campaign etc.

Bible Scriptures Warnings on TFI's Practices

"Now the works of the flesh are evident, which are: adultery, fornication, uncleanness, lewdness, idolatry, sorcery, hatred, contentions, jealousies, outbursts of wrath, selfish ambitions, dissensions, heresies, envy, murders, drunkenness, partying and the like; of which I tell you beforehand, just as I also told you in time past, that those who practice such things will not inherit the kingdom of God."

Galatians 5:19-21 NKJ

"The cowardly, unbelieving,abominable, murderers, sexually immoral, sorcerers, necromancers (those that contact the dead) and those that practice magic arts, idolaters, and all liars, shall have their part in the lake which burns with fire and brimstone, which is the second death."

Revelation 21:8 NKJ

"You shall not learn to follow the abominations of the pagan nations. There shall not be found among you anyone who makes his son or his daughter pass through the fire, or one who practices witchcraft, or a soothsayer, or one who interprets omens, or a sorcerer, or one who conjures spells, or a medium, a spiritist, or one who calls up the dead. For all who do these things are an abomination to the LORD, AND BECAUSE OF THESE ABOMINATIONS THE LORD YOUR GOD DRIVES THEM OUT FROM BEFORE YOU."

Deuteronomy 18:9b-12 NKJ

"But you—come here, you children of a sorceress, you offspring of adulterers and prostitutes! Who are you mocking? At whom do you sneer and stick out your tongue? Are you not a brood of rebels, the offspring of liars? You burn with lust among the oaks and under every spreading tree; you sacrifice your children in the ravines and under the overhanging crags."

Isaiah 57:3-5 NIV®

The Pride and Arrogance of TFI

David B. Berg claimed he was *'The End Time Prophet sent by God; The Father of a New Nation'* with special rights to set aside the Scriptures and replace them with his own updated version. This allowed him to do whatever his heart desired. *He wanted to be 'The light' and voice of God to TFI who belonged to him—and he demanded their loyalty!*

The Scriptures remind us of where pride leads. In Isaiah Chapter 14 we gain insight into the Angel Lucifer who was not satisfied or content with his place as one of God's top angels. No longer satisfied with being the 'Bearer of the Light of God,' he wanted to be 'The Light.' He desired to be like the Most High; he desired to be something he was not. In his quest for power and authority his heart was corrupted by pride.

The Fall of Lucifer aka Satan, the Devil

Hell from beneath is excited about you, to meet you at your coming; it stirs up the dead for you, all the chief ones of the earth; it has raised up from their thrones, all the kings of the nations. They all shall speak and say to you:

Have you also become as weak as we? Have you become like us? Your pomp is brought down to Sheol, at the sound of your stringed instruments; the maggot is spread under you, and worms cover you. How are you fallen from heaven, O Lucifer, son of the morning! How you are cut down to the ground, you who weakened the nations!' For you have said in your heart: 'I will ascend into heaven, I will exalt my throne above the stars of God; I will also sit on the mount of the congregation, on the farthest sides of the north; I will ascend above the heights of the clouds, I will be like the Most High.' Yet you shall be brought down to Sheol, to the lowest depths of the Pit. Those who see you will gaze at you, and consider you, saying: 'Is this the man who made the earth tremble, who shook kingdoms?'"   Isaiah 14:9-16 NIV®

Paul aka 'Aaron' Berg (David Berg's Son)

Some believe Aaron died of a broken heart over his father's bizarre and ungodly behavior and teachings. Aaron's conscience was active and he verbalized his concerns to his dad. This interfered with David Berg's dismissal of Godly standards and resulted in Aaron being rejected by his dad for being disloyal. Emotional and mental distress and depression followed. While on a hike in France Aaron fell to his death. No one knows any details other than his body was discovered several weeks after the fall.

Linda Berg

When I think of Linda Berg as a late teen and what unfolded in her life as a result of her dad taking a nose dive by yielding to the influence of the evil one, it's so sad. The same trusting innocence was present among many Children of God and 'Family' members who in good faith joined a group that looked so promising, only to find they'd been deceived by a host of evil spirits.

Clearing Up Any Murky Water

In 1969 *David Brant Berg* and *Karen Elva Zerby aka Maria became lovers.* Berg was married at the time and Zerby was a young female in Berg's band of followers. While alone in a motor home in Canada the two claimed they received prophecies about Berg and Maria's new roles as Prophet and Queen of a New Nation. According to Berg, only Maria could interpret the prophecies they received. From this time forward Zerby became Berg's mistress lover and Queen of the movement.

What followed was an expansion numerically, comprised of hundreds of young followers of Jesus Christ—*with Berg and Maria at the top, leading from behind the scenes, living in secret locations.* The group 'Teens for Christ' soon to be renamed 'The Children of God,' *took a detour away from the Christian faith in belief and practice, but only Berg and Maria and Berg's immediate family members and their spouses and a handful of secondary leaders knew about it.*

Gradually and systematically, in incremental steps, Berg and Zerby were able to steer hundreds of young Christ-followers (approximately 1,800) to *transfer their primary loyalty to Berg and Maria.* Mo Letters were the vehicle used to accomplish this. Members were encouraged to place Berg's Mo Letters above the Bible. In an earlier Mo Letter 'Old Bottles,' Berg plants seeds for his writings to take precedence over the Bible.

> "I want to tell you frankly: If there's a choice between your reading the Bible, I want to tell you—you had better read what God says today in preference to what he said 2,000 or 4,000 years ago!"
>
> - *David B. Berg*

The COG and Family under its different names have continued to use Christian terminology, but their deeds and teachings have nothing to do with God or Jesus Christ! Discerning members left. Those who stayed had no choice but to get on-board with undivided complete obedience to God's End-Time Prophet!

Having seen and read hundreds of Mo Letters and many Maria Letters, I'm 100% confident in saying *there is no similarity between God, Jesus Christ and the Word of Truth found in the Bible, when placed next to Berg and Maria's Spiritist and immoral teachings.*

Since the inception of this group with all its name changes to the present, there has been no semblance of Godly character manifest in Berg or Zerby. *By writings ranging in the thousands from Berg and in the hundreds from Zerby, a different spirit is present.* To the discerning, Berg was a rogue self appointed prophet. The movement he spawned was overtaken by a legion of demonic spirits. *Berg reveled in having his words replace moral and ethical directives in the Bible as he exalted himself as 'The Voice of God' on this earth.*

His grand-daughter, Merry Berg saw through Berg's hypocrisy and described him as a sex-driven, drunken false prophet. Others would add, "Berg was a man obsessed with evil-spirit inspired lust of the flesh and visions of greatness. He loved micro controlling this movement as one he owned. He also enjoyed punishing or destroying people openly who challenged him.

Berg and Zerby share equal blame for the evil they embraced and disseminated to thousands of followers. The two polluted the entire Family with demonic poison, while vehemently denying their Satanic alliance to outsiders.

A day of reckoning for the evil TFI has perpetrated in the name of God will be here soon enough! God is not mocked!

The Act of Leaving and Recovery

When leaving a religious cult, there's a huge sense of relief for most, but an equally gaping hole when thinking about family and friends left behind.

Emotional ties and the absence of those you love and care about are real; not easily dismissed. Separation is never easy when there's a bond of love.

Those born into cults have to dig and claw their way out. The cost of escaping might entail being labeled a traitor. Cults like TFI plant fear about leaving; warning of punishment and judgment for turning your back on God's prophet. In some cases, anger and reproach may come from your own biological family or close friends who choose to stay behind.

The book by X-Family members Celeste and Kristina Jones and Juliana Buhring entitled "Not Without My Sister" is an example of devoted determination to leave together. Sadly, this isn't always possible.

If you end up leaving alone like I and many others have, be strong. Your example of courage to do what's right will often nudge others to follow, or you may find a way to help a friend or biological family members once you're out.

Everyday, cult members are doing the seemingly impossible by leaving. We stand with each of you and applaud your strength of heart! We know how important this first step is.

Gradual Restart

I'd pushed the restart button by leaving physically, but suddenly was hit by an avalanche of emotions about my family, recent events, the tribunal and what I needed to do immediately to avoid being found by cult members. Fear and paranoia about the latter was tangible. I couldn't let them find me, knowing I would be a threat to them because of what I knew.

Whatever functioning I did during the first few months was like walking in a blurry surreal dream. The weight of guilt for my mistake of inviting the COG to Atlanta and deep concern for my family and friends still in the group bounced back and forth. Life and ministry in Atlanta had been shattered into hundreds of pieces. I felt numb, in a daze of sorts with emotions of depression, anger, paranoia, fear and guilt. The need of finding shelter and food was the first priority.

I wondered if I dare pray for help, but in desperation did, offering to God my best weakest prayer. Thankfully God's in the business of answering contrite calls for help no matter how terrible and difficult the situation may be.

This prayer was heard and I was led to a small group of Good Samaritans who came to my aid. They sensed the gravity of my predicament of having a young family trapped in a group who was now a cult.

These new friends extended practical assistance and personal support over a period of several years. For these acts of love and compassion I will always be grateful!

Recalling my journey and listening to others who've left, getting back on our feet is a slow process of small steps. *Being patient with ourselves is important. We cannot simply erase the emotional roller coaster of abuse or intensive indoctrination we've been subjected to. It will take time.*

It took eight months for me to be able to begin to function socially in a limited manner. I couldn't be around people who were hyper or asked a lot of questions. I began working in the same time frame. It might have been earlier if I was in my home country.

People said I looked in a state of shock, like a ghost. I felt like it! I wanted to feel normal, but couldn't. Sleep was a welcome escape. A flood of bad memories would randomly play like a movie in my head. Not wanting to, my mind would bring up episodes, or a series of them that brought back fresh emotions of anger hate, revenge, or disgust related to what I'd experienced. I'd rehearse what I could have said or done differently to protect myself, my family and others. Inner healing was slow.

Regiment & Indoctrination Debriefing

The intensity of regimentation and control in 'closed cults' (mostly isolated from the outside world) is strict and oppressive. Consider TFI's 40 year history of manipulating each member's movements microscopically during every waking hour and monitoring some as they slept.

It was like a horror movie but worse—since it was real—with thousands of victims! Hundreds are still struggling with terrible memories of being physically, sexually, mentally and spiritually controlled with no choice but to submit or be humiliated and punished!

The overbearing trait in all cults is their obsession with indoctrination. TF used this in back to back lengthy teaching sessions. In the early days slogans were yelled sporadically to keep members awake and alert. In time TF imposed punishments on its members for not paying attention, mental drifting, or sleeping.

Rebellious and troubled group members were required to listen to Berg or other leaders on cassette tapes with earphones when sleeping, for subliminal programming. Younger Family tweens and teens who were incorrigible were required to document their thoughts during the day and make this available to be read by local leaders at night. This was TF's attempt to get ahead of rebellion in the ranks.

This structure of unnatural control and indoctrination needs to be understood by those who leave TF. *The hundreds of rules imposed on family members were never for their benefit, but to control them.*

TF also went on an unsuccessful exorcism spree. Hundred of rebellious adults, teens and kids were exorcised to *remove doubts, or any disloyal thoughts or behavior.* The notoriously abusive, *Macao, Teen, Combo and Victor Camps* led the way for these experiments in exorcism. The dilemma for Family leadership was their inability to cast evil spirits out because the entire group was riddled with demons from the top down. If demons did leave in fear of the name of Jesus—they'd be right back!

Exorcism of doubters in a cult is ridiculous! To doubt is to practice discernment, a gift of the Holy Spirit. I hope there will be more and more doubters who come to their senses and see through the evil cults impose.

Initial R&R

Knowing the rigors of the COG/Family and the rigid demands placed on members, I'm recalling how it was for me and what worked after I left. I realize these comments are subjective, but hope they'll be helpful.

Finding a few supportive friends can be an emotional lifesaver. For those who've read my COG-Family departure account, Mr. Ken Burnett, the Frampton family and the Steare family provided compassionate down-to-earth friendship in a Christian context. I didn't feel I had to talk unless I was willing or able. The same applied to attending religious activities, which I didn't feel up to during the first six months. I was OK with sharing a meal, light visiting, a short prayer time and that was about it.

My initial need was rest, a safe place to be, a non-stressful setting and no expectations placed on me. My inner world was crushed. As mentioned earlier, I could only be around a few people for limited periods of time. I couldn't be in any setting where people were happy and laughing. The natural joys of life were out of context to what I felt. When in public, a combination of anxiety, stress, emotional pain and depression made me want to retreat.

Facing the Nightmare Little by Little

Revisiting my experiences in the COG/The Family when my immediate family and friends were still in, was draining and depressing. I rarely did so except with the Frampton family because they shared my anguish with two of their own boys still trapped in the group. We chatted and debriefed on any new developments and prayed for each other's family members.

One day while visiting Mr. Frampton at the Deo Gloria Trust offices, a staff member offered to lend me a book from their library. titled 'Kingdom of the Cults,' by Walter Martin. After perusing this book I knew it would help me better understand what had happened to the COG.

The book described the germination process of cults and how their new beliefs were shaped by revelations that swerved away from Biblical Christianity. Reading this book was a confirmation. 'Kingdom of the Cults' assists readers in seeing when human or satanic teachings or revelations are introduced to a leader or leaders— who then begin the work of convincing their followers to believe this is a special revelation from God that no one else has.

It was filled with Scripture quotes, so I kept my Bible handy and looked up all the verses. *I quickly learned, The contrast between the Christian Faith and that of a cult is significant.* The progression into error and the making of a cult is always accompanied by *a leader or leaders adopting the belief they are the 'chosen ones' on planet earth.*

In my brief tenure in the COG I experienced what deception looked and felt like. I didn't like the 'School of Hard Knocks,' but couldn't change what happened. Because of the severity of my error—this lesson would be burned on my soul. This is what I learned:

> Never put anything, anyone, or any group before
> God the Father, His Son Jesus Christ or the Holy
> Spirit. God does not share His glory with sinful men
> or women!

Post Traumatic Syndrome Battles

We're each wired differently, but a common occurrence among those who've had horrific life experiences, are strong emotions and flashbacks which can be triggered by any number of things.

Out-of-the-blue feelings of anger, rage, revenge, hate, fear, regret, guilt, depression, hopelessness or some other negative emotion may surface. This can be very disturbing—scaring us and others. A flashback can cause an outburst reaction and take us back to some crisis that happened years ago making it seem fresh. The bottom line is, we've been wounded internally. It usually takes time for these emotional tapes to subside and stop replaying. The initial emotions I felt were *Fear* of the COG finding me, *Anger* at cult leaders who manipulated everything and were boldfaced liars. And, feelings of *Great Loss, Helplessness and Depression.* These thoughts and feeling were triggered when I thought about my family and friends still trapped. In the immediate, I didn't know what to do. I felt overwhelmed. Replaying what I could have done differently or sooner wasn't going to help, but I did it anyway.

Many X-Family members have been bummed for ignoring conscience indicators and felt terrible for trusting Moses David and leaving God and Jesus Christ in the dust! Strong regrets.

Nightmares about strict control, sexual or discipline abuse and abusers may surface. We might wrestle with intense anger towards our parents or cult leaders for not protecting us from sexual or physical abuse. Or, parents might feel extreme guilt for not protecting your children from predators, or for not leaving TF sooner.

The intensity of negative memories is unique to each individual and what they experienced. Almost all former members have been exposed to *false doctrines and Spiritism.* Those that lived in TF *during the sexual and physical abuse years* will have more error and bad things to subdue and deposit with God.

Leaving the worst of our pain and confusion with God is not a cop-out or easy to do. We will never forget—but reviewing the tormenting tapes in our head hundreds of times will not help us move forward. This is what we need help with.

A Time to Tear Down and a Time to Rebuild
Ecclesiastes 3:3b

What went wrong with the COG/TFI?

Early obsessions: Berg writes about being fixated on and desiring to have sex with his Mom for many years. Berg's daughter Deborah documents in her book, her dad's persistent attempts to have sex with her when she was a teen, which she resisted. Deborah suspected he was making the same sexual advances toward her sister Faith. What happened is unknown. Running parallel to these incest desires, was a rebellious streak toward the broader Christian church and society as a whole—which Berg grew to despise.

After Berg's self-appointment to Prophet status, and all restraints were lifted, his sexual appetites and longstanding hatred toward the church increased. In addition to unbridled lust and hate gripping his soul, he invited departed spirits from the dead to be his guides. These influences spread like a wildfire throughout TF infecting the entire population. This is the short version of what progressed and became worse.

This is why X-Family members should be firm about renouncing all doctrines they've been taught and rebuild a new foundation using Truth. God and His Son Jesus Christ are The Truth (John 14:6). The Holy Spirit is the Spirit of Truth and the Words of the Bible are the true revelation of God's Truth.

Tearing down a crumbling foundation is non-negotiable. *Extensive structural damage is not salvageable.* Berg and Maria disseminated a disease that spread to thousands of members, who were coerced to accept and participate in these abusive directives, or leave the group, if able.

Each X-COG/Family member had their own experience with physical, mental and sexual abuse, or witnessed it happening to others. *There were victims, participants and abusers and various combinations of these.* Acknowledging your part is important in beginning to put this chapter of your life behind.

You know what happened. Bring it to God and ask for forgiveness. Most X-Family ignored their conscience for numerous reasons and *accepted living within TF's abusive culture.* In regret, hundreds could have and should have done or said something, but gave in to group pressure and manipulation. Failure to stand against blatant bad teachings, abuses and deviant behavior went on for years. Take care of these sins and omissions by going directly to God and confess them to Him. Listen to your conscience and pay attention to His guidance in these matters.

Recalibrating your conscience about truth is essential when rebuilding your spiritual life. Differentiating between Good and Evil is primary. Cults are notorious for working in the gray areas and avoiding God's absolutes. Berg systematically introduced his teachings as superior to undermine God's clear instructions in the Scriptures.

God's teachings throughout the Bible instructs us to seek and do what is good and *stay away from evil. Jesus Christ reinforced this truth by including "deliver us from evil" when teaching the disciples how to pray.* Choosing God's guidance in the Bible above the doctrines of cult leaders helps sever an evil indoctrination chord. The Bible verse below is 100% true!

Your Word, O Lord is eternal; it stands firm in the heavens."
Psalm 119:89 NIV®

God can always be trusted to lead us in the right direction. TFI has muddied the waters since its inception by casting aside God's absolute principles. Berg and Zerby welcomed departed spirits that were evil and became conduits for them. Their conscience about Good and Evil was infiltrated by the 'father of lies—the devil' and died. The Scriptures describe it this way:

They "spoke lies in hypocrisy, having their conscience seared with a hot iron."   1 Timothy 4:2 KJV

An Active Conscience is essential in securing soul recovery. Studying the Old and New Testaments Scriptures and other literature that differentiates between what is true and false will help clean out the poison of error..

I did this by carefully re-reading the entire New Testament, Psalms and Proverbs, a variety of Old Testament books and the 'Kingdom of the Cults' book by Walter Martin. This input solidified what was true, exposed error and realigned my spiritual compass and foundation.

While studying, I saw numbers of mis-steps I was responsible for in interacting with the COG. I'd overlooked some questionable things, while self righteously standing against more blatant errors. My personal sins and a lack of wisdom led to the bad decision of inviting the COG to Atlanta. When the dust settled a year later, I'd lost family, friends and an entire Southern ministry into the COG. After my tribunal and exiting the group, I had a lot to deal with internally. Gradually, I was able to bring this pain and guilt to God.

The hardest thing any cult-survivor will do is, come to terms with the unhealthy things they've learned, supported and practiced.

Getting bad stuff out of our head and heart is a cleansing process that requires willing-ness, time and God's help. All cult lies must be expelled and God's Truth taken in.

The sooner we come to grips with the fact, TFI does not represent the True and Living God of the Scriptures, the better.

A Review: Who Can Absorb My Pain and Sin?

After leaving a cult, disturbing emotions usually linger. Some are: anger, rage, revenge, hate, fear, regret, guilt, depression, despair and hopelessness. The intensity varies as does the length of time it takes for them to begin to subside. A question we should ask, "What can I do to help relieve some of this distress?"

This depends on what you feel up to. You may not want to share anything about your cult experience. You may view the Bible as negative if the cult used it to manipulate and abuse you. Prayer might seem like a use-less religious ritual *the cult ruined with their insincere rote expressions filled with hypocrisy.*

Recalling Jesus Christ's crucifixion, plotted by religious leaders and carried out using extreme torture by Roman soldiers—I hope you will believe God and His Son Jesus know a lot about human suffering.

With this in mind, lessening emotional distress is often accomplished sooner if we are willing to access God's help. This can happen in a number of ways simultaneously. Rereading the New Testament, speaking with God in prayer, meeting with a godly Christian pastor or counselor with cult-recovery experience, joining a cult recovery group, or a more generic Christian support group like Celebrate Recovery, developing new friends and reconnecting with trusted family and old friends. Any combination will help.

Your Internal Work

Cult victims, perpetrators and those who did nothing to protect those being abused are all in God's sight. No one is perfect or sinless. Your work is to acknowledge and confess your own sins and omissions related to being in a cult and to believe God can heal you.

Nothing is beyond God's scope of forgiveness. His love and grace is greater than our worst sins and deepest emotional pain. With great kindness and patience God waits for us to ask for His help. Present yourself to God, so He can pour His Peace, Love and Truth into your brokenness.

> "I, even I, am he who blots out your transgression,-
> for my own sake, and remembers your sins no
> more."   Isaiah 43:25 NIV®

Soul Recovery

The relief of being freed from TFI's 24/7 monitoring and indoctrination is a huge welcomed change. In spite of many challenges— leaving has been one of the best decisions hundreds of X-Family members have made!

The specifics of how each of us left and started over by securing food, shelter, work and deciding where to live more permanently came first. The second internal phase is sorting through emotions, feelings and cult memories; initially coping and over time moving past them.

I think it's wise to accept your recovery will probably be slow and gradual. The trauma cults cause cuts deep into our soul. The wounds and scars don't vanish in a month or two. We are going to be thinking about this ordeal on and off for the rest of our lives. Hopefully it will become less and less, but it will still be on a back burner as a difficult life lesson. We've been through a serious ordeal and have invisible wounds that need plenty of time to heal.

Rediscovering Good Things

Finding or rediscovering and then engaging in doing things that help us in this process is essential. It's not complicated, but requires thinking and reflection on what brings us enjoyment, inspiration, hope and peace.

Some *Artistic examples are:* music, art, dance, acting, singing, sculpting, photography, writing, crafting, painting, making or inventing things. *A few Activity examples are:* sports, hiking, walking, swimming, gardening, serving others, volunteering, restoring, making or building things.

What are you interested in doing or learning about? A vocation, a skill, returning to school, taking classes, securing a coach or mentor, joining a club?

Regaining a spiritual appetite for God's Word is incredibly helpful in clarifying the difference between what a cult is and what a relationship with God is intended to be. I dived into the Bible and other books on cults to understand what happened to those of us who were swept up into TF. I'm glad the right resources came my way and I was willing to invest the time needed so they could work their way into my soul.

Writing or talking out your experience can be a cleansing exercise that is extremely helpful. Some who've left TF have accessed the X-Family website to debrief, find help, or to tell their stories to aid others. Merry Berg did so in a concise manner without rehashing all the gory details of her abuse. Telling your story could be part of your healing, but I recommend allowing a reasonable span of time before doing so. This suggestion is for your well being, as hurtful memories will surface when writing. I know something about this.

A Time for Peace—Ecclesiastes 3:8b

A time of 'Peace' is welcomed for any cult survivor. Jesus' words "Peace be with you" are what our soul longs to experience (John 20:9). To bring calm to the disciples' distress, Jesus greeted them in this way after He rose from the dead. *It is 100 % God's wish to bring peace to our heart.* He confirms this in this Scripture:

> Jesus said, "Peace I leave with you; my peace I give you. I do not give to you as the world gives. Do not let your hearts be troubled and do not be afraid."   John 14:27 NIV®

When we take steps into the unknown of a new life, we need to know God will be at our side. He will give us His peace and guidance if we remain open to Him.

I've grown to love the peace of Silent Prayer in the presence of The True and Living God. I treasure these opportunities to meditate on the greatness of God and His glory that fills the universe. I confess my sins, forgive others, renounce all evil, meditate on The Word of God, slowly review the words of the 'Our Father' or '23rd Psalm.' I listen quietly to the Lord's voice, intercede for all types of needs around the world and for those I know and give thanks to The Living God in all things!. It is not unusual to spend 1-2 hours during each prayer time.

A relationship with God is possible if we'll take the time to cultivate it. He is the one who restores our soul, gives us wisdom and understanding and fills us with His Spirit of Love, Truth and Peace.

Capsule Summary

New Online members in TFI today are much like the early COG. They only know what their leaders want them to know. A big chunk of TFI's history including thousands of Mo Letters and hundreds of Maria letters have been destroyed to avoid prosecution. TFI would like to bleach *The Crime Scene* of any record of massive sexual child abuse, teen torture and extreme member abuse, but it's not possible. *Hundreds of us have saved incriminating Mo Letters to prove TFI's white-washed history is just another Public Relations lie!*

Peter and Maria would like to be viewed as wonderful ambassadors for Christ, but it's simply not true. Their source of inspiration comes from the spirit-world of demons.

For Family & Friends of Cult Members

The helplessness parents, family members and close friends feel when a loved one is in a destructive cult is overwhelming. It's heightened when their whereabouts is unknown, and the cult's practice is to cut off all contact with the outside world. A sense of powerlessness is difficult to accept when we're used to working through problems within a reasonable time frame.

I gradually learned to place this terrible burden in God's hands, knowing He can accomplish 100% more than I can by worrying, or trying to do things in my own steam. I learned to pray in faith and keep believing. Persistently, I prayed for my family and friends, believing they would be released! It took about eight years before my prayers were realized and my oldest children, x-wife and new husband left the 'Children of God,' 'Family of Love!' Many friends from Atlanta also found their way out at different times.

Waiting for the release of a family member or friend from a cult is a heart-rending, anguishing experience. It saps our emotional energy and stretches our patience to the limits. *This kind of Trauma can divide parents; don't let it!* Blaming one another for parenting mistakes and choices hinders the effectiveness of your prayers at a time when unity in prayer and mutual support is needed. All parents make thousands of mistakes. The best thing we can do is make the needed changes and keep moving forward.

The freedom desired for your loved one, mandates warfare against counterfeit evil spirits embedded in cults, posing as The Truth (I Timothy 4:1). The surface reasons for individuals joining are numerous, but at the core, *The lure and hold of 'deceiving evil spirits' is the deeper problem.*

Prayer is the most effective means of spiritual warfare we can engage in on behalf of a cult victim. Ephesians chapter six is a good chapter to read and familiarize yourself with. Ask The Father and Jesus Christ to 1.) Bind the evil spirits control over your family member(s) or friend. 2.) Expose the cult's deception to them. 3.) Reveal the truth. And 4.) Give them the courage to leave.

This type of prayer is fully in harmony God's will. You cannot go wrong by praying specifically for these things!

For your ongoing personal well-being it's incredibly helpful to seek out a support system. It could be a few friends, a small group from a church, a prayer partner, a counselor, mentor, a cult support group or something similar. The reality is, there will be low spots and hurdles to overcome when a loved one is still in a cult and there seems to be no signs of them leaving.

I recommend being prepared to wait as long as it takes and keep believing, bringing and leaving this difficult heart-burden with the Lord. If you are able, release your loved ones by name into God's hands, asking Him to work deeply in their hearts. This will help you cope and continue to do the things you need to do in your own life.

Any direct contact you have with your loved one, in person, or by phone is one of the best things that can happen. If this occurs, **work at building trust by listening and not reacting,** be sensitive to doubts they may have about the cult and reconfirm your unconditional love. Let the Holy Spirit guide you. *Believe it is possible for your loved one to have their eyes opened and the courage to leave when they are ready.*

"What is impossible for man is possible for God!"
- Jesus Christ Luke 18:27 GNB

A Few Reminders:

- Cults separate, indoctrinate, control and seek to isolate members from their biological family and friends. They want to usurp these roles and gain undivided member loyalty.

- It's best for a close family member or trusted friend to speak with a cult member when contact, openness or dialogue opportunities arise. Bonds of love with those on the outside are life-lines for cult members who may in time see through any part of the lies these groups dispense and *want to leave.*

- *In the interim, find out what the cult is about,* what they teach, believe, how they operate and some of the nuances of how they lure, or keep members in.

- Do your best to *keep hope alive.* All over the world cult-member-victims of deception are exiting the control of destructive cult groups.

- When any contact is made, *show you care by actively listening* in spite of any distress or nervousness you may feel. Stay calm, listen more than talking and don't react to things they say or believe that are troubling. Gently ask open-ended questions and give your full focus to their answers.

- Keep in mind it's embarrassing and hard for any cult member to voice their doubts (when they're taught not to), or admit they've made a terrible mistake by joining this group. Be sensitive to this.

- *Aiding anyone exiting a cult requires sensitivity, wisdom and patience.*

- Cult teachings are often complex; with built in deterrents to prevent deserters. For 35 years TFI had thousands of members trapped in distant locations with no resources to leave. Many were only able to escape because *someone on the outside helped them* with airfare and other practical needs.

- The prayer of faith to the True God for a loved one to find their way out of a cult is one of *the best behind the scenes gifts we can give.* By doing so, we are engaging in spiritual battle on their behalf, appealing to God the Father and His Son Jesus Christ to rescue and deliver them from a destructive group.

- Preparing our heart in advance to come alongside a family member or friend who leaves a cult is another important way of showing love in a tangible way. Those who leave a cult usually feel disorientated and in an emotional and mental fog. The majority will struggle with coping with all the changes of starting over.

- *A caring support system of family and friends is an incredible resource.*

Ideally, parents and friends will be in a good place spiritually to set an example of God's unconditional love, compassion, patience and understanding. Reminder: Pray intensely with faith. This is an incredible tool for good.

X-cult members will have a lot to deal with and need time and space to recover. Almost all of those exiting a cult agree, leaving and then finding healing of heart, mind and spirit is one of the hardest things they've ever done.

If family members or friends want to help in the recovery of someone you care about and love, a right-attitude is a must. *Avoid placing undue expectations on them to conform to what you think they should 'Do or Be.'*

Those recovering will move at their own pace, make new friends, discover their own interests and make their own choices as they rebuild their lives. Encouragement and help is important without inserting an agenda of control. They've already had plenty of that! Our job is to love them, be available when they want to talk and keep trusting God in prayer for their well being.

Suggested Reading

Not Without My Sister– by *Kristina Jones and Celeste Jones and Juliana Buhring*

Born Into the Children of God – by *Natacha Tormey*

The Family: The shocking true story of a notorious cult- by *Chris Johnson and Rosie Jones*

The Children of God, The Inside Story - by *Deborah (Linda Berg) Davis*

Kingdom of the Cults – by *Walter Martin*

Take Back Your Life – by *Janja Lalich and Madeleine Tobias*

Combating Cult Mind Control – by *Steven Hassan*

Terror, Love and Brainwashing –by *Alexandra Stein*

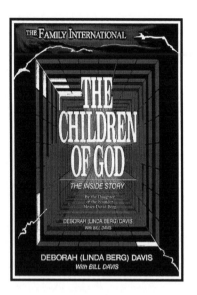

Research Resources:

CBC News, Ottawa Canada, "COG Sex Cult Survivors Come Out of the Shadows," Simon Gardner,

Telegraph Co. UK, "How a Cult Stole my Life" by Julia Llewellyn Smith / article about Smith www.telegraph.co.uk/culture/books/11184489/taylor-stevens-joaquin-phoe-nix- david-berg-children-of-god.html

Timeline, https://timeline.com/children-of-god-5245a45f6a2a Stephanie Buck- A 'Family' you don't want to join

Crime Feed.com, Twins tell their story, http://crimefeed.com/2015/06/children-of-god-cult-twins/

ABC Nightline, video Interview with Twin Sisters Inside Controversial Sect, 'Flor & Tamar' Rebelcircus.com, "Inside the World's biggest Celebrity Sex Cult"

New York Times World, "Sex Cult Enslaved 268 children in Argentina", Nathaniel Nash 10-3-93

Cult Education Institute, "FBI investigates Coast Sex Cult" The Courier-Mail / Australia

Daily Mail UK – Natacha Tormey's Story, by Naomi Greenaway, July 28, 2014

Daily Mail UK, Rose McGowan Story, by Ellie Genower, Aug 26, 2011

Pornographic Art of the COG, Family of Love, Family, The Family International www.vice.com /en_us/article/av44za/the-bizarre-and-terrifying-propaganda-art-of-the-children-of-god-666

Final Report on the Activities of the Children of God to Hon. Louis J. Lefkowitz, At-torney General of the State of New York

The Sun a UK Co. 'Life as a child inside the Children of God cult' update April 6, 2016

Article: No Real Changes in the Children of God Cult, xfamily.org

The Children of God – The Inside Story, by Deborah Linda Berg Davis, Zondervan 1984

X-Family - Encyclopedia about "The Family International COG cult - https://www.xfamily.org/

X-Family website - http://www.exfamily.org/

Family International –IPFS, Information site on timeline history and facts: https://ipfs.io/ipfs/QmXoypizjW3WknFiJnKLwHCnL72vedxjQkDDP1mXWo6uco/wiki/Family_International.html

Califia's Children, "The Children of God/The Family

http://califias.blogspot.com/2014/12/the-children-of-godthe-family.html

The Family International.com (TFI site)

Countercog.org

The Family International, Wikipedia.org

 "The Family International" indoctrinated teens sing to aging Berg / Video https://www.youtube.com/watch?v=585DbY4gy1s - 281k

Merry Berg and other 2nd Generation Family members speak out on Abuse / Video https://www.youtube.com/watch?v=7W5rANQ9hD0 - 318k

Ricky Rodriguez Abused & Tormented Video, https://www.youtube.com/

+ Phone & Personal visits with active Family members, X-Family and parents

I said, "Have mercy on me, Lord; heal me, for I have sinned against you."   Psalm 41:4

Restore us, God Almighty; make your face shine on us, that we may be saved.   Psalm 80:7

This resource is written for those who find themselves trapped in
a self-destructive lifestyle and the fall-out of these choices.

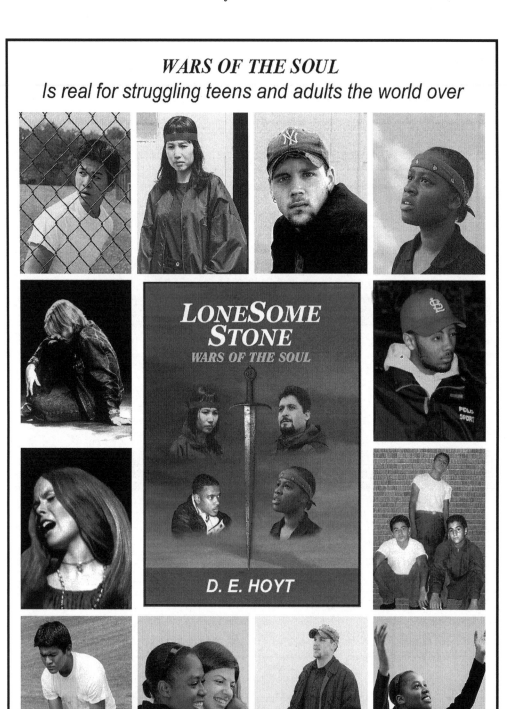

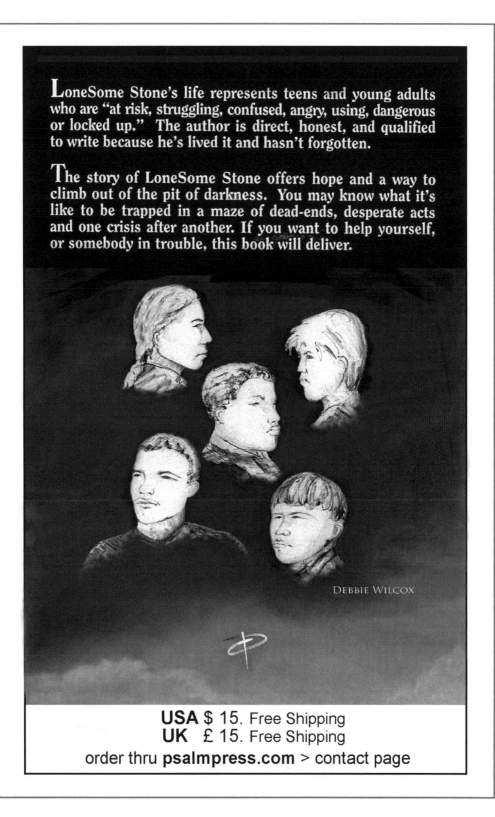

Printed in Great Britain
by Amazon

33176972R00441